Exploring Direct Marketing

Exploring Direct Marketing

Lisa O'Malley,
Maurice Patterson,
Martin Evans.

Australia ¥ Canada ¥ Mexico ¥ Singapore ¥ Spain ¥ United Kingdom ¥ United States

Exploring Direct Marketing

Copyright © 1999 Lisa O'Malley, Maurice Patterson and Evans

First published by International Thomson Business Press
Reprinted 2001 by Thomson Learning
The Thomson Learning logo is a registered trademark used herein under licence.

British Library Cataloguing-in-Publication Data
A catalogue record for this book is available from the British Library

First edition 1999

Typeset by LaserScript Limited Mitcham. Surrey
Printed in Croatia by ZRINSKI d.d.

ISBN 1-86152-402-1

Thomson Learning
Berkshire House
168-173 High Holborn
London WC1V 7AA
UK

http://www.thomsonlearning.co.uk

Table of Contents

Dedications

Lisa O'Malley: Phyllis and John.

Maurice Patterson: My parents.

Martin Evans: My father and Anne.

Preface

There are many books available on the subject of direct marketing. This particular book is different. From the very beginning our intention was to write a book for students, rather than for practitioners in direct marketing. That is not to say that this book will not be of interest for direct marketers, but rather that it was conceived and developed with students in mind. As such, we have attempted to ensure that this book is suitable for students who have no prior knowledge of direct marketing by covering the basics well. We have also incorporated both theoretical and practical discussions of how and why direct marketing works. This involved utilizing relevant underpinning theories and references supplemented with illustrative examples from the marketplace. Indeed, fundamental to making this book student-friendly is the inclusion of cases and examples throughout and, in particular, providing a dedicated chapter which deals with in-depth case discussions.

This book is different from other direct marketing texts in a number of other respects. It does not peddle a two, three, five or seven step process for effective direct marketing. On the contrary, it attempts to present developments in direct marketing from an informed and objective perspective, warts and all!

The book begins by outlining what it is we understand by the term *direct marketing* (a contentious issue in itself) and by identifying the factors which have contributed to the phenomenal growth of UK direct marketing in recent years. Next the book deals with issues of planning and strategy which are informed by strategic decisions within the firm generally. Discussions in the book are influenced not only by existing coverage of direct and database marketing, but also by wider marketing issues. As such, our treatment of some topics is broader than might otherwise be expected. For example, our discussion of segmentation involves more than just list segmentation and customer profiling. Similarly, in addition to testing, a wide variety of other marketing research approaches are also addressed. Coverage of the marketing database underlines its importance for direct marketing and indeed for contemporary marketing generally and highlights the power afforded to organizations by data fusion and profiling.

Direct marketing communications are increasingly being employed by mass marketers to encourage loyalty and build customer relationships. Consequently, this text includes two chapters devoted to discussing loyalty and relationship issues. Not only do these chapters concern themselves with the techniques employed in building loyalty and fostering consumer relationships, they also involve more in-depth treatment of conceptual and strategic issues such as the nature of loyalty and the determinants of relational exchange.

Increasingly, the Internet is being proposed as a contemporary means by which organizations can communicate with their customers. As with all innovative technologies, rather more rhetoric is in evidence than serious coverage and practical advice. To this end, the book contains a guest chapter by Linda Peters detailing the structure of the Internet and the possibilities it affords direct marketers in terms of interactive communications.

In dealing with creativity for direct marketing this book goes beyond the usual illustrative examples of what might be considered creative and provides a very real foundation upon which creative work can be built. Furthermore, the necessity for co-operation between the creative team and those in production and fulfilment is underlined.

Within the market-place today there is greater pressure for organizations and their employees to do business in a socially responsible manner. Discussions of ethical issues and social responsibility are controversial within a direct marketing context but are none the less deserving of attention. The chapter which focuses on these issues is significantly influenced by our own research in this area and while students may disagree with our position on privacy issues, they will at least have had an opportunity to develop an informed view. Indeed, it is encouraging to note that many direct marketing practitioners and some industry bodies now acknowledge consumer concerns regarding privacy issues, and are attempting to proactively address the underlying problems. This chapter is further supported by a guest chapter by Paul Sampson which introduces students to the relevant legislation with respect to the direct marketing industry.

Acknowledgements

Many thanks to all our colleagues and students for their inspiration and help in writing this book, and to Linda Peters and Paul Sampson for their valued contributions.

To Jennifer Pegg for being such a tremendous champion of our work.

Thanks also to the many contributors of case material including:

Aardman; Brann Software; CACI; Craik Jones; Direct Response; Dunn Humby; Experian; HHCL; Land Rover; Mail Marketing; Marketing Direct; Reputations Managers; Revolution; Royal Mail; BMW; CIGNA Healthcare; Scandinavian Seaways; Data Protection Registrar; SITEL Corporation; Evans, Hunt, Scott and Flying Flowers Group.

Also deserving acknowledgement for technical, administrative and mental support (not necessarily in that order) are the Direct Marketing Association, the Institute of Direct Marketing, Lloyd Harris, Stella Warren, Donna Watson, and Lee, Andrew, Sian and Amy who kept at least some of us sane while writing this book. Gúna, Geansaí and Oscar also warrant thanks for keeping us entertained during meetings.

List of Figures

List of Tables

Foreword

The DMA research centre estimates that expenditure in the UK economy on Direct Marketing in 1997 approached £7 billion. This expenditure influenced the sales of goods and services to the tune of £25 billion, and has in turn had a profound effect on UK employment. By way of comparison, the US DMA recently reported expenditure levels of some $135 billion, influencing US sales of $1.1 trillion, directly and indirectly influencing 9 million jobs in the US.

Growth levels of 12 to 15 per cent compound have been achieved by the industry over the last few years, and the indications are that there is no sign of any let up.

This phenomenon is attributable to a number of interwoven factors:

Changing consumer demands (with customer service now seen as a given) combined with consumer price pressures, are forcing manufacturers to find alternative ways of meeting profitability targets. This has created a process of disintermediation where companies bypass intermediaries – salesmen, distributors and retailers – and create direct relationships with their customers. The motor insurance industry, for example, has been revolutionised as a result of this process.

Retailers have responded by creating their own customer information channels through the adoption of added value promotions, using smart card technologies and creating new products in the process.

In our daily lives, we are all under increasing time pressures, some created by the information overload. This forces consumers to seek more time efficient methods of buying. The convenience and accessibility afforded through the direct marketing telephone revolution is meeting this demand.

Marketing, sales and customer service departments that were once separate have been fused to create holistic customer relationship strategies. Attracting new customers is an expensive process: increasing profits from an existing client base through relationship marketing programmes is the way forward.

In addition this we have the benefits of all the technology that the information revolution promises. We can now hold, manage, overlay and mine customer information on a massive scale, opening new direct marketing opportunities.

This revolution places strains on the pool of talent available to satisfy the insatiable appetite of companies practising direct marketing.

I therefore welcome the publication of Exploring Direct Marketing. This book will serve its readers well, and will add an important cornerstone to increasing the knowledge base of professionals in our industry enabling them to meet the Direct Marketing talent needs of the future.

Colin Lloyd
Chief Executive
Direct Marketing Association

The Rise of Direct Marketing

This Chapter:

▶ Reviews The Origins Of UK Direct Marketing.

▶ Delineates A Definition of Direct Marketing.

▶ Provides An Overview of Direct Marketing Media.

C H A P T E R

1

The Rise of Direct Marketing

It All Started With The Kids!

Although many business-to-business marketers, and a few mass market consumer companies such as Readers Digest and Time Life have utilized direct marketing for some time, its widespread use in consumer markets is a relatively recent phenomenon. So how did it all start?

Heinz and Procter and Gamble are among the consumer giants who initiated the foray into direct marketing. Originally both companies confined their direct marketing efforts to their markets for baby foods and products that are limited to about 3 per cent of the population. Indeed, the impetus for Heinz's 1994 decision to invest £10 million in a direct marketing campaign for its whole range of products came as a direct result of their experience in the baby foods market. The company issued baby packs to women who had just given birth and then collected data from these packs. Using this information Heinz was able to communicate tailored messages to the families involved by post, at different stages of the infant's life. Different messages were appropriate at different stages from weaning onto first foods to solids. Over the period of the campaign, Heinz's share of infant foods rose from 50 per cent to 59 per cent.

Procter and Gamble also attributes its success in marketing Pampers to its use of a database. Like Heinz they used such tactics as 'individualized' birthday cards for babies, and reminder letters to move up to the next size.

On the basis of their success with direct communications in the baby sector, Heinz believed that the same approach would work across all their product categories. As Heinz Marketing Director Laurence Balfe said 'We see a rapid and efficient means of speaking to our key customers as essential to develop our consumer franchise'. The announcement of their £10 million campaign in 1994 sent shock waves through the consumer goods marketing community. Other manufacturers have dashed to jump on the bandwagon of database and direct marketing. The Oxo brand quickly rolled out a 2.5 million-strong questionnaire survey soliciting detailed information regarding purchasing habits. This they attribute to a need to become involved in relationship marketing, and as a direct result of the hype surrounding the Heinz move.

(Source: *The Economist* 1995; *Marketing* 1994a)

Introduction

The term 'direct marketing' is reputed to have been used for the first time in the 1960s, by Lester Wunderman. For many years direct marketing was synonymous with direct mail and mail-order, probably because these were the most common approaches utilized by direct marketers to sell their products. However, today's direct marketers have a plethora of approaches at their disposal including direct mail, telemarketing, direct response television advertising, door-to-door and the Internet among others. Direct marketers are not confined to the important, though mundane, objective of generating sales. As this chapter will show, while the range and volume of products sold directly to consumers has increased, the number of companies who use direct marketing to achieve other objectives has also increased. Because of the variety of applications encompassed by direct marketing it is increasingly being employed by organizations who are not 'direct marketers' in the traditional sense. However, it is also this range of applications which makes developing a generic definition of direct marketing so difficult. Any definition is going to be problematic as it must incorporate both direct distribution and direct communication. A second problem is identifying what media and methods are appropriate to include in any definition. This chapter will first review the origins of direct marketing, and then move towards delineating an appropriate definition. Next the rapid growth of direct marketing in recent times will be reviewed, and finally the chapter will briefly comment on the media of direct marketing.

The Origins of Direct Marketing

Contemporary UK direct marketing has evolved from rather humble beginnings in the field of direct distribution. In an effort to reach consumers who were geographically dispersed some companies began to offer direct distribution services. In order to let consumers know the kinds of products they sold, these companies developed lists of products with their associated prices. These lists were then mailed to prospective customers. As competition grew, many of the lists became more detailed. Descriptions and, in some cases, pictures of the products were included. After choosing from these catalogues, consumers would place an order by mail, and wait until the product was delivered. Thus, the idea of purchasing directly from a company was associated with ordering by mail – or mail order.

In the UK mail order began to develop at the beginning of the 20th century. The Freemans catalogue, which is still around today, was launched in 1905 (McCorkell 1997). However, it was not until after the war that mail order really took off. Indeed, the share of retail sales accounted for by direct channels grew steadily between 1950 and 1970 (McGoldrick 1990). During this period mail order companies relied upon a network of local agents who circulated catalogues and collected payments. Agents were paid through a combination of commission and discounts off catalogue prices. Consumers themselves were attracted to mail order (Stewart Howe 1992) shopping because of:

▶ the convenience of shopping from home;

▶ the convenience of free home delivery;

▶ the wide product choice within a single catalogue;

▶ the ability to order goods on approval and return them if they were unsatisfactory;

▶ the availability of 'free' credit over an extended payment period.

Mail order was traditionally targeted toward the lower socio-economic groups, and the availability of credit terms was its main attraction. Even in the 1980s this downmarket bias was still evident with 50 per cent of adults in the C_2D categories purchasing through mail order, as opposed to only 37 per cent of AB consumers (McGoldrick 1990).

The proportion of total sales accounted for by mail order declined from 4 per cent in 1976 to 3.3 per cent in 1985 (Stewart Howe 1992). The sector experienced a number of problems during the early 1980s, partly because of its dependence upon lower income groups, and partly because of its inability to keep pace with general social change and with developments on the high street. These problems included (McGoldrick 1990):

▶ Rising unemployment and recession increased the number of bad debts and the returns rate (a major cost).

▶ Mail order had acquired a rather dull image.

▶ Many agents began to use catalogues primarily for their own purchases.

▶ The widespread availability of credit from other sources.

Indeed, it was probably the widespread availability of credit which had the biggest impact on the declining fortunes of mail order. Credit terms had always been the sector's greatest selling point but by the mid-1980s many of the larger high street stores also began to offer credit facilities, and high street prices were often perceived as being more competitive than mail order (Stewart Howe 1992). As the population became more affluent, and the range of products and services available in the high street increased, mail order continued to lose ground.

In the latter part of the 1980s mail order began a process of revitalization, which led to 'a blurring of the distinctions between mail order, direct response selling, and traditional retailing' (McGoldrick 1990:60). The sector was stimulated in the latter part of the 1980s by the entry of Marks & Spencer with their home furnishings catalogue, and the Next chain's launch of Next Directory. These companies had a number of advantages over traditional mail-order marketers. First, their high street image was up-market and innovative. Second, they had ready-made mailing lists created from the information given by customers who applied for store cards. Their target customers were similar to those shopping on the high street, and the quality of the catalogues clearly reflected this. For example, when the Next Directory was produced in 1988, it used high quality photography, graphics and paper. Although it was much more expensive to produce (at £9 each) than other catalogues, it succeeded in appealing to a more up-market clientele (primarily ABs). Next Directory also enhanced the convenience of home shopping by allowing orders to be placed by telephone, with calls charged at lower rates, and products delivered within 48 hours. Thus, the proposition offered by Next was quality, choice and convenience rather than easy credit. 'Not surprisingly, other companies have responded by improving catalogue design, reducing delivery times and encouraging telephone ordering with credit card payment' (McGoldrick 1990:61).

The ability to order by telephone has vastly improved the convenience of catalogue shopping, while the product range and credit terms continue to attract customers. As a result mail order is firmly back on the agenda, although today customers are more likely to order by phone, fax or e-mail. Today's consumer can buy practically anything from home (e.g. domestic appliances, videos, books and more recently financial services). Indeed, home shopping for financial services is intriguing given that many experts said it couldn't be done. They believed that face-to-face contact between company and customer was vital for success in this market. The success of financial services direct marketers is testimony to the importance of direct marketing today.

What is Direct Marketing?

The concept of direct marketing overriding traditional marketing mix boundaries of distribution and communications has contributed to problems in accurately defining the term. However, direct marketing clearly falls within the realm of marketing communications, irrespective of its use as a vehicle for distribution or dialogue. Shimp defines marketing communications as representing 'the collection of all elements in an organisation's marketing mix, that facilitate exchanges by establishing shared meaning with the organisation's customers or clients' (Shimp 1992:10). Furthermore, this definition recognises that a marketing organisation is both a sender and a receiver of messages, therefore highlighting the importance and relevance of direct marketing facilitating two-way exchanges of information. This interaction or dialogue is made possible through a wide range of media, each of which can be utilized on its own or as part of a battery of media. Thus, although direct marketing developed from mail order and was thus considered to be a means of direct selling, it is increasingly playing an important role in marketing communications. On this basis it is clear that direct marketing can be used for both communication and distribution.

The most comprehensive and accepted definition is that offered by the American Direct Marketing Association (ADMA) (Cited in Lindgren and Shimp 1996:520).

> *Direct marketing is an interactive system of marketing which uses one or more advertising media to effect a measurable response and/or transaction at any location.*

This definition isolates a number of issues which distinguish direct marketing from other forms of marketing and communication.

- ▶ *An interactive system.* Unlike advertising which speaks to people *en masse*, direct marketing can isolate and communicate with customers as individuals (Bird 1993). Direct marketing also ensures feedback from the customer, and thus facilitates interactive dialogue.

- ▶ *One or more communication media.* Although the ADMA definition uses the specific term advertising, we believe that the more general term 'communication' is more apt given the increasing range of media and approaches within the direct marketing repertoire. Direct marketing can utilize not only direct mail, but also telephone, fax, Internet, and press, TV and radio advertising with a direct response element.

- ▶ *Effects a measurable response.* This is one of the distinguishing factors of direct marketing. The response to a direct marketing offer can be a request for further information, or the placing of an order. Either way, direct marketers can capture and measure individual responses, and in this way more effectively measure their programmes.

- ▶ *At any location.* Direct marketers do not need high-street premises. More importantly, the range of options for customers is not limited to any one location. They can respond by phone, by mail, by fax or e-mail (and all this from either home or work). They may also have the option of responding at a kiosk, or by initiating a personal visit.

Although widely accepted, the above definition has attracted criticism, mainly because it 'focuses attention primarily on *using* a particular type of advertising to effect a measurable response' (Bauer and Miglautsch 1992). This seems to categorize direct marketing as simply an element of the communications mix. As we saw earlier, direct marketing is both a distribution and a communication method, and as such may be seen as a wholly distinct marketing system, with its own separate marketing mix (Schofield 1995). As a result, a very different definition is offered by Bauer and Miglautsch (1992), which has become accepted by the UK Direct Marketing Association.

> *Direct marketing is a cybernetic marketing process which uses direct response advertising in prospecting, conversion and maintenance.*

The authors qualify this definition by providing a more detailed description of the terms they use:

▶ *Direct response advertising* is defined as advertising that contains a definite offer, a response device and tracking code or other means of tracing responses to individual consumers and/or media source.

▶ *Prospecting* means seeking out and targeting new customers, beginning usually by generating enquiries or making introductory offers.

▶ *Conversion* refers to upgrading respondents (enquirers, trialists, non-paid orderers) to fully fledged paid-up customers.

▶ *Maintenance*, in this case, means maintaining custom or interest. In other words, maintaining loyalty.

▶ *Relational marketing* means developing on-going dialogue between marketer and customer. It implies feedback, a two-way communication process.

▶ *Cybernetics* is the science of control and communication. A cybernetic system is one in which there is feedback of information on the deviation of output from goal. A cybernetic system contains a control mechanism which compares output (actual result) to system goal (forecast). In direct marketing, micro-control is practised through the use of tracking codes allowing deviation of actual response from forecast response to be recorded – and allowing the actual response to inform future decisions.

The main strength of the Bauer and Miglautsch definition is that it makes clear that direct marketing is not just another element of the communications mix, that it is a marketing system in its own right. Despite this, it has also received some strong criticism, including (Schofield 1995):

▶ that Bauer and Miglautsch define direct marketing as a concept rather than a field of study;

▶ that certain terms are not defined absolutely unambiguously (e.g. relational, prospecting, conversion, and maintenance);

▶ that their definition espouses an ideal type rather than being based on reality.

It is the latter criticism that is most important in terms of having a good working definition. By identifying the elements included in direct marketing, the Bauer and Miglautsch definition excludes other elements. 'Such a definition excludes much marketing work which employs individual direct marketing techniques on a pragmatic and eclectic basis, alongside nondirect marketing elements, and in which the use of such techniques is normally seen as direct marketing' (Schofield 1995:36). In other words, it excludes marketers who believe themselves to be using direct marketing unless they use tracking devices, intend to maintain a relationship etc. The nub of the problem seems to be that the Bauer and Miglautsch definition includes too many elements, and all of these together are not necessarily always evident in the practice of direct marketing. In a sense then, this definition is attempting to define what would be the *ideal* or *most effective* direct marketing, especially where a product or service is marketed exclusively through that system.

> ❝ *This is quite illegitimate: Direct marketing with tracking codes (or lifetime value calculations, or the use of a database) would undoubtedly be more effective, but direct marketing without it would still be direct marketing. The concern of definers should be to define the reality of the subject or business as it really exists, not to 'define out' any direct marketing which is imperfect, or ineffective, of falls below the highest standards.* ❞
> (Schofield:37)

On the basis of these criticisms, Schofield proposes that two definitions of direct marketing may indeed be needed (pp. 37–8):

1 The first would be a general, inclusive definition of *direct marketing*, which would allow any use of any direct marketing technique to be recognized as an instance of direct marketing as in the earlier DMA definition.
2 The second definition needed would be a definition of a *direct marketing system*, covering cases where a product or service is marketed exclusively by direct marketing methods. Bauer and Miglautsch's definition is adequate for this purpose.

The Growth of Direct Marketing in the UK

The direct marketing industry has been the fastest growing sector of marketing communications for more than a decade. According to the 1996 DMA census direct marketing expenditure within the UK has reached £5.5 billion, a 22 per cent rise on the previous year's figures, testament to its rapid growth.

The recent growth of direct marketing in the UK has been impressive, both in terms of volume and expenditure. The range of companies that now makes use of direct marketing's services has also seen dramatic expansion, with many fast moving consumer goods (FMCG) marketers gradually moving into the area, as outlined in the opening *vignette*. Direct marketing is currently employed in business-to-business and consumer markets, by charities, and even by the government. Such is its flexibility, that it easily lends itself to campaigns outside the domestic market. On the back of recent growth, many industry experts predict continued success in the future. However, in order to understand the extent and direction of future growth, the forces which combined to initiate and fuel the dramatic success of the industry thus far, must first be appreciated.

Forces of Change

The marketing environment has witnessed tremendous change in the last two decades, and it was as a result of these changes that direct marketing was to become the force it is today (see Figure 1.1). This growth can be attributed on a general level to a combination of demand and supply side factors (Evans, O'Malley and Patterson 1995). Indeed, as Fiegenthaler states (Fletcher, Wheeler and Wright 1991):

> ❧ *In the early 1980s, two things began to happen simultaneously. Electronic data processing costs declined and marketing costs climbed, both dramatically. These two curves crossed and this was the catalyst for European direct marketing growth.* ❧

Demand for more effective targeting resulted from increasing marketing costs, caused by significant changes in market behaviour. These changes also adversely impacted the effectiveness of traditional media. However, satisfying this demand for improved targeting would have been impossible without the accompanying technological revolution which facilitated data access, storage, manipulation, and targeting. Not only was the availability of technology significant, but substantial cost decreases continue to allow more and more companies to harness the power of database technology in developing individualized marketing communications.

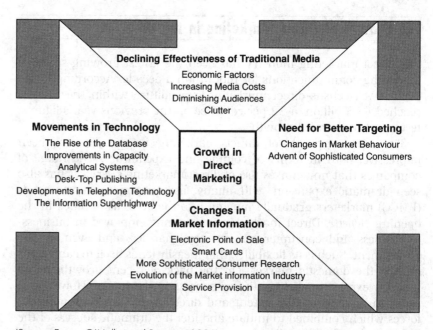

Declining Effectiveness of Traditional Media
Economic Factors
Increasing Media Costs
Diminishing Audiences
Clutter

Movements in Technology
The Rise of the Database
Improvements in Capacity
Analytical Systems
Desk-Top Publishing
Developments in Telephone Technology
The Information Superhighway

Growth in Direct Marketing

Need for Better Targeting
Changes in Market Behaviour
Advent of Sophisticated Consumers

Changes in Market Information
Electronic Point of Sale
Smart Cards
More Sophisticated Consumer Research
Evolution of the Market information Industry
Service Provision

Figure 1.1 Catalysts of Change

(Source: Evans, O'Malley and Patterson 1996)

Changes In The Marketing Environment: The Need For Better Targeting

A number of transformations have taken place within the marketing environment which have resulted in the increasing desire of organizations to communicate with consumers in a more individualized fashion. The most important of these transformations include:

▶ changes in market behaviour;

▶ the advent of sophisticated consumers who value convenience.

Changes in Market Behaviour

A number of key issues have altered the structure of the modern consumer market-place, and the behaviour and expectations of contemporary consumers. The fragmentation of consumer markets has exacerbated the difficulties of communicating with customers through traditional channels. Market fragmentation may be partially explained by an increasing trend towards individualism. In fact, there is evidence to suggest that people are becoming more interested in expressing their individuality rather than following mass social movements. Individualism has led to a proliferation of subcultures or segments within society based on a variety of criteria (e.g. music, fashion, religion, hobbies, interests and employment), in addition to the traditional demographic variables of age, sex and income. This has led to greater pluralism in society, which can clearly be observed in the diversity of fashion trends evident in the high street.

Demographic and lifestyle shifts have also led to substantial changes in household composition. Increases in careerist couples and single parent families, for example, mean that the concept of a household containing a working father, a housebound mother and 2.4 children is fast becoming a thing of the past.

> ❧ *Although the family remains the basic unit in society, the shape of the family within the household is changing, so that it is not so much 'nuclear' as a collection of individual cells, each with its own tastes and needs.* ❧ (Henley Centre 1995)

One implication of this is that consumers have increasingly specialized requirements for the products and services they use. It is also clear that individuals within the household will often express their individuality through their choice of products and brands. Within a single household a variety of brands in each product category may be purchased (e.g. several brands of breakfast cereal, shampoo, and snack food). In parallel, consumers have become more experienced and cynical about advertising, and less likely to accept branding at face value. They want to know why they should be expected to pay a premium price for certain products. Companies are thus required to communicate more and more with household members as individuals, rather than as homogenous family groups.

Manufacturers must also take some responsibility for the fragmentation of markets. As many consumer products reached maturity in the late 1970s and early 1980s, manufacturers began to purposely fragment markets through segmentation, as a means of obtaining growth. In effect, manufacturers 'demassified the market' (Achenbaum 1992). The development of niche marketing, where products are aimed at limited segments of consumers, resulted in making traditional advertising more wasteful and less effective. Having said this, it is likely that traditional advertising will continue to have a role in building brands, while direct marketing, using a variety of channels, will be used to communicate different, detailed messages to specific individuals and groups of individuals.

The dramatic shift in the balance of power within the traditional marketing channel, from manufacturers to retailers (McGoldrick 1990) has also increased manufacturers' desire to communicate directly with their target audience. Retailers are no longer simply distributors, and through the growth of own-label brands, they now represent serious competition for manufacturers in a variety of product categories. This has also added to the proliferation of products and services available to consumers, further complicating consumer choice. Retailers have utilized their unique position within the channel to profile their customers and detail and record purchasing behaviour. At the same time they have inhibited access to consumers for many manufacturer brands through the reduction of available shelf space. As a result, many marketers need to find more direct methods of reaching their customers. Indeed, many consumer goods companies now use direct marketing (through customer clubs and couponing) as a way of supporting retailers and increasing their shelf space.

Market fragmentation has increased the wastefulness of traditional advertising. This has had the effect of making direct marketing's targetability a very attractive proposition. Whether 'demassification' of markets occurred as a result of changes in the composition and behaviour of society, manufacturers' segmentation strategies, or the development of retailer power, remains unclear. The most likely scenario is that 'demassification' is a consequence of all three. To combat the situation, many companies have now begun to reorganise on the basis of markets rather than products in order to overcome some of the problems of excessive segmentation. For example, Apple Computers is now reorganized on the basis of its three primary markets – business, education, and consumers.

The Advent Of Sophisticated Consumers Who Value Convenience
The growth of direct marketing was also greatly influenced by changes in the way people purchase products. The increasing incidence of women in the workforce, growing work commitments and the pursuit of leisure interests meant that consumers constantly found their time restricted. In order to satisfy the demands placed on their time, many shoppers began to buy through direct media as outlined earlier. Furthermore, they began to seek information from companies either via mail or phone, rather than by visiting the company's premises in

person. Such behaviour was encouraged and facilitated by vast improvements in customer service provision.

The convenience of direct marketing was enhanced by the advent of the cashless society. Consumers moved from carrying out mainly cash transactions to using credit and debit cards, and direct marketing was in the ideal position to take advantage. This was due largely to the ease with which such transactions could now take place, either via mail, telephone, fax, or more recently via home computer and modem. Moreover, deregulation of the financial services industry resulted in intense competition, with service development and direct marketing being used in the fight for competitive advantage. Initially, it took a lot to convince the financial services market of the merits of direct marketing. Companies questioned who would consider buying their services through the post. Yet now they are the second biggest users of the medium. The success of financial services direct marketing has much to do with modern consumer sophistication and the search for greater convenience. Vernons, a subsidiary of the Ladbrokes Group Plc, decided to sell insurance by direct mail when an independent survey revealed that 43 per cent of men would rather do housework than shop for insurance. The company believed that consumers who bought through the new medium would no longer view buying insurance as an intimidating or wearisome experience.

Declining Effectiveness Of Traditional Media

Lord Leverhulme of Unilever, the Anglo-Dutch consumer product giant, is reputed to have said 'I know that half the money I spend on advertising is wasted, but I can never find out which half.' Few marketers were excessively concerned with this issue while markets grew, disposable income increased and the consumer hungered for new products. However, the consumer marketplace has changed. It is now crowded, many product categories are saturated, and few opportunities exist for growth. The increasing costs of advertising, combined with diminishing audiences, have forced marketers to confront the problem of marketing inefficiencies. There are four broad areas of concern:

▶ economic factors;

▶ increasing media costs;

▶ diminishing audiences;

▶ clutter.

Economic Factors

Both the boom of the 1980s and the recession of the 1990s have contributed to the growth of direct marketing. Buoyant consumer spending, particularly in the latter part of the 1980s, was reflected in greater advertising expenditures generally. Companies that could not afford to keep pace looked to direct marketing, and to direct mail in particular, as a cost-effective alternative. Budget rich marketers also began to use direct marketing to supplement their existing communications strategies, as evidenced by the degree to which in-bound customer carelines became utilized.

The latest recession in the UK has brought with it a distinct air of consumer and company caution (*Marketing* 1992a). In order to induce consumer spending, companies have had to turn to more forthright means of communicating with their customers. The recessionary climate has also forced many companies to focus more on customer retention and to consider the 'lifetime value' of their customers (Payne 1993). Having recognised that advertising is less accountable, post-recession marketers are reluctant to invest without a solid return. This has brought the concept of relationship marketing, and the utility of direct marketing in maintaining relationships, to the fore.

Increasing Media Costs

Given that there was only a finite space available across the various media, competition among advertisers was fierce during the 1980s. This had the inevitable effect of driving costs upward. Increased printing costs have continued to push up the cover prices of magazines and newspapers, thereby reducing circulation and making them less attractive to advertisers. Although the advent of digital and satellite television and the separation of Channel 4 from ITV have helped to make television advertising in the UK more competitive (Pearman 1992), it remains an expensive business. Radio advertising, although relatively inexpensive, accounts for less than 5 per cent of all UK advertising spend, mainly because of questions regarding its effectiveness (Prager 1993). Factors such as these serve to make direct marketing that much more attractive.

Recession is in many ways responsible for growing concern among companies that marketing expenditure needs to show quantifiable returns. It is no longer acceptable to be unaware which half of the money spent on advertising is wasted. Companies have begun to demand accountability, and direct marketing is fortunate in that it can truly accommodate this demand. The ability to be measured, predominantly by tracking response inquiries and sales as a result of direct campaigns, is a distinct advantage which direct marketing has over other forms of promotion.

Diminishing Audiences

The cost effectiveness of traditional media was further reduced by diminishing audiences. Television, in particular, suffered from a reduction in reach and share of voice. Daily viewing of TV fell to 3.40 hours in 1991 from 3.77 hours in 1985. Commercial stations accounted for 1.78 hours down from 2.04 hours over the same period (DMIS 1995). The introduction of the video recorder and the remote control has meant that customers can now limit their exposure to commercial breaks (Kitchen 1986). Furthermore, audiences are becoming fragmented as numerous satellite and cable TV channels become available, national radio stations are forced to compete with local commercial stations, and there is a burgeoning in the availability of different newspapers and magazines.

Clutter

> ❧ *Mass-marketing or segment based advertising is highly unfocused. It reaches millions of non-customers and the messages are untargeted, resulting in high advertising costs and questionable sales effects.* ❧ (Blattberg and Glazer 1994)

As the amount of non-programme material grows, much of which holds no interest for consumers, the problem of advertising clutter will intensify. The average duration of each advertisement is falling with the result that more companies are vying for the customer's attention but spending less time doing so. Clutter is also increasingly problematic in press advertisements. Consequently, in order for an individual company to stand out, the method of communication it utilises must free the message from immediate competition. Direct marketing is seen to overcome the difficulties posed by clutter, as the message is free from direct competition at least for a short period of time.

The Ability To Improve Targeting

Against this despairing background of increasing costs, media proliferation and market fragmentation, the development and constant improvement of technology suitable for use in direct communications was the 'get out of jail card' for many marketers. Instead of marketing products indiscriminately to fuzzy segments of the population, marketers could now speak directly to individuals. In effect, the 'shotgun' of mass advertising had been replaced by the 'rifle' of the database. These movements in technology are typified by the following:

▶ the rise of the database;

▶ improvements in capacity;

▶ analytical systems;

▶ desk-top publishing;

▶ developments in telephone technology.

The Rise of the Database
One of the most influential events in terms of industry growth has been the sensational reduction in the cost of collecting, holding, and using customer data. Utilising technology became cost-effective as a result of the significant cost reductions in computing hardware and enhanced processing capabilities that were developed. Marketing databases became more widespread and have provided the most significant impetus to industry growth. Indeed, today's direct marketers see the database as a vital element in their communications strategies. In fact,

to many the two are inseparable, with the terms 'direct' and 'database' marketing often being used interchangeably. The use of a database allows companies to gather huge amounts of data on individual customer needs and preferences. Database marketing provides companies with four distinct abilities (Vavra 1992):

▶ *Addressability* – being able to identify every customer and reach each one on an individual basis. This could also be referred to as targetability.

▶ *Measurability* – knowing exactly what and where every customer purchased, along with his or her purchase history.

▶ *Flexibility* – having the opportunity to appeal to different customers in different ways at different times.

▶ *Accountability* – having precise figures on the gross profitability of any marketing event and qualitative data showing the type of customers who participated.

On this basis, database marketing is:

> ❝ *the ability to use the vast potential of today's computers and telecommunication technology in driving customer-orientated programmes in a personalised, articulated and cost-effective manner.* ❞ (Rapp and Collins 1987)

Databases can be compiled in-house or, alternatively, they may be purchased from any number of database suppliers. While the move from manual files to computer files greatly increased the amount of information which could be stored on customers, and facilitated easier access to data, the technology was initially inflexible. However, the introduction of relational databases, and reductions in the cost of holding and using information, have greatly enhanced the propensity for data manipulation (Fletcher 1990). Additionally, there is increasing pressure upon companies to invest, simply because competitors are doing so. It is already clear that many consumer-goods firms are investing heavily in databases. Kraft, the food division of Philip Morris Inc., has addresses of 30 million customers culled from free sample offers and other promotions, whilst Unilver has centralised all of the customer data held by its British subsidiaries.

Information held on databases can provide an important input into creative strategy, with even the simplest piece of information facilitating greater targeting precision. Using the database for a direct campaign can radically increase the effectiveness of that campaign. By accessing the data held, companies are able to identify those consumers with whom a relationship is held. Proper utilisation of this information can lead to increased response rates for the campaign. Scotland Direct is a group of mail order companies specialising in Scottish crafts, gourmet foods, and collectibles. The company is a successful example of effective database marketing. Having perfected the database, which now holds information on over 200,000 customers on its files, it uses this database, not just for storage and mailings, but also for analysing and measuring response rates to different products and approaches.

The ability to layer names, addresses, purchasing behaviour, geodemographic and lifestyle information all together onto one record allows companies to build a comprehensive picture of consumers. Database linking occurs on two levels. First, on an industry level, census data, geodemographics and lifestyle data build up a broad picture of the population, ideal for segmentation purposes. Second, at the individual company level, matching this data to credit history, actual purchasing behaviour, media response, and the recency, frequency, and monetary (RFM) value of purchases, can create pretty detailed pictures of an organisation's customers.

Over £500 million a year is spent on marketing databases, as more and more companies embrace database marketing and customer care continues to zoom up the corporate agenda. Without a database to manage it, maintaining contact with customers becomes random and less effective.

Improvements In Capacity

Marketers have for some time yearned to develop tighter targeting in the search for increased profits. This was partly recession-induced and partly a recognition of the lifetime value of customers. Whether the objective was to build relationships with new prospects, or enhance existing customer relationships, marketers became hungry for customer information. Technology provided part of the answer, particularly because of increased data processing and analysis capabilities. Increasing processing capacity led to one of the most data rich sources to emerge in the last 20 years. This was the geodemographic classification system, initially based only on census information and later supplemented with other data. The term *geodemographics* describes the combination of geographic and demographic data to profile individuals. In short, geodemographics is a targeting system, based on the theory that where someone lives says a lot about their lifestyles and the types of products and services they buy (this is something that thieves have always known). Essentially, geodemographics attempt to describe people by where they live, which is represented by their postcode. Richard Webber developed the first geodemographic data system in 1979 for government purposes, and its first commercial application was based on the 1981 census. This has subsequently resulted in a proliferation of 'geodemographic' databases, supplied by specialised companies, which generate customer typologies based on postcode data and demographics. Marketers now have information on all households. Admittedly, names and addresses cannot be revealed from the census by the OPCS; however, the statistics for enumeration districts can be revealed. Such data can be linked with the postal code database (there is one postcode for approximately 16 households) and with the electoral register, and ultimately it may be possible to identify individual households and their characteristics. More sophisticated consumer typologies later emerged from the 1991 census.

Another significant data source for information hungry marketers emerged in the mid-1980s in the form of lifestyle data. Again, the potential was unlocked by the increasing capabilities of computers to analyse vast amounts of data. In contrast to geodemographic data which is based on aggregate census data, lifestyle data is based on questionnaires completed by individuals on their personal character-istics and purchasing behaviour. Since its inception, many companies have entered the field, and a number of specialist lifestyle databases have been launched onto the commercial market.

Although initially perceived as being in competition, a spirit of co-operation developed between geodemographics and lifestyle database suppliers. From a client perspective, the synergy which resulted in combining both approaches soon became apparent. The major limitation of both approaches is that they do not necessarily deal with known individuals. Their enormous potential is unleashed only when combined with actual data on individual known consumers. Thus internal data sources based on the behaviour of known customers or prospects was all that was needed to make the marketers' dream come true.

The marketers' dream has indeed come true! Although it has always been perceived that retailers, of all the channel members, are closest to customers, they could not know each of their customers as individuals. During the 1980s as more and more high-street retailers began to offer credit, they began to amass data on customers' purchasing behaviour. However, the primary use of databases at that time was to record data for credit and not marketing purposes. More recently the capacity of databases has allowed data to be recorded on a much greater scale, and in much greater detail.

Retailers are the most recent and probably the most sophisticated users of individual level behavioural data. Having developed a system where customers would voluntarily provide purchasing details through card-based loyalty schemes, retailers can combine geodemographic, lifestyle and behavioural data to build an accurate picture of a customer's behaviour. This can be used for store location and merchandising decisions, for manipulating customer behaviour, and for cross-selling. Indeed, many retailers have utilized their databases to offer financial services to their customers (e.g. Marks & Spencer and Sainsbury's).

Analytical Systems
In addition to database technology, developments in sophisticated analytical and visual techniques have further enhanced targeting efforts. The technology now exists, not only to access data, but also to analyse it. Geographic Information Systems (GIS) – specifically designed to access, manage and link geographical data and to visualise the spatial patterns inherent in many sets of data – represent the most important framework for the handling of geographic information since the invention of the map. Since postcode data is widely used in database management, GIS are clearly an important contribution. For example, Geopin 2 launched in 1983 by Pinpoint Analysis had the ability to analyse consumers and their purchasing habits; it could

cross-reference datasets with census information, road maps or standard industry research. The system had many applications including the identification of the most appropriate location for a new retail store. This would be based on retailers' knowledge of the geodemographic profile of its more successful stores. Using a GIS, the retailer could ask the computer to identify all of the areas in the country where this geodemographic profile exists. These locations could then be displayed on screen. Databases holding information on road networks or competitor locations can also be included, providing the decision maker with a visual analysis of the opportunities. Similarly, a GIS could identify the locations of all the company's customers based on their postcode data. The analytical potential of GIS is enormous. The falling costs of such systems has led to the development of specialist in-house systems, and today many of the UK's larger retailers have their own GIS department, where employees can access internal databases, analyse that data based on a number of external data sources including geodemographics and lifestyle, and use their GIS to predict the outcomes of various courses of action. Responses to direct mail campaigns can be displayed on screen, as can replies to direct response advertisements.

Furthermore, the wide availability of advanced statistical techniques, such as logistic regression and discriminant analysis, and the development of neural networks (which search, like the human brain, for patterns in a mass of data), have improved the marketer's ability to optimize customer response by using internal database information. For a mailing for the World Wildlife Fund (WWF), the starting point was a list of 2.4 million seemingly appropriate names. The modelling which was carried out prior to the mailing reduced this list to 1.4 million people. Although expensive, the modelling more than paid for itself with improved response rates. The model is continually refined based on the analysis of previous mailings in order to improve cost-per-response. This is important because the more accurately a company targets, the more it can spend per individual mailing and in this way, higher response rates can be achieved. Porsche's database contained around 30 000 names, 20 000 of which were current Porsche owners. In an attempt to make more use of the database, a modelling system was utilized to target 1 000 top executives with a mailer. The pack included a video, and the objective was to tempt prospects to test-drive the new £70,000 928GTS. The additional spend per individual mailing resulted in the company's targets being surpassed.

Relational databases, GIS systems, and sophisticated analytical tools have therefore combined to improve the targeting ability of direct communications, and in this way have fuelled industry growth. Technology continues to improve while costs continue to fall. As a result, an increasing number of companies are gaining access to this sophisticated and cost effective technology.

Desk-Top-Publishing (DTP)

In June 1985 a revolutionary new technology, desk-top-publishing, was introduced to the market. This advancement was to have a terrific effect on the direct marketing industry, as it greatly facilitated the production of quality publications for marketing purposes, in-house. Once the initial investment in training and equipment had been made, companies were able to significantly reduce their costs while maintaining the quality of their direct marketing output.

Developments in Telephone Technology

The potential of the telephone as a customer service and information dissemination tool was largely ignored until the mid 1980s. Although used to a limited extent for *outbound telemarketing* as a sales tool, inbound calls were not encouraged, as companies could not cope either in terms of the capacity of their telephone systems, or staffing requirements. However, as a result of advances in telecommunications and data management, the telephone has come to be recognised as a strategic business tool. Telecoms can now link departments, sites and even suppliers in a dynamic information network. One of the already noticeable benefits is the apparently effortless ability to transfer calls between remote sites. This has facilitated the use of the growing numbers of call handling agencies. High volumes of in-bound traffic can be successfully handled either using an external agency or using an automated call distributor (ACD). Some of these have an interactive voice response (IVR) facility. This allows callers to choose between a menu of options using touch tones on their phones. Before the advent of computer-based interactive response handling mechanisms, in-bound calls using freephone numbers and trained operators cost between £1 to £3 each, depending on the size and rate of response. Technology has halved these costs, clearly making the medium more accessible to smaller companies without access to large budgets.

Consumers were also seen to be reluctant to use the telephone for inbound calls because of the costs involved. However, a revolution in *inbound telemarketing* occurred in 1985 when British Telecom launched LinkLine and Callstream services. BT's LinkLine, incorporating 0800 (free) and 0345 (local) numbers, and Mercury's 0500 Freecall, encouraged increased use of such services by advertisers, and promoted acceptance among consumers (Young 1994). The overall impact of such developments was a growth of 40 per cent per annum in telemarketing usage for the remainder of the decade.

Although after its launch BT's LinkLine was generating 12 million calls in 1991, vast potential remained untapped. Less than 10 per cent of UK television advertising carried a phone number compared with 54 per cent in the USA. The biggest problem lay in handling the number of inbound calls which peak immediately after the ad is broadcast. The computerized response mechanisms outlined above alleviated this problem resulting in exponential growth of the medium since 1992. More recently this has been enhanced by the provision of additional information on Teletext. For example, Tropical Places invites callers to get additional information on teletext, before booking a holiday via the Freephone number. Similarly, in an advert, British beef viewers are invited to consult Teletext for a set of recipes.

Sun Express's Multilingual Station

From its tele-centre in the Netherlands, Sun Express handles in the region of 11 000 calls a month. These calls are currently taken in four different languages and come from the UK, France, Germany, Switzerland, and the Netherlands itself. Coverage will soon extend even further as Sweden is included.

Operations at the centre involve taking orders and enquiries from consumers, with regard to the computer peripherals offered by parent company, Sun Microsystems. These enquiries are generated by a direct mail campaign which encourages consumers to dial a telephone number in their home country, free of charge. These calls are then automatically routed to the tele-centre in the Netherlands. At this stage the calls pass through a computerised call-distribution system, linking the consumer with an operator speaking in the same language.

A further computer link with Sun Microsystems's distribution centre in the US, means that once an order is taken, delivery is guaranteed within five days. On receiving confirmation of the shipment, an invoice is produced back in the Netherlands.

The system has enabled the high-value workstation salesforce to concentrate on their main area of business, as enquiries regarding peripherals are handled by the tele-centre. It has also improved the company's performance in the peripherals market.

(Source: *Marketing* 1994b)

Changes In Market Information

Given the changes already outlined in the composition and behaviour of markets, it becomes more and more important that marketers have access to detailed, accurate and up-to-date information. Significant technological developments have revolutionised the ability to acquire more timely and accurate information, often at individual customer level. These developments include:

► electronic point of sale;

► smart cards;

► more sophisticated consumer research;

► service provision.

Electronic Point of Sale (EPoS)

Widespread acceptance by retailers of point-of-sale technology has resulted from technological developments which led to smaller, faster, and more reliable EPoS (Electronic Point of Sale) terminals. There has also been a parallel development in the area of product codes which are standardized between manufacturers, distributors, and retailers. The

European Article Number (EAN) is compatible with the Universal Product Code (UPC) in the USA. Thus, it is possible for any retailer with an EPoS system to access product purchasing data. More importantly, this data can be downloaded daily producing a wealth of market information. The marketing application of bar-codes (EAN/UPC) in retailing includes the ability to record who buys what. One system currently being used by Asda is Catalina. Essentially, Catalina monitors every purchase scanned at the till and will print out a coupon based on individual purchases. Therefore, if a consumer has bought Pepsi the system can immediately print out a coupon for a competing brand such as Coke. Other applications include producing incentives for multipurchase and for related category buying. Catalina is thus highly targeted and very precise, and provides detailed information on individual purchases for Asda's database. One limitation of the Catalina system is that it does not recognise who the customer is, merely that they have bought certain products, which then trigger the coupon. While Asda's was one of the first systems on the market, the more recent loyalty programmes such as Tesco's Clubcard are capable of matching purchases with individuals. Coupons are not delivered at the point of sale, but later through direct mail in the home.

Smart Cards

Smart cards are essentially credit-card-sized cards with a computer chip embedded on them. They can read, write and store information, and form a link between the cardholder and the organisation's central computer. Gone are the days when consumers had to keep till receipts in order to take part in promotions. Now it's simply a matter of using the smart card and the computer takes care of the rest. The information provided through the use of the card allows an operator, such as a shop or bank, to communicate in an individual fashion with all of its customers and gather more information on them at the same time.

Smart cards offer immense opportunities for marketers. They can be used for customer loyalty schemes, database, and direct marketing and the possibilities they offer are limited only by the imagination. Shell launched a smart card scheme in 1994, and although it is only using 10 per cent of its capacity, the card still allows Shell to run its incentive scheme and build a comprehensive customer database. Shell believe that it will be possible at a later stage to use the card for direct or credit payments, telecoms facilities and even for interactive shopping purposes. Although the smart card is far more expensive to produce than conventional storecards, it does have a greater capacity and far more potential. Despite this, it has, as yet, achieved limited uptake among consumers.

More Sophisticated Consumer Research

Consumer panel research has been revolutionized in recent years. In the past, set meters were used within consumer panels to study TV audiences. The major drawback of such systems were that they were notoriously inaccurate. Technological improvements have meant that collection of this type of data is easier and much more accurate. New set meters are currently being used in the US which reduce the amount of effort required from panel members and also reduce the likelihood of inaccuracies (Evans and Mouthino 1992). Together with modern scanning technology, these meters allow individual household media and purchasing habits to be studied in increasingly detailed, reliable and even individual ways.

Service Provision
Ten years ago there were only three or four specialist direct marketing agencies in the UK; now there are well over 50. In addition, many mainstream agencies have expanded their operations and are now able to offer direct marketing expertise. However, many companies have developed their own in-house direct marketing departments or, where the investment does not warrant a full direct marketing team, a smaller team is used to co-ordinate the use of several specialist suppliers. The phenomenal growth in supplier services has made this a viable option.

Trends, Prospects and Challenges for UK Direct Marketing

Direct marketing has been growing rapidly in the UK since 1980. It is now considered to be among the most sophisticated in Europe, primarily because of the quality of its postal and telecommunications services.

Direct Mail

Throughout the 1980s, the impetus for market growth was provided by the direct mail sector. Between 1988 and 1990, expenditure on direct mail increased by 75 per cent, an increase which has since been sustained, albeit at a slower rate. In 1996 3.173 billion items were mailed in the UK at a cost of £1.4 billion. The recent growth of direct mail is largely accounted for by non-traditional users such as FMCG companies. Core sectors also increased mailings with mail order up 8 per cent to 859 million, and banks up 25 per cent to 264 million (*Marketing Direct* 1997). However, the majority of direct mail is still prospecting in nature, with only approximately 13 per cent sent as a result of requests from customers (Henley Centre 1995). Direct mail will continue to be important in the future. Of the UK's top 1500 companies 83 per cent envisage direct mail being integrated into their advertising strategies in the future. However, it is clear that direct mail has lost its dominance as the range of media available to direct marketing increases.

Telemarketing

Since 1990, industry growth has been driven by increases in the market value of telemarketing and door-to-door distribution (Keynote

1994). The growth in telemarketing may be due in part to the increasing use of in-bound systems by companies, and by the fact that telemarketing has traditionally been underutilized in this country.

According to the 1996 DMA census, telemarketing now accounts for an expenditure of £1175 million. In general, outbound telemarketing is most apparent in the business-to-business sector. It is commonly believed that consumers in this country (as opposed to the US) are not receptive to unsolicited sales calls interrupting their family meals or favourite TV show. Clearly, there are those companies who do not agree – in particular kitchen and double-glazing sales people – and it is many of these who have given the sector a bad name.

Inbound telemarketing will continue to grow much faster than its outbound counterpart, fuelled in particular by customer carelines, and direct response advertising. Furthermore, the role of automated inbound call handling will become increasingly important as technology advances, and consumers show increasing willingness to talk to answering devices (*Marketing* 1992b).

Door-To-Door

Household distribution has been strongly criticized in the past as being largely a broadbrush medium. Now, however, postal areas can be effectively targeted using geodemographic classification. This improved targeting accuracy has encouraged companies to use the medium. Statistics derived from the BMSSB's monitoring show that households receive twice as much unaddressed letterbox advertising as direct mail (Titford 1994). In 1992-93 the relative figures were an average of 10.4 unaddressed items and 4.1 direct mail pieces per month. The medium is now enjoying rapid growth because of lower costs relative to mail, and the 1994 figure for expenditure on the medium was £180 million. BCA (book club) used household distribution for the first time in 1993. The campaign exceeded the objectives set, and resulted in an impressive 15 per cent cost reduction per recruit in comparison to direct mail. More recently some TV ads, instead of carrying a telephone number are asking audiences to look out for imminent leaflet drops. Thus, household distribution is likely to continue to play an important role in the future.

Direct Response

Direct Response advertising has also experienced exceptional growth in the last few years. A 1995 DMIS survey found that 90 per cent of all advertising in print media carried a direct response mechanism (DMIS 1995). In addition, the DMA census estimates that direct response TV commercials accounted for £398 million in expenditure. On this basis, direct marketing is becoming increasingly important to the mainstream media. In 1989, British direct marketers were responsible for 18 per cent of press and TV ad revenue. By 1992, this figure had risen to 28 per cent, more than a quarter of the total.

In support of more widespread utilisation, TGI found that nearly 35 per cent of the UK population had made telephone calls as a result of advertisements seen on TV and in the press over the previous 12 months (Young 1994). Direct response advertising is clearly set to grow. As more commercial airtime becomes available over the next few years, through satellite and cable, there will be more scope for reaching tightly defined audiences at highly competitive rates. QVC the shopping channel is already available within the UK, and has paved the way for further industry growth.

Some industry experts claim that the cost-per-enquiry (CPE) ratio of DRTV makes it very attractive *vis à vis* other media. DRTV is clearly the biggest success story so far, and combines the image building impact of TV, with the personalized and measurable advantages of direct marketing. Although currently handled by existing agencies, it may become a truly specialized service in the future.

The Information Superhighway

The electronic superhighway has been hailed as being the biggest advance in media since the invention of the television. It could create a radical change in retailing, distribution of brands and access to services. The information superhighway is simply an infrastructure that allows high-speed access to incredible amounts of information, and facilitates data sharing. A 200-strong company survey carried out by 3Com in Britain during 1994, found that 68 per cent of managing directors were unclear as to what the information superhighway was, and yet 64 per cent believed it could help them improve their businesses (*Computer Buyer* 1994). The information superhighway may play an increasingly important role in direct marketing as many services move on-line, and the possibility of interactive advertising becomes a reality. The value of the information superhighway has been realised to some extent through the widespread use of Internet sites by a variety of different organisations.

Integrated Marketing Communications (IMC)

Direct marketing has experienced rapid growth. While some of this growth is within traditional 'mail-order' companies, much has come from organisations that have traditionally relied on mass media advertising. Indeed, 'mass marketing advertisers are now very enthusiastic about direct marketing, so much so that it has already ceased to be shock news if an FMCG company of the stature of Heinz announces its intention to beef up below-the-line' (Dwek 1995). These companies have not completely abandoned traditional media, but rather began to include direct media in their communications repertoire. The strategic use of different communications and marketing techniques has become known as integrated marketing communications (IMC).

A simple description of integrated marketing communications is: selling with a consistent voice and message. A more thorough definition is provided by the American Association of Advertising Agencies:

> ❧ *A concept of marketing communications planning that recognises the added value in a programme that integrates a variety of strategic disciplines, e.g. general advertising, direct response, sales promotion and public relations – and consistency and maximum communication impact.* ❧

There are many reasons that IMC has become popular. For example, as we identified earlier, it is often very difficult to measure the return on investment from traditional advertising. Equally, there is greater emphasis today on customizing communication to achieve different objectives in different target markets. Marketers have recognised the implications of this (Stewart 1996):

▶ there will be different costs associated with reaching particular customers;

▶ there will likely be a differential return on investing in these customers.

Both of these principles have long been recognised by direct marketers, and the ability of direct marketing to measure the associated costs and returns has indeed been one of the reasons for its increasing success. But IMC is more than simply measurability. Consumers absorb information from many different sources, and to avoid inconsistent images, the whole of marketing and communications needs to generate a consistent image and voice. As such, a good IMC programme focuses first on the consumer, and then the communication is assessed in terms of the consumer response it generates (Schultz 1996).

IMC thus represents the integration of different strategic disciplines to create a coherent strategy. 'IMC planners attempt to identify the best times, places, or situations where marketing communications are most likely to reach different target audiences' (Englis and Solomon 1996:184).

What The Future Holds

In view of the tremendous success experienced so far by the industry, one would clearly expect growth to continue. Indeed, the European Commission believed that direct marketing expenditure in Europe would exceed that of above-the-line advertising by 1998. The trend is already moving away from direct marketing as a stand-alone tactical element of the promotions mix towards integration and a more strategic role. The move toward direct response has dual benefits: it will facilitate more accurate targeting as a result of requests from consumers, thereby reducing 'junk' mailings and it will allow marketers to move from prospecting to relationship building, an approach which will require a totally integrated marketing and communications mix. Companies will need to relate their communications and actual consumer behaviour, as opposed to relying on inferential data such as geodemographics or psychographics, as they have done in the past.

Traditionally, direct marketing has been presented as an inexpensive alternative to above-the-line communications. However, this is unlikely to be the perception in the future. Targeting will clearly need to improve and in order to be effective, companies will need to build a database; a sizeable investment both in terms of time and money. Research indicates that lower than average response rates occur with cheaply produced mailings (DMIS 1995) and therefore costs are likely to escalate as higher response rates are sought. Indeed, in 1996 there was a 34 per cent increase in production costs, reflecting the improved quality of mailings (*Marketing Direct* 1997). The move to integrated marketing communications and direct response mechanisms also implies that marketers will continue to bear the costs of traditional above-the-line approaches (although perhaps at reduced rates due to the choice of off-peak slots).

The current trends indicate that direct marketing can no longer be considered cost-effective if it is merely a tactical appendage to a company's communication policy. Successful companies will truly attempt to build relationships through increased use of direct response mechanisms, investment in in-house databases, and integration of the whole marketing communication mix with the company's total offerings. This approach is more likely to facilitate future growth and acceptance of direct marketing.

STUDY 1

First Direct

The Immaculate Conception

Integration is defined thus:

... combine parts into whole; bring or come into equal membership of society ...

Under the traditional marketing banner it is very rare that the various parts that go to make up a campaign ever come together as a whole, and even more unlikely is that their status and input within any one campaign will be doled out in equal measures.

For integration to work well it is therefore logical that the entire marketing process should be approached afresh, from the very beginning.

The First Direct campaign was an ideal candidate for an integrated approach, being entirely new and original, with no previous image or track record. Jan Smith was initially appointed marketing director of Project Raincloud – the codename under which the First Direct project was conceived. In taking on the position she found herself facing the challenge of not just one, but two unknown quantities:

1 A brand new briefing for a brand new company.

2 A totally new concept.

If the project worked, it was going to revolutionise both the consumer vision of the telephone as a commercial tool, and the traditional concept of the high street bank.

Smith decided to take the brave route – an unusual kind of bank called for an unusual kind of promotion. Her first steps toward building this new vision were to work closely with Paul Jarvis of Wolfe Olins on the brand positioning, brand personality and corporate identity of the bank. Jarvis then worked with Smith and Sean Perkins (also of Wolfe Olins) to conceive the striking, minimalist, black and white images that are so firmly associated with First Direct. The name of the bank was also established at this point, giving the team a strong identity to work with, and finally enabling them to set the level of Midland Bank endorsement the new venture required. These decisions made, the team were free to work through the initial formalities with the Bank of England.

Smith was then ready to set about the

● ● ▶

process of 'cherry-picking' the team that she wanted to work with. Rather than going for a 'One-Stop-Shop' agency, who could handle the entire campaign 'under one roof' she opted for an entirely different selection procedure.

Inviting a number of specialist agencies from each marketing sphere to pitch for the business, she decided to plump for the advertising firm first. Having selected HHCL (Howell Henry Chaldecott and Lury), she then included representatives from the agency in the pitches from the direct marketing agencies. Together they selected Option One, as their direct marketing team. In a similar manner, the Quentin Bell Organisation was chosen to handle the PR, while the Media Business, who were to play in the planning and strategy of the campaign, were chosen as the media buyers.

What Smith was aiming to achieve was a commitment to the new company. This selection of the team *by* the team meant that a strong chemistry was experienced by the various agencies from the outset.

Allowing all the individuals involved to have some input into the final decision resulted in a team that actively wanted to work together. Smith was also aware that a meeting of unfamiliar minds and fresh faces would spark a huge flow of diverse creative input, giving the team a good chance of creating just the unusual approach she was looking for.

The fact that all the teams were largely unfamiliar to one another individually also meant that the potential 'One-Stop-Shop' clash of personalities with old axes to grind was avoided. Therefore the focus would be on the campaign, and not on point-scoring.

From this point onward Smith insisted that every single instance of communication and interaction was important. She arranged for every member of the team to be present at regular weekly meetings, during which the current situation and day-to-day business of running the campaign was officially reviewed. These also gave the team the chance to hold any presentations of new work, and discuss

them as a unit. To complement the weekly meetings the key senior team members also gathered at a strategic meeting once a fortnight.

With the agencies selected, and the working processes in place, the time had come for the whole team to sit down with the new vision, brand positioning and identity in front of them and begin to develop a strategy. The overriding need was to establish the brand and concept behind the new bank. The strategy was to run in three almost distinct stages: First to achieve a spectacular launch, secondly to build a strong brand identity, and finally to actively start to recruit customers when stages one and two had been completed. A six month time-frame was specifically set-aside to build the brand before turning to more conventional routes to promote banking products and services.

During the entire decision-making process Smith acted as a referee to the discussions. She wisely recognised that each agency would have its own vision for the campaign, and each was liable to speak out strongly for the way in which they saw the new bank being best represented.

Smith allowed every member of the team to have their head at strategic points, and to push for their side of the argument, thus ensuring that the creative potential of each individual was brought to the forefront and that all potential approaches were considered. However, anyone becoming too dominant was brought back to the main body of the debate, rather than being left to overwhelm the discussions. Integration's main stumbling block is the reality that any one campaign will usually contain several overwhelming personalities who, inevitably, dominate. Smith's action as a good mediator defines one of the fundamental building blocks behind the success of the First Direct Campaign.

The team decided that, in order to get over their point that this was a new kind of banking concept, they would need a new kind of promotion. They didn't simply want to say 'We're different' – it literally had to *be* different.

Advertisements for banking services traditionally have a very defined, safe format in keeping with the way they assume people like to feel about their banks. First Direct went for a unique approach. The initial advertisements were therefore to be intentionally designed to provoke and gain attention – to make the audience ask 'What the hell is all this about?'

The ground-rule for any good integrated campaign is to find one strong, simple idea as a peg to hang the whole campaign on. Having discarded the 'We're different' approach as not different enough, the team opted for a very simple solution; the bank would have no strap-line, or at least not in the traditional sense. Instead they made the telephone number their trademark. This was designed to make people think and then pick up the telephone, and it worked. This being secured, the team set about defining next steps in the campaign.

Details of the launch were kept under wraps so well that the entire body of journalists present at the first official press conference were under the impression that they were there for the launching of a new Midland Switch card. Considering the large number of agencies involved in the project, and the ease with which one of them could have let something slip out, this is a remarkable further demonstration of the loyalty that was shown to the project by all involved.

The first target – creating attention-grabbing intriguing ads – had already been achieved. Next followed the role of the public relations. This also received an unusual treatment, the PR role being solely to support and echo the advertising. They planned to literally talk *about the ads*, discussing and explaining the totally new concept and taking it out into the national media and other supporting media. There was a real need to do this, because the banking concept itself was so new – no branches and 24 hour service was a huge departure from the norm. Vast research into the number of customer visits to branches had conclusively persuaded the team that

● ● ▶

the concept could be successful, but they still had a serious re-education job to do on the public – especially as several banks had started telephone banking systems that relied on automated voice activated systems, and these had been received unenthusiastically. Explaining the concept that this was a one-to-one genuine personal banking service was a major task. Therefore throughout the launch they sustained their plan to talk about the ads and nothing else.

Fitch & Co. were brought in to design the bank cards and the cheque books at this point, and a melding of their input and the black and white design put together by Paul Jarvis resulted in a striking product that has remained a trademark of the bank. Here, again, the First Direct team had managed to pull off the creation of a successful working relationship between two leading corporate identity firms, who should under any natural circumstances have been in direct competition with one another.

The ads themselves were unusual in their content (one TV ad featured a happy gent in a pink suit dancing around the Broadgate Centre alone and singing in a high-pitched voice – not the sort of image you would normally associate with banking services), and also in their delivery. The team used the concept of taking the audience forward into the future. To establish that this was a bank from the future the initial launch ad was set in 2010. The television suddenly started to fuzz as though the audience were receiving interference from another time. To enhance their futuristic vision the team then used the innovative notion of 'channel hopping' – so long the bane of advertisers – to their advantage. The Media Business, by using unprecedented tact and subtlety, managed to persuade ITV and Channel Four to cooperate in scheduling their ads to run simultaneously, meaning that First Direct could 'leak' from channel to channel. The ad running on ITV stating, 'If you're happy with your bank – fine. If you're not, switch to Channel 4 now!'

On changing channels the viewer was presented with a further ad for First Direct,

this time offering a direct response number to call. This number carried with it the staggering news that a bank was contactable 24 hours a day. Interactive channelling was being seen for the first time – the thought in itself had been creative, but actually managing to implement the process of co-ordinating two slots of ads on two different channels was a major feat. All banks were obviously not the same! Press ads (in the form of unusually folded 'tip-ons') and posters were designed by Option One to depict stills from the ad, and these went out in both the national papers, and in a very carefully targeted selection of magazines. A further run of 'image' based TV ads were also repeated in poster format and tip-ons. Both echoed the current advertising theme and also provided the direct response number. Therefore each medium played nicely off the other, increasing First Direct's exposure considerably.

During the initial burst of advertising activity the PR team were carefully 'leaking' news of the latest advertisements. This served two important purposes. The first was to provide the intended publicity. The second was to afford the team a chance to explain the rather way-out and intentionally thought-provoking advertisements to the media and public alike, thus guaranteeing that everyone understood what the bank were trying to achieve. All this promotional activity ensured that all eyes were glued to the advertising, gaining just the attention that First Direct was seeking. PR had yet another, more subtle, advantageous role to play. First Direct was bound legally to display in its advertisements the fact that they were affiliated to Midland Bank. The PR campaign, however, had no such restrictions placed upon it. The team were free to talk about First Direct in its sole identity as a new bank, thus helping to hold the endeavour up as an new concept in its own right – not as an add-on to an old system that they wanted to stand quite apart from.

By March 1990, the six-month brand-building period the team had set themselves was ending. Having captured the public's imagination and attention the team were poised to start recruiting customers for real

– a radical new concept had become a reality. When they felt satisfied that they had established their potential audience, the team were ready to hit the public with their sales promotion activity. Their ad campaign had defined an initial sample of interested parties and the team then continued to extend their ever-growing customer base on a member-get-member basis.

Recognising the vital role that internal communications had to play Smith specifically requested that the activities of the various disciplines, and the decisions they had taken, were compiled onto video – a project which was taken on by Willow. They kept a record of all the internal communication from the beginning of the campaign right through the entire launch and brand-building period, eventually building an internal employee's 'bible' from the information. Each agency that had been involved donated a piece for the project, explaining exactly what their involvement in the campaign had been, and how it had come together. This project was designed to keep everyone on the First Direct staff informed and interested, from start to finish – a task which Smith felt was vital for morale, as one chunk of the new staff were in Leeds, another was in London. She wanted to retain the air of involvement and oneness that she had worked so hard to build with the creative teams, and Willow's 'bible' and their following video allowed new employees to understand exactly what the process behind the building of the brand had been.

The First Direct launch was a model example of integration. The team was drawn together in a way that was designed to inspire absolute commitment from every member throughout the entire process.

This commitment has run from the original core to the end result, and has radiated out to touch every aspect of the company. It has undoubtedly been the cornerstone on which First Direct have built their outstanding reputation.

(Source: The Sitel Corporation)

Review Questions

1　What environmental factors resulted in the need for more effective targeting of marketing communications?

2　What technological developments have fuelled the growth of the direct marketing industry over the last 15 years or so?

3　Why have many FMCG companies, which have traditionally been heavy users of mass communications media, recently embraced direct marketing?

4　What kinds of marketing information are particularly important to direct marketers?

5　What sources of marketing data have emerged in recent years?

6　Explain what is meant by the following terms:

　(a)　geodemographics;
　(b)　geographical information system;
　(c)　automated call distributor;
　(d)　interactive voice response;
　(e)　the information superhighway.

7　Direct marketers now have a broad repertoire of media to choose from What trends are evident in the following media over the last 10 years?

　(a)　direct mail;
　(b)　telemarketing;
　(c)　door-to-door;
　(d)　direct response advertising.

Discussion Questions

1　Industry experts predict that the phenomenal growth currently being experienced by the UK industry is likely to continue unchecked into the future. What factors do you think might promote future growth? What factors might have an adverse impact upon future success?

2　What will be the future impact of the Internet on marketing communications?

3　Will direct marketing communication replace mass advertising in the coming years?

References

Achenbaum, A. (1992) 'The advertising environment of the nineties', *American Regional Managers Meeting*, Lincoln Centre, April 27.

Bauer, C. and Miglautsch, J. (1992) 'A Conceptual Definition of Direct Marketing', *Journal of Direct Marketing*, 6 (Spring), pp. 7–17, pp. 10–11.

Bird, D. (1993) *Commonsense Direct Marketing*, London, Kogan Page.

Blattberg, R. and Glazer, R. (1994) 'Marketing in the Information Revolution', *The Marketing*

Information Revolution, Blattberg, R. and Glazer, R. (eds.), Boston, Harvard Business School Press.

Computer Buyer (1994) 'What Superhighway?', October, p. 93.

DMIS (1995) *DMIS FACTBOOK*. Direct Mail Information Service, London.

Dwek, R. (1995) 'Positive Positioning', *Campaign*, July 7, p. 29.

The Economist (1995) 'How to turn junk mail into a goldmine – or perhaps not', 1 April, pp. 81–82.

Englis, B. and Solomon, M. (1996) 'Using Consumption Constellations to Develop Integrated Communications Strategies', *Journal of Business Research*, 37, pp. 183–91.

Evans, M.J. and Mouthino, L. (1992) *Applied Marketing Research*, Addison Wesley.

Evans, M.J., O'Malley, L. and Patterson, M. (1995) 'Direct marketing: rise and rise or rise and fall?', *Marketing Intelligence and Planning*, 13(6), pp. 16–23.

Evans, M.J., O'Malley, L. and Patterson, M. (1996) 'Direct Marketing Communications in the UK: A Study of Growth, Past, Present and Future', *Journal of Marketing Communications*, 2, pp. 51–65.

Fletcher, D., C. Wheeler and J. Wright (1991) 'Database Marketing: A Channel, A Medium, Or A Strategic Approach', *International Journal of Advertising*, 10, pp. 117–27.

Fletcher, K. (1990) *Marketing Management and Information Technology*, Prentice Hall.

Henley Centre (1995) *The DMA Census of the UK Direct Marketing Industry*, Henley Centre.

Keynote (1994) *Direct Report*, Keynote, London.

Kitchen, P. (1986) 'Zipping, Zapping and Nipping', *International Journal of Advertising*, 5, pp. 343–52.

Lindgren, J. and Shimp, T. (1996) *Marketing: An Interactive Learning System*, Florida, Harcourt Brace.

McCorkell, G. (1997) *Direct and Database Marketing*, London, Kogan Page.

McGoldrick, P. (1990) *Retail Marketing*, Maidenhead: McGraw Hill.

Marketing (1992a) 'The Miserable Life of the Careful Consumer', September 17, p. 9.

Marketing (1992b) 'Telemarketing Moving into the Future', February 13, p. 22.

Marketing (1994a) 'Souped-up for Direct Attack', 29 September, pp.18–19.

Marketing (1994b) 'Dial direct for marketing' August 25, pp. 26–32.

Marketing Direct (1997) 'Volume of Direct Mail Hits Three Billion Mark', March, 6.

Payne, D. (19??) 'Old Customers: Interesting New Profits – How to Grasp the Dynamics of Customer Service Marketing', *Admap*, July/August, pp. 35–7.

Pearman, C. (1992) 'Winning Ways with TV Buying', *Marketing*, July 16, p. 13.

Prager, I. (1993) 'The Media: New Opportunities Different Criteria', *Admap*, July/August, pp. 37–9.

Rapp, S. and Collins, T. (1987) *Maxi Marketing*, New York: McGraw Hill.

Schofield, A. (1995) 'The Definition of Direct Marketing: A Rejoinder to Bauer and Miglautsch' *Journal of Direct Marketing*, 9(2), Spring, pp. 32–8.

Schultz, D. (1996) 'The Inevitability of Integrated Communication', *Journal of Business Research*, 37, pp. 139–46.

Shimp, T.A. (1992) *Promotion Management and Marketing Communications*, 3rd edn, Fort Worth, TX: Dryden Press.

Sitel Corporation *A Guide to Integrated Marketing*. For a copy of the 'Guide' call the SITEL Communications Centre on (+44) 01789 200336.

Stewart, D. (1996) 'Market-Back Approach to the Design of Integrated Communications Programs: A Change in Paradigm Need a Focus on Determinants of Success', *Journal of Business Research*, 37, pp. 147–53.

Stewart Howe, W. (1992) *Retailing Management*, London, Macmillan.

Titford, P. (1994) 'Self Regulation in Direct Marketing', *Journal of Database Marketing*, Vol. 2, No.2, pp. 141–50.

Vavra, T. (1992) *Aftermarketing*, Homewood, IL: Irwin.

Young, M. (1994) 'Direct Response Television', *Journal of Targeting, Measurement and Analysis*, 2(2), pp. 125–38.

Further Reading

Bauer, C. and Miglautsch, J. (1992) 'A Conceptual Definition of Direct Marketing', *Journal of Direct Marketing*, 6 (Spring), pp. 7–17.

Meuller-Heumann, G. (1992) 'Market and Technology Shifts in the 1990s: Market Fragmentation and Mass Customisation', *Journal of Marketing Management*, Vol. 8 pp. 303–14.

Fletcher, D., Wheeler, C. and Wright, J. (1991) 'Database Marketing: A Channel, A Medium, Or A Strategic Approach', *International Journal of Advertising*, Vol. 10, pp. 117–27.

Rapp, S. and Collins, T. (1987) *Maxi Marketing*, New York: McGraw Hill.

Planning for Direct Marketing

This chapter:

▶ Introduces The Student To The
Importance Of Direct Marketing
Planning.

▶ Identifies The Stages In The Planning
Process.

C
H
A
P
T
E
R

2

Planning for Direct Marketing

❝ Plans are nothing, planning is everything ❞ (Eisenhower)

The Importance of Planning

The environment in which firms operate is exceedingly complex, and subject to rapid change. Within such an environment it may seem pointless to engage in planning. However, the purpose of planning is to reduce uncertainty, to assist in the identification of strategies which maximize strengths and opportunities, and minimize weaknesses and threats, to identify a coherent action plan, and to evaluate the effectiveness of the committed resources. On this basis, 'planning is essential when we consider the increasingly hostile and complex environment in which firms operate' (McDonald 1992:78). Thus direct marketing strategies must occur within well thought-out frameworks, and with the required resource allocation in place if they are to be successful.

Models of planning can be divided into roughly two types; the conventional and the alternative (Piercy and Giles 1989). The conventional view dominates popular texts and 'presents the process of planning as a logical, rational and sequential management activity' (Harris 1996). Direct marketers argue that conventional strategic planning models can be adapted to plan for direct marketing:

> ❝ The only differences are that the microchip has empowered us
> to consider customers at a micro, not just a macro, level and,
> even more importantly, to study the dynamics of customer
> relationships. ❞ (McCorkell 1997)

Essentially, the argument is that given the detailed level of knowledge about individual customers and their relationship to the organization which direct marketers possess, precise objectives can be developed which are then subject to rigorous measurement criteria. In this sense, the value of planning to direct marketers is perhaps greater than its value to strategic planners. Direct marketers can accurately measure

35

the success of their planning, and thus can identify their contribution to the profitability of the business. This in turn increases the legitimacy of direct marketing within the organization.

In putting together direct marketing plans it is important that managers ensure that they are easy to understand, that they are detailed and precise, that they are sufficiently flexible to allow for sudden changes in circumstance, that they are realistic given current resources and capabilities, that they cover all relevant market factors and that they clearly delineate the responsibilities of various members within the organization (Holder 1993a).

The Direct Marketing Planning Process

Various authors have identified what is involved in the planning process, although few would agree on the exact steps involved. Despite debate over the terminology or the number of steps involved, the process of planning is similar whether for the organization's strategic plan, the marketing plan, the communications plan, or even the direct marketing plan. We envisage the direct marketing planning process as consisting of 12 steps, which we call the Direct Marketing Planning Wheel (see Figure 2.1).

Although the process of direct marketing planning is presented here as sequential, this is over-simplified purely for pedagogic purposes. In reality, 'the process is highly iterative – requiring constant doubling

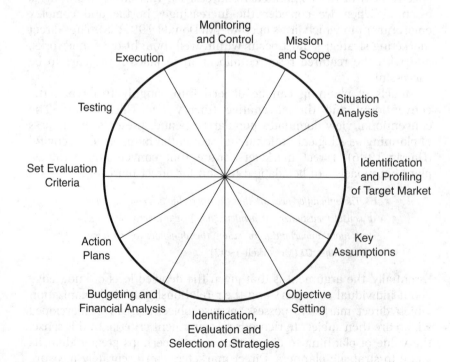

Figure 2.1 The Direct Marketing Planning Wheel

back to earlier parts of the situation assessment as new insights about customers, competitors and competencies are introduced, issues are clarified, and new strategic directions are contemplated' (Day 1984:66). Thus, although the process appears sequential, planners are likely to be involved in several stages simultaneously, and are free to alter earlier decisions based on more current analysis and information. That said, the written plan should deal with these headings within this logical sequence.

Mission and Scope

Mission and scope relate to the attitudes and expectations within the organization with regard to the business that the organization is in, how the organization rates against competition and how it fits in to its environment. Piercy (1992) divides mission analysis into two separate components: customer missions and key value missions. Customer missions focus on the customer needs which the organization aims to satisfy and the competitive domain in which the organization is going to operate. Key value missions on the other hand centre on what aspects of the business the organization deems important. Delineating the mission and scope of the organization is an important step in defining the market in which the organization operates. This in turn should go some way towards deciding who its customers are and how best it should go about satisfying customer needs.

Business Objectives

Business objectives should be included at this stage in the plan. This is to ensure that direct marketing planners know what the priorities of the business are. At the business level, it is common to find objectives relating to profitability (ROI, £ profits); cash flow; utilization of resources; market share; growth (revenue, units); contribution to customers (price, quality, reliability, service); and risk exposure (reliance on specific products, markets or technologies) (Day 1984). While at any time the business may have objectives in all of these areas, it is common practice that only the most important three or four are stated. This indicates management priorities, and facilitates the development of coherent plans. From the direct marketer's point of view, a thorough understanding of the business objectives will guide the formulation of direct marketing objectives and strategies, and ensure that they play their part in achieving organizational objectives.

Situational Analysis

The situational analysis is the bedrock upon which the planning process is built. Broadly, it involves an assessment of the company's present position within its market(s). Thorough knowledge of the current situation is critical to the success of any plan, primarily because it helps the organization to identify exactly what position it currently holds and what positions it might like to hold in the future. The situational analysis involves a detailed analysis of four individual elements; an analysis of the external marketing environment, an analysis of the company itself in terms of internal resources and capabilities, an analysis of trends in the particular market(s) in which the company operates and of product performance within that market and, an analysis of customers. These elements can then be combined into a summary statement of the company's internal strengths and weaknesses, and a review of its opportunities and threats. Given this information it then becomes possible for the company to identify its critical success factors. 'The major challenge of the situation assessment phase is to piece together a comprehensive picture of the prospective business environment in the face of inherent uncertainty' (Day 1984:51).' In this way, the subsequent direct marketing plan is built upon very solid foundations, with due consideration given to any flaws or weaknesses that become evident during the planning process.

Environmental Analysis

'A knowledge of the business environment must precede the acquisition of any degree of control over it' (Brownlie 1987:102).' The problem is, however, that the business environment is in a constant state of flux. Moreover, the vast majority of changes in the business environment are not dramatic and happen over time, thus they are difficult to spot. As a result firms have had to develop structured processes in order to monitor the marketing environment. These processes have become known as environmental scanning, the purpose of which according to Jain (1990) is to enable the firm to deal with environmental change. Many environmental scanning models have been proposed though they all more or less share similar characteristics (see Figure 2.2).

The environmental factors that make up the wider marketing environment are essentially beyond the control of the organization. Thus it is that the organization must adapt to or account for changes in the environment. Based on the work of Kast and Rosenzweig (1974) these environmental factors include those shown in Figure 2.3.

Obviously, some of these environments have particular relevance for direct marketers given the nature of direct marketing. Changes in technology have been increasingly evident in recent years and have had a dramatic effect upon the industry, especially in terms of factors such as the evolution of the database, analytical systems and the emergence of desk-top-publishing. Equally, given the targeted nature of direct marketing, changes in demographics or sociocultural factors are likely to have a profound effect on how a direct marketer conducts business. The legislation which governs direct and database market-ing is currently evolving, and direct marketers clearly need to keep up-to-date with any relevant changes. Changes in the economic

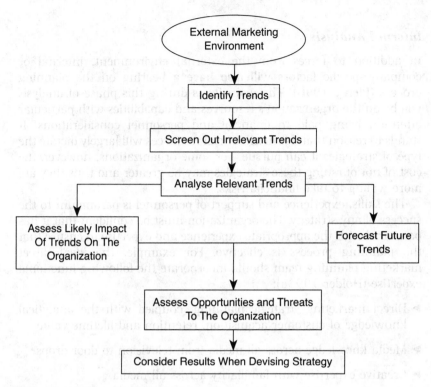

Figure 2.2 The Environmental Scanning Process

(Source: Adapted from Jain (1990))

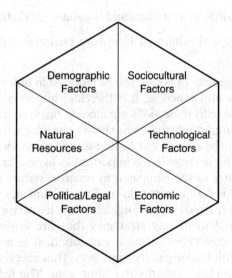

Figure 2.3 The Macro-Marketing Environment

environment may also have implications for marketers, and direct marketers in particular. For example, the resources available may be dependent upon economic conditions, target markets may become more or less appealing in times of economic crisis, and the product or service offerings may need to be adapted to offer unique value to customers.

Internal Analysis

In addition to forces from the external environment, internal or company-specific factors will also have a bearing on the planning process (Piercy 1990). The main focus during this phase of analysis will be on the organization's resources and capabilities with particular attention being paid to financial and personnel considerations. It stands to reason that a firm's financial resources will largely dictate the type of strategies it can pursue. For some organizations, however, the cost of not pursuing these strategies may be greater and thus they are more willing to take financial risks.

The skills, experience and support of personnel is paramount to the success of any strategy. The organization must be confident that it has personnel with the appropriate experience and expertise to ensure that the planning process is effective. For example, the ideal direct marketing planning team should incorporate the following functional expertise (Holder 1993a):

► Direct marketing strategic planning, coupled with the analytical knowledge of customer acquisition, retention and lifetime value.

► Media knowledge across all media from television to door drops.

► Creative expertise with familiarity across all media.

► Production talent to be abreast of the latest techniques and processes.

► Systems specialists who understand database marketing.

► Manufacturing and fulfilment to ensure customer satisfaction and service.

It is likely that a number of people will be required in order to cover all of the required skills and expertise. It is therefore important to identify at this stage if people with these skills are already involved in the planning process. Equally important, the team should consider what elements of the campaign can be carried out in-house, and what elements will be contracted out to an agency. This is important as agency briefs need to be developed very early in the campaign in order to ensure that sufficient time is available for design, artwork, mailing, fulfilment, etc.

An organization needs to be confident that its personnel have the capabilities to implement any strategies that are outlined. Furthermore, in a truly customer-centred organization, it is imperative that the firm has the full backing of its employees, that everyone within the organization is working towards the same goal. The field of internal marketing has been developed whereby employees are treated as internal customers in an effort to smooth the path towards successful implementation of external strategies (Berry 1981; Piercy and Morgan 1993). This is particularly important if direct marketing is to be used as part of a relationship building programme.

Internal analysis should also help to clarify the organization's competitive advantage and core competencies. Any strategy which an organization pursues should enable it to identify its competitive advantage(s) and to focus on these to the benefit of the organization (Jain 1990). According to Jüttner and Wehrli (1994) the majority of explanations of the origins of competitive advantages focus on what they refer to as 'resources' and 'competencies'.

For the direct marketer, the following resources are important (Roberts and Berger 1989):

▶ An extensive and accurate mailing list.

▶ A detailed database providing relevant and up-to-date information on customers and prospects.

▶ Analytical techniques and models capable of extracting from the database the critical information with which to make managerial decisions.

Finally, internal analysis should take account of the structures and systems within the firm in terms of organization, training and development, and intra- and interdepartmental communication. Key questions will centre on the ways in which decisions are made, the degree of autonomy at functional levels, and the process of internal communication.

Market Analysis and Product Performance

Market analysis refers to the process of monitoring changes in the markets in which the organization operates. Factors for consideration will include the size of the market, whether the market is growing or shrinking, and any trends or developments that may be occurring within it.

Market analysis will also include a focus on the organization's competitors. Given the intensely competitive nature of contemporary markets this competitive focus is becoming increasingly important. Not only must the firm consider which organizations are competitors at the present time, but must also try to gauge whether new competitors are likely to emerge in the near future. This is becoming ever more difficult, particularly with the move toward scrambled merchandising by many high-street retailers. For example, the major supermarkets have, in recent years, moved into the competitive domains of clothing, petrol, DIY and even financial services. The move by Marks & Spencer into financial services several years ago and Sainsbury's more recently indicates the power of the customer database, and the role of customer relationships. It promotes further evidence that as we move toward the millennium customer relationships as opposed to product development will be the key to success. Despite the associated difficulties, the direct marketer needs to ascertain what its competitors' likely objectives are and above all how they are likely to react to any strategies his company pursues. While future competitive actions are probably the most important to consider, they can be gauged to some extent by reference to past actions and performance. Continuous environmental scanning will also be of significant benefit here.

Next the organization will have to assess the performance of its product mix within these markets. The firm will need to identify the level of success that these products enjoy, the degree of funding and support they require, and the role each of them plays in customer acquisition and retention.

Customer Analysis

A business can increase value in two ways: customer acquisition and customer development. In planning direct marketing strategy, the role of direct marketing in both these areas must be addressed. As such, customer analysis is critical to understanding a company's current situation. This is because ultimately it is customers and not products which generate profit (McCorkell 1997), it is through the behaviour of customers that the business will grow or decline. Traditionally, assets of the business included property, capital equipment, new product patents. Ironically customers were not included in such an assessment. However, today, the existing customer base is viewed as one of the organization's most critical assets. This is primarily because research suggests that existing customers are at least five times more profitable than new customers. Thus, an analysis of current customers is particularly important. Customer analysis broadly deals with the following questions:

1 Who are our customers?

2 What do they look for in a product or service in this market?

3 How well do our products or services match their particular needs?

On the face of it these questions appear overly simplistic. However, identifying the customers of a company may be quite difficult in practice. Even if we only deal with current customers, they may be classified in a general fashion into loyal customers, promiscuous customers, frequent customers and occasional customers.

Loyal customers may be further classified by the level of revenue each customer or group of customers generate. With customers, as with most other things, the Pareto principle suggests that 80 per cent of revenue will come from only 20 per cent of customers. That is not to suggest that an organization should only focus on its most profitable customers, but it does suggest that different customers may have different requirements, and that the organization is satisfying some customers more than others. As a result, classification of loyal customers may in itself suggest a number of strategic directions which the company might take.

Promiscuous customers are those that will purchase the organization's product or service but will also purchase those products and services offered by competitors. Frequently, they switch allegiance due to the existence of a discount or special offer. What the organization must decide is what lengths to go to in order to win their custom, or what might be required to convert them to loyal customers.

Frequent and occasional customers can also pose difficulties for the organization. Frequent customers may purchase the organization's product or service on a regular basis but they may only purchase small amounts. On the other hand, occasional customers may purchase large enough amounts of a product or service to warrant special consideration.

Although the emphasis today is on 'keeping customers', that it not to suggest that finding new customers is no longer important. The suggestion is simply that existing customers should not be ignored in a constant search for new business. After all, new customers are the lifeblood of any business, and thus prospecting continues to be important. In identifying potential customers many organizations look to customers of competing firms. Similar to the analysis above, these customers can be broadly classified as loyal and promiscuous and the organization needs to identify which of these customers in prospecting terms represents a worthwhile investment.

Most product markets also have a stream of consumers entering for the first time, consumers who have not purchased in this product category before. Because these consumers do not already have loyal affiliations, these may be worth targeting in the search for new business. For example, banks and building societies generally have very attractive packages available for first-time buyers and college students. The logic is that if the customers are happy with the offering they are unlikely to switch to a competitor. Equally, they can be tied in to one organization for a period of time. For example, the average mortgage is set for 25 years, and the average college student is repaying student loans for some years after graduation.

This analysis of the customer base leads to a number of qualitative descriptions of who the customers are and who the company's potential customers are. Although this description is useful to the company, it is far more valuable for direct marketers to try to quantify the customer analysis in relation to a number of elements. These include:

▶ Identify revenue streams from existing customers.

▶ Categorize customers, in terms of the amount of revenue they generate (Pareto analysis is useful here).

▶ Carry out a customer lifetime analysis. Essentially this is an assessment of how much a customer is likely to spend, and over what period. Customer lifetime analysis is thus the anticipated profitability arising from each customer. It is similar to a product sales forecast, but in this case the focus is upon individual customers rather than individual products. An understanding of customer lifetime value assists the company in forecasting turnover, profit and resource implications. This topic is dealt with in greater detail in Chapter 4.

▶ Analyse customer gains and customer losses. This helps identify the relative value of new business, and the profitability of lost customers. Such an assessment will help the organization identify if additional profit is to be gained from existing customers, or from growing the customer base.

► Evaluate if any trends are evident in terms of losing or gaining customers. Can lost customers be attributed to aggressive competitive activity? What about new customers, did the company run a successful acquisition campaign at some point?

► Identify the rates of success of cross-selling or up-trading customers. Such an analysis is particularly useful for future programmes which aim to increase revenue from existing customers.

Direct marketers argue that the customer database is an invaluable source of information relating to customers, and that we can virtually ignore traditional market research techniques. 'Conventional market research methods are sometimes too slow and almost always too imprecise to provide the right quality of planning information' (McCorkell 1997:149). While we agree that the customer database is invaluable, we would caution against completely eliminating conventional research methods, especially in situations where a new market, a new target group, or a new product are involved. In such cases, basing future predictions entirely on past behaviour may be somewhat dangerous. The organization has a vast array of research techniques, and sources of research at its disposal, and it should make use of whatever sources of information are appropriate for a given situation. For example, Heinz considers research to be the cornerstone of its success. It employs exhaustive research that involves product tests, group discussions, and consumer surveys in addition to database analysis (Smyth 1996).

This summary should also note where the company already performs well, and where there is room for improvement. The SWOT analysis should make it relatively easy for the organization to identify what the critical success factors in its market are likely to be. For example, from the following SWOT analysis in Table 2.1, the critical success factors would include:

► Customer retention is one of the company's critical strengths.

► The inability to profile customers effectively is a critical weakness.

► Increasing the value offered to existing customers (through broadening the product line) represents a critical opportunity.

► Competing loyalty schemes may attract our customers if we don't respond very quickly.

Critical success factors represent areas that are crucial for success in a particular market. However, many organizations make the mistake of believing that these factors will not change (Day 1984). Change is likely to be slow and difficult to identify and this makes constant re-evaluation imperative. Identification of these critical success factors is the first step in preparing appropriate strategies. The company knows its strengths and weaknesses, and is aware of potential opportunities and threats. However, before this information becomes really useful, the company must really understand who its customers are, and what it is they want.

Strengths	So What?
Customer lifetime value is high. Trend analysis suggests that the company has a good record of customer retention.	This means that customer retention is particularly important to us, and so far we're pretty good at it.
Weaknesses	**So What?**
The customer database is not very sophisticated.	We cannot capture a great deal of information about our customers. This affects our ability to target customers effectively, and leads to a great deal of waste.
The organization does not have the resources to deal with high volumes of in-bound telephone calls.	Promoting telephone direct response may not be a viable option at this time.
Opportunities	**So What?**
Research indicates that customers are more likely to purchase products via the mail or telephone if the organization has an established returns policy.	We might make purchasing more attractive for customers if we used our existing distribution system to collect returns. Although this will involve additional costs, it also represents additional value.
The majority of our customers use the credit facilities we offer. There might be an opportunity to diversify into financial services.	We could use the information we already hold on our credit customers to offer them financial services products. We can also use this data to profile credit customers, and extend our target base.
Threats	**So What**
Environmental scanning suggests that financial services are being offered by a wide variety of organizations.	It's becoming increasingly difficult to identify competitors. The number of new entrants suggests that the firm will lose market share unless action is taken.
All of our competitors now run loyalty schemes.	We don't. Our competitors know more about their customers, and offer their customers more value.

Table 2.1 SWOT analysis

Identification and Profiling of Target Market

Gaining knowledge of customers is extremely important for marketers in general, but even more so for direct marketers. Comprehensive customer knowledge allows the direct marketer to choose which approaches to use in future acquisition and retention drives and, as a consequence, to make valued judgements with regard to acquisition and retention costs.

Customer profiling is the process whereby the customer base is categorized into distinct groups according to customer characteristics. These characteristics may then be used in the search for future prospects and to tailor future communications and offerings to existing customers. According to Holder (1993) the characteristics of greatest use in customer profiling are likely to include:

► socio-demographics;

► geographics;

► lifestyle;

► method of customer acquisition;

► customer behaviour (especially in terms of recency, frequency and monetary value of purchases);

► responsiveness to promotions.

Many of these characteristics have long been used by marketers in general for market segmentation purposes. What sets direct marketers apart however, is the ability to use the database to develop extremely accurate profiles. Other marketers have traditionally relied on generalized profiles which are of dubious value.

Unfortunately, having access to such detailed information about customers simply isn't enough. It is imperative that the direct marketer learns how to use this data effectively. Hansotia (1997:351–2) indicates that successful utilization requires:

► Having access to the right data.

► Using that data to develop knowledge and insights about customers.

► Applying the knowledge gained in designing creative marketing programmes.

► Testing acquisition and retention programmes that focus on the right customers.

► Utilizing advanced analytical systems to aid decision making.

► Creating a customer oriented learning organization.

One of the keys to understanding customers is to learn from experience. Developing meaningful dialogue with customers and generating feedback enables the direct marketer to strengthen future efforts. Even in the area of creativity it is customer knowledge that holds the key much more than witty and clever headlines and images. Creativity is borne of knowing who the customer is, what benefits he is looking for, and which approaches appeal to him most. Prospect management, according to Hansotia (1997:352–3) begins with answering the following questions:

► To what degree are prospects aware of the organization and its offerings?

► How knowledgeable are prospects about the benefits on offer?

► What is the process by which prospects seek out product or service information?

► What is the nature of the purchase decision process in this market?

► How are these prospects segmented?

► How do these prospects rate and evaluate the products attributes?

Key Assumptions

The strategic planning literature suggests that it is important to challenge key assumptions *before* developing strategies in order to avoid a situation where a lot of time and effort have gone into formulating a plan which is unacceptable to the organization for a number of reasons. For example, it may be that the proposed strategy requires additional personnel or technology which will not be made available (Piercy 1992). In direct marketing terms, key assumptions which must be challenged include the following:

1 Is there an assumption that an external agency will be used for creative, fulfilment, media buying, or data capture? To what extent is this assumption valid? Will the required finance be available? Is it common practice to use external agencies or is the majority of work normally done in-house?

2 Does the campaign depend upon the purchase of new mailing lists? Is more research required in order to refine strategies? Will the media choice be acceptable to the organization? If so, is it safe to assume that the organization will support such requests?

3 Is there a need to access other datasets within the organization in order to profile or generate a mailing list? Can you presume automatic access to such data?

4 Is the assumption that the campaign will be fully stand-alone, with no need to ensure the compatibility of either the offer or the message with other strategies? How valid is this assumption? Given the growing trend toward Integrated Marketing Communications (IMC) who is the person or people with whom you should confer?

5 Will there be an incentive offered to increase response to the campaign? If this is based on the use of specific products or brands, is it safe to presume that this will be acceptable?

6 Does the campaign seek to secure direct sales? If this involves supplementing or by-passing retail channels will this contravene existing policy?

7 If any of the financial analysis is based on the sale or sharing of mailing lists with other departments or organizations, is it a valid assumption that this will be supported within the organization?

The assumptions that are made will differ greatly from company to company, and indeed, from campaign to campaign, and therefore the above list is illustrative rather than definitive. There are no hard and fast rules which determine which assumptions are valid and which may lead to criticism from others within the organization, and the ultimate failure of the plan. The following is a rough guide:

▶ *Identify the assumptions which you have made.* This is easier said than done, because assumptions are often subconscious. However, it is worth looking at your proposed plan asking yourself the following questions; Is anything that you are proposing likely to have an impact on any other functional areas, on any specific products or customer groups? In other words, do you imagine that some of your ideas might involve stepping on someone else's toes?

► *Challenge your assumptions.* Is it valid to assume that the finance will be available for this plan, that differentiated offerings can be made to different customer segments, or that specific products can be discounted as an incentive? Is it likely that clearance will be required from higher up in the organization, or from other managers within the organization?

► *If in doubt, check it out.* If at any stage doubt arises then consultation should be sought. It is best to get confirmation at an early stage, rather than wait until the plan is finalized. This way, if there is a problem, alternative strategies can be developed.

► *Get appropriate support and confirmation at the earliest possible stage.* If your suspicion is confirmed that you do not have sufficient authority to request additional resources, or authorize other elements of the plan, then it is important to get the appropriate people involved at the very earliest stage. Where possible (and where critical resources are involved) try to get written authority as early as possible.

If you are happy at this stage that the appropriate resources will be available, and that in principle your strategy is compatible with the business mission, then you are in a position to formulate a detailed plan. It is now appropriate to identify the specific objectives for the direct marketing campaign.

Objective Setting

Setting objectives is another critical element of the direct marketing plan. Indeed, if objectives are inappropriate, unrealistic or inconsistent, then everything that follows is of little value. The first question to ask is what is an objective? George Day (1984) states that objectives are 'desired or needed results to be achieved by a specific time period.' This suggests that objectives are simply statements of the results that a business should achieve. However, it is important to note that objectives are hierarchical in many ways. We outlined earlier that the business mission and overall objectives should be stated in the Mission and Scope stage of the plan. This is because direct marketing objectives should go some way toward achieving the overall business objectives. Objectives can be developed in a number of ways which will be discussed shortly. However, before looking at the process of objective setting, it is first important to identify what makes a good objective, and what are the elements which all objectives should incorporate. We suggest that objectives should **C**ommunicate **A**spirational but **R**ealistic goals, with each objective having a **P**recise focus (market share, product sales, increased retention), which is capable of **E**valuation (quantifiable measures), within a specific **T**ime period. This has led us to suggest the mnemonic CARPET, described in Table 2.2.

Communicate	The purpose of a written objective is to communicate with other members of the organization. This suggests that the language used should not be open to interpretation – it should communicate a clear message. Because objectives are written they are less open to subjective interpretation than objectives which are verbally stated.	**Table 2.2** CARPET Objectives
Aspirational	Objectives need to challenge and focus effort, particularly because businesses generally wish to grow, increase profitability etc. Essentially business objectives focus upon improving on previous achievements. As a result, objectives should include some aspirational element. In this way, objectives act as motivators, and allow the organization to strive to do better than in previous years, and/or in previous programmes.	
Realistic	Although there is some element of aspiration included within an objective, it is also important that objectives are achievable with the appropriate strategies, within budget, environmental and competitive constraints. Otherwise, objectives are just pipe dreams. If managers do not believe that objectives can be achieved, then there is no motivational element involved.	
Precise Focus	Objectives should focus on a specific element (e.g. share of customer, percentage of sales, product penetration). Where the company has objectives in more than one of these areas, then several objectives are required. This results in clear, specific objectives which will subsequently provide more guidance for strategic and tactical choices.	
Evaluation	Objectives must be written to include clear evaluation criteria. If not, they become no more than a wish list, and it is impossible to determine if objectives have been met, or if strategies have been successful. These evaluation criteria refer to the precise focus of the objective. These could relate to volume, value, margin, market share, or profitability. In order to facilitate objective evaluation, the use of loose terms such as 'maximize', 'minimize', 'penetrate', and 'increase' should be avoided unless they are qualified by specific targets. Thus, the objective may be to increase market share by 10 per cent, to increase customer retention by 20 per cent, to reduce customer defections by 50 per cent etc.	
Time	For an objective to be useful in terms of measuring performance, there must be a time limit involved in order for managers to determine if targets have been met or missed. If objectives do not have a specified time limit then it becomes unclear when evaluation is appropriate. Thus all objectives should specify the time period involved – this may be within one year, within one month of running an advertisement, or within two weeks of sending out a direct mail shot.	

To reiterate, objectives are intended to communicate required results to managers and others. Objectives should focus upon single precise issues (market share etc.) should be capable of evaluation, and should identify a specific time period. Given the focus upon customers in direct marketing, it is common practice for separate objectives to be set down for each target group – loyal users, competitive users, and promiscuous consumers (McCorkell 1997). Indeed, in some markets, objectives may be established for individual customers, particularly where those customers account for a large proportion of sales.

Objectives can relate to a number of different results. For example, the objective may be to build awareness, or to inform or educate. Although direct marketing can assist in achieving such objectives, on its own, direct marketing tends to focus upon generating direct sales, generating sales leads, and/or creating a database of key prospects:

▶ *Generating direct sales.* Appropriate if the product can be sold through direct channels, and/or if the organization wishes to bypass or supplement a retail network.

▶ *Generating sales leads.* Appropriate if a salesforce is required, a new market sector is entered, or new prospects are needed. In this case, further work is required to make a sale. For example, double glazing and financial services generally require a sales visit – however, the job of the salesperson is more effective if they can spend time dealing with clients rather than trying to generate sales leads.

▶ *Creation of a database of key prospects.* The objective here is not only to generate a database containing key information but also to make this information accessible in order that it can be used to support and drive marketing initiatives.

▶ *Build Awareness/Educate/Inform.* Although traditionally the domain of mass communications, direct marketing can also play a role in achieving these objectives. For example, although direct marketing of pharmaceutical products is prohibited in India, direct marketing is used to build awareness. Mailings discuss patients symptoms in general, in the hope that recipients will be encouraged to ask their doctor for further details (Linton 1995).

The Objective-Setting Process

The process of setting objectives is particularly important. This is because a business will have several objectives, and indeed direct marketing may itself have several objectives. If the process is not taken seriously, then objectives may not be consistent. That is, one objective may invalidate another. For example, objectives to increase customer retention may directly impact upon an objective to reduce costs (especially where cost reductions occur in customer service or product development). Because strategies are developed to meet objectives, there is a need to carefully think through the objectives to ensure that strategies are not counter-productive. Equally, objectives need to be acceptable to management. This is more likely where they have been actively involved in the objective-setting process, and where they believe that objectives are realistically achievable within the given budget and environmental conditions. Thus, 'one of the roles of the objective-setting process is to provide a structured basis for developing objectives that can be embraced by managers' (*Business World* 1997:49). There are three broad approaches to setting direct marketing objectives: derive from business objectives; develop from database and; combine, negotiate, formulate.

Derive from Business Objectives
Within most businesses, senior managers are responsible for setting business objectives over time periods of one, three, and perhaps five years. These objectives are generally set having taken into considera-

tion stakeholders' expectations, environmental conditions and internal resources. Stakeholders include investors, unions, employees, and perhaps even government. Senior managers are expected to weigh the often conflicting expectations of these groups, and to identify what is achievable within given business resources. On this basis, business objectives are set, which subsequently form the basis for marketing, financial, production and other functional objectives. These objectives then become the basis for lower-level objectives. For example, within this approach, direct marketing objectives are derived from distribution and communication objectives, which are derived from marketing objectives, which are derived from business objectives. The strength of this process is that lower level objectives aim to achieve higher-level objectives, and as a result strategies should be compatible, and higher-level objectives should be achieved. The major criticism of this process is that middle management are not involved in the objective setting process, that objectives are handed down with no thought to the extent to which they are achievable.

Develop from Database

This approach to planning has also been called outside-in planning (Schultz *et al.* 1993; McCorkell 1997). Within this approach, objectives are based upon information derived from the database. Essentially, direct marketers 'work out what it will cost, using their back data and forecasting models as a guide, to achieve any given volume of sales and cut off their plan at the optimum level' (McCorkell 1997:155). This approach leads to the formulation of direct marketing objectives which are clearly achievable. Indeed, some argue that this approach is far superior to top-down approaches, in that it is 'based on the reality of what previous customer behaviour suggests is achievable, not the pipe dreams of stakeholders' (McCorkell 1997:158). Thus, this approach to setting objectives results in more realistic objectives. However, its main limitation is that such objectives do not include an aspirational element, and thus are limited in their ability to motivate managers to exceed previous performance. Second, objectives may be set unrealistically low – within this scenario objectives may be continually met – but the extent to which they contribute to business objectives is increasingly questionable.

Combine, Negotiate, Formulate

Both of the above approaches to setting objectives are commonly used in business today. It has been shown that each have particular strengths, and that each have particular weaknesses. By combining both approaches it is possible to maximize the strengths of each, and to minimize weaknesses. That is, the aspirational element is provided by top-down business objectives derived approaches, while the realistic element is provided by reference to information held on the database. Of perhaps greater importance, however, is that negotiation involves managers in the objective-setting process. In this way, they begin to take ownership of objectives, and they are motivated by aspirational but realistic objectives. Where this process takes place, even business objectives may be changed to reflect the reality of what is achievable within the available resources. As a result, stakeholder expectations are more likely to be achieved.

In an ideal world, the preliminary objectives set by senior management will be achievable, and as a result all lower-level objectives will also be achievable. However, in practice the world is far from ideal, and business objectives often incorporate politically desirable objectives, or reflect stakeholder wish lists. Thus, there is a clear gap between business objectives, and what previous information suggests is achievable. Negotiations are generally about compromise – compromise over what is required and what is achievable within budget and other constraints. This is likely to result in changing objectives, for example, by reducing the level of aspiration, changing strategies, and/or increasing resources available in order to improve the expected performance of a strategy. Because it is more firmly based in reality, the negotiated strategy is probably best for most organizations. Within this process, unrealistic objectives are not imposed top-down, although there is some aspirational element involved. Equally, objectives are not just the same or incrementally higher than previous campaigns. Most importantly, management are aware that these objectives are clearly achievable. The combination of aspirational and achievable objectives is a powerful motivator for management. Furthermore, because managers have been actively involved in the objective-setting process, they have 'bought-into' the plan at an early stage. Thus, in summary a negotiated process of objective setting results in a number of valuable benefits:

▶ Objectives are both aspirational and realistically achievable.

▶ Management have ownership of objectives, and thus motivation is likely to be higher.

▶ The level of focus and discussion should also ensure that objectives are precise, capable of evaluation, and specify appropriate time periods.

Identification, Evaluation and Selection of Strategies

Strategy is 'the major link between the goals and objectives the organization wants to achieve and the various functional area policies and operating plans it uses to guide its day-to-day activities' (Hofer and Schendel 1978:13). Marketing strategies therefore, outline the path or approach to be taken by an organization in allocating resources towards achieving its objectives (McDonald 1992).

Day (1986) indicates that a strategy's applicability may be evaluated according to the following criteria:

▶ *Suitability.* Is there a sustainable advantage? Any strategy should enable a company to identify its strengths and competitive advantage(s) and to focus on these to the benefit of the organization.

▶ *Validity.* Validity refers to the consistency a strategy has with assumptions held about the external product/market environment (Jain 1990) and on whether those assumptions are realistic.

▶ *Feasibility.* Does the company have the skills, resources and commitments? In selecting strategies an organization will have to make a decision regarding their willingness to commit to a particular way of doing things (Ghemawat 1986) which will inevitably involve the matching of resource requirements to strategic proposals.

▶ *Internal Consistency.* Internal consistency, what Yee (1990) refers to as 'strategic alignment', relates to the degree of fit between proposed strategies and current operations.

▶ *Vulnerability.* What are the risks and contingencies? The degree of risk associated with any strategy is a reflection of the resources allocated to it.

▶ *Workability.* Can the company retain its flexibility? Ideally the workability of any strategy should be subjected to quantitative analysis (Jain 1990). In the absence of such measures recourse to managerial consensus is advisable. Littler and Leverick (1994) suggest that in markets where new technology is the driving force, detailed and structured marketing planning becomes difficult. As a consequence it is likely that under such conditions decisions will be made quickly, managerial judgement and guesswork will be the order of the day, and decisions will be bold and sweeping.

▶ *Appropriate Time Horizon.* 'A viable strategy will have a time frame for its realization' (Jain 1990).

The process of strategy evaluation can be quite difficult at first but becomes easier with experience. Using the criteria set out above, management should be able to test and refine the strategic options that lie before them. Some options can easily be eliminated as they clearly fail to meet the criteria. However, it is rare for one clear option to emerge. Instead, management are likely to be forced to choose between a range of options on the basis of the balance between the risks and opportunities they offer. Constant refinement and re-evaluation of the options against the evaluation criteria should eventually highlight the strategies to be pursued. This process of strategic evaluation is outlined in Figure 2.4.

In direct marketing strategy terms there are three main areas for consideration: media strategy, creative strategy and contact strategy.

Media Strategy

According to Bird (1993) media considerations in direct marketing differ from those in traditional advertising in a number of important respects. Direct marketers assign the various media different weightings. Television, for example, does not play as significant a role in direct

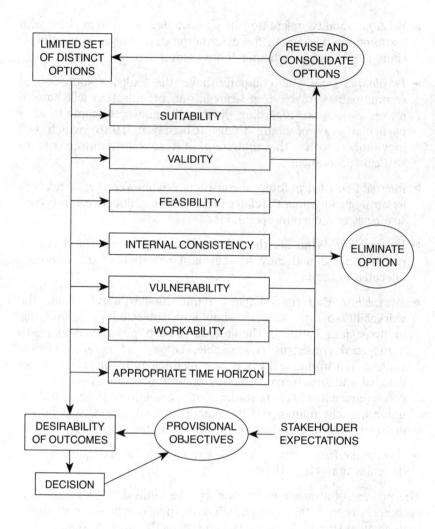

Figure 2.4 The Strategy Evaluation Process

(Source: Adapted from Day 1984)

marketing as it does in traditional advertising. That said however, direct response television is growing in importance year on year. Direct marketers also evaluate the different media at their disposal not only in terms of cost but also in terms of individual impact and generation of response. Furthermore, scheduling and budgeting need to be flexible in order to allow for testing. Direct marketers also need to be wary of repetition and should take into account factors such as the size of the ad, the human appeal the product or service generates and the circulation of the medium. In direct marketing the effect of space size is also viewed differently in that larger sizes are not considered to be proportionately more effective. Like traditional advertising, however, media selection in direct marketing owes a lot to the effectiveness of various media in reaching the desired audience and in communicating the message.

Creative Strategy

Development of the creative strategy, according to Roberts and Berger (1989) incorporates five basic steps.

1 *Develop the Key Selling Concept.* The key selling concept relates to the core benefit on offer to consumers. Because consumers buy on the basis of product or service benefits rather than attributes, using the core benefit as the basis of the creative strategy makes good sense.

2 *Define the Primary Marketing Problem.* Building on the key selling concept this second stage moves from the customers point of view to the perspective of the organization. The organization needs to identify what, in terms of the campaign at hand, is its major marketing problem.

3 *Specify the Desired Action.* The creative strategy will differ depending on which particular action is desired of consumers.

4 *Create the Message Strategy.* What is the creative platform on which the message will be built. This will be expressed in general terms at this stage to be broken down later on into specific types of appeal, wording of the appeal etc.

5 *Take Account of Mandatory Requirements.* Creative strategy must be consistent with the requirements laid down at organizational or divisional level.

Contact Strategy

The information required to develop a contact strategy should come initially from a communications audit (Linton 1995). The communications audit compares customers' views of previous communications by the organization and by competitors and identifies key communications actions needed to generate the desired result. Management will need to decide at which points in the relationship between the organization and the consumer communication is going to take place (Bird 1993). General decisions will also need to be made here with regard to when the customer or prospect is to be contacted and by which means.

Budgeting and Financial Analysis

Setting budgets is one of the most detailed parts of the planning process. Essentially, the budget reflects the allocation of resources to strategies, and ultimately becomes a benchmark by which performance is measured. As such developing budgets is also one of the most important parts of the planning process. The purpose of budgeting is to:

▶ communicate and motivate;

▶ allocate resources and accountability;

▶ control and co-ordinate activities;

▶ report results and provide feedback on performance. (Stone *et al.* 1995)

Setting Marketing Budgets

Within marketing there are many different ways in which companies go about allocating resources to strategies. Indeed, many of these methods can also be used in budgeting for direct marketing. These are briefly outlined below:

▶ *Percentage of Sales.* Budgets can be allocated either as a percentage of last year's sales or as a percentage of expected future sales. This method has received strong criticism in that sales form the basis of expenditure, rather than direct marketing expenditure resulting in sales. As such, budgets are either too low or too high, and tend to have little bearing on the stated objectives of a particular campaign.

▶ *Competitive Parity.* This budgeting method has little to offer direct marketers, primarily because direct marketing is a below-the-line activity and thus it is difficult to determine how much competitors are actually spending. In any case, competitors spend to achieve *their* objectives which may be very different from those stated in the direct marketing plan.

▶ *Objective and Task Approach.* Essentially, rather than starting with a fixed budget, direct marketers look at the objectives which have been agreed, and identify what tasks are required in order to achieve these stated objectives.

The first two methods (together with a number of others) work on the basis of allocating a fixed budget for a specified period of time. 'The very idea of a fixed sum to be spent each financial year or season is not sensible for direct marketers. The issue is: how much can I afford to spend to acquire a prospect, or to produce a sale for a customer?' (Bird 1993:138) Furthermore, the criticisms outlined above suggest that these methods are not particularly useful for direct marketers. As a result, the objective and task approach is much more applicable for developing direct marketing budgets. Additionally, because of the capacity to calculate the costs of direct marketing fairly accurately, this approach can be further refined (and improved) using the concept of allowable costs (Kruegar 1996; McCorkell 1997). Thus, we call this refined approach 'objective and task within allowable costs'.

Objective and Task Within Allowable Costs

There are a number of stages involved in budget allocation using this method. These include:

1 Determine projected lifetime value of customers and prospects.

2 Financial analysis of previous direct marketing campaigns.

3 Determine Allowable Costs.

4 Review Objectives and Tasks, and allocate Costs.

5 Ensure that the budget is feasible given the available financial resources.

Determine Projected Lifetime Value of Customers and Prospects
The first step in the process is to determine the anticipated lifetime value from different target prospects, and to rank them accordingly. The direct marketer needs to be aware which prospects are likely to generate a high lifetime value and which are not. This will then allow the direct marketer to decide how much it is worth spending to attract certain prospects, and this will feed in to allocating allowable costs.

Financial Analysis of Previous Direct Marketing Campaigns
Unless this represents a company's first direct marketing campaign, there will be information available on the success or otherwise of previous campaigns. It is important that this information be analysed thoroughly in order to enhance the effectiveness of the current process of budgeting, and indeed the overall planning process. The main performance measures used by direct marketers are (Stone *et al.* 1995):

▶ *Customer acquisition costs.* Essentially a review of the average cost of acquiring customers as indicated by previous data. This will be an important input into determining the allowable costs of acquisition.

▶ *Break-even volumes.* This indicates the minimum level of sales required in order to break-even on campaigns to particular target segments.

▶ *Attrition rate.* This is a measure of the rate at which customers are lost by the business. Further analysis is required to establish the reasons why customers defect.

▶ *Lifetime values.* This may be further broken down to reflect the different lifetime value potential of different customer segments.

▶ *Profit potential.* Based on previous data, calculate the expected profits of the campaign.

▶ *Resource allocation.* Data on how all of the marketing resources have been deployed, and how effective resource allocation has been with different customer groups.

Determining Allowable Costs
Direct marketers are in a position to calculate the costs associated with different methods of customer acquisition by analysing previous campaigns. By comparing the costs associated with different approaches, and the results of these approaches, they can identify average costs of customer acquisition. This method can be further refined by looking at the profile of customers acquired through

different methods or media, that is, looking at acquisition costs in relation to anticipated lifetime values. In this way, a direct response advertisement in a newspaper might have a low acquisition cost, but result in acquiring customers with low anticipated lifetime value, while a video mailing might have high acquisition costs and yet yield more profitable prospects. Because objectives are likely to have been set for both existing customers and new customers, the allowable costs can be reflected accordingly.

McCorkell recommends that direct marketers start with an analysis of the business that can be derived from existing customers, as the cheapest sales will result from this. Next consider customer acquisition initially using the prospect file, then the suspect file, and finally using more speculative approaches. He further suggests that experience will help to identify the costs of acquisition using all of these means, but in general, highly targeted prospects will cost substantially less per acquisition than more speculative prospects. At some point, it will no longer be profitable to attempt to attract more customers or to make more sales.

Review Objectives and Tasks, and Allocate Costs
Stages four and five of the planning process require that realistic objectives are set, and that the strategies chosen are capable of achieving the desired results. Because the availability of the budget is crucial to achieving success, setting objectives, choosing strategies and allocating budgets are highly interactive stages of the process. Essentially, budgets are structured plans for the financial aspects of the campaign. Therefore costs need to be allocated to the various tasks which combine to form strategies. This requires a thorough assessment of the costs involved, because these will vary significantly depending on strategies chosen (see Table 2.3).

Ensure that Budget is Feasible within Available Financial Resources
One of the potential problems with the objective and task approach is that the required budget may be far higher than expectations, and

Table 2.3 Costs Related to Direct Marketing Implementation

Media Costs	Press, TV, radio, billboard etc.
Agency Costs	Design, copy, artwork, consultancy etc.
Mailing	Envelope, brochure, postage etc.
Cost of Handling Response	Freepost, Freephone, maintaining and staffing a call centre, data capture etc.
Cost of Meeting the Response	Supplying and distributing the material that is required.
Cost of Servicing the Response	Sales or telemarketing costs in dealing with the potential volume of new business.
Testing	Separate budgets are required for testing format, publications, mailing lists etc. Test budgets generally show a loss because of fixed costs which cannot be allocated over a large volume.

indeed far higher than the business can afford at this particular point in time. Thus, this last stage is essential to ensure that the resources will be available to implement the chosen strategies. If the required resources will not be available, then this is the stage to rethink the objectives, strategies or other elements of the plan.

Action Plans

Action plans provide the means by which the organization's ideas are turned into reality by being given a structure and a format through which they can be implemented. This involves not only the communication of ideas on a general level, but also the specific detail of any changes to be made and the programmes to be pursued. Piercy outlines a process by which action planning should occur (see Figure 2.5).

Essentially, management's task is to identify the most critical areas for consideration, decide how any solutions should be accomplished and communicate these plans to the relevant people within the organization. The general objectives and strategies outlined earlier must now be developed into precise objectives 'supported by more detailed strategy and action statements, with timings and responsibilities clearly indicated' (Christopher and McDonald 1995:303).

Set Evaluation Criteria

Measurability is the key attribute of response generating activities, and the type of measurement to be used must be planned in advance.

Effective measurement involves five key stages (Brannon 1993):

1 Every objective must be quantified and timed. If it is response you seek, of what kind, from whom, how many, at what rate and over what period of time?

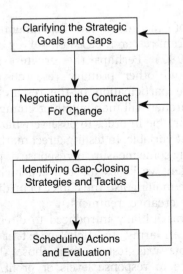

Figure 2.5 The Action Planning Process

(Source: Adapted from Piercy 1992)

2 Define what analyses will be used in evaluating the campaign and thus define the information needed for effective evaluation.

3 Identify how every response will be captured. Ensure that there are systems in place which allow every response to be logged, and identify the source of response. Such a system must also be capable of collecting all of the data deemed to be necessary for evaluation

4 Identify how progress on each response will be tracked through to the final action dictated in your objective.

5 Identify how the results will be analysed.

Set Target Response Levels

The simplest and most immediate measure of a direct marketing campaign is the response levels it achieves (Linton 1995). The organization should aim for a realistic figure that is within the organizational budget, and that has taken into account the industry average, and any other variables which might impact upon performance. In a 1995 DMIS survey it was found that general mailings achieved 3-6 per cent response, while on-pack promotions with a direct response element achieved up to 15 per cent (*Marketing Week* 1995). However, average responses tend to vary by industry, with a response rate of 1-2 per cent regarded as the norm in some industries, and regarded as appalling in others. Thus, there is a need to identify the average within the relevant industries. Other variables may also impact upon the level of response. For example, factors such as the price, the offer, the quality of the mailing list and the quality of the copy and design are all likely to have an impact (Linton 1995).

Testing

Testing is a form of experimentation. Experimentation differs in some essential respects from research based on survey or observation (Cook and Campbell 1997). Perhaps the greatest difference between experimentation and other primary research methods is that it involves the active participation of the researcher in the process. Basically, the researcher will manipulate or change what is known as the independent variable in order to observe what effect this will have upon the dependent variable. In testing direct marketing the dependent variable is inevitably some measure of response or profit while the most common independent variables to be tested include the product or service on offer, the mailing list, the choice of media, the offer or price, timing, format and creative treatment.

When testing was initially introduced to direct marketing it was embraced with open arms, to such an extent that almost every conceivable variable was tested, even those things which made negligible difference to response levels or profit. Due to increasing costs however, direct marketers have been forced to concentrate on the variables that matter, the things that will make a major contribution to success.

'The pragmatic defining characteristic of testing is the desire to minimize downside financial risk' (Nash 1986:195). Furthermore, according to Forshaw (1993), testing has led to continuous improvement in direct marketing efforts thereby contributing to the relative success which the industry has enjoyed. This occurs because testing distinguishes which activities work and which do not. In 1997 Mitsubishi Motors launched three different mailings, in order to test which were most effective in encouraging test drives for the Carisma and the Space Wagon. The results of the test mailings will form the basis for developing long term direct marketing strategy (*Precision Marketing* 1997). Testing also helps to reduce costs by isolating the most cost effective approaches and stimulates the creative process by identifying new goals. Above all testing is customer centred because it recognizes what it is exactly that consumers want from the direct marketing approaches they receive.

One of the benefits of a direct marketing campaign is that it can be tested without committing full resources. Tests can be carried out on relatively small groups of consumers, which has the added advantage of being relatively inexpensive compared with other forms of research. Equally, testing is easy to set up, quick to conduct and results tend to have a high degree of reliability.

Roberts and Berger (1989:188) outline three criteria for the successful use of tests:

▶ All tests should be measured against the criterion of expected profit.

▶ Decisions about the content of the test should be based on sound marketing judgement.

▶ Decisions about the design of the test should be based on statistical theory.

The Royal National Institute for Deaf People has utilized its testing and profiling procedures over the years to build up a detailed picture of their typical donor. This information has proved vital in donor recruitment drives which are necessary to keep the charity running. Because few charities can manage to break even just from initial donations, it is imperative that they hold on to their donors and maximize lifetime value. Central to this process is the constant evaluation and re-evaluation of campaigns which are used to monitor response, identify ideal donor candidates and highlight successful approaches.

Execution

'Most marketing plans are killed by inaction, rather than by deliberate rejection' (Nash 1986:52). This suggests that when the time comes to execute the plan it is important that everybody knows what they have to do, everybody is fully committed to making the plan work, and above all everybody actually *does* what they are required to do. The process of planning can be seductive, in that it is generally easier to plan, and to keep on planning, than it is to actually do something. Procrastination occurs because those involved are attempting to develop the *perfect plan*. However, it is important to remember that the objective of the planning process is *not* to develop the perfect plan, but rather to execute strategies capable of achieving agreed-upon objectives. As Drucker (1974) states:

> 💬 *The best plan is only a plan, that is, good intentions, unless it degenerates into work. The distinction that makes a plan capable of producing results is the commitment of key people to work on specific tasks.* 💬

Thus, in a sense execution signals the end of the planning process. Specific action plans have been developed, budgets and resources allocated, evaluation criteria laid down and testing completed. The direct marketer is now ready to execute the plan, that is to take the required action. Taking action involves:

1 Reviewing implementation problems.

2 Organizing for implementation.

3 Promoting customer response.

4 Fulfilling orders.

5 Managing customer service.

Reviewing Implementation Problems

Piercy (1992) argues that managers need to anticipate implementation problems as early as possible and prior to implementation should ensure that:

▶ Strategies are coherent and complete.

▶ Strategies are capable of being implemented by the company at this time – e.g. structures are in place, and key resources are available – for direct marketers, these include database facilities, distribution channels, and fulfilment operations (Stone *et al.* 1995).

▶ The required support exists within the organization.

Organizing For Implementation

Organizing for implementation involves:

▶ Mobilising the required resources.

▶ Allocating responsibility for tasks to individuals.

▶ Co-ordinating the activities of in-house and agency personnel.

▶ Initiating an effective communication process.

▶ Establishing reporting process.

The direct marketing manager is now confident that the strategy is capable of being implemented, that the resources and budgets are in place, that personnel are aware of their roles and responsibilities, and that communication and reporting procedures are in place. He or she is now ready to implement the action plans developed earlier in the planning process.

Promoting Customer Response

The next step for the direct marketer is to initiate the activities intended to promote the customer response. These activities should be detailed in the action plans developed earlier in the planning process. Essentially, these should state *what* needs to be done in order to implement the chosen strategies. Such plans will include a schedule of activities indicating *when* tasks need to be initiated or completed. Because action plans translate strategies into structured frameworks each action plan for each organization will indicate different tasks and different dates. As such, there is no such thing as a generic action plan. However, action plans are likely to detail the following activities:

▶ creative activities;

▶ production;

▶ purchase or rent of mailing lists;

▶ generation of customer target list;

▶ purchase of media space;

▶ placing of advertising, conducting mailing, beginning telemarketing.

The above list is not exhaustive, and could conceivably involve other activities. Essentially, what we are talking about here is all activities required to induce customer response. When the customer responds, the fulfilment process begins.

Fulfilment

Fulfilment involves all of the activities required to fulfil a customer order after it has been received (Roberts and Berger 1989). It includes:

▶ handling responses;

▶ data capture;

▶ order processing;

▶ order shipment.

Handling Responses

For many customers, their first contact with the organization occurs when they respond to a mailing, a telephone call or a direct response advertisement. Because the organization will not get a second chance to make a first impression, customer responses must be handled professionally. Additionally, there are a number of opportunities to collect data which will be invaluable in evaluating direct marketing, enhancing the customer database, and identifying opportunities for future strategies. Response handling includes:

▶ Managing initial contact (via mail or telephone).

▶ Collecting and recording relevant data (source of enquiry, order, method of payment, and additional profile information if required).

▶ Responding to queries (customer service is not something that happens *after* the order is placed, but is something which should occur throughout the process).

Data Capture

The information provided by customers must be recorded in such a way that it is available for order processing, enhances the customer database, and can be used to monitor and evaluate strategy implementation. Most organizations have developed appropriate procedures and forms designed to capture and record this data on the database. Because the direct marketer has the capacity to communicate with individual customers in an individual way, capturing and recording the data become particularly important. For example, the database can be used:

▶ To make differentiated offers to prospects who respond to the advertising campaign.

▶ To provide information for planning telemarketing or sales follow-up.

▶ To target mailings precisely.

▶ Provide telesales staff with customer information so that they can handle customer calls more effectively and productively.

▶ Ensure that the salesforce has access to comprehensive customer information (Linton 1995).

Order Processing/Order Shipment

In order to respond to the customer request, the order must be processed. Where this involves the sale of merchandise, two forms are generally raised: one goes to the warehouse to initiate fulfilment, and one to finance to request payment. When the warehouse receives the orders it will sort, pick, pack and ship the required merchandise to customers. Many organizations will guarantee shipment within a 30-day period, and thus, processing and shipment must be able to respond quickly.

Customer Service

Customer service must permeate the entire fulfilment process. In the initial stages personnel must be capable of dealing with customer queries and establishing customer expectations. Where guarantees are made they must be adhered to. Where a goods return policy exists, this must be available to all customers. Where problems occur, sorting these out must become an organizational priority. Above all, the organization must be able to respond to customers quickly and professionally whatever the problem may be.

The execution process is both sequential and cyclical. It is sequential in that response-generating activities precede customer contact, and that the processes of data capture, order processing, shipment, etc. must follow in a linear fashion. However, the execution process is also cyclical. This is because direct marketers can design activities so that customer response can be managed effectively. For example, mailings can be staggered to ensure that the organization is not overwhelmed with responses in a particular time period. As a result, methods of generating customer response may be undertaken periodically throughout the campaign, and each time a response is initiated a sequential fulfilment process occurs. The timing of response generating activities should be identified in the action plan prior to implementation. However, it is not always possible or even desirable to implement action plans exactly as laid out in the plan. For example, responses may be far higher or lower than expected, media or production costs may be subject to change, or the strategies themselves may need to be adapted. As Day (1984:39) points out, 'Strategies are constructed in ambiguous environments in which many significant events cannot be forecast and planned for in their entirety. Some events will not even be contemplated when the strategy is chosen.' There is therefore a need to review if the chosen strategies are still feasible, if specific targets are being met, if the campaign is within budget, and if objectives are likely to be achieved. This suggests that execution needs to be continually monitored, in order to provide the necessary management information. Where problems or opportunities arise, management are then in a position to respond, and to maintain control of the process. Monitoring and control activities must therefore take place throughout the execution process. These activities are discussed below.

Monitoring and Control

> ❝ In a world where it is increasingly difficult to control anything, direct marketing makes a considerable appeal because when properly conducted it is very controllable compared to less disciplined marketing activities. ❞ (Day 1984:39)

Monitoring and control of a direct marketing programme is particularly important because it allows managers to identify the effectiveness and efficiency of the resources deployed. It compares performance levels to the objectives and strategies that have been set out and questions whether key assumptions still hold true. Furthermore, it provides a learning forum which can then be used to formulate more effective strategies in the future. Essentially, if actual performance is below expectations, the role of monitoring and control systems is to determine whether under-performance is a result of poor execution, unrealistic budgets or unexpected events. Success can be measured in a number of ways which include identifying the response rate to a campaign, tracking the number of resulting leads or sales on the database and tracking changes in purchasing patterns resulting from the campaign.

Monitoring is an on-going process, which aims to provide management with information about the campaign. Monitoring occurs throughout the campaign, flags up unexpected results and is necessary to assist with the control of the execution process. Measurements taken during and after the campaign allow management to evaluate the whole campaign, and to feed this information into the next planning cycle. Monitoring involves:

▶ Reviewing results on a regular basis (as laid out in the evaluation criteria).

▶ Comparing actual with planned results.

▶ Comparing actual spend with planned budgets.

▶ Communicating with key personnel (orally or by report).

The database can assist in the monitoring process by:

▶ Tracking responses generated, sales enquiries, sales.

▶ Recording speed of fulfilment.

▶ Tracking responses in different sectors.

▶ Comparing conversion to response statistics.

▶ Assessing which media were most effective in reaching the target audience.

▶ Comparing response levels in different media.

▶ Recording customer data capture through the campaign.

Such information can be useful, not only in measuring the effectiveness of a single campaign, but can be used to enhance future direct marketing programmes. For example, Rover's 1991 Conquest direct marketing programme yielded the following information:

▶ best media in which to advertise for leads;

▶ best method of trawling for quality leads;

▶ most attractive incentives (through analysing gift take-up);

▶ levels of incentives according to model purchase (through analysing gift take-up).

▶ the effectiveness of telemarketing (through analysing voucher returns).

Thus, direct marketing managers need to continually monitor execution in order to ensure that all is going according to plan. However, the real world is far more dynamic than planners can accommodate, and thus it is most likely that changes will have to be made to ensure than campaign objectives can ultimately be met. Regular reports will assist in identifying whether targets are being met. The use of 'exceptional' reporting procedures (where extraordinary results are flagged up as a matter of course) provides particularly timely information. Where targets are not being met, management can make the required adjustments. Adjustments can vary from relatively minor issues like adapting action plans (increasing frequency of advertising, size of mailing, number of re-calls etc.), to quite serious changes involving strategies. In deciding what changes are to be made, management will find that information from the database will be invaluable.

When the campaign is complete, it is usual to write a final report. This should include:

▶ Statements of expectations (targets, objectives).

▶ Statements of anticipated expenditure (budget allocations).

▶ Statement of actual performance (response, conversion rates, sales, profitability, share).

▶ Evaluation of actual versus expected performance.

▶ Evaluation of actual versus expected expenditure.

▶ Managerial justification (if there is a variation between actual and expected).

▶ Recommendations.

The direct marketing manager should continually learn from his or her experiences. Thus, this report should be used as an input into the next planning cycle, and the whole process begins again.

STUDY 1

Banking on a sure thing?

The man who brought you the Sex Pistols now wants to handle your pension. Ian Darby reports

Virgin Direct was set up two and a half years ago. Unlike Richard Branson's ballooning career, it's founded on something more than hot air.

Initially, Virgin Direct sold PEPs, but it has since diversified into life insurance, pensions and health insurance. It recently passed £800 million of funds under management, an increase of £500 million in a year.

The impetus for Virgin Direct came from Branson himself. Frustrated with wading

through ineptly managed PEPs, he decided to steal a march on existing players such as M&G to become the first supplier to sell them direct.

'When we launched, the accepted wisdom was that PEPs and pensions were things you had to sell to people, they would not voluntarily go looking,' says Tony Wood, marketing director of Virgin Direct.

Virgin has worked on attracting people who, Wood says, are 'put off by the horror

● ● ▶

of dealing with sales people and jargon.' Its marketing, while strongly branded, is not hard sell. Customers respond to a mix of direct response press and television ads. Cold mailings have never been used.

Turning up the volume

An on-site call-centre of 120 workstations handles 10,000 calls a day from Virgin Direct's new prospects and its 160,000 existing customers. Wood says that it sells between 600 and 700 PEPs a day, plus 50 pensions.

Wood argues that the Virgin brand is ideally suited to financial services: 'The Virgin qualities – of good value, cutting costs, not making things more complicated than is needed and of bringing flair and life to any market - all of those applied in financial services,' he says.

PEPs were chosen as a launch pad for the operation because they were the most high-profile product available. Virgin also sought to cut through the morass of gobbledegook spouted by many of the PEP suppliers.

Wood concedes that, as a marketer, he has been handed advantages because of the strength of the Virgin brand and the immense amount of PR it generates. But it would be unfair to underestimate the work put in by his team.

Playing on brand values

'We've added more to the Virgin brand than we've taken away,' stresses Wood. 'My task was to broaden things. To make people think "If that's what it's like buying financial services, what's it like to fly to Orlando with them".' Of course, if things go wrong, this could become a double-edged sword.

Key features of the Virgin Direct 'experience' are service and price, but it also seeks to supply extra value by demystifying financial services and by offering a strong product.

Virgin Direct's £6 million annual marketing spend, dominated by responsive press and

TV, has developed an in-house database of 160,000 customers.

However, this is used carefully. Customers can 'opt in' to receive a six monthly newsletter and selective mailings about new products. Around 90 per cent have chosen to do so. The database is not used to market other Virgin companies.

'What people object to is crap dropping through their letter box,' says Wood. 'We don't exploit the database in the negative sense, but the way we've built it has made it as good as our competitors.'

Marketing support has focused on a twin approach – the perceived popularity of Branson himself and the oblique selling tactics of PEP firms and independent financial advisors (IFAs).

Wood concedes that he has been helped by the obscurity of his competitors: 'If you transport the names like Perpetual, M&G and Save & Prosper out of the finance pages then you just get blank looks', says Wood. 'Our challenge was to use the brand as leverage to take the product to a wider audience.'

'Rival attempts to build brands have failed' says Wood. He claims M&G spent £9 million on its Nigel Lawson ads but gained only £20 million in funds as a result. There are 17 firms selling index tracking products. The other 16 sell 50 per cent. Virgin alone sells the other half.

Keeping ahead of the competition

'We have single focus distribution with no historical baggage', says Wood. The problem for companies such as Eagle Star and Scottish Widows is that while they have launched direct arms they are tied to the old system of selling through IFAs. If they go too heavily into direct selling they isolate themselves from this system: if they don't, they give Virgin a few years head start.

But does Wood see the competition catching up in the PEPs market: could Virgin see its profits squeezed as Direct Line did?

'Their proposition was a combination of convenience and price,' he argues. 'There were no real barriers to entry and other competitors could undercut while following the same philosophy. Because of the associations with our brand. and what we've built up with the customers, it's something companies can't replicate. And there is far more to a PEP and a pension than a low price.'

Having said this, Virgin is putting increased efforts into its diversification away from PEPs. Wood sees pensions as the future and predicts that in ten years Virgin will have more money under management in pensions than in PEPs.

Partners for life?

Currently just 10,000 of Virgin Direct's 160,000 customers are in pensions and life. But its ambitions are supported by its partner Australian Mutual Provident Society, which replaced Norwich Union last year. AMP provides the administrative support, fund management and financial experience: Virgin a brand and skilled marketers.

This summer Virgin will go on the attack to market its pensions and insurance. It will target a young audience through a variety of music and lifestyle titles. Some £250,000 of its £2 million pension ad budget is committed to a press campaign warning of other companies mis-selling pensions.

After this activity thoughts will turn to the launch of direct banking at Virgin. Wood is still not certain of timing, but he says Branson and his team want to go live with a direct banking service by the end of this year. He says that nothing is concrete yet, though Virgin is talking to potential partners.

'Now we've got the main building block products in place we are thinking about it much more seriously,' says Wood. 'And Richard would like, by the end of this year, to have firmed up the plans for a bank.

● ● ▶

Everyone here is really excited about doing that. We are up for it so it's just a question of tying the deal up.'

Virgin is not resting on its laurels – it keeps a close eye on new entrants to the direct PEPs and pensions market. While Wood doubts the tactics of the major grocers will be a significant threat, he is impressed by the potential of Marks & Spencer in financial services. 'The big insurance companies will step actively into direct and the IFAs will like it or lump it,' he predicts.

The sense of laid-back triumphalism you associate with Branson pervades the Virgin Direct office. Though the marketing team is serious about its objectives, it's also having fun: 'We tend to be slightly anarchic in the way we work,' Wood says. 'We all have strong ideas.'

(Source: Marketing Direct, June 1997)

Review Questions

1 Identify the major components of a direct marketing plan and explain how they are interrelated.

2 In what way does a clear business mission aid direct marketing planning?

3 Outline the process of environmental scanning. For what purpose is environmental scanning utilized?

4 What trends in the macro-environment are likely to have the greatest impact on direct marketers?

5 Why is the existing customer base currently viewed as one of the organization's most critical assets.

6 What advantages do direct marketers have in terms of developing profiles of their target markets?

7 What are the characteristics of good objectives?

8 On what bases can we evaluate a strategy's applicability?

9 What are the advantages of testing in direct marketing?

Discussion Questions

1 'The best plan is only a plan, that is, good intentions, unless it degenerates into work', (Drucker 1974). Discuss with reference to the process of plan execution.

2 A charity has established the following objective for its next direct mail campaign: Increase donations by 8 per cent. Comment on the suitability of this objective. What changes if any would you make?

3 Discuss why, with reference to budgeting for direct marketing 'the very idea of a fixed sum to be spent each financial year or season is not sensible for direct marketers', Bird (1993).

References

Berry, L.L. (1981) 'The Employee as Customer', *Journal of Retail Banking*, 3(March), pp. 33–40.

Bird, D. (1993) *Commonsense Direct Marketing*, 3rd edn, London: Kogan Page.

Brannon, T. (1993) 'The Profitable Power of the Response', *Marketing Business*, December-January, pp. 41–2.

Brownlie, D. (1987) 'Environmental Analysis', in M.J. Baker (ed.) *The Marketing Book*, London: Heinemann, pp. 97–123.

Business World (1997) 'Developing a New Bedside Technique', May 22, p. 49.

Christopher, M. and McDonald, M.H.B. (1995) *Marketing: An Introductory Text*, London, Macmillan.

Cook, T.D. and Campbell, D.T. (1979) *Experimentation: Design Analysis Issues for Field Settings*, Chicago: Rand McNally.

Day, G.S. (1984) *Strategic Marketing Planning: The Pursuit of Competitive Advantage*, St. Paul, MN: West Publishing Company.

Day, G.S. (1986) 'Tough Questions for Developing Strategies', *Journal of Business Strategy*, Winter, pp. 60–8.

Drucker, P. (1974) *Management: Tasks, Responsibilities, Practices*, New York: Harper & Row.

Forshaw, T. (1993) 'Testing - The Direct Route to Continuous Improvement', *Direct Response*, July, pp. 28–9.

Ghemawat, P. (1986) 'Sustainable Advantage', Harvard Business Review, September/October, pp. 53–8.

Hansotia, B.J. (1997) 'Enhancing Firm Value through Prospect and Customer Lifecycle Management', *Journal of Database Marketing*, 4(4), pp. 351–52.

Harris, L. (1996) 'The Impediments to Initiating Planning', *Journal of Strategic Marketing*, 4, pp. 129–142.

Hofer, C.W. and Schendel, D. (1978) *Strategy Formulation: Analytical Concepts*, St. Paul, MN: West Publishing Company.

Holder, D. (1993a) 'Planning a Direct Marketing Strategy', *Direct Response*, May, pp. 24–6.

Holder, D. (1993b) 'Customer Acquisition and Retention', *Direct Response*, June, pp. 39–40.

Jain, S.C (1990) *Marketing Planning and Strategy*, 3rd edn, Cincinnati, OH: South-Western Publishing Co.

Jüttner, U. and Wehrli, H.P. (1994) 'Competitive Advantage: Merging Marketing and the Competence-based Perspective', *Journal of Business and Industrial Marketing*, 9(4), pp. 42–53.

Kast, F.E. and Rosenzweig, J.E. (1974) *Organisation and Management: A Systems Approach*, New York: McGraw Hill.

Kruegar, J. (1996) 'Developing a Marketing Budget' *Target Marketing*, 19(10), pp. 118–22.

Linton, I. (1995) *Database Marketing: Know What Your Customer Wants*, London: Pitman.

Littler, D. and Leverick, F. (1994) 'Marketing Planning in New Technology Sectors', in J. Saunders (ed.), *The Marketing Initiative: Economic and Social Research Council Studies into British Marketing*, London: Prentice Hall, pp. 72–91.

Marketing Week (1995) Direct Marketing Supplement, July 14, pp. 33–6.

McCorkell, G. (1997) *Direct and Database Marketing*, London: Kogan Page, p. 147.

McDonald, M.H.B. (1992) *Strategic Marketing Planning*, London, Kogan Page.

Nash, E.L. (1986) *Direct Marketing: Strategy, Planning, Execution*, 2nd edn, New York: McGraw Hill.

Piercy, N. (1990) 'Making Marketing Strategies Happen in the Real World', *Marketing Business*, February, pp. 20–1.

Piercy, N. (1992) *Market-led Strategic Change*, Oxford: Butterworth-Heinemann.

Piercy, N. and Giles, W. (1989) 'The Logic of being Illogical in Strategic Marketing Planning', *Journal of Marketing Management*, 5(1), pp. 19–31.

Piercy, N. and Morgan, N. (1993) 'Internal Marketing – The Missing Half of the Marketing Programme', *Long-Range Planning*, 24(2), pp. 82–93.

Precision Marketing (1997) 'Mitsubishi Test Drives Three Mailings for Data Acquisition', June 2, p. 2.

Roberts, M.L. and Berger, P.D. (1989) *Direct Marketing Management*, Englewood Cliffs, NJ: Prentice Hall.

Schultz, D.E., Tannenaum, S.I. and Lauterborn, R.F. (1993) *The New Marketing Paradigm*, Lincolnwood, Ill: NTC Business Books.

Smyth, E.D. (1996) 'Integrated Marketing Communications: H.J. Heinz Company', *Irish Marketing Review*, 9, pp. 28–33.

Stone, M., Davies, D. and Bond, A. (1995) *Direct Hit: Direct Marketing with a Winning Edge*, London: Pitman Publishing.

Yee, D.K. (1990) 'Pass or Fail? How to Grade Strategic Progress', *Journal of Business Strategy*, May/June, pp. 10-14.

Further Reading

Day, G.S. (1984) *Strategic Marketing Planning: The Pursuit of Competitive Advantage*, St. Paul, MN: West Publishing Company.

Nash, E. (1990) *Direct Marketing Strategy, Planning and Execution*, New York: McGraw Hill.

Segmentation and Direct Marketing

This chapter:

► Demonstrates That Segmentation Is Becoming Increasingly Individualized.

► Examines The Relevant Dimensions Of Social Stratification, Lifestyle, Self-Concept Theory And Family Influence As They Apply Within A Direct Marketing Context.

► Examines Some Approaches To Segmentation Such As Geodemographics Which Have Acted As Catalysts For More Individualized Marketing.

► Provides An Understanding Of Issues Related To Targeting And Positioning.

CHAPTER

3

Segmentation and Direct Marketing

Introduction

The very essence of the marketing concept leads to an inevitable consideration of market segmentation, because marketers are concerned with satisfying consumer needs and wants. In order to do this, marketers must first understand these needs and wants. Second, although as humans we all have a similar need structure, all humans will not have the same consumption needs and wants, nor will these needs be salient to every person at the same point in time. Indeed, it is the notion of varying salient needs and values (or other buying factors) in different individuals (or in organizations) which provides the rationale for market segmentation. Those with similar salient needs and values may be grouped together to form a market segment if their buying behaviour is seen to be sufficiently homogeneous and at the same time different from those of other groups. Indeed, if buying behaviour within a group is homogeneous, a potential market segment exists. Market segmentation therefore helps organizations to identify marketing opportunities more successfully. Companies can develop the right offering for each target market and they can adjust their prices, distribution channels and communications to reach the target market efficiently. Instead of scattering their marketing effort (shotgun approach) they can focus it on buyers whom they have the greatest change of satisfying (rifle approach).

Market segmentation is usually considered to be the act of dividing a large market into smaller, distinct groups of buyers who might require different products and/or marketing mixes. In a mass marketing context, the company identifies different ways to segment the market, and develops profiles of the resulting market segments. Segmentation remains important for direct marketers, because in the current marketplace products and offerings are normally most cost-effective when they meet the needs of groups of customers (Stone *et al.* 1995). That said, direct marketers often approach segmentation very differently to mass marketers. This is because, traditionally, segmentation 'is a top-down approach. The marketer starts with a mass market and divides it into micromarkets' (Shani and Chalasani 1992:45). In contrast, direct marketers can begin the process with information held on their database on known individuals. This results in more precisely defined market segments which have meaningful implications for the marketer in terms of appropriate offers and messages, and which further assist in identifying appropriate targets for future prospecting activity. As a result, many of the variables traditionally used in segmentation remain useful for direct marketing purposes, but are supplementary rather than core segmentation variables. However, such actions are perhaps more correctly termed customer profiling, which refers to the process whereby the customer base is categorized into distinct groups according to customer characteristics. Those characteristics may then be used to identify segments, choose relevant segments, and develop appropriate offerings and messages for these segments. It can also be used in the search for future prospects. As a result, 'effective targeting stems directly from successful profiling' (Holder 1993:24). However, traditional segmentation approaches remain important, particularly when entering new markets, or when seeking new customer groups. Additionally, these segmentation bases play an important role in profiling customers more accurately.

This chapter looks first at the progression from mass production through product differentiation to market segmentation. Then we discuss bases for segmentation, beginning with traditional demographic and geographic segmentation variables. However, these are no longer considered to be good discriminators of consumer purchase behaviour, and as a result we consider geodemograhpic, geolifestyle and psychographic segmentation bases as more recent alternatives and/or complementary to traditional approaches. Next, an especially relevant segmentation theme for direct marketers is analysed and illustrated, namely the trend toward increasingly individualized targeting. This theme is introduced with a discussion of transactional and behavioural data which allows direct marketers to identify who is buying what, when, how frequently and in what quantities, and has led to the development of *biographics*. Through the application of information technology and databases there are clear moves toward targeting individuals. The essence, for the direct marketer then, is to identify segments in ever more focused ways and for them to target markets not only in terms of niches but increasingly as *individual* customers and potential customers.

From Mass Production to Mass Customization

When we talk about marketing today, we invariably think of mass marketing and mass production. However, it has not always been like this. Henry Ford's famous quote, that customers could have any colour as long as it was black, was a reflection of the mass marketing focus at the turn of the century. Great economies of scale were achieved through long production runs aimed at satisfying an apparently homogeneous market. However, as mass production and consumption continued, many organizations developed product differentiation strategies in an effort to gain some competitive advantage (Smith 1956). Product differentiation was conducted so as to offer variety to consumers; it was not however, an attempt to tailor production for different market segments. Perhaps such product differences do indeed appeal to different groups within the overall market, but if they do it is mainly due to coincidence. True segmentation starts with identifying the requirements and behaviour of segments and varying marketing mixes accordingly in order to more deliberately match marketing offerings with consumer behaviour.

Product differentiation clearly represents a product orientated approach in that it is an 'inside-out' management attitude to marketing planning. Greater market orientation starts with market understanding and the identification of market needs and behaviour and thus is an 'outside-in' planning approach. Thus, segmentation accepts that marketing offerings cannot generally hope to be all things to all people and that differences between groups and similarities within groups, may be analysed for marketing planning purposes.

The emphasis on mass production, mass marketing, market segmentation and advertising is increasingly viewed as being less effective than in the past. As outlined in Chapter 1, market changes have already proved challenging for marketers (Shani and Chalasani 1992; McKenna 1988). Indeed, '... it is increasingly difficult to build marketing activities on the notion of a market. 'Markets' are fragmenting rapidly and we are moving towards a time when the only relevant segment is the individual customer' (Storbaka 1997:479). Direct marketers are well placed to deal with market segments of one, primarily because they have the opportunity to identify and communicate with their customers as known individuals.

The result of market segmentation appears to be a dividing of the market into smaller groups. However, rather than seeing the process as divisive, it is more helpful and appropriate to consider it as one of aggregation. In this way segmentation groups customers together as far as it is meaningful for them to be targeted with distinct marketing mixes. Having said this, there is always a danger of segmenting 'too far'. Market 'fragmentation' or 'over-segmenting' may create too small and unprofitable segments and thus becomes less efficient.

Bases for Segmentation

Segmentation involves aggregating consumers into segments with homogenous buying behaviour within a segment, but heterogeneous buying behaviour between segments. The organization then builds up profiles of the different types of customer within the various segments using sophisticated data fusion and analysis. This is now relatively easy for direct marketers, because in addition to the existence of powerful database technology in-house, a whole industry dedicated to the provision of information on customers and prospects has developed since the early 1980s.

This section discusses the wide range of segmentation variables available to the direct marketer. These range from traditional demographic and geographic segmentation bases to more recent developments in geodemographic, psychographic and geolifestyle segmentation bases. Finally, we discuss behavioural indicators because the direct marketer already holds the relevant data on the in-house database.

Demographics

Demographic criteria include age, gender, family size, family life cycle, income, occupation, social grade, education, religion, ethnicity and nationality and have long been used in segmentation. Indeed, such demographic criteria have been relied upon heavily in the past primarily because it has always been relatively easy to access such information. For example, Table 3.1 outlines a profile of the drinks market on the basis of age, social grade and gender.

Demographics remain important as an element of customer profiling. However, they are increasingly considered to be less discriminating than other variables. As a result demographic data is generally combined with other data as we will see later in this chapter. This section discusses the main demographic segmentation bases, including age, gender, social grade, family lifecycle and ethnicity.

Age

Age is an important segmentation base in numerous markets. For example, 'young adult' and 'teenage' segments have long been considered to be significant spenders. Indeed, the 18-24 year-old market has traditionally been considered important because of its size and the high disposable income among individuals within this age group. However, the size of this market has declined in relative terms in the UK through the 'demographic time-bomb' of the mid to late 1980s.

Table 3.1 Typical Demographic Profile of the Drinks Market

	Beer (%)	Wine (%)	Whisky (%)
Age			
18-24	58	23	7
25-34	50	29	8
35-49	45	28	14
50+	30	15	17
Social Grade			
AB	39	40	17
C1	40	30	14
C2	48	20	13
D, E	38	9	10
Gender			
Male	65	22	19
Female	21	22	8

Despite this, they remain an important target market for many products today (Evans 1989).

One complicating factor in targeting these young adults (labelled Generation X) is that they have been found to be particularly individualistic in their behaviour and are generally sceptical of marketing activity (Coupland 1991; Ritchie 1995; Ritson 1995). This doesn't necessarily make it any more difficult to reach them, but influencing them is proving harder. However, it is possible that direct marketing can provide some of what Generation X might be looking for, in terms of greater interactivity and participation in marketing communications. These issues are further explored in Chapter 10.

At the other end of the age spectrum, it is noticeable that the size of older age segments have been increasing. The 'baby boom' generation (i.e. people born just after World War II) has long been a very important target market. This is the biggest single generation of the twentieth century. The first baby boomers turned 50 in 1996 and estimates suggest that, in the USA, a baby boomer will turn 50 every 6.8 seconds in 2001, suggesting that they will remain important to marketers for some time to come.

Research amongst the over-50s market has revealed several characteristics. For example, they don't like to be portrayed as 'old' but at the same time would see through attempts to portray them as 'young', so caution is needed. There has certainly been a move toward using older models and stereotypes in marketing to these older segments (e.g. the use of Joanna Lumley in advertising) and these are generally welcomed. Those in their 60s generally prefer to use cash and are rather cautious consumers. Those over 70 are perhaps even further along this continuum.

Indeed, it seems that although the over-50s are generally grouped as a single market, it is important to be aware that not all of the over-50s are baby boomers. For example, those in 60s, 70s and 80s are from other generations with lifestyles and attitudes of their own. Taken together, however, it is clear that the over 50s represent an important market segment. They account for about a third of the population (in the late 1990s) and are some 18 million strong, in the UK. By 2020 they will represent about half of the UK population.

As a result, profiling should not be carried out simply on the basis of age. Social grade and geodemographics are also being used and there is a trend toward overlaying this with attitudinal research. An example of this comes from the analysis of the TGI in 1993 (reported in Cummins 1994), which identified, based on shopping attitudes and behaviour, segments including: 'astute cosmopolitans', discerning consumers constituting about 19 per cent of the 50-75s; 'temperate xenophobes' (20 per cent of 50-75s) who are less likely to go abroad or eat foreign food; 'thrifty traditionalists' make up 20 per cent of this age group; a further 19 per cent are 'outgoing funlovers' and; the largest group are the 'apathetic spenders' (21 per cent) who use credit cards to extend their purchasing power beyond what they can really afford. It is therefore important not to treat all over 50s as a single group, and this should be reflected in the targeting of direct marketing.

An area of particular relevance to direct marketers is the reaction of the over-50s to being individually targeted. There is strong evidence to suggest that the over-50s do not, generally, like direct mail or telesales as much as younger generations (Evans *et al.* 1996), and therefore direct response advertising is likely to be most appropriate in prospecting within this market.

Gender

Gender is a long-established segmentation variable, not only in the sense of there being products for men and for women, but also because consumption was traditionally confined to the feminized sphere of household duties and as a consequence, much marketing activity was directed towards women. However, female stereotyping has been the focus of much criticism over the last couple of decades. In the mid 1970s there was a general reliance on either the 'mother' or 'mistress' images of women in advertising. Towards the end of that decade criticisms centred on these approaches becoming less and less realistic (Scott 1978; Women in Media 1981; Hamilton *et al.* 1982). During the 1980s a new stereotype emerged, characterized by the 'career woman', but even this was limited and not always appropriately implemented.

One important trend for the 1990s is the continued change in respect of the 'Feminal Consumer' (Henley Centre for Forecasting 1992). Increases in the divorce rate and the singles market have added to the more general changes in sex roles, with women becoming more individualistic through their own careers rather than being house-wives *per se*. Marketing to women, however, may still be in need of updating. There are new female roles such as the independent assertive woman, independent passive woman and independent sexual woman. Some of these clearly relate to what in popular culture has been termed 'girl power'. Understanding of these issues may influence development of appropriate offers and messages to women.

The concept of the 'new man' emerged towards the end of the 1980s and we saw the manifestation of this in the advertising of cars. For example, Audi's 'caring-sharing' man who holds the baby was quite different from the aggressive and selfish boy racers of earlier periods. Whether the 1990s will really see a significant shift towards the caring and sharing new man is debatable. What is clear is that, as female roles change, so inevitably do male roles. The increase in the divorce rate affects both sexes and produces sizeable singles markets, some male, some female, all requiring greater independence in buying terms.

In direct marketing terms, there is an increasing amount of evidence to suggest that targeting needs to be either male or female in tone, style, wording and design. Work by Pidgeon (1997), for example suggests that direct mailings of different styles appeal in differing ways to men and women. This suggests that personalization needs to go further than addressability, but message content and tone may also need to be adapted on the basis of gender. There may also be creative implications in targeting men and women. For example, with regard to direct mail in the automotive industry, men appear to be less concerned with practical details than their female counterparts, and conversely are more interested in the artwork (Nairn and Evans 1998).

Social Grade

Marketers have, especially in the past, adhered to the basic principle of social stratification but have long avoided researching possible segments on the basis of social class in any true sociological sense. This would involve a rather complicated assessment of income, wealth, power and skill. So instead, in the UK and many other European countries, social grade is used. In the UK the occupation of the chief income earner in the household is the determinant and a sixfold classification results: A, B, C_1, C_2, D, E. The occupational basis for social grade in the UK is summarized in Table 3.2.

The traditional justification for the continued use of social grade is basically twofold. First, it is simple to research. All that is required is for data to be analysed according to the occupation of the chief income earner in the household (Market Research Society 1981). Second, social grade appears to have been a reasonably good discriminator of buying behaviour, as identified in Table 3.3. This suggests that ABs are more likely to buy toothpaste and baked beans than are D and E social groups. Similarly, C_2s drink far more tea than all of the other social groups.

However, during the 1980s, a number of significant criticisms of social grade were made, in particular that there are inevitable anomalies in its use. For example, nearly a third of those earning over £21,000 are C_2DE and half those earning £15,000-£21,000 are C_2DE. Thus, the traditional strong correlations between social grade and income have been destroyed. Some in C_2, such as highly skilled manual workers, will be earning more than some middle managers in group B. Furthermore, it was also shown that of 400 respondents to

Social Grade	Social Status	Head of Household's Occupation	Percentage
A	Upper Middle Class	High managerial, administrative or professional.	2.7
B	Middle Class	Intermediate managerial, administrative or professional.	15.2
C_1	Lower Middle Class	Supervisory, clerical, junior managerial or administrative	24.1
C_2	Skilled Working Class	Skilled manual workers	17.8
D	Working Class	Semi and unskilled manual workers	17.8
E	Lowest levels of subsistence	State pensioners, widows, casual or lowest-grade workers	13.0

Table 3.2 Social Grade in the UK

Table 3.3 The Discriminatory
Power of Social Grade

	Toothpaste	Tea	Baked Beans
AB	140	78	89
C₁	119	90	95
C₂	123	108	128
D, E	52	103	40

Note: Indices of usage (national average = 100).
(Source: Market Research Society 1981)

earlier surveys who were re-interviewed to confirm their social grade,
41 per cent had been allocated to the wrong group and this is an
indication of instability of the system (O'Brien and Ford 1988).
Similarly, Coleman drew a distinction between the 'underprivileged'
segments and the 'overprivileged' segments of each social grade. The
most economical cars are not bought by the really poor, but rather by
'those who think of themselves as poor relative to their status
aspirations and to their needs for a certain level of clothing, furniture
and housing which they could not afford if they bought a more
expensive car' (Coleman 1961). Finally, such socio-economic groupings have lost their power to discriminate because of the increasingly
diverse lifestyles in existence today. Despite this, social grade continues
to be used as a convenient descriptor of target markets.

Family Life Cycle

As outlined above, social grade overly relies on stereotypes when
inferring interests, opinion and attitudes. As a result, it is perhaps a
significant indicator of the end of marketing's love affair with social
grade that from 1988 Granada TV replaced social grade as one of the
profiling characteristics in its audience research with family life cycle
(they call it 'life stage') (O'Brien and Ford 1988).

Family life cycle is a framework that to some extent combines age
and gender variables, and attempts to show a family unit's interests
and buying behaviour changes over time, particularly in terms of the
progression from the single bachelor stage, to newly married, married
with children, married with children who no longer live in the parental
home ('empty nest'), and finally to the solitary survivor stage. Buying
needs, values and behaviour clearly differ for the various stages. An
updated life cycle model for the UK is shown in Table 3.4 (Lawson
1988).

A recent promotional campaign by Barclays Bank depicted the life
stages through which their customers go, by picturing a young single
man, then a couple with a family and an older couple whose children
had left home. The overall suggestion is that Barclays Bank has
financial service products to suit not just each stage now, but each
individual as they progress through these stages of the life cycle.
Similarly, the Prudential used a caterpillar to reflect how we

Lifecycle Stage	Percentage of Households
Bachelor	1.7
Newly Married Couples	3.8
Full Nest 1 (With Pre-School Children)	14.6
Full Nest 1 (Loan Parent)	1.5
Middle Age, No Children (Aged 35-44)	1.5
Full Nest 2 (School-Aged Children)	2.1
Full Nest 2 (Loan Parent)	2.4
Launching Families (With Non-Dependent Children)	7.8
Empty Nest 1 (Childless Aged 45-60)	11.6
Empty Nest 2 (Retired)	11.7
Solitary Survivor (Under 65)	3.3
Solitary Survivor (Retired)	17.42
Total	100

Table 3.4 Modernized Family Life cycle

metamorphose through life stages, promising equally evolutionary financial products to match each life stage.

From a direct marketing perspective it is also important to identify who to target within the family. It has been found that some product categories, like life assurance, are predominantly chosen by the husband, while other categories, like food and children's clothing, are 'wife dominated' and yet others, such as choice of holiday and housing, are based on joint decision making, including the children to some extent (Davis and Rigaux 1974). This suggests that direct marketers need to be cognisant of these different roles in targeting decisions.

Children can also have a tremendous effect on family purchasing behaviour. In one survey (BBC2 Money Programme October 1997) it was found that 72 per cent of parents admitted that £20 of their weekly spending was influenced by their children, 22 per cent of parents thought that up to £50 of weekly spending resulted from pester power, and 4 per cent thought that up to £100 of their weekly spending was child influenced. This would amount to £5bn per year if averaged across the UK. Although children clearly have an important influence on family consumption, there are ethical issues associated with targeting children. Despite this children are already heavily targeted by traditional advertising, and there is evidence to suggest that direct marketers may also be considering this market. The Royal Bank of Scotland obtained details of children from subscriptions to the Disney Book Club and sent them offers for a credit card. Children as young as five received the mailing offering at 9.9 per cent APR! (*Sunday Times* 1997).

Most UK marketing trade bodies outlaw practices which exploit minors. But there are usually ways around some of these. The Direct Marketing Association has a clause concerned with avoiding direct appeals unless the product is 'affordable' and of 'interest' to children. However, this can clearly be interpreted liberally. The DMA, does, however, ban the use of lists of under 14s unless there is parental consent. Having said this, in the lead up to Christmas 1997, Lego promoted its kindergarten brick, Duplo, with a £5m campaign through direct mail, plus advertisements in magazines sent to mothers. This is a pre-school market!

Current direct marketers often consider segmentation by life stage. An example is the Tesco Clubcard which results in transaction analysis based initially on life stage, then overlaid by other characteristics such as vegetarianism, diabetes etc. In February 1996 Tesco, via their data analysts Dunn Humby, identified 12 different segments and targeted each with a different version of their club magazine. By November 1996 the figure had risen to 5 000!

The concepts here have been extended and applied within practical market analysis programmes such as SAGACITY which combines an abbreviated family life cycle with income and occupation. The result is a series of 12 categories based on life stage, whether both partners are working or not, and on 'blue collar' or 'white collar' occupations (Table 3.5) (Research Services Ltd 1981).

Ethnicity

Traditionally, ethnic origin has not been a popular demographic segmentation variable (Piper 1997). However, the relevance of ethnic origin in consumption is increasingly being recognized (Tynan and Drayton 1987). For example, ethnic segments may have their own culture, language, religion and distinct product and service requirements.

Table 3.5 Twelve SAGACITY Categories

1	Dependent			1.1	White Collar
				1.2	Blue Collar
2	Pre-Family			2.1	White Collar
				2.2	Blue Collar
3	Family	3.1	Better Off	3.11	White Collar
				3.12	Blue Collar
		3.2	Worse Off	3.21	White Collar
				3.22	Blue Collar
4	Empty Nest	4.1	Better Off	4.11	White Collar
				4.12	Blue Collar
		4.2	Worse Off	4.21	White Collar
				4.22	Blue Collar

Furthermore, attitudes may be significantly different both within ethnic segments, and between ethnic segments and the indigenous population. Indeed, one study demonstrated that attitudes to direct mail were very different between respondents of Pakistani origin and those from the indigenous population (Chudry 1998).

The difficulties associated with accessing ethnic segments for research purposes is arguably the main reason why this has not traditionally been a popular segmentation variable. However, there are now market research agencies which specialize in different ethnic segments, thus making data collection far easier. Furthermore, because of developments in ethnic media, it is increasingly possible to reach distinct segments. One important outcome of this is the availability of mailing lists on the basis of ethnicity. Different message, tone and style of writing may be appropriate for different groups, and direct marketers should be sensitive to this.

In summary there has been much controversy about the use of demographics in general, and social grade in particular for segmentation purposes. The difficulty with using demographics is that they are limited in their explanatory power and are constantly changing. Despite this, demographics continue to be important, particularly because of their ease of use. However, they are increasingly being supplemented by other data types like geodemographics and psychographics.

Geographics

Geographics involves dividing the market into different geographical units such as nations, regions, cities, etc. The company may then decide whether to operate in one or a few geographic areas, or operate in all but pay attention to variations in geographic needs and preferences. Direct marketing is less concerned with targeting different geographic areas than traditional marketers primarily because geography is less of an issue with direct marketing. However, local geography is often very important when considering door-to-door leaflet drops.

The European market is clearly an important opportunity for UK direct marketers. However, rather than assuming that there is a single homogeneous market across Europe, there is evidence to suggest that for many products and services geographic market segments will stay and even become more heterogeneous at regional and even local level (Henley Centre for Forecasting 1992). Any direct marketing campaign that travels across borders must be cognisant of such differences. In Spain, for example, many young people remain at their parental home until they are well into their 20s and 30s. Some don't pay rent and as a result are able to afford more expensive cars and other products than their parents! Thus, direct marketers must be careful of making generalizations on the basis of age or gender across national boundaries.

Later in this book we discuss the impact of the Internet on direct marketing and it is worth mentioning at this stage that although the

Internet provides for personalized marketing internationally, the sensitivities and culture of different nations must be taken on board because it is all too easy to offend, and indeed to break national laws. We deal with these issues later in our coverage of the Internet (Chapter 9) and direct marketing law (Chapter 12).

Geodemographics

Geodemographics describes the combination of geographic and demographic data to profile individuals, and was introduced in Chapter 1. Geodemographics is a targeting system, based on the theory that where someone lives says a lot about their lifestyles and the types of products and services they buy. Put succinctly, the assumption is that 'birds of a feather flock together' (Leventhal 1995). Essentially, geodemographics is based upon small geographical areas, which are grouped into types based on the characteristics of their residents. These areas are represented by their postcode. Unlike sample surveys, geodemographic classifications are based on the UK census (over 55 million people). As a result marketers now have information on all households, and although names and addresses cannot be revealed from the census by the OPCS, the statistics for enumeration districts can be. Such data can be linked with the postal code database (there is one postcode for approximately 16 households) and with the electoral register, and ultimately it may be possible to identify individual households and their characteristics.

As outlined in Chapter 1, Richard Webber developed the first geodemographic data system in 1979 for government purposes. The first commercial application of geodemographics by ACORN was based on the 1981 census, where 40 discriminating variables were identified, and after being cluster analysed resulted in the creation of 39 neighbourhood types. As competitors entered the market, several clones of the original ACORN system were developed. Richard Webber himself set up one of the newer competitors after he left CACI to join another similar agency, CCN (Consumer Credit Nottingham, now called Experian), and developed MOSAIC which analyses the census data together with credit company records and a database on county court bad debt cases.

The most recent Census was carried out in 1991. This resulted in a whole host of different systems being made available to direct marketers including: ACORN; MOSAIC; Super Profiles; DEFINE; Portrait; and Neighbours and Prospects. All of these systems vary to some extent in terms of the data used, the number of variables employed from these sources and the number of clusters of area types which have emerged (Leventhal 1995). For example, the updated versions of ACORN resulted in 54 different neighbourhood types some of which are outlined in Table 3.6.

Because there has been a full geodemographic analysis of the Target Group Index (this is an annual report in 34 volumes of buyer profiles in most product-markets based on samples of over 20 000) it is easy to

Table 3.6 Updated ACORN profiles based on 1991 Census

Categories	Population %	Group	Types
A Thriving	19.7	1 Wealthy Achievers in Suburban Areas	1.1 Wealthy Suburbs, Large Detached Houses
			1.2 Villages with Wealthy Commuters
			1.3 Mature Affluent Home Owning Areas
			1.4 Affluent Suburbs, Older Families
			1.5 Mature, Well-Off Suburbs
		2 Affluent Greys in Rural Communities	2.6 Agricultural Villages, Home Based Workers
			2.7 Holiday Retreats, Older People, Home Based Workers
		3 Prosperous Pensioners in Retirement Areas	3.8 Home Owning Areas, Well-Off Older Residents
			3.9 Private Flats, Elderly People
B Expanding	11.6	4 Affluent Executives in Family Areas	4.10 Affluent Working Families with Mortgages
			4.11 Affluent Working Couples with Mortgages, New Homes
			4.12 Transient Workforces, Living at their Place of Work
		5 Well-Off Workers in Family Areas	5.13 Home Owning Family Areas
			5.14 Home Owning Family Areas, Older Children
			5.15 Home Owning Family Areas, Younger Children
C Rising	7.5	6 Affluent Urbanites in Town & City Areas	6.16 Well-Off Town & City Areas
			6.17 Flats & Mortgages, Singles & Young Working Couples
			6.18 Furnished Flats & Bedsits, Younger Single People
		7 Prosperous Professionals in Metropolitan Areas	7.19 Apartments, Young Professional Singles & Couples
			7.20 Gentrified Multi-Ethnic Areas
		8 Better-Off Executives in Inner City Areas	8.21 Prosperous Enclaves, Highly Qualified Executives
			8.22 Academic Centres, Students & Young Professionals
			8.23 Affluent City Centre Areas, Tenements & Flats
			8.24 Partially Gentrified Multi-Ethnic Areas
			8.25 Converted Flats & Bedsits, Single People

Categories	Population %	Group	Types
D Settling	24.1	9 Comfortable Middle Agers, Mature Home Owning Areas	9.26 Mature Established Home Owning Areas
			9.27 Rural Areas, Mixed Occupations
			9.28 Established Home Owning Areas
			9.29 Home Owning Areas, Council Tenants, Retired People
		10 Skilled Workers, Home Owning Areas	10.30 Established Home Owning Areas, Skilled Workers
			10.31 Home Owners in Older Properties, Younger Workers
			10.32 Home Owning Areas with Skilled Workers
E Aspiring	13.7	11 New Home Owners, Mature Communities	11.33 Council Areas, Some New Home Owners
			11.34 Mature Home Owning Areas, Skilled Workers
			11.35 Low Rise Estates, Older Workers, New Home Owners
		12 White Collar Workers, Better-Off Multi-Ethnic Areas	12.36 Home Owning Multi-Ethnic Areas, Young Families
			12.37 Multi-Occupied Town Centres, Mixed Occupations
			12.38 Multi-Ethnic Areas, White Collar Workers
F Striving	22.7	13 Older People, Less Prosperous Areas	13.39 Home Owners, Small Council Flats, Single Pensioners
			13.40 Council Areas, Older People, Health Problems
		14 Council Estate Residents, Better-Off Homes	14.41 Better-Off Council Areas, New Home Owners
			14.42 Council Areas Young Families, Some New Home Owners
			14.43 Council Areas Young Families, Many Lone Parents
			14.44 Multi-Occupied Terraces, Multi-Ethnic Areas
			14.45 Low Rise Council Housing, Less Well-Off Families
			14.46 Council Areas, Residents with Health Problems
		15 Council Estate Residents, High Unemployment	15.47 Estates with High Unemployment
			15.48 Council Flats, Elderly People, Health Problems
			15.49 Council Flats, Very High Unemployment, Singles
		16 Council Estate Residents, Greatest Hardship	16.50 Council Areas, High Unemployment, Lone Parents
			16.51 Council Flats, Greatest Hardship, Many Lone Parents
		17 People in Multi-Ethnic, Low Income Areas.	17.52 Multi-Ethnic, Large Families, Overcrowding
			17.53 Multi-Ethnic, Severe Unemployment, Lone Parents
			17.54 Multi-Ethnic, High Unemployment, Overcrowding

determine each geodemographic category's interest in the product concerned. In fact the TGI sample design is now based on geodemographic categories. In addition, the National Readership Survey is similarly analysed by geodemographics and this can provide readership profiles for media selection purposes. Table 3.7 summarizes some of the dimensions of ACORN, while Table 3.8 provides a detailed profile of ACORN Type 22.

Geodemographic systems are not restricted to the UK and a number of similar systems around the world are listed in Table 3.9.

In the future, geodemographic databases may prove even more worthwhile. For example, some additional questions which are likely to be of interest to direct marketers may be added to the 2001 census. A selection of additional questions being tested prior to that census are outlined below (Rees 1997):

Category and Label	Description
Category A Group 1 Wealthy Achievers, Suburban Areas	The majority of people in this Group live in a large detached house and have access to two or more cars. They are typically well-educated professional people, corporate managers in their middle-age, enjoying the fruits of their labour. These are the consumers with the money and the space to enjoy very comfortable lifestyles.
Category A Group 2 Affluent Greys, Rural Communities	This Group covers Britain's better-off farming communities - residents here are twelve times more likely than average to be involved in agriculture. Many are self-employed and work long hours. The very high incidence of visitors and households which are not the main residence show that these areas also include many holiday homes.
Category A Group 3 Prosperous Pensioners, Retirement Areas	The better-off senior citizens in society are to be found in Group 3. Living in flats, detached houses or bungalows, these are old folk who can enjoy their retirement in pensioned comfort after their professional or executive careers. They are likely to own their home outright, so they have the disposable income to enjoy themselves.
Category B Group 4 Affluent Executives, Family Areas	These are the well qualified business people, successfully juggling jobs and families. There are lots of working women in this Group. With mortgages, young children and often two or more cars to support, these busy people need their incomes but aren't having too hard a time making ends meet. They are likely to have large, modern detached houses and generally enjoy a good standard of living.
Category B Group 5 Well-Off Workers, Family Areas	In a wide range of well-paid occupations, people in Group 5 are likely to be in couples, often with children aged 0-14. Both Mum and Dad are working hard to pay off the mortgage on their detached or, more probably, semi-detached home. While they are not as highly qualified as people in Group 4, they still have an agreeable lifestyle, often with more than two cars per household.
Category C Group 6 Affluent Urbanites, Town & City Areas	These are the young couples or single people starting out in life, a few years and a couple of kids behind the people in Group 4! They tend to live in flats, terraced houses or bedsits. There are quite a number of students in this Group. Car ownership is average, reflecting the urban setting.
Category C Group 7 Prosperous Professionals, Metropolitan Areas	People in Group 7 share many characteristics with Group 6. However, they live in more cosmopolitan areas with a high ethnic mix. They take the train or underground to the office each day, working long hours in fairly senior roles and making the most of their high qualifications.

Table 3.7 Dimensions of ACORN

Table 3.7 Continued

Category and Label	Description
Category C Group 8 Better-Off Executives, Inner City Areas	These are well-qualified people over a third of whom are single with no dependants. The age profile here is younger than for Groups 6 and 7 and there are many more students and other characteristics of academic centres. This Group also has a relatively high proportion of professionals and executives and shares many of the cosmopolitan features of Group 7.
Category D Group 9 Comfortable Middle Agers, Mature Home Owning Areas	Mr and Mrs Average are to be found in these areas - they are close to the national "norm" on just about every key characteristic. Living in a detached or semi-detached house with at least one car, likely to be an older married couple, Group 9 represents middle-of-the-road Britain. They are not particularly well-off but have few problems with unemployment or health.
Category D Group 10 Skilled Workers, Home Owning Areas	People in this Group are likely to be found in manufacturing areas, working in skilled occupations. They tend to live in terraced homes and are more likely to be couples with children aged 0-14. Most are homeowners and the majority are buying with a mortgage. Although not quite as comfortable as Group 9 - car ownership is lower - people in these areas are also around the midpoint on the social ladder.
Category E Group 11 New Home Owners, Mature Communities	These areas are characterized by people who have bought up their semi-detached or terraced council houses. They are likely to be older couples, often pensioners. Those still at work tend to be involved in craft or machine-related occupations. Unemployment is only slightly above the national average.
Category E Group 12 White Collar Workers, Better-Off, Multi-Ethnic Areas	The relatively high incidence of people from diverse ethnic groups - especially Afro-Caribbean and Indian - characterizes these multi-ethnic family areas. Accommodation tends to be either terraced houses or flats. Unemployment is slightly higher than in Group 11, but overall living conditions are reasonable.
Category F Group 13 Older People, Less Prosperous Areas	These are the areas of older couples aged 55+ who find the going quite tough. The incidence of limiting long-term illness is high. The majority do not have a car. People are generally living in small terraced houses or purpose-built flats, typically from housing associations. Those still at work tend to be in manual or un-skilled occupations; unemployment is above average.
Category F Group 14 Council Estate Residents, Better-Off Homes	These areas are typified by young couples with young children. Housing tends to be council or housing association terraces, often with cramped living conditions, though families tend to be better off than those in other Groups in this Category. Unemployment is relatively high and there are many single parents.
Group15 Council Estate Residents, High Unemployment	Group 15 has a greater ethnic mix and higher unemployment than Group 14. This Group has an older age profile and the highest incidence of limiting long-term illness - almost double the national average. People live mainly in purpose built council flats. Car ownership is lower in these areas than anywhere else.
Category F Group 16 Council Estate Residents, Greatest Hardship	Two key features characterize this Group: single parents and unemployment, both of which - at roughly three times the national average - are higher in this Group than in any other. Overall, living conditions are extremely tough. There are lots of young and very young children, with large households in small council flats.
Category F Group 17 People in Multi-Ethnic, Low-Income Areas	The greatest ethnic mix in Britain is found in this Group, especially of Pakistani and Bangladeshi groups which account for over 40% of the population. Single parenting and unemployment are very high. Many people are living in extremely cramped conditions in un-modernised terraced housing or council flats. Whilst these areas are relatively poor, there is evidence to suggest small pockets of more affluent residents.

Overview	These are predominantly student areas. In addition to students, there are people who work in higher education and young professionals. They are cosmopolitan areas located near universities. ACORN Type 22 neighbourhoods are found all over Britain, but the highest concentration is in Oxford.
Demographics	These areas have 80% more people than average in the 15-24 age group. There is also an above average level of 25-44 year olds, but below average representation of all other age groups. There are above average proportions of ethnic minorities - twice the national proportion of people from the Afro-Caribbean ethnic group, over 3 times the national proportion of people from the Asian ethnic group and, within this, over 5 times the national level of people from the Pakistani ethnic group. In terms of household structure, there are 2.2 times the average proportion of single non-pensioner households.
Socio-Economic Profile	The socio-economic profile of ACORN Type 22 is dominated by education. Almost 47% of the adult population are students based in these neighbourhoods in term time. The non-student population is also highly educated, with 3 times the average proportion of people with degrees. The proportions of women, both with and without children, who work are below average. The level of professionals is over twice the average.
Housing	The housing structure of ACORN Type 22 is a mix of terraced homes (37% more than average), purpose built flats (twice the national average proportion), converted flats (2.7 times more than average) and bedsits (5.2 times more than average). The key feature of the tenure profile is the level of furnished rented accommodation - almost 7 times more than average. The proportion of households sharing amenities is 3 times greater than average.
Food & Drink	People living in ACORN Type 22 neighbourhoods are more than twice as likely as average to do their grocery shopping on foot, though less likely than average to do daily food shopping. The typical student diet is reflected in the range of foods purchased regularly. Consumption of frozen ready meals is high, though consumption of other frozen foods such as beefburgers is below average. Other popular products are brown sauce and ketchup, tinned steak, boxed chocolates and fruit juice. Beer consumption is extremely high, especially of bottled lager, but consumption of wines and spirits is only just above average.
Durables	Car ownership levels are low, reflecting the socio-economic profile of the population. Twice as many people as average walk to work. Although car ownership is very low the car profile is biased towards new, large and expensive cars. Company car ownership is 75% lower than average. 66% more people than average are buying home computers and 83% more people are buying tumble dryers. Purchase rates for other household durables are extremely low.
Financial	The average income in these areas is very low, as might be expected given the large numbers of students. Almost a quarter of people earn less than £5,000 per annum, and only 3% earn over £30,000 per annum. Almost twice as many people as average are opening new current accounts but virtually no one is opening new savings accounts. Ownership of all financial products is very low except debit cards which are owned by 48% more people than average.
Media	The penetration of cable television in these neighbourhoods is 46% higher than average. The Financial Times, The Guardian and The Independent all have much higher than average readership levels. Amongst the Sunday newspapers, The Observer and The Independent on Sunday are read by 2-3 times more people here than average. Both ITV viewing and commercial radio listening are very light.

Table 3.8 Type 8.22 Academic Centres, Students & Young Professionals

Table 3.8 Continued

Leisure	The proportion of people taking holidays is average, but 82% more people than average take long holidays. 2.5 times more people than average go camping and destinations outside Britain and Europe are 82% more popular than average. There is a very high propensity to visit pubs regularly. The proportion of people eating out regularly is slightly above average. Burger bars are popular, as are Chinese, Indian and Italian restaurants. Sports which have very high participation rates are running and training, cricket, tennis, cycling, squash, table tennis, skiing and climbing. Attendance at cinemas, theatres and art galleries is very high.
Attitudes	People here are less likely than average to be happy with their standard of living. They are much more likely than average to search for the lowest prices when shopping. They are over twice as likely as average to be vegetarian. They like to take holidays off the beaten track, but are happy to return to the same holiday destination.

Table 3.9 Geodemographic Systems Around The World

	Vendor	Turnover band*	Data Source
USA			
► Prizm	Claritas	3	Census
► Microvison	Equifax	3	Census
► Cluster plus	Donnelly	2	Census
► Niches	Polk	2	Census
► Acorn	CACI	1	
Canada			
► Cluster	Compusearch	3	Census
UK			
► MOSAIC	Experian	3	Census & others
► Acorn	CACI	3	Census
► Super-profiles	CDMS	1	Census
► Define	Infolink	1	Census & others
► Neighbours & Prospects	EuroDirect	1	Census
Ireland			
► MOSAIC	Experian	1	Census
Spain			
► Regio	Bertlesmann	1	Various
► MOSAIC	Experian/PDM	1	Various
Belgium			
► MOSAIC	Sopres	1	Various
Netherlands			
► MOSAIC	Experian	2	PTT, CARS, Surveys
► GEO	Geomarktprofiel	1	Various
Finland			
► Acorn	Gallup/Post Office	1	Census
Sweden			
► MOSAIC	MarknadsAnalys	1	Personal Registers

* Turnover Band: 1<£1m pa; 2=£1m-£5m pa; 3>£5m pa.

► Are you in receipt of unpaid personal help?

► Do you provide substantial unpaid personal help for a friend or relative with any long term illness, health problems or disability?

► Does your household's accommodation have a garden or yard?

► Do you consider you belong to a religious group? (list of categories provided)

► What is your total gross income from all sources?

These questions could provide some additional data for geodemographics/lifestyle databases. For example, income is a useful measure of potential disposable income; the possession of a garden would be of interest to direct marketers of garden products; levels of personal help might be of interest to service providers; religion could be used to target individuals by church organizations, which are increasingly turning to direct marketing. The 1991 census included a controversial question about ethnic origin, and the questions above may prove equally controversial.

Consumer Psychographics

Psychographic segmentation is not a new concept. Indeed, markets have been segmented on the basis of psychographics since the early 1980s. Psychographic segmentation includes personality, self-concept and lifestyle.

Personality

Personality is a superficially attractive variable for segmenting markets. Personality refers to 'all those relatively permanent traits, dispositions or characteristics within the individual that [give] some measure of consistency to that person's behaviour' (Feist 1990:70). The use of personality as a segmentation variable is based upon the logic that we buy products and services that in some way reflect or extend our personality traits. Indeed, a classic study in the US supported this proposition to some extent in that it revealed Ford owners to be more independent and go getting than their Chevrolet counterparts (Evans 1959).

Various personality traits have proved useful to marketers in deciding how best to approach consumers. Consumer innovativeness relates to how receptive consumers are to new products. Dogmatism is a personality trait that measures the degree of rigidity individuals display toward the unfamiliar and toward information that is contrary to their own personal beliefs. Self-monitoring is the degree to which persons adapt themselves to their social environment. Persons high in self-monitoring behave in a chameleon-like manner and are always trying to make good impressions on others. It is important for them to be accepted by others. They tend to buy products and brands that contribute to making favourable impressions on their reference group. Affinity marketing taps into this, for example by targeting a credit card at members of professional or social groups (e.g. The Law Society). Persons low in self-monitoring behave more in accordance with their own beliefs and attitudes and are less influenced by the perceived or actual approval of their social environment. Different consumers also have different stimulation thresholds in that some people prefer a simple uncluttered and calm existence, while others seem to prefer an environment crammed with novel, complex and unusual experiences. Finally, social character is a trait that ranges on a continuum from inner-directed to other-directed. Inner-directed people tend to rely on their own judgement and standards while other-directed consumers look to others for direction.

Research reported by Publicis (Block 1992) suggests that from 1973 to 1989 there had been a shift in motivators from functional and rational factors (40 per cent to 27 per cent of the population) and other-directedness (static at 35 per cent) to more inner-directedness (25 per cent to 38 per cent of the population). A specific example centres on some group discussions conducted for Levi Strauss in the mid 1980s which revealed general praise for Levi's advertising in which rock music soundtracks were used. Many group members, however, expressed their own personal music tastes to be orientated towards different specific music styles of the time. The result was a poster campaign that showed 12 head shots of different young people who clearly had different fashion tastes, many of them music based. The copy headline of 'we cut our jeans the way you cut your hair: blue jeans cut 12 ways' was the result. Thus, direct marketers may target certain types of individuals for new or innovative products.

Psychographic segmentation is further based on the premise that consumer personalities should match brand personalities. It may seem odd to think that brands have personalities, after all they are inanimate objects. However, because brands are often used by consumers to signal personal values, or to identify with social groups, these consumers feel a need to project their values, traits and emotions onto brands (Goodyear 1993). Brand personality then, is the brand's essential characteristics, expressed in human terms (Restall and Gordon 1993). Just as people have friends and colleagues who play different roles in their lives, they have brands that serve the same purpose across different product categories (Lannon 1992; Woodward 1996). One problem however, it that consumers do not necessarily match their own personalities with the personalities of the brands they buy (Lannon 1992). This only really happens during situations of high involvement where product choice comes as a direct result of personal values, etc. but this just isn't true for the majority of packaged goods.

Unfortunately, personality has had a mixed reception in research programmes. Even replications of the Ford study produced conflicting results, so personality appears to be a less reliable segmentation variable than other variables. Perhaps one of the problems with personality as a segmentation variable is that although an objective personality test might reveal our true personality, we might not know that this is how we are, or we may not agree with it. Indeed, in many cases we might want to disguise our true personality and therefore buy brands that in some way extend those traits we want to portray, and perhaps different traits at different times in different social circumstances. This leads us to a consideration of how we might *want to be* and *how we think we are*, rather than how we *actually* are, according to some externally determined tests and criteria. This is self-concept theory.

Self-concept

This variation on the personality theme in psychographic segmentation is based not on what sort of personality traits consumers possess, as identified through administering standardized personality inventory tests, but on how consumers perceive themselves to be. Indeed, it has been suggested that 'of all the personality concepts which have been applied to marketing, self-concept has probably provided the most consistent results and the greatest promise of application to the needs of business firms' (Foxall 1980).

Self-concept is indeed an alternative worthy of consideration. It is based on the premise that we buy those brands which extend the personality characteristics that we think we possess, or that we would like to possess or that we want others to think we have. The self-concept approach is usually based on semantic differential scales showing series of bipolar adjectives (Figure 3.1) for which respondents may be asked to position how they see various brands, and/or themselves and/or their ideal self-concept. The brand preferred would then be the one closest to (greatest degree of congruence with) the segment's self image or ideal-self image. With distance scores this degree of congruence is calculated and this helps to identify appropriate brand images to create and project. Questions of this type could be included in questionnaires sent to customers or could be sponsored on large lifestyle surveys.

	1	2	3	4	5	6	7	
Sophisticated	A	B	S					Plain
Appealing	S	B				A		Reserved
Daring		S	B			A		Cautious
Sensitive	A	B		S				Insensitive

Note:	
S = self image;	
A = brand image of A	DA = distance between S and A: $DA = \sqrt{\{(3-1)^2 + (6-1)^2 + (6-2)^2 + (4-1)^2\}} = 7.3$
B = brand image of B	DB = distance between S and B: $DB = \sqrt{\{(3-2)^2 + (2-1)^2 + (3-2)^2 + (4-2)^2\}} = 2.6$

Figure 3.1 Self-Concept Distance Scores (Seven Point Scale)

The variants of 'self' are based on the actual self and the more aspirational ideal self and also on whether consumption is private or more conspicuous (i.e. having social connotations) (Table 3.10). Perhaps the most appropriate variants of self for the respective buying contexts are the actual self in the private context and the ideal self in the social context. The smaller the distance score, the greater the degree of congruence between brand and self images. Brand preferences can be predicted on the basis of such congruence. More support for this approach comes from the change in social attitudes outlined in Chapter 1. These include the trend towards greater individualism and self-expression, which may be manifested in the purchasing of products and services which more closely match brand image and self image.

Although self-concept theory has been well established in the behavioural sciences, it has only been since the late 1960s that it has been employed to explain buyer behaviour. For instance, the semantic differential methodology has been used to compare self-image with car images (Birdwell 1968). Generally congruence is found, although not at the lower end of the socio-economic scale due to financial constraints. The matching of self-image with car image is even greater after purchase, perhaps as a way of reinforcing the purchase choice (Kassarjian 1971).

Lifestyle

An example will demonstrate this approach to segmentation. In the 1980s Levi Strauss in the USA went through a new product development programme concerning a range of up-market men's suits. The market research programme revolved around an attempt to discover 'lifestyles'. This is concerned with investigating activities, interests and opinions, sometimes referred to as AIO analysis. Such lifestyle data is then cluster analysed to produce groupings of respondents which are relatively homogeneous and at the same time heterogeneous *between* clusters in terms of their activities, interests and opinions. Each cluster is then allocated a somewhat glib title. In the lifestyle research programme, Levi Strauss developed the following titles: 'classic independent'; the 'main-stream traditionalist'; the 'price shopper'; the 'trendy casual' and so on (BBC 1984). This sort of profile will help determine appropriate product/service features, and will help to arrive at a communications message which is congruent with the segment's lifestyle.

This traditional form of lifestyle (AIO) segmentation provides useful insights into what makes people 'tick'. It is traditional market research

Table 3.10 Actual and Ideal Self in a Private and Social Context

Context	Actual Self	Ideal Self
Private Context	How I see myself now	How I would like to see myself.
Social Context	How I think others see me	How I would like others to see me.

and therefore the data is anonymized and the resulting profiles are very useful for determining the style and mood of promotional messages. Lifestyle segmentation is typically based on respondent answers to a series of lifestyle statements (Likert scales). Table 3.11 reproduces a short selection of the (246) lifestyle statements used in the Target Group Index annual research programme (British Market Research Bureau 1988). However, a recent development in life style research and segmentation is the 'life style survey' which works on a somewhat different basis. These surveys are designed by companies such as NDL and CMT and they essentially ask respondents to 'tick' those responses that apply. A UK lifestyle typology was named Taylor Nelson's Applied Futures and Table 3.12 shows some extracts from this version. Some of these questions may be sponsored by specific companies.

Although the industry has claimed there is now a life style *census*, the reality is somewhat different. Admittedly a large number of individuals (around 20 million in UK) have responded, but the survey is by definition a self selected sample and it is known that some respondents do not tell the whole truth in completing the questionnaire (Evans *et al.* 1997). The difference between the more traditional form of life style segmentation and the current approach is that the former builds psychographic profiles of segments from relatively small data sets and expands these to generalize patterns within the larger population. The latter, however, has the ability to list names and addresses of those who claim to be interested in specific products, brands and services and it is this, of course, that direct marketers value. It provides data on what respondents claim they buy, but doesn't in itself reveal the same type of *affective* data on opinions and 'outlook on life' that can be derived from traditional AIO analysis.

	Definitely Agree	Tend to Agree	Neither Agree nor Disagree	Tend to Disagree	Definitely Disagree	Not Applicable
I buy clothes for comfort, not for style						
Once I find a brand I like, I tend to stick to it						
I always buy British whenever I can						
I dress to please myself						
My family rarely sits down to a meal together at home						
I enjoy eating foreign food						
I like to do a lot when I am on holiday						

Table 3.11 Examples of Lifestyle Statements

Table 3.12 Taylor Nelson's Applied Futures

Lifestyle Category	Characterized by	Percentage of Population
Belonger	Place great store by home, family, country, the establishment etc.	19
Survivor	Disposed towards identification with groups and accepting of authority. Self-expression and creativity are irrelevant.	16
Experimentalist	Attracted to all that is new and different, always looking for new ideas, items and experiences.	12
Conspicuous Consumer	Energy is directed toward the consumer dream via material possessions, take their cues from reference groups, not critical of advertisers, followers of fashions.	18
Social Resistor	Seeks to maintain the status quo, controlling self, family, society, suppressing self in favour of duty and moral obligation.	15
Self Explorer	Self-aware and self-concerned people, self-expression important.	14
Aimless	Uninvolved and alienated, aggressive towards the system, resentful of its failure to provide employment.	6

(Source: McNulty and McNulty 1987)

Geolifestyle

Geodemographic databases have traditionally relied upon the Census as the main data source. The major limitation of Census data relates to the difficulties associated with updating information, particularly because in the UK the Census is only carried out every ten years. In the past, database developers had no other option than to rely on Census data. However, recent developments in 'geolifestyle' databases now provide an alternative. These databases are aggregated to unit postcode level and are available as a result of the development of large lifestyle databases by companies such as NDL and CMT. There are a number of benefits associated with these new 'geolifestyle' databases (Leventhal 1995; Gorski 1995).

▶ In contrast to census data which is collected every ten years, lifestyle data are collected continually. Thus, direct marketers can maintain up-to-date information on customers and prospects.

▶ Unlike the census, geolifestyle databases provide data on named individuals. Thus, geolifestyle databases can assist in targeting of individuals for direct marketing offers. For example, a company selling dog food can target individuals who own dogs, as opposed to targeting neighbourhoods where people *are likely* to own dogs.

▶ Geolifestyle databases can be constructed at unit postcode level, which are ten times smaller than census enumeration districts (EDs). Thus, the resulting neighbourhood profiles are far more precise.

▶ Individuals can be asked to provide additional information relating to personal interests and household income. Such data is not available from the census because the census is designed for public service planners *not* consumer marketers.

▶ However, geolifestyle databases provide less information than the census, and furthermore are not compulsory. In contrast, the census is compulsory and every household responds at the same time.

As a result, 'it is too early to say whether the new 'geolifestyle' approach is superior to the conventional geodemographic route' (Leventhal 1995:174). In any case, the drawbacks outlined previously that lifestyle survey participants are self-selecting, and may not always be truthful suggests that there may be some biases or distortions in 'geolifestyle' databases generally.

Behavioural Indicators

Direct marketers are in the enviable position of being able to use information on specified individuals rather than simply relying on generalizations about market segments. Identification of valuable customers can easily be achieved through segmenting the customer database on the basis of the recency, frequency, monetary value, and product category. Additional information on occasion, person-situation, loyalty status and attitude can also be extracted from existing data.

Recency, Frequency, Monetary Value and Product Category

Frequency
This is a traditional profiling variable in direct marketing, and relates to the frequency of purchase. In direct marketing 'frequency' is used together with the other purchase variables (recency, monetary value, and product category) to identify profiles of heavy, medium and light users.

Recency
This relates to how recent the customer's last purchase was. This will assist the marketer in determining the user status, e.g. lost customer, lapsed customer, recent customer which will have further implications for individualized targeting. Recency is particularly important in profiling customers because customers who have bought most recently are considered to be most valuable to the organization. Additionally, recency is relevant in targeting customers. For example, additional communications can be triggered if customers have not purchased for some time.

Monetary Value
There may be many customers who buy regularly and indeed have bought very recently. However, some of these may be less important to the organization by virtue of the limited amount they spend. As a result, monetary value assists in distinguishing heavy users of the product and service, and contributes to the profile of high spending customers.

Product Category

This involves identifying what products the customer has purchased. Through an understanding of what the customer has purchased, the organization can develop profiles of customers for different product categories. Furthermore, product category information provides some guidance for future cross-selling or up-selling efforts.

Data on recency, frequency, monetary value and product category is useful to direct marketers for a variety of reasons. For example, it can assist direct marketers in identifying their most profitable and loyal customers. Additionally, the customer database can be segmented on the basis of heavy, medium and light users for different product categories. Heavy users have generally been found to be profitable customers, and direct marketers may wish to target new prospects who have similar characteristics. Traditional marketers also target heavy users. For example, beer advertising is generally directed at heavy users. Similarly airlines attempt to build loyalty among heavy users by allowing them to accumulate air miles which can lead to discounts. However, because direct marketers can identify their heavy customers by name in their databases, the resulting profile is far more accurate than traditional marketers could expect to achieve.

Person-Situation

Dickson (1982) argues that different consumers may seek different benefits from the same product, and that desired benefits may alter depending upon the situation in which the product is being used. Thus, Dickson proposes that we move toward person-situation segmentation which essentially is an amalgamation of individual-level or personal attributes and characteristics of the usage situation tied in to the benefits required by consumers (Figure 3.2). Direct marketers will consider the circumstances of their targets. For example, is the customer a young mother, a student, or a recently retired individual? Direct marketers may also consider relevant occasions for product or service purchase. For example, depending on the product category, critical life events such as birthdays, marriages, deaths, graduation, etc. might be relevant. Another aspect of occasion which is relevant to direct marketers is the timeliness of offers, including, for example, renewal dates for household insurance or magazine subscription, the purchase of a car, the birth of a baby, etc. Other information may be provided by customers in response to a questionnaire. For example, customers or prospects may provide information on renewal dates for home or car insurance, when they are likely to move home or buy a new car, when they next intend to take a holiday. This information can be particularly important in both profiling and targeting. Indeed, such 'transactional information gives you an accurate record of response and is a key discriminator' (Stone *et al.* 1995:62). Information can also be accessed via other sources. For example, Kimberly Clark spent over $10 million setting up a database of names of 75 per cent of expectant mothers in the USA. Much of this information was gleaned from hospitals and local doctors.

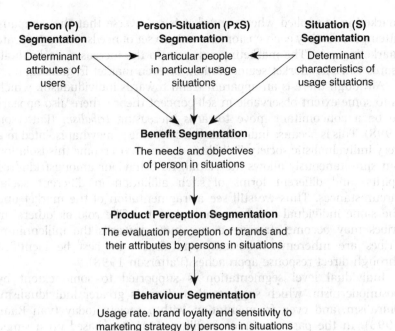

Figure 3.2 Person-Situation Segmentation

The best profiles are those of customers who have purchased recently, bought frequently, have a high monetary value and buy a variety of products' (Stone et al. 1995:62). This information can be gleaned from the in-house database. However, although it may identify who the best customers are, it does not explain why this is so. As a result, profiling on purchase related attributes alone is insufficient. Luckily, most of the segmentation variables already discussed are available to direct marketers, and are a useful supplement to internal data.

Markets are now being analysed in ever more sophisticated and detailed ways and this is leading to the identification and targeting of smaller but better defined segments. Markets themselves are fragmenting, not least because of a trend toward individualism which in turn provides support for smaller but more individualistic or tribal segments. Technology is facilitating this segmentation through more sophisticated, but easier, analysis of marketing databases and it is also facilitating targeting, via mailings, telemarketing, cable and interactive TV and the Internet. Already traditional television advertising is losing ground to techniques that can focus attention on those who are more likely to be interested in specific products or services. It might fight back, though, because it is now possible to target an individualized TV message, analogous to personalized mailing, to a unique address via fibre optic cable (Channel 4 1990). The linking of variables via direct marketing databases is also a significant trend. The move toward using transactional data and overlaying it with a variety of profiling data is moving us to another segmentation category, *biographics*. This might lead to the ultimate form of segmentation – the individual! Custom marketing is applied when a market is so diverse that the company attempts to satisfy each customer's unique set of needs with a separate marketing mix. The marketing response to the increasing individualism is extreme market segmentation, or even market fragmentation.

Although there is an apparent trend towards individualism, which is to some extent observable in self-concept theory, there also appears to be a concomitant move towards increasing *tribalism* (Patterson 1998). This is because individuals have become somewhat isolated in a very individualistic society. Tribalism is seen to overcome this isolation but simultaneously allows individualistic behaviour amongst kindred spirits, and different forms of such affiliation in different social circumstances. Thus we still see a fragmentation of the market and the same individual can have multiple roles. The role of 'others' in tribes may become stronger as we move towards the millennium. Tribes are inherently transient, and thus may best be identified through direct response approaches (Patterson 1998).

Individual level segmentation is supported to some extent by postmodernism, which suggests that there is greater individualism, pluralism, and even fragmentation within society today (van Raaij 1993). In the past, customer profiling was often based on a single attribute, perhaps age, gender, value of purchase. However, such segmentation is not as effective as it used to be, primarily because the resulting segments often consist of consumers with a variety of needs, aspirations and motivations. As a result, segmentation based upon multi-attribute profiling is clearly the direction of the future.

'The segmentation approach is still the method most commonly used in the database marketing industry to target audiences for promotion, and to predict mailing response' (Levin and Zahavi 1996). One of the primary benefits of segmentation is that it allows the organization to 'determine the state of the existing customer base in terms of the degree of homogeneity over a number of variables describing the documented patronage and background data about customers' (Storbaka 1997:480). Because direct marketers will usually have an in-house database or list, segmentation is based upon 'carving up the house file by likelihood of purchase', (Levin and Zahavi 1996) with the resulting segments treated as separate units for decision making. Segmentation is critical for direct marketers, because the resulting information is used to ensure that the right segments are targeted, and bad segments are ignored. For a potential segment to be considered as a target for a distinct marketing mix, it should satisfy a number of criteria, including that it should be measurable, accessible and of strategic value to the organization.

Targeting

Within a traditional segmentation strategy, targeting refers to the process involved in evaluating segment attractiveness and choosing appropriate segments for marketing campaigns. This involves looking first to the mass market, dividing that market into different segments, choosing relevant segments and targeting appropriate consumers within those segments. In direct marketing, targeting is much more of an 'inside-out' strategy. It is based on profiling existing customers, performing cluster analysis on the database, and as a result the segment emerges. It is not forced. Direct marketers often do it the other way around, that is, they begin with the customers they already have on their database. This can result in very accurate profiles, but may exclude potential segments which have not yet purchased. Either way, the target market then represents the defining characteristics of the segments the marketer wishes to gain access to. As a result, important marketing decisions relating to the timing, the creative treatment, the offer and positioning can be informed by information already known about customers (Holder 1993).

There are a number of important decisions to consider in targeting including: which segments to target; how best to gain access to these segments; how to communicate with individuals within those segments; determining which offers and messages to use.

Which Segments to Target

Having identified a number of segments in the marketplace the marketer will have to decide which (and how many) of these segments to target. There are a number of criteria which will help in choosing appropriate segments (Frank *et al.* 1972). These criteria are related to typifying the segments, homogeneity, usefulness, and strategic use in marketing management. The four main and nine subcriteria are (van Raaij and Verhallen 1994):

Typifying the Segments

▶ *Identification*. Differentiation of segment from other segments.

▶ *Measurability*. Identification of segments in terms of differences in individual and household characteristics or other 'measurable' characteristics should be possible.

Homogeneity

▶ *Variation*. Heterogeneity between segments in terms of behavioural response (Engel *et al.* 1972).

▶ *Stability*. The segments should be relatively stable over time. Also, switching of consumers from one segment to another should not be frequent. There should be stability at the individual level.

▶ *Congruity*. Homogeneity within segments in terms of behavioural responses.

Usefulness

▶ *Accessibility.* Segments should be accessible in terms of the use of media and distribution outlets. Segments are being reached in a 'communicative and distributive' manner. Segments should react consistently to communicative, promotional, distributional and product-related stimuli. This means that it must be possible to reach the segment, for example selecting appropriate approach methods and media which are compatible with the segment's media profile and/or purchasing behaviour. These factors have traditionally been in demographic terms, but increasingly since around the start of the 1980s other more sophisticated market profiling and targeting dimensions have been explored and used.

▶ *Substantiality.* Segments should be of sufficient size to enable specific marketing actions. This does not mean that segments need to be especially large, but profitable enough to have distinct marketing mixes aimed at them.

Strategic Criteria

▶ *Potential.* The segments should have enough potential for marketing objectives, e.g. profitability.

▶ *Attractiveness.* Segments should be structurally attractive to the producer, e.g., create a competitive advantage for the company (Porter 1979).

These criteria can be met using a proper segmentation methodology including a pre-test study to investigate the stability of the segments. The discriminative power of the segmentation can be assessed by comparing the segments on specific criteria in the market such as brand choice, brand evaluations and brand attribute importance ratings. This provides the researcher with an independent criterion for the validity of the obtained segments. However, it is important to note that research methods used may determine segmentation. If some variables of market behaviour are difficult, time consuming, or costly to research, sometimes the market will be segmented according to those dimensions that are more conveniently analysed, such as age, gender and socio-economic variables. Indeed, many direct marketers rely on their internal data as a basis for segmentation. Although the profiles of internal customers may be more accurate and reliable than profiles based on external data sources, there is a potential and significant drawback in that the direct marketer may be excluding important customers and segments simply because they have not previously purchased from the company.

It is not always necessary that a different product be developed for each segment. Although this might occur, it is equally probable that there might be different prices charged in different segments for the same product or service (e.g. gas, electricity and train travel) or for different segments based on levels of repeat purchase and loyalty. Similarly, there could be differences in promotion. For example, Levi's advertise on television for a fairly wide market but the same product lines are also promoted with quite different images and themes in the 'style' press (e.g. The Face) targeted at 15-19-year-old fashion opinion leaders (Edmonson 1993). There are also examples where distribution might be the main mix difference between segments. A women's clothing manufacturer might produce a range of dresses but have alternate batches go into different catalogues and department stores. There would probably be branding and price differences here as well but the primary difference would be based on retail outlet and catalogue and hence segment targeted.

The major criteria of measurability, substantiality and accessibility inform the research process. For example, the measurability criterion gives research direction in identifying primary or active segmentation variables. The substantiality criterion indicates market size, potential and share as dimensions to research. Accessibility suggests the importance of secondary or passive characteristics. It is important to note the distinction between active and passive variables: active variables are the variables that are used in forming the segments whereas passive variables are used afterwards to characterize the formed segments more completely.

Which Customers Within Each Segment?

Because traditional marketers use mass communication approaches, it is usual that *all* customers within that segment are targeted. In contrast, direct marketers can choose how many customers to target and, depending on the approach, even which customers to target. The number of customers targeted within any segment should be determined by the campaign objectives as outlined in Chapter 2. In some cases, all customers within a segment may be targeted, or alternatively only those customers who fit a particular profile within that segment might be contacted. These customers might be considered to have a high probability of responding, or they may be heavy users of the company's or competitor's products. This is important where, for example, the costs of targeting (e.g. mailing costs) are high.

Cloning is the process of replicating customer characteristics in non-customers in order to select the best prospects for a direct marketing programme. It is obvious that the more complete a picture which exists of current customers, the better attempts at cloning will be. This complete picture of the customer can be achieved through data fusion and data enhancement as we outline in Chapter 4. Additional data could include demographic, geographic, geodemographic and psychographic data. Indeed, given the existence of sophisticated databases and a whole industry dedicated to providing information on consumers, many organizations already profile their customers on this basis. For example, if Diet Coke wished to find new users, it might look for lists which include people who have been heavy drinkers of sugared soft drinks, but who have recently begun to buy artificially sweetened foods and beverages. This list would form the basis of its strategy. However, it would first need to remove the names of those on this list who are already drinkers of regular Coke, in order to avoid inappropriate offers. All that is required is to match the external list with the house list, and remove names already held on the house list (Blattberg and Deighton 1991).

How to Communicate with Customers

'Effective communications with customers is critical to the successful functioning of any organization, business or otherwise' (Shimp 1993:5). The purpose of marketing communications should not only be to provide product or service information but also to foster positive associations with the brand and to create a product positioning which builds upon competitive advantages and taps into the needs and wants of consumers (Park *et al.* 1986). Having decided which segments, and which customers within those segments to target, the direct marketer must then assess whether direct methods are the most appropriate form of communications. Such decisions can be more easily made because the marketer understands the characteristics of the target audience. For example, if the marketer has difficulty identifying prospects through external mailing lists, it might consider a direct response press or television campaign. This would enable customers to self-select themselves. The response to the campaign would then form the basis of future in-house mailing lists, and response might even automatically trigger direct mail or telemarketing activity. Indeed, it is this ability of direct marketers to communicate directly with their customer base that sets them apart from traditional marketers. Traditional marketers rely almost exclusively on broadcast media which 'targets its audience much as a battleship shells a distant island into submission; addressable media initiates conversations' (Blattberg and Deighton 1991:5). However, as outlined in Chapter 1, direct marketers can now use broadcast media to initiate the conversation (direct response) and then use the database to maintain that conversation.

Content Personalization

Addressability imbues commercial speech with the character of a conversation, through enabling the marketer to respond to what the customer has just said. It is the ability to engage in conversations with customers that distinguishes dialogue from monologue. The customer database plays an enormous part in this process: 'To appreciate the power of a customer database, one must see it not merely as a mailing list, but as a record of the customer relationship: a record of every message and response between the firm and each address' (Blattberg and Deighton 1991:6). Indeed, the data held on customers and prospects can be used to enhance marketing activity, especially when that data is 'orientated towards creating practical solutions as to how to approach customers, how to communicate with them, and how to influence their behaviour' (Storbaka 1997:481).

The system can be used to drive the personalized content of communications. 'Add artificial intelligence and the system can design new messages, and even product offerings, at the individual level to reflect everything learned from past interactions' (Blattberg and Deighton 1991:6). For example, computers can be used to assemble different catalogues for each customer, and magazines can also be developed for each individual customer. Earlier in the chapter we identified that Tesco had identified 5 000 different segments on their ClubCard Database. Their intention is to increase personalization and to eventually to develop a different version of their magazine for every single one of their customers as soon as printing capabilities allow.

In summary, the customer database is fundamental to effective targeting of both customers and prospects. It holds a record of all previous conversations between the organization and its customers, it facilitates customer profiling, it allows offers and messages to be adapted in line with customer behaviour and expectations, and it facilitates assessing the effectiveness of these offers and messages. Blattberg and Deighton sum up the importance of technology in direct marketing targeting:

> **▮▮** *When a low cost computer drives a two-way communications medium in this way, the result is an electronic marketer with as much flexibility as the average human salesperson, a better memory, and a talent for the most numblingly repetitive tasks.* **▮▮** (Blattberg and Deighton 1991:6)

Positioning

'Positioning is the process of establishing and maintaining a distinctive place in the market for an organization and/or its product offerings' (Lovelock 1991). Product positioning is not actually something that is done to the product, rather it is something that marketers do to the minds of consumers. It relates to how consumers perceive the product in terms of image relative to competing offerings (Ries and Trout 1986). In other words, positioning is about making the product or service distinctive (or seemingly distinctive) from its competitors. In doing this, the company is stating to customers what the product or service means and how it differs from current and potential competing products or services. Most marketers consider product differentiation and positioning to be the biggest contributor to success in the marketplace. Minolta, for example, is positioned in the copier market with a differential advantage based on high-volume, low-cost performance and reliability. British Midland is positioned in the business executive segment of the air travel market with a differential advantage based on perceived value-pricing and better in-flight service. Some organizations make a strong position even when they are not the biggest in the market, as evident, for example, in the Avis positioning strategy of: *'We're number two. We try harder'*. Similarly, the AA have positioned themselves away from other breakdown services by suggesting that they are *the fourth emergency service*. In other words they are more important than a breakdown service – they rank as highly as the police, the fire service and the ambulance service.

Positioning is a fundamental element of the marketing planning process, since any decision on positioning has direct and immediate implications for the whole of the marketing mix. In essence, therefore, the marketing mix can be seen as the tactical details of the organization's positioning strategy. For example, when an organization like Marks & Spencer is pursuing a high-quality position, this needs to be reflected not just in the quality of the product or service, but in every element of the mix including price, the pattern of distribution, the style of advertising and the after-sales service. Without this consistency, the believability of the positioning strategy reduces dramatically.

For some organizations the choice of a positioning strategy proves to be straightforward. Where, for example, a particular positioning strategy and image has already been established in a related market, there are likely to be synergistic benefits by adopting the same approach in a new market or with a new product. For other organizations, however, the choice of position proves to be more difficult or less clear and the company ends up by pursuing the same position as several other competitors in the market. Where this happens the degree and costs of competition increase substantially. There is a strong case therefore for the marketing manager to decide in detail on the basis of differentiation. In other words, the organization must identify and build a collection of competitive advantages or benefits that will appeal to the target market and then communicate these benefits effectively.

It should be recognized that very different positioning strategies need to be followed depending upon whether the company is a market leader, follower or challenger, and that as a general rule market followers should try to avoid positioning themselves too closely or directly against the market leader. The reasoning behind this is straightforward, since a smaller company is most likely to succeed if it can establish its own position within the market and develop its own customer base. To compete head-on against the market leader is to invite retaliation and a costly marketing war.

Product attributes and benefits that are important to consumers provide a way to describe the structure of a market. These characteristics relate to the benefits sought by the buyers and the needs served by the sellers. Competing products or brands have positions within the market structure that are based on the degree of each important characteristic buyers perceive these brands to possess. Each consumer has a location in the market structure that corresponds to the characteristics of the buyer's ideal product.

Although a given product possesses many characteristics, only a few will be important in the consumer's decision-making process. These critical attributes are used to differentiate among the competitive offerings. The remaining characteristics/attributes are often related to basic product performance and are presumed to be equal among all brands.

Every market has a structure that can be expressed in terms of these critical attributes. Within this structure, the locations of products/ brands are determined by the strengths of the attributes they are perceived to possess. The closer products/brands are in this space, the greater the likelihood that consumers will perceive them as similar. These multidimensional configurations are called perceptual maps.

Every consumer respondent in a survey can be placed in multi-dimensional space denoting a position on each scale. That space becomes a perceptual map. By identifying consumer characteristics, marketers can learn what kind of product they have. For the strategic planner, the empty space may represent a marketing opportunity. These perceptual gaps in the market can only be pursued if the segments have a substantial size of potential consumers and if they represent profitable holes in the market. Psychological maps can help strategic planners locate markets that are not being serviced, or where two brands are competing for the same segment.

Positioning tends to be based on the characteristics of the product class which consumers value most highly – these could include price or value for money, level of service, quality etc. The normal way of depicting product positioning is through the use of perceptual mapping (Figure 3.3).

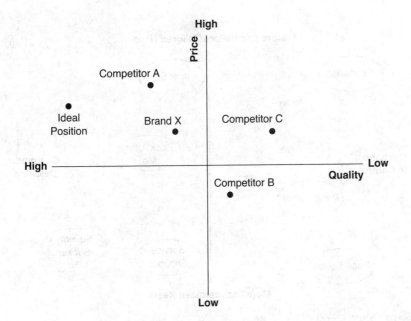

Figure 3.3 A Typical Perceptual Map

Probably the most frequently used positioning strategy is associating a product with an attribute, a product feature, or a customer benefit. For example, Volvo has stressed safety and durability, showing commercials of crash tests and citing statistics on the average long life of their cars. BMW has emphasized handling and engineering efficiency, using the strap line, *'the ultimate driving machine'* and showing BMW performance capabilities at a race track. Figure 3.4 shows an example of positioning for travel agencies. This suggests that the segments of customers labelled 'specialist', 'price buster' and so on, require differing degrees of (a) control over the travel/tour buying process and (b) with the degree of specialized or standardized 'package' the agency provides. Whether this approach would be adopted by travel agencies is debatable, but it could be a significant and worthwhile change in how different *known* customers are treated in store; a good example of one-to-one marketing.

Conclusions

To conclude this chapter, the synergy between the trends towards smaller segments, individualization and direct marketing have been explored. Related to this is that marketers have personal and purchase characteristics of customers in their database and are using this information for personalized propositions. Rather than relying exclusively on general characteristics such as age, social grade and gender, the trend away from profiling characteristics is evident, as is the trend to using transactional data for targeting those who are known to buy in that product category.

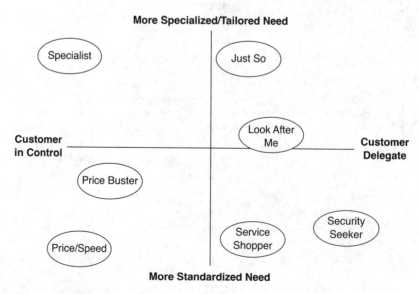

Figure 3.4 Travel Agencies: Service Needs

(Source: Forster 1997)

As we will see in the next chapter, the customer database is fundamental to effective targeting of both customers and prospects. It holds a record of all previous conversations between the organization and its customers, it facilitates customer profiling, it allows offers and messages to be adapted in line with customer behaviour and expectations and it facilitates assessing the effectiveness of these offers and messages.

Some of the *techniques* for analysing and identifying segmentation data, such as regression and CHAID, are discussed in our coverage of marketing research and testing, in Chapter 5.

CASE
STUDY 1

The China syndrome

When the client pulled out, launching a direct mail china business seemed perfectly logical for WWAV. Neill Denny gets fired up

It's a common fantasy for people in advertising, confronted with a client who just won't listen. Buy them out, and then show them how to run things.

Sadly, or perhaps fortunately, such dreams never become reality. Except, that is, in the case of WWAV and Royal Doulton.

In the early eighties WWAV worked on the Lawleys By Post account, part of Royal Doulton, which sold china plates and figurines using direct response advertising.

Royal Doulton decided to pull out of the mail order market, but, instead of walking away from the account, the agency decided to have a go itself.

Compton & Woodhouse was started by WWAV in 1984 with a staff of two: today it is an independent company with a £25m turnover and a staff of 100. Early next year it will be floated.

But the most interesting thing is that the entire business has been built using classic direct marketing techniques.

Put up or shut up

'You've got to put your money where your mouth is', says Rhinalda Ward, now managing director of Compton & Woodhouse. She was one of the quartet that founded WWAV in 1981, working on account management.

(Michael) Compton and (Elizabeth) Woodhouse were, respectively, the marketing manager of Doulton and the designer. They moved across to WWAV, successfully launching their first product — a china figurine called the Goosegirl — in 1985. The agency provided an account team handling media, production and advertising.

Right from the outset Compton & Woodhouse was defined as much by its products as by its off the page advertising. The marketing it choose to specialise in was china figurines and, more recently, plates. Some may find their chocolate box colours a little too rich, but they struck the right note with a significant number of consumers.

By 1987 the operation was turning in a profit of £250,000 — but the next year it hit losses of £500,000 as too much management time was devoted to design, not enough to distribution. Accordingly, Ward was brought in to run the business day to day.

For the next four years the operation was run in-house at WWAV, concentrating on English china figurines. By 1992 the operation, with a £13m turnover, had outgrown the agency. Ward, with the backing of 3i and of the agency management, staged a management buy-out.

Link remain: there are some cross-holdings and directorships and WWAV still handles much of Compton & Woodhouse's creative and media-buying.

The media budget alone is £7m, making the business WWAV's largest media client, but Ward is firm in her denial that the relationship is a cosy one. Because she has inside knowledge of the way the agency runs, she claims: 'it's probably tougher for them'.

Since the buy-out, the business has doubled, but the strategy has remained consistent. There are no shops, no agents, no third-party distribution: the business is entirely direct, with all orders generated from mailings, inserts and press. So media selection is critically important.

There are two main product lines: plates and figurines, with distinctive customer profiles. Figurines are more upmarket, at between £135 and £500; plates range from £20 to £35.

● ● ▶

Anatomy of a collector

Figurines are bought, or rather collected, by a group of middle-aged women described by Ward as 'Mrs M&S': middle middle class or lower middle class. They buy the figurines and display them, with some obsessively collecting the whole series. These women (and some men — 20 per cent are male) wear real jewellery, like flowers and are 'neat rather than flashy'.

They contrast with the plate collectors, who, to extend the retail analogy, are more Iceland than M&S. There are fewer passionate collectors of the plates, partly because they are larger and harder to display. Some collect whole sets of 12, even leaving them in the original packaging to enhance their value.

Both sets of customers are quite distinctive, with strong lifestyles. Could potential customers be identified from lifestyle indicators? Ward says they have considered this approach, but ruled it out on cost grounds. Off the page press still remains far cheaper in costs per response terms.

TV has been explored as a media option, with ads on satellite and Channel 4, and it tends to attract a different type of customer, but press remains the favourite. However, cost per response between TV and press is broadly similar. Telemarketing has been considered, but ruled out on the grounds that the customers are of the generation happier to respond by post rather than by phone. But the Internet has been looked into.

Over the years a substantial customer database has developed, which is mailed regularly, with packs rolling out to selections within it on average every seven days.

Why aren't the products sold through retailers? 'People wouldn't buy from a shop' explains Ward, 'because they need the detail contained in a press ad to convince them'.

The company is a large direct response advertiser. Has it built a brand in addition to its business this way? 'Yes, we have a brand, a distinctive look, that comes from the ad as well as the product. Everything has to be consistent,' she says.

On the product side, Compton & Woodhouse still concentrates on the figurines that made its name. They are designed in house, with colours and themes decided on first, and then a sculptor is commissioned to produce the figure. All are made in fine bone china from one of the three great English china houses, Wedgwood, Royal Worcester and Royal Doulton.

The art of the deal

A recent diversification into fine art prints has proved successful. So successful, in fact, that in November Compton & Woodhouse bought Collingbourne Fine Arts, its main rival in the direct marketing of fine arts prints. These are more upmarket products, costing over £600 for the set, advertised off the page in the *Sunday Times*. Other new product areas under consideration are jewellery and china tea sets.

But the major development is the float, pencilled in for a year's time. Ward will start talking to brokers this autumn, with a view to an AIM listing after the next set of figures — the financial year runs from April to April, with the last quarter always the best-performing.

And when that happens, Compton & Woodhouse will find itself firmly on the front pages, rather than hidden away at the back.

(Source: *Marketing Direct*, September 1997, pp. 32–3)

Success on a plate

Growth of the database (indexed)		Turnover	£ millions
1987	100	1987	£3.4m
1988	138	1988	£3.4m
1989	207	1989	£6.3m
1990	321	1990	£10.3m
1991	433	1991	£12.2m
1992	528	1992	£12.6m
1993	647	1993	£15.8m
1994	783	1994 (annualized)	£17.1m
1995	914	1995/6	£19.4m
1996	1086	1996/7	£22.9m
1997 (half year)	1211		

Source: Compton & Woodhouse

Review Questions

1   What are the differences between product differentiation and market segmentation and why has the latter become more favoured than the former?

2   What sort of market segments might a scheme like Heinz at Home or the Tesco Clubcard produce and from which types of data?

3   What are the implications for direct marketing of targeting:

(a) women;
(b) ethnic groups;
(c) different age groups.

4   Discuss the relative contributions to direct marketing of demographics, psychographics, geodemographics and transactional data.

Discussion Questions

1   What are the direct marketing implications of the market trends of individualism and tribalism?

2   How would you go about segmenting and targeting a market for life assurance products?

3   What are the implications for direct marketing activity on behalf of a car manufacturer, of increased globalization of marketing on the one hand and on the other hand the suggestion that different markets are increasingly localized?

References

BBC (1984), *Not By Jeans Alone*, Commercial Breaks.

Birdwell, A. (1968), 'Influence of Image Congruence on Consumer Choice', *Journal of Business*, January, pp. 76–88.

Blattberg, R.C. and Deighton, J. (1991) 'Interactive Marketing: Exploiting the Age of Addressability', *Sloan Management Review*, Fall, pp. 5–14.

Block, R. (1992), *Sales Talk*, BBC Radio 4, January.

British Market Research Bureau (1988) The Target Group Index.

Channel 4 (1990), *Direct Marketing*, Equinox Series.

Chudry, F. (1998) 'Attitude Toward Direct Mail: A Comparative Study of UK's Indigenous Population and the Pakistani Community', Proceedings of the 1998 Annual Conference of the Academy of Marketing, Adding Value to Marketing, Sheffield Hallam University, pp. 112–16.

Coleman, R. P. (1961) 'The Continuing Significance of Social Class to Marketing', *Journal of Consumer Research*, 10 (December), pp. 265–80.

Coupland, D. (1991) *Generation X: Tales for an Accelerated Culture*, London: Abacus.

Cummins, B. (1994) 'Time Pundits', *Marketing Week*, 8 April, pp. 29–31.

Davis, H., and Rigaux, B. (1974) 'Perception of Marital Roles in Decision Processes', *Journal of Consumer Research*, 1, pp. 51–61.

Dickson, P. R. (1982) 'Person-Situation: Segmentation's Missing Link', *Journal of Marketing*, 6 (Fall), pp. 56–64.

Edmonson, R. (1993), reported in 'Levi Zips into Youth Market with Hip Ads', *Marketing*, 17 June.

Engel, J.F., Fiorillo, H.F. and Cayley, M.A. (1972) *Market Segmentation. Concepts and Applications*, New York: Holt, Rinehart & Winston.

Evans, F.B. (1959) 'Psychological and Objective Factors in Predicting Brand Choice: Ford versus Chevrolet', *Journal of Business*, October, pp. 340–69.

Evans, M.J. (1989) 'Consumer Behaviour Towards Fashion', *European Journal of Marketing*, 23(7), pp. 7–16.

Evans, M.J., O'Malley, L., Mitchell, S. and Patterson, M. (1997) 'Consumer Reactions to Data-Based Supermarket Loyalty Schemes', *Journal of Database Marketing*, 4(4), pp. 307–20.

Evans, M. J., O'Malley, L. and Patterson, M. (1996) 'The Growth of Direct Marketing and Consumer Attitudinal Response to the Privacy Issue' *Journal of Targeting, Measurement and Analysis for Marketing* 4(3), pp. 201–13.

Feist, J. (1990) *Theories of Personality* (3rd Ed.), Fort Worth, TX: Holt, Rinehart & Winston.

Forster, S. (1997) 'Direct Marketing in the Travel and Tourism Sector', *IDM Lecture*, UWE, Bristol, May.

Foxall, G.R. (1980), *Consumer Behaviour: A Practical Guide*, London: Routledge.

Frank, R.E., Massy, W.F. and Wind, Y. (1972) *Market Segmentation*, Englewood Cliffs, NJ: Prentice-Hall.

Goodyear, M. (1993) 'Reviewing the Concepts of Brands and Branding', *Marketing and Research Today*, May, pp. 75–9.

Gorski, D. (1995) 'Systems for Geodemographic and Lifestyle Analysis and Targeting', *Journal of Targeting, Measurement and Analysis for Marketing*, 3(4), pp.372-380.

Hamilton, R., Haworth, B. and Sadar, N. (1982), *Adman and Eve*, Department of Marketing, Lancaster University.

Henley Centre for Forecasting (1992), Presentation to Market Research Society, 5th March, Bristol.

Holder, D. (1993) 'Planning a Direct Marketing Strategy', *Direct Response*, May, pp. 24–26.

Kassarjian, H.H. (1971) 'Personality and Consumer Behaviour', *Journal of Marketing Research*, November, pp. 409–18.

Lannon, J. (1992) 'Asking the Right Questions: What do People do with Advertising?', *Admap*, 27(3), pp. 11–16.

Lawson, R.W. (1988) 'The Family Life Cycle: A Demographic Analysis', *Journal of Marketing Management*, 4(1), pp. 13–32.

Leventhal, B. (1995) 'Evaluation of Geodemographic Classifications', *Journal of Targeting, Measurement and Analysis for Marketing*, 4(2), pp. 173–83.

Levin, M. and Zahavi, J. (1996) 'Segmenation Analysis with Managerial Judgement', *Journal of Direct Marketing*, 10(3), Summer, pp. 28–47.

Lovelock, C.H. (1991) *Services Marketing*, 2nd edn, Englewood Cliffs, NJ: Prentice Hall.

Market Research Society (1981), *Working Party Report on Social Grade*, London: MRS.

McKenna, R. (1988) 'Marketing in the Age of Diversity', *Harvard Business Review*, September/October, pp. 88–95.

McNulty, C., and McNulty, R. (1987), *Applied Futures, Social Value Groups*, Taylor Nelson.

Nairn, A. and Evans, M.J. (1998) 'Direct Mailshots: The Gender Effect', Proceedings of the 1998 Annual conference of the Academy of Marketing, Adding Value to Marketing, Sheffield Hallam University, pp. 214–18.

O'Brien, S., and Ford, R. (1988) 'Can We at Last Say Goodbye to Social Class?', *Journal of the Market Research Society*, 30, pp. 289–332.

Park, C.W., Jaworski, B.J. and MacInnis, D.J. (1986) 'Strategic Brand Concept-Image Measurement', *Journal of Marketing*, 50(October), pp. 135–45.

Patterson, M. (1998) 'Direct Marketing in Postmodernity: Neo-Tribes and Direct Communications', *Marketing Intelligence and Planning*, 16(1), pp. 68–74.

Pidgeon, S. (1997) 'The Success and Future of Gender-Specific Fund-raising Propositions', *Journal of Not for Profit Marketing*, 2(1) pp. 22–34.

Piper, J. (1997) 'Britain's Ethnic Markets', *Marketing*, January, pp. 18–21.

Porter, M.E. (1979) 'How Competitive Forces Shape Strategy', *Harvard Business Review*, 57(2), pp. 137–145.

Rees, P. (1997) *Questionnaire to Users of Census Data: Views about the 2001 Census of Population*, ESRC/JISC, Summer.

Research Services Ltd. (1981) *SAGACITY*.

Restall, C. and Gordon, W. (1993) 'Brands – The Missing Link: Understanding the Emotional Relationship', *Marketing and Research Today*, May, pp. 59–67.

Ries, A. and Trout, J. (1986) *Positioning: The Battle for Your Mind*, New York: McGraw Hill.

Ritchie, K. (1995) *Marketing to Generation X*, New York: Lexington Books.

Ritson, M. (1995), 'Marketing to Generation X: Strategies for the Measurement and Targeting of Advertising's Lost Generation', Second Annual Henry Stewart Conference on *Advances in Targeting Measurement and Analysis for Marketing*, 7 June, London.

Scott, R.. (1978), *The Female Consumer*, Associated Business Programmes.

Shani, D. and S. Chalasani, (1992) 'Exploiting Niches Using Relationship Marketing', *The Journal of Services Marketing*, 6(4), pp. 43–52.

Shimp, T.A. (1993) *Promotion Management and Marketing Communications* (3rd ed.), Fort Worth, TX: The Dryden Press.

Smith, W.R. (1956) 'Product Differentiation and Market Segmentation as Alternative Marketing Strategies' *Journal of Marketing*, 21(July), pp. 3–8.

Stone, M., Davies, D. and Bond, A. (1995) *Direct Hit: Direct Marketing With A Winning Edge*, London: Pitman.

Storbaka, K. (1997) 'Segmentation Based on Customer Profitability – Retrospective Analysis of Retail Bank Customer Bases', *Journal of Marketing Management*, 13, pp. 479–92.

Sunday Times (1997) 'Taking Advantage of Children', September 28th, p. 6.

Tynan, A.C. and Drayton, J. (1987) 'Market Segmentation', *Journal of Marketing Management*, 2(3), pp. 301–35.

van Raaij, W.F., and Verhallen, T.M.M. (1994) 'Domain-Specific Market Segmentation', *European Journal of Marketing*, 28(10), pp. 49–66.

van Raaij, W.F. (1993), 'Postmodern Consumption', *Journal of Economic Psychology*, 14, pp. 541–63.

Women in Media (1981), *Women in Advertising*, London: WIM Video.

Woodward, S. (1996) 'Competitive Marketing', in D. Cowley (ed.), *Understanding Brands*, 2nd edn, London: Kogan Page.

Further Reading

Evans, M. J. (1994) 'Market Segmentation' in M. Baker (ed.) *The Marketing Book*, London: Heinemann.

Evans, M. J. (1994) 'Domesday Marketing', *Journal of Marketing Management*, 10(5), pp. 409–31.

Evans, M. J. (1998) 'From 1086 and 1984: Direct Marketing into the Millennium', *Marketing Intelligence and Planning*, 16(1), pp. 56–67.

The Marketing Database

This chapter:

► Analyses Some Of The Technological
Developments Which Facilitate Greater
Customization Of Marketing.

► Explores The Nature And Implications
Of The Marketing Database Within A
Direct Marketing Context.

► Examines Some Of The More
Significant Developments In Databases.

► Demonstrates The Power Of Data
Fusion And Data Mining.

The Marketing Database

STUDY 1

Mercury Communications and Database Marketing: Flowing with the current of information

It's morning, and you're running the bath, but for some reason this morning things just aren't proceeding the way they should. The water is on full force, but the plug doesn't seem to fit right; nearly as fast as the water is pouring in it's draining away, and a successful bathing experience is looking less and less likely. But is the problem the amount of water, or the plug?

In this decade, and no doubt in decades to come, the simile that compares the inexorable flow of water with the torrent of information that we live with and process every day, is an increasingly apt one. Businesses that are collecting and analysing all manner of data in order to improve their value to their customers face an Olympian task if they are to gather and manage all the appropriate information. If the amount of water in the analogy above stands for the acquisition of data or customers, and the plug represents their efficient retention, then it's clear that sheer volume of information by itself is virtually meaningless if the method of retention

doesn't 'fit'. Like the flow of water, data must be harnessed, dammed, channelled, if it is to be of any use. Enormous volumes of either water or information have no inherent value – and can even be a hazard.

The drive to refine and harness data has been vital to Mercury Communications throughout its 15 year history. However, exceptional customer growth in the early 1990s prompted Mercury to undertake a large-scale data cleaning project. Working with database marketing specialists Dunn-Humby Associates, rules were developed for recognizing any faults in the incoming data, such as duplicate entries and a resulting 'master system' was set up. Using data regarding households, business sites or subsidiary offices, pictures and information were slowly built up from Mercury's 1.2 million customer-records. This programme helped illuminate the ongoing complexities involved in collecting, analysing and applying customer data.

Data cleaning is now ongoing at Mercury, but as Sarah Rowe, Mercury Communications' Database Marketing Manager points out, 'Database marketing and telecommunications are both extremely fast-moving industries. We needed more efficiency and more power on a daily basis – not just for the occasional project. We also had to be able to offer different services to different customers and needed a database system sophisticated enough to allow us to achieve this'. In 1995, Mercury decided to build itself a new database. The challenge – and the demand from all Mercury's depart-

ments – was to be able to collate the data effectively, and to use it intelligently for a whole range of purposes. To this end, an internal team was assembled that consisted of representatives from many different departments, with the task of agreeing on a supplier to look after both the acquisition and the retention of data – a package to include marketing strategy, data processing, technological compatibility, and top of the mark quality. After an extensive tendering process, DunnHumby was awarded the contract.

The data cleaning project at Mercury meant that DunnHumby was already on board, with an insider's knowledge of Mercury's particular market and the challenges the company faced; the relationship was to become even more intimate as the design and implementation of the database commenced. 'Like a marriage,' is how Rowe characterizes it, and describes the attendant changes, demands, honeymoon periods, peaks and valleys as the two companies began to work more and more as a team. With the size and scale of Mercury, the complexity of the data, and sites all over the country offering all combinations of partial and complete services – both companies were under enormous pressure to, as Rowe puts it, 'Glue all the information together, and maintain the right knowledge at the right level.'

Water and information are again invoked as Rowe describes the initial stages of the partnership: 'If we use what we call the

● ● ▶

'swimming pool analogy', DunnHumby was building the swimming pool, or the database. Meanwhile, lots of other information was flowing into different 'holding tanks' around the Mercury network, while Mercury's Information Systems department was simultaneously building the 'pipeline' to the database. The objective was that the database would be of real value to all Mercury's departments, and that responsibility for the system's evolution would be a shared endeavour between these departments. 'At the outset of the database's design,' recalls Rowe, 'we specified everything we needed, everything we wanted, and everything we could possibly dream of ever wanting – and still, we're adding, changing, growing.... The database is adaptable and allows us to do this – to change direction, to add products, services, customer classification. There's a constant stream of new demands on the system.'

Mercury considers itself to be unreservedly customer-driven which meant that one of the main issues the company wanted to address was that of lapsed customers: those who sign up for a service but never use it; and those who used it regularly but have inexplicably stopped. The range of reasons why a customer may lapse is wide and very individual – whether the customer is domestic or business. The database now provides Mercury with the capability to identify lapsed customers: in fact sometimes to identify them before they lapse, and to take appropriate action: a single well-timed and informed telephone call to a customer can identify whether there's a problem and offer some solutions.

Edwina Dunn of DunnHumby Associates remarks that the revenue generated from reactivation can be phenomenal. The database is also a valuable tool in assessing which media source yields the best revenue stream in terms of different advertising campaigns; customers can be tracked from origin through to outcome – how they were signed up and what kind of customer they turned out to be – and the conclusions fed into marketing strategy. Says Dunn, 'Most companies traditionally have measured their success by how much of a certain service they are selling and how much revenue is generated from each area. We believe, instead, that the vitally important information is: How many customers spend how much money with you and on which combinations of services? It's sales by customer that count – not by product.'

Rowe concurs. 'We're using the database to identify similarities between groups of people, to respond to the fact that not all businesses within a certain industry are identical. It seems obvious that a large commercial dairy farm will have different telecommunications needs than a small family-run concern in the same field and now we can reflect this in our services.' The service can be as simple as identifying which customers consistently pay their bills late, and offering them a different billing date in a more convenient time of the month. Or it can be more specialist: last year on France's 'phone day' Mercury had already identified those customers who regularly phone that country and sent an informative mailing only to this select group. By taking this approach rather than sending out a blanket mailing, Mercury not only saved itself time and money, but offered a truly useful service to an appropriate segment of its customer base.

But it has grown even more sophisticated since then, through the 'what-if' scenarios that the database enables. 'Now' says Rowe 'in a similar circumstance we might wonder 'If we did a promotion regarding France what kind of return would we get?' and be able, very quickly, to have a reliable figure in front of us. No matter how many variables to a particular equation we can dream up, the database can respond. We never used to have the luxury of having even simple business decisions supported by concrete evidence and actual information.'

Both Rowe and Dunn share the deeply-held belief that customers are eager to offer their information and opinions, provided they are convinced that someone is listening. Rowe expands, 'We owe our customers the respect of actually recording what they've told us. Our customers know and understand us to be caring and innovative, and database marketing lets us listen more effectively. I would hope that we are being useful to our customers – not just giving them a service, but helping them do something with it.' Adds Dunn, 'Telecoms is the marketplace of the future -very few industries can respond as quickly in terms of analysing data, looking at the ways in which customers are using telecommunications, and then swiftly providing new tariffs and products accordingly. And customers today are sophisticated enough to know this, and to look for the proof that a supplier can give them what they need.' Mercury has used analysis of customer call patterns to develop and target telecommunication packages appropriately. It has developed attractive tariff packages for UK or international calls which separately address the consumer and business market. In fact, by linking information across departments, by supplying important supporting evidence for market research and product development, and by allowing the anticipation of customers' needs – database marketing is turning out to be a vital 21st century tool that will help give Mercury the competitive edge.

© Dunn Humby Associates

■

Introduction

In Chapter 1 we outlined that the growth of direct marketing was facilitated by both demand and supply changes in the market. On the demand side we pointed to consumers' desire to be treated more as individuals, while marketers required more effective media to target consumers. On the supply side, there have been opportune technological developments over the last decade or so which have influenced the way in which market information can be collected, stored and utilized. Technology has clearly been a factor in the growth of the direct marketing industry, with the most significant developments being the increasing capabilities of computers and advances in relational databases. Indeed, the power, speed, memory and storage capacity of computers has been continually improving over the last ten years. There was also a related decline in the costs associated with the acquisition of technology. As a result of both increases in capacity and cost reductions more and more organizations have been able to avail of database technology in running their marketing operations. Indeed, nine out of ten companies in a DMIS survey claimed to have a marketing database and 92 per cent of these say they plan more database activity (DMIS 1997). The sectors in which marketing databases are more prevalent are automotive, mail order, publishing and charity, while pharmaceutical and DIY sectors have less of a database presence.

There are now a proliferation of databases in existence, including geodemographic, lifestyle and purchase data, all of which improve the targetability of direct communications. These developments have been important because 'direct marketing depends on customer information for its effectiveness' (Stone *et al.* 1995:70). This information needs to be accurate and easily accessible to managers if the benefits are to be maximized. The existence of a customer database enhances the speed and efficiency of accessing and utilizing customer data. Equally, the database plays an important role in measuring response to direct marketing programmes.

In terms of the in-house utilization of databases the move from manual files to computer files greatly increased the amount of information which could be stored and thus facilitated easier access to data. Furthermore, the introduction of relational databases has greatly enhanced the flexibility of manipulating data (Fletcher 1990). Further developments allow marketing databases to reside on the mainframe, allowing 'virtually unlimited access to data at any time' (Burnett 1994:68). Database technology facilitates the capture, storage, retrieval, analysis and manipulation of detailed customer data 'not only for the purpose of improving operational efficiency, but also for "fine-tuning marketing programmes"' (Uncles 1994). Furthermore, the wide availability of advanced statistical techniques, such as regression, discriminant analysis, CHAID and the development of neural networks, has enhanced marketer's 'ability to optimize customer response by using internal database information' (Bickert

1994:153). We discuss GIS in greater depth in the later section on Data Fusion.

This chapter concentrates on the means of storing and retrieving individual data – the marketing database. The database lies at the heart of much direct marketing though it should not be the central focus; this position should still be reserved for the customer.

Database Marketing: An Overview

> ❧ Database marketing is the process of systematically collecting, in electronic or optical form, data about past, current and/or potential customers, maintaining the integrity of the data by continually monitoring customer purchases and/or by inquiring about changing status and using the data to formulate marketing strategy and foster personalized relationships with customers ❧
> (De Tienne and Thompson 1996).

Database marketing involves the use of computer systems and data to generate the information required for marketing decisions in a timely and structured manner. Direct marketers rely on data in order to personalize, segment and profile customers in their target market. Implicit in the idea of personalized communications is that direct marketers target individuals, by name, at their known address. However, a more strategic use of the data is to ensure that the communication is relevant to the recipient by acknowledging previous transactions, personal circumstances, etc. Profiling involves using the data held on one group of customers to identify other, potential customers (prospects) with similar characteristics. Direct marketers therefore need to ensure that accurate and reliable data is available in a flexible and cost effective manner. The database is therefore central to successful direct marketing. The information held on the database is also very valuable in planning for direct marketing as identified in Chapter 2. It can help the organization to understand its target market, its competitors and its customers. It can assist in identifying trends and opportunities within the market. Customer information is particularly important in both strategic and tactical terms, and it has a number of important uses (Linton 1995):

▶ To improve customer handling by making information available to staff responsible for sales, enquiries, help-lines, order processing, complaints, service or other customer facing activities.

▶ To improve understanding of the customer's purchasing life-cycle.

▶ To identify opportunities to offer customers a range of other products or services tailored to their needs. Taken to its logical conclusion, this could enable a company to deal with its customers on a one-to-one basis.

Database Basics

What makes a good database?

A good database is one which allows for flexible, accurate and quick access to the records held. Flexibility implies the ability to interrogate the database in new ways as new questions or opportunities present themselves. The key to flexibility is data structure. Accuracy results from quality name and address management, while the ability to generate information quickly relates to the power and speed of the technology being used. This is particularly important when we consider the vast amount of data held on databases today.

Information on a database is usually structured on the basis of files, records and fields. In order to understand how a database works, a simple analogy is a manual filing system. A manual system is made up of filing cabinets, within which there are individual suspension files. The database is the equivalent of the manual filing system, individual files are the filing cabinets, records are the suspension files (which might pertain to individual customers), and fields the different pieces of information held within those files. Files could hold information on all customers, products or transactions. These files are composed of a series of 'records'. Each record contains data about someone or something, for example, a customer or potential customer. Each record is then further divided into 'fields' which store particular data items such as post code, name, age, gender and so on.

The reason why 'field' data is held separately is because a marketer may want to extract those customers in a particular age category, or of a particular gender for analysis or targeting purposes. Marketers therefore need to be able to identify those categories in a discrete way while taking care to avoid having too many data fields jumbled up together, as this would not allow us to be as selective as individual targeting requires. For example, although key word searches extract the relevant records, without separating these records into fields the search time would be greater because all of the data in the homogenized record would have to be searched. Conversely when records are divided into fields this means that only those fields in which the relevant characteristics are stored would need to be searched. Also, if all of the individual field data were jumbled together and a life style category of the 'Hooray Henry' was to be extracted for the targeting of trendily styled and fluorescent yellow mobile phones, we might extract everyone whose name is also Henry (indeed first name or surname!).

Types of Database

There are a number of different types of database available to organizations. These include:

▶ Hierarchical

▶ Network

▶ Relational

Hierarchical databases

These are the oldest form of marketing database. They store information in a structure similar to that of an organizational chart where they are analogous to 'parent' and 'child' relationships. Consequently they are somewhat inflexible, because the routes of access are embedded in the data. As a result, hierarchical database systems are best suited for large, transaction-orientated databases in a mainframe environment. They can be designed for very high performance for specific queries, but this performance comes at the cost of fixing views of data. For example, while alternative views are possible, they are difficult to create once the primary structure has been created. Most bank databases have traditionally been hierarchical, and can process data on transactions (of which there are potentially millions) very quickly. However, it has proven difficult to utilize the database for marketing purposes. For example, it may be possible to access data by account number or name, but exceptionally difficult to generate a list of all 18-year-olds for direct marketing purposes.

Network databases

These are similar to the hierarchical model in that there are owner and member relationships. The system also uses pointers to identify records needed for analysis purposes. Such a system allows multiple access points to exist, and is therefore more flexible than a hierarchical database. However, it is also more expensive and complex to run. For example, routes to accessing data are embedded in its structure and therefore the user will need to understand the data structure in order to effectively manipulate the data. This makes its use difficult for many routine marketing analysis purposes.

Relational databases

These are currently the dominant database architecture (or design) for systems developments. Relational databases store data in two-dimensional tables of rows and columns. A single row represents all attributes (data) for a given entity (such as a customer), while a column represents the same attribute for all records. Thus, routes of access are independent of the data and files can easily be joined in new logical structures. The tables are linked together by a common key, such as a customer number. This link allows users to create dynamic views of data and to add new data with minimum difficulty. Relational databases have provided a huge boost for direct marketing applications.

An example will illustrate how relational databases are more useful than traditional hierarchical databases for direct marketing purposes. Hierarchical databases only deal with one file at a time. Think of a mail order business operating in the music market. This business would need to be able to store a customer's order and to update stock records when the music CDs are transferred from stock to customer. A hierarchical database would only be able to deal with either the stock or the customer record at one time – they can't 'talk to each other'. On the other hand, the relational database allows both records to communicate with each other. The catalogue code for the customer's order for The Beatles 'Abbey Road' might be '28 1F' and the relational database allows the stock level of this CD to be checked and updated as the sale is made. The customer record is also updated so we now have a field containing purchased CDs against each customer from which a pattern of their music preferences can be analysed, together with whatever other data is being stored – quantities purchased, time of year when orders are usually placed, profile characteristics, method of payment and so on.

Figure 4.1 demonstrates the appearance of a database and shows there can be customer 'records' with the separate 'fields' for name, gender, address (with a different field for each component of the address) and so on. The figure also shows how entries might appear for data entry – for keying in data collected from some source or indeed for a telemarketing operator at time of collection. Also shown is the same data in tabular form, for many customers. Each row represents a 'record' (one for each customer) and the columns are the specific 'fields'. We would also need to have other 'tables' – for 'orders', 'stock levels' and 'stock reordering'. The figure also indicates how links can be made between such databases and demonstrates how linked data can be retrieved for personalized communications. Thus, it becomes clear that a relational database allows for a variety of links between different tables. These include:

▶ *One to One.* Where each record in one table can be linked with one record on another table. This is typical of list management applications.

▶ *One-to Many.* Where each record in one table can be linked with many records in another table.

▶ *Many-to-Many.* Where each record in one table can be linked with many records in another table and each record in that table can be linked with many records in the first table.

The customer table stores customer details – name, address, geodemographic profile. The order table stores all orders by date together with delivery and invoice dates, delivery address and delivery company. The stock level table stores each product in stock together with quantities and the stock reorder table stores order number and stock number together with quantity of the order. One-to-many links will be needed between each of these tables.

Increasingly even the most powerful and sizeable databases are available on the humble desk top PC. The advent of hard drives in excess of 8 gigabytes, for storage; and RAM sizes over 64mb for analysis and CD ROMs for even larger storage purposes, has made it possible to hold – and analyse – very large databases on the PC.

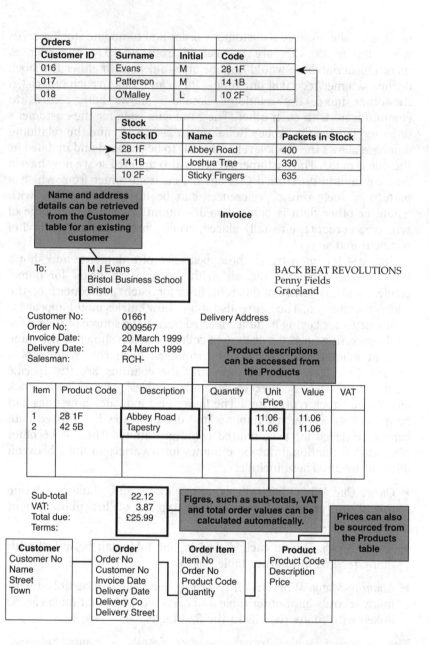

Orders

Customer ID	Surname	Initial	Code
016	Evans	M	28 1F
017	Patterson	M	14 1B
018	O'Malley	L	10 2F

Stock

Stock ID	Name	Packets in Stock
28 1F	Abbey Road	400
14 1B	Joshua Tree	330
10 2F	Sticky Fingers	635

Name and address details can be retrieved from the Customer table for an existing customer

Invoice

To: M J Evans
Bristol Business School
Bristol

BACK BEAT REVOLUTIONS
Penny Fields
Graceland

Customer No: 01661
Order No: 0009567
Invoice Date: 20 March 1999
Delivery Date: 24 March 1999
Salesman: RCH-

Delivery Address

Product descriptions can be accessed from the Products

Item	Product Code	Description	Quantity	Unit Price	Value	VAT
1	28 1F	Abbey Road	1	11.06	11.06	
2	42 5B	Tapestry	1	11.06	11.06	

Sub-total 22.12
VAT: 3.87
Total due: £25.99
Terms:

Figres, such as sub-totals, VAT and total order values can be calculated automatically.

Prices can also be sourced from the Products table

Customer	**Order**	**Order Item**	**Product**
Customer No	Order No	Item No	Product Code
Name	Customer No	Order No	Description
Street	Invoice Date	Product Code	Price
Town	Delivery Date	Quantity	
	Delivery Co		
	Delivery Street		

Figure 4.1 Database Appearance of Relational Data

Millions of lifestyle records, for example, can easily be manipulated in this way and even the national census is now available on CD. Costs have also dropped – in 1973 the cost of storing 125 bytes was $7.13 but had dropped to $0.002 by 1995 (Hughes 1996:119).

In House or Outsourced?

Building and maintaining a customer, prospect or marketing database represents a significant investment for companies today. As such, it is important that the company carefully considers how the database will be used. Linton (1995:22) suggests that managers should address the following issues in order to assist them in selecting the appropriate database.

► How will the database support business objectives?

► What is expected from the system?

► What are the main requirements?

► What applications will it be used for?

Having answered these questions, managers should be in a better position to identify the type of database they need. It will also allow them to ensure that they have the appropriate computer power, speed, memory and processing capacity to run such a database.

A second issue which needs to be addressed is whether the database will be developed and maintained in-house, or whether an external supplier will be used. Keeping the database in-house certainly ensures that the organization has more control, but it is often a more expensive option, particularly for smaller companies. Indeed, one of the current problems in the direct marketing industry is a skills gap (Mitchell 1996). There are all too few people with a strategic marketing vision coupled with the more technical database and analytical skills. As a result it is often recommended for the database to be run by an outside company (Hughes 1996).

The database needs to be capable of storing large amounts of data and of doing analyses in sophisticated ways. It has to be constantly updated, de-duplicated, purged and merged. Sometimes the software may also need to link directly into automated telephone contacts and so on. The software for these activities takes more than a couple of in-house seminars to learn and the company may not be able to afford to commit the time and resources internally to this. Outside database companies operate for multiple clients and therefore there are some economies of scale in the area in which they specialize. As a result, there may be certain advantages associated with out-sourcing database management (Linton 1995) including:

► The database will not affect the capacity of the organization's internal systems.

► There will be no need to recruit or train additional staff.

► The database will be managed by specialists.

► Out-sourcing can be more cost-effective because the organization can choose the most appropriate service option.

Populating the Database

The type of data used to 'populate' the database is of course a key consideration. There are some 'off the shelf' databases which can be purchased, including lifestyle databases (e.g. from NDL and CMT) and there are geodemographic databases (e.g. from Experian (formerly CCN) and CACI). In addition there is a vast number of lists, thousands in fact. There are also more in-house sources of data from which to populate the database. For example there are a company's own customer records, results from sales promotion campaigns (coupons, competitions, etc.) also from our market research and from transactional data – the latter being one of the major growth areas for database population and which we explore shortly. Internal records usually represent the best place to start searching for suitable data. Put simply, there are four general sources of data open to an organization that broadly encompass 'internal' and 'external' data, generating the kind of records outlined in Figures 4.2 and 4.3:

▶ *Performance Data.* Internal data on sales, enquiries, competitions, customers, complaints – in fact any data generated as a result of interacting with customers.

▶ *Primary Research.* Companies may carry out market research among customer or non-customer groups and this information may be recorded in the database.

▶ *External Data Sources.* This includes any external database containing compiled lists as a result of research. It includes lifestyle databases such as NDL and geodemographic databases such as ACORN or MOSAIC, and financial databases and County Court Judgements (CCJs).

Identification Data	Demographic Data	Financial	Lifestyle
▶ First Name	▶ Gender	▶ Homeowner	▶ Holiday Preferences
▶ Last Name	▶ Age	▶ Home Value	▶ Leisure Interests
▶ Title	▶ Occupation	▶ Car Owner	▶ Reading Habits
▶ Address	▶ Income Level	▶ Car Value	▶ Viewing Habits
▶ Postcode	▶ Marital Status	▶ Credit Card Holder	
▶ Account Number	▶ Number of Children	▶ Insurance Status	

Shopping Behaviour	Other	Special Markers
▶ Shopping Patterns	▶ Length of Time at Current Address	▶ VIP Customer
▶ Brand Preference	▶ Responses to Questionnaire	▶ Do Not Promote
▶ Recent Purchase History	▶ Customer Service History	▶ Shareholder
▶ Life-Time Value		▶ Frequent Complainer
▶ Loyalty Category		

Figure 4.2 Customer Lists

Identification Data	Business Data	Transaction Data
▸ Company Name ▸ Key Contact ▸ Address ▸ Postcode ▸ Account Number ▸ Region ▸ Sales Territory ▸ Name of Salesperson	▸ Size of Business ▸ Annual Turnover ▸ Number of Employees ▸ Head Office/Local Purchasing ▸ Budget Authority ▸ Financial Year End	▸ Account Number ▸ Purchase History ▸ Purchase Frequency ▸ Annual Expenditure ▸ Average Order Size ▸ Service History ▸ Responses to Promotions ▸ Method of Customer Acquisition ▸ Response to Questionnaire
Sector Data	Key Contact	Special Markers
▸ Type of Business ▸ SIC Code	▸ Name ▸ Job Title ▸ Telephone ▸ Fax Number ▸ E-mail ▸ Relevant Information	▸ VIP Customer ▸ Links with Other Companies ▸ Do Not Promote ▸ Frequent Complainer

Figure 4.3 Business Lists

Performance Data

The best place to begin the search for relevant data is the company's internal records. Most companies hold records of products, customers and marketing activities either on a database or databases, or indeed manually in filing cabinets. Such information could include data on sales records, accounts records, customer enquiries, customer complaints, etc. However, unless this information is integrated the company will be unable to get a single view of their customers as a basis for marketing planning. As a result, when building a marketing database, companies should plan to ensure that the system is capable of linking records held on different files.

'Computers work best with information that is well organized to start with. That is why database marketing puts a strong emphasis on the structured collection of data' (Stone *et al.* 1995:74). Thus, in dealing with customers it is imperative that the organization captures relevant data in a formal structured way. Staff who deal with telephone enquiries often use a pre-structured checklist in order to ensure that they collect the relevant data. Furthermore, this data must be recorded in such a way that it is available for order processing, enhancing the customer database, and as an input into monitoring and evaluating strategy. There are a wide variety of important internal data sources which are a valuable input into the marketing database. These are outlined in Figure 4.4.

Internal data is probably the most economical way to build a list, and should therefore be the first source of data considered by the company. However, there are several disadvantages of relying solely on internal data (Linton 1995), including that:

Customer Records	Transaction Records	Promotions
▸ Customer Correspondence ▸ Customer Complaints ▸ Market Research Survey	▸ Sales ▸ Returns ▸ Application forms (insurance, credit etc.) ▸ Service	▸ Campaigns ▸ Response rates ▸ Contacts Generated ▸ Sales ▸ Profits
Products	**Prospect Records**	**Geodemographics**
▸ Products Sold ▸ Price ▸ Distribution	▸ Enquiries ▸ Sales Prospect File ▸ Market Research Survey	▸ Postcode

Figure 4.4 Internal Sources of Data

▸ the information may not be held in an appropriate format;

▸ the information may not be comprehensive;

▸ the data may be out of date;

▸ reliance upon internal lists may limit the company from expanding the market for its products.

Primary Research

Primary research is a fairly good source of database information. However, when conducting research it is important to be aware of the issues raised by Fletcher and Peters (1996) with respect to the use of market research data to populate databases. The main problem is one of using marketing research data for selling purposes (selling under the guise of research; SUGGING). The Market Research Society has long outlawed this practice but has now compromised over the issue by having dual codes of conduct for the two 'reasons' for data collection.

In our later coverage of fulfilment, in Chapter 10, we show that there is an iterative process of database maintenance, because data from customer enquiries and orders together with payment details and invoicing data all need to be fed back into the database. Table 4.1 identifies the difference between a database and a file, Figure 4.5 summarizes the link between the database and customer list segmentation, fulfilment and accounts, and Figure 4.6 identifies a number of possible sources of data and their possible uses.

External Data Sources

As outlined earlier, external data sources include mailing lists and databases compiled on the basis of lifestyle, geodemographic or financial information. A 'list' is a set of names and how to contact them. It is the simplest form of marketing database (Stone *et al.* 1995). A basic list of customers or prospects can be enhanced by adding

Characteristic	Database	File
Type of Data Held:	Contains many types of data which can be linked together.	Usually contains only a single type of information.
Sources of Information:	Derives information from multiple sources.	Usually derives information from a single source.
Number of Applications Supported:	Supports multiple applications.	Supports a very limited number of applications.
Ability to Access Information:	Can be accessed easily and in multiple ways.	Often allows a single method of access, making ad hoc queries difficult.
Strategic or Tactical Value:	Generally strategic. Is viewed as a major corporate resource (or asset).	Generally tactical value only.

Table 4.1 Differences Between Databases and Files

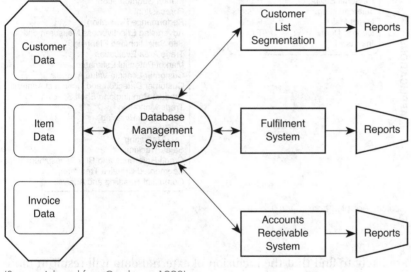

(Source: Adapted from Courtheoux 1992)

Figure 4.5 Data and Files

further information on buying patterns, lifestyle, geodemographic classification etc. Thus, the list is the basic requirement of a database system, while the other information provides a valuable role in data enhancement (i.e. making the data more accurate and relevant). Thus, we will first discuss lists.

Lists

Clever list building is the key to successful direct marketing (Stone et al 1995). Therefore it is important to ensure that customer and prospect lists are accurate, up-to-date, and contain as much information as possible. Organizations may initially consider using internal data, but

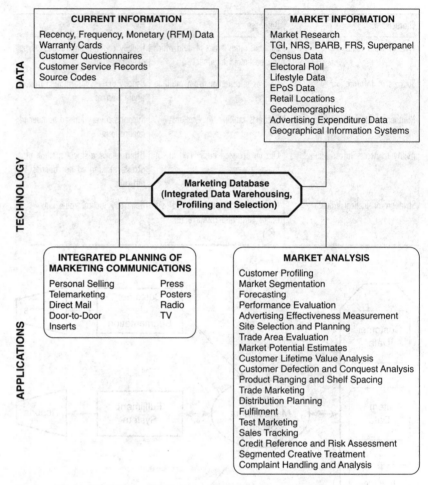

Figure 4.6 Data Sources

(Source: Adapted from Patron 1996)

are likely to find that the inclusion of external data will result in more effective direct marketing. As a result, the organization may need to consider external sources of data. This is relatively easy as there are numerous external list sources. These include (Linton 1995):

▶ list brokers who offer different categories of lists;

▶ magazine publishers who offer lists to their readers;

▶ directory publishers;

▶ trade associations or professional institutes which offer lists of their members;

▶ commercial organizations (including retailers) who offer lists of their customers.

External lists can be rented or purchased (or licensed) and can be for consumer, industrial or international markets. It is generally the case that internal lists (if accurate) will perform better than external ones, but externally acquired lists will be modified on the basis of the company's personal experience, so becoming more tailored to their market requirements. It is also generally true that lists of people who have already shown a willingness to respond will produce better response rates than lists of non responders.

It is therefore clear that there are a wide variety of lists available. Some have been specially compiled for marketing (though not necessarily for each client company), while some exist as a result of other marketing activity. Examples of the latter would include lists compiled from magazine subscribers, store card applicants, attendees at exhibitions, responders to DRTV advertisements, mail order, telephone and direct mail responders. Examples of 'compiled' sources include Lifestyle Questionnaires (e.g. NDL/CMT lists) and geodemographics linked with Electoral Roll and Business lists from Companies House. Lifestyle lists are constantly expanding due to the increase in the number of sponsored questions added to the questionnaire. Individual companies pay to have a question included that is relevant to their products as is the case with omnibus surveys (Figure 4.7).

Because answers are personalized, those with cats for whom the company might have a relevant product become known by name and address and can be further geodemographically profiled via postcode. Equally, customers with particular problems with their hair also become known by name and address. These customers thus represent good prospects.

Lists are obviously available from the list owners but because they are tied to those lists they will not be able to sell other lists. A list broker on the other hand can recommend what they consider to be the best list and there is evidence that the majority of direct marketers use brokers (DMIS 1997). Most lists are supplied in a format which allows for deduplication and for cleaning against the Mailing Preference Service (MPS) list to exclude those who do not wish to receive unsolicited mail. As for list prices, there is obviously a wide range but a fairly typical figure would be around £100 per thousand names.

It is important to consider the appropriateness of the lists purchased and our coverage of testing in Chapter 5 shows how sample sizes should be determined. One simple approach is to check how closely the external list matches the company's customer profile. This ensures that direct marketing will be targeted to similar types of customer. If the list is very different from the 'profile' of good prospects then it is likely that many recipients will not respond, and there will be a high degree of

---

Does your cat frequently suffer from:		
Flaking Skin ☐	Flatulence ☐	Constipation ☐

Does anyone in your household have a problem with:		
Dandruff ☐	Lank Hair ☐	Split Ends ☐

Figure 4.7 Examples of Questions Included on an Omnibus Survey

wastage associated with the mailing. There is also the option of commissioning the building of an appropriate list by an external supplier. Again, individuals or companies are sought who closely match the internal customer profile. According to Sargeant (1996) the factors contributing most to producing a high response list are:

▶ recency of data;

▶ similarity to customer profile;

▶ relevance of selection;

▶ previous/future use (how often mailed, level of competitive usage and overlapping mailing dates);

▶ quality of the data;

▶ integration of list with creative/offer/timing;

▶ impact of external factors.

He also suggests that although there is no universal rule relating to cost/responsiveness, the framework depicted in Figure 4.8 is worth considering.

Take a hypothetical consumer list – one based on consumers who have purchased from a mail-order catalogue. Lists of names and addresses could be provided for each of the product categories serviced by the catalogue: photography, car accessories, gardening, hi-fi, fashion, health aids and so on – individual categories can usually be bought and often run to several hundred thousand names. There will usually be other profiling factors included from the original purchase from the catalogue, such as age, gender, payment method, marital status, home ownership and income. Many of these factors derive from customers' applications to the catalogue for credit arrangements.

Business lists can provide as much detail, for example, a hypothetical list of marketers. This might have been compiled from

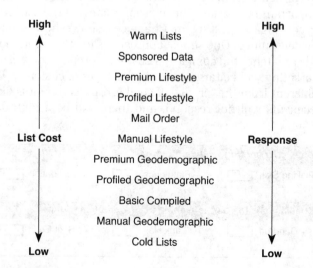

Figure 4.8 Cost-Responsiveness of Lists

attendees at conferences and seminars and could include name, job title, company and even secretary's name, drink preferences and dietary requirements.

Figure 4.9 summarizes the features of just one list and it clearly shows the wealth of useful profile characteristics that can be made available. Figure 4.10 reviews a selection of lists within just one category – holidays/travel – there are many other lists classified according to dozens of other categories ranging from animals and charity to music, hobbies and even church attendees and 'ethical/green people'! If you are wondering from where this last category derives its data, some comes from responders to 'green' catalogues, subscribers to relevant magazines and investors in 'ethical' financial products and stocks. All in all, there are literally thousands of lists available. It is possible to cross select thus ensuring targeting those affluent individuals even more finely. The holiday list has worked well for higher priced consumer goods including travel accessories, clothing and wine, publications and books, financial services, insurance and charities.

The use of a list must comply with the Data Protection Act 1984. That is, clear notification of uses must be given to the source of the data before the data is provided. An opportunity to opt-out of receiving further marketing material from the company (or if necessary third parties) must also be given. This is the first principle of the Act, namely that the obtaining and processing of personal data must be fair and lawful. In addition, lists must satisfy MPS (Mailing Preference Service) cleaning and of course the list owners' own terms.

There are, unfortunately, examples of inept or unethical use of lists, such as the instance concerning a bank which used a list of subscribers to the Disney Book Club for their targeting of an offer relating to a new low cost credit card. Several parents were somewhat upset when their five- and seven-year olds received mailshots for a credit card with no annual fee and a low APR! (*Sunday Times* 1997)

Data Enhancement

By adding additional data to a customer or prospect list the company can enhance the value of the data. For business lists this could include adding industry codes (SIC); yellow pages classification; number of employees; telephone number; contact name etc. For customer lists, data from credit reference agencies, and census or postcode data is often used for data enhancement.

Data Profiling

Data profiling involves classifying records held on the database into a number of different categories. There is a merging of lifestyle and geodemographic databases, providing a combination of profile and behavioural data. The list below shows that although the base source of geodemographic data is the census, there are now many more sources integrated into the analysis.

GARDENING DIRECT
OF SOUTH WOODHAM FERRERS

LIST NUMBER: **21149**
LIST NAME: **Gardening Direct**
LIST QUANTITY: **358041**

EXCLUSIVELY MANAGED
BY THE MAIL MARKETING GROUP

Brand new onto the market, Gardening Direct is one of the fastest growing lists of UK mail order buyers available today!

Customers have initially responded to a wide range of promotions in the National Press, Gardening magazines, and Women's magazines. All have purchased products including a wide range of annual bedding plants, as well as traditional garden hardware.

Customers receive a new catalogue after each order, to encourage repeat purchases, while the list owner also mails the list regularly, further improving the accuracy and responsiveness of the list. Average order values are in the region of £10-£30, depending on the offer. All customers have purchased during the last 12 months, and the list is expected to grow at a high level.

The list has recently been profiled (NDL), and indicates the following:-

Customers are typically married, and in the older age groups - in fact most are aged 45 and over. With nearly 50% retired, children have in general 'flown the nest'.

Household income levels are evenly spread across the board, although it should be noted that over 20% earn in excess of £20,000 pa. Many others have lower levels, as they will be living off their investments and savings.

Over 75% are homeowners, with ownership of credit and charge cards matching the national average.

Main interests and hobbies include gardening, grandchildren, needle-work, DIY, and puzzles/crosswords/doing the pools, holidays, reading, and other sporting/leisure pursuits.

Typically, they read the mid market press, such as the Mail, Express and Telegraph, and drive a small to medium sized car.

The list is expected to be a prime responder for non-competing offers, charities, selected financial and insurance offers, collectibles, publishers, selected gardening and mail order promotions suitable for Gardening Direct's mature customers.

For more details, call John Walker or Tim Proudman on 0117 966 6900.

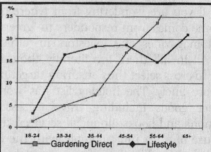

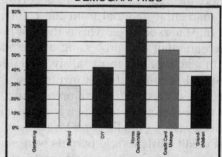

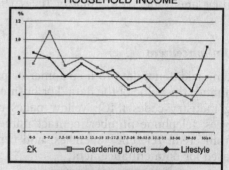

SPRINGFIELD HOUSE
WEST STREET
BRISTOL BS3 3NX
TEL: 0117 966 6900
FAX: 0117 987 2043
www.listbroker.com

Figure 4.9 Gardening Direct

M LISTS

STATISTICS
Enquire for others	0
Males	144603
Females	195748
Unknown sex	17690

GENERAL INFORMATION
Total size:	358041
Lead time:	7 Days
Minimum rental quantity:	5000

STANDARD CHARGES
Basic rental price:	85.00	/000

EXTRA FORMAT CHARGES
Magnetic tape:	25.00	Flat
Self-adhesive labels:	5.00	/000
Cheshire labels:	5.00	/000
Disk:	15.00	Flat
Key coding:	5.00	/000
Tape deposit:	0.00	

SELECTIONS
Nth Name	FOC
Recency	6.00 /000
Geographic/Postcode	6.00 /000
Sex	6.00 /000
Mailsort	6.00 /000
Method of payment	6.00 /000

SPRINGFIELD HOUSE
WEST STREET
BRISTOL BS3 3NX
TEL: 0117 966 6900
FAX: 0117 987 2043
www.listbroker.com

Reproduced courtesy of Mail Marketing and of Flying Flowers Group Ltd.

LIST NO.	TITLE	QUANTITY
00520	ATAB Travel Database	500000
00350	BBC Holidays	21704
10521	Beautiful British Columbia Magazine – UK	40731
00515	Bon Viveur Club Members	27880
00434	Business Traveller	13000
00557	Christian Hols Books/Enq & Mag Subscriber	37849
10194	Country Holiday Customers	763423
00905	Craigendarroch Owners/Visitors	27823
10538	Direct Holidays	112985
00870	English Tourist Board Promotions	460000
10200	F/T Travellers	2897
00849	Flightbookers Names	65000
10866	French Property News	55000
10906	French Railways Database	87000
10409	Gatwick High Fliers	21000
00137	Holiday Makers Database	300000
00282	Holiday Property Bond Enquirers	204856
00150	Hoseasons Holiday 1993 Buyers	121407
10396	IAPA Active Members	87772
00816	IAPA Expires	190087
10447	IAPA Prospects	212711
10876	Johansen Hotel Guides Purchasers	41630
00261	John Fowler Holidays	171732
10755	London Luton Airport	30000
10301	Look at LeisureBase	690000
00189	Lotus Supertravel/Holidays	99856
10490	Outlook	1000000
00934	Page & Moy	458973
00485	Practical Caravan	37000
00238	Skiing Enthusiasts	27522
00095	The ICD Holiday Database	2500000
00664	The UK Airports Park n' Fly File	200000
00023	Wexas International	168948
10336	YHA Members File	138776
00361	Yorkshire & Humberside Tourist Board	254378

HOW WOULD
MAIL MARKETING
MANAGE YOUR LIST?
WHY NOT DISCUSS IT WITH
LAURIE ORME
ON 0117 966 6900

Figure 4.10 Holiday/Travel Lists

Reproduced courtesy of Mail Marketing

► Census statistics (Source: OPCS)

- socio-economic data
- housing
- household and age

► Demographic data (Source: Electoral Registers)

- age
- household composition
- population

► Financial data (Source: Lord Chancellors Office; CCN Credit Database; Companies House)

- county court judgements
- CCN consumer searches
- directors

► Retail Data

- accessibility

(Source: Experian)

We now provide a few examples of how geodemographic databases can be analysed. Plate 1 profiles the Bristol area and Table 4.2 shows the penetration of stylish singles around Bristol. Having identified these profiles, names and addresses can be produced for direct mailings of relevant target groups in relevant locations. Equally, a map of the penetration of student drinkers in the Bristol area can also be generated (Plate 1). This demonstrates the linking of data from more than just the census and electoral roll. Apart from catchment area analysis for bars, this sort of analysis could be used for direct targeting within areas – via direct mail because the analysis can produce list of names and addresses or even through door drops based on newspaper or milk rounds (as we discuss later).

Catchment area analysis for a car dealer is shown in Figure 4.11 based on ACORN groups. The dealer can determine which groups are the best prospect and acquire names and addresses for direct mailings.

Another interesting development is the linking of 'old style' life style with geodemographics. Taylor Nelson lifestyle groups, based on the old 'activities, interests, opinions' style of research rather than the NDL/CMT type of self completion questionnaires, now appear in Experian's 'Psyche' system and every postcode in the UK is assigned to one of the social value groups. As we have said, geodemographics are not based exclusively on the census but the census does provide the 'base'.

Database Maintenance

Ensuring Data Accuracy

'Without constant updating, any database will be a wasted asset' (Linton 1995:17). This is because accurate data is critical to the

Table 4.2 Penetration of Stylish Singles Around Bristol (Top 25 Postal Sectors)

	Stylish Singles	Target %	Total household estimate 1996	Base %	Penetration	Index
BS 8 2 Chantry Road, Bristol	3142	8.12	3147	0.81	0.9984	997
BS 8 1 Buckingham Pal, Clifton, Bristol	1780	4.60	1845	0.48	0.9648	963
BS 6 6 Cotham, Bristol	4917	12.70	5157	1.33	0.9535	952
BS 1 4 Colston Avenue, Bristol	228	0.59	242	0.06	0.9421	941
BS 8 4 Hotwells, Bristol	3393	8.77	3660	0.95	0.9270	926
BS 1 1 Baldwin Street, Bristol	162	0.42	183	0.05	0.8852	884
BS 6 5 Cheltenham Road, Bristol	3758	9.71	4433	1.15	0.8477	846
BS 1 5 Park Row, Bristol	549	1.42	681	0.18	0.8062	805
BA 1 2 James Street, Bath	2047	5.29	3093	0.80	0.6618	661
BS 6 7 Westbury Park, Bristol	2407	6.22	3716	0.96	0.6477	647
BS 8 3 Clifton, Abbots Leigh, Bristol	1450	3.75	2487	0.64	0.5830	582
BS 2 8 Jamaica Street, Bristol	1368	3.53	2583	0.67	0.5296	529
BA 1 5 Sion Hill, Bath	1209	3.12	2337	0.60	0.5173	517
BS 7 8 Redland, Bristol	2039	5.27	3991	1.03	0.5109	510
BS 1 6 Redcliffe Way, Bristol	757	1.96	1780	0.46	0.4253	425
BA 1 1 Avon Street, Bath	429	1.11	1011	0.26	0.4243	424
BA 2 4 Beechen Cliff, Bath	951	2.46	2611	0.68	0.3642	364
BA 1 6 Larkhall, Bath	1181	3.05	3604	0.93	0.3277	327
BS 7 9 Down Road, Bristol	1761	4.55	5674	1.47	0.3104	310
BS 3 1 Coronation Road, Bristol	897	2.32	3682	0.95	0.2436	243
BS 1 3 Newbridge, Bath	610	1.58	2653	0.69	0.2299	230
BS 1 3 Broadmead, Bristol	76	0.20	387	0.10	0.1964	196
BA 2 3 South Twerton, Bath	565	1.46	3291	0.85	0.1717	171
BA 2 6 Claverton, Bath	466	1.20	2958	0.77	0.1575	157
BS 16 3 Speedwell, Bristol	400	1.03	2834	0.73	0.1411	141

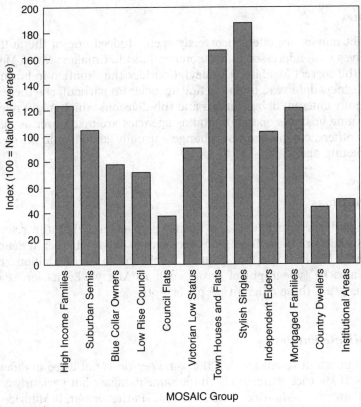

© Experian Ltd

Figure 4.11 30-minute Off-Peak Drivetime Around Bristol By MOSAIC Group

effective use of a marketing database. In particular 'list accuracy has a very close correlation with the profitability of a mailing. The more accurate the list, the better the likely response' (Bradford 1995:33). The importance of continually checking the accuracy of the data held becomes obvious when we consider how many details are likely to change in a single year. Indeed, Linton suggests that about 48 per cent of data held on business lists changes annually (Linton 1995). Equally, consumers' circumstances alter – they marry, they move house, they have children, they die. Thus, there is a need to continually update the data held on customer and prospect databases. Indeed, one of the most important tasks associated with running a database is to make sure it remains relevant and up to date. This can be achieved through list cleaning and list enhancement. Data cleaning involves checking the accuracy of data held, and ensuring that addresses are correct.

Common Inaccuracies Found on Mailing Lists

Although it is not possible to identify all potential list inaccuracies, there are a number of quite common ones identified below:

Names

Target names are often incorrectly spelt. (Indeed one of the authors receives mail addressed to Mrs. omaly; Miss L. Omalley; Mr. O'Malley and the correct Ms. Lisa O'Malley). Consider the situation in business-to business databases on marketing agencies (in particular) – there can be many different abbreviations and sub-divisions which might refer to the same business operation and as agencies are taken over or merge with others, company names change – usually get longer in the case of marketing agencies!

Salutations

One problem which exists is the need to ensure that the relevant salutations are used. The need is therefore to check whether M Evans is Mr, Mrs, Ms, Prof., Dr, Rev., Captain, Rabbi and so on. In addition, there can also be typographical errors such as Martyn Evans for Martin Evans – are these different people or not?

Duplicate Entries

It is important to ensure that the same person is not listed in different ways. If Maurice Patterson is on the same database but variously as M. A. Patterson, Maurice Patterson, M. Patterson and Maurice A. Patterson, and is targeted with the *same* mail shot separately under *all* of these names, then it is no wonder if he feels that rather more trees have been used than is absolutely necessary.

Gone Aways

Mail continues to be sent to a named recipient months or years after they have moved. Even more distressing, people who have died also receive direct mail.

As a result of data inaccuracies, regular cleaning of the data becomes particularly important. Indeed, 'regular cleaning is the only way to ensure that money is not being thrown away on people who have moved' (Bradford 1995:33). Luckily, industry standard software such as the Postal Address File (PAF) and the Electoral Roll are available. The PAF contains details of all domestic addresses in the UK, of which there are over 20 million. Indeed, matching lists with data available from the Electoral Roll can enhance customer details, for example through providing customer initials, sex, or first name. Other software can be purchased which verifies addresses, deduplicates records, and removes gone-aways. As a result, use of such cleaning software can offer very significant savings through reduced postage and brochure print costs, and indeed the subsequent improvement in response rates to mailings.

Up-Dating

With around 640,000 people dying in the UK per annum direct marketers know full well that their databases need to be updated and cleaned. However, as Darby (1997) states, there is a cost attached to this – 20p for every name matched against suppression files of those who have moved house or died – and in any case there has been no requirement for them to do so at present. If customers change their circumstances in any relevant way – for example if they move, or die – then it is not only a waste of scarce resources to target inaccurately but it can be very annoying and even distressing if a loved one who has recently died is sent a direct mailing for life assurance – or anything, for that matter. Consider the following experience of Martin Kettle, a writer for The Guardian:

> ❧ *My patience snapped when, 18 months after her death my mother received a reprimand for her lack of generosity in failing to respond to the latest appeal letter. So I wrote a seventh letter, this time a personal one to the general director, pointing out that his company might not lose so much money if it stopped sending mail to the dead.* ❧ (Kettle 1997:10)

In 1997 the Direct Marketing Association was proactive in lobbying for a change in legislation allowing the direct marketing industry access to the Register of Deaths. This encouraging example of voluntary regulation means that within two weeks of death, the industry will have to remove the deceased's name from their databases and will not be allowed to use the knowledge for any 'selling' purpose (for example targeting the widow with a savings policy for inherited money). Having said this, there are those who are more sceptical: 'using suppression files is about ethics and morality. Ethics and morality don't come into capitalism' (Adalbert 1997:10). If individuals ask about what personal data are held about them, on an organization's database then if all the data pertaining to them is not easily accessible in one record there could be breaches of the Data Protection Act.

Deduplicating

Duplicate records often occur because data is input from a variety of sources. Furthermore, names and addresses are not always listed in exactly the same way, and details are often incomplete. Therefore, deduplicating avoids multiple incomplete entries, and attempts to generate complete details on the individuals listed. Mander (1993) describes a six stage de-duplication process developed as a basis for a de-duping software programme:

▶ *Stage 1.* Identify and examine key elements of name and address.

▶ *Stage 2.* Form 'access keys'.

▶ *Stage 3.* Develop a scoring system for potential duplicates.

▶ *Stage 4.* Identify the acceptable level of duplication.

▶ *Stage 5.* Prioritize duplicates.

▶ *Stage 6.* Change records.

Stage 1

Each name and address is examined and the key elements identified: for example, title, initials, surname, occupation, each line of address and so on. There will be some standard references for some of these, built into the programme, such as addresses. Mander gives an example of a company name and address 'Smith Moulded Fittings Company Ltd., Unit 9, Broadway Industrial Estate, Kingsbury Road, Rugby, Warks., CV22 5AB' and lists the key elements of this as shown in Figure 4.12.

Stage 2

'Access keys' are formed – for example from combinations of parts of names and addresses and where two or more records share the access key they are potentially duplicates. For example, a search through other records might find the following 'matches':

▶ 1st word/address/post town   SM1 BRO

▶ Alternative initials/address/post town   SMF BRO

Full Company Name	Smith Moulded Fittings
Company Name – 1st word	Smith
Company Name – 2nd word	Moulded
Company Name – 3rd word	Fittings
Company Initials	SMF
Alternative Company Initials	SMFC
1st Address Element (Number)	9
1st Address Element (Name)	Broadwater
1st Address Element (Qualifier)	Industrial Estate
2nd Address Element (Number)	–
2nd Address Element (Name)	Kingsbury
2nd Address Element (Qualifier)	Road
Post Town	Rugby
Post County	Warwickshire
Post Code	CV22 5AB

Figure 4.12 Key Address Elements

▶ 1st word address/address2/post town   SM1 KIN

▶ Alternate initials/address2/post town   SMF KIN

Some of the matching elements in these other records may well turn out to be false duplicates but stage 2 is concerned with identifying all that *might* be duplicates.

Stage 3

A scoring system is used for each of the potential duplicates – for example, ranging from -99 to +99 (the higher the score, the greater the degree of similarity). '0' means that the matched records have as many similar elements as different elements. Some of the more obvious similarities and differences can be weighted in an appropriate way – for example, although it is very likely that ABC Engineering is different from DEF Engineering, the word 'Engineering' would highlight a potential duplicate. If 'Engineering' is given a weighting score of (say) 80 per cent less than other words, then ABC and DEF Engineering would not be flagged as high probabilities of duplication.

So far, the software programme analyses the database but the following stages involve the human touch.

Stage 4

This stage requires a rule of thumb for determining the level of score that we take to be the threshold for duplication. A very high score would be taken to represent clear duplication and the programme would deal with this automatically. Low scores would be ignored but those in the grey area would require someone to check manually. Table 4.3 shows how such thresholds might be set.

The value of this is that different weighting can be attached to different elements of the record according to experience and logical judgement.

Stage 5

Here, operators can prioritize duplications. For example, if only one mailing per household is to be sent, priority can be given to title, such as Mr, Dr, Sir, etc. and if none of these is present, then priority goes to Lady, Mdme, Mrs and so on.

Stage 6

This is finalizing the process by changing the records in the database, flagging changed records, deleting unwanted ones, merging data from different records and so on. The process also helps to add detail to addresses and in that way 'address enhancement' takes place.

Table 4.3 Thresholds

Address Element	Probable Duplicate Score Threshold	Possible Duplicate Score Threshold
Title:	+50	+30
Initials:	+50	+10
Surname:	+70	+50
Street Number:	+90	0
Street Name:	+80	+50
Post Town:	+99	+99
County:	+99	+99

Sources for identifying matching elements include the Royal Mail's PAF file but because this contains few names (rather than addresses) the Electoral Register, Companies House and others would often be used to identify matching elements.

Database Analysis

A number of techniques can be used to analyse the database, essentially to customize it for our organization and purpose. Even with geodemographic databases, these have traditionally been off-the-shelf systems from which we can profile our existing customers according to postcode – or select a sample of certain geodemographic clusters for research or testing purposes. There is the suggestion, however, that if the raw data were made available to clients, they could analyse it in ways which would be more appropriate – and customized – for each client (Oppenshaw 1997). The criticism being that geodemographics are too generic and that direct marketing, by its very nature, requires something more tailored.

Data Fusion and Data Warehousing

These lists and databases are being linked to provide the consecutive overlaying of information. Data fusion is the linking of data between databases and a data warehouse is the merged database.

Data warehousing is the process of creating one large collection of data in a single location. Typically, this requires gathering and storing data from multiple sources which then becomes the single focal point for all types of data analysis. The data warehouse allows fast queries on potentially any data attribute it contains. 'The data warehouse ...can be defined as a system that collects data from various applications throughout an organization, integrates that data, stores it and then exploits it to deliver information throughout the organization' (Read 1997:64). This definition by the director of marketing at the SAS Institute – one of the world's largest software companies – shows that it goes beyond the marketing function and is an integrator of a variety of business functions. We will restrict ourselves to the direct marketing context here, though.

Humby (1996a) describes the interrogation of data from a variety of sources but also states that it is not worth including 'everything'. There is always the danger of 'paralysis by analysis'! Humby goes on to suggest that 'it is not the detailed transaction data that is of interest, but patterns in transactions, such as an increasing balance over time or the range of products purchased over a period of time' (Humby 1996b). He also reiterates the problem that the industry has over a lack of staff to fill the IT-Marketing gap.

T-Groups

This is another version of the data fusion concept. In Chapter 5 we discuss the difference between traditional market research and testing. This is relevant here because *testing* – and much database data, such as transactional data and profiling data – provides valuable information on who is buying what, when, how and where, but it is market research that can get beneath the surface even further and discover reasons and 'why' behaviour is as it is.

As a result some direct marketers are linking their databases with market research data. In this way, for example, consumer panels are linked with geodemographic or lifestyle databases. The 'T' means that 'horizontally' database data provides tremendous breadth of data over millions of consumers but the 'vertical', from market research (e.g. panels) provides greater depth of information over a period of time (because panels are 'continuous' data sources). Figure 4.13 summarizes the characteristics of the T-Group.

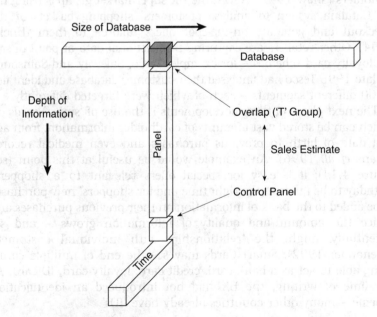

Figure 4.13 T-Groups

It was from such research that the claimed levels of purchasing in lifestyle surveys have sometimes been found to be extremely over or under represented in actual buying behaviour – as we discuss in our coverage of consumer panels in Chapter 5. One version of linking panel data with lifestyle database is the SMARTbase system developed by Taylor Nelson/Calyx. The former running a number of different consumer panels and the latter, lifestyle surveys (Walker 1996).

Biographics

There has been a progression from profile data to transactional data. Profiling has moved through demographics, geodemographics and various forms of psychographics to the most recent version of lifestyle data (as collected by NDL and CMT surveys). The important development facilitating the collection of transactional data has been the installation of point-of-sale (POS) computers. Widespread acceptance by retailers has resulted from technological developments which led to smaller, faster, and more reliable EPoS (Electronic Point of Sale) terminals. Closely allied to this progress has been the development of product codes which are standardized between manufacturers, distributors and retailers (McGoldrick 1990). European Article Number (EAN) is compatible with the Universal Product Code (UPC) in the USA. This implies that any retailer with an EPOS system can access information. More importantly this can be downloaded daily – giving rich market information.

The marketing application of bar-codes (EAN/UPC) in retailing includes the ability to record who buys what. Products can be matched with customers via credit, debit (switch) and loyalty cards numbers. Retailers will therefore be able to match special offers with individual customers (Shaw 1991). ASDA, the UK supermarket group is using the US Catalina system to analyse customers' shopping baskets at the checkout and generate on-the-spot offers tailored to them (Uncles 1994). Other retailers are capturing transactional data at point of sale via loyalty card schemes – for example, Tesco, Safeway and Sainsbury. By late 1996 Tesco had analysed their customer database and identified 5 000 different segments – each of which were targeted differently.

The next phase of these developments is the use of 'smart' cards on which can be stored vast amounts of cardholder information, from age and date of birth to previous purchases and even medical records (Evans *et al.* 1996). An example would be useful at this point (see Figure 4.14); it is easy for special offers relevant to a shoppers' birthday to be made at the right time and for shoppers' new purchases to be added to the bank of information on their previous purchases and hence the amount and quality of information grows – and so, potentially, might the 'relationship' with individual customers (Foenander 1992). Smart Cards may see the end of multiple cards, being able to act as a bank card, credit card, loyalty card, ID card. At the time of writing, the UK had not introduced an identification scheme – many other countries already have 'IDs'.

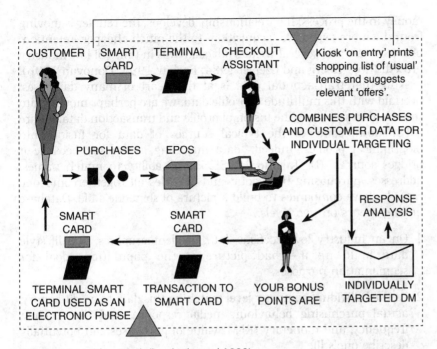

Figure 4.14 Bar Codes, Scanners and Cards

(Source: Adapted from Mitchell and Littlewood 1992)

There is clear evidence of a trend toward the creation of strategic alliances between non-competing companies based on sharing data. For example, an insurance company has a ten year agreement with motor companies, a vehicle breakdown service and a satellite TV company. There is clearly synergy to be had between these, if data is shared, with respect to complementary business (for 'cross selling) and for advertising purposes. Unilever, Kimberley Clark, Cadbury, Bass have joined to form the Consumer Needs Consortium which aims to reduce research and database costs. 'It is difficult to make the numbers work on expensive database building and direct marketing strategies, which provide the framework for ventures such as direct shopping, when you are churning out low purchase price items' (Richards 1998:18). An issue that is likely to be raised in the future is how to assess which companies should join such partnerships – corporate culture will be as important as product-market synergy. If some form of unified loyalty scheme is offered, customers will have to be researched on the basis of the total amalgam of the grouping rather than a single 'brand'.

With reference to the type of transactional data emerging from EPoS systems linked with individual shopper's loyalty or smart cards, an inspection of a resulting retail loyalty scheme database revealed, for a certain Mrs 'Brown', her address and a variety of behavioural information including: she shops once per week, usually on a Friday, has a baby (because she buys nappies), spends £90 per week on average and usually buys two bottles of gin every week (Mitchell 1996). By knowing what individual consumers buy, the retailer might be able to target them with relevant offers whilst the consumer saves money in the process. If a 'relationship' develops, the retailer is moving from the more expensive 'acquisition' to the much cheaper 'retention' of consumers and several writers advocate this in times of low industry growth (Rossenberg and Czepiel 1984; Barlow 1992; Donovan 1996).

Now that transactional data is at the heart of many databases, overlaid with this multitude of profile data, we are perhaps moving into the era of *biographics* – the fusion of profile and transaction data. Figure 4.15 shows some of the typical sources of data for fusion into biographical profiles. Indeed, 'data matching is the key because it bridges sources' (Di Talamo 1995:25), the ability to match names, addresses, purchasing behaviour, and lifestyles all together onto one record allows companies to build a picture of someone's life. Database linking occurs on two levels:

1 On an industry level, census data, geodemographics, and lifestyle data build up a broad picture of the population ideal for segmentation purposes.

2 At the individual company level matching this data to credit history, actual purchasing behaviour, media response, and the recency, frequency, and monetary (RFM) value of purchases can potentially describe one's life.

In 1997 the DMIS found that 53 per cent of a sample of companies matched their internal customer record data with external geodemographics and 57 per cent with external lifestyle profiles (DMIS 1997).

However, fusion doesn't always take place, in studies by Long *et al.* (1992), it was suggested that synergy is needed between marketing,

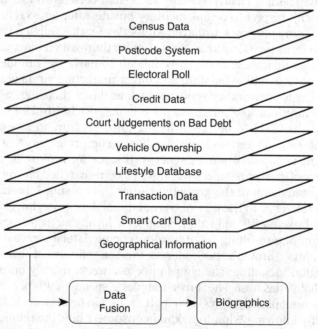

Figure 4.15 Layers of Database Marketing

(Source: Adapted from Evans 1994)

operations, information technology and database literacy before the power of such systems will be unleashed in practice. In a follow-up study a clear message emerges, namely a call for organizations to 'move away from using technology to do things to and for customers, to doing things with customers by giving the customer a voice in the process of building relationships' (Long et al. 1992).

Just as consumers in the 1980s became 'advertising literate,' the 1990s consumer is more sophisticated in the use of direct marketing. Companies will be judged by their communication and communication judged in terms of the 'relationship' held with a company, the purpose of the contact, and the quality of that contact. Increasingly, customers will require dialogue with marketers and will become less tolerant of being talked at. The current trends indicate that the direct marketing database can no longer be considered cost-effective if it is merely a tactical appendage to a company's communication policy, as we discussed earlier in this chapter.

Geographical Information Systems

Often it is very useful to be able to picture, geographically, what our database information tells us. The key to this is address and postcode because from this there are geographical information systems (GIS) which allow any linked database to produce map overlays.

Another application of GIS-linked data is in the siting of posters for direct response, based on the profile of the neighbourhood or even on the through traffic (Leggit 1997). A related software solution is 'Drivetime', (offered by The Data Consultancy, Reading) because this calculates drive times as *isochrones* (the distance one can drive in a given time along roads).

Data Mining

Data mining is a 'process of extracting hidden or previously unknown, comprehensible and actionable information from large databases' (Antoniou 1997). From this there are two approaches that data mining can adopt. The first is *verification-driven*; 'extracting information to validate an hypothesis postulated by a user' (Antoniou 1997). The second approach refers to the digging around in databases in a relatively unstructured way with the aim of discovering links between customer behaviour and almost any variable that might potentially be useful. This second approach is *discovery driven*: 'identifying and extracting hidden, previously unknown information ... (to) scour the data for patterns which do not come naturally to the analysts' set of views or ideas' (Antoniou 1997). There is a parallel with market research versus environmental scanning, because the former focuses on specific problems and the latter has a wider ranging brief to identify anything in the marketing environment which might have a relevant impact upon the marketing operation.

Direct marketers have tried a variety of unusual or unexpected areas in which to mine. For example some have examined consumers' individual biorhythms and star signs as predictors of their purchasing patterns (Mitchell and Haggett 1997) and others have linked their transactional and profile data with meteorological databases to predict, perhaps months ahead, what demand there might be for ice cream or woolly sweaters!

Another example of data mining is afforded by the linking with a GIS database to target down to newspaper round! This is usually around 150–200 households and by linking transactional data with lifestyle, geodemographics and panel data, a very accurate picture of individual buying patterns emerges. The newspaper round – or milk round – can be used for door drops or direct mail as well as for local catchment area analysis. This has been rather more formalized by Unigate who have advertised a door-step delivery service based on MOSAIC geodemographic profiles at local level. In addition to product delivery they offered a delivery service for samples and vouchers and a delivery and collection service for questionnaires.

Database Interrogation

A number of dedicated tools are available for analysing databases. One such 'product' is VIPER which is a software package developed by Brann Software. This tool allows very fast linking and analysis of different databases. Plate number 4 demonstrates some of the prints-out from VIPER processed queries on a lifestyle database, linked with a geodemographic database and a geographical information (GIS) system. The questions asked might have been: select those (name and address) who claim to be readers of books on post-modernism, like underground music, drink above average quantities of Guinness and live in the South Wales. The graphical print out combines data from all of the databases interrogated and shows in both topographical form, where these people live and also in tabular form the actual names and addresses of the individuals concerned. VIPER is not the only database interrogator on the market but it does reflect the sort of capability that is now available – the speed with which the analysis is completed is indeed impressive – and on what is now a relatively standard desktop PC.

CASE
STUDY 2

Parlez-vous Database?

Does the parlance of database technology hold *about as much significance as a Klingon car manual for you? Fear not, MICHAEL COLLINS of the Database Marketing Council can explain it all....*

A couple of months ago the *Direct Response* Awards spawned some novel products which were described in the July issue as 'innovative' (fitting for finalists for Innovation Awards) if not 'a bit complex for those of us not fluent in database jargon'. In the same issue I attempted to establish an understanding amongst marketers that one does not have to speak fluent SQL in order to use the front end data manipulation tools that will become the basis for every marketer's

● ● ▶

tactical and strategic data driven marketing activity.

The ability to define segments of the campaign, to define cells of activity and manage the triggering of further events at the drag and click of a mouse button is all very well but will you understand when your systems specialist asks whether your campaign will need to account for controlled and uncontrolled response, whether your strategic communications are to be single or multi stream or how your prioritisation hierarchy should be defined and managed? What???? Slow down.

These, however, are the terms of the new data driven marketing. They strive to define, in terms that the techies will understand, how you, the marketer, wish to have your requirements addressed and what information you want to have access to. The more access the marketer has to hands-on use of the data tools, the more he or she will have to define in these terms in order that they will maximize the power offered to them.

Understanding these terms will assist in deciding whether a particular application package is appropriate. In order to assist in this, here is a first glossary of database terms which will be added to in an occasional series of updates.

Attribute: An element of a data record, for example, fields holding name, address, age and so on.

Boolean operators: A series of universally accepted generic symbols used chiefly for defining extract criteria. Often data manipulation tools expect you to be au fait with these. For example, you can indicate all companies on the database with more than 100 employees by entering '>100' in the 'employees' field.

Cell: A discrete element within a mailing file to receive variations in proposition, creative treatment, or timing and so on. Especially applicable to testing.

Controlled activity: Campaign activity where the marketer has control over

which segment or cell a particular individual is included in (in order to achieve relevance, test validity or volume quotas) or is suppressed from, to maintain the strategic communication process or to comply with data protection requirements.

CHAID (CHI-square Automatic Interaction Detector): Provides an automated approach to response modelling, segmentation and test cell performance analysis. An established, proven statistical technique, it is often the only straightforward way to analyse response data.

Chronographics: Time parameters with regard to an individual's life cycle, for example: student, newlyweds, empty nesters, grey panthers.

Database Marketing: Also (and more appropriately) referred to as data-based marketing or data-driven marketing. This is a generic strategic concept that describes the creative application of information to drive product development, the selection of individuals, the tailoring of proposition and the direction for presentation when applied to marketing communications. Often confused with direct marketing or even direct mail which are in themselves often functions of data-based marketing. The message can be delivered to an individual from a database via direct communications or can be used to drive media selection and ad design to address above the line initiatives.

Data Mining: The ability to enquire on specific elements of data that contribute to summarized or aggregated information at the higher levels. Using appropriate software tools, a data analyst can drill down through data and follow a specific thought process by focusing on those aspects, in a report or chart for instance, that warrant investigation.

Demographics: Attributes pertaining to clusters of people with similar age, gender, occupation, marital status, number of children, income, education, ethnic background and so on. Often census based and most usually extrapolated across neighbourhoods or groups of households using

proprietary products such as Mosaic, Acorn and others.

Event: An occurrence that has direct impact on the relationship between the marketing company and the contact such as response to a mailing, visit to a dealer, purchase, enquiry or complaint.

Event-tree: A map of causes and effects of triggers and communications. For instance, a graphical representation of the communication strategy.

GIS (Geographical Information Systems): The use of mapping techniques to clarify the presentation of distribution or analysis data.

Hierarchical database: A straight sequential file of data with all information normally in one table keyed on one attribute (such as a customer reference number). It is therefore difficult to use if you do not have the key and prone to duplication, since all the record attributes are repeated each time that contact appears on the database.

Hierarchy Management: The automatic prioritisation controls by which individuals are suppressed from inclusion in either strategic or tactical marketing activities, thereby protecting the relationship between the company and the customer or to address data protection compliance.

Indexing: The establishment of key sortations criteria against a selection of prime attributes, to enhance the speed of data access.

Lifestyle: Criteria determining the personal tastes and preferences that make up the individual's profile, for example: enjoys swimming, prefers caravanning to package tours abroad, is a keen gardener, uses his credit card or is a member of a loyalty programme. Overlaid on demographics, the combination provides a powerful selection profile to be applied to a customer or prospect database and the key to sourcing new prospects with propensities similar to the house file.

Multi-stream communication strategies: A strategic programme of communications whereby there is the opportunity to manage a number of strands of the relationship between the marketing company and the contact. A contact may be both a customer for one range and a prospect for another, therefore both statuses may require parallel communication strategies to maintain this double relationship.

MPP (Massive Parallel Processing): For the marketer, just think of it as a whole bunch of large PC's strapped together, each handling a part of the task, to provide high speed processing of queries and extracts against very large databases.

Normalisation: Ensuring that a piece of information appears only once in the database.

Post-relational database: The lines of information relating to a record appear in the same table as the attributes they relate to by nesting one table of information within another. This reduces the complexity of accessing data with databases with a large number of data tables and thus improves response speeds.

Psychographics: Sometimes confused with lifestyles, however, psychographics are very different. While lifestyles describe what the individual actually does in his life, psychographics describe what he would like to do in his life. It is the emotive, aspirational profile that often drives purchase decision in the light of how ownership of the product would fit in with the image the purchaser aspires to for themselves.

Query: A query, or targeting function, enables marketers to structure and develop the right proposition and deliver it to evaluation target market sectors with absolute precision. It combines fast data selection, counts and highest level analysis with the facility for precise database sampling, allowing the marketer to define a selection of customers and/or prospects that conform to a pre-determined description such as geography, age, frequency of custom, spend and so on. Each field on the database may normally be used to define the

Use it wisely

Managing director of database marketing specialist, Conduit Communications, Gerald Chertavian, outlines issues which require attention prior to any investment in database marketing.

The first question to ask is what are you trying to do more effectively as a result of utilizing the database. This ensures you do not become lost in the technical considerations, which after all are unlikely to be your forte. Rather, you draw on your understanding of your business and the environment in which it operates to make a commercial decision which will bring maximum benefits to your organization.

Assuming you have a business case for investing in databases, you must then acknowledge that this is a project which is both IT and marketing related. Both these skills sets, in full co-operation, are required for success so bring them into the thinking and decision making early.

Finally, the issue of cost. Bear in mind costs should be relative to the gains you can achieve. Databases are no different to any other capital expenditure – your decision should be supported by a cogent business case offering a reasonable payback period.

Remember, information lies at the heart of every business process – nowhere more so than in the process of managing and developing customer relationships. An organization failing to manage its information assets effectively will fail to prosper.

parameters for the query, however, depending on the structure limiting the definitions to indexed fields may assist speed.

Relational Database: A database where data is split into logical groupings so that different attributes belonging to the same customer are only stored once in specific tables that are linked by keys.

Segment: A definable element within a database or extract containing data discernible by a set of criteria such as all customers for a particular product who live

within the M25. A segment is also an application within the definition of direct marketing campaigns to determine cells.

Single-stream communication strategies: A strategic programme of communications whereby there is only a single strand of relations between the marketing company and the contact managed by the system.

Strategic activity: Time or event driven communications. Normally initiated to address a long term relationship building objective, communications are generated automatically as the result of either an action by the contact, an action by the company relevant to all or a particular element of the contact-base or the passing of time without any event. Aimed at building and maintaining a relationship between the company and the contact, strategic activity is capable of both soft sell (customer care letters/calls, newsletters, magazines and so on) and hard sell approaches (special offers, personalized propositions and tailored packages) driven by the trigger.

Suppression: The exclusion of one or more individuals from extracts, models, reports etc, either automatically or manually.

Synchrographics: Another time-oriented element. This time it describes the point the individual is within the purchase cycle for any particular product or service. Knowledge of this will assist the marketer in the targeting of prospects as they enter their renewal or subsequent purchase window.

Tactical activity: Marketing activity, normally discrete campaigns, initiated to address short term, ad-hoc objectives outside the strategic programme. Care must be taken to ensure that such activity does not impact on the relationship being developed via the strategic programme, either through over-mailing or through conflict of proposition, hence the need for both automatic and manual suppressions.

(Source: Direct Response Magazine, September 1996, pp. 51–2.) © Direct Response Magazine, London.

Consider the following case. As it shows, much can be gleaned from a few small pieces of data.

What's In It For Me?

A motor car dealer attended a direct marketing course. As a result, he discovered that he has much more information about his customers than he previously realised. Before attending the course he was really rather *reactive* in his marketing – waiting for customers to book services/repairs for their vehicles and apart from some co-operative local advertising with his supplying motor manufacturer, generally waited for people to come into the showroom. Now he realises that he can be *proactive* and understand his customers and potential customers much more – and on an individual basis.

He was shown that every time a car was purchased he actually gathered significant amounts of information on the purchaser – name, address, telephone number etc. Also, when there was a credit agreement, information on the customer's financial and occupational circumstances was revealed. As a result, he began to send letters (and sometimes even telephone calls) asking about the new customer's evaluation of how well he/she was treated during the purchase process, thus potentially starting a relationship with that customer. He also used this process to gather a little bit more information about the customer – including lifestyle details which he realised could help with the targeting of relevant offers.

At regular intervals, he began to mail his customers to remind them about servicing. After several 'services' he had information on the usual mileage of each customer, thereby making the reminders more timely. He also began to send out reminders regarding MOTs by simply checking the purchase date in the log book. At appropriate intervals he could send out mailings with news about new car launches and modifications, therefore offering up-selling opportunities for his dealership. Wine and cheese evenings were arranged for selected customers at appropriate launches.

Cross selling was also possible because he could contact the customer with details of car alarm systems and other accessories. The customer's partner became an important target as well – the second family car might be a used vehicle and targeting for cross and up-selling was approached in a similar way. He also became aware of the ages of the couple's children and was able to target them when they reached the age of 17.

He found that an analysis of address locations of customers, geodemographically profiled, was particularly helpful in defining his catchment area, and identifying where his customers lived. As a result, he mailed prospects in similar areas with regard to launches and other events.

Over time, the dealer found that with regular contact a relationship developed and he realised that if he was able to retain this customer and his family, over several years, the 'lifetime value' of their business would be quite significant and at the same time cheaper than new customer acquisition. This dealer also now has a 'list' which he is considering selling on to, for example, warranty or 'breakdown' companies, thus making money out the process itself!

Such data can also be used to 'score' customers. Most items of data are scorable. For example, we might know from previous campaigns that we have had a greater success rate when marketing to those with the 'Mr' title rather than Mrs or Ms, in which case we can give a quantitative weight to 'title'. Postcode is especially revealing because we can profile geodemographically from this and again compare with previous success/failure rates to score the geodemographic cluster and the postcode itself, at different levels. For example, do we have more success in Cardiff (CF) or Bristol (BS)?

This is an example of scoring from two of the most basic elements of data. By adding lifestyle and transactional data and scoring all those in our database on a weighted index which incorporates all of these variables, we can produce very useful league tables for targeting purposes.

RFM Analysis

Our database 'data' also becomes 'information' when we identify the 'recency, frequency and monetary value' (RFM) of customer orders.

▶ *Recency.* Just knowing that a customer has purchased from the organization in the past is important but not sufficient. Marketers are clearly more interested in a customer who has purchased in the last six months, than a customer who last bought from the organization in 1984.

▶ *Frequency.* A one-off purchase may also make a customer less attractive (depending, of course, on the product-market in which we operate). So knowing how often they buy from the organization is an important measure.

▶ *Monetary Value.* The value of orders from the customer.

Small orders are usually less attractive than larger ones, so this is yet another measure of significance. Indeed, as has already been discussed marketers are increasingly concentrating on their 'better' customers – those who have the highest monetary value (and frequency) of purchase and are segmenting on the basis of 'volume' because in this way they are more cost effective, because they concentrate on those who bring greater returns. Vilfredo Pareto's theory of income distribution has been transferred and borrowed by direct marketers to support the proposition that 80 per cent of sales come from just 20 per cent of customers – in many markets the ratio can be even more polarized (95:5 is not uncommon). The Pareto principle is often quoted by direct marketers and is certainly relevant to this discussion of RFM analysis.

RFM analysis clearly, by the nature of the variables involved, means that transactional data must be tracked by the database – actual purchase history is needed. In addition to leading to the identification of volume segments and best prospects, the RFM information also contributes to the calculation of 'lifetime value' – another of the direct marketer's cornerstone measures.

Lifetime Value Analysis

'Lifetime' is perhaps a little of an overstatement – it doesn't mean the lifetime of the customer, but rather a designated period of time during which they are a customer of your organization. Depending on the type of products or services on offer, lifetime might be as little as six months (as in purchases for baby products) or as long as 10 years (as in the automotive market). Essentially, different sectors have worked out the probable lifetime value of the 'average' customer and calculate accordingly. Whatever period is relevant, however, the concept of what that customer is worth to the organization in sales and profit terms over a period of time is a critical concept within direct marketing.

To take an extreme example, if a car company is only concerned with acquiring customers and does nothing to retain them, there is a fair chance that each customer who buys one of their cars this year will go on to buy another make next time – and the time after that and so on. The value of the sale might be £10,000 but subtracting acquisition costs, production and other costs could mean a net profit of a just a few pounds.

With a more dedicated retention programme the company could expect that customer to buy one of their cars every third year for, perhaps, 12 years – not just at £10,000 but as they progress through their life stages they may be able to buy more expensive models. So, with lower costs of retaining a customer than acquiring him/her in the first instance, together with repeat buying and the prospect of up-selling over a period of time, the sales value could be as high as, say, £70,000 (£10k + £12k + £14k + £16k + £18k).

Consider the smaller case of a home delivery curry business – Farooq's Tandoori. Assume 3000 customers per year with overall sales amounting to £180,000. His costs of running the business were about 60 per cent of sales so profit was £72,000.

The business, because it 'delivers', is able to record customers' names and addresses and the amount they spend. After the first couple of years of such recording Farooq was alarmed because he discovered that only 30 per cent of his home delivery customers ever returned. Farooq decided to apply some of the material he had recently learnt by reading this book!

He analysed his database of customers. With 3000 customers and revenue of £180,000 the first simple calculation was that the average spend per customer was £60 per year (on average this represents two orders per year, each order being for three meals averaging £10. Taking the 3000 customers from year 1, only 30 per cent returned and this we take as the 'retention rate'. Table 4.4 shows the initial calculations.

Table 4.5 demonstrates how Farooq extended this basic analysis into the second and third years and Table 4.6 shows how, from these calculations, he ultimately calculated the lifetime (after 3 years) value of his customers. Because only 30 per cent of customers were retained, the decline in returning customers is shown under years 2 and 3 as 900 and 270 respectively.

Table 4.4 Lifetime Value
Calculation – I

	Year 1
Customers	3,000
Retention Rate	30%
Average Spend	£60
Revenue	£180,000
Costs as % of Sales	60%
Costs	£108,000
Profits	£72,000

Table 4.5 Extended Analysis

	Year 1	Year 2	Year 3
Customers	3,000	900	270
Retention Rate	30%	30%	30%
Average Spend	£60	£60	£60
Revenue	£180,000	£54,000	£16,200
Cost as % of Sales	60%	60%	60%
Costs	£108,000	£32,400	£9,720
Profit	£72,000	£21,000	£6,460

With these smaller numbers of customers, but assuming the same average spend of £60, total revenue from the 'loyals' falls in year 2 and in year 3. The 'knock-on' effects for costs and profits are also shown in Table 4.5.

Because the value of profit is less in years 2 and 3 than in the current year 1, Farooq made an adjustment to the figures to take account of this – the calculation is the 'net present value'. This essentially converts tomorrow's money to today's value. The starting point for this calculation is the interest rate – which Farooq knows has just moved to 10 per cent. However, to be prudent, he bases his calculations on double this rate – all sorts of things might happen over the next three years – another home delivery service might start up, or the town by-pass that has been discussed for years might eventually be built.

Having decided on a rate of interest of 20 per cent he now has to 'do the sums'. The formula for calculating the rate at which to 'discount' future money to today's level is:

$$D = (1+i)^n$$

Where i = the selected rate of interest (in this case 20 per cent) and n = the number of years beyond the current first year that we are considering.

So, for Farooq:

$$\text{For year 2, } D = (1 + .20)^2 = 1.44$$
$$\text{For year 3, } D = (1 + .20)^3 = 1.73$$

What this means is that in order to discount future profit (in years 2 and 3) to today's value, we need to divide the actual profit figure by 1.44 in year 2 and 1.73 in year 3. The first year's profit is not discounted because today's money is at today's value! Table 4.6 shows the effect of the discount rate on profit. In years 2 and 3, the rates for discounting those year's profit to today's value produces 'net present values' of £15,000 and £3746 respectively. Cumulatively, this means profit figures amount to £87,000 by the end of year 2 and to £90,746 by the end of year 3.

Dividing these figures by the number of customers Farooq started with (3,000) produces the estimate of lifetime value per customer per year. As can be seen, the lifetime (over 3 years only, in this case) value of the loyal customer is £30.25.

The reason why the original 3000 customers is used to divide into the cumulative NPV is because Farooq is concerned with the lifetime of each new customer – based on certain assumptions regarding retention rates and cost structures. The resulting lifetime value can be used in predictions about alternative marketing strategies and is therefore an immensely valuable planning calculation. To demonstrate some of this, assume Farooq decides to be a little more proactive in retaining customers – he has seen the increased value to be gained from the return of regular customers and now wants to implement a retention strategy.

Farooq develops a reward card scheme whereby his returning customers get a 10 per cent discount and either a free onion bhajee or

	Year 1	Year 2	Year 3
Number of Customers	3,000	900 (30% of 3,000)	270 (30% of 900)
Retention Rate	30%	30%	30%
Average Spend	£60	£60	£60
Revenue (Spend x No. of Customers)	£180,000	£54,000	£16,200
Costs as % of Sales	60%	60%	60%
Costs (60% of Revenue)	£108,000	£32,400	£9,720
Profit (Revenue – Costs)	£72,000	£21,600	£6,480
Discount Rate	1.00	1.44	1.73
NPV (Profit/Discount Rate)	£72,000	£15,000	£3,746
Cumulative NPV	£72,000	£87,000	£90,746
Lifetime Value per Customer (NPV/ 3,000 customers)	£24.00	£29.00	£30.25

Table 4.6 Lifetime Value Calculation II

banana fritter for each main meal ordered. He sends all of his customers a questionnaire asking for their views on his home delivery service and the food. On the questionnaire he also asks for some additional personal details. He asks for their date of birth and names and dates of birth of others in the household. He now sends birthday cards to those on his database together with a birthday menu of 'special occasion' meals. Also enclosed with these mailings is an offer if they recommend Farooq's service to others who purchase a meal (and of course for every new customer he is able to add them to his database because the home delivery system means name and address are essential prerequisites for delivery). The other side to the offer is half-price meals for the first order after a referral makes a purchase. Farooq thinks that this 'member get member' scheme will lead to about 5 per cent of his existing customers 'recruiting' new customers – he bases this on the experience of some friends in the direct marketing industry. In addition to birthday cards he also sends Christmas cards with a special 'winter curry' menu with the aim of increasing ordering at Christmas and New Year – and a calendar for the next year. He calculates that the additional costs are as shown in Table 4.7:

Farooq thinks that the entire scheme will have a positive effect on retention rates such that rather than the mere 30 per cent of customers returning, he will now see 50 per cent retained. The above programme, he estimates, will increase the number of orders per year from each customer – after all, he is offering discounts and other incentives for them to buy more frequently. The home delivery service is made more salient because of the regular mailings, tailoring to birthdays and promotional offers. Overall, Farooq estimates that the value of each customer's orders over the course of a year will now rise from £60 to £120 (each *order* will still be for an average of three meals

Table 4.7 Additional Costs of Marketing Activities

Marketing Activities	Cost
Discounts (10% of order value per customer per year) £120 x 10%	£12.00
Free Item (50p per meal per year: 3 meals per order & 4 orders per year' 12 meals)	£6.00
Birthday Cards (average 3 per household @ 50p)	£1.50
Christmas Cards (1 per household @ 50p)	£0.50
Special Menus (average 4 per household @ 20p with one for each of 3 birthdays plus Christmas)	£0.80
Mailing Costs (4 @ 26p per year)	£1.04
Total (per household per year)	£21.84

@ £10, but now four times per year rather than just twice) – but this does not take account of the discounts and free items from which they will benefit. In addition, the MGM scheme will cost a further 50 per cent of one order for the 5 per cent of customers who make a referral.

Table 4.8 summarizes the effects of the above retention programme on Farooq's sales, costs, profits and lifetime values. The referral rate from the MGM scheme has no effect in year 1 and then is based on an extra 5 per cent of customers on those retained (after the effect of the 50 per cent retention rate has impacted).

In addition, different lifetime values can be calculated for each segment we might be targeting differently (e.g. by postcode, or age and so on). The point here will be to identify the effects of our different marketing strategies for each segment, in order to modify our approach. In this way, such calculations are not merely 'nice to know' but make a real contribution to the iterative nature of direct marketing planning and evaluation.

It must be pointed out, however, that several estimates – and even guesses – contributed to the above calculations – for example in terms of referral rates and increased spend. These could be inaccurate and the whole scheme could produce negative results. As the scheme moves along, revised figures can be built into the calculations, iteratively, to improve accuracy, but the risks should not be swept under the carpet. Direct marketing is full of 'try it and see' programmes

	Year 1	Year 2	Year 3
Referral Rate	5%	5%	5%
Referred Customers from MGM Scheme	0	150 (5% of 3,000)	83 (5% of 1650)
Retention Rate	50%	50%	50%
Customers Including Retention	3,000	1,500 (50% of 3,000)	825 (50% of 1650)
Total Customers Including Referrals	3,000	1650 (1500 + 150)	908 (825 + 83)
Average Spend	£120	£120	£120
Revenue	£360,000	£198,000	£108,960
Costs as % of Sales	60%	60%	60%
Costs	£216,000	£118,800	£65,376
Additional Costs (£21.84 per customer)	£53,520	£36,036	£19,831
Total Costs	£269,520	£154,836	£85,207
Profit	£90,480	£43,164	£23,753
Discount Rate	1.00	1.44	1.73
NPV	£90,480	£29,975	£13,730
Cumulative NPV	£90,480	£120,455	£134,185
Lifetime Value per Customer: (Based on cohort of 3,000 customers: NPV/3000)	£30.16	£40.15	£44.73

Table 4.8 Lifetime Value Calculation III

– not all succeed by any means, but if you never try you never succeed! Lifetime (or 'long time') values can be calculated for each segment targeted; our calculations have aggregated any possible segments into one, to make it easier to follow the logic. Indeed lifetime values can even be calculated for each individual customer and perhaps this should be the ultimate aim.

A problem with the LTV concept in practice is that marketers very often analyse their databases as they are *now*. Many segments, however, are extremely dynamic. Take an extreme case of the 'best' customers at a DIY store. There may only be about 5 per cent of these who are also 'best' customers in the 4th quarter of a year compared with the 1st quarter. This can easily be explained by DIY projects at home that they may be involved with at the beginning of the year, but as soon as it is completed, their store patronage dies, yet they might be targeted as high LTV customers with a relationship marketing programme.

Allowable Cost

For this calculation a 'mini' profit and loss account is created for the 'average' sale. Promotional costs are excluded (because we are attempting to estimate these) but other costs and the desired profit are included. Table 4.9 shows a simple example in which the selling price of a directly distributed computer is £1000, its cost of production is £600, order handling is £40, 'p&p' is £20 and the desired profit is £250. Costs total £660 so the 'contribution' is £340. If the selling price is £1000 and the sum of costs and profit for the average sale is £910 (£660 costs + £250 profit) then the allowable cost is £90 (£1,000–£910).

As an average figure this means that we can afford to spend £90 on each sale and that the resulting profit will be £250. This figure can now be used to calculate the response rate that would be needed from a mailed promotion. Table 4.10 shows that if the mailing costs are £26,000 and we allow £90 per order, then we need to get 289 sales

Table 4.9 Allowable Costs

Selling Price of Computer			£1000
Costs	Cost of Product	£600	
	Order Handling	£40	
	Postage & Packing	£20	
Total Cost		£660	(£660)
Contribution: (selling price – cost)			£340
Desired Profit			(£250)
Allowable Cost per order (selling price – costs – desired profit)			£90

Mailing Cost	£26,000
Allowable Cost Per Order	£90
Sales Required (25,000/90)	289
Size of Mailing	28,000
Response Rate (Required sales/size of mailing expressed as percentage)	1.03% (289 ÷ 28,000) x 100

Table 4.10 Response Rates

(26,000 ÷ 90). If the mail shot is to 28,000 people a response rate of 1.03 per cent will be required.

There is an additional use of these two calculations. From Table 4.9 it was shown that the 'contribution' was £340 and if we divide this into the cost of the promotion (£26,000) we can see that the break-even point is at 76 orders. That is, once there have been 76 orders, the costs of the mailing will be covered.

This analysis can be done for different selling prices and different promotional campaigns and shows again how direct marketing can be measurable and accountable. We have not delved into the intricacies of different costing structures because our intention is to show the allowable cost principle and how it can be used.

Cost Per Thousand

If we have been given quotations from different mailing companies; A costs £26,000 for a mailing of 28,000 and B costs £30,000 for a mailing of 32,500, there is a standard measure to compare cost effectiveness though this does not take into account any difference in likely response rate from the two mailings (Table 4.11).

The message here is not to go for the cheaper mailing or, conversely, for the one that reaches more people, but rather to combine these factors in the 'cost per thousand' calculation.

Cost Per Order

Here, the cost per order is found by dividing total cost by total orders:

Cost Per Order   Total Cost ÷ Total Orders

Cost per thousand	(Cost ÷ Size of mailing) x 1000
Mailing A	(£26,000 ÷ 28,000) x 1000 = £928.57 per thousand mailed
Mailing B	(£30,000 ÷ 32,500) x 1000 = £923.08 per thousand mailed

Table 4.11 Cost Per Thousand

Response Per Thousand

This is found by dividing total response by the total mailed:

Response Per Thousand (Total Response ÷ Total Mailed) x 1000

Note that 'cost per thousand' divided by 'orders per thousand' will also give 'cost per order'.

Strategic and Tactical Use of Databases

Organizations can use the database for both tactical and strategic issues. Although tactical utilization is very widespread, it is usually only through consideration of strategic issues that the database is truly a source of competitive advantage for the organization.

Tactical Utilization of the Database

If used merely tactically, the nature of the marketing database does not need to refer greatly to corporate strategy or organizational structure (Cook 1994). Under such circumstances the database is more concerned with 'the next event' than with a longer term view of customers (Bigg 1994). Cook (1994) suggests that it is actually more usual for organizations to employ the database at tactical rather than at the strategic level, for the purposes given in Figure 4.16 below.

If the database is used only for tactical issues, this will ultimately relegate direct marketing itself to a tactical appendage of a broader, more strategic marketing function. Thus, strategic uses of database marketing need to be considered.

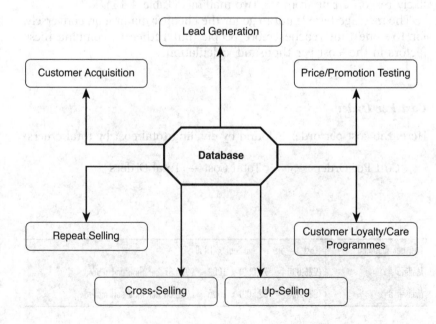

Figure 4.16 Tactical Uses of the Database

Strategic Utilization of Databases

At a strategic level, decisions will need to be taken with respect to direct marketing planning, and in particular, segmentation and targeting as outlined in Chapter 3. In this sense the marketing database can focus on a whole range of different categories (e.g. new prospects, best prospects, loyals, etc.) which are then utilized for acquisition or retention strategies. In this way, the creation and use of marketing databases will be quite selective.

Once created, the database has a variety of uses. It can clearly be used as a list from which to target customers via direct marketing activity. But in addition it can also provide a wealth of information on the market and on customers and potential customers within it. In this context, the database provides data for both planning and analysis purposes: the database can be analysed for most attractive segments, for campaign planning and predicting campaign response. Strategically, the database can be used to change the basis of competition, strengthen customer relationships, overcome supplier problems, building barriers to entry and developing new products (Shaw and Stone 1988). Table 4.12 examines these further.

For example, Holiday Inn clearly believes in a positive strategic role for their marketing database which they see as allowing them '...to more accurately define strategies for the future and concurrently maximize short term marketing efforts' (Durr 1989). A new strategic use of the database which potentially could transcend all five categories is the sharing of data with other organizations in strategic alliances. We discuss this development in the section on *biographics* and the authors believe it will be a significant trend for the future. Shaw and Stone (1988) take this further by proposing a four stage process of development of the marketing database. These phases are outlined below:

▶ *Phase One*. The database is merely a sales database originating from accounting systems and focusing more on product sales rather than customers.

▶ *Phase Two*. Occurs when a company has multiple databases for different sales territories or retailers and although they can be well used within the sector they cover, there can often be overlapping effort due to lack of communication and co-ordination – customers might receive direct mailings from the same company, but different and even conflicting ones from different parts of that company!

▶ *Phase Three*. There is evidence of a greater customer focus, with one database co-ordinating all communication with customers. Analysis is according to profiles, transactions and other relevant factors in order to determine how to target segments and individuals.

▶ *Phase Four*. There is evidence of true integration, with different organizational functions, not just the marketing one, linked with the marketing database.

Table 4.12 The Role of Database Marketing as a Competitive Tool

Competitive Opportunity	Marketing Strategy	Role of Information
▶ Change Competitive Basis	▶ Market Development or Penetration ▶ Increased Effectiveness ▶ Better Margins ▶ Alternative Sales Channels ▶ Reducing Cost Structure	▶ Prospect/Customer Information ▶ Targeted Marketing ▶ Better Control
▶ Strengthen Customer Position	▶ Tailored Customer Service ▶ Providing Value to Customers ▶ Product Differentiation ▶ Create Switching Costs	▶ Know Customer Needs ▶ 'Individual' Promotions ▶ Response Handling ▶ Identify Potential Needs ▶ Customers as 'Users' of Your Systems
▶ Strengthen Buyer/Supplier Position	▶ Superior Market Information ▶ Decreased Cost of Sales ▶ Providing Access to Supplier ▶ Pass Stockholding onto Supplier	▶ Internal/External Data Capture ▶ Optimization of Sales Channels ▶ Measure Supplier Performance ▶ Identify Areas of Inefficiency
▶ Build Barriers	▶ Unique Distribution Channels ▶ Unique Valued Services ▶ Create Entry Costs	▶ Knowledge of Market Allows Improved Service/Value ▶ 'Lock In' Customers, Suppliers and Intermediaries ▶ Immediate Response to Threats
▶ Generate New Products	▶ Market-Led Product Development ▶ Alliance Opportunities ▶ New Products/Services	▶ Market Gap Analysis ▶ Customer Dialogue ▶ User Innovation ▶ Information as Product

(Source: Fletcher *et al.* 1990)

In parallel with this analysis, Parkinson (1994) identifies three levels of IT application within marketing. The first is concerned with the management of transactions, the second is concerned with profiling, targeting and developing effective direct marketing, while the third level is concerned with marketing productivity analysis, modelling and strategic planning.

If the organization is not truly customer orientated then there will only be a tactical role for the marketing database but if used strategically, then it has a central role to play – as outlined in the definition of database marketing offered earlier. Indeed, De Tienne and Thompson (1996) propose that the 'customer database is an opportunity for organizations to mechanize the process of learning about customers' and for this to be iterative because 'the database transcends the status of a record keeping device and becomes an implement of ever-increasing organization knowledge'.

Conclusions

Technological change is facilitating database development and as we discussed in Chapter 1, there is demand for a more individualized marketing approach. The database provides a vehicle for understanding and analysing markets and customers and the merging of data sources leads to the development of *biographics*.

This 'biographical' analogy is perhaps paralleled with another analogy, the Domesday Book, for which, in the UK in medieval times, William the Conqueror collected personal information (though rather more brutally than the database industry of today does!) about each of his subjects. In this sense we have seen the birth of what might be termed 'Domesday Marketing' (Evans 1994). This raises a variety of ethical issues concerning the acquisition and use of personal data as are discussed in Chapter 11 and indeed have been discussed to some extent in the current chapter.

The database provides direct marketing with one of its main reasons for claiming to be more measurable and accountable than more traditional forms of marketing. The calculation and strategic use of lifetime values and allowable costs are examples.

STUDY 3

Tor Line
– Freight Shipping

This brief covers the consumer database for Scandinavian Seaways UK based passengers only.

Scandinavian Seaways – Marketing Database Brief

Background

DFDS Group

Scandinavian Seaways is the passenger division of the Danish public company DFDS A/S who operate passenger ferries between the UK and Northern Europe and within Scandinavia. The DFDS group is divided into 3 divisions:–

Passenger Division
– Scandinavian Seaways

Transport Division
– DFDS Transport whose activities include:
  (i) Freight transport and forwarding
  (ii) Freight shipping
  (iii) Haulage
  (iv) Logistics

Scandinavian Seaways route network

Route Network:	Harwich to	Esbjerg	(Denmark)	Year
		Gothenburg	(Sweden)	round
		Hamburg	(Germany)	services
	Newcastle to	Amsterdam	(Holland)	Seasonal
		Gothenburg	(Sweden)	summer
		Hamburg	(Germany)	services
	Copenhagen to	Oslo	(Norway)	
		Gothenburg	(Sweden)	

Scandinavian Seaways product

Products are divided into four categories:

1 Transportation (port to port crossing);

2 ITs (inclusive tours which are packaged holidays for either groups or individuals);

3 Mini-Cruises (2 night short breaks which include a sightseeing tour at the destination city);

4 MIC (meeting incentives and conferences using the ships' conferencing facilities).

The on-board product concept (which is referred to as the '*Liner Concept*') combines nautical tradition, high standards of service and good facilities in order to make the journey an integral and equally enjoyable part of the holiday/trip.

● ● ▶

Some of the features of the on-board product are:

(i) All passengers have cabins except during the Summer period when a few airline style reclining chairs are installed on some ships.

(ii) Sailing departures and arrivals are at sociable times.

(iii) All sailings are over-night crossings which vary in length from 15 to 24 hours.

(iv) The on-board catering includes a range of restaurants, a café and bars.

(v) Entertainment includes a band in the main lounge, cinemas, children's play area and children's club.

(vi) Retailing includes duty-free shop (which uses a shop within shop concept with franchise areas such as Tie Rack and Red & Green) and a gift shop on some ships.

(vii) Other facilities vary according to ship but include:
- Casino
- Sauna
- Swimming Pool
- Pianist in the bar
- Disco

(vii) Conference facilities are available; scale varies by ship

Scandinavian Seaways have 3 main unique selling propositions:

1 All services offer direct connections. There are no direct competitors on the routes from UK to Denmark, Sweden or Germany.

2 You can take your car.

3 Large groups can be accommodated (unlike airlines who will often not accept large groups because they displace higher fare paying passengers).

Direct Marketing Objectives

Strategic Activity

Strategic DM objectives are:

1 To launch new holiday, Mini-Cruise and transportation brochures using the marketing database;

2 To develop transportation customer loyalty through the Seaways Club and through relationship marketing;

3 To improve understanding of our target groups in order to:

(i) improve the targeting of database marketing activity to gain increased cost efficiency in terms of cost per passenger and life-time value.

(ii) improve the delivery and phasing of above the line advertising creative messages and media planning and buying;

(iii) development of new and existing products;

(iv) improve the relevance of brochures and the products in them;

(v) develop the onboard product and sailing schedules.

This should include the ability to undertake lifestyle, geographic and demographic analysis.

4 To increase the size of the marketing database with high quality prospects who will be of the right profile. It is particularly important to attract customers who will not only travel with us but who will also spend on-board.

5 To increase the conversion of brochure enquirers to bookers through effective post-fulfilment follow-up.

6 To provide cost effective access to the database for staff in Harwich and to provide pro-active support in terms of identifying new business opportunities.

Tactical Activity

Tactical DM objectives are:

1 To identify, from our database, households who are likely to book products which satisfy our tactical needs, which may include:

(i) Generating cost effective volume on problem sailings;

(ii) Driving business into specific cabin types in order to improve berth utilization;

(iii) Producing large or small volumes of business on specific routes during defined periods;

(iv) Selling higher revenue products during more busy periods;

(v) To encourage early booking.

2 To identify tactical general and special interest product opportunities for promotion via the marketing database;

3 To identify key geographic areas for door drops or regional inserts;

4 To identify cold DM opportunities.

General Objectives

1 To maintain household information which is accurate and up-to-date;

2 To obey all laws relating to direct marketing and to follow industry best practise;

3 To provide accurate, timely and user-friendly management information. As an indication of the sort of information which will be needed, the monthly reports should show (in addition to other elements identified with the agency):

(i) A summary of the main segments on the database;

(ii) Summary of additions and deletions during the month;

(iii) Geographic, demographic and travel history summaries;

(iv) A summary of the ICD survey;

(v) An analysis showing conversion of enquiry to booking.

4 To prepare the database for revenue generation from 3rd party list rental.

The Marketing Database

The marketing database currently contains 584,000 customer records, which is made up of:

12,000 bookers
473,000 enquirers

● ● ▶

There are four main sources of data:
(i) Scandinavian Seaways reservations systems for bookers;
(ii) Brann Contact 24 for consumer brochure requests;
(iii) The Seaways Club database (loyalty club);
(iv) ICD survey responders (survey handed out at check-in in Harwich and Newcastle

Additionally, there are ad hoc sources of data such as tourist boards and other business partners.

The volume of records added to the database each year is approximately

(i) Scandinavian Seaways booking data	25,000
(ii) Enquiry data	30,000
(iii) Seaways Club members	2,000
(iv) ICD Survey	10,000

The Brief

In your presentation, you should address the following question:

How can Scandinavian Seaways manage its marketing database in order to optimize the booking opportunities available across the product range in the most cost effective manner?

Specifically, you should cover:
(i) Data analysis, targeting and profiling.
(ii) Identifying marketing opportunities from the database.
(iii) Mailing selection and database 'housekeeping' and reporting.

Your presentation should give a clear breakdown of costs.

The team who would be working on this account should be present at the presentation.

■

Review Questions

1 A motor car dealer has been on a direct marketing course and discovered that he has much more information about his customers than he previously realized. Before attending the course he was really rather reactive in his marketing – waiting for customers to book services/repairs for their vehicles and apart from some co-operative local advertising with his supplying motor manufacturer, generally waited for people to come into the showroom. Now he realizes that he can be proactive and understand his customers and potential customers much more – and on an individual basis. He has realized that he has a very useful database already and can supplement this in significant ways. How and with what benefits?

2 What is meant by 'RFM' and the 'Pareto Principle'. What is their value to direct marketers and customers?

3 What is meant by 'lifetime value' and what is its value to direct marketers and customers?

Discussion Questions

1 For a consumer market of your choice, consider the sources of information which might be relevant for data fusion (including the range of existing databases which could be relevantly linked). What could each source contribute to a direct marketing operation?

2 Select two organizations with which you are familiar and analyse in which stages of database development they currently are. Discuss how they reached that stage and how they might progress further.

References

Adalbert, T. as reported in Darby, I. (1997) 'Direct Mail's Night of the Living Dead', *Marketing Direct*, September, p.10.

Antoniou, T. (1997) 'Drilling or Mining? Handling and Analysis of Data Between Now and the Year 2000', *Marketing and Research Today*, May, pp.115–120.

Barlow, R. (1992) 'Relationship Marketing: The Ultimate in Customer Services', *Retail Control*, March, pp.29–37.

Bickert J. (1994) 'Database Marketing: An Overview', in E.L. Nash (ed.) *The Direct Marketing Handbook*, New York: McGraw Hill.

Bigg, A. (1994) 'Techno Tactics', *Campaign* July 8th, pp.37–38.

Bradford, G. (1995) 'Targeting Technology', *Admap*, January, pp.32–4.

Burnett, E. (1994), 'A faster, better way to access marketing information', *Journal of Database Marketing*, 2(1), p.68.

Cook, S. (1994) 'Database Marketing: Strategy or Tactical Tool?' *Marketing Intelligence and Planning*, 12(6) pp.4–7.

Courtheoux, R. (1992) 'Lists and Databases', Iin Brown, H. and Buskirk, B. (1992) *Readings and Cases in Direct Marketing*, Lincolnwood, IL: NTC Business Books.

Cowling, A. B. (1996) 'Big Issues for the Next Five Years: Data Fusion, Reach the Parts Others Don't', *IDM Symposium*, May.

Darby, I. (1997) 'Direct Mail's Night of the Living Dead', *Marketing Direct*, September, p10.

DeTienne, K. B. and Thompson, J. A. (1996) 'Database Marketing and Organizational Learning Theory: Toward a Research Agenda', *Journal of Consumer Marketing*, 13(5), pp.12–34.

Di Talamo (1995) cited by Reed, 'Jumping on the Bandwagon', *Marketing Week*, 24 March, pp. 25-6.

DMIS (1997) *Consumer Databases: A Study of External Lists and In-House Database Usage*, London.

Donovan, J. (1996) 'The True Price of Loyalty', *Marketing Week Customer Loyalty Supplement*, February 8th, pp.XI–XIII.

Durr, J. L. (1989) 'The Value of the Guest Register', *Direct Marketing*, September, pp.48–55.

Evans, M. (1994) 'Domesday Marketing' *Journal of Marketing Management*, 10(5), pp.409–31.

Evans, M., Patterson, M. and O'Malley, L. (1996) 'Direct Mail and Consumer Response', *Journal of Database Marketing*, 3(3), pp.250–262.

Fletcher, K. (1990) *Marketing Management and Information Technology*, London: Prentice Hall.

Fletcher, K. and Peters, L. (1996) 'Issues in Consumer Information Management', *Journal of the Market Research Society*, 38(2), pp.145–60.

Fletcher K., Wheeler, C. and Wright, J. (1990) 'The Role and Status of UK Database Marketing' , *Quarterly Review of Marketing*, Autumn, pp.7–14.

Foenander, J. (1992) 'The Use of Smart Card Technology for Target Marketing in the Retail Sector', *Journal of Targeting, Measurement and Analysis for Marketing*, 1(1), pp.55–60.

Hughes, A.M. (1996) *The Complete Database Marketer*, Irwin, p.119.

Humby, C. (1996a) 'Opening the Information Warehouse', *Marketing*, September 18th, pp.34–7.

Humby, C. (1996b) 'Digging for Information', *Marketing*, November 21st, pp.41–2.

Kettle, M. as reported in Darby, I. (1997) 'Direct Mail's Night of the Living Dead', *Marketing Direct*, September, p.10.

Leggit, D. (1997) 'Putting Posters on the Map', *Marketing*, July 3rd, pp.23–25.

Linton, I. (1995) *Database Marketing: Know What Your Customer Wants*, London: Pitman.

Long, G., Angold, S. and Hogg, M. (1992) 'Who Am I?: A Preliminary Investigation into the Extent to which Data Collected via EPoS and EFTPoS Systems is Incorporated into Customer Databases Accessible through the Provisions of the Data Protection Legislation', in J. Whitelock *et al.* Proceedings of the Marketing Education Group Annual Conference, *Marketing in the New Europe and Beyond*, Salford, pp.596–606.

Mander, G. (1993) 'De-Duplication', *Journal of database Marketing*, 1(2), pp.150–61.

McGoldrick, P. J. (1990), *Retail Marketing*, London: McGraw Hill.

Mitchell, A. (1996) 'You and Yours', *Interview transcribed from BBC Radio 4*, January.

Mitchell A. and Littlewood, S. (1992) 'Marketing's Smart Transformation', *Marketing*, May 21st.

Mitchell, S. (1996) 'Training and Support Given to Users of Marketing Databases', *Journal of Database Marketing*, 3(4), pp.326–430.

Mitchell, V. W. and Haggett, S. (1997) 'Sun-Sign Astrology in Market Segmentation: An Empirical Investigation', *Journal of Consumer Marketing*, 14(2), pp.113–131.

Oppenshaw, S. as reported in Walker, N. Savage, M. and Fiddick, P. (1997) 'A Top Level Look at the New Geodemographics', Research, January, pp.10–11.

Parkinson, S. (1994) 'Computers in Marketing', in M.J. Baker (ed.) *The Marketing Book*, London: Butterworth Hienemann, pp.18–19.

Patron, M. (1996) 'The Future of Marketing Databases', *Journal of Database Marketing*, 4(1), p.8.

Read, G. (1997) 'The Future of Data Warehousing', *Business and Technology*, February, p.64.

Richards, A. (1998) 'Can Unity Beat the Retailers?', *Marketing*, February, p.18.

Rosenberg, L. and Czepiel, J. (1984) 'A Marketing Approach for Customer Retention' *Journal of Consumer Marketing*, Spring pp.45–51.

Sargeant, P. (1996) 'The UK List Industry', Guest Lecture, UWE, Bristol, November 18th.

Shaw, R. (1991) 'How the Smart Card is Changing Retailing', *Long Range Planning*, 24(10), pp.111–14.

Shaw, R. and Stone, M. (1988a) *Database Marketing*, Aldershot: Gower.

Shaw, R. and Stone, M. (1988b) 'Competitive Superiority through Database Marketing', *Long Range Planning*, 21(5), pp.24–40.

Stone, M., Davies, D. and Bond, A. (1995) *Direct Hit: Direct Marketing With A Winning Edge*, London: Pitman.

Sunday Times, (1997) 'Taking Advantage of Children', September 28th, Business Section, p.6.

Uncles, M. (1994) 'Do you or your customers need a loyalty scheme?', *Journal of Targeting, Measurement and Analysis for Marketing*, 2(4), pp.335–50.

Walker, J. (1996) 'SMART Move but will it deliver the goods?', *Precision Marketing*, May 6th, pp.18–21.

Further Reading

Davies, J. (1992) *The Essential Guide to Database Marketing*, London: McGraw Hill.

Evans, M. J. (1998) 'From 1086 and 1984: Direct Marketing into the Millenium' *Marketing Intelligence and Planning*, 16(1), pp. 56–67.

Hughes, A.M. (1996) *The Complete Database Marketer*, Chicago: Irwin.

Jackson, R. and Wang, P. (1996) *Strategic Database Marketing*, Chicago: NTC Business Books.

Kelly, S. (1997) *Data Warehousing: The Route to Mass Customization*, Chichester: Wiley.

Shaw, R. and Stone, M. (1988) *Database Marketing*, Aldershot: Gower.

Market Research and Testing

This Chapter:

► Provides The Student With An
Understanding Of The Basics Of
Researching Markets.

► Reviews Sources Of Marketing
Information.

► Contextualizes Primary Research
Methods Along A Continuum
Comprising Observation, Interview &
Experimentation.

► Provides The Student With An
Understanding Of 'Testing', As A Form
Of Experimentation.

► Introduces A Structured Framework For
Designing & Implementing Marketing
Research Programmes.

C
H
A
P
T
E
R

5

Market Research and Testing

Research or Test?

A company sends out two versions of a mailing as a split run (or A/B split) on a purchased list. Version A produces a response rate of 8% but B manages only 2%. The company decides to continue with version A and is content with the response.

Later, however, response falls significantly to only 1% and the company becomes concerned. Version B is tried again but with an equally disappointing response. The company decides to investigate further and employs a market research agency which recommends a research programme to include group discussions. In the groups the alternative versions of the mailing are presented to the participants (who have been screened to reflect the characteristics of the original list).

The finding is that version B was generally seen to be boring and unappealing but version A produced more interesting reactions. The participants considered it to be rather frightening (it was indeed using a fear appeal on behalf of a charity). Many participants also thought that the initial reaction might be one of horror and concern for the cause and that many would, themselves, feel inclined to donate. However, they also felt that they would easily recognise the mailing again and that its shock tactic would probably prompt them to 'bin it'.

This over-simplified story demonstrates some of the difference between market research and testing, namely that testing can tell us which version works but it doesn't explain the reasons why it did or did not work. It is this deeper explanation that some of the more qualitative forms of market research can contribute.

Introduction

Although the opening case makes a distinction between research and testing, we will be treating testing as part of research. The reason for the separation in the case is that the direct marketing industry, and most direct marketing books, tend to view them as different and separate entities. Our recognition of this is reflected in the chapter title rather than the content! The direct marketing industry has perhaps concentrated more on the immediate campaign and has been concerned more with 'what works now' than with a longer term understanding of market behaviour. On this basis, experimental tests have formed the bulk of direct marketing research efforts.

We view the variety of research tools as constituting a continuum that reflects the degree of control that can be exerted over the subject of study. The continuum is shown in Table 5.1 and incorporates testing under the 'experimentation' category.

This chapter reflects the view that a more holistic approach should be taken to research/testing. It outlines a general framework of the research process and introduces examples of secondary and primary data sources. Furthermore, details are provided of the role and nature of observation, interview and experimentation (testing) in a direct marketing context while the mechanics of sampling, sample size and 'testing' are also explained as are a variety of statistical tests.

Table 5.1 The Research/Testing Continuum

Observation	Interview	Experimentation
Little control over what is being studied. Highly objective because actual behaviour is recorded as opposed to what the researcher thinks is important.	Degrees of control depending on the method used. In group discussions participants can veer off into areas of little interest, whereas more structured surveys restrict the range of answers to what the researcher feels to be the relevant issues.	High levels of control over variables (e.g. mailing list or content and style of mailing) but require complicated and expensive experiments to cover all the factors which might account for the relative success of one variant.

STUDY 1

The brains trust

Consumer data is one thing, but does it reveal how your customers really feel about you? Laura Field reports

Knowing intimate details about your customers is key to targeting them. But so many companies have gone down this route, how do you keep your edge? The next step is to get inside your customers' minds — aspirations, values, opinions and beliefs — and use this 'soft' psychological data to provide a greater insight to their future behaviour.

A bank, for example, may identify two types of customer. Customer A has held a current account for ten years, banking his salary and paying any extra into the bank's savings account. He is deemed extremely loyal. Customer B, however, has held a current account for the same time, but deposits cash into a building society, and so is considered less committed. In fact, the reverse may be true.

Blind prejudice

Customer A may act purely out a lack of awareness of alternatives or because he sees all banks and building societies as equally evil. He could, therefore, switch at any time. If the bank took commitment and intensity of ambivalence into account

● ● ▶

instead of previous behaviour, it could predict a possible defection and act to prevent it.

It is true that traditional transactional and lifestyle data doesn't provide enough depth, particularly when you are dealing with specific markets, says Huw Davis, senior director at Data By Design. 'You really need to dig deeper.'

This was borne out on an assignment for BMG Records. Instead of concentrating on how often customers purchased records and which format they preferred, it gathered data on how important music was in their lives and related it back to the database.

Gathering this kind of data is very popular, says Caroline Kimber, director of direct marketing at CACI. In its work with BT a couple of years ago, CACI found that people identified by psychological questioning to be early adopters were particularly hot prospects for mobile phones.

Psyche from Experian (formerly known as CCN) was one of the first attitudinal products on the market. It asked a UK sample various psychographic questions relating to politics, social trends, innovation, experimentation, excitement, health and security. The product is now being updated and is called Experian RISC.

Trend Spotting

As the data goes back over a decade, says Richard Webber, managing director of the marketing division at Experian, the updated Psyche can identify emerging trends. For example, we are now less motivated by ads depicting conspicuous consumption than we were in the 1980s and more influenced by social responsibility.

The trouble is that, to obtain good information, according to Kimber, you need extensive samples, but if the information is to be gathered responsibly people have to be interviewed face-to-face.

'It's easy to answer 'yes' or 'no' to 'Do you buy X-brand dog food?', but more difficult to state on a scale of one to five how important security is in your life,' says Tony Cowling, chairman of Taylor Nelson AGB. 'For example, an individual's attitude to savings may not follow logically from their views on cheques or credit cards. Questions have to be posed very carefully, which is where market researchers can help.'

It is dangerous to generalise, warns James McKenzie, planning director at Interfocus. It is no good chucking a few attitudinal questions on the end of a questionnaire. The information gathered can be too superficial to be useful or require so much data that nobody wants to complete it.'

Soft data is more difficult to model than 'hard' factual data, as Barry Leventhal, vice chairman at Berry Consulting, discovered. Its segmentation system, FRuiTS, uses demographic information to set up segments which are mapped on to customer databases and prospect lists to pick out best customers. It looked at softer variables, experimenting with them along with the 'harder' data, but found that they clouded the picture.

'We found the 'soft' data did not fit in well with the categories when we mapped it on to external data,' says Leventhal. 'I can only surmise that two people with similar incomes, types of house and spending patterns will not share the same views.'

Not only is it tricky to model, there is a certain amount of resistance to spending money on gathering this kind of data. Direct marketing is a numbers game and although one to one relationship marketing is a goal, hard practicalities come into play.

There are various dangers in soft data which can catch out the naive. Firstly, because this data cannot be proved right or wrong, it leaves the market open to opportunists, who simply gather information to tell a company what it believes it wants to hear.

'Soft data needs to be treated with respect,' says Barry Hudson, business development director at Lexicon Marketing Services. 'Sophisticated data mining tools are needed to ensure the data is correctly modelled. Marketers should be wary of new whizz-kid outfits who don't have the experience or knowledge.'

Another restraint is the Market Research Society's code of conduct, where information gathered from the public using market research should always be anonymous — providing general indications, not individual names and addresses.

'Obviously, companies would love to overlay this data on to their databases,' says Dave Phillips, client services director at Research International. 'Because of this demand, some market researchers have got into trouble for 'Sugging' (Selling Under the Guise of market research). The Data Protection Act, among others, will stop this.'

If there was a contest between the value of hard and soft data, hard data would win hands down with direct marketers.

'Whenever we've looked at our panels and our own usage behaviour alongside direct marketing databases we've always found that people's recent behaviour is the most reliable way of targeting,' says Cowling. 'The best predictor of what you are going to do next week is to look at what you did last week.'

Davis confirms: 'I would hesitate before I put a psychographic code on to a database. We tried it once with a Zodiac system dividing our database into astrological signs — we certainly didn't find that Pisceans were more into water sports!'

(Source: *Marketing Direct* September 1997)

The Marketing Research Process

'Marketing Research involves the diagnosis of information and the selection of relevant inter-related variables about which valid and reliable information is gathered, recorded and analysed'. Zaltman and Burger's (1975) definition indicates that marketing research is both 'systematic' and 'formalized' and it introduces a sequence of research events, from diagnosing marketing information requirements through data collection to data analysis. This leads to the structuring of research programmes around a series of stages in the research process as shown below in Figure 5.1. Such stages can be of great help in both the planning of research programmes and in their control and evaluation.

Stage 1: Defining and Clarifying the Marketing Problem

It has been suggested that of all the stages in the research process, it is often this one that can be riddled with error and bias in practice. Although error and bias can occur at any stage of the process if this first stage is not fully explored and agreed between decision maker and researcher, the entire programme can waste time and money.

Consider the difficulties created by poor definition and clarification of the marketing problem as evidenced by a direct response advertising research programme. A brewery wanted to evaluate a direct response poster campaign for a new beer. Response rates were monitored, but the brewery also wanted to investigate levels of awareness and attitudes using a questionnaire and street interviewing. The results were gratefully received by the brand manager concerned. However, feedback received at a later stage from the organization revealed that the decision maker resided in general marketing management and

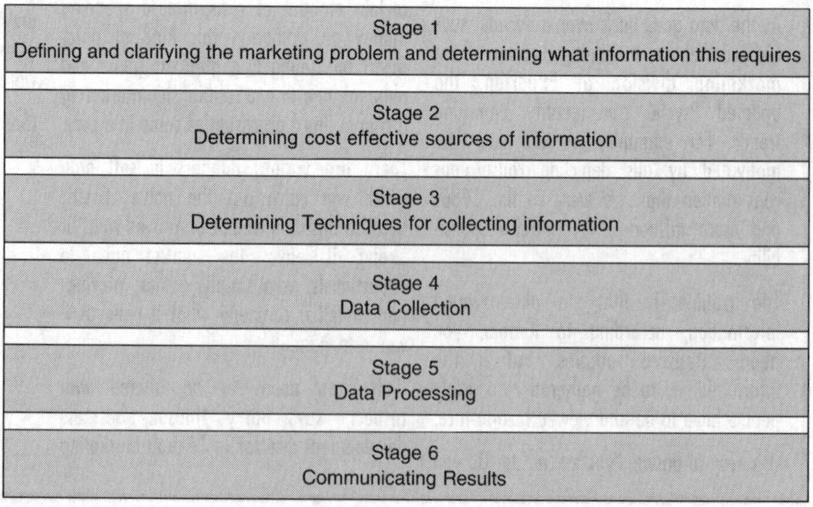

Stage 1 Defining and clarifying the marketing problem and determining what information this requires
Stage 2 Determining cost effective sources of information
Stage 3 Determining Techniques for collecting information
Stage 4 Data Collection
Stage 5 Data Processing
Stage 6 Communicating Results

Figure 5.1 The Marketing Research Process

while the research results were relevant and useful, they had their limitations. The problem turned out to be one of poor communication. While the brand manager briefed the researchers in line with *his* perception of the problem, the marketing manager wanted to use the information to decide whether to use a direct response poster campaign to support the launch of the new lager. Many of the research findings were relevant but the decision makers were less interested in the reaction to this specific poster than to the wider concept of direct response mechanisms in poster advertising new products in the drinks market.

Other instances of difficulties caused by faults in problem analysis and the briefing of researchers are provided by England (1980) and the dangers are generalized by Millward, the joint managing director of the Millward Brown Agency:

> 🔳 *The utility of any research project is critically dependent upon the quality of the original brief . . . too often research is neither communicated effectively to the decision takers nor relevant to their decisions . . . make sure that the real decision makers attend key presentations . . . the best briefing session is a two-way discussion which both crystallises and challenges current management thinking.* 🔳 (Millward 1987)

The problem definition stage should lead naturally to the listing of appropriate informational requirements (the 'data list') in the context of the decision areas concerned.

Exploratory vs. Conclusive Research

Developing a clear formulation of the scope and nature of a research problem may be referred to as exploratory research. Exploratory research explores the parameters of the problem in order to identify what should be measured and how best to undertake a study. Exploratory techniques are usually relatively unstructured. Sometimes they are merely discussions of the problem with knowledgeable people or the study of case histories of similar projects which could suggest a methodology. Group discussions with consumers are popular, as they are not constrained by highly structured questionnaires and enable the problem to be seen from a 'market' perspective. Group discussions are covered in greater detail later in this chapter.

In contrast, conclusive research is conducted through the main research design and is aimed at measurement of the variables identified from the exploratory exercises. It provides the information, specified on the data list, which management requires.

Stage 2: Determine Cost Effective Sources of Information

The list of specific informational requirements (the data list) should have been built up during the problem definition phase. Now it is necessary to determine where the data can be found. There is a popular misconception that marketing research is no more than an interviewer in the street with a questionnaire and clipboard. While this image is appropriate to some research programmes, there are others where the interviewing is conducted in a hall, or someone's home; others that require no interviewer at all (e.g. postal surveys); some that involve no questioning (e.g. observation studies); and yet others that rely exclusively on existing reports or other documentation (i.e. secondary data sources).

Secondary Data Sources

The range of data sources can be broadly categorized under the headings of secondary and primary. Secondary sources involve information that already exists, such as customer lists, internal company records or previous reports, government statistics, newspaper and journal articles and commercial market research agency reports. Table 5.2 lists some examples of the wealth of information that exists and serves to demonstrate that it is always worth exploring the possibilities of using secondary sources as a *first* resort before commissioning what would usually be a more expensive and time consuming programme of collecting new information using primary research methods.

Because of the heavy use of secondary sources, there is a need to adopt a critical perspective in using them. The researcher should evaluate such sources for impartiality in order to be reasonably sure that there is no bias in the information resulting from the source provider or compiler attempting to make a case for or against something. The researcher should ensure that sources are *valid*. That is, he or she should check that the information provides the researcher with what he or she wants to know. The researcher should also clarify the *reliability* of sources. In other words, the information should be representative of the group it purports to describe (e.g. a sample of 12 consumers is unlikely to reflect all consumers in a national population). Finally, the researcher should make sure that sources provide information with *internal homogeneity* (e.g. consistency within a set of figures).

So great is the amount and variety of secondary sources that quite large books are published which do nothing other than list possible sources of information related to various topics and areas of concern. The Government's Statistical Service publishes an annual booklet entitled '*Government Statistics: A Brief Guide to Sources*' together with another guide, '*Profit from Figures*' which illustrates some of the main uses of government statistics.

Many of these are free (either because they are to be found in most public libraries or because they are available from Government Departments). Even some of the expensive commercial reports can be found in some libraries.

KOMPASS	Names & addresses of companies (possible competitors) by country & by product category.
Kelly's Guide	Addresses & description of main activities of industrial, commercial & professional UK organisations. Listings are alphabetical according to trade description & company name.
Key British Enterprises	Register of 25,000 top UK companies providing company name, address & basic data (e.g. sales, number of employees & Standard Industrial Code – SIC).
UK Trade Names	Trade names & parent company.
BRAD (British Rate and Data)	Costs of advertising in press, radio, poster, cinema, TV & all other mass media.
The Retail Directory	Details of Retail trade Associations & lists retail companies according to type (co-op, Multiple, Department Store etc.) & according to geography (e.g. lists the retail outlets within many towns).
MEAL (Media Expenditure Analysis)	Information on competitors' advertising spend on specific brands per month. Also gives ad agency concerned.
Business Monitor	Statistics for different products (e.g. number of manufacturers, industry sales & import levels).
Henley Centre for Forecasting	Projected future social attitudes, life-styles, income and expenditure.
Target Group Index (TGI)	34 volume annual profile of most product-markets in terms of who buys what. The research uses a geodemographically determined sample design and analysis is demographic, geodemographic and now psychographic.
Regional Trends	Plots population size & structure trends through the regions, together with regional income & expenditure.
Electoral Register	Useful to help define catchment areas of retail outlets & to calculate number of potential customers. Also used to draw samples for market research. Links can be made with post codes to identify potential targets by name and address.
National Readership Survey	Profile of readers of newspapers & magazines. Useful for direct response & other advertising media selection when matched with profile of target market.
Who Owns Whom	Firms & their parent organization.
Trade Associations	Usually have information on numbers of competitors & size of market.
Family Expenditure Survey	Average weekly expenditure on many products & services according to different regions, size of household, age of head of household & household income levels. Useful for estimating market size & potential sales levels.
Market Intelligence (MINTEL)	Monthly profiles of different markets (both customers and competitors). 'Special' Reports investigate particular issues such as direct marketing itself.
Local Chambers of Trade	Have statistics on companies in their trading area & information on trading conditions.
Retail Business	Monthly profiles of different retailing markets (both customers and competitors).
Internal Database	It mustn't be forgotten that one's own database can provide a wealth of data for analysis purposes – for profiling and targeting customers and potential customers and for evaluating the effectiveness of alternative direct marketing campaigns via the tracking of split run tests.
On-line databases	Including some market and company information. Others are more specialised (e.g. TEXTLINE provides a 'key word' search of many newspapers and journals for information and articles on the topic concerned). INTERNET sources continue to proliferate and offer databases, even mailing lists, as well as market and marketing information in a variety of forms.

Table 5.2 Secondary Data Sources

Primary Data Sources

Primary sources, on the other hand, involve collecting new information, first hand, for the particular research programme. We have already suggested (in Table 5.1) that primary data can be considered along a 'control continuum', which extends the simple listing of *'observation', 'interview'* and *'experiment'* to a framework which takes into account the degree of control that the research approach can exert over what is being researched. We do not explore the elements of this continuum here, because they are explored in greater depth in the next section of this chapter.

However, it is worth raising an ethical issue here because direct marketing has changed the nature of collecting details about individuals. Traditional marketing research was more concerned with respondents' buying behaviour, attitudes, characteristics and so on, but direct marketing wants names and addresses as well, in order to target relevant individuals. The Market Research Society's Code of Conduct used to outlaw the collection of personal details for selling purposes (SUGGING: Selling under the guise of research) and indeed most marketing research was based on more anonymised statistical analysis of data. But direct marketing needs to be able to identify individuals. Even if direct marketers do not use the personal details for immediate selling, they are keen to develop databases of personal information – 'DUGGING' (data under the guise of research), as proposed by Santry (1994). These issues are well explored by Fletcher and Peters (1996) and their research revealed practitioners to be reasonably comfortable with the situation. Researchers and sellers were keen to make clear to their informants the purpose to which personal details might be put. However Fletcher and Peters show that privacy issues are highly relevant here and have not been resolved. We delve more deeply into direct marketing privacy concerns in Chapter 11.

As it stands at present, however, the 1997 MRS Code overcomes the conflict with the phrase:

> **❝** *members shall only use the term confidential survey research to describe projects which are based upon respondent anonymity and do not involve the divulgence of names or personal details of informants to others except for research purposes.* **❞** (Market Research Society 1997:3)

The new code excludes, from its 'confidential research' principles, the collecting of personal data for sales or promotional approaches to the informant and for the compilation of databases which will be used for canvassing and fund-raising. In such circumstances the data collector should not claim to be involved in a confidential survey and should make this clear to the informant.

Continuous Research

A distinction worth making within primary data collection methods is between *ad hoc* and *continuous* research. When the *same* respondents are observed or interviewed repeatedly over a period, then this is referred to as continuous research as opposed to an *ad hoc* study, which would only collect data on one occasion from the same respondents. Repeated surveys, therefore, even if they use the same questionnaire and the same sample design would only be continuous if exactly the same respondents were interviewed each time.

The *retail audit* is an example of continuous research. A sample of retail outlets allow sales patterns to be analysed and sold. The main benefit is to discover customer activity with respect to *competitor* stores and brands, on a regular, continuous basis. Sales of specific brands are recorded, often this used to be by means of physical stock checks by observers at regular intervals. The replacement of manual stock and shelf counts by laser scanning is now commonplace, as we discussed in our coverage of EPOS and EDI in Chapter 4.

The other example of continuous research is the *consumer panel* (not to be confused with a group discussion). Here, respondents – often in the form of 'households' – agree to report on their buying behaviour or media habits over a period of time. The original method was for respondents to complete a type of diary every week and to post this to the research agency concerned. For example, in a panel for media studies, the radio stations listened to would be noted on a pre-printed chart for each day of the week, and a grocery panel would require the brands, pack sizes, prices paid and stores used to be recorded, for the product categories being studied. The Royal Mail operate a panel (the *Mailmonitor*) with the research agency RSGB, to study the receipt of different types of mail, from a variety of sources and in a variety of source categories including of course from direct marketers:

> ❝ the panel consists of a clustered, stratified sample of some 1350 households made up of around 2700 individuals recruited on a nationally representative basis according to gender, age, social class, size of household and TV region. In each of these households, everyone over the age of 16 completes a daily diary. The data is collected weekly but analysed on a 4 weekly basis. ❞
> (Francis 1995)

One of the advantages of a panel such as this is that it facilitates the running of *ad hoc* surveys with the panel respondents. There are significant economies of scale since the infrastructure is already in place with respect to sampling, mailing and data analysis. The research into 'gender effects in direct mail' mentioned in the market segmentation chapter employed the Mailmonitor panel to test the main hypotheses 'for real', which emerged from group discussion research.

It is increasingly the case, however, that panels do not involve any form of interviewing. Some, for example, use a special audit bin, in which the packs of products are placed for a researcher to monitor. Measuring TV viewing is now conducted by means of a set meter (e.g. for exposure to DRTV commercials) and in this form can be categorized as a form of observation research.

Households are commonly selected on the basis of random sampling (using electoral registers and/or geodemographic lists and multi-stage sampling of the type discussed shortly) rather than quota sampling. The major problem with panels is the high mortality rate of panel members. That is, the withdrawal rate due to boredom (and indeed because of members moving home and so on) is high – perhaps up to 40 per cent after the first interview. Clearly, the aim is that replacements should be as representative as possible. However, the problem of recruiting replacements, together with the need to offer members some form of inducement or payment provides a constant danger of panel composition being unrepresentative. For example, once recruited new members sometimes change their behaviour, so it might be appropriate to exclude the results from these households for some time until their behaviour reverts to normal.

The basic working of the panel system involves operators compiling reports (e.g. consumer profiles, matching behaviour with names and addresses and other aspects of their buying behaviour, such as stores used, brands preferred, times of purchase and so on) and selling these to their clients. These firms can thus monitor their competitors' direct marketing activity, as well as their own, with the additional advantage that a time series of information is built up, allowing the identification of trends over time. This is important because direct marketers would get a biased reading of their customers' loyalty if they relied exclusively on their own transactional data – repeat purchase rates for *their* store or brand might be encouragingly high – but panel data might reveal even greater repeat patronage of competitors' brands or stores. Thus, as discussed in Chapter 4, direct marketing is increasingly using consumer panel data in the 'layering' of databases because it adds even greater richness to the tapestry. Not only is this a significant benefit it its own right, but because one of the characteristics of direct marketing is that marketing activity is less obvious to competitors (mailings and telephone contacts are less observable than are media advertising campaigns), the analysis of panel data can reveal competitor activity.

There are a couple of points made in Chapter 4 concerning database analysis that are worth remembering in this context. First, T-Group research (Figure 4.13) will be of benefit to direct marketers because 'research' adds depth of understanding to market data and panels offer a longitudinal view of market data. The importance of this latter point is that it is all too easy to rely on one-off analysis of the database for such analyses as lifetime value.

Overall, then, direct marketers are linking panel data with other databases to provide additional richness to their data. It has also been found that during lifestyle and other surveys some respondents are economical with the truth with regard to buying patters, but the panel, being a record of actual buying, can be used to weight some of these responses.

Today, panels are generally conducted with even more sophisticated technology. The typical approach is for panel households to be equipped with TV *set meters* which identify which programmes and channels have been watched. These link the TV with a phone line and the research agency is able to download the data stored unobtrusively during the night. The problem of whether people are actually watching the television when it is switched on has also been addressed, though only partially. *People meters* allow panel members to press a coded button whenever they enter and leave the room, one of which is dedicated to each household member (even visitors can be coded). One of the authors was a panel member and although it is far from scientific to base conclusions on a sample of one – indeed oneself !- the reader will no doubt be thinking about the likelihood of every panel member *always* indicating when they enter and leave the room.

Another piece of equipment often provided to panel members is a hand held *bar code reader* and households in relevant panels are asked to scan all their groceries, key in prices of every item, scan a bar code on a card to indicate from which store it was purchased and whether there was a special offer involved. They may also be asked to scan bar codes which indicate the newspapers and magazines that were read that day and to which radio stations the household had listened. Again the reader might wonder whether those willing and able to perform all these tasks daily are really representative of the population!

The panel in which one of the authors was a participant provides a good example of the uses of this technique. The ITV region of concern was HTV which is a 'split' region, there being HTV Wales and HTV West. The panel was set up in South Wales where many households tune in to one or the other transmitter. The panel was funded in association with retailers and split run experiments were possible, with different versions of the same DRTV advertisement being broadcast via the different transmitters. The results could be tracked through analysis of viewing, response to the DRTV commercial and subsequent purchase via the scanned shopping baskets. The author may not have been an ideal panellist due to the lack of dedication to the scanning tasks, but the household concerned was able to receive both HTV Wales and West and occasional 'channel hopping' did indeed reveal different versions of some commercials being transmitted at the same time!

This example provides a forerunner to our discussion in a later section on experimentation and testing because it demonstrates a practical way of sending out alternative DRTV commercials to different, but matched, audiences. All in all, this review of the consumer panel has introduced all three forms of primary data collection method; observation, interview and experimentation.

Once it has been determined what information (Stage 1) should be collected and from where it would be found and indeed whether it should be pursued (Stage 2), it then has to be determined how it should be collected.

Cost Effectiveness

In terms of determining cost effective sources there are practical, but constraining influences of time and money, expertise and politics, and research designs are really based on a compromise of some sort.

Secondary sources are often cheaper and less time consuming than primary ones though some are very expensive in absolute terms. If secondary sources only provide exploratory results, or if there are problems due to invalidity and/or reliability, then firsthand data collection is likely to be the next stage, if time and money warrant.

A rule of thumb in assessing cost effectiveness is the extent to which research results provide benefits exceeding their costs and this approach has been refined by the use of *Bayesian Analysis* (Churchill 1979), which helps by using probability theory to estimate the value of decisions made without research information, compared with decisions made with information derived from different types of research design, sample size variations and so on (Figure 5.2). Direct marketing can claim to be measurable, so the importance of measuring the cost effectiveness of research proposals is entirely appropriate.

There are four possible 'outcomes' with a financial value of:

A = £10,000   B = £80,000   C = £40,000   D = £28,000

From the 'outcomes' column it can be seen that the *expected value* of marketing version 1 is £7,500 + £20,000 = £27,500, while the expected value of marketing version 2 is £24,000 + £11,200 = £35,200. Thus, marketing version 2 would appear to be the more favourable course of action.

The presentation of research alternatives in the form of decision trees is useful to both research and research user and, as discussed earlier, the more the decision maker is involved in the preliminary stages of research programmes the more likely is the resulting programme to produce information which is appropriate to the specific decision context.

Some managers use subjective probability scales to help them in their decision making process. One scale measures the level of combined disagreement among them with regard to a specific project's final decision. Another, the profit-consequences scale is intended to measure the expected monetary value in terms of the overall

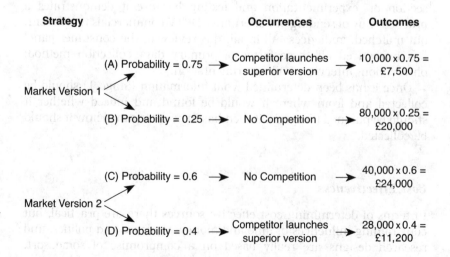

Figure 5.2 Decision Tree for Launch of Direct Banking Product

profitability of the project. Combining these two 5-point subjective scales (combined disagreement and profit consequences) in a summated 10-point scale will help managers in the process of choosing a decision alternative.

When there is a situation where the management disagreement level/profit consequences scores suggest delaying a decision to obtain additional information to increase the likelihood of selecting the correct alternative, increased costs become a factor to consider. Decision delay is not without some cost; the reduction of uncertainty is not free of charge. This cost must be compared to the expected gain resulting from increasing the probability of selecting the best course of action; that is to say, the cost of such added information should not exceed its value.

If additional information is deemed necessary, how can the decision makers determine the amount of money to allocate to the marketing research unit that will gather it? If marketing research is the only cost associated with decision delay, the marketing manager could, in theory, allocate any amount that does not exceed the estimated profit consequences of a wrong decision. In other words, if additional research data improve the chances for a more profitable decision, then the maximum amount that should be expended for such data is the difference between the expected profit consequences of the decision taken without additional data and the expected profit consequences of the decision taken with additional data. This difference is sometimes referred to as the expected value of added information.

The cost of marketing research is only one cost element in decision delay. Opportunity cost is another. For example, delaying the introduction of a new direct mail pack pending the results of extensive consumer research may improve the chances of making the right decision. However, the expected benefits from such a decision should be compared to the amount of predicted sales revenue that would be lost during the testing period.

A third cost in decision delay stems from the reduction of lead time over competitive counteraction. Less and less frequently do companies enjoy long periods of competitive product advantage. A new direct banking product, even when a competitor is caught by surprise, can often be quickly duplicated. To test a contemplated direct banking product in the marketplace over a long period of time will alert competitors. They can analyse the product and produce a similar one while the originator is still seeking additional data for the reduction of uncertainty. To illustrate these points Table 5.3 presents a payoff table for a marketing decision on the introduction of a proposed new direct banking product.

The marketing alternatives in Table 5.3 have been evaluated in terms of the established monetary criterion, namely, expected profit. The expected profit for each alternative was obtained by multiplying the probabilities of the outcomes by the payoffs for each alternative and summing up. At this point, the principal decision maker was reluctant to pass up a chance to make £4 million, and was wondering if more information should be gathered before taking action, thus incurring delay. In terms of the combined disagreement (say, level 3) and profit consequences (say, level 5) on the ten-point (combined disagreement

Table 5.3 Payoff Table for Decision on Introduction of a New Direct Banking Product

	Marketing Alternative Payoffs		
Predicted Sales	Probability of Outcome	Introduce Direct Banking Product	Do Not Introduce Direct Banking Product
£40 million	0.3	£4.0 million	£0
£20 million	0.7	−£2.0 million	£0
Expected Profit: (0.3) (£4) + (0.7) (−£2) = −£0.2 million			£0

and profit consequences) scales used by the top management of the company, this situation 'scored' between 8 and 9.

These 10-point scales are designed to measure (initially on a separate basis):

1 The degree of combined disagreement achieved by a group of managers when evaluating a specific issue related to a particular problem-solving situation.

2 The estimated profit consequences attached to the assessment of the same managerial issue confronted by the company.

The scales range from low level of combined disagreement (1) to high level of combined disagreement (10) and from low profit consequences (1) to high profit consequences (10). The subsequent stage of analysis involves merging the rating scores from both scales into a final 10-point scale which should reproduce the final assessment rating of the managers' combined disagreement and perception of profit consequences associated with a particular decision-making area. Due to the composition of the group of decision makers and intra-group variability, different weights can be placed alongside the rating scores in order to maximize the effectiveness of this scaling procedure. It would thus meet the criterion for deciding to delay the marketing decision and gather more information.

In the context of the decision analysis framework, the following could be noted regarding the marketing decision situation shown in Table 5.3:

1 The agreed-upon marketing alternatives are (a) to introduce the product and (b) not to introduce the new direct banking product.

2 The criterion may be stated: if the expected profit is greater than some specified amount, say £0.1 million, then the new direct banking product will be introduced.

3 Profit consequences are high for a decision to introduce the new direct banking product (a £2 million loss on sales of £20 million) and high for a decision not to introduce the new direct banking product (£4 million foregone).

4 The estimate of 0.7 for low sales and 0.3 for high sales is decidedly stronger for low sales, but the high-sales estimate may come from the most experienced members of the decision group.

5 The expected monetary result (-£0.2 million) indicates that the appropriate action is to abandon the new direct banking project (i.e. not to introduce the new direct banking product).

Since the indicated values of the expected profit criterion are zero and negative for the two alternatives, the proper decision is clearly not to introduce the new direct banking product.

If the marketing manager authorized an expenditure of £0.2 million for a market survey and the results of this survey convinced the decision makers to revise their original estimates of the probabilities of the outcomes given in Table 5.3 to 0.6 for high sales and 0.4 for low sales, then the expected profit for the new direct banking product introduction alternative would be £1.6 million, as illustrated in Table 5.4.

Based upon the evaluation of the alternatives in this case, the decision is plainly indicated to introduce the new direct banking product, since the expected profit is £1.6 million. When the cost of the survey, which was stated to be £0.2 million, is included, the net expected profit is £1.4 million. Since this is preferable to the zero profit from not introducing the new direct banking product, the decision is to introduce the new direct banking product. Of course, one does not know in advance which direction the probability revisions will take, but conducting the research produces a known out-of-pocket cost.

Stage 3: Determining Techniques for Collecting Information

This stage is concerned with the instruments and procedures for data collection; secondary data has to be found, interpreted and summarized, so the main focus of discussion at this stage is on primary data collection. The following elements of a research design are the major concerns here though not all of these of course will be part of every research programme:

▶ the techniques of observation, interview and experimentation;

▶ questionnaire and observation form design. (We do not cover questionnaire or observation form design in this book but refer the reader to relevant references at the end of this chapter);

▶ sample design.

Marketing Alternative Payoffs			
Predicted Sales	Profitability of Outcome	Introduce Direct Banking Product	Do Not Introduce Direct Banking Product
£40 million	0.6	£4.0 million	£0
£20 million	0.4	−£2.0 million	£0
Expected Profit: (0.6) (£4) + (0.4) (−£2) = −£1.6 million			£0

Table 5.4 Payoff Table for Decision on Introduction of a New Direct Banking Product After Market Survey

These elements, as with aspects of all other research process stages, are sources of error and bias which may invalidate the whole programme. An inappropriate research instrument, for example asking interview respondents for information they cannot or will not give accurately, or an inappropriate sample asking questions of the wrong people or too few of the right ones, will seriously affect the utility of research results. As we have stated, we consider the 'observation-interview-experiment' continuum to be highly relevant to the direct marketer and in this section we outline some of the issues involved with each together with direct marketing examples. We will start with observation.

Observation Techniques in Market Research

Direct marketers employ observation techniques in a variety of ways. For them there is less of the physical observation by a human than the use of machines to record customer behaviour for humans to analyse later.

Structured or Unstructured

In a formalized research programme, observation may be used in an unstructured form to record aspects such as general purchasing behaviour, as opposed to the more structured observation of such factors as the gender of purchasers of a specific brand of toothpaste. Indeed, a fairly unstructured observational approach may serve as exploratory research in attempting to explore and clarify the focus that is needed in conclusive research. Direct marketers will record the behaviour of customers via loyalty cards – which products they buy, in what quantities, when and through what payment method. In more specific terms, such as a direct marketing test, response rates to different mailing creative will be monitored (observed).

Natural or Contrived

It is usually more realistic to observe in actual or real conditions, such as recording the number of people who respond to a mailing. Sometimes this is not always possible, for instance, when evaluating new direct mail creative – reactions are required before roll-out and the direct marketer might use an eye camera with a sample of respondents to check which colour combinations for the direct response mechanism attracts most attention. This research would be an example of the contrived category because respondents would not be viewing the mock advertisements in a real environment but more typically in a research room.

Disguised or Undisguised

Perhaps the greatest potential problem of observation is that of modified behaviour – people who know they are being watched may not act as they otherwise would. For example, some continuous studies record respondents' television viewing habits and record the grocery products they purchase. It has been found that some respondents watch different programmes, or buy different products, during the first few weeks of such recording, until reverting to their more normal habits.

Human or Mechanical Observation

Various mechanical and electronic devices offer alternatives to a human observer watching an event. The direct marketer can use checkout EPOS and EFTPOS scanning linked with loyalty cards to record customer purchase behaviour. This is observation research, because no questions are asked of the customer.

We have already considered the use of set meters to observe television viewing habits and other examples include the digital recording on the Internet of which web sites are visited and by whom. Mechanical observation techniques may use devices like the psychogalvanometer, or lie detector, one version of which records changes in perspiration rates as a result of emotional reaction to stimuli such as test advertisements. Similarly, the tachistoscope allows an object, such an advertisement or a product package to be illuminated for a fraction of a second to test it for initial impact, legibility, recognition and so on. The direct marketer can use such techniques to pre-test alternative colour combinations or positions for their brand name, response mechanism, copy headline and so on. Another machine being used to great effect by the direct marketer is the eye camera – as mentioned earlier. Direct mail can be checked for how the reader's eye moves over the copy (RSCR 1997). This can also check for how different colour combinations might lead the eye to desired points on the mailshot or direct response press advertisement.

The advantage of observation is objectivity because what actually happens is recorded, compared with the subjectivity of questioning approaches, which, as will be shown shortly, by the very nature of question wording and interviewing, can introduce some bias. However, as discussed above, such objectivity is lost if subjects are aware of the observation and modify their behaviour. In practice, the researcher may be unable to even approach the ideal of effective data collection through observation. The fact that the researcher does not have to gain respondent co-operation poses an ethical problem, but direct marketers generally feel that there are sufficient safeguards to consumer privacy in this regard.

Interview Survey Methods

There are, in fact, various types of interview used in research surveys and typically a distinction is made between personal, telephone and postal interviews. Further distinctions can be made between structured and unstructured interviews, and the personal interview can be of a depth or group variety. Indeed, new technology provides another kind of interviewing, where the computer provides a vehicle for asking questions and collecting responses, in some cases using the Viewdata facilities of domestic television sets. Each form of interviewing merits a brief outline, as the basis for a choice of methodology.

Postal Interviews

Postal questionnaire studies have the obvious advantage over personal interviews of being able to cover a very large geographic area usually with little increase in postal costs. The major characteristic of postal surveys is the absence of an interviewer, which eliminates interviewer bias but at the same time provides little scope for respondents to query the meaning of the questions. The lack of personal contact also means that when a questionnaire is sent to an address, there is no guarantee that the respondent is the addressee since the questionnaire may be completed by another member of the family, or another member of the organization.

However, on the positive side, where a survey requires the respondent to consult with others, or with filed information, the postal survey provides the necessary time and freedom, and additionally some respondents may be less inhibited about answering certain questions. On the other hand, without an interviewer, misunderstood questions cannot be explained, open questions cannot be probed, and the non-verbal communication of the respondents (facial expressions, intonation and the like) cannot be observed.

The single most significant problem associated with postal surveys is the low level of response they tend to generate. Without a carefully constructed covering letter, emphasizing such factors as how useful (and confidential) the respondent's replies will be, or without a reminder, response rates can be as low as single figures. Even with these and the obvious enclosures such as stamped addressed return envelopes, response rates may be so low as to be unrepresentative of the selected sample. The point is, of course, that non-response may not be a random factor. The characteristics of those who do respond may be significantly different from the characteristics of these who do not respond, a factor for which survey results should be tested where possible. Once such limitations have been identified for a particular study then avoidance may be planned. Despite such problems, postal surveys are used extensively in practice, perhaps often because it is an acceptable compromise between reliability and validity, and cost considerations.

Postal interviews are widely used by direct marketers, generally because they can be included with planned mailings to customers. They can be included with promotional mailings, utility bills, bank statements and so on. However, the length of the questionnaire can cause difficulties. Birmingham Midshires Building Society carefully planned their questionnaire to be as concise as possible: it consisted of only one page, with five service propositions on the front and free space for comment on the back. Additionally the Society highlighted the importance of customer response by including the home telephone number of the Chief Executive on the form (Vlier 1997). A variation on the postal questionnaire is the 'inserted' questionnaire. As we saw in the chapter on segmentation the use of self completion lifestyle surveys has become an established component of database construction. These questionnaires are usually inserted in newspapers or magazines or with warranty details on new purchases and the consumer is asked to post the completed form.

Telephone Interviews

Although not used as much as other interviewing approaches, nor as much in the UK as in the USA, the telephone interview is becoming more important and merits consideration in research design, as long as the sampling can be restricted to those with telephones. Indeed, the Market Research Society in a major report confirms that most telephone interviewing is just as appropriate as personal interviewing, but much more convenient because of the easier and cheaper access to respondents (no waiting in cold and wet streets for the 'right' people to come along when a quota sample is being used – or no more futile multiple call-backs to a name and address when the sample design is random and the interviewing is face to face) (MRS 1994).

As in the case of postal surveys, there is a geographical advantage although it is less pronounced than with postal questionnaires because of long-distance telephone rates, time-related call charges and the inability in many cases to make use of cheap rate times (phoning companies at the weekend or in the evenings promises little success). Telephone interviews are often appropriate for industrial or organizational surveys because most companies have telephones and the chances of contacting someone from the organization during office hours are reasonably good, although it may be more difficult to contact the relevant respondent within the organization due to the actions of gatekeepers such as personal assistants. Once the problems of organizational switchboards are overcome, telephone interviewing can be the quickest of all the interviewing methods because the interview is made from the researcher's desk so no travel is involved, and the replies are immediate. Telephone interviewing can also be used in consumer markets. For example, BT conducts some 13,500 telephone interviews monthly. Interviewees are chosen from those customers who have asked for a service or fault repair, made a request or complaint (Vlier 1997). Birmingham Midshires Building Society make further use of the telephone option to contact every single customer who completed the questionnaire mentioned above, to thank them for praise or apologize if they criticize. This involves about 36,000 people per year (about 25 per cent of the sample). The Society's use of research, together with its commitment to excellence, won it the 1997 Management Today/Unisys Service Excellence Award (Vlier 1997).

There can also be a misuse of the telephone for bogus 'research' purposes. Consider the car exhaust and tyre company which made telephone contact with its customers on the basis that they had been recorded in the database as having purchased new tyres, batteries or exhaust systems in the last month. The questioning commenced with satisfaction with the service according to a 5-point scale with no request for further feedback. Soon, however, the questions moved on to cover aspects of car insurance such as renewal dates. The research was clearly an attempt to cross-sell another service because when a customer tried to provide reasons for their degree of dissatisfaction, the questioner was very reluctant to pursue this and admitted there was no provision to record such information!

There have been many calls to use applications of new information technology in marketing research and Hyett (1982) pointed to the link between telephone interviewing and the use of mini computers and main frame computer terminals as long ago as 1982. He suggested that the computer be used to store the questionnaire and as the interviewer goes through the interview over the telephone, the computer can select and display the appropriate questions for each respondent, and the replies can be keyed directly into the computer for immediate analysis. This is now common place and is referred to as Computer Assisted Telephone Interviewing (CATI).

There are, however, clearly some questions that cannot be asked over the telephone, such as those asking the respondent to look at something like a product or package, or the type of attitude scales discussed below and telephone interviews are of necessity restricted to questions which are capable of instant reply. On the other hand, the telephone can sometimes hide the existence of a questionnaire and the interview can appear more like a conversation to the respondent, and thus more relaxed and less inhibited. The more sophisticated interactive TV technology will allow questions to be sent down the line to households possessing such a system, and after being displayed on people's television sets, their answers can be keyed in via a keypad, or via a home computer keyboard and sent back along the line to the researcher for analysis, although such systems are as yet in their infancy. However, already tested and used is a compromise between the above approaches, involving the use of a computer visual display unit, presenting the respondent with a self-completion questionnaire – as reported by Shugan and Hauser (1977). The future is likely to see the Internet being used more as an interviewing vehicle and appropriate respondents can be identified through records of their web-browsing or other lists. They can be 'e-mailed' questionnaires and any responses can be analysed rapidly because the data is communicated on-line in an already coded form.

Personal Interviewing

The distinguishing feature of personal interviewing is, of course, face to face communication between respondent and interviewer, which poses problems of bias and error as well as offering flexibility and control. However, it is the fieldwork cost of interviewing that provides the main disadvantage of this type of data collection. In fact, the sample design employed is of some importance here, because different fieldwork problems occur when using different sampling methods. For example, with a quota sample the interviewer has to select respondents who possess the required characteristics, while with random sampling the interviewer must contact a specific name and address.

The presence of an interviewer offers the opportunity for varying degrees of structure. For instance, questions might be open-ended to allow the respondent to answer in their own words without the constraints of pre-determined optional answers in closed question. Also, the interviewer can ask the respondent to expand on a point with various probing techniques. In unstructured interviewing, there is more of a conversation because, although certain broad topics are to be explored there is no set sequence of pre-worded questions. This is sometimes referred to as a depth interview and is an example of qualitative, as opposed to quantitative, research. 3M has moved from surveys to depth interviews in recent years. The manager of Customer Loyalty Measurement, Tim Hewston, explains that 40–50 one-and-a-half-hour interviews are conducted at the premises of key customers (companies) because this results in greater understanding of what the customers actually want. These interviews are then followed by an action plan to improve value, which is implemented and monitored (Vlier 1997).

Group Discussions

A variation is the group discussion (or focus group) which is generally unstructured and qualitative. With this method several respondents (possibly between six and ten in number) are brought together and the interviewer guides the discussion through relevant topics, leaving most of the talking to members of the group. This method is widely used to pre-test advertisements. While the costs per respondent may be high with group discussion work, as a result of the degree of skill required by the interviewer and the time that a group discussion takes, group discussions may still prove cost effective relative to large scale sample surveys. The cost of one group discussion can exceed £1000, which would include screening participants for relevant characteristics, devising the interview schedule, paying group participants, organizing an appropriate venue, recording and transcribing events and analysing results. Since groups revolve around the sociology of group dynamics, it is not surprising that the interviewer must possess skills necessary in dealing with issues such as the different roles respondents adopt as described by de Almeida (1980) (see Table 5.5).

The Competing Moderator	The Complier
The Rationalizer	The Conscience
The Choir	The Rebel
The Super Ego	The Pseudo-Specialist

Table 5.5 The Personas Which Group Discussion Participants Can Adopt

Using Group Discussions to Investigate Consumer Reactions to Supermarket Loyalty Schemes.

The authors undertook this study in the mid 1990s. The choice of a qualitative methodology was predicated on a desire to explore consumers' reactions to loyalty schemes with minimal prompting from the researcher. Six discussion groups were conducted within an exploratory and relatively unstructured framework that was group orientated rather than moderator influenced. A highly structured discussion guide was not used since the purpose of the group was to 'experience the experience of respondents' (Calder 1977). The use of a flexible guide promoted the maintenance of a good rapport with respondents, facilitated interaction between group members, and provided the opportunity to improvise, 'to pursue unexpected but potentially valuable lines of questioning' (Basch 1987). In terms of analysis, emphasis was placed on extensive verbatim quotes from group members, as the objective was to communicate respondents' perspectives in their own words (Calder 1977).

By way of introduction, the groups were given a brief scenario dealing with the introduction of a hypothetical supermarket 'loyalty scheme' as a way of initiating discussion. The subsequent agenda was determined largely by respondents who were encouraged to explore their experiences of the rewards, satisfactions, dissatisfactions and frustrations of loyalty schemes within a wider context of direct and database marketing. Respondents were recruited by professional recruiters on the basis that they had received some direct marketing communication in the last three months. The groups (eight respondents per group) were split as follows:

The scenario presented was: "Your local supermarket launches a 'loyalty scheme' which will allow you to accumulate points based on how much you spend. These points will then be redeemable in terms of money off future purchases. In order for you to participate in this scheme you are required to fill out an application form regarding your personal details".

To demonstrate the additional richness to emerge from 'groups', this particular project found that nearly all of the group participants or their partners were members of a retail loyalty scheme but many participants volunteered comments like

► *'If you shop in that store anyway – it's a good idea.'*

► *'It's a bit bloody cheeky I think really, they can obviously bring the prices down because they can operate the scheme, so just bring the bloody prices down.'*

► *'People shop because of convenience.'*

So alongside general participation, there are concerns about the low level of discount and that such schemes don't result in much switching behaviour. A more structured survey approach to these issues would probably lack this richness of comment.

There are a number of commonly cited criticisms of group discussions which must be acknowledged. The method is seen to lend itself to providing evidence to support preconceptions and relies heavily on the moderator's interpretation.

Motivation Research

We make no apology for including these more specialized approaches in a book on direct marketing because we believe that they provide something of an antidote to direct marketers' concentration on testing.

It is these more qualitative techniques which can provide the direct marketer with explanations as to *why* a certain approach works or doesn't work. We have already discussed *depth interviewing* and *group discussions* and so now turn to *projective techniques*.

Projective techniques

If persons are relieved of direct responsibility for their expressions, they will tend to answer more freely and truthfully. Projective tests are designed to achieve this end. These are called projective tests because respondents are required to project themselves into someone else's place or into some ambiguous situation. Consider the following examples of projective tests:

THIRD-PERSON TESTS

The respondent is encouraged to reply through some third party. The rationale is that there are both 'good' and 'real' reasons for behaviour. 'Good' reasons are socially acceptable, (e.g. to buy environmentally friendly products). 'Real' reasons are sometimes not socially accepted. While 'good' reasons will probably be given in response to a direct questioning approach, such as 'Why did you buy this?', these answers may only be partially true. There may be a 'real' reason for behaviour that either the respondent is unwilling to admit or unable to recognize. An indirect question, for example 'What sort of people buy this?' or 'Why do people buy these?', might be sufficient to reveal 'real' reasons for behaviour.

WORD ASSOCIATION TEST

This type of test, also known as free association, involves firing a series of words at respondents who must state immediately which other words come into their minds. Word association tests can be used to determine consumer attitudes towards products, stores, advertising themes, product features, and brand names. The response 'junk mail' to 'direct mail from Evans Direct' but not to 'Patterson Direct' would suggest a lower level of accurate and relevant targeting by Evans Direct.

SENTENCE COMPLETION TEST

Here the respondent is asked to complete a number of sentences. This test can provide more information than word association. The following are some examples: 'Patterson Direct's mailings are . . .', 'Evans Direct sends details of products I have not bought from them, but from Patterson Direct and I think this is . . .'.

STORY COMPLETION TEST

This is an extension of the sentence completion technique. Consider the following example: 'A man buys petrol at his regular petrol station which sells a nationally advertised brand. The petrol attendant who knew the man from the company database says, '*Mr Smith, your battery is now nearly two years old. We have just got in a new product which, when added to the water in your battery, will prolong its life by about a year. It's a bargain at £50'. What is the customer's response? Why?* This technique can provide the seller with data on the images and feelings that people have about a particular product. Another example might be where a group of housewives are asked to complete a story in which the opening sentence is related to supermarket shopping using a loyalty card.

PSYCHODRAMA

Here, the respondent is asked to play a role and, to do so, he or she is given a complete description of the circumstances. For instance, the role playing of respondents to depict two alternative pain killers with other respondents playing the role of the pain. How 'the pain killer' tackles 'the pain' might lead to the copy strategy in direct response and other advertising campaigns (Cooper and Tower 1992).

THEMATIC APPERCEPTION TEST (TAT)

In the TAT test, a series of related pictures are shown to respondents who are then asked to describe what conditions gave rise to the situation, what is happening, and what the outcome will be. The assumption is that in explaining the picture, subjects will tell something about themselves. For example the pictures might show a young housewife looking at a direct response TV advertisement for a charity, or the same housewife casting her eyes over a personalized mailing from the same charity. The respondent would be asked to comment on the person in the cartoon and the likelihood of donating to the charity.

CARTOON TEST

The cartoon test is a variation of the TAT method and is commonly referred to as a 'balloon test'. Informants are presented with a rough sketch showing two people talking. One of them has just said something represented by words written into a 'speech balloon' as in a comic strip. The other person's balloon is empty and the informant is asked what he or she is replying (see Figure 5.3).

Issues and problems involved in motivation research

It should be noted that motivation research is not without its own special problems and issues. A major problem is the fact that all the above mentioned techniques require the use of highly skilled interviewers and analysts trained in psychology. This, of course, is a problem which can be overcome, albeit at a cost. Potentially more serious issues and problems relate to the extent to which these techniques are scientific and ethical. With regard to scientific status, the controversy continues. Critics argue that the techniques are shaky to say the least, with little comparability between various research studies. On the other hand, confirmed advocates of motivation research suggest that the techniques are powerful marketing tools. With regard to ethical status, critics have long argued that the use of such techniques is tantamount to an invasion of the privacy of the consumer's mind and lays the customer open to manipulation. No doubt the debate will continue, although it must be said that in recent

Have you got Smith's new loyalty card?

Figure 5.3 Cartoon Test

years the use of these techniques in consumer research has probably declined somewhat. The direct marketer would perhaps be best advised to keep an open mind, picking and choosing from the techniques available, as and where appropriate.

Attitude Measures

Very often marketers try to discover consumer attitudes toward their and their competitors' offerings. Attitude measurements require special consideration because it is far too easy and superficial to ask a respondent questions like: 'What is your attitude towards Smith Direct?' only to receive a reply along the lines of 'I like it', or 'It's all right'. While such feelings may be important, it would be of greater use to uncover the reasons for such feelings and the type of actions in which they are likely to result. This perspective views an attitude as more than a global evaluation, and considers its structure to be composed of the:

▶ *Cognitive component* which includes what is known, the beliefs about the topic concerned, even if part of this is a misperception.

▶ *Affective component* which are the feelings and evaluations about these beliefs resulting from what is known about the topic.

▶ *Conative component* which includes the behavioural intentions resulting from the cognitive and affective components.

If intentions are based on specific elements of knowledge (beliefs) and evaluations, these beliefs and evaluations need to be discovered if the results are to be meaningfully used. Furthermore, such attributes are perceived by respondents with varying degrees of strength, so that the concept of degree in measuring attitudes is unavoidable. While some form of scale is required, the straightforward like/dislike continuum would be of only limited value. A more useful approach is to compile a series of scales, each measuring a different attribute of the same attitude. If a department store wishes to identify any scope for improvement on the one hand and perceived strengths to accentuate on the other hand, there are a variety of attitude scaling methods that can be employed and these are outlined below.

Semantic Differential

The semantic differential incorporates a set of 5 or 7-point bipolar scales (see Figure 5.4). The scales are characterized by opposites such as good/bad, active/passive, hot/cold, rough/smooth and strong/weak. One advantage of the semantic differential is that it provides a convenient way of comparing attitudes to different elements (e.g. direct mail, telemarketing, leaflets, inserts, direct response television), on the same scales and on the same pictorial representation.

Repertory Grid

However, using the semantic differential requires some way of identifying the aspects that are of importance to customers and non-customers, to avoid including irrelevant aspects. Group discussions can be used for this purpose, as could another technique which is called the repertory grid. This technique involves asking the respondent how he or she perceives two items of a triad to be similar and different from the third. In Figure 5.5 similar items are identified by a tick and the different item by a cross. While some of the reasons given are likely to be of little use, some might provide bipolar adjectives that the researcher would not otherwise have considered for the semantic differential. For example the triad Telesales, DRTV and Off the Page Ads might produce a response which differentiates the latter because it is printed and the other two are not. While this is undoubtedly true it is unlikely to be of any use or relevance.

Alternative attitude measurement techniques use statements rather than adjectives, and the scaling is in terms of either the strength of each statement (Thurstone scales), or the strength of respondent's

For the direct mail you receive, in general do you think it is:						
Interesting	1	2	3	4	5	Uninteresting
Informative	1	2	3	4	5	Uninformative
Intrusive	1	2	3	4	5	Not Intrusive
Entertaining	1	2	3	4	5	Not Entertaining
Damaging to the Environment	1	2	3	4	5	Not Damaging to the Environment
Relevant to You	1	2	3	4	5	Not Relevant to You

Figure 5.4 Semantic Differential

	Direct Mail	Telesales	Inserts	DRTV	Off The Page	
Informative			✗	✓	✓	Uninformative
Intrusive	✓	✓	✗			Not Intrusive
Relevant			✗	✓	✓	Irrelevant
Printed		✓		✓	✗	Not Printed

Figure 5.5 Repertory Grid

agreement with each statement (Likert scales). Thurstone scales are not very popular or useful because they are extremely restricting in the range of responses allowed, as Figure 5.6 suggests. It presents respondents with a series of statements and requires them to pick out the one statement that most accurately reflects their attitude. The difference between statements should be of a uniform degree to allow the scaling approach to be effective.

The scoring here could value the first statement +2, the last statement -2 and the others accordingly. It is often difficult to compile a series of statements that facilitates the choice of just one statement by the respondent, whilst at the same time maintaining the same distance between them.

Likert Scales

Respondents may be presented with a series of statements about the topic concerned, and asked to indicate their degree of agreement with each, according to a five-point scale ranging from 'strongly agree' to 'strongly disagree'. It is important, though difficult in practice, for the range of statements offered to cover the range of cognitive, affective and conative aspects that the topic involves. Figure 5.7 shows a version of the Likert scaling technique, where a mixture of positive and negative statements allows respondents' consistency to be checked.

Both the semantic differential and the Likert scale can be used quantitatively by assigning values to each scaling position, and average scores for all respondents' replies can be calculated, either for each scale, or in an overall summation.

Fishbein provided another useful approach by suggesting that respondents might be able to score brands or products along each semantic differential scale (belief) but that they might not regard all bi-

I think Smith Direct is the best direct bank

I think Smith Direct could be improved

I have no feelings one way or the other about Smith Direct

I don't think Smith Direct is the best bank

I think Smith Direct should close because it is so bad

Figure 5.6 Thurstone Scale

Please indicate your level of agreement or disagreement with the following statements:					
	Strongly Agree				Strongly Disagree
I like having product or service information communicated to me by organizations	1	2	3	4	5
I like to decide for myself when and where to look for product or service information	1	2	3	4	5
The more that organizations know about me, the better they can meet my needs	1	2	3	4	5
I really don't mind about marketers having my personal details	1	2	3	4	5
There is a need for strong laws to control the sharing of personal information	1	2	3	4	5
For the direct mail I receive, marketers have generally got my details correct	1	2	3	4	5
I like to deal with organizations over the phone	1	2	3	4	5
I like to deal with organizations through the post	1	2	3	4	5

Figure 5.7 Likert Scales

polars with equal importance or favourableness. So the idea is to elicit not only a rating along each belief scale, but also a favourableness rating of each scale. Multiplying the two for each scale and aggregating the scores provides a more meaningful analysis. The attitude is the summation of the weighted belief scores.

Attitude Toward Object Model
An example of the use of the Attitude Toward Object Model comes from the authors' own experience (Evans *et al.* 1997) through a research project into consumer attitudes toward direct marketing. Figure 5.8 summarizes the identified contributors to 'attitude' and the relationship with 'intention'. Our later coverage of statistical analysis techniques reviews the results we obtained from this model.

Other Survey Approaches

Omnibus Surveys
Omnibus, or shared surveys are becoming increasingly popular in the UK. The research design of an omnibus survey is constant, but the questions included vary according to which clients 'buy in', thus providing a quick and inexpensive survey approach. As long as the

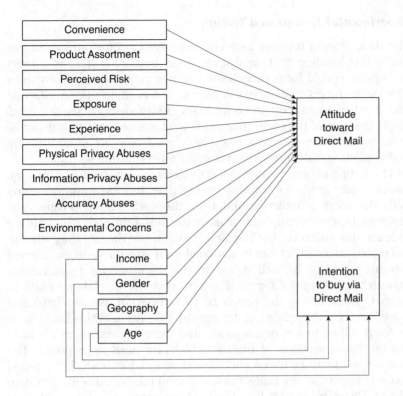

Figure 5.8 Fishbein and Ajzen Multi-Attribute Model: Used for Investigating Consumer Attitudes Toward Direct Mail

research design and methods are satisfactory, the advantage is that costs are shared among all clients. Omnibus surveys vary in the specialization of their samples, different operators offering for example, samples of 4000 adults nationally, 1000 motorists nationally or 2500 managers of small businesses. Clearly the operators do not alter their designs for a single client, but repeat a survey of the same design at regular intervals. Because the research design is the constant there is a minimum of administration in planning and fieldwork and some major sources of error and bias can be removed.

Omnibus surveys can be used in a number of ways. For example, if the same questions are asked in consecutive surveys, the results can either be combined to give a larger sample size, with the aim of reducing sampling error or, analysed to measure change over time. However, this last example should not be equated with continuous research since the same respondents would not be interviewed in consecutive surveys in spite of the same sample design being used. The direct marketer could use omnibus surveys for a variety of projects: surveying consumer attitudes to direct banking services, awareness research concerning a DRTV advertising campaign, surveying small business managers on their use of marketing databases and so on. Providing only relatively few questions are involved, the omnibus survey can be an inexpensive and quick alternative.

Experimental Design and Testing

The third form of primary data collection is experimentation and it is under this heading that we discuss direct marketing 'testing'. Direct marketers tend to focus their testing on five major elements (Forshaw 1993): the target audience; the offer or 'proposition'; timing; format and creative treatment; in some cases the product or service itself. Given that one of the cornerstones of direct marketing is that it can be '*measurable*', there can be a reasonably good prospect of quantifying and predicting outcomes which is what makes testing so useful.

The testing of target audiences centres largely on the use of lists and media. Direct marketers need to ensure that they are communicating with the correct audience and thus the customer or prospect list assumes paramount importance as do the media through which we try to reach this audience. In Chapter 4 we discussed the fact that lists can be created internally or can be obtained from external sources. Internal lists are likely to be well suited to the organizations requirements though the testing of different segments within those lists may still be needed. There are in the region of 3000 external lists available and these are likely to require greater testing. No external list is going to be perfectly suited to the organization and therefore testing will help to identify those sections of the list which are most appropriate. The number of lists to be tested and the degree to which each list is tested depends largely on the budget available and time constraints (Purdom 1996). Direct marketers also have a large number of media at their disposal and media choices can be tested for each individual campaign.

The offer or proposition relates to that element of the direct communications campaign which encourages the target audience to respond. Direct marketers are fortunate in having a great deal of flexibility in this area and there are a number of characteristics of the offer which can be tested and which include (Stone *et al.* 1995: 240):

► price levels;

► benefits;

► exclusivity;

► ways of using the product;

► competitive comparison;

► newsworthiness;

► image;

► drawback of non-use;

► celebrity endorsement.

For many direct marketers the timing of the offer is crucial to such an extent that high levels of non-response are usually attributed to poor timing. While issues such as seasonality are general aspects of timing which need to be accounted for, timing, more often than not, is specifically related to the product or service in question (Forshaw 1993).

MOSAIC GROUPS AROUND BRISTOL

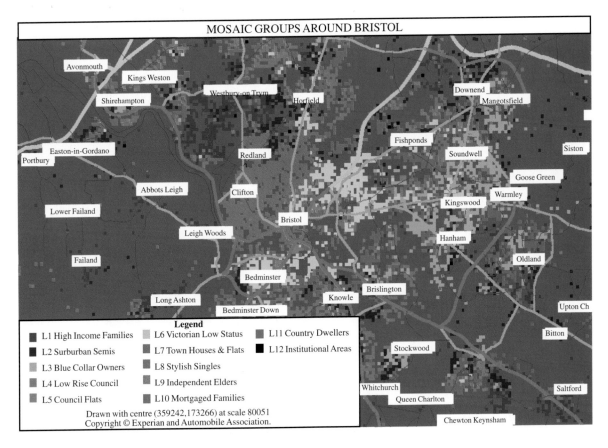

Legend

- L1 High Income Families
- L2 Surburban Semis
- L3 Blue Collar Owners
- L4 Low Rise Council
- L5 Council Flats
- L6 Victorian Low Status
- L7 Town Houses & Flats
- L8 Stylish Singles
- L9 Independent Elders
- L10 Mortgaged Families
- L11 Country Dwellers
- L12 Institutional Areas

Drawn with centre (359242,173266) at scale 80051
Copyright © Experian and Automobile Association.

PENETRATION OF STUDENT DRINKERS AROUND BRISTOL

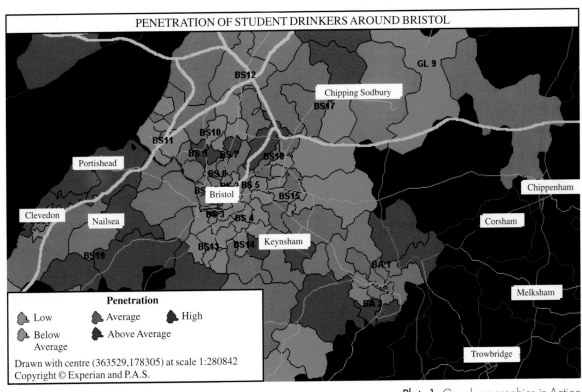

Penetration

- Low
- Below Average
- Average
- Above Average
- High

Drawn with centre (363529,178305) at scale 1:280842
Copyright © Experian and P.A.S.

Plate 1 Geodemographics in Action

Plates 2 & 3 Creativity
in Direct Marketing:

Customers and prospects who attended the launch afterwards received a video of highlights from the Range Rover expeditions in Patagonia, Japan, Vermont and other locations

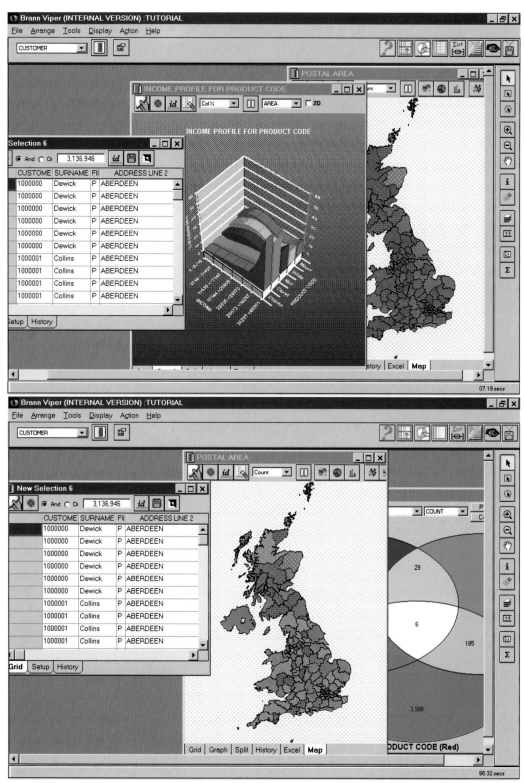

Plate 4 Database Interrogation: Viper Software

The testing of different formats is also commonplace among direct marketers and it tends to centre on issues such as size, number of components, quality and types of envelope, etc (Forshaw 1993). In addition to making sure that the format is appropriate for the target audience the direct marketer must also strive to maintain consistency between each of the elements in the communication; they must come together as a coherent whole. It is in this area that testing plays a major role.

Most organizations will already have decided upon the product or service and thus there will be no need for testing. However, in developing new products/services or in tailoring them to suit the needs and requirements of specific market segments some testing may be required.

Two general types of testing can be distinguished; first, when we want to compare the results from different lists or creative and second, when we want to test a direct marketing approach on a small scale in order to predict how it work in full. The former type is a comparative test and the latter is a predictive test.

Comparative tests
In such tests direct marketers test response rates to:

▶ *Different lists*. NDL versus CMT lifestyle lists.

▶ *Timing of campaigns*. Whether business-business customers are more likely to spend their budgets at the beginning or end of a financial year.

▶ *Different creative treatment*. Whether different wording for men and women produces different response rates.

▶ *Response mechanisms*. Coupon versus telephone.

▶ *Production/Print*. Whether a C5 envelope in green produces a better response than a C4 in orange and so on.

It is also possible to test combinations of these, so we are not restricted to a single experimental variable and the structure of experimental design is discussed in a later section.

Predictive tests
A predictive test is where the direct marketer wants to estimate the future impact/response of a full roll-out based on a test sample. This might be where a test sample from a mailing list is being used to predict the level of response if the full list is used.

A/B Splits
When inserts in different newspapers or magazines can be tested or where different copy can be tested in the same newspaper, these are often referred to as 'A/B Splits' because version A is inserted into one batch of the newspaper, version B into another batch, either in an interleaving way or stacked in groups of each version. The interleaving method is based on printing machines which print two copies

simultaneously. For these, one half of the output is geared up for version A and the other half for version B. The result is each alternative copy of the publication contains 'A' or 'B'. Although this sounds very good there can be problems of unequal numbers of 'A' and 'B' going out, due to machine breakdowns which would not always be notified to the client. This could destroy the reliability of the test because response rates would not be based on equal (or even known) sample sizes. There might also be restrictions on the style of insert – in terms of size, shape and material – if the publisher is not able to handle such differences. As well as testing copy in this way, though, if different publications are used, then the medium can also be tested.

Sample Size

Clearly in the practical world, the cost effectiveness criterion is of paramount importance in determining how many people should be contacted in a test mailing, interviewed or observed. The fact is that while decision makers want results to be accurate, generally increased accuracy comes with increased sample size (for the same sample design). Indeed, there is normally a trade-off between possibly dramatic increases in research costs and increased research accuracy or other benefits. According to Bayesian principles (discussed earlier) the difference between research benefits (in expected financial payoffs) and research costs provides the criterion for deciding whether or not to proceed and theoretically this yardstick can be used to assess whether extra benefits from a larger sample are worth the extra cost. However, other resources such as time and human resources are also important. If a larger sample cannot be resourced, or if it would push the estimated completion date too far, then the smaller sample may be acceptable. The size of the list or market segment concerned is not relevant to sample size determination.

Where levels of accuracy are important in determining sample size, the relationship can be summarized in the following way. For example, if we are designing a predictive test for a new mailing list we are not going to use the full list until we have the results of a mailing of 'n' names from it. But what is the size of 'n' ? The aim here is to reveal results in percentage terms, that is, the response rate percentage and the formula for helping to determine sample size in such cases is:

$$\text{Sample size} = \frac{R \times (100 - R) \times Z^2}{E^2}$$

where R is the estimate of what the response rate percentage (the 'population' percentage) might be, E reflects the degree of accuracy desired in the estimated percentage and Z, a parameter which reflects the degree of confidence we desire in the result. For 95 per cent confidence Z is 1.96 and for 99 per cent confidence it is 2.58.

This model is based on the characteristics of the normal distribution (see Figure 5.9). To briefly explain this, if many test samples are taken from a population (say, the mailing list) their results would vary but would be normally distributed. For such a distribution, about 34 per cent of test samples would be one standard error away from the mean on either side and approximately 48 per cent would be two standard errors of the mean. Adding these divisions together, it can be seen that 95 per cent of the items will be between +1.96 and −1.96 standard errors (or 'Zs') of the mean. An element in this context would be what each sample estimates the response rate (population percentage) to be.

In our example, we feel that based on previous experience of similar lists, the response could be around 5 per cent and we decide that we want to be 95 per cent confident that our findings will be within a range of + and − 0.6 per cent of the projected response. In this case:

$$\text{Sample size} = \frac{R \times (100 - R) \times Z^2}{E^2}$$

where:

R = our estimate of the response rate being about 5 per cent
Z = our 95 per cent level of confidence identifies 1.96 'Zs' or standard errors from the mean
E = our requirement for the result be in the range of ± 0.6 per cent of the projected response.

In our example this produces:

$$\text{Sample size} = \frac{5(100 - 5) \times 1.96^2}{0.6^2}$$

$$= \frac{475 \times 3.84}{0.36}$$

$$= 5067$$

That is, if, for the mailing list, the response rate *will be* 5 per cent, a sample of 5067 from our list (irrespective of the size of that list) would

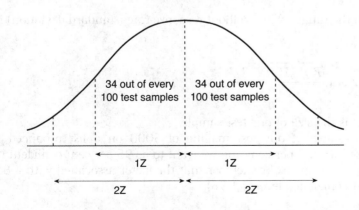

Figure 5.9 Normal Distribution Characteristics

mean that we would be 95 per cent confident that when we 'roll out' the campaign that the response would be within the range 4.4 per cent to 5.6 per cent ($\pm$ 0.6 per cent).

Let us suppose that the test mailing produces 233 responses. This would be 4.6 per cent of our sample of 5067 and is within the range of 4.4 per cent to 5.6 per cent ($\pm$ 0.6 around 5 per cent) for which there is a 95 per cent confidence level. It is likely, therefore that the full roll-out would produce a response rate within this range. In probability terms our sample/test result does *not* challenge the proposition that the full roll-out response rate (population percentage) will be 5 per cent.

If, however, our test mailing produced a response of 172 (that is, 3.4 per cent of our sample from the list) it would fall outside of the range for which we could be 95 per cent confident of the full roll-out response being 5 per cent. That is, although not ALL tests would produce the same response rate, the chances of a *sample test* producing a 3.4 per cent response if the *overall* response rate is actually 5 per cent would be so rare that we would question whether the 5 per cent response rate is a realistic one to expect. In that case we could conclude that it would be *likely* (not *definitely*, because all of this is based on *probabilities* not *certainties*) to be significantly less than 5 per cent.

If we want to be 99 per cent confident of our test results being within ± 0.3 percentage points of the test response rate, then the size of the test sample would have to be:

$$\text{Sample size} = \frac{5(100 - 5) \times 2.58^2}{0.3^2}$$

$$= \frac{475 \times 6.66}{0.09}$$

$$= 35\,150$$

This demonstrates how increases in accuracy can lead to extremely large increases in test sample size required and point again to the 'compromise', in practice, between the variables of accuracy, time and resources. The above analysis can used in a slightly different way to estimate the range for the response rate during roll-out, from the test sample.

Then the range for the roll out response rate (standard deviation) is given by:

$$E = Z \times \sqrt{\frac{R \times (100 - R)}{n}}$$

where n is the size of our test sample.

For example, if our test mailing of 5000 on a list produced a response rate of 2 per cent and we want to be 95 per cent confident of the range of response (remember that the factor associated with a 95 per cent confidence level is 1.96):

$$\text{Range (E)} = 1.96 \times \sqrt{\frac{2 \times 98}{5000}} = 0.39$$

We can therefore be 95 per cent confident that the range of roll-out response is therefore 1.61 per cent to 2.39 per cent.

Test Designs

A simple example demonstrates some of the considerations involved in designing direct marketing experiments or *tests*. Suppose a direct marketer believes sales are low because of an ineffective direct mail 'creative' and wants to establish what will happen if another 'creative' is used. A new creative execution is developed and sales are monitored and compared with sales from the earlier mailing. In terms of experimentation this would be a simple *before-after* design in the following manner (see Table 5.6).

The difference between the two levels of sales is taken to be the effect of the new creative. So, if X1 is 5000 units per month and X2 is 6000 units per month, the organization might conclude the new creative to be effective. Clearly, this would not necessarily be valid. If, for example, competitors' direct mailing systems delayed delivery of competing products to consumers during the time of this new campaign, the customers may be purchasing the organization's product, not because of an effective creative, but because of the lack of availability of alternative brands. It is clearly impossible to control competitors' marketing activity when conducting marketing experiments and there are many other uncontrollable variables to take into account when designing and analysing experiments. For example, there might be a general trend of increasing sales and sales might have been even higher if the old campaign had continued. There are dangers of simply comparing sales before and after the introduction of an experimental variable. The effect of time has to be considered, and it might be that the time delay before achieving any influence might be substantial (e.g. with direct response poster advertising). Another problem with the experiment above is that the wrong dependent variable (that is, the variable that is measured to judge the effect of the experimental variable) may be selected. Much depends on what the campaign is trying to do of course, and it may therefore be more valid to measure changes in attitudes, or perceptions rather than response rates or sales. This is related to the point we made earlier concerning greater use of qualitative research techniques alongside testing.

Another way of improving an experimental design like the one above would be to include a *control group*, that is to measure the

Before measure	YES (initial sales = X1)
Experimental variable	YES (new direct mail creative)
After measure	YES (new level of sales = X2)

Table 5.6 Before-After Test Design

same dependent variables in the control group in the absence of the experimental variable. This allows some degree of assessment of uncontrollable variables. For example, if for the experimental group (that is, those exposed to the experimental variable), the *before-after* calculation showed increased sales from 5000 to 6000 units per month, but for a *control* group sales rose from 4000 to 4800 per month, then the 20 per cent increase for both groups might mean that there had been little effect of the experimental variable. This type of design is referred to as *before-after* with control as shown in Table 5.7.

In direct marketing it is often relevant to be able to test several variables at the same time. Under such circumstances a test matrix would be developed, like the one in Figure 5.10.

Each cell is a independent variable and referred to as a factor and this form of experimental design is a *factorial design*.

In addition to measuring the effects on dependent variables, the direct marketer can also identify any effects of *interaction* between the variables (factors). This could be important because if two variables might affect each other – they might be *interdependent* – but if they were tested separately this would not be identified. Direct marketers can employ a great variety of factorial designs such as in Figure 5.11.

Marketing experiments can use data from consumer panels or retail audits, with the advantage of being able to demonstrate changes over time more effectively than ad hoc research. The test market is the largest marketing experiment because the whole direct marketing 'mix' is tested, rather than just one of several variables. Panel data are

Table 5.7 Before-After With Control Test Design

	Experimental Group	Control Group
Before measure (initial sales)	X1	Y1
Experimental variable (new direct mail 'creative')	Yes	No
After measure (new level of sales)	X2	Y2

Therefore, effect of experimental variable = (X2-X1)-(Y2-Y1)

Mailing lists	Versions of 'Creative'		
	Version 1	Version 2	Version 3
List 1			
List 2			
List 3			

Figure 5.10 Test Matrix

▶ 2 × 2 FACTORIAL DESIGN

	Direct Mail	No Direct Mail
Free Newspaper Inserts	1	2
No Inserts	3	4

Test sample 1 receives direct mail shots and inserts in their free newspaper. Sample 2 receives only inserts, 3 gets only direct mail and 4 receives neither.

▶ 2 × 3 FACTORIAL DESIGN

	Direct Mail	No Direct Mail
Free Newspaper *Colour* Inserts	1	2
Free Newspaper *Black & White* Inserts	3	4
No Inserts	5	6

Test sample 1 receives *colour* direct mailings and inserts in their free newspaper. Sample 2 receives only *Colour* inserts, 3 gets *B&W* inserts AND direct mail, 4 receives only *B&W* inserts, 5 gets only direct mail and 6 receives none of these.

▶ 2 × 2 × 3 FACTORIAL DESIGN

	Direct Mail		No Direct Mail	
	Telesales	No telesales	Telesales	No telesales
Free Newspaper Inserts	1	2	3	4
No Inserts	5	6	7	8

Test sample 1 receives direct mailings, inserts and a telesales call, sample 2 receives inserts, direct mail but no telesales, 3 gets inserts, telesales but no direct mail, 4 receives only inserts, 5 gets direct mail, telesales but no inserts, 6 receives direct mail only, 7 receives telesales only and 8 gets none of these.

Figure 5.11 Types of Factorial Design

particularly useful in test markets, because not just sales, but customer profiles (and 'by name and address') new and repeat buying levels, attitudes, retail preferences, and so on, are analysed over a period. As mentioned earlier, this data is now being used as an overlay to other sources of individual records in marketing databases.

Sample Design

There is an inevitably close relationship between the choice of data collection method and research instrument, and the selection of respondents or sample design. Actually, the ideal plan would be to include all relevant people in the study, which would make the study a census. Indeed, this is sometimes possible if the relevant population is small, and perhaps geographically concentrated, as is sometimes the case in industrial markets. It is more usual, however, for populations to be larger, and thus less suitable for a census. In these circumstances, something less than the whole population will be observed or interviewed, and it is necessary to select a sample from the total population. Samples will also be used by direct marketers in the 'testing' context as discussed above, but this section discusses issues of sample *design*.

Probability vs. Non-probability Sampling
The main choice in sample design is between those samples based on the laws of probability (probability samples) and those based more on subjectivity (non-probability samples). The various choices under each of these headings are highlighted in Table 5.8.

RANDOM SAMPLING
When a complete list exists of all individuals or elements in the relevant population (i.e. sampling frame), it is possible to design a sample that gives each a calculable chance of being selected. This principle provides the basis of random sampling. There is a popular misconception that random is something rather vague and haphazard, like interviewing anyone available in the street, while in fact it is extremely precise. If a population were composed of 12 people and each could be listed, then the following are ways of selecting a random sample of three:

▶ Reference to mathematical tables of random numbers, three are selected, for example 5, 6, and 8. Items labelled 5, 6 and 8 would then be the sample.

▶ With a large sample a more convenient approach would be to divide the population size by the sample size to calculate the sampling interval (n) and every 'nth' item can be selected. In this example the sampling interval would be $12/3 = 4$. Thus, every 4th item could be taken: 4, 8, 12 or 3, 7, 11 or 2, 6, 10 or 1, 5, 9. This is referred to as *systematic random sampling* and provides a practical method of selecting random sample items.

When there are subdivisions in a population there are four ways of designing a random sample. Take as a common example for all four, a mailing list purchased by a direct mail company. Assume that the company knows that their most relevant customer groupings are within two geodemographic categories (e.g. MOSAIC categories 'High Income Families' and 'Stylish Singles') and these are included – and

Table 5.8 Probability and Non-probability Samples

Probability Samples	Non-probability Samples
Simple Random Sampling	Quota Sampling
Systematic Random Sampling	Judgement Sampling
Stratified Random Sampling	Convenience Sampling
Multi-stage Sampling	
Cluster Sampling	

coded as such – on the newly acquired list. These groups, within the list, might represent the 10,000 potentially most lucrative customers. High Income Families are further sub-divided in the MOSAIC system into 'Clever Capitalists', 'Rising Materialists', 'Corporate Careerists', 'Ageing Professionals' and 'Small Time Business'. 'Stylish Singles' are divided into 'Bedsits and Shop Flats', 'Studio Singles', 'College and Communal' and 'Chattering Classes'. In total the two main MOSAIC groups divide into nine sub clusters.

Assume that a random sample of 1000 people is to be taken from the new list. The alternative approaches would be as follows. *First*, select the same number from each of the nine clusters, that is 111 from each. Selection could employ the *systematic* approach described above. This is referred to as *stratified random sampling* using a *uniform sampling fraction*. A second method would be to select that proportion of the sample from each sub cluster that reflects the proportion of the cluster that live in each. This is again a stratified sample, but this time with a *variable sampling fraction* (see Table 5.9).

Thus, for the sample we select from each sub group we would select the percentages shown in Table 5.10.

However, it is not always essential to include respondents from each sub group and it may not be convenient if, for example, the study required personal rather than postal interviewing and the fieldwork costs of covering nine geographically dispersed areas are high. Then, it is possible to randomly select only some of the clusters and the choice of which to select is itself based on random sampling. It might be decided, for example, to concentrate the fieldwork in just three clusters (see list below) where a random selection of three from nine has been identified.

	% of High Income Families and Stylish Singles in each sub cluster
High Income Families	
Clever Capitalists	10%
Rising Materialists	8%
Corporate Careerists	6%
Ageing Professionals	20%
Small Time Business	12%
Stylish Singles	
Bedsits and Shop Flats	6%
Studio Singles	8%
College and Communal	5%
Chattering Classes	25%
Total	100%

Table 5.9 Mailing List Profile

Table 5.10 Sample Selection

	Sample Proportions	Sample Size (1,000)
Clever Capitalists	10%	100
Rising Materialists	8%	80
Corporate Careerists	6%	60
Ageing Professionals	20%	200
Small Time Business	12%	120
Bedsits & Shop Flats	6%	60
Studio Singles	8%	80
College & Communal	5%	50
Chattering Classes	25%	250

► Clever Capitalists
  – Rising Materialists
  – Corporate Careerists
► Ageing Professionals
  – Small Time Business
  – Bedsits and Shop Flats
► Studio Singles
  – College and Communal
  – Chattering Classes

Clever Capitalists, Ageing Professionals and Studio Singles have been selected by *systematic sampling* and either 333 people from each would be selected, according to a *uniform sampling fraction*, or a proportion of each according to a *variable sampling fraction*. This approach is referred to as multi-stage sampling and there can be many more stages than in this example.

Finally, further concentration of fieldwork is possible if only a very few sub groups are selected, but the sample includes everyone in these sub groups. In the example, if only Ageing Professionals are selected, the sample of 1000 might be fulfilled by interviewing everyone in this category from the list. This is referred to as cluster sampling and can again be implemented through selection at two or more levels, though it is probably better suited to a situation in which the strata are equal in size, since a random selection of very few sub groups producing exactly the desired sample size, is unlikely to occur. The question of what the sample size should be in the first instance, is discussed shortly, but first we look at a very popular sample design approach in marketing research – quota sampling.

QUOTA SAMPLING

With many marketing research programmes no suitable sampling frame exists (e.g. there is no complete list of baked beans buyers despite a good start made through the 'Heinz at home' programme). Typically, such markets are segmented according to characteristics like age, sex and socio-economic groupings, where there is no accessible sampling frame. Quota sampling allows for such factors, as the following example demonstrates. Assume that a market is segmented according to age and socio-economic group, producing four quota sampling *cells*, as follows.

1 15–34 year olds in socio-economic group ABC_1;

2 15-34 year olds in C_2DE;

3 35 years and older in ABC_1;

4 35 years and older in C_2DE.

Sufficient data is available for marketing regions (for example, ITV areas) to estimate the incidence of these characteristics in regional populations. For example, 70 per cent of an ITV region might be C_2DE, and 67 per cent might be 35 years and older. Assuming that a sample of 500 is required, this type of sample design would produce cells of the relevant sampling characteristics with quotas allocated to each in proportion to their incidence in the population, as shown in Figure 5.12. In this case, because 70 per cent of the population are C_2DE and 67 per cent are 35 years or older, the quota of 35 years and older C_2DE's is 70 per cent of 67 per cent of 500 (the sample size), and this produces a total of 235.

It is then up to the interviewer to select the correct quotas of respondents with each set of characteristics. This would very often be the basis for street interviewing and hopefully, the misconception (indeed, oxymoron) of selecting people *at random in the street* is now apparent.

Stage 4: Data Collection

Having discussed some of the issues that the direct marketer may need to consider in terms of data collection techniques – observation, interview, experimentation (or testing) and sampling, we now turn briefly to data collection itself. Our coverage will concentrate on

ABC_1 (30 per cent) 15-34 (33 per cent) 30 per cent of 33 per cent of 500 Quota = 50	C_2DE (70 per cent) 15-34 (33 per cent) 70 per cent of 33 per cent of 500 Quota = 115
ABC_1 (30 per cent) 35+ (67 per cent) 30 per cent of 67 per cent of 500 Quota = 100	C_2DE (70 per cent) 35+ (67 per cent) 70 per cent of 67 per cent of 500 Quota = 235

Figure 5.12 Quota Sampling

interviewing procedures. Indeed, in collecting data the main types of error and bias occurring are due to poor interviewing.

Interviewing Techniques

Kahn and Cannel (1968) propose three conditions necessary for successful interviewing:

1 Accessibility of the interviewer to the respondent, and of the information to the respondent (both physically and psychologically).

2 Cognition on the respondent's part, in understanding what is required.

3 Motivation on the part of the respondent to answer – and to answer accurately.

They also describe five symptoms of inadequate response that can occur during interviewing (Kahn and Cannel 1968):

▶ Partial response, where the respondent gives a relevant but incomplete answer.

▶ Non-response, which is either refusal to answer or a silent response.

▶ Inaccurate response, which is a biased or distorted answer.

▶ Irrelevant response, where the question asked is not answered.

▶ Verbalized response problem, where a respondent explains why he or she cannot answer the question.

To encourage respondents to reply more fully and accurately, experienced interviewers develop skills such as using neutral questions, like 'How do you mean?' and 'Could you say more about that?'. Sometimes aided recall (indicating some of the possible answers) can be used, as can the explanation of questions to respondents. The danger of explanation, however, is that the interviewer actually changes the meaning of questions, so there is a thin line between interviewer bias and interviewer help. Non-verbal behaviour can also be exploited during interviews, with interviewers employing expectant pauses, glances and nods to elicit more information. Indeed, non-verbal communication is two-way because respondents' intended meanings can be interpreted through their gestures and intonation. However, interviewers should be aware of the dangers of misinterpreting what respondents are trying to say. For this reason it is usual to require interviewers to record verbatim everything a respondent says. This last point introduces further interviewing problems, since responses have to be recorded as well as questions asked. Open ended questions, especially, create recording difficulties because each word of sometimes lengthy replies has to be taken down. Interviewers have to repeat their task with many different respondents, but with the same questionnaire, so the resulting boredom and fatigue should be taken into account when setting the number of interviews, or interviewing time, for each interviewer. The repetition can eventually lead the interviewer to take short-cuts by paraphrasing questions, which provides another source of interviewer bias.

Interviewers should be given time to become acquainted with the questionnaire before using it, to avoid errors over question sequencing and poor recording of answers. They also have responsibilities beyond asking questions and recording answers. There is the initial task of making contact with appropriate respondents and the need to gain sufficient co-operation for the interview to proceed. When quota sampling is used, interviewers are provided with a list of the characteristics they must look for in potential respondents and errors often occur when interviewers become tired of waiting for the 'right' people to come along. Close supervision, by checking that some of those interviewed do indeed possess appropriate characteristics, can go some way to overcoming this problem. This encourages interviewers to select more carefully and, if a quota cell is difficult to complete, to discuss this with a supervisor rather than attempting to cover up. An alternative interviewing point might be decided upon or they may just decide to try again later. The same could apply in poor weather when no one wants to stop to be interviewed !

The problem of gaining the co-operation of respondents can be eased by explaining the purpose of the survey and providing evidence of being a bona fide interviewer, which has been made easier for those organizations that have joined the Market Research Society's scheme of allocating identity cards to interviewers. One obstacle that this can overcome is the equating of market researchers with salesmen, which is usually due to salesmen posing as researchers. We have already discussed the problems for direct marketing of the combined research/ selling use of individualized data. If respondents can remain anonymous then this can be emphasized to gain their co-operation.

Stage 5: Data Processing

Once the data have been collected they have to be analysed, edited and tested, before communication to the decision maker. It is all too easy for the planning stages of a research programme to revolve around designing samples and questionnaires and little else. When this happens the researcher can be shaken by the problems of data analysis. The key is to plan in advance and this is another reason for the general division of the research process into a series of stages. A valuable discipline is to list all the data processing requirements in Stage 1, at the time of compiling the data list. It is more likely, then, to be reasonably sure that the data list is accurate.

Statistical Analysis

Statistical tests of research and test data are based on the characteristics of sampling distributions and on the laws of probability, as introduced in the discussion of random sampling and sample size earlier and the following sections use the concepts introduced in that coverage.

Significance Testing

We use an example to provide a practical point of reference for the first type of statistical analysis relevant to direct marketers. Suppose that last time your direct mailing on a full list produced a response rate of 5 per cent. You now carry out a test of a new mailing list, randomly selecting 10,000 consumer names and this produces a response of 5.7 per cent. Does the new list perform significantly better than the old one? To answer this basic question, a significance test can be used to provide information on the chances, of 5 per cent still being the true response rate. That is, we test the 'population percentage' (not the 'sample' percentage of 5.7 per cent). If the test suggests that 5 per cent is *not* likely to be the true response rate then the response rate for the new list is said to be significantly different from 5 per cent.

If (say) 100 different mailing tests of the same size were taken to discover the response rates, then we could expect that from such a large number of separate tests the average of these 100 tests would be pretty close to the true figure. Due to sampling variations, we would not be surprised to find some of these test samples producing slightly better response rates and other test samples producing slightly worse response rates. The distribution of the response rate measurements for the 100 test mailings could be described as Figure 5.13 with the mean being five, if the response rate from the full mailing list (i.e. the 'true population percentage') is five. The distribution of sample results does not, however, give any indication of how much of a spread there is of individual test mailing response rates. For this, the standard error is required. One standard error away from the mean would contain approximately 34 per cent of all the test results. (This figure is taken from normal distribution tables – when reading the figure in the table against one 'z', 0.3413 is identified, which means that the probability of an item in the distribution taken at random being between the mean and one standard deviation away from the mean is 0.3413).

The standard deviation is the measure of the spread of a normal distribution and normal distribution tables provide the size of the area

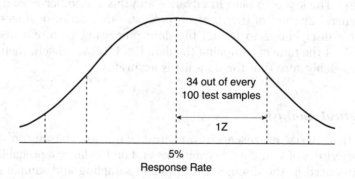

34 out of every
100 test samples

1Z

5%
Response Rate

Figure 5.13 Sampling
Distribution I

under the curve between the mean and various numbers of standard deviations away from the mean. When dealing with distributions of sample (in our case, test) results, the same tables and logic apply, but the measure of spread is referred to as the standard error.

For the example given at the beginning of this section, the mean of the sampling distribution is taken to be five, and its standard error (SE) is calculated by:

$$SE = \sqrt{\frac{\Pi(100 - \Pi)}{n}} = \sqrt{\frac{5 \times 95}{10\,000}} = 0.22$$

Π is the population percentage (response rate from the full mailing list, in our example) being tested, which is 5 per cent in this case, and n is the size of sample taken, given in the example as 10,000. This has converted one standard error into 'response rate' percentages. Thus, if Z is 0.22 (in 'response rate' terms), it can be useful to label the horizontal axis of the sampling distribution as $\pm$ Z (from left to right) being 4.78 and 5.22 respectively. The results so far can be summarized as follows. If 5 per cent is the true response rate from using the full mailing list, 34 out of every (similar sized) 100 tests would probably produce response rates to be something between 5 per cent and 5.22 per cent and another 34/100 tests would produce response rates of between 4.78 and 5 per cent.

It is necessary to calculate how 'rare' our test result of 5.7 per cent is, if the true response rate is 5 per cent. To do this we need to relate it to the probabilities as described by the sampling distribution in Figure 5.14.

The approach is to position our 5.7 per cent somewhere along the horizontal axis. That is, we must convert our 5.7 per cent into standard errors and this is done by employing the following calculation.

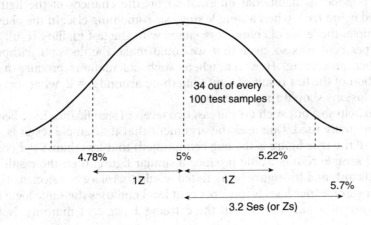

Figure 5.14 Sampling Distribution II

$$Z = \frac{p - \Pi}{SE}$$

Here, p denotes the sample percentage as found by our test and Z is used to denote the number of standard errors that our sample percentage figure (5.7 per cent) is away from the mean (5 per cent) of the sampling distribution. The logic of this calculation is that it is not merely the actual difference between the two percentages $(5.7 - 5)$ that matters – but this difference relative to the sampling distribution as described. In this case:

$$Z = \frac{5.7 - 5}{0.22} = 3.2$$

Therefore, 5.7 per cent is 3.2 standard errors away from 5 per cent, and from the normal distribution tables it can be determined that, if 5 per cent is the true figure, the probability of a test estimating the response rate to be 5.7 per cent or more would be about 0.0001 (i.e. when $Z = 3.2$, the area under the curve from the mean to this point = 0.4999 per cent , and because the area to the right of the mean = 0.5, then the area to the right of $Z = 3.2$ is: $0.5 - 0.4999 = 0.0001$, or 0.01 per cent). Thus, if the true response rate from using the full mailing lists is 5 per cent, due to sampling variations of test mailings we could expect only *one* out of every *ten thousand* (!) similar sized test mailings to estimate it to be 5.7 per cent or more – technically possible but somewhat rare and we would probably conclude that the true response rate for our new list is likely to be significantly greater than 5 per cent. Note that the conclusion is not that the true figure is 5.7 per cent or any specific figure at all, just that it is significantly different from 5 per cent – that is, it is statistically significant. At first sight the difference between a hypothesized response of 5 per cent and a test response of 5.7 per cent might not appear too great, but this example demonstrates the value of conducting statistical significance tests.

It is tempting to use the significance test as a 'decider', that is to allow the test to make a decision, but it cannot validly do this. All the test provides is additional information on the chances of the figure tested being true, when a sample suggests something else. In the above example, the levels of chance associated with the test mailing result of 5.7 per cent was so clear that we could make the decision without further processing. However, where such calculations produce a Z position of the test result of (say) something around $Z = 2$, what sort of conclusions should then be drawn?

To help sort out such grey areas, two levels of significance have been traditionally used. One uses the argument that if a sample result is so rare (if the true figure is the one being tested) that less than 5 per cent of all sample results would produce a similar figure, then the result is significant, and the figure being tested would therefore be rejected. The other significance level is the 1 per cent level and uses the same logic in the case of a sample result in the extreme 1 per cent minority. Note

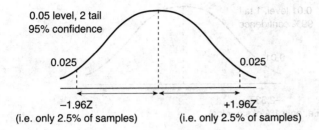

0.05 level, 2 tail
95% confidence

0.025

0.025

−1.96Z
(i.e. only 2.5% of samples)

+1.96Z
(i.e. only 2.5% of samples)

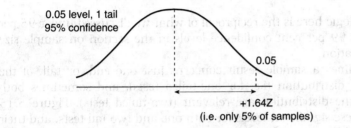

0.05 level, 1 tail
95% confidence

0.05

+1.64Z
(i.e. only 5% of samples)

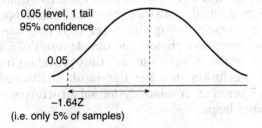

0.05 level, 1 tail
95% confidence

0.05

−1.64Z
(i.e. only 5% of samples)

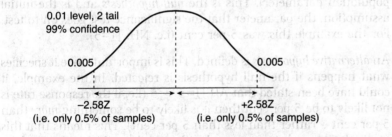

0.01 level, 2 tail
99% confidence

0.005

0.005

−2.58Z
(i.e. only 0.5% of samples)

+2.58Z
(i.e. only 0.5% of samples)

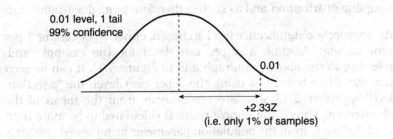

0.01 level, 1 tail
99% confidence

0.01

+2.33Z
(i.e. only 1% of samples)

Figure 5.15 Significance
Levels

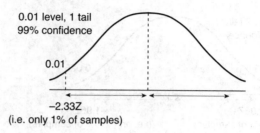

0.01 level, 1 tail
99% confidence

0.01

−2.33Z
(i.e. only 1% of samples)

Figure 5.15 Continued

that the logic here is the reciprocal of what we discussed under 95 per cent and 99 per cent confidence levels in the section on sample size determination.

Sometimes a sample result concerns just one end, or tail, of the sampling distribution (i.e. for one-tailed tests), and sometimes both ends of the distribution are relevant (two-tailed tests). Figure 5.15 shows these significant levels for both one and two tail tests, and their associated Z values which give the beginning of the rejection areas – that is if the sample result Z is further away from the mean than this, the NH may be rejected. To demonstrate how this might operate, referring back to the example testing the 5 per cent response rate whichever significance level were chosen, the sample result of 5.7 per cent would fall in any of the 'rejection areas', thus providing further justification for our conclusion that the test result challenged the population figure of 5 per cent. A relatively formal structure such as the following sometimes helps:

1   An hypothesis is set up (e.g. an assumption about the value of a population parameter). This is the *null hypothesis* and is the initial assumption, the parameter that the significance test goes on to test. For the example this was 5 per cent (i.e. NH: $\Pi=5$).

2   An *alternative hypothesis* is defined. This is important since it specifies what happens if the null hypothesis is rejected. In the example, it could have been stated that AH $\Pi=5 > 5$ (i.e. if the response rate is not likely to be 5 per cent then it is likely to be something *more* than 5 per cent – rather than less than 5 per cent). This means that this particular example is concerned with only the right hand side of the sampling distribution and as such is therefore termed a 1 tailed test.

3   An appropriate significance level is chosen, either 5 per cent or 1 per cent usually. Assume a 5 per cent level for the example and, referring to the above paragraph and to Figure 5.15 it can be seen that for a one tailed test using the 1 per cent level, the 'rejection' level begins at 2.33 standard errors away from the mean of the distribution. Thus if the sample result is calculated to be more than 2.33 'Zs' away from the population parameter being tested (which is tested by being the mean of the sampling distribution) then it could indicate that the chances are that the population figure being tested is wrong and, in this instance, is likely to be something *greater*.

4 The standard error of the sampling distribution (which has a mean equivalent to the population parameter being tested) is calculated according to:

$$S.E. = \sqrt{\frac{(100 - \Pi)}{n}}$$

Types of significance testing other than the one appropriate for this first example require different formulae and these are described in some of the sources listed at the end of this chapter.

5 The position of the sample result in the sampling distribution under test is found from the following calculation:

$$Z = \frac{P - \Pi}{SE}$$

This value is compared with the 'Z' value for the rejection of the null hypothesis as specified in stage 3 and if it is further away from the mean than this figure, the null hypothesis can be rejected in favour of the 'alternative' hypothesis.

In the example, we test 5 per cent (response rate) being the mean of the sampling distribution in which our sample result is 5.7 per cent (response rate). Because this is over three standard errors away from the mean, and well into the 'rejection area', which starts at 2.33 standard errors from the mean, we would indeed reject the null hypothesis and accept the alternative hypothesis, that because our test sample produced a response rate of 5.7 per cent we could expect the use of the full list to deliver a response significantly greater that 5 per cent.

It should be pointed out, however, that these tests are strictly only applicable to research based on some form of random sampling, because only these are in turn based on the laws of probability. Indeed, it is generally taken by purists that only simple random sampling allows such testing, but in practice most surveys use some other sampling method, and many depart from randomness and employ non-probability techniques like quota sampling. Koerner (1980) has discussed the compromises that can be made in order to conduct data tests. He suggests that once the standard error has been calculated according to the appropriate statistical test, it should be weighted by a design factor (e.g. this might be 1 for a simple random sample, and perhaps 1.5 for a quota sample).

COMPARING TEST AND CONTROL SAMPLE RESULTS

When we want to compare response rates from two sub samples, for example when a control group is used, against which the test sample response rate is to be compared, a variation on the statistical formula is needed.

For example, one sample from a mailing list tested the new version B of the copy and another sample from the same list used the established version A of the copy. In this case there would be two sample results each of which is an estimate of the true response rate for each version of the copy. If a randomly selected test of 5000 consumers from a list produced a 5 per cent response rate version A (the one mailed to them) and a sample of 6000 from the same list produced a response rate of 6 per cent to version B, then there is a significance test which helps determine whether there is likely to be a difference in response rate between the two versions of the mailing copy tested.

The starting point for this test is that the NULL hypothesis assumes NO difference between the actual levels of response for the two versions. Thus the response rate (population percentage) for version A is the same as the response rate (population percentage) for version B.

Working through the steps:

1 The null hypothesis is that $\Pi_1 = \Pi_2$

2 If (1) is rejected the ALTERNATIVE hypothesis is that $\Pi_1 \# \Pi_2$
Here the concern is with a difference which could be either side of the mean, therefore it becomes a two tailed test.

3 A significance level is selected for example 0.05 which, for a two tailed test identifies the beginning of the rejection areas as 1.96 standard errors either side of the mean.

4 If there is NO difference between the response rates for the two versions of copy and if a large number of (pairs of) tests were conducted then it is likely that, on average, the difference between these pairs of test results would be NIL.

Thus where P1 and P2 refer to response rates (sample percentages) for version A and B respectively, this significance test tests the likelihood (rarity) of our pair of samples producing a difference of 1 per cent (6 per cent-5 per cent) if there is no difference between the population percentages in reality.

$$SE = \sqrt{\frac{P1(100 - P1)}{n1} + \frac{P2(100 - P2)}{n2}}$$

(where n1 and n2 denote sample sizes for version A and B respectively)

$$\text{Thus } SE = \sqrt{\frac{5 \times 95}{5000} + \frac{6 \times 94}{6000}} = .095 + .094 = 0.44$$

From this, IF there is NO actual difference between the two versions in terms of response rate it could be expected that 34 out of every 100 pairs of test samples taken might estimate a difference of between nothing and 0.44 per cent as shown in Figure 5.16.

Our pair of test samples produces a difference of 1 per cent (6 per cent-5 per cent), so the 'Z' value of this has to be found – from:

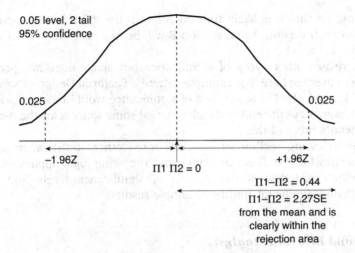

0.05 level, 2 tail
95% confidence

0.025

0.025

−1.96Z

+1.96Z

Π1 Π2 = 0

Π1−Π2 = 0.44

Π1−Π2 = 2.27SE
from the mean and is
clearly within the
rejection area

Figure 5.16 Testing Two Sample Percentages

$$Z = \frac{(P1 - P2) - (\Pi1 - \Pi2)}{SE}$$

$$= \frac{1 - 0}{0.44} = 2.27$$

This shows that the 'Z' value is not merely the difference between P1 and P2 but the difference between THEIR difference – with a difference of NIL (ie the assumption that there is no difference between the two versions) and this is 'relative to' the spread of the distribution as described by its standard error.

Because our pair of test samples produce a difference that is within the rejection area (the 'Z' value for a difference between response rates for the two versions (of 1 per cent) is further away from the mean (ie a difference between the two versions of 0 per cent) than the beginning of the rejection area (at 1.96) as defined in stage 3, a conclusion might be that this is such a rare event if there really is a significant difference between the two versions of copy. That is, we challenge the validity of our initial (null) hypothesis and accept the alternative hypothesis – in other words, it is likely that there IS a significant difference between the two copy versions in terms of response rate.

Calculating likely results for roll-out can now take place. If our test samples produced a difference of 1 per cent (6 per cent-5 per cent) and we want to operate at the 95 per cent confident level, the range for the difference between the two versions of copy will be :

$$\text{range(E)} = Zx\sqrt{\frac{P1(100 - P1)}{n1} + \frac{P2(100 - P2)}{n2}}$$

$$= 1.96 \times \sqrt{\frac{5 \times 95}{5000} + \frac{6 \times 94}{6000}} = 0.86$$

This means that it is likely that on roll-out, the *difference* in response rate between version A and version B will be from $1 - .86 = 0.14$ to $1 + .86 = 1.86$.

There are other types of significance but space does not permit further coverage here. For example, where a Factorial Design of several 'cells' is used, the *Chi Square* test of significance would be appropriate. The references at the end of the chapter list some sources for the reader who wants more of this !

The following section summarizes some other statistical analysis approaches for the direct marketer and the same logic applies to the following, in terms of the nature of significance levels and the statistically significant nature of sample results.

Uni- and Bivariate Analysis

The statistical analysis of the data collected with Osgood, Likert and Thurstone scales may be uni-, bi- or multivariate. Univariate analysis is concerned with the frequency distributions, means, and standard deviations of the variables. Testing the significance of differences between means and nonparametric tests are all part of univariate data analysis.

Bivariate analysis is concerned with the relationships between variables in terms of correlations and regression coefficients. These coefficients are measures between variables in terms of correlation of the variables. Correlation coefficients indicate to what degree variables vary in the same or in the opposite direction. For instance, a positive correlation between the level of response to a mailing and social grade indicates that persons in higher social grades tend to respond more to the mailing. If this correlation is 0.60, social grade explains the variance of response for 36 per cent: $(0.60)^2 = 0.36$.

Regression coefficients indicate to what degree a variable is a predictor for another variable. Social grade may be a predictor for response rate. With only one predictor, this is called simple regression, but with more than one predictor it is called multiple regression. For instance, apart from social grade, other variables such as previous purchasing from similar mailings, age and geodemographic category, may be other predictors of responding to the mailing. With more predictor variables it is often possible to explain more variance of the dependent variable (response rates). The correlation and regression coefficients are examples of metric coefficients. There are also non metric coefficients, used with non metric data. These are called similarity or proximity coefficients and are used as input data for non metric multidimensional scaling.

Multivariate Analysis

The direct marketer might use a number of multivariate techniques for market segmentation. The main categorization of these techniques is the distinction of structural and dependence analyses. A second distinction is based on the level of input data: metric or non-metric data.

Structural Analysis

In structural analysis the interrelations between variables are explored in order to create a structure that is simpler than the original variables. Typical examples of structural analyses include factor analysis, cluster analysis, multidimensional scaling, and correspondence analysis. With factor analysis a battery of one hundred lifestyle statements may be reduced to six or seven underlying factors. This is much easier and relevant to report than the scores on all one hundred statements. Structural analysis is used by direct marketers for simplification of complex structures as in lifestyle research, attitude and image analysis in categorization and positioning.

Dependence Analysis

In dependence analysis a relationship between a dependent or criterion variable and a set of independent or predictor variables is studied (e.g. the variables that predict or explain the market share of a brand). Typical examples of dependence analyses include multiple regression, multiple discriminant analysis, analysis of variance, and conjoint analysis.

Metric and Non-metric Data

Another important distinction is between the types of data that can be analysed: metric and non-metric data. Metric data are interval-level data (for example, where the 'rating' reflects a standard distance between categories, such as temperature or distance) and ratio (for example, where 'rating' is based on standard distances between categories but where there is also a true zero, such as with income). Metric data are often based on correlations and variances. Most multivariate analyses are possible if the data input consists of metric data. Non metric data are ordinal (for example, a rating scale) and nominal-level (for example, the mere coding of variables such as gender or postcode) data, often based on similarity coefficients and preference ratings. Only non-metric techniques are allowed with non-metric data input. In Table 5.11 the types of multivariate analyses are classified according to these two distinctions.

	Structural Analysis	Dependence Analysis
Metric Data	Factor Analysis LISREL	Regression Analysis Discriminant Analysis LISREL
Non-metric Data	Cluster Analysis Multidimensional Scaling Correspondence Analysis	Analysis of Variance Conjoint Analysis AID, CHAID

Table 5.11 Classification of Types of Multivariate Analysis

Factor Analysis

Factor analysis is a multivariate technique to structure a large array of variables into a smaller set of factors. These factors are underlying constructs that summarize the set of variables. Variables are often highly intercorrelated. These sets of intercorrelated variables are then summarized by one factor. Attitude questionnaires are often factor analysed to reduce the large set of questions to a meaningful small set of factors. This is an exploratory application of factor analysis, called principal components analysis.

Factor analysis is useful to direct marketers because it can 'reduce' large amounts of data by identifying more meaningful relationships. Factor analysis may also be applied to test for the number and type of underlying factors in a data set. The researcher may have an idea about how many factors and what type of factors could be expected. This is called confirmatory factor analysis.

Cluster Analysis

Cluster analysis provides a set of procedures that seek to separate the data into groups. The goal in such applications is to arrive at clusters of objects, cases or persons that display small within-cluster variation relative to the between-cluster variation. The goal in using cluster analysis is to identify a smaller number of groups such that objects belonging to a given group are, in some sense, more similar to each other than to objects belonging to other groups. Thus, cluster analysis attempts to reduce the information on the whole set of n objects, to information about, say, g subgroups where $g < $ n.

One of the major problems in direct marketing consists of the orderly classification of the myriad data that confront the researcher. Clustering techniques look for classification of attributes or subjects on the basis of their estimated resemblance. Cluster analysis is an exploratory method that seeks patterns within data by operating a matrix of independent variables. Usually objects to be clustered are scored on several variables and are grouped on the basis of the similarity of their scores. The primary value of cluster analysis lies in the pre-classification of data, as suggested by 'natural' groupings of the data itself. The major disadvantage of these techniques is that the implicit assumptions of the researcher can seriously affect cluster results. Cluster analysis can be applied in direct marketing for clustering buyers, products, markets, as well as key competitors. It has been found to be a particularly useful aid to market segmentation (such as in analysing and reducing data for geodemographic or lifestyle clusters) or experimentation and product positioning. Several questions need to be answered with respect to a given cluster solution, including:

▶ How do the clusters differ?

▶ What is the optimal (i.e. correct number of clusters)?

▶ How good is the fit of the solution for a pre-specified level of clusters?

The first question concerns the distinctiveness of cluster profiles. The second question concerns the trade-off between parsimony, in the sense of fewer clusters, and some measure of increase in within-cluster homo-geneity resulting from having more clusters in the solution. The third question concerns cluster recovery which can be viewed in terms of the fit between the input data and the resulting solution – this should be high.

Multidimensional Scaling
Multidimensional scaling (MDS), unlike other multivariate methods, starts with non-metric data pertaining to perceived similarities or dissimilarities among a set of objects such as products, buyers, competitors, etc. The main objective of using the technique is to obtain a configuration showing the relations among the various objects analysed. The attitudinal or perceived similarities (or dissimilarities) among a set of objectives are statistically transformed into distances by placing these objects in a multidimensional space. Two types of MDS exist: perception and preference scaling. Perception scaling needs similarity data and provides a single space of objects/stimuli. Preference scaling needs preference data of the type: A is preferred to B and B is preferred to C: A > B > C. Preference scaling may be projected into a similarity space to provide a joint space of objects/stimuli and preference vectors or ideal points.

Multidimensional scaling has been applied in direct marketing in areas such as product positioning, market segmentation, large-scale new product development models, the modelling and evaluation of buying behaviour and the determination of more effective marketing mix combinations. MDS may also be applied in the product development process by finding consumer attitudes towards various product attributes. In such applications the technique can:

▶ Construct an object configuration in a product space (perception).

▶ Discover the shape of the distribution of consumers' ideal points in this space. This is a joint space of perceptions and preferences.

▶ Identify likely opportunities ('market gaps') for new or modified products or different levels of service that a telephone banking service could offer.

Correspondence Analysis
Correspondence analysis is a robust, yet relatively simple method of enabling multi-variate data to 'speak for itself' in the form of maps. These maps provide user-friendly, global snap-shots of the patterns of, for example, consumers' perceptions in terms of the significant factors within a particular area, and the relationships between those factors. Participants are allowed to contribute at whatever level they feel comfortable and can avoid areas that they don't feel qualified to comment upon. As they are unaware of the fact that they are creating a map they don't feel pressurized into giving the 'right' answers. Correspondence analysis is a particularly useful means of revealing patterns of association without the need for *a priori* speculations.

Correspondence analysis is a visual or graphical technique for representing multidimensional tables. It is in fact a picture of a table of figures. It can often be impossible to identify any relationships in a table and very difficult to account for what is happening. Correspondence analysis unravels the table and presents data in an easy-to-understand chart. This technique is particularly useful to identify market segments, track brand image, position a product against its competition and determine who non-respondents in a survey most closely resemble. Correspondence analysis provides a joint space (i.e. a configuration of both objects/stimuli and attributes of these stimuli) whereas multidimensional scaling of similarity data provides a single space with only objects/stimuli.

The authors conducted a research programme into consumer attitudes toward direct marketing, employing group discussions and respondents were asked to complete a questionnaire detailing their perceptions of various forms of direct marketing prior to and after the group discussions. Using correspondence analysis a series of maps were produced for the total sample and for various segments reflecting class, gender and age. The 'before' maps provide pictures of where 'they were coming from', while the 'after' maps showed how perceptions had changed, if at all, following exposure to the group discussions. Analysis of the maps revealed a surprisingly high degree of unanimity across the sample and the before and after comparison revealed that perceptions were resistant to change (see Figure 5.17).

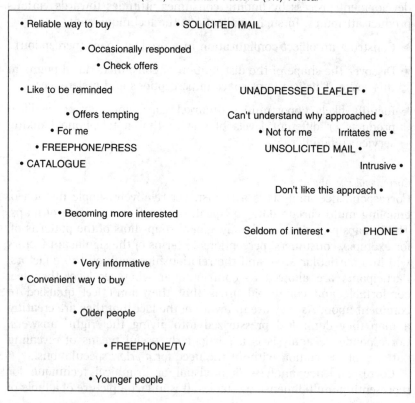

Factor 1 (88%) Horizontal / Factor 2 (4%) Vertical

- Reliable way to buy   • SOLICITED MAIL

    • Occasionally responded
        • Check offers

- Like to be reminded   UNADDRESSED LEAFLET •

        • Offers tempting   Can't understand why approached •
    • For me   • Not for me   Irritates me •
        • FREEPHONE/PRESS   UNSOLICITED MAIL •
- CATALOGUE   Intrusive •

                                            Don't like this approach •

    • Becoming more interested

                                    Seldom of interest •   PHONE •

        • Very informative
- Convenient way to buy

            • Older people

            • FREEPHONE/TV

            • Younger people

Figure 5.17
Correspondence Map

The analysis explained 92 per cent of the data in the first two factors, making it unnecessary to represent the data any further. The horizontal axis (which explains 88 per cent of the data) is very important in determining perceptions, and the map is graphically divided between favourable (left) and unfavourable (right) sides. In addition, the further from the centre of the map a factor is, the more distinctive or discriminated it is. The list below shows the percentage influence of each form of direct marketing in shaping the whole map. Each of the direct marketing methods are clearly relatively distinctive (i.e. none of the methods are viewed as being typical of all direct marketing communications methods).

▶ Phones   34%

▶ Catalogues   22%

▶ Freephone Press   16%

▶ Unsolicited Mail   12%

▶ Unaddressed Leaflets   08%

▶ Freephone TV   05%

▶ Solicited Mail   03%

Catalogues (22 per cent) and freephone/press (16 per cent) clearly organized favourable perceptions on the left, while phones (34 per cent), unsolicited mail (12 per cent) and unaddressed leaflets (08 per cent) had little influence. The next list displays the percentage influence of each attribute in shaping the whole map:

▶ Intrusive   12%

▶ Don't Like This Approach   11%

▶ Irritates Me   10%

▶ Seldom of Interest   10%

▶ Offers Appealing   08%

▶ Convenient Way to Buy   08%

▶ Reliable Way to Buy   06%

▶ Can't Understand Why Approached 06%

▶ For Me   06%

▶ Not For Me   06%

▶ Occasionally Respond   05%

▶ Check Offers   03%

▶ Very Informative   02%

▶ For Older People   02%

▶ For Younger People   02%

▶ Becoming More Interested   02%

▶ Like to be Reminded   01%

The top four influential attributes: intrusive (12 per cent), don't like this approach (11 per cent), irritates me (10 per cent) and seldom of interest (10 per cent) are all negative and are closely associated with phone, unsolicited mail and unaddressed leaflets (Patterson *et al.* 1997). Attributes with positive associations clearly had less influence in organizing the map.

Multiple Regression Analysis
Multiple regression is the best known and most frequently used type of dependence analysis. Metric data are needed, both for the dependent and the independent variables. For the independent variables, dummies may be used: variables with only two values (e.g. the presence or absence of an attribute). With a set of independent or predictor variables a proportion of the variance in the dependent variable may be explained. The dependent variable may include sales, response rates and attitude. Independent variables may include previous use of a direct mail service, profile characteristics such as age, gender, income, geodemographic and lifestyle group, distance from the nearest 'physical' supplier of the product concerned, number of households in a catchment area, and other factors that may explain or predict the dependent variable.

Regression analysis may be used in an explanatory and predictive sense. Regression may be used to explain variations in a dependent variable (e.g. to explain which of a number of variables to 'attitude toward direct mail' contributes most significantly). Table 5.12 shows a summary of the results for the authors' survey mentioned earlier in connection with attitude research models (Evans *et al.* 1997). Based on our earlier discussion of significance testing it can be seen that the more significant contributors (where the significance level is 0.05 or less) to attitude toward direct mail are (positive contributors): convenience; ease; product assortment (choice); relevance; previous exposure. The more negative contributors are risk, with inaccurate details and intrusion approaching significance. Both convenience and product assortment were discussed in the literature as being the most important perceived advantages of direct mail. Perceived risk is also significant as a contributor, indicating that purchase through direct mail remains a risk for some consumers. Where p is < 0.05 and at a similar level for several factors, the higher the t value, the greater the 'contribution' toward the dependent variable. Overall model fit is assessed by the R^2 and F statistics; we observe that (a) the independent variables explain 50.8 per cent of the variation in identification and (b) the postulated model is significant ($F = 46.04$, $p < 0.000$).

Linear Structural Relations
A combination of structural and dependence analysis is LISREL, linear structural relations. LISREL is a combination of factor analysis, multiple regression and other types of multivariate analyses. Depen-

Table 5.12 Regression Analysis

Dependent Variable: How do you feel about buying products and services as a result of direct mail – is it 'appealing – unappealing'? (five point scale).

Variable	Regression	Coeff.	T Value	Sig.
Convenience: is buying as a result of direct mail:				
'convenient – inconvenient'	Q5.1	0.30522	9.61	0.000
'difficult – easy'	Q5.4	0.08669	2.80	0.005
'quick – time consuming'	Q5.5	0.09780	3.13	0.002
Product assortment – how important is it for you to get products that aren't in the high street 'very – not'	Q35.4	0.10358	3.46	0.001
Perceived Risk – how do you feel about buying products and services as a result of direct mail – is it 'risky – safe'	Q5.6	–0.11449	–3.31	0.001
Experience – For the direct mail you receive is it 'interesting – not interesting'				
'informative – not informative'	Q7.1	0.06513	1.37	0.171
'entertaining – not entertaining'	Q7.2	0.05897	1.37	0.171
'relevant – irrelevant'	Q7.4	0.03187	0.88	0.381
Exposure – do you buy as a result of organizations contacting you through the mail: 'often – never'	Q7.6	0.11518	2.91	0.004
Physical privacy:				
– do you consider the amount of direct mail you receive to be – 'too little – too much'	Q3	0.16055	2.97	0.003
– is the direct mail you receive 'intrusive – not intrusive'	Q1	–0.05850	–1.40	0.161
Information privacy:				
– personal details are being kept by organizations for reasons unknown to me	Q7.3	–0.04966	–1.67	0.096
– I really don't mind about marketers having my personal details	Q22.6	–0.03157	–1.05	0.293
– there is a need for strong laws to control the sharing of personal information	Q22.4	0.04857	1.60	0.110
– marketers should inform me before selling on my details	Q22.5	–0.00570	–0.14	0.888
– there are sufficient safeguards to my personal details	Q22.13	0.02837	0.66	0.509
– direct marketing shouldn't share my details with other organizations	Q22.14	0.04235	1.35	0.177
Accuracy:				
– for the direct mail I receive the marketers have generally got my details correct	Q23.4	0.01831	0.50	0.620
Environmental concerns:				
– for the direct mail you receive, does it 'damage the environment – does not damage the environment'	Q22.7	–0.06144	–1.82	0.070
	Q7.5	–0.02638	–0.92	0.359
	R-Sq = 50.8%			

dence analysis is used for explanation and prediction of a dependent variable, such as response rate, attitude and evaluation of direct marketing operations. Linear Structural Relations (LISREL) is an overall, both structural and dependence, multivariate technique. All types of metric multivariate analysis may be regarded as specific cases of LISREL. With LISREL the researcher should have an *a priori* model of how the variables and factors are related. This model or a number of models can be tested with LISREL. The model with the best fit is then assumed to be the 'best' model to represent the data. Usually it is recommended to do single regression and/or factor analysis, whichever is appropriate, before testing the developed model with LISREL. An example is a study of consumer attitudes toward direct mail. In such a study a number of survey questions can be reduced to two underlying factors, which is similar to factor analysis. These factors can then be used to predict the dependent variables: attitude toward direct mail and intention to buy by direct mail, in a similar way to our discussion of regression analysis. The current SPSS package that deals with structural equations is called AMOS.

Multiple Discriminant Analysis
Discriminant analysis is a useful technique to differentiate within groups and predict group membership characteristics. Applications include uncovering characteristics of groups most likely to purchase products and determining the qualities of first-time customers to predict repeat business. Discriminant analysis may be used to validate the clusters obtained from cluster analysis.

Discriminant analysis involves deriving linear combinations of the independent variables that will discriminate between *a priori* defined groups in such a way that the misclassification error rates are minimized. It is the appropriate statistical technique when the dependent variable is categorical (nominal, thus non metric distinction between groups) and the independent variables are metric. Discriminant analysis is very similar to regression, with the only difference being that the dependent variable is categorical rather than metric. Discriminant analysis is widely used by direct marketers in market segmentation and credit scoring but can also be used in studies of the diffusion and adoption of new products, and consumer behaviour analysis.

Analysis of Variance
Analysis of variance (ANOVA) is another well-known type of dependence analysis, related to experimental test designs as discussed above. In an experimental design, differences are studied between

Table 5.13 A 2 × 2 Experimental Design

	Standard Creative	New Creative
Standard Prices	Group A	Group B
Lower Prices	Group C	Group D

conditions. For instance, in some mailings from a list the creative is changed (group B), in another mailing from the list prices are lowered (group C) and in a third mailing batch from the list, nothing is changed (group A). If the three mailings are similar with regard to other factors, ANOVA may be used to test the significance of the response rates differences between the three mailings. In a more complex 2×2 design, four types of mailing may be distinguished, according to the four groups in Table 5.13. In group D, both the creative and the prices are changed. In an ANOVA analysis, the significance of the effects of creative and prices may be tested, as well as the effect of a combination of both effects (interaction effect). In order to study the interaction effect, the inclusion of group D is necessary.

Conjoint Analysis

Conjoint analysis is concerned with the joint effect of two or more independent variables on the ordering of a dependent variables. It is rooted in traditions of experimentation. A definition of conjoint analysis must proceed from its underlying assumption that a composition rule may be established to predict a response variable from two or more predictor variables. Conjoint analysis, like multi-dimensional scaling, is concerned with the measurement of psychological judgements, such as consumer preferences.

For conjoint (trade-off) analysis products are essentially bundles of attributes such as price and colour. Conjoint analysis software generates a deck of cards, each of which combine levels of these product attributes. Respondents are asked to sort the cards generated into an order of preference. Conjoint analysis then assigns a value to each level and produces a 'ready-reckoner' to calculate the preference for each chosen combination. Conjoint analysis can be used to design packaging, establish price, rank a hypothetical product against existing competitors already in the market and suggest modifications to existing products which would help to strengthen a product's performance.

It seems that various types of direct planning models and other procedures using judgmental estimates in a formal manner might benefit from the utilization of conjoint models in additive form. Moreover, buyer preferences for multi-attribute items may also be decomposed into part-worth evaluations in a similar manner. Potential areas of application for conjoint analysis include product design, new product concept descriptions, price-value relationships, attitude measurement, promotional congruence testing and the study of functional versus symbolic product characteristics. The output of conjoint analysis is frequently employed in additional analyses. Since most studies collect full sets of data at the individual respondent level, individual utility functions and importance weights can be computed. This fosters two additional types of analyses:

1 market segmentation;

2 strategic simulation of new factor-level product combinations.

AID and CHAID

Most types of cluster analysis start with single cases and form clusters by adding similar cases to an existing cluster. These types of cluster analysis are of a 'growth form'. Automatic Interaction Detection (AID) is a type of cluster analysis in which large samples are broken down into homogeneous subsets. AID and Chi AID (CHAID) are cluster techniques with a dependent variable. Based on scores on the dependent variable, clusters are formed that differ maximally between clusters on the dependent variable. The programme develops clusters in which the objects or cases differ minimally. At the same time, the differences between the clusters should be large. Large samples are needed to apply AID or CHAID. The clustering stops if the clusters become too small or if the differences between the clusters become too small. The AID programme can only split a group into two subgroups. With CHAID other splits are also possible, based on a Chi-square criterion.

An example of a dependent variable is the response rate to a direct mailing in a large sample. In the total sample this response rate may be 6.5 per cent. With the AID programme subgroups are distinguished with significantly lower or higher response rates. AID and CHAID are useful techniques for market segmentation and are becoming very popular amongst direct marketers.

If, for example, a direct mail operation is building a predictive model on the basis of length of time customers have been on the database, geodemographic category and age. The direct mail company analyses response rates to a large test mailing (say, 20,000). CHAID will produce a tree-like analysis which identifies different segments based on the variables themselves but also on the effects of the variables interacting with each other (regression doesn't automatically do this). Where there is no significant difference between some of the variables, such as age categories, CHAID will combine these into a larger 'segment' (see Figure 5.18).

For example, there may be six age groups (1 to 6) but CHAID might detect no significant difference between some and is able to group then into just two – say, under and over 50 (1,2,3 and 4,5,6). If there were 11 geodemographic groups involved in the overall response, CHAID might combine them as shown in the 'tree', thus reducing data to more meaningful groups on the basis of statistical significance. Length of time on the database might be classified according to four periods (less than six months, six months to a year, one to two years and more than two years) and again CHAID could reduce these to more significant groupings. The programme will calculate response rates for each category/segment (shown in Figure 5.18) and numbers of responders (not shown). The resulting reduction of an enormous amount of data to just seven significant segments, based on different combinations of factors, is clearly of tremendous value to the direct marketer. Without this, there would have, potentially, been 264 (6 x 11 x 4) segments but without much significant value. CHAID is also able to do this on data for which regression might have produced an overall low level of explanation (low R^2) of the dependent variable

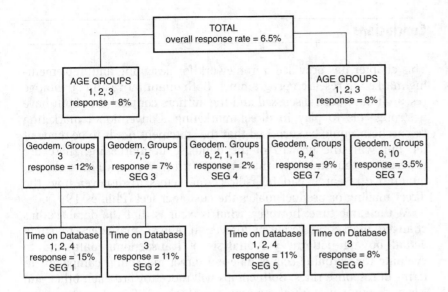

Figure 5.18 CHAID Tree

(response) by the independent variables (age, geodemographics and length on the database).

Stage 6: Communicating Results

A research programme is manifested in its final research report and it is usually possible to use it to some extent in evaluating other stages of the process. For example, any questionnaire used should usually appear in an appendix and the researcher can scrutinize this. Also, the sample design and size should be explained and the reader is also given the opportunity to evaluate this. The manner in which the data has been analysed and reported can also be studied in the report, but although the project objectives may appear reasonable to a reader who is not the person responsible for making decisions on the basis of this report, they may be wholly inadequate for the actual decision area concerned.

In the same way that it was suggested in Stage 1 that communication between decision maker and researcher is important for the research objectives to be clarified and agreed, so the same applies at the end of the process. Results have to be communicated to the users of research in such a way that their meaning is not distorted and so that they answer the brief as originally agreed. We are not going to delve into the procedures for report writing or for making presentations because these are amply covered in a variety of other more specialized sources, some of which are listed at the end of this chapter.

Conclusions

This chapter has provided a framework for designing and implementing marketing research programmes. Both quantitative and qualitative research have been discussed and the authors contend that both have a strong role to play in direct marketing. Conventional marketing researchers would be surprised that the statement needs to be made at all, but with the growth of the database in marketing, there are suggestions that that is all that's needed. However, as we have shown, qualitative research can help direct marketers to discover how the direct mailing or product makes the customer feel (Phillips 1997).

At the same time, however, what is clear is that the database has changed marketing research forever. It allows marketers to study actual buying patterns via analysis of transactional data and to evaluate the actual effects of different direct marketing campaigns in terms of response rates. Both camps will move toward each other and learn through a mutual synergy. As Dunn (1995) suggests 'some purist market researchers are sticking their heads in the sand . . . database marketing isn't going to go away.'

We have provided a framework and the techniques for determining sample sizes for surveys and direct marketing tests have discussed different designs for direct marketing experiments as have a variety of statistical analysis techniques.

Direct marketing has raised some issues, however, because marketing research has long prided itself on the ethic of not using research to sell products. The database is used to store data about specific individuals and the resulting lists of names and addresses used to target those individuals. This issue has been well addressed by Fletcher and Peters (1996). The Market Research Society itself has redrawn its Code of Conduct and this provides differently for what would be classed as traditional market research and what is clearly database driven.

The chapters so far have covered direct marketing planning, segmentation, databases and research. We now move on to look at acquisition and retention strategies, which use many of the strategic and tactical issues raised so far.

STUDY 2

Ford opts to keep it plain and simple

Ford in Europe was a relatively late entrant to the web. But when the company made its debut last October, it did so big-time. The same web site template was rolled out simultaneously across the UK and France, with six other European markets following suit over the following six months.

As might be expected from the company that pioneered assembly-line manufacturing, economies of scale were foremost in Ford's mind – hence its use of a single template which allowed for a consistency of design. Inherent within that design is the capacity to capture data.

'Data capture is certainly not the primary reason for having a site but looking at the size and quality of the response we've received, it's a very important aspect,' says Jeremy Thomson, Ford's UK manager of direct marketing.

● ● ▶

'Ford is encouraged by the positive response from the internet. It equates favourably with the cost of other media,' says Gavin Bayliss, account director for new media at Wunderman Cato Johnson – the agency maintaining Ford's UK web site.

In the six months that the web site has been live, Thomson claims it has attracted tens of thousands of impressions. Whether or not any cars have been sold as a direct result of this interaction, Ford is not saying. Certainly the site has served as the first point of contact with the company for a number of buyers. However with the URL now appearing on much of Ford's above-the-line work, most buyers may have first been wooed by other media.

'Simple but functional' sums up the design approach to Ford's site. Its simplicity is a result of the need to arrive at a format that can be reinvented for different markets.

The main route by which customers are invited to part with information – on income bracket, current car driven, intended replacement date etc – is a competition to win a Ford Probe. This is flagged-up on every page of the site. Clicking on this link takes the visitor to a three-page questionnaire.

After the first page, respondents are divided into existing Ford owners and prospects, with their responses fed into different databases.

The number of questions asked seems prodigious, though Thomson claims this has not proved a deterrent.

'I'm constantly surprised by the predisposition of the British public to complete lengthy data capture forms,' he says.

The other data capture route lies in a simpler two-page brochure request. 'On screen there's not much copy,' says Bayliss. 'So where is the copy? It's in the brochure.'

No mail-shot is automatically dispatched to those people whose data is captured on the site. Instead prospects are mailed when marketing activity appropriate to them begins – for example a new model launch, or promotion on an existing model.

The hottest prospects – in other words, those expressing the intention to replace their vehicle in the near future – may be recruited directly into an existing Ford loyalty programme. This would mean receiving regular contact via mail including issues of the quarterly Ford Magazine.

(Source: *Revolution Magazine*, June 1997, p. 56)

CASE
STUDY 3

Vauxhall's relaxing approach

Vauxhall, arch-rival of Ford, is also tentatively trawling the web for data. The company has had a site since August 1995.

Vauxhall captures data via a brochure request form on its site. However, it does not adhere to Ford's minimalist principles. It puts much of the vehicle data online, believing that this remains true to the web's tenet of being an on-demand environment.

Vauxhall requires a minimal amount of data from prospective customers. Areas such as income are neglected in favour of simple details such as name and address, and information on the current car driven.

'No-one's going to fill out a three-page form, because it's their telephone time being eaten into,' says Vauxhall new-media manager, Matthew Timms.

Vauxhall's preferred data capture method is currently a competition run via banner ads placed at other sites. Its most ambitious project to date was the sponsorship of the ITN election site by the Vauxhall Omega.

The ITN site offered a variety of advantages, claims Charlie Dobres, head of digital communications at Lowe Howard-Spink, Vauxhall's ad agency: 'It was a spot-on audience of ABC1 males, and ran for a limited time, which promised high site-traffic over that period.'

The campaign took the car's virtues as a relaxing mode of transport as its theme – in stark contrast to the stressful subject matter of the site. This was flagged up in two banner ads at the top and bottom of the site's opening page. A competition offering a suitably relaxing reward – such as a weekend break – was used to elicit basic demographic and motoring data.

The hottest prospects from this data-trawl receive a follow-up e-mail offering a test drive. Other leads are contacted nearer their declared date for replacing their current car.

To assess the effectiveness of the media, respondents will be tracked to find out which went on to take test drives, and which converted to Omega buyers.

(Source: *Revolution Magazine*, June 1997, p. 57)

Review Questions

1   What is the rationale behind determining sample sizes and significance testing?

2   What is the role of motivation research in direct marketing?

3   What is CHAID and how can it help the direct marketer?

Discussion Questions

1   What are the issues involved with collecting individualized data for database marketing, from a market researcher's perspective, a direct marketer's perspective and the consumers' perspective?

2   What is the difference between market research and testing? What are the implications of this difference for direct marketers?

References

Basch, C.E. (1987) 'Focus Group Interview: An Underutilized Research Technique for Improving Theory and Practice in Health Education', *Health Education Quarterly*, 14(4), pp. 411–48.

Calder, J. (1977) 'Focus Groups and the Nature of Qualitative Marketing', *Journal of Marketing Research*, XIV, pp. 353–64.

Churchill, G.A. (1979) *Marketing Research: Methodological Foundations* (2nd Ed.), Hinsdale, Ill: The Dryden Press.

Cooper, P. and Tower, R. (1992) 'Inside the Consumer Mind', *Journal of the Market Research Society*, 34(4), pp. 299–311.

de Almeida, P.M. (1980) 'A Review of Group Discussion Methodology', *European Research*, 3(8), pp. 114–20.

Dunn, E. (1995) Summers, D. in 'A Point in Question', *Financial Times*, 29th June.

England, L. (1980) 'Is research a waste of time?', *Marketing*, 16 April, pp. 5–7.

Evans, M., O'Malley, L. and Patterson, M. (1997) Direct Mail Attitudes: A UK Perspective, in T. Meenaghan (ed.), Proceedings of the American Marketing Association Special Conference, *New and Evolving Paradigms: The Emerging Future of Marketing*, Dublin, CD-ROM.

Fletcher, K. and L. Peters (1996) 'Issues in Customer Information Management', *Journal of the Market Research Society*, 38(2), pp. 145–60.

Forshaw, T. (1993) 'Testing: The Direct Route to Continuous Improvement', *Direct Response*, July, pp. 28–9.

Francis, N. (1995) *Panel Data Friend or Foe? How the Royal Mail Use the Panel*, Portsmouth: Royal Mail.

Hyett, P. (1982). 'Should we be having more of IT?', *Market Research Society Newsletter*, 196(3).

Kahn, R. L. and Cannell, C.F. (1968) 'Interviewing', *International Encyclopaedia of the Social Sciences*, 2(2), pp. 118-35.

Koerner, R. (1980) 'The Design Factor: An Under-Utilised Concept?', *European Research*, 8(6), pp. 266–72.

Market Research Society (1994) *The Opinion Polls and the 1992 General Election*

Market Research Society (1997) *Proposed Revised Code of Conduct*, London.

Millward, M. (1987) 'How to get better value from your research budget', *AMSO Handbook and Guide to Buying Market Research in the UK*, pp. 6–10.

Patterson, M., O'Malley, L., Evans, M.J. (1997) 'Database Marketing: Investigating Privacy Concerns', *Journal of Marketing Communications*, 3(3), pp. 151–74.

Phillips, D. (1997) Miller, R. in 'The Human Face of Data', *Marketing Direct*, May, pp. 52–6.

Purdom, N. (1996) 'Lists: The Best Way Forward', *Marketing Direct*, September, pp. 73–8.

RSCR (1997) 'Focal Points: Eye Flow Research Centre', *Academy of Marketing Annual Conference*, Manchester.

Santry, E. (1994) *Research*, June, p. 337.

Shugan, S.M. and Hauser, J.R. (1977) 'P.A.R.I.S.: An Interactive Market Research Information System', *Discussion Paper 292*, Northwestern University: Center for Mathematical Studies in Economics and Management Science.

Stone, M., Davies, D. and Bond, A. (1995) *Direct Hit: Direct Marketing With A Winning Edge*, London: Pitman.

Vlier, A. (1997) 'Are They Being Served?', *Management Today*, February, pp. 68–71.

Zaltman, G. and Burger, P.C. (1975) *Marketing Research*, Illinois: The Dryden Press.

Further Reading

Alreck, P.L. and Settle, R.B. (1995) *The Survey Research Handbook*, 2nd edn, Chicago: Irwin.

Chisnall, P.M. (1992) *Marketing Research*, 4th edn, Maidenhead: McGraw Hill.

Crouch, S. (1988) *Marketing Research for Managers*, London: Heinemann.

Hawkins, D.I. and Tull, D.S. (1994) *Essentials of Marketing Research*, New York: Macmillan.

McDaniel, C. and Gates, R. (1995) *Marketing Research Essentials*, St. Paul, MN: West.

Miles, M.B. and Huberman, A.M. (1994) *Qualitative Data Analysis*, 2nd edn, London: Sage.

Moutinho, L. and Evans, M.J. (1992) *Applied Marketing Research*, Wokingham: Addison-Wesley.

Proctor, T. (1997) *Essentials of Marketing Research*, London: Pitman.

Silver, M. (1992) *Business Statistics*, London: McGraw Hill.

Silverman, D. (1993) *Interpreting Qualitative Data: Methods for Analysing Talk, Text and Interaction*, London: Sage.

Tesch, R. (1990) *Qualitative Research: Analysis Types and Software Tools*, New York: The Falmer Press.

Tull, D.S. and Hawkins, D.I. (1980) *Marketing Research: Measurement and Method*, New York: Macmillan.

Webb, J.R. (1992) *Understanding and Designing Marketing Research*, London: The Dryden Press.

Customer Acquisition, Retention and Loyalty

This Chapter:

▶ Discusses The Relevance Of Acquisition To Direct Marketers And Identifies Various Prospecting Approaches.

▶ Introduces The Importance Of Customer Retention In Today's Marketplace.

▶ Discusses The Concept Of 'Loyalty' And Introduces A Framework To Classify Loyalty.

▶ Identifies The Objective(s) Of Customer Loyalty Programmes And Discusses Their Value.

CHAPTER

6

Customer Acquisition, Retention and Loyalty

From Acquisition to Retention in Retail Banking

By the end of the 1980s, most retail banks had transferred their information onto massive databases. However, the value of such data was limited. In particular, though bank marketers knew how many accounts they had, they knew very little about their customers. For example, they did not know how many customers they had, nor did they know anything about the income, lifestyle or life-cycle stage of their customers (Croft 1995a). Because information was held on *accounts* not *customers*, it was difficult to tell if a customer held more than one account (current, savings, loan). The banks' strategies also tended to be product focused rather than customer focused, with many new products being developed. As a result, limited knowledge of the customer base resulted in poor targeting efforts.

The focus on customer acquisition was also misleading. For example, most new cheque accounts are unprofitable for the first three years. The importance of this fact becomes evident if we look at the student market. The cost of attracting 150,000 new student/youth accounts in the UK could be as much as £3,000,000 in advertising, and another £20 per head in incentives, mailings literature, computer costs and administration. In the first few years when students operate these accounts it is likely that they will maintain low balances, and initiate a high number of transactions (all those trips to the cash machine next to the students' union!). From the banks' point of view, this business will be unprofitable. "Profit comes with customer maturity, through higher income, higher balances, lending services, deposit products and insurance commissions. The proposition is only viable where the customer is retained" (Cram 1994:44). Thus, the bank needs to keep student customers for at least six years in order to recoup the initial investment costs (Murphy 1994). Furthermore, in these later years, account balances are likely to be much higher, and there are a number of additional possibilities in terms of credit cards, loans or even mortgages.

This has led to a greater focus on customer retention with banks attempting to engender greater loyalty among their customers. New customer acquisition continues to be important, but now the banks are aware that they must manage both acquisition and retention of customers, if they are to continue to be profitable in the long term.

Introduction

Organizations throughout the world have for a long time focused on acquiring new customers. Customer acquisition is based on the rationale that the more customers an organization has, the bigger the organization will be. Being big, in turn is assumed to positively impact upon economies of scale, market share and profitability. 'As a result, the front-end function of customer *getting* commands a substantial portion of budgets, top management attention, and talented marketing personnel. The back-end efforts of customer *retaining* generally are neglected' (Rosenberg and Czepiel 1984:45). However, the opening vignette suggests that retail bankers at least have realized that while acquiring new customers remains important, retaining these customers is the key to profitability. The retail banks are not the only sector to have come to this conclusion. Today most business sectors have reached the same conclusion, with the back-end activity of retaining customers no longer so neglected. This chapter will discuss the importance of both acquisition and retention strategies to ensuring success for organizations in the 1990s, and indeed, into the twenty-first century.

Essentially, organizations can build their business in three ways (Ainslie and Pitt 1992):

1 obtain new customers;

2 get more business from existing customers;

3 reduce customer defections.

Although, many organizations have traditionally put most of their marketing effort into acquiring new customers, the competitive marketing environment of the 1990s has led to a renewed focus upon customer retention. As identified above, reducing customer defections and increasing the value of the business generated from existing customers are also valid growth strategies. Today's organizations have developed strategies in each of these three areas. Before looking at how and why customers can be retained, we will first examine customer acquisition in greater detail.

Customer Acquisition

Prospecting is considered to be the life-blood of any business. It involves searching for appropriate new customers. This often requires the purchase of names and addresses from outside sources. Ideally, in addition to being interested in the product on offer, prospects should represent a high life-time value to the company. Acquisition occurs when the message and offer are appropriate to the prospect.

Traditional communications media can be used for prospecting. However, many argue that direct strategies are more effective because they are targeted to the most likely parts of the market. Over 90 per cent of direct marketing in the UK is prospecting in nature, and because of ineffective targeting, much of this is viewed by consumers simply as 'junk'. As a result, many companies are now turning to non-intrusive prospecting methods. These include the use of press, radio and TV direct-response advertising, which invites customers who are interested to contact the company.

Marketers have recently become dissatisfied with traditional mass market approaches. Consumers have become more demanding and sophisticated. Mass communications are increasingly losing the ability to target effectively as a result of increasing market fragmentation. At the same time, advances in technology have presented marketers with new ways of connecting with customers (Copulsky and Wolf 1991). Essentially, it has been argued that 'broadcasting targets its audience much as a battleship shells a distant island into submission; addressable media initiates conversations' (Blattberg and Deighton 1991:5). Thus, direct marketing offers the possibility of targeting new customers with specific information and offers.

Cost-effective acquisition of new customers depends, in part, upon an organization's ability to efficiently target prospects. A prospect is any individual, household or business who is not a current customer, but who is worth considering for acquisition. These include (Hansotia 1997):

▶ households, individuals and businesses with no prior relationship with the company;

▶ lapsed customers;

▶ customers of a parent or sister company;

▶ customers of strategic partners;

▶ enquirers.

These categories of prospect may not be relevant to every organization (for example, a small company may not have a parent or sister company), however, every organization will identify at least some of the above categories as a source of prospects. Depending upon which source of prospect is identified, it is likely that the organization will have varying amounts and types of information on each. For example, if prospects are already customers of the parent company, then it is likely that the database will hold fairly detailed information, including transaction data. This may also apply to lapsed customers. Enquirers are likely to provide a limited amount of information, but it will certainly be more than the organization knows about consumers who have no prior relationship with them. Prospects can be categorized rather crudely as cold, warm, and hot (see also Table 6.1).

▶ A *cold prospect* has not purchased from the organization previously, and the degree to which they are interested in the product or service is generally unknown.

▶ *Warm prospects* may have similar characteristics to existing customers of the organization, may be customers of competing organizations, or may have expressed an interest in the product or service through their purchasing behaviour. For example, subscribers to Anglers' Weekly, are likely prospects for organizations which sell heavy-duty rain wear. By purchasing the Anglers' Weekly mailing list the organization has a ready-made list of warm prospects.

▶ To an organization which sells fishing-rods or angling holidays, the same Anglers' Weekly mailing list may represent *hot prospects*. They have clearly displayed sufficient interest in the area to regularly purchase a magazine. That said, the hottest prospects self-select. For example, if Anglers' Weekly carried a direct response advertisement for angling holidays, those customers who returned the coupon, or telephoned for further information, would be 'hot' prospects. Equally, existing or previous customers may represent 'hot' prospects for new offers. As we identified in Chapter 2, converting 'hot' prospects will be the cheapest option for the organization.

Hansotia (1997:353) identifies that the key decisions in customer acquisition are:

▶ Which prospects should the firm target for acquisition?

▶ With what offer, message/positioning and creative/look?

▶ Through which media?

▶ Should the communication unfold through a series of contacts?

▶ Should the firm try and create inquiries, so that the sale is the result of a multi-stage process?

Effective targeting of prospects depends upon the organization's ability to evaluate new prospects. This information is then used to target prospects for acquisition whose expected net present value (after acquisition costs) is greater than zero (Hansotia 1997). The acquisition cost of a new customer depends upon the cost of marketing and the attractiveness of the customer. This has already been discussed in greater detail in Chapter 4, however it may be useful to recap here. Where direct marketing is used to acquire a new customer, the acquisition cost per customer is:

$$\frac{\text{Marketing cost per prospect}}{\text{Response Likelihood}} = \text{Acquisition cost per customer}$$

Table 6.1 Categories of Prospect

Cold Prospect	Warm Prospect	Hot Prospect
Has not indicated an interest.	Behaviour may suggest interest. Characteristics may suggest interest.	Previous customer. Behaviour suggests interest. Customer self-selects.
Targeted prospecting expensive.	Testing will indicate how worthwhile prospecting may be.	Hot prospects represent the least expensive acquisition costs. Prospecting should start here.

Response likelihood depends on how attractive the offer is and how well the product or service offered is positioned to meet the needs or wants of the prospect. Different prospects will have different response likelihood because of the utility of the offer to them and because of the impact on them of different marketing communication methods. As a result, direct marketers attempt to predict response to different marketing treatments, and evaluate the costs associated with different methods.

However, there is no science to acquiring new customers: 'Techniques for the acquisition of new prospects rest almost exclusively on subjective or experientially based judgement' (Lix *et al.* 1995:9). That said, there are a few ground rules that can be followed successfully by most organizations. The first step in the process is to understand existing customers. This will go a long way toward identifying the profile of likely responders, by looking at the characteristics of the customers already held by the organization. The direct marketer will be able to access the customer database for this rich source of information. For example, direct marketers have learned that certain segments of their customer lists are more likely to respond than others. This has led to the RFM rule, that is, the likelihood of a response to a particular mailing is influenced significantly by the *recency* of the last purchase, the *frequency* of purchases in the past, and the *monetary* value of a customer's purchase history. Thus, as a first step, the organization should:

1 Use in-house lists to segment customers most likely to respond based on the RFM rule.

2 Define segments and rank them from most likely to least likely to purchase.

3 Identify factors which distinguish different segments.

4 Examine new mailing lists, and extrapolate targets with similar characteristics with high purchase probability segments on internal databases.

The second step in the process is to generate an understanding of the prospects which the company intends to target. While the internal database may generate profiles of likely prospects, this may not be enough information to develop the offer. Thus, understanding prospects involves identifying the following (Hansotia 1997:352):

▶ What is the awareness level of the company and its brands?

▶ How knowledgeable are prospects about the product's fundamental benefits?

▶ How do prospects seek out product information?

▶ How are purchase decisions made?

▶ What are the different prospect segments?

▶ How does each segment evaluate products (i.e. how do different segments rate product attributes on importance)?

Finding all of the above information generally involves conducting primary research among the different target groups. Although this may be expensive, surveys provide important information, which can be used to evaluate prospects, design creative and assist generally with direct marketing planning. Where possible the organization can conduct large consumer surveys and merge the resulting data with externally available databases (a good review of the use of surveys combined with commercially available databases in the USA can be found in Lix *et al.*1995). Predictive models which are built upon this detailed level of prospect information are likely to be far more reliable than those without. Despite this, many direct marketers do not spend a great deal of time evaluating prospects, but simply target all prospects on a particular list. Although this may work, it is more through luck than judgement and therefore is of little benefit in refining long-term planning for the organization.

Prospects can be targeted individually, or can be attracted through the use of direct response mechanisms in either press, radio or TV. Individual targeting can be via mail or telephone (although mail is generally cheaper for 'cold' prospecting). The advantage of personalized targeting is primarily that the 'offer' can be designed to appeal to different segments or types of people. This will require some information on individual prospects, and the success is dependent upon how well the organization understands its prospects, the quality of the mailing list, the offer, and the success of testing. McCorkell (1997) suggests that there are six factors which lead to success:

▶ product;

▶ targeting;

▶ offer;

▶ format;

▶ copy;

▶ timing.

Ensuring success therefore requires not only having the right product and the right offer, but also relies upon the effectiveness of targeting, the format, the offer and the timing of communication to individuals. In order to get these elements 'right' for each prospect, direct marketers rely heavily on testing various combinations of the offer, to different customer segments. Only when they are satisfied with the results will they implement their strategies.

The use of a direct response mechanism through mass media has the advantage of reaching a potentially larger audience than a mailing and, more importantly, produces hot prospects. That is, prospects have self-selected themselves by showing interest in the offer. When using direct response in non-personal (broadcast) media it is important to make it easy for the prospect to respond, for example by using an 0800 number or Freepost facility. If an immediate response is required, the suggestion of a 'one-time-only-offer' or availability for a limited period may prompt warm prospects to become 'hot prospects'. The inclusion of a free gift, or opportunity to enter a free draw have also proved useful in this regard. For some products or services, initiating a request for further information is likely to be a less risky option for a customer than a straight purchase, and therefore is likely to prompt a higher response rate. Whether the offer is one-stage (buy the product) or multi-stage (request information or receive a catalogue) will depend greatly on the nature of the offer, the company and the target prospects. (For a more detailed review of one-stage versus multi-stage prospecting see McCorkell 1997). Thus, testing is equally important when generating a direct response through non-personal media.

Problems with Focusing on Acquisition

The short-sightedness of focusing all of the marketing effort on getting new customers is typified by the following statement from a marketing executive (cited in Rosenberg and Czepiel 1984:45):

> ❝ *The many ways companies relate to customers is akin to looking for a needle in a haystack, finding it, and then throwing it back to look for it again.* ❞

Because some marketers have assumed that growth can only be obtained from attracting new customers, they have often unwittingly minimized the importance of satisfying old ones. As a result, existing customers are treated as though they were prospects. They often receive conflicting information and their value to the company is continually undermined. Additionally, the company has little information about its customers and this limits the ability to target customers with appropriate offers. Furthermore, such companies are often unaware which customers they have lost, and have no information as to why customers defect. This prevents the organization from improving its strategies in the future.

All this suggests that while customer acquisition is certainly important, it has received a disproportionate amount of attention, often to the detriment of satisfying existing customers. The competitive climate has now changed, radically new products are few and far between, and in any case, 'me-toos' are on the market much more quickly than in the past. Added to this, population growth has slowed down in many developed countries, making new customers more and more difficult to find. Thus, companies today must find the right balance between acquisition and retention strategies, and must develop different propositions for potential and existing customers.

Customer Retention

As outlined in the previous section, much marketing activity is about constantly finding new customers. Indeed, 'some companies seem hooked on steady doses of fresh customers to cover up regular losses of existing ones' (Rosenberg and Gzepiel 1984:46). Traditionally marketing efforts have ended with the sale. Recent business trends suggest that a continual focus on acquisition is expensive, and led Ted Levitt (1983) to emphasize 'after the sale is over . . .'. The suggestion, metaphorically, is that a focus on a single sale (transaction) is equivalent to a one-night stand, and that in today's volatile business environment, firms should endeavour to enter wedlock with their customers. Thus, today there is a new emphasis on retaining existing customers.

In looking at customer retention the first step is to analyse the organization's customer 'scrap heap': that is, the customers who leave the company and don't come back (Reichheld and Sasser 1990). In this 1990 Harvard Business Review article, Reichheld and Sasser predicted that marketers would strive for 'zero defections' where organizations would try to keep every customer that they could profitably serve and thus reduce the scrap heap. This prediction was based upon some startling results from their research, which suggested that 'as a customer's relationship with the company lengthens, profits rise. And not just a little. Companies can boost profits by almost 100 per cent by retaining just 5 per cent more of their customers' (Reichheld and Sasser 1990:105).

Marketers, have indeed, placed customer retention high on their agenda throughout the 1990s, and presumably, will continue to do so into the twenty-first century. The rationale for the focus on customer retention has come from management realization of the impact which customer defection has upon profitability. Indeed, in many industries, customer defection can have a far more powerful impact than market share, unit cost, scale and a host of other factors generally associated with competitive advantage. It is not uncommon for a business to lose 15–20 per cent of its customers each year. Reducing such defections can lead to phenomenal increases in profitability. This is because, served correctly, customers generate increasingly higher profits each year they stay with a company. Existing customers are a lot cheaper to sell to and, as their purchases rise, operating costs decline. This, together with the amount of spend required to attract a new customer, implies that retention is a more profitable option. Estimates vary between studies, but in many industries it costs between five and ten times more to acquire a new customer, than to sell to an existing one. Furthermore, these loyal customers will provide free advertising, through positive word-of-mouth. Thus, there is a link between loyalty, value and profits (Reichheld 1988). When an organization improves its retention rates its revenues and market share grow because the best customers generate repeat sales and referrals and the costs associated with acquiring and developing new customer relationships shrink. Equally, by understanding the economics of defection, the marketer can justify investments in existing customers, can emphasize improvements in service quality over cost reduction and can focus on new ways to grow the business.

It makes sense to argue that an organization's ability to retain customers will be directly proportional to its understanding of why customers defect, and its ability to make appropriate changes in the future. Therefore, before discussing the issue of customer retention in greater detail, it is first appropriate to deal with the whys and hows of customer defection analysis. Hirschman argues that after experiencing a decline in quality, a customer (citizen or member) could opt to leave, complain or stay. Hirschman uses the terms 'exit', 'voice' and 'loyalty' to refer to these phenomena (Hirschman 1970). Using this (EVL) framework, Stewart (1994) has conducted research in the UK into customer's exit from retail banking. Understanding why customers leave (exit) can be an invaluable source of information for organizations and thus customer defection analysis is being increasingly used.

Customer defection analysis is about developing an understanding of the sources of failure (i.e. why do customers defect?). This information is invaluable to an organization in terms of preventing future defections. The importance of 'failure analysis' is highlighted if we consider why airlines spend millions of pounds trying to retrieve the flight recorder (Black Box) after a crash: The 'Black Box' holds the key to why the crash occurred. If the cause was instrument failure, then more will be spent on designing and servicing instruments in the future; if the cause was pilot error, then more training and scenario planning will be required. Thus, by understanding why something has happened, management are better able to prevent similar events in the future. The same principle applies to direct marketers. If a customer defects, a lot can be gained by analysing the reasons why this occurred. At the very least the customer should be asked why they no longer wish to do business with the organization. Where possible the organization should attempt to win these customers back (where it is profitable to do so). Information from individual customer defections can then be aggregated to identify if there are any trends in the reasons for defection. This may allow the organization to identify possible future defectors by looking at recent complaints, or highlighting customers who are spending less money or even spending less frequently than previously.

Defining Loyalty: Conceptual Issues

Some marketers have mistakenly assumed that satisfied customers will automatically be loyal, and therefore measures of customer satisfaction have been widely used as proxy measures for loyalty. However, the use of satisfaction (or attitude) in measuring loyalty poses certain problems for marketers. While it certainly makes sense to suggest that dissatisfied customers are unlikely to be loyal, it seems that the corollary – that satisfied customers will be loyal – is not true. Indeed, the link between a customer's words and actions in this case may only be tenuous; despite being satisfied with current offerings, customers may still defect. Research from the Ogilvy Loyalty Centre confirms that marketers incorrectly believe that a satisfied customer is a loyal customer. For example, 85 per cent of automative industry users report being satisfied but only 40 per cent repurchase, while for packaged goods, 66 per cent of people who identified a 'favourite brand' admitted to have bought 'another brand' most recently (McKenzie 1995). As a result, satisfaction measures have proved to be ineffective measures of loyalty (Reichheld 1988). In order to overcome this problem, loyalty is increasingly being measured by behaviour rather than attitude. Measures include share of wallet, purchase sequence, and probability of purchase. In this way, marketers can identify the RFM of individual customers.

However, behavioural measures have been also been criticized for only capturing static outcomes, and having no theoretical or conceptual basis. 'These definitions make no attempt to understand the factors underlying repeat purchase. High repeat purchase may reflect situational constraints, such as brands stocked by retailers, whereas low repeat purchases may simply indicate different usage situations, variety seeking, or lack of brand preference within a buying unit. The behavioural definitions, consequently, are insufficient to explain how and why brand loyalty is developed and/or modified (Dick and Basu 1994:100).

As a result of these deficiencies, Dick and Basu proposed a framework which conceptualizes loyalty as 'the relationship between the relative attitude toward an entity (brand/service/store/vendor) and patronage behaviour' (Dick and Basu 1994:100). This definition combines both approaches, and results in four categories of loyalty, each of which have managerial implications. These four categories of loyalty provide a far richer conceptualization of loyalty then previously existed (see Table 6.2). In order to understand the categories used, it is important to understand the dimensions on which these categories are based.

▶ *Relative attitude.* Relative attitude focuses not only on attitude to the entity, but also incorporates comparison to other organizations or brands. For example, a customer may have a favourable attitude toward First Direct, but may prefer to deal with a high street bank.

▶ *Patronage Behaviour.* Traditional retention measures, share of wallet, purchase sequence etc.

The four categories of loyalty are briefly explained below:

No Loyalty

There is an absence of loyalty where the consumer's relative attitude is low, and there is no evidence of purchase behaviour. For example, research carried out by Shell in the early 1990s suggested that 85 per cent of petrol buyers were not loyal to any brand or location (Dignam 1996). Motorists tended to stop for petrol whenever it was most convenient for them to do so. In this and similar cases, the best that management can do is attempt to generate spurious loyalty through such means as in-store promotions, loyalty clubs and special offers.

Category	No Loyalty	Spurious Loyalty	Latent Loyalty	Loyalty
Relative Attitude	Low relative attitude.	Low relative attitude.	High relative attitude.	High relative attitude.
Patronage Behaviour	Low repeat patronage behaviour.	High repeat patronage behaviour.	Low repeat patronage behaviour.	High repeat patronage behaviour.
Manifestation	Does not patronise the company, and does not wish to.	Patronises the company, but does not have a high relative attitude. This may be as a result of other factors, including location, convenience, lack of alternatives.	In this case, the customer wishes to patronise the organization, but perhaps is not able to do so — store location may be inconvenient, favourite brands not stocked etc.	The individual enjoys a high relative attitude, together with high repeat patronage behaviour.
Implications	Management may attempt to generate 'spurious loyalty'.	'Spurious loyalty' cannot be relied upon. The customer is clearly open to better offers.	Managerial efforts are best focused on removing the obstacles to patronage for the customer.	Loyalty must be continually reinforced, and the value offered must remain acceptable.

Table 6.2 Four Categories of Loyalty

(Source: Adapted from Dick and Basu 1994)

Spurious Loyalty

Spurious loyalty is very similar to the concept of inertia. That is, although behavioural data indicate that there is high repeat patronage, in reality the customer does not believe that the alternatives are highly differentiated. In such cases, repeat purchase may be based upon the availability of deals, special offers, convenience or the influence of other people. As a result, the consumer may only temporarily display such loyalty, and is likely to be very open to competing offers. The management objective in this case is to convert spurious loyalty into loyalty. This can be done by enhancing the customer's relative attitude by communicating specific advantages. Alternatively, where competing offers are generally undifferentiated, the manager can attempt to increase switching costs (effectively erecting a barrier to exit), that is, making it costly for a customer to switch between competing offers. One effective method of achieving this is through 'point accrual programmes' as used within many existing loyalty programmes. For example, petrol retailers have for a long time run point accrual programmes such as Tiger Tokens and Premier Points. These programmes aim to tie the customer into a particular supplier through the promise of future rewards. In this case, the points already accrued represent switching costs, because the customers lose the benefit of previous purchases if they switch suppliers. Given the importance of loyalty programmes to today's marketers, these will be looked at in greater detail later in this chapter.

Latent Loyalty

This suggests that a consumer has a high relative attitude toward the company or brand, but this is not evident in terms of purchase behaviour. This is probably as a result of situational influences – including inconvenient store locations, out-of-stock situations, or the influence of other people as in the case of restaurant patronage. Using the previous example, a motorist might have a preference for Shell, but it may be more convenient to purchase from BP, or his or her company may have a credit account at a Texaco station. In this case, despite a higher relative attitude for Shell, the motorist would exhibit low patronage behaviour. In the case of latent loyalty, managerial efforts are best focused upon removing the obstacles to patronage, for example by extending the branch network, or developing credit accounts with local businesses who provide company cars.

Loyalty

When true loyalty exists, the customer regularly buys and does so because of strong preferences (high relative attitude). As such, this is clearly the most preferred of the four categories. Where loyalty exists, managerial efforts are best aimed at continually strengthening relative attitudes, particularly as the customer may be the focus of aggressive marketing by competing organizations. This may involve maintaining a price advantage, and/or offering additional services which are of value to the customers. In the case of petrol retailing, these might include car wash, valeting or even oil-change facilities.

Managing Loyalty

Consumers have never had more choice. There are now a myriad similar products and services to choose from. Competition is intense, not just nationally but also globally. Additionally, population growth has slowed considerably, resulting in more and more companies chasing the same consumers in order to maintain market share. As a result, the task of managing loyalty has emerged as an important challenge within the present business environment (Dick and Basu 1994). Managing loyalty is impossible if the organization has not developed effective measures of loyalty. As Reichheld succinctly puts it – 'if you can't measure it, you can't manage it' (Reichheld 1988:15).

On a practical level, the organization must identify what measures of loyalty it will use. Using the earlier discussion, we caution against using either satisfaction measures or behavioural measures *on their own*. Rather, we suggest combining both measures to identify relative attitude and patronage behaviour. Equally important, however, is identifying the unit of measure, or the focus of loyalty. For example, if Rover were attempting to measure loyalty, would it be appropriate to measure loyalty to the company, or loyalty to individual brands (e.g. the Rover 200)?

Individual organizations will need to identify which is the correct definition for them to use, and then make every employee aware of this. It is important in any definition of loyalty to consider what the customers perceive as value and loyalty. For example, if customers trade up from a Rover 200 to a Rover 400, company figures might indicate defections from the Rover 200 series (when in fact, satisfaction with the 200, combined with changing needs and/or financial circumstances might be the cause of trading up within the Rover portfolio). Inappropriate definitions of loyalty in this case might have substantial implications for management activity.

Having defined the appropriate focus of loyalty within the organization (brand, company, etc.) and identified the measures which it will use, the organization should look first to its internal data. Most organizations routinely capture transaction data in the course of doing business. This data should be used to generate customer knowledge, which can be further utilized in strategy development and budgeting decisions. 'Customer knowledge includes insights into the drivers of customer behaviours as well as predictions of customers' future behaviours under different marketing scenarios' (Hansotia 1997:351). Although many organizations have the relevant data on their databases they are unclear as to what to do next. Having the right data is clearly important, but it is only a first step in creating customer knowledge. Converting data into customer knowledge and insights involves looking first at aggregate data on existing customers, and then analysing the data at the individual customer level. Aggregate company data will help the organization to identify how well (or badly) it is doing at serving existing customers and attracting new ones. Aggregate data can be used to:

▶ Analyze customer acquisitions and defections.

▶ Identify the average length of time customers remain with the organization.

▶ Estimate the average lifetime value of customers to the organization.

▶ Develop profiles of high lifetime value customers (i.e. customers who represent the best value to the organization).

This aggregate data should assist management in identifying objectives for acquisition and retention. 'Once retention measures have been quantified, it is finally possible to determine how much it is worth investing to increase loyalty and retention' (Reichheld 1988:16). It should also assist in identifying the type of prospects the organization wishes to attract and which existing customers should be the focus of retention strategies. Because direct marketers have access to individual level data, it would be a serious mistake to base all its models, predictions and strategies on aggregate data. Individual level data can be both behavioural and attitudinal.

Individual behavioural data is captured routinely in recording customer transactions with the organization. From this, the organization can identify the following:

▶ date of last purchase (recency);

▶ frequency of purchase in the past (frequency);

▶ the value of purchases (monetary value);

▶ lifetime value (calculated from the above);

▶ length of time with the organization;

▶ responsiveness to different types of offer.

As we identified earlier, behavioural data on its own may be insufficient to determine loyalty. As a result, it is useful for marketers to also collect information on customers' attitudes toward the organization and their levels of satisfaction with different elements of the offer. This often requires primary research, which may be *ad hoc* (i.e. a periodic survey of a sample of the customer base) or continuous (e.g BT continually interview all customers who have made a complaint, reported a fault or requested a service). As outlined in Chapter 5, customer surveys do not have to be lengthy, and they can be conducted in a variety of ways. The research methods used will be dependent on the company, their business, and the research questions they have set. 'Some leading service and information-intensive companies also conduct census surveys of new customers to understand their purchase motivations, product knowledge, level of sophistication, attitude toward risk, service expectations, etc. so that the company can anticipate their needs, exceed their expectations and truly delight them' (Hansotia 1997:353). Equally, a census survey of all defectors will facilitate understanding of why the organization is failing. 'If a company honestly invests in finding out why defections occur, defecting customers will tell the organization exactly where its value proposition is deficient. Because value is the key to loyalty, defections eventually lead back to that fundamental concern' (Reichheld 1988:20). This level of attitudinal information can make the difference between success and failure for many companies.

Marketing Techniques to Retain Customers

McCorkell (1997:241–7) identifies a number of retention devices, primarily pioneered by direct marketers, but increasingly being used by more mainstream organizations. Most devices attempt to make staying loyal the easy option for customers. These include:

▶ negative option;

▶ credit accounts;

▶ automatic payment;

▶ lease/rental;

▶ loyalty programmes.

Negative option marketing was pioneered by book and record clubs. Essentially, rather than requiring the customer to do something in order to remain loyal, negative option implies that doing nothing keeps the customer loyal. A simple example is a book club. The customer responds to press advertising (perhaps via a coupon) which offers four popular books at a significant discount. In order to purchase the books at this price, the customer is required to become a member of the book club. As a member, they are required to buy at least four books per year. Each quarter the customer is sent out a catalogue to make their order. If the customer does not respond with an order within the required period of time they are automatically sent the 'editor's choice' and invoiced for this. Thus, the negative option implies that even when customers do not place an order, they still make a purchase. The customer will generally have the right to cancel (after a stated minimum period) but cancellation of membership will generally be required in writing. However, this requires some effort on the part of the consumer, who through inertia continues to remain a customer.

Catalogue retailers have traditionally offered to deliver the goods ordered within a specific period of time. They also offer a full refund if the goods are returned within, for example three weeks. While many customers may wish to return the goods – this again requires effort on their part – repackaging, posting (and its associated costs) – and as a result, due to customer inertia, they retain the goods and pay in full. Therefore negative option agreements operate on the principle that customer inertia can be used in their favour. The 'do nothing' option keeps the customer, while the 'do something' option is the opt-out. Although very successful from the direct marketers point of view, negative option has attracted criticism in that it is not a very 'customer centred' approach to marketing. Also, customers who eventually 'do something' may be less inclined to enter similar agreements with other organizations. As a result, this method of retaining customers (although still quite prevalent) may be losing ground to more customer orientated methods. For example, a customer who wishes to return a product purchased from Next Directory simply has to telephone the company and arrange for the unwanted merchandise to be collected. Although this is an expensive service for Next Directory to operate, it considerably reduces the perceived risk for customers buying mail-order. The easy return service may be one of the reasons why Next Directory has achieved so much success.

Customers who have credit accounts tend to spend more and stay loyal to the organization offering the account. Many accounts offer customers the option of paying the balance in full each month, or simply paying a percentage of the amount outstanding (usually 5 per cent or £5 whichever is the smaller). Customers who pay the minimum amount each month are the best customers from the marketers' point of view. They remain loyal to the organization while they are making repayments, they pay interest (often quite high) on the outstanding balance, and they continue to make purchases, thereby maintaining a balance. Although credit options still retain these benefits, they are becoming less effective, primarily because of the number of organizations with whom a single customer will have credit. For example, it is not unusual for a customer to have an M&S account, a Debenhams account, a House of Fraser account (and possibly a number of others). Although the customer may continue to buy at each of these outlets, the share of customer which each achieves does not vary significantly. Thus, credit accounts are primarily an advantage when competitors do not offer them. This is an increasingly rare occurrence. Today, customers expect to have a credit option for most purchases, so it becomes a requirement of doing business, rather than a differential advantage.

Credit accounts are most effective when the customer pays by direct debit. Although direct debit is more expensive to operate for the organization, there is less likelihood of the customer paying their balance in full and closing the account. The minimum is paid each month via the direct debit, and therefore the 'do nothing' option is to maintain payments in this manner. Continuous authority mandates have a similar impact. For example, one of the authors pays for AA Relay annually by credit card. Each year notification arrives that the AA will debit the account by a specified amount. In this way, even if the cost of the service increases the AA does not have to get permission to take a higher amount. The option to cancel the agreement clearly exists, and the customer can look for alternative quotations. However, both of these require effort, and therefore without a strong reason to change, the customer remains a customer. Lease and rental agreements have a similar effect to credit accounts when retaining customers.

Loyalty programmes are another device used to retain customers. These are proving increasingly popular with organizations today, and therefore are deserving of greater attention.

Customer Loyalty Programmes

> **▲▲** *The Loyalty card is now one of the most successful marketing tools of the 90s. A descendant of the Tesco 'lick and stick' Green Shield stamps that offered rewards to loyal customers, it has transformed the marketing battle across a range of sectors.* **▼▼**
> (Dignam 1996:51)

Loyalty card marketing has grown as the technology has developed to allow detailed and extensive databases to be built. A whole range of organizations have introduced loyalty programmes in one form or other over the last five years, and consumers also appear to be interested in such programmes, with UK consumers in 1995 having on average 3.2 loyalty cards each (Reed 1995). Datamonitor estimates that at the present rate of launch, there will be 3.8 billion cards in operation by the year 2000 (Dignam 1996). On the surface, however, the card appears to be nothing more than Green Shield stamps without the glue. Despite criticisms, it has been argued that frequent buyer programmes are powerful relationship builders (Blattberg and Deighton 1991). This is because they generate information that can be used by retailers and manufacturer's to develop individually tailored marketing programmes.

Many loyalty programmes are now card-based. There are essentially three types of cards used in such programmes (Croft 1995b):

▶ magstrip (e.g. Tesco or Sainsbury cards);

▶ credit-card based (GM's card);

▶ smart-card based (Shell programme).

Loyalty programmes are used to both acquire and retain customers. In terms of retention, such programmes are seen to be a significant extension on traditional sales promotion discounting programmes (Uncles 1994), because these programmes not only provide customers with cheaper shopping, but also provide the sponsoring organization with a great deal of information about individual customers. This information can be used to target relevant offers via direct marketing mechanisms, either at the point of sale or later in-home. Loyalty programmes are developed for a variety of reasons including:

▶ to generate information;

▶ to reward loyal customers;

▶ to manipulate consumer behaviour;

▶ to increase switching costs.

To Generate Information

One of the advantages a loyalty programme can offer is that it provides information about the company's customers which, if used appropriately, result in highly specific targeting. In 1995 Tesco was reputed to have five million names on its database at a cost of £10 million, generating management information and names at only £2 each (Reed 1995). The information generated by a loyalty programme is much more precise than any other data which a supermarket might have. The programme will provide information on the recency, frequency and monetary (RFM) value of purchases. This information can also be linked with customer data from a variety of other sources (geodemographic; lifestyle; credit history), in order to build up a fairly accurate picture of someone's life. The next phase of these developments is emerging, in the use of 'smart' cards on which can be stored vast amounts of cardholder information, from age and date of birth to previous purchases and medical records (Shaw 1991; Reed 1994).

Smart Shell

Shell has developed one of the most technically sophisticated programmes in operation in the UK, and is believed to have invested almost £40 million on its smart Promotion. The programme is based on the use of a smart card, with each card having a computer chip capable of storing data on up to 500 transactions. This incorporates information about shopping patterns, spending habits, its holders and the outlets they use. The programme was launched in October 1994, and since then Shell is believed to have amassed a database of around four million customers. More recent reports suggest that one out of every six motorists now carry a Shell Smart Card. Points collected against purchases can be held on the card and redeemed against gifts, cinema tickets, air miles or donated to charity.

In 1995 Shell was only using 10 per cent of the card's capacity, and was still building the database. This is what techies call a 'dumb smart card', an under-achieving Einstein. Even in the early stages data were transferred to a central computer via electronic readers at each outlet. This could then be analysed geographically, by outlet, type of product, frequency of purchase, and rewards redeemed. This information could then be used for direct marketing purposes. In 1997 Shell announced a landmark development with news that a consortium of retailers, including Dixons, Currys, Victoria Wine, Vision Express, John Menzies, the RAC and Hilton Hotels was to join the scheme. If customers use the card for purchases in all of these outlets, the card promises to provide retailers with one of the most comprehensive pictures of customers' shopping habits and lifestyles. This is likely to result in even more effective targeting in the future.

(Source: Dignam 1996; Dye 1996; Hollinger and Taylor 1997; *Marketing* 1995a and b)

Reward Loyal Customers

Most programmes offer either a direct discount based on the amount of purchases, or allow customers to accumulate points which can be redeemed against a range of products. Both options aim to give a tangible reward to frequent shoppers. Other programmes offer more intangible rewards. For example, British Airways has segmented its customers according to the potential value of their business, and enrols them as members of a hierarchy of 'clubs'. Members of these clubs are offered a package of benefits and privileges related to their frequency of flying. Club membership is recognized at all points of contact with the customer, through booking to on-board service.

Manipulate Consumer Behaviour

With a sophisticated system, the retailer and/or manufacturer can build a detailed matrix of demographic and behavioural data for each of its customers. On this basis, individualized communications can be generated and incentives and coupons can be specifically tailored to individuals. These may be used to expose customers to products they have not tried, to encourage payment of premium prices, and to prevent switching to competing brands. Many loyalty programmes also aim to increase the amount spent by each customer. For example, the Tesco ClubCard is credited with encouraging members to spend as much as £3 more every time they visit the store than would normally have been the case (Dignam 1996).

Increase Switching Costs

Ultimately these programmes have the aim of increasing customer loyalty in order to retain a higher proportion of existing customers. They achieve this by developing higher relative attitudes through positively differentiating the offer from competitors, and/or enhancing value to the customer. Although financial rewards may represent value for some customers, these are most easily copied by competitors, as evidenced by the proliferation of similar programmes in the market-place. Thus the programmes which focus on using the information generated to truly understand their customers, and who then respond by continually enhancing value (often through intangible rewards) are likely to be most successful.

Other than the initial gathering of data, all of the other objectives are likely to take time to be realized. Loyalty programmes are also highly visible, so back-end failure can be particularly harmful (Hochman 1992). Entry costs are high, and pay-off is unlikely to occur until the second or third years. As such, loyalty programmes should be seen as a long-term investment, and not simply as the ultimate solution to customer retention – the direct marketing panacea of the 1990s. There are a number of limitations which must be acknowledged. Criticisms include (McKenzie 1995; Dye 1996):

▶ They are little more than sophisticated sales promotions.

▶ They overemphasize data collection.

▶ Loyalty is exhibited toward the programme, not toward the brand.

Sophisticated Sales Promotions

The comparison to sales promotion is as a result of the emphasis on discounts – although in this case the discount is on total spend over time, as opposed to offers on individual products for a short period. Loyalty programmes are seen as being more sophisticated than sales promotion because of their potential to target individuals and their dependence upon the database.

The Loyalty Paradox Report described many loyalty programmes as 'mechanical hard sell promotions' (Henley Centre:12). Although loyalty programmes have attracted a great deal of membership, many customers may simply be signing up because they patronize the organization anyway. In this sense, programmes have been criticized for subsidizing existing business. Furthermore, the emphasis on discounting may ultimately reduce profitability, and limit the ability to use price as a tactical weapon in the future (Dye 1996). Indeed, one commentator has suggested that using loyalty programmes as sophisticated sales promotions has been likened to the taking of drugs – 'constant discounting is the commercial equivalent of snorting cocaine – where an illusory short-term benefit leads to long-term disaster' (Bird 1991).

Despite the high numbers who have enrolled, customers are not entirely fooled by these programmes. For example, many consumers believe that the discounts offered are not large enough to warrant modifying their behaviour. Indeed, an NOP survey carried out in 1995 found that 43 per cent of non-cardholders thought the savings too small to merit joining the programme (NOP 1995). Many supermarket programmes offer one per cent discount on shopping over £10, and some participants in group discussions carried out by the authors were unhappy about the minimum expenditure required to be eligible for 'points' (Evans *et al.* 1997). This problem has been addressed by some retailers with lower purchase requirements for students and the elderly, although the one per cent discount still applies. Furthermore, despite statements about the ability of programmes to generate targeted offers, many consumers feel that the offers they receive are based more on what the retailer wants to 'shift' rather than being determined by their needs. This equally applies to in-store offers, where for example, Sainsbury's offer 'extra reward points' on certain products.

Sales promotions themselves have been criticised for encouraging promiscuity among customers, where customers shop for the best 'deal' rather than being loyal to any one brand. Loyalty programmes may also suffer from this problem, where one programme attempts to attract customers of a competing programme. For example, in 1995 the battle among UK retailers for market share manifested itself most strongly in loyalty programmes. Tesco was the first to introduce its Club Card, and was quickly followed by Sainsbury's. This sparked off a loyalty battle among the larger supermarkets. In late 1995 Tesco began to poach customers from other supermarkets with free turkeys and offers to redeem the accumulated points from other stores. It has been suggested however, that 'if these programmes are to go beyond sales promotions they need to offer more than a bigger turkey than the next programme' (Evans et al 1997).

Data Overload

The most important element in loyalty programmes is not data capture but the subsequent use of that data. Despite this, many programmes have emphasized the data gathering benefits, so much so that many programme organizers find themselves suffering data overload. Rather than using the data to improve service, target offers, or design new products, limitations of data processing systems have resulted in very basic uses of the information generated. For retail programmes, this is primarily manifested in untargeted money-off coupons. However, it is the ability to further utilize the information that will allow loyalty programmes to fulfil their initial promise.

Loyalty Toward the Programme, Not the Brand

'From a customer perspective, many loyalty programmes offer me-too benefits which may be nice to have (most people like to get something for nothing) but there are no guarantees of continued loyalty' (Uncles 1994). Too much emphasis on promoting the programme to consumers may result in a shift from loyalty to the company or brand toward loyalty toward the programme itself (McKenzie 1995). This suggests that rather than developing 'loyalty' to the company or brand (as defined earlier in the chapter), 'spurious loyalty' toward the programme itself is developed. An analogy can be drawn here to the fairly unquestioning loyalty of a dog (being loyal to the brand or company based on inherent brand properties) compared with the more cupboard love of cats (where loyalty is less pronounced and customers will switch brands if other 'offers' are seen to be more attractive) (Jones 1994). Failing to move beyond spurious (cat) loyalty, could result in the destruction of any form of meaningful loyalty over time. One suggestion here is not to judge programmes simply by the scale of participation, but rather to focus upon measuring the impact on brand loyalty (Fitzgerald 1994).

Today many organizations are being forced into running a loyalty programme simply because their competitors are offering them. However, as we stated, loyalty programmes represent a considerable investment and take at least two to three years to achieve any return on investment. That said, loyalty programmes are a very good way of developing a customer database, but this is only a first step in the process. Information must be carefully collected, and must then be used to provide added value for customers. Many existing programmes are data rich but information poor and as a result are little more than sophisticated sales promotions. Given the earlier categories of loyalty, it seems that most of these programmes can achieve little more than spurious loyalty. That said, if organizations use the data they have, loyalty programmes can achieve their potential and may engender real loyalty in the future.

It's Good To Talk

An Evolving Loyalty Programme

BT has now become well known for its – It's Good to Talk – advertising. In addition to its TV advertising, BT also makes use of promotional programmes designed to engender loyalty among its customer base, and to attract new customers. BT's programmes are not static, but are evolving based on feedback from customers and changes in the competitive marketplace.

BT initially offered customers Option 15. This was essentially a promotional programme which gave participants 10 per cent off calls for a quarterly fee. Next BT introduced Friends & Family which linked the discount programme with phone numbers which have personal relevance for customers. As a result, the programme was found to have high levels of emotional involvement. Initially based on five customer selected phone numbers (one of which could be international and one a mobile) BT later expanded Friends & Family to ten phone numbers. BT used their database to help customers, by identifying the ten numbers they most frequently phoned.

> In addition to Friends & Family, BT followed up on the original Option 15 programme, with Premier Line. This offered customers further discounts, the option to pay by telephone, and a point collection mechanism. Initially points could be collected for BT products (Talking Points) or for air miles. However, based on customer response to the air miles the Talking Points were discontinued.
>
> These programmes continue to be backed up with improvements in customer service and reductions on the cost of calls. The latter is epitomized in its 'The Cost of Calling Keeps on Falling' national advertising campaign.

When To Consider A Loyalty Programme

The previous section discussed some of the benefits and limitations of loyalty programmes. This suggests that organizations should very carefully consider developing their own programme. It also seems that loyalty programmes are not necessarily appropriate for every single organization. Hochman (1992) suggests that they are most effective for organizations who meet the following conditions:

1 Where the organization has a product that is purchased *frequently*, enabling the customer to work actively toward a level of reward.

2 Where the product *margin* enables the organization to support the programme.

3 Where the product is a *parity item*, that is where it is just as sensible and convenient for your customers to purchase a competitor's products.

4 Where the product has a history of *brand switching*.

5 Where the organization is in a position to *commit all the resources* – money plus marketing systems and service staff support – required to sustain the programme.

6 Where the company has a *service culture* in which concern about the customer is integral to the business.

7 Where the company has an aggressive *commitment to excellence*.

Conclusion

The future cash flow of a firm is generated by purchases from existing customers and purchases from new customers. 'Hence, if a firm makes sound investments in acquiring only the right customers and in developing existing customers, it should over time, continually enhance its value' (Hansotia 1997:351). This chapter has shown that both acquisition and retention are important for survival, and that marketers who focus only on the former are ignoring exciting opportunities and essential information. Although the customer battle in the 1990s may be raging in the area of customer retention, acquisition remains the lifeblood of all organizations. As a result, organizations must develop differentiated strategies to deal with existing customers and new prospects. This chapter outlined the basics of the customer acquisition process. It then discussed the importance of retaining customers, and outlined the elements of successful retention strategies. Given the proliferation of customer loyalty programmes within the UK at the present time, the objectives, problems and future direction of such programmes were discussed.

The lesson, from this chapter if there is one is that marketing alone cannot engender loyalty. As Frederick Reichheld (1988:15) said

> ❝ *marketing – acting alone – cannot create sustainable loyalty. Customers remain loyal, not because of promotions and marketing programmes, but because of the value they receive. Value is driven by a full array of features, such as product quality, service, sales support and availability.* ❞

The issue of 'value' will be dealt with in the next chapter because of its relevance to developing sustainable relationships with customers.

STUDY 1

The Thoughtful Supermarket Loyalty Scheme:

Tesco Harnesses the Power within the ClubCard Data Explosion.

Dateline: 1995. The launch of the original supermarket loyalty programme was met with a mixture of amazement, enthusiasm, criticism and disparagement; it sparked immediate factions of supporters and naysayers, all keenly awaiting the scheme's evolution or demise. That Tesco's ClubCard became an unqualified success and spawned a host of imitators was, however, not a surprise nor just a lucky chance for the Tesco team who had spent 18 months engaged in the exhaustive and unbelievably complex task of coaxing ClubCard from planning to launch. Two years on, ClubCard remains the best, most

thoughtful and most thorough of the supermarket loyalty schemes; it was a combination of careful planning, honest evaluation, and a hand-picked team of experts in the field which made the near-impossible appear effortless, and kept ClubCard at the cutting edge of marketing technology and customer service.

Nine months prior to launch, a 17-store trial of the card was well underway; Tesco and database marketing experts Dunn Humby Associates put their heads and their expertise together to ascertain whether the preliminary data could prove, in clear financial terms, that ClubCard was worthwhile. Straight data analysis was the name of the game at this stage, as customer transaction data was taken directly from the trial stores and manipulated to illustrate sales before the card and how subsequently, week by week, the card was affecting sales. The results were extraordinary.

'We were invited to present our findings directly to the Board of Tesco,' reports Simon Hay of Dunn Humby 'who were not prepared to just accept our findings at face

value; they grilled us, looking for a weak link in our conclusions. Amazed though they were, they finally believed how well we knew their customers — and we were away. I was impressed by the fact that Tesco were so open to a new way of looking at their business; they were receptive and interested, not frightened by the possibilities.' One possibility — now a near-apocryphal tale — would have seen Tesco actually buying up the world's supply of Chardonnay if one extremely popular trial card promotion had gone national! The Board came back with some more tough questions based on the original findings, and the Tesco/Dunn Humby team set to work on the near-Herculean task of preparing the national launch.

The proportions of the project that Tesco had set itself simply cannot be understated. The scheme was unprecedented; there was no industry model and no proven timeline to work from. The co-ordination of a nationwide technology and marketing effort was added to the logistical complexity of preparing each and every Tesco store

● ● ▶

to implement the scheme at the same moment on the same day, and training every member of staff to understand and promote the Card's benefits. Tesco's IT department tackled each store's ability to issue and swipe cards, plus the in-store system's capacity to pull the data from the card and channel the data to a central location. Here, at this headquarters, Dunn Humby were busily working out what data should be analysed, and preparing load routines of unheard-of speed and capacity for the enormous quantities of data that were anticipated; in a record nine weeks, Dunn Humby had tailored their generic systems to fit Tesco's requirements. Simultaneously, Tesco's marketing department was planning the logistics of printing seven million cards and promotional material whilst buying up the world's available supply of plastic and overnight becoming one of Royal Mail's biggest-ever customers!

The risks, the potential hitches, the timing, the technology – everything had to be perfect, and everyone was on the edge of their seat. Because of this, the entire project remained virtually speculative until the eleventh hour; it was only in late December that the final go-ahead came for February's launch. It was a phenomenal, top-secret and potentially disastrous project – despite 110 per cent effort from everyone involved, too much was out of Tesco's direct control for a successful launch to be assured. But on 10th February 1995, thorough planning and exhaustive research triumphed and Tesco ClubCard made a graceful – and earthshaking – debut.

ClubCard was instant dynamite – the uptake had been tremendous, but if the follow-through and support weren't in position the momentum could have ground to a halt. 'Our biggest job' confides Hay, 'came in those next three months, preparing for the first statements and vouchers to be posted in May. A personalized letter had to be accompanied by coupons and offers which were specifically tailored for the customer – would the coupon uptake show that our

analysis had been correct?' In fact, in an industry that normally counts 1—2 per cent coupon redemption as wholly respectable Tesco ClubCard's first batch of coupons notched up an unbelievable 30 per cent redemption; distributors and suppliers of these first coupons were scrambling to provide stock.

Since then, the coupons have gradually become even more targeted. After all, the main purpose of any loyalty scheme is simply to identify and also cultivate valuable customers, and treat them accordingly. The customer transaction data has given rise to some rather entertaining and telling anecdotes – the frequent marriage of prunes and Battenburg cake in the average OAP's shopping trolley, for example – but the real use of the data has been for 'segmentation' – finding out who Tesco's customers really are. At the initial card sign-up, customers gave only their name, address, and the ages of all the members of their household; however, this information combines with data from their card transactions – what each customer buys, when and where they buy it, how far they travel and how much they spend – to engender extraordinarily useful information that is far more than the sum of its parts.

The true purpose of a loyalty scheme being to identify and reward a company's most valuable customers, Tesco knew that no loyalty scheme on any scale could reasonably be considered without the use of database marketing, which is simply the application of technology to the dictum, 'know-your customer,' and allows the fast analysis of data for marketing purposes. In order to feel loyal to any organization, a customer must feel that all his needs and desires are not only satisfied, but intelligently predicted and understood. Before an organization can expect loyalty, then, it must inspire loyalty – by demonstrating that it cares about its customers. The data about each customer that the card scheme collects sets the stage for establishing a dialogue between organization and customer. And with skill

and expertise, loyalty does blossom, and bear fruit.

For months Tesco stood alone in the marketplace while competitors waited for ClubCard to come crashing down. Rumours and criticism were rife, but the company kept its head down and trusted that the results would speak for themselves. And in the meantime Tesco and Dunn Humby set about ensuring those results: the segmentation of customers enabled the development of a range of 'lifestyle' magazines which are sent with the coupons and targeted at a specific group of customers; shelf layout can be planned and adjusted to reflect the combinations of items that certain groups of customers buy; coupons can be virtually personalized as the spending characteristics of for example, young couples, vegetarians, young families and older families are seen as distinct and recognizable. And yet what sounds like 'Big Brother' is really just the logical modern, continuation of the old-fashioned village store where the proprietor knew his customers, their families, their spending habits and their tastes. And database marketing has turned the village store global.

Tesco's customers have 'voted with their ClubCards' – in fact, credit card insurance services even report their customers trying to register Tesco ClubCards! As Hay explains 'This is marvellous evidence of ClubCard members coming to see their Card as inherently valuable. However, it's not the card or the scheme that's important – it's being able to recognize customer value; the commitment is the company's not the customer's. After all, as 30 per cent coupon redemption clearly demonstrates, if you understand your customers, your company is more efficient, and wastes less money.' Recognizing how different people shop means that Metro stores may be stocked with some significantly different items than suburban stores; equally, particularly valuable customers may find certain favourite and unusual items stocked just for them. In the future, customers may

● ● ▶

© Craik Jones Watson Voelkel Ltd

Plate 5 Direct Marketing Creative – The 'Freelander' Mail Pack: Fast Active Relief from the Humdrum!

Durex is a trademark of the LI group

Plate 6 Marketing via the Internet: Example from Durex.

The Wallace & Gromit website receives 3000 visitors per week generating 5000 orders in 18 months (Clarke A, 1998, 'Taking business on line' *Marketing Direct*, July/August, p.43)

Plate 7 Marketing via the Internet: The Wallace and Gromit Case Study

Clever Capitalists
Corporate Careerists
Average Families
Smart Singles
Problem Families
Low Rise Pensioners
Christian Grey Families
Roman Families
Conservative Young Fams
Farmer Families

UTRECHT

BARCELONA

El Prat del Llobrega

Elite
Well To Do
Conspicuous Consumers
Blue Collar Metropolitans
Tourist Class
New Industrial Areas
Smokestack Classics
Breaking Away
Mixed Sector In Transition
Living Off The Land
Remote Rural, Rejected Reg
Unclassifed

© Experian Ltd

Plate 8 International Geodemographics: MOSAIC Profiles of Utrecht and Barcelona

find wheel-in gondolas that change during the day as, for example, peak time for young families ends and peak time for elderly couples begins. One local Tesco branch even extended the range of its courtesy bus when it found out how far its customers were travelling to shop there!

ClubCard's success can also be measured in its auxiliary programmes; the overwhelming demand for the initial Card made specialist ventures not only feasible but sensible. The 'Mother & Baby Club' was launched in January of this year communicating with new mothers and mothers-to-be at key stages of pregnancy and motherhood via mailings, magazines and vouchers. The Club communications are personalized and carefully selected for the appropriate stage of each baby's life, and the project expects a first full year membership of 300,000, expanding to 450,000. ClubCard Plus is a 'budget account', a high interest deposit for the grocery budget. This card simultaneously debits the account when the customer shops and records ClubCard 'points'; data analysis has shown that ClubCard Plus customers spend more than ClubCard customers – and ClubCard customers spend more than customers without either card. So, this information can in turn help Tesco target its financial services more effectively. Tesco's third-party alliance with B&Q has also been fruitful; a purchase at B&Q gives the customer ClubCard points for use at Tesco – an arrangement that provides for three-way satisfaction. Finally, an electronic service that provides for ordering by e-mail, 'Tesco Direct' is currently being tested.

It's not at all what Tesco's competitors expected, back in 1995. The ClubCard project was enormous, ambitious and unprecedented; the fact that it succeeded on such a grand scale can be attributed to good luck, shrewd timing, expert planning and very hard work. All these plus the cutting-edge management and application of data mean that Tesco ClubCard is still out in front of what is now a very crowded loyalty-scheme marketplace – and that Tesco customer satisfaction is second to none.

© Dunn Humby Associates

Review Questions

1 Identify the three different ways in which organizations can grow the business.

2 What do you understand by the following:

   (a) hot prospects;
   (b) marketing 'scrap heap';
   (c) multi-stage offer;
   (d) exit, voice and loyalty.

3 Why has customer retention become such an important managerial challenge?

4 What are the different categories of customer loyalty and what are the characteristics of each?

5 Identify five devices commonly used by direct marketers to retain customers.

6 Specify three objectives of a customer loyalty programme.

Discussion Questions

1 'Some companies seem hooked on steady doses of fresh customers to cover up regular losses of existing ones' (Rosenberg and Czepiel, 1984:46). Discuss the implications of this statement for business organizations in the 1990s.

2 What needs to be done by organizations in order to overcome criticisms that their loyalty programmes are nothing more than sophisticated sales promotions?

3 What impact has any of the retention devices used by organizations, had on *your* behaviour?

References

Ainslie, A. and Pitt, L. (1992) 'Customer Retention Analysis: An Application of Descriptive and Inferential Statistics in Database Marketing', *Journal of Direct Marketing*, 6(3), Summer, pp. 31–43.

Bird, D (1991) 'Targeting Consumer Loyalty' *Marketing*, June 27, p. 13.

Blattberg, R.C. and Deighton, J. (1991) 'Interactive Marketing: Exploiting the Age of Addressability', *Sloan Management Review*, Fall, p. 5.

Copulsky, J.R. and Wolf, M.J. (1991) 'Relationship Marketing: Positioning for the Future', *Journal of Business Strategy*, July/August, p. 18.

Cram, T. (1994) *The Power of Relationship Marketing – Keeping Customers for Life*, London: Pitman.

Croft, M. (1995a) 'The Bill to Change', *Marketing Week*, November 17, pp. 29–30.

Croft, M. (1995b) 'It's All in the Cards', *Marketing Week* (Customer Loyalty Supplement), March 24, pp. 4–6.

Dick, A.S. and Basu, K. (1994) 'Customer Loyalty: Toward an Integrated Framework', *Journal of the Academy of Marketing Science*, 22(2), pp. 99–113.

Dignam, C. (1996) 'Being Smart Is Not the Only Redeeming Feature', *Marketing Direct*, September, pp. 51–56.

Dye, P. (1996) 'Don't Let Them Get Away', *Marketing Direct*, December, pp. 65–71.

Evans, M., Patterson, M. O'Malley, L. and Mitchell, S. (1997) 'Consumer Reactions to Database-based Supermarket Loyalty Programmes', *The Journal of Database Marketing*, 4(4), pp. 307–20.

Fitzgerald, J. (1994) 'The Database Argument', *Marketing Week* (Loyalty Supplement), November 18, pp. 7–8.

Hansotia, B. J. (1997) 'Enhancing Firm Value through Prospect and Customer Lifecycle Management – Part 1', *The Journal of Database Marketing*, 4(4), pp. 350–60.

Henley Centre (1995) Loyalty Paradox.

Hirschman, A.O. (1970) *Exit, Voice and Loyalty: Responses to Decline in Firms, Organizations and States*, Cambridge, MA: Harvard University Press.

Hochman, K. (1992) 'Customer Loyalty Programs' in Nash, E.L (ed.) *The Direct Marketing Handbook*, 2nd edn, New York: McGraw-Hill, pp. 781–99.

Hollinger, P. and Taylor P. (1997) 'Shell launches Smart card revolution: Retailers join discount scheme for shoppers', *The Financial Times*, March, p. 12.

Jones, M. (1994) 'It's a Dog's Life Being at the Beck and Call of Marketers', *Marketing Business*, February, p. 48.

Levitt, T. (1983) 'After the Sale is Over' *Harvard Business Review*, 61, pp. 87–93.

Lix, T.S., Berger, P.D. and Magilozzi, T.L. (1995) 'New Customer Acquisition: Prospecting Models and Use of Commercially Available External Data', *Journal of Direct Marketing*, 9(4), pp. 8–18.

Marketing,(1995) 'Smart Cards on the table', February 9, p. 27.

Marketing, (1995) 'Bright Future for Smart Cards', April 6, pp. III-VI.

McCorkell, G. (1997) *Direct and Database Marketing*, London: Kogan Page.

McKenzie, S. (1995) 'Distinguishing Marks', *Marketing Week*, November 17, pp. 13–15.

Murphy, J.A. (1994) 'Retail Banking', in F. Buttle (ed.) *Relationship Marketing: Theory and Practice*, London: Paul Chapman Publishing Limited, pp. 74–90.

NOP (1995) 'NOP Poll Proves Shoppers are Taking Part in Loyalty Programmes', *Loyalty*, November, p. 7.

Reed, D. (1994) 'System Shakedown', *Marketing Week* (Loyalty Supplement), November 18, pp. 25–6.

Reed, D. (1995) 'Many Happy Returns', *Marketing Week*, November 17, pp. 7–11.

Reichheld, F.F. (19888) 'Loyalty and the Renaissance of Marketing', *Marketing Management*, 2(4), pp.10–21.

Reichheld, F.F. and Sasser, W.E. (1990) 'Zero Defects: Quality Comes to Service', *Harvard Business Review*, September/October, pp. 105–111.

Rosenberg, L.J. and Czepiel, J.A. (1984) 'A Marketing Approach for Customer Retention', *Journal of Consumer Marketing*, 1(Spring), pp.45–51.

Shaw, R. (1991) 'How the Smart Card is Changing Retailing', *Long Range Planning*, 24(1), pp. 111–14.

Stewart, K. (1994) 'Ex-customers: Did They Jump or Were They Pushed?' *Marketing: Unity in Diversity*, Proceedings of the Marketing Education Group Annual Conference, University of Ulster, p. 906.

Uncles, M. (1994) 'Do You or Your Customers Need a Loyalty Programme', *Journal of Targeting, Measurement and Analysis for Marketing*, 2(4), pp. 335–50.

Further Reading

Hochman, K. (1992) 'Customer Loyalty Programs' in Nash, E.L (ed.) *The Direct Marketing Handbook*, 2nd edn, New York: McGraw-Hill, pp. 781–99.

Dick, A.S. and Basu, K. (1994) 'Customer Loyalty: Toward an Integrated Framework', *Journal of the Academy of Marketing Science*, 22(2), pp. 99–113.

Dowling, G.R. and Uncles, M. (1997) 'Do Customer Loyalty Programs Really Work?', *Sloan Management Review*, Summer, pp. 71–82.

Relationship Marketing

This Chapter:

► Introduces The Student To The Concepts Of Relationship Marketing, In Particular How RM Differs From A Marketing Mix Strategy.

► Discusses The Role Of RM In Consumer Markets.

► Suggests A Framework For Implementation Of RM In Consumer Markets.

► Highlights The Role Of Direct Marketing In Relationship Building.

**C
H
A
P
T
E
R

7**

Relationship Marketing

Chinese Delivery Service

In a village in ancient China there was a young rice merchant, Ming Hua. He was one of six rice merchants in that village. He was sitting in his store waiting for customers, but the business was not good.

One day Ming Hua realized he had to think more about the villagers and their needs and desires, and not only distribute rice to those who came into his store. He understood that he had to provide the villagers with more value and not only with the same as the other merchants offered them. He decided to develop a record of his customers' eating habits and ordering periods and to start to deliver rice to them.

To begin with Ming Hua started to walk around the village and knock on the doors of his customers' houses asking how many members there were in the household, how many bowls of rice they cooked on any given day and how big the rice jar of the household was. Then he offered every customer free home delivery and to replenish the household rice jar at regular intervals.

For example, in one household of four persons, on average every person would consume two bowls of rice a day, and therefore the household would need eight bowls of rice every day for their meals. From his records Ming Hua could see that the rice jar of that particular household contained rice for 60 bowls or approximately one bag of rice, and that a full jar would last for 15 days. Consequently, he offered to deliver a bag of rice every 15 days to this house.

By establishing these records and developing these new services, Ming Hua managed to create more and deeper relationships with the villagers, first with his old customers, then with other villagers. Eventually he got more business to take care of and, therefore, had to employ more people: one person to keep records of customers, one to take care of bookkeeping, one to sell over the counter in the store, and two to take care of deliveries. Ming Hua spent his time visiting villagers and handling the contacts with his suppliers, a limited number of rice farmers whom he knew well. Meanwhile his business prospered.

(Source: Gronroos 1996)

Introduction

The opening *vignette* is a story told to Christian Gronroos by some visiting students from China. This story demonstrates how Ming Hua, the rice merchant, changes his role from a transaction orientated channel member to a value enhancing relationship manager. By doing this, he creates an advantage over his competitors who continue to pursue a traditional strategy. This ancient story illustrates that developing and maintaining relationships has always been important in doing business. However, since the 1950s, in particular, this approach to marketing has been de-emphasized as a result of developments in mass marketing approaches. However, recent changes in the business and marketing environment, together with advances in technology, has led to a renewed focus on relationships as the core of marketing strategy.

> ❝ *In the business environment and marketing situation that is emerging in more and more industries and an ever-growing number of markets, a relationship marketing strategy is becoming a necessity for survival.* ❞ (Gronroos 1996:13)

What is Relationship Marketing?

Relationship marketing (Berry 1983) is a term which is currently in vogue. Originally intended as an approach to service and industrial markets, it has recently begun to attract the attention of consumer goods marketers. This is primarily as a result of developments in direct and database technology, which not only allow individualized communications, but are also seen to facilitate the development of one-to-one interactive relationships with customers. Relationship marketing emphasizes customer retention through developing relationships. Indeed, sometimes the ideas of retention and relationship are used to mean the same thing. This is not accurate and this chapter will show how relationship marketing is much more than a customer retention strategy and yet, at the same time, contributes greatly to customer retention.

Relationship marketing is an approach which views marketing as 'relationships, networks, and interaction' (Gummesson 1987). This is in contrast to traditional views of marketing which see marketing as identifying, anticipating, and satisfying customers' needs and wants through the tools of the marketing mix (for an excellent review of these different perspectives see Gronroos 1994). The distinction between the mix management and relationship management views of marketing is fundamental to truly understanding and implementing relationship marketing. We will now briefly review the meaning of the terms, relationship, network and interaction.

Relationship

A relationship is different from a transaction in terms of the time frame involved, the existence of a past, and the expectation of a future. For example, in a relationship there is a history of previous transactions and the possibility of more transactions in the future. In traditional marketing (4Ps) every interaction between the customer and the organization is treated by the organization as though it were a one-off transaction. Traditionally, this was because the size of many consumer markets rendered it impossible for the organization to recognize existing customers, or to deal with them as individuals. As a result, mass communications techniques, sales promotion and price became important tools in attracting customers. Existing customers, ex-customers, potential customers and non-customers were all treated in the same way, and with the same message. This lack of recognition of individual customers resulted in a transactional view of marketing. In contrast, within a relational perspective, previous interactions (history) are acknowledged, and the message is changed not only for different types of prospect, but also in response to customers' actual behaviour.

Networks

Networks will not concern us greatly in this chapter. A network is made up of a number of different relationships involving customers, competitors, suppliers, distributors, advertising agencies and others. As a result of participating in a number of different relationships certain benefits accrue to the organization. For example, supplier relationships are seen to improve value or reduce costs through more efficient ordering systems, whereas relationships with distributors are expected to accommodate new product introductions. Collectively, the network of relationships in which the organization is involved will enhance its competitive position. That is, all of these relationships in some way contribute to adding value, reducing costs, increasing innovation, etc. As a result, this combination of relationships should ultimately help the organization to enhance its relationships with its own customers.

Interaction

Interaction refers to how relationships are developed. Within the mix management model it is argued that transactions are facilitated by the provision of an optimum marketing mix (i.e. the right product, in the right place, at the right time and at the right price). In contrast, in a relationship perspective, relationships develop as a result of interaction between the organization and the customer. Interaction can be person to person, or it can be through the organization's technology or other systems. Every interaction has an impact upon the customer's perception of the organization, and thus in every interaction there is a possibility that the relationship will deepen, or that the relationship will become weaker. Clearly, the organization wishes to deepen the relationship in order to gain a number of benefits. This view of marketing as interaction is fundamental to implementing a relationship approach (Gronroos 1997).

This conceptualization of marketing as relationships, networks and interaction has evolved over the last 20 years primarily within the context of services and industrial marketing. The motivation for developing this new approach resulted from the limited applicability of mass marketing techniques within these contexts. For example, industrial buyers (customers) needs are often diverse (heterogeneous) and some customers are more important to the firm than others. As a result, a standardized mix targeted to different segments is often inappropriate. Furthermore, relationships between firms often develop over time, and the relationship, rather than just the price can become an important factor in choosing suppliers. Marketing consultant Regis McKenna (1986:15) argues that personal relationships are often more lasting than product brand loyalties. 'Those relationships are more important than low prices, flashy promotions, or even advanced technology. Changes in the market can alter prices and technology, but close relationships can last a lifetime.' Similarly, in services markets the standardized 4P approach is limited because services have a number of unique characteristics (heterogeneity, intangibility, perishability and inseparability). Intangibility means that a service (unlike a product) cannot be touched, tasted, or otherwise evaluated *prior* to purchase. Heterogeneity refers to problems with standardising a service. In essence, the quality of a service may vary depending on who the service provider is, the time of day, etc. Perishability simply refers to the idea that a service cannot be stored. For example, when an aeroplane takes off, unfilled seats cannot be sold again for that particular trip. Finally, inseparability suggests that it is nearly impossible to separate the service from the provider in many cases.

An example will serve to highlight these issues and to understand how they have resulted in the move of services marketers toward a relational perspective. Consider a situation in which you wish to have your hair styled. First of all you cannot evaluate that hairstyle until after it has been cut (intangibility). You have an idea that some hair salons have a better reputation than others, and that even within a particular hair salon some stylists are likely to be better than others (heterogeneity). You choose a hair stylist and have your hair cut. It is difficult to imagine that you could get a good haircut from a bad stylist (inseparability). Also, it is unlikely that you would only evaluate the haircut itself. You would probably evaluate the whole 'experience' of having a haircut. Were the surroundings pleasant? Did the stylist engage in conversation? Did you want to have a conversation? Were you offered a coffee? Did you have to wait a long time? All these and perhaps a number of other issues will influence how you rate the service. Equally, you and a friend may not give the same stylist or salon the same rating.

Customers tend to evaluate a service on two general criteria. First, the *technical quality* refers to the quality of the service (the haircut, a meal, advice given by financial consultant), whereas *functional quality* refers to how the service was delivered (staff competence, staff friendliness, waiting time etc.) (Gummesson 1987). In practice it is often difficult to distinguish between the two. However, in today's competitive environment more and more attention is being paid to enhancing functional (also called relational) quality.

As a result of these characteristics, services marketers emphasize the importance of the interaction between the customer and service provider, and refer to the service encounter as a 'moment of truth'. That is, each encounter (interaction) can make or break the relationship, because each will influence the customer's evaluation of that service. In the earlier example it is clear that interactions can occur, not only with different personnel (the hair stylist, receptionist, junior), but also the customer may interact with the organization's technology or systems. For example, traditionally customers would have had no choice but to interact with a member of banking staff if they wished to withdraw or deposit funds. Nowadays, however, customers may choose to interact with staff or with technology. Indeed, more and more customers choose to interact with bank technology in the form of ATMs (Automated Teller Machines). Thus, the emphasis shifts from personnel to technology in terms of the primary means of interaction for many banking establishments.

The interaction is seen to influence the functional quality (how the service is delivered), whereas the service itself (e.g. hairstyle) is evaluated in terms of 'technical quality' (the quality of the service). When customers experience high technical *and* functional quality they are more inclined to return to the same provider. As a result, over time a 'relationship' develops between the customer and the firm. When such relationships exist they are seen to benefit the organization in terms of enhancing organizational effectiveness and efficiency.

What is an Exchange Relationship?

An exchange relationship is thought to be similar to an interpersonal relationship. Indeed the most common analogy used to describe exchange relationships is that of marriage (see for example Levitt 1983). The suggestion is that organizations should enter wedlock rather than one-night stands. In order for exchange relationships to develop a period of courtship is required where both parties learn to understand the other, and identify what pleases and does not please the other. Furthermore, the elements of exchange relationships and interpersonal relationships are seen to be similar. Indeed, 15 variables have been identified as key relationship success factors (for a thorough review of the elements of exchange relationships, see Wilson 1995). Of these factors, trust, commitment, co-operation and respect are often acknowledged to be the most important.

Focusing on trust and co-operation as elements of marketing lies in stark contrast to the adversarial view of marketing which currently exists. Customer satisfaction is viewed as highly important, as are relationships with the organization's other stakeholders and network partners. Based on this broader, co-operative understanding of exchange relationships, the following definition is offered:

> ❝ *Relationship marketing involves the identification, specification, initiation, maintenance and (where appropriate) dissolution of long-term relationships with key customers and other parties, through mutual exchange, fulfilment of promises and adherence to relationship norms in order to satisfy the objectives and enhance the experience of the parties concerned.* ❞ (O'Malley et al. 1997:542)

This definition incorporates the purpose, process, focus and key elements of the relational paradigm. The purpose of relationship marketing is to satisfy the objectives and enhance the experience of the parties involved; the focus is on key customers and other parties; the process involves the identification, specification, initiation, maintenance and dissolution of relationships; while the elements include mutual exchange, fulfilment of promise and adherence to relationship norms.

Given this definition of relationship marketing it is important to understand how (a) it differs from direct and database marketing, and (b) how direct and database marketing can be used to implement a relationship strategy in consumer markets.

Is Direct Marketing Relationship Marketing?

> ❝ *Because relationship marketing combines elements of other communications disciplines, a natural question arises: How is it different from direct marketing, general advertising, or sales promotions? In some ways, it is all these and more. What distinguishes relationship marketing is its purpose: to build a long-term connection between company and consumer.* ❞ (Copulsky and Wolf 1990:17)

A review of the popular press would seem to suggest that direct marketing, database marketing and relationship marketing are closely related, if not synonymous terms. However, it is unlikely that the majority of direct marketing today could be described as 'relational'. That is not to say that direct marketing is not important in relationship building, but only that direct marketing and relationship marketing are not the same thing. 'More often that not, database marketing is used interchangeably with relationship marketing. Database marketing is a necessary tool to implement relationship marketing, but it is not, in itself, relationship marketing'. (Shani and Chalasani 1992:46)

The motivation for direct marketing is to generate a customer response of one form or another. The motivation for relationship marketing is to build a mutually beneficial relationship with customers. Where it is used simply as a synonym for direct marketing, or for developing loyalty schemes, it becomes just another marketing tool (Gronroos 1991). Used as intended, it has the potential to transform marketing strategy.

Database marketing, simply put, involves the collection of information about past, current and potential customers to build a database to improve the marketing effort. This information is likely to include demographic profiles, consumer likes and dislikes, taste, purchasing behaviour and lifestyles as we have seen in Chapter 4. Relationship marketing is much more than this. It seeks to build a lasting bond with each customer. It centres around developing a continuous relationship with consumers across a family of related products and services. It is seen to encompass database marketing, advertising, public relations and direct marketing. In consumer markets relationship marketing is believed to be 'an integrated effort to identify, maintain, and build up a network with individual consumers and to continuously strengthen the network for the mutual benefit of both sides, through interactive, individualized and value-added contacts over a long period of time' (Shani and Chalasani 1992:44).

It is therefore important to be clear about the differences between database marketing and relationship marketing. Database marketing is information driven and centres on efficient reach of consumers that are likely to represent good targets for a particular offer. Relationship marketing, on the other hand, concentrates on differentiating individual customers from each other. Using the information stored in a database, the marketer individualizes a series of offers and messages to each member in the target market in order to build and maintain a mutually satisfying relationship between the organization and its customers.

The use of the database in database marketing is consistent with a transaction-orientated marketing strategy. That is, the marketer focuses all of his or her efforts on making the sale. Market share is improved through constantly increasing the number of customers that the firm has. This approach to marketing has prevailed since the 1950s and is reflected in the way in which marketing is implemented and taught. The underpinning tool of this managerial approach to marketing is the marketing mix, of product, price, place and promotion. Recently this approach to marketing has attracted avid criticism and thus relationship marketing has been suggested as an alternative approach (Gronroos 1994).

When is Relationship Marketing Appropriate?

Until recently, it was generally accepted that a relationship strategy is appropriate in service and industrial markets, whereas a transaction marketing strategy (mass marketing techniques) continue to be most appropriate in consumer (especially fast moving consumer goods) markets. This is depicted in Figure 7.1.

Traditional mass marketing techniques were considered most appropriate for consumer goods markets because many organizations,

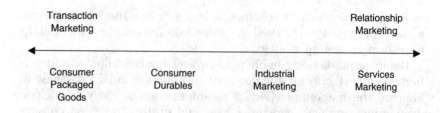

Figure 7.1 The Marketing Strategy Continuum

(Source: Gronroos 1994)

although aware that they had customers somewhere 'out there', did not really know who their customers were at all. As a result, companies marketed products to unknown individuals who comprised idealized market segments. Marketing occurred at arm's length, with many marketers never actually encountering a real customer. In such cases marketers rely on data from market research to develop strategy (Gronroos 1994). This is less effective that basing strategy on the actual behaviour and responses of customers.

Arm's length marketing frequently implies that the organization does not know who its customers are. The organization is likely to have a working description of its 'typical' customer, which tends to be an amalgam of the attributes of different customers. Since the organization does not actually know its customers, it must treat each one as if they were non-customers and attempt to persuade each prospect to try the product. Thus, the customer profile and the message are used as the basis of marketing communication strategy. Within this approach to marketing, emphasis is placed on maintaining or increasing market share. Consequently, customer acquisition is stressed within the organization to the exclusion of customer retention. As a result, existing customers of the organization often do not get the attention they deserve as valued patrons of the organization. As identified in Chapter 1, one consequence of this has been increasing market fragmentation and escalating consumer promiscuity. Together they have limited individual organizations' ability to retain valued customers and increase market share.

Marketers are now increasingly interested in turning individual transactions with anonymous masses of potential and existing customers into interactive relationships with well-defined customer groups. Thus, relationship building and management is one of the leading new approaches to marketing. 'The new marketing does not deal with consumers as a mass or as segments, but creates individual relationships, managing markets of one, addressing each in terms of its stage of development (Blattberg and Deighton 1991:5).' Thus, it is an approach that stresses the building of relationships rather than the production of products. As a result, it is now believed that 'every firm, regardless of its business, can benefit from a relational approach (Gronroos 1996:13).' This said, it is likely to be far easier in business-to-business and services marketing than in most consumer goods industries.

Industrial and business-to-business firms often have more to gain from interactive marketing because they typically have fewer customers. As such, their databases tend to be smaller and more manageable. The salesforce can gather relevant data from customers to develop profiles and the pay-out of database marketing is often higher because the value of a single transaction is much larger. In consumer markets, a relationship marketing strategy is seen to be appropriate for premium brands (Rolex watches), for products with high potential lifetime value (financial services), for product categories where a high volume is consumed over a short period of time (baby products) and in markets where there are restrictions placed on the media vehicles available to marketers (alcohol and tobacco) (Shani and Chalasani 1992).

Organizing for a Relationship Marketing Strategy

There are a number of important elements inherent in implementing a relationship marketing strategy. First and foremost, the organization must be able to make direct contact with its customers. In order to do this, it must clearly be able to identify them. Since a single individual within the organization cannot possibly remember all relevant details, it was not until recently that a relationship strategy became possible for organizations with a large number of customers. Indeed, if a database does not exist for firms with large numbers of customers, then 'customer contacts will be handled only partially in a relationship orientated manner (Gronroos 1996:11).' Thus, it is likely that a database will be required to store the necessary information. In such situations, 'customer databases invoke, in part, the bygone days of personalized customer relationships'(DeTienne and Thompson 1996:31). Detailed customer information should be used to track and monitor consumer purchasing and to respond appropriately to customers' requirements. Thus, it is almost a certainty that a database will be required to store the information necessary to pursue a relationship strategy. This translates into the following five points:

1 The organization must identify, build, and continuously update relevant information about current and potential customers on their database. The information required will vary depending on the organization and the type of products/services it offers. However, it is likely that the information held will include demographics, lifestyle data, purchase history and data relating to customer preferences, etc.

2 The organization must communicate with individual customers on a one-to-one basis. This requires utilizing the database to enhance dialogue with customers, and is likely to embrace different communication media including mail, telephone, personal contact, and electronic media.

3 The organization should monitor their relationship with each individual customer, through recording and evaluating their purchase behaviour over a specified period of time, and through

assessing their relative attitude. This will allow the organization to identify the extent to which it is satisfying the requirements of individual customers.

4 A relationship strategy requires a high level of customer service. Thus, it is necessary for the organization to develop a customer orientated service system. This implies that the organization should endeavour to provide high levels of service across all interactions with the customer (personnel, technology and/or systems). This signals to customers that they are important to the organization.

5 The final element of a truly relational strategy involves treating customers as individuals. This requires a detailed understanding of customers' needs and preferences (through the database), communication based upon personalized, differentiated messages, and ultimately the customization of product and/or service offerings to suit individual requirements where possible.

Customer Database and Relationship Marketing

The roots of a successful relationship marketing programme lie in understanding customers, their individual preferences, expectations and changing needs. As a result, the customer database is important because it allows the organization to retain key information on its customers. This is necessary if the firm is to truly respond to customers' individual requirements. Thus, it should not merely be seen as a mailing list, but should be viewed as a record of every response between customer and organization.

Developing a database, and using it for customer acquisition and retention have already been addressed in earlier chapters. For a relationship strategy the information contained on the database is particularly important. For example, if the firm is to be in a position to cater to a customer's individual needs, it is important that the database contains information relating to benefits sought, needs, preferences, purchase occasions, etc. This may seem self-evident but many firms who espouse a relationship perspective do not hold this kind of data. For example, a recent survey of financial services organizations found that 80 per cent of respondents claimed to have information on source of business, products held by individual customers, and the duration of the relationship. However, less than 30 per cent had information on customers' needs and preferences (Abram Hawkes 1995). This suggests that databases are designed to suit organizational requirements, not customer requirements. That is, many organizations only see their data in terms of relating to transactions (e.g. most recent order, bank account balance, etc.), and not in terms of describing some aspects of the lives of real people. In reality, therefore it is questionable how committed such firms are (or can be) to a relationship-building strategy.

Customers' needs, preferences, domestic and financial situations can clearly change over time. It is therefore important to update and amend data held on the database to reflect the dynamic nature of customer-related information. It should be monitored and updated periodically, preferably with information provided directly by the customer. For example, two years after establishing its database of 4.7 million customer names, Heinz recognized the need to update this information. Therefore each customer on the database was asked to complete a detailed questionnaire. Because of the length of the questionnaire, customers were offered an incentive to reward them for the time and trouble involved. In addition to maintaining data on customers, the database should also be able to retain information on all the interactions which occur between an organization and its customers. Such a comprehensive approach to collecting and holding customer information is the first step in developing a relationship approach. The information held on the database should allow the organization to do the following:

▶ Identify whether the products and services it offers fit well with the needs and preferences of individual customers.

▶ Identify what products and services it offers, which are not currently used by the customer, but which might fit his/her requirements better than the products/services already being used.

▶ Identify the recency, frequency, and value of purchases.

▶ Identify individual customer responsiveness to mailings, offers, etc.

▶ Identify lapses which might suggest a defection, or which identify the possibility of a future defection.

▶ Identify any complaints, suggestions or information required by the customer.

▶ Monitor the organization's responsiveness to customer initiated interaction.

The organization should actively use this kind of information to enhance customer relationships. That is, the organization must learn from the data it holds in terms of responding to the needs of individual customers. Thus, in markets where a large number of customers exist, the database must be viewed as a *key learning tool* for the organization as a whole (Pearson 1994). 'The customer database is an opportunity for organizations to mechanize the process of learning about customers' (DeTienne and Thompson 1996).

In learning relationships, individual customers teach the company more and more about their preferences and needs, giving the company an immense competitive advantage. The more customers teach the company, the better it becomes at providing exactly what they want and the more difficult it will become for a competitor to entice them away. Even if a competitor were to build the exact same capabilities, a customer already involved in a learning relationship with the company would have to spend an inordinate amount of time and energy teaching the competitor what the company already knows. Because of this major competitive advantage, a company that can cultivate learning relationships with its customers should be able to retain their business indefinitely. Thus, organizational response to customers can (and should) refer to previous communication; the organization can learn which types of offering the customer is (and is not) interested in and can adapt communications to reflect this information. Indeed, even the offering itself (product/service) can be adapted to suit customers' requirements.

In order to develop a relationship with customers, it is necessary to understand them. This has led some companies to collect more information than they are likely to need. For example, the questionnaire used by Heinz to update its customer database involved 18 sections which included a request for information on frequency of purchase, age, number of children living at home, and ownership of cable and satellite television. Organizations will have to identify very carefully what information they need, how that information will be used, in order to avoid problems of data overload as discussed in Chapter 6. Many commentators suggest that where incentives are given, consumers are likely to be happy to provide information. That said, the collection of appropriate information on a database is only the first step in building a relationship strategy. Using that information to create dialogue between the organization and the customer is the next integral element of a relationship marketing strategy. Thus, communication strategies need to be carefully designed in order to encourage interaction, enhance mutual understanding and facilitate relationship building.

Interactive Communications

All communications should be well designed and relevant to the recipient if they are to be effective. Communications are particularly important in a relationship strategy because the objective is to build on-going interactive relationships with customers over time. As a result all communication from the company must be relevant. For each individual communication, the organization must identify if the purpose is to inform, persuade or educate. This includes monthly statements, bills and all other customer correspondence. Second, communications have to be truly interactive and should aim to establish a shared understanding. The organization can communicate through traditional media, personal contact, direct mail and/or telephone. Indeed, all of these different approaches should be integrated in order to promote a coherent image and message.

Interaction implies that the organizational responses should be based on the actual behaviour or preferences of customers. It should not deal with the requirements of the 'average' customer (as would be the case in a segmentation strategy). Ultimately, relationship marketing aims to deal with customers on a truly individual basis.

Interaction also occurs when the firm answers a phone call, or when service engineers meet a customer. All of these are important in contributing to the customer's perception of the organization.

Technology can facilitate interactive communication. While different people may interact with the customer, the database allows each of them access to relevant data in order to effectively deal with the customer. The database can also be used to customize written communication. Recent technology is facilitating the development of computer generated catalogues. These catalogues can be completely designed to meet the preferences of each individual customer.

Dialogue is not just a two-way or parallel monologue, but involves interaction. When an organization responds to its customer and makes reference to previous correspondence or behaviour, it is holding a dialogue. That is, it is having a conversation. Facilitating dialogue is a simple concept to understand, but in reality is difficult to execute (Blattberg and Deighton 1991). For example, it is not the approach which traditional marketers are familiar with and they may therefore need to develop additional skills in order to do it well. One area which is often ignored is to make it easy for customers to initiate conversations with the organization, to make the organization more accessible to the consumer. That is, rather than the organization trying to get close to the customer, it aims to allow the customer to get close to it. The increase in provision and use of free-phone numbers in recent years is evidence of the growing emphasis on customer service.

There are many different communication techniques that are used to build individual customer relationships. For example, conversation can be initiated through direct mail, telephone, and/or personal contacts. These are likely to be supplemented by traditional techniques such as advertising, publicity, public relations and sales promotion. In particular, traditional approaches are appropriate in creating and presenting a consistent corporate or brand image.

Monitoring the Exchange Relationship

There is some dispute as to whether it is important to identify customer lifetime value in order to implement a relationship marketing strategy. Direct marketers would tend to argue that it is important to identify your best customers and then to develop a relationship with them. In contrast, relationship marketing would suggest that all customers should have an equal opportunity to be relationship customers and, as such, all should be dealt with in a professional manner. However, not all customers will wish to be relationship customers, something which is important for the organization to accept. Thus, opportunities for relationship building exist only with those customers who, for one reason or another, wish to be relationship customers. There is little concrete evidence on why customers may wish to participate in exchange relationships. While studies vary, it is often considered to be a factor of reduced risk and/or simplified decision making (Sheth and Parvatiyar 1995). That is, when the customer is satisfied with a particular provider, they may be open to developing an exchange relationship.

In a customer retention strategy, the purpose of tracking and monitoring customer behaviour is primarily to identify opportunities for up-selling or cross-selling. In contrast, in a relationship strategy, the database is used primarily to monitor customer satisfaction and to facilitate the development of an understanding of customers. This is because, in a relationship strategy, the company aspires to facilitating a mutually satisfying exchange. Thus, the company aims to give customers exactly what they want. As a result, there is a continuous feedback loop in a relationship marketing strategy, which makes it a learning system as well as a selling system (Pearson 1994). This initially requires careful analysis of the database. Furthermore, the organization must use technology to become two things: a mass customizer and a one-to-one marketer.

Developing a Customer-Orientated Service Strategy

The most important element in a customer-orientated service strategy is that it is the customer's perceptions of quality that is important, and not the organization's perception of service quality. The definition which is gaining acceptance is that quality equals customer-perceived quality, or 'quality' is in the eye of the beholder (Gummesson 1987). This is a market-orientated approach to quality. As outlined earlier, the two important elements of quality are technical quality (the service/ product itself) and the functional quality (quality of the interaction). In order to provide high levels of customer service, the organization needs to fully understand customer needs. This implies a need to utilize customer data in designing customer service. According to Berry and Parasuraman (1991) there are five key dimensions that influence customers' evaluation of a service:

1 *Reliability*. Reliability refers to the ability of the company to perform the service dependably and accurately. Thus, the company is expected to be able to keep any promises it makes.

2 *Responsiveness*. This indicates a willingness to help customers, to provide prompt service, to respond to their problems. The time frame is particularly important here.

3 *Assurance*. Assurance refers to the knowledge and courtesy of staff. When staff have the required knowledge and deal with customers in an acceptable manner, this invariably earns customers' trust and confidence.

4 *Empathy*. This exists when customers feel that their situation is understood, and that they are getting the level of attention which they deserve.

5 *Tangibles*. This refers to the physical facilities, equipment, personnel and communication materials the company uses.

Tangibles are very important within the context of direct marketing. 'Tangibles' could relate to the length of time a customer is waiting to deal with a member of staff in the customer service department when they phone up (equipment and personnel) and to the quality of the communication material they receive. For example, when a customer gets a letter from an organization and their name is spelled incorrectly, the result could be a simple case of annoyance, or it could reflect quite badly on the company, in that the customer believes if the organization can get something as simple as this wrong, what else could be wrong? (O'Malley *et al.* 1997). Of equal importance are customers' perceptions of the reliability, responsiveness, assurance and empathy of staff. These are issues which can be addressed very effectively in training and which are very important to developing a customer service strategy.

As outlined earlier interactions can occur via people, technology or systems, and each of these interactions will contribute to the customers' evaluation of quality (Gummesson 1987). Thus, there is a need to integrate all aspects of the company's strategy, structure and systems which are likely to influence the customers' experience with and evaluation of the organization.

This discussion of service quality applies equally to products and service organizations, because in today's marketplace, even products offer a high service component to the customer. It is also important to remember that the customer evaluates each interaction with the organization and thus each can influence their perceptions of quality, or indeed lack of quality. These interactions include marketing communications, and in particular direct mail and telephone.

Dynamic companies try to maximize the value they offer to customers through the skills of their staff, the effectiveness of their supporting technology and through the way they use the information they have on customers.

People

The attitude, commitment and performance of employees is one of the key aspects of successfully implementing a relationship strategy. Ultimately, what must be remembered is that 'relationships are individual and they should be personal. People buy from people (Pearson 1994:34).' Everyone in the organization can impact upon a customer's perception of product and service quality. It is the people in a company who are best placed to communicate the company's values to customers. Therefore, 'ultimately, it is people who develop and achieve an RM strategy.' (Murphy 1996:84). This suggests, that all staff who interact with the customer (in any way) should be trained to provide a high level of service. Many of these personnel will not be marketing people, but may be telephonists, engineers, credit controllers, etc. The impact of such personnel is often far greater than the impact of marketing personnel, and therefore Gummesson (1987) coined the term 'part-time marketers' in recognition of their importance. 'For employees acting as part-time marketers it is not enough to smile, but rather to be fair and to take responsibility for their actions.' (Holmlund and Knock 1996:292).

This highlights the importance of internal marketing in terms of training, motivating, and recruiting appropriate staff. For example, First Direct select banking representatives on the basis of their telephone manner and customer empathy. Each of these employees are then given six weeks' intensive training in order to deal with customers effectively. Clearly this kind of investment in people is needed in order to build lasting relationships with customers (Gronroos 1996).

Technology

Technology also has a role in the building of relationships. For example, the fax machine helped build stronger marketing relationships between lunch-time customers and deli-shops in Manhattan (Kochak 1989). Using fax technology, customers no longer needed to wait on hold on the phone to place their lunch time orders; a simple faxed request took care of it. Since employees spent less time taking orders on the phone, they could serve customers more quickly. This was particularly important for lunch-time requests. The Internet is also having a profound effect on the ability of organizations to build exchange relationships with consumers. For example, in 1996 Levi Strauss & Co. launched its own web site as a means of communicating with its customers (15 to 24-year-old men). The company believe that this type of communications medium has the ability to enhance brand image. The Internet can also be used to collect information on customers. This information will eventually be used to improve the organization's offering to individual customers.

Knowledge

Knowledge is also important in effectively implementing relationship marketing. While the acquisition of information is important, the emphasis should be placed on how knowledge will be used. For example, information which results in added value for the customer is particularly important in a relational perspective. This is because relationships are enhanced when the organization or the customer can add value. Adding value includes the provision of additional services which would be difficult or expensive for customers to provide themselves. The provision of such value forges a bond between the customer and the organization. Thus, the firm must identify extras that are valued by customers, not easily copied by competitors and which are financially and operationally feasible to offer. This again reiterates the importance of using the database to learn about the requirements of individual customers. Another approach to adding value is to customize the service to the unique needs of the particular customer. This suggests that the organization can utilize the database to enhance exchange relationships by (a) adding value for the customer, or (b) customizing the relationship.

This discussion might suggest that high service quality is all that is required to implement relationship marketing. This is not the case.

Service quality is a necessary, but not sufficient condition for relationship quality. This suggests that a high-quality service in itself will not automatically lead to a good relationship, but that it is an important component of a good relationship. As outlined earlier, a relationship strategy is also dependent on the availability of up-to-date, accurate information on customers' individual requirements and an emphasis on interactive communications. The fourth element is that the service should become increasingly personalized or customized. This is an important aspect of a relationship strategy and is based on the organization's ability to learn from customer interaction, and its flexibility and desire to accommodate individual customers. Indeed, it is the flexibility and desire to accommodate customers which truly distinguishes relationship marketing from other strategies.

In a relationship marketing strategy, therefore, the organization should know the names of each and every one of its customers. These should be recognized as individuals, and, where possible, their individual requirements should be catered to. Customers are not just statistics. They are not nameless entities. Recognition of customers as *customers* rather than units is one element of the change in perception required by managers in relationship strategies. When customers are recognized as individuals, they are more likely to believe that they have a personal relationship with the organization. For example, American Airlines gives its flight crew a list of every platinum and gold customer on the plane, along with their seat numbers. In such cases, they have no reason to look elsewhere for better deals and the relationship itself becomes a good reason for staying with the organization.

The strength of relationship marketing is that a market segment is an individual. There is therefore potential, to adapt not only the message, but to customize the product or service to suit individual customers' requirements. Personalized service recognizes the importance of treating each customer as an individual, and in a totally customized fashion (Vavra 1992). Customized service provision facilitates the building of bonds between customers and the organization (Christopher *et al.* 1991). This further enhances the building of long-term relationships. Personalising the service is necessary in order to maintain the relationship.

Implementing Relationship Marketing

Organizations need to harness the people, technology, knowledge and processes they use in order to enhance the customers' experience. This involves investing in two strategic systems, a customer support system and a customer contact system. 'The customer support system and customer contact system are the hardware which support the management of relationships with customers.' (Pearson 1994). Given the importance of such systems in the implementation of relationship marketing, these two elements will now be discussed in greater detail.

Customer-Support System

We have already talked much about the need for organizations to develop a customer database. This is an integral part of a customer support system, which, when used properly, allows the organization to begin to know its customers and to understand their requirements. Ultimately, the database should be used to facilitate customization, and to enhance communications with customers. 'A well-prepared, updated, easily retrievable and easy-to-read customer information file is needed in such cases to make it possible for the employee to pursue a relationship orientated strategy' (Gronroos 1996:11). Basically, the customer database allows the organization access to information on customers. What is required in a customer-support system is a facility which allows the customer access to information on the organization.

The ability to help customers is enhanced by supportive expertise. Thus, a second integral element of a customer support system, is a database which holds information on the company, its products, its suppliers and distributors. This should be available to all staff who deal directly with customers, whether in person, or through non-personal means (phone, e-mail, written communications). This will allow the organization to be responsive to customer queries, provide additional information where necessary and identify potential problem areas such as delivery times, stock outs, price increases, etc. In 1997 the Bank of Ireland implemented a relationship manager system. Essentially, certain staff are trained as relationship managers, and these people have sufficient knowledge of all of the bank's products and services that they can advise customers on the best products or services to suit their needs. Thus the focus moves from simply making the sale to solving customers' problems. This is one sure way to retain customers in the long-term. Similarly, First Direct attribute some of their success to developing systems and technology which enable the company to provide service quality and deliver the information necessary to manage the business better than the competition. This description closely resembles the idea of a 'customer delivery system'.

Customer-Contact System

The customer contact system ensures that the organization is accessible to the customer and not just the other way around. It is based upon telephone response systems, automated call distribution and electronic media (Pearson 1994). Customers need to have access to the organization for a number of reasons. For example, it is likely that for some customers either minor or serious problems may occur after purchase. The company should be willing to hear about and deal with these. It should actively encourage customers to initiate contact whenever the need arises – to inform the organization of problems, to request information, to place an order, or even to comment on positive issues. Therefore, a channel of communication must be provided which allows an easy dialogue to take place. Many organizations provide inbound telephone lines. Some of these numbers are free, which suggests that the organization is openly available to customers. Today, many organizations also provide e-mail addresses, which appeal to a large number of consumers.

Customer-contact systems should be staffed by trained personnel, who are in a position to deal with customer problems themselves (or at least know who the customer should deal with). In cases where customer problems are likely to take some time to sort out, commitment to the customer would suggest that the company, and not the customer, should bear the cost. Especially when that problem initiates with the organization's products, services, communication material etc. Relationship marketing therefore involves a continuous feedback loop from the customer to the company and the company to the customer (Pearson 1994). Over time, and through interaction, the organization learns to improve the amount of value inherent in its offering to its customers.

Mass Customization

> ❧ Given markets close to saturation and consumers who now regard very wide choice, low cost, high quality and fast delivery as the norm, what could possibly add more value and continue to stimulate demand? Answer: the widest variety of all – to personalize the product for each customer. ❧ (Westbrook and Williamson 1993:40)

In traditional marketing the customer is often not completely satisfied. That is, there is a difference between what each customer really wants and what the company is offering. This has been called a customer sacrifice gap (Gilmore and Pine 1997). This is the difference between a company's offering and what each customer truly desires. Increasingly, it is being recognized that it is possible (and profitable) to customize products/services to the needs of individual customers. Indeed, this is seen as a major opportunity to add value to the offering, and thus enhance the relationship between the organization and its customers.

For mass customization to work, the company needs to be really tuned into its customers' requirements. Allied to this, it needs to have a responsive and flexible production system. The company must decide in association with its customers whether a wide choice or a customized production system is required. The decision should incorporate the extent to which value can be added, the costs involved, and the production and technological developments required. There are four different types of customization (Gilmore and Pine 1997):

1 *Collaborative customization* is closest to what is often referred to as mass marketing. It refers to situations where the organization and the customer work closely together in order to design the product.

Collaborative customization thus requires interaction, and results in a truly individualized product or service. This type of customization is now possible with the assistance of technology in product categories such as clothing.

2 *Adaptive customization* is where the product or service (offering) is standard, but can be altered or adapted by the customer to suit his/her requirements. For example, a lighting company.

3 *Cosmetic customization* is simply where the same product is presented differently to different customers. The customization of the presentation offers value in this case.

4 *Transparent customization* is one of the hallmarks of the learning organization (referred to earlier). Transparent customization involves learning about individual customers' preferences through interaction, and using this information to customize the offering over time (e.g. high-class hotels).

Mass customization is a relatively new concept. It is the merging of mass production and individual marketing and as such, holds much promise for relationship marketing. Indeed, many would see it as a natural progression toward more mutually satisfying exchange relationships. However, there are a number of other issues which must be considered in terms of fulfilling the potential offered by relationship marketing.

Other Issues to Consider in Implementing a Relationship Marketing Strategy

A number of authors have indicated concern at the speed with which consumer goods marketers have embraced relationship marketing. There are a number of specific concerns. First, the extent to which consumers actually want relationships with organizations is still unknown (for a thorough review see Barnes 1994 and 1995). Secondly, the emphasis on information acquisition has resulted in consumer privacy concerns being exacerbated (Chapter 12). Such concerns reduce the utility of direct and database marketing in relationship building, because they reduce the opportunity for trust and commitment to develop (O'Malley *et al.* 1997). The literature suggests that an atmosphere conducive to trust must exist. This involves putting the interests of the customer *before* the interests of the company. It also requires that the people, technology and systems of the company are all orchestrated to engender trust. Finally, it should be recognized that any process which damages the relationship with the customer is not worth the cost. Organizations interested in pursuing a relationship strategy must thus evaluate their people, technology and systems, not only in terms of cost (as is traditional) but also in terms of the impact it has upon all of its customers.

In order to truly engender trust an organization must (Jackson 1994):

▶ *Be Dependable*. Set realistic expectations for customers. In particular, do not make promises that the company cannot deliver. Make sure that deeds match words.

▶ *Be Honest*. Honesty is important. Do not overstate the benefits of the product or service. Do not tell lies about what it can or cannot do. Be open about both the advantages and disadvantages of the product or service over those of competitors.

▶ *Be Competent*. It is insufficient to be honest and dependable, if the company is not competent. All staff who deal with the customer should have the required knowledge and communication skills. Competence also means being available to the customer.

▶ *Be Customer Orientated*. This implies that the company should not only be interested in getting the sale, but should consider the customer and the relationship as being more important.

▶ *Establish Rapport*. Staff should be friendly, polite and courteous. The company should listen to its customers.

In order to establish trust in the current business environment, organizations will need to change their behaviour in terms of how they pursue and initiate customer relationships. One of the problems, as identified at the beginning of this chapter, is that the terms direct marketing, database marketing and relationship marketing are often used interchangeably. Although, we identified the differences between these terms, it seems than many organizations are still missing the fundamental point:

> 🕮 *In particular, rather than viewing the database as simply an enabling technology, far too many firms have focused their energies on database building rather than relationship building.* 🕿
> (O'Malley *et al.* 1997:553)

Organizations need to recognize that a database is an essential tool in assisting relationship building in consumer markets. A relationship marketing strategy involves a greater emphasis on engendering trust, demonstrating respect for consumers, engaging in dialogue and ultimately enhancing the value offered to each individual customer. As a result, marketers must be careful in how they go about initiating and managing customer relationships. Relationship marketing is not just an add-on to the organization's current strategy. It is fundamentally different from mass marketing approaches and requires a tangible investment in people, technology, systems and customers. Although substantial, such investment should improve marketing effectiveness and efficiency and, as a result, enhance profitability.

Implications of a Relationship Marketing Strategy

'Marketing that builds customer relationships can be treated as a long-term investment with a high rate of return.' (Pearson 1994:38). For many organizations, relationship marketing offers the possibility of creating a stable customer base. This is particularly important in today's dynamic and competitive environment. In particular, when implemented appropriately, relationship marketing offers the possibility of improving both the efficiency and the effectiveness of marketing strategy (Sheth and Parvatiyar 1995).

Marketing Efficiency

If the organization knows who its customers are, where they live, what they like, etc. then clearly there is less need for a traditional pull strategy (i.e. less emphasis on mass advertising to pull the products through the marketing channel). There is less need to create latent customer demand because it is possible to produce products as and when customers require them (resulting in less stock and as a result less money tied up in stock) and in the variations required by customers (where the offering is customized). Because the organization doesn't need to guess what customers might want in the future (strategy based on predictive market research) only products which are required are produced. Thus less stock is held and marketing generally becomes more efficient. Within this approach the emphasis shifts from profitability as a result of economies of scale to profitability from economies of scope (Blattberg and Deighton 1991). That is, as the firm gets to know each customer well, there are greater opportunities to get involved in new product lines etc. (largely without risk). For example, Marks & Spencer used its customer database to introduce its financial services products. Similarly, Virgin has moved into diverse markets from records to airlines to financial services. Both of these organizations have earned customers' trust, and both have worked hard to offer value to customers. Finally, as co-operation develops between customer and marketer, 'the customer will be willing to undertake some of the value creation activities, such as self-service, self-ordering, and co-production (Sheth and Parvatiyar 1995:264).'

Marketing Effectiveness

Given the tenets of the marketing concept, increases in marketing effectiveness are of even greater importance. Because the organization does not have to guess what customers will want in the future, it will not have to off-load unwanted stock. As a result of really understanding its customers, it can truly cater to their needs and preferences (within profit and capability requirements of course). Thus, where the organization employs a customization strategy it can offer the customer exactly what he or she wants. Since the organization is providing exactly what the customer wants, there is less need for the customer to look to competitors' offerings. This in turn increases customer retention. Increases in customer retention reduce the emphasis on acquisition strategies, again limiting the need for wasteful mass communication strategies. As a result marketing efficiency is once more increased.

Conclusion

Relationship marketing is a strategic response to dealing with diverse markets, and offers a number of significant possibilities. For example, the organization can identify its customers and therefore can communicate with them as individuals. This would allow the firm to rely less on market research. Firms are now able to monitor the customer base directly (e.g. the firm will know what customers it has lost and which ones it had gained). Equally important, in theory at least, the organization can respond to the requirements of individual customers. Using the same rationale as in services marketing this is likely to encourage loyalty and de-emphasize promiscuity. Thus relationship marketing offers a number of exciting possibilities in consumer goods markets. It echoes the type of relationship that may have existed between a small businesses and their customers prior to the growth of mass marketing. 'The complexity of today's market may preclude such commercial intimacy, but modern marketers seem to be trying to recapture a sense of connectedness to the customer.' (DeTienne and Thompson 1996:31)

Direct and database marketing can be employed within either a traditional transactional strategy or within a relationship strategy. In terms of the former, the role of direct and database marketing is to identify and attract prospects and to retain those with high lifetime value. As part of relationship marketing, direct and database marketing become tools to help build lasting relationships. Used in a relationship strategy, the database becomes an important element of organizational learning. It enhances the organization's ability to identify customers, record and monitor their needs and preferences, and to adapt the organizational offering to achieve a better match with customers over time. The database will also maintain a record of the history of an individual relationship and record and influence interaction between the organization and its customers. Direct marketing is only one possible source of interaction between an organization and its customers. However, it is often the primary means of communication in markets where there is little or no direct personal contact. In such situations the use of mail and telephone in particular is important in establishing shared understanding, building rapport and creating bonds. Personalized direct marketing must be evaluated from the point of view of the customer. Mailings should be monitored in order to gauge the customers response/attitude. The history of the relationship must be recognized and thus no customer should be treated as Mr or Mrs Average. Mistakes should be avoided at all cost because they show lack of commitment to the relationship. When mistakes are made they should be rectified and appropriate apologies should be made. Above all, customers should be treated as individuals, as real living people and not simply as addresses on a database.

Review Questions

1   What do you understand by the following:
    (a) transactional view of marketing;
    (b) relational view of marketing;
    (c) customer support system;
    (d) customer contact system;
    (e) customer sacrifice gap.

2   Why is managing interaction fundamental to a relationship marketing strategy?

3   What are the purpose, process, focus and key elements of the relational paradigm?

4   Why are consumer goods marketers moving from a transaction-orientated strategy toward a relational one?

5   In what kinds of consumer markets is a relationship strategy *most* appropriate?

6   List and explain the five process elements required to implement a relationship marketing strategy.

7   How does a relationship marketing strategy enhance marketing effectiveness and marketing efficiency?

Discussion Questions

1   How different is relationship marketing from direct marketing, database marketing, and loyalty marketing?

2   Discuss the extent to which relationship marketing is appropriate in consumer goods markets as in services and industrial markets. It may be helpful to first identify how these markets differ.

3   Can customer databases invoke the bygone days of personalized customer relationships?

4   For a department store, what kinds of information might be included in a customer support system?

References

Abram, Hawkes (1995) *Relationship Marketing in the Financial Services Industry*, London: Abram, Hawkes, pp. 16–17.

Barnes, J.G.(1994) 'Close to the Customer: But is it Really a Relationship?', *Journal of Marketing Management*, 10, pp. 561–70.

Barnes, J.G. (1995) 'Establishing Relationships – Getting Closer to the Customer May be More Difficult Than You Think', *Irish Marketing Review*, 8, pp. 107–16.

Berry, L.L. (1983) 'Relationship Marketing' in Berry, L.L. Shostack, G.L. and Upah, G.D. (eds) *Perspectives on Services Marketing*, Chicago: American Marketing Association, pp. 25–28.

Berry, L.L., and Parasuraman, A. (1991) *Marketing Services – Competition Through Quality*, New York: Free Press.

Blattberg, R.C. and Deighton, J. (1991) 'Interactive Marketing: Exploiting the Age of Addressability', *Sloan Management Review*, Fall, pp. 5–14.

Christopher, M., Payne, A. and Ballantyne, D. (1991) *Relationship Marketing: Bringing Quality, Customer Service and Marketing Together*, Butterworth-Heinemann: Oxford.

Copulsky, J.R., and Wolf, M.J. (1990) 'Relationship Marketing: Positioning for the Future', *The Journal of Business Strategy*, July/August, pp. 16–20.

DeTienne, K.B. and Thompson, J.A. (1996) 'Database Marketing and Organizational Learning Theory: Toward a Research Agenda', *Journal of Consumer Marketing*, 13(5), pp. 12–34.

Gilmore, J.H. and Pine III, B.J. (1997) 'The Four Faces of Mass Customization', *Harvard Business Review*, January/February, pp. 91–101.

Gronroos, C. (1991) 'The Marketing Strategy Continuum: Towards a Marketing Concept for the 1990s', *Management Decision*, 29(1), pp. 7–13.

Gronroos, C. (1994) 'From Marketing Mix to Relationship Marketing: Towards a Paradigm Shift in Marketing', *Management Decision*, 32(2), pp. 4–20.

Gronroos, C. (1996) 'Relationship Marketing: Strategic and Tactical Implications', *Management Decision*, 43(3), pp. 5–14.

Gronroos, C. (1997) 'Relationship Marketing: Interaction, Dialogue and Value', *Centre for Relationship Marketing and Service Management*, Swedish School of Economics, Finland, Working Paper 344, March.

Gummesson, E. (1987) 'The New Marketing – Developing Long-Term Interactive Relationships', *Long Range Planning*, 20, pp. 10–20.

Holmlund, M. and Knock, S. (1996) 'Relationship Marketing: The Importance of Customer-Perceived Service Quality in Retail Banking', *The Service Industries Journal*, 16(3), p. 292.

Jackson, D.W. (1994) 'Relationship Selling: The Personalisation of Relationship Marketing', *Asia-Australia Marketing Journal*, 2(1), pp. 34–53.

Kochak, J. (1989) 'Get the Fax', *Restaurant Business Magazine*, 88(7), pp. 123–28.

Levitt, T. (1983) 'After the Sale is Over', *Harvard Business Review*, 61, pp. 87–93.

McKenna, R. (1986) *The Regis Touch*, MA: Addison-Wesley, p. 15.

Murphy, J.A. (1996) 'Retail Banking', in F. Buttle (ed.) *Relationship Marketing: Theory and Practice*, London: Paul Chapman Publishing, p. 84.

O'Malley, L., Patterson, M. and Evans, M.J. (1997) 'Intimacy or Intrusion: The Privacy Dilemma for Relationship Marketing in Consumer Markets', *Journal of Marketing Management*, 13, pp.541–559.

Pearson, S. (1994) 'Relationship Management: Generating Business in the Diverse Markets of Europe', *European Business Journal*, pp. 28–38.

Shani, D. and Chalasani, S. (1992) 'Exploiting Niches Using Relationship Marketing', *The Journal of Services Marketing*, 6(4), pp. 43–52.

Sheth, J.N. and Parvatiyar, A. (1995) 'Relationship Marketing in Consumer Markets: Antecedents and Consequences', *Journal of the Academy of Marketing Science*, 23(4), pp. 255–271.

Vavra, T.G. (1992) *Aftermarketing: How to Keep Customers For Life Through RM*, New York: Irwin.

Westbrook, R. and Williamson, P. (1993) 'Mass Customization: Japan's New Frontier', *European Management Journal*, 11(1), p. 40.

Wilson, D.T. (1995) 'An Integrated Model of Buyer-Seller Relationships', *Journal of the Academy of Marketing Science*, 23(4), pp. 335–45.

Further Reading

Gronroos, C. (1994) 'From Marketing Mix to Relationship Marketing: Towards a Paradigm Shift in Marketing', *Management Decision*, 32(2), pp. 4–20.

Gronroos, C. (1996) 'Relationship Marketing: Strategic and Tactical Implications', *Management Decision*, 43(3), pp. 5–14.

Sheth, J.N. and Parvatiyar, A. (1995) 'Relationship Marketing in Consumer Markets: Antecedents and Consequences', *Journal of the Academy of Marketing Science*, 23(4), pp. 255–71.

Direct Marketing Media

This Chapter:

▶ Introduces Students To Addressable
And Non-addressable Direct Marketing
Media.

▶ Discusses Direct Mail, Telemarketing,
Direct Response Advertising And The
Internet.

Direct Marketing Media

That'll Be The Daewoo

Perhaps the best known and most successful interactive kiosk operation in the UK is run by Daewoo Cars. A subsidiary of the Korean industrial giant Daewoo, the company entered the UK market in early 1995. Right from the very beginning the interactive kiosk was central to its marketing strategy. Working in conjunction with Halfords and to a small extent with Sainsbury's, the company has now placed in the region of 140 kiosks around the country.

The kiosks were all part of what the company views as an emphasis on customer service. They envisage themselves as being closer in orientation to high-street retailers than car dealerships. They wanted to take the pressure out of buying cars and kiosks provided them with the means to carry it off. But kiosks were not the only direct marketing element of the Daewoo campaign. The launch of the cars in the UK was supported by an £11 million direct response television advertising campaign. The original direct response television advert offered UK drivers 200 year-long test drives of the new cars. Response to the offer was phenomenal and the company was able to build a list of 200,000 individuals. These individuals were then mailed a follow-up questionnaire which generated a 60 per cent response. Daewoo has been able to use the information from these activities to build up its own comprehensive database.

The strategy has clearly worked. Daewoo has witnessed unprecedented success in the short time it has been operating in the UK. It has taken 1 per cent (18,000 units) of the UK car market in its first year of operation.

(Sources: Lord 1997; Fletcher 1996a)

Addressable Media

Direct Mail

Direct mail is personally addressed advertising that is delivered through the post. It has traditionally been the mainstay of UK direct marketing efforts and in recent years has provided the impetus for growth within the industry. One positive side-effect of this growth in the volume of direct mail is that it has become a more accepted medium within marketing generally and consumers may also be more accepting of it. However, while direct mail continues to be a major weapon in the direct marketer's armoury, it no longer dominates, as the range of media available to direct marketing increases. Direct mail can be used for many purposes (Taylor 1995)which include:

▶ generating leads and enquiries;

▶ building customer loyalty;

▶ improving image;

▶ generating sales;

▶ building brand awareness;

▶ cross- and up-selling;

▶ building a database;

▶ supporting the trade.

The strategic use of direct mail means that organizations no longer use the medium simply to generate sales. Direct mail is also useful in terms of data collection and can be used to collect a wealth of information particularly about existing customers. Furthermore, the medium plays a significant role in building and maintaining customer relationships because it is ideally suited to facilitating the meaningful dialogue so important to such relationships. At a strategic level direct mail can be used to promote the image of the organization and its brands.

Direct Mail and Response

Research conducted by Ogilvy and Mather Direct and The Qualitative Consultancy (TQC) in 1991 indicates that response to direct mail communications depends upon four factors: subject matter, brand relationships, personality types and creative execution (Figure 8.1). Perhaps the most powerful contributor to consumer response to direct mail is the subject matter of the direct mail piece itself. Having the right offer at the right time is paramount to success. This further emphasizes the importance of ensuring that consumers receive direct marketing which is relevant to their lives. Having a brand relationship is also viewed as necessary for the successful implementation of direct mail programmes. Consumers seem to be far more willing to accept and respond to direct mail which comes as a result of the relationship between them and the organization.

Personality type basically refers to whether the consumer has a positive or negative attitude toward direct mail in general and this also contributes to the level of response. The TQC/Ogilvy and Mather research further details personality types in this regard as can be seen in Table 8.1. Finally, excellent creative execution will engage the recipient's attention and interest and may also encourage them to respond.

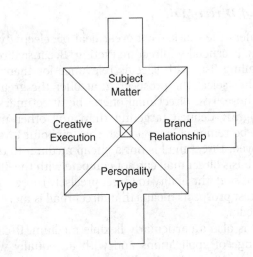

Figure 8.1 The Determinants of Consumer Response to Direct Mail

(Source: TQC/Ogilvy and Mather Direct, cited in Henley Centre 1991:80)

Type	Basic Attitude	Motivation	Characteristics
Compies	Very Positive	Entering Competitions 'Something for Nothing'	Not interested in subject matter Small/extreme group
Librarians	Positive	Value Information Like Storing Things	Little compulsion to respond now Like Financial Services
Adults	Balanced	Look for Things of Value Ability to Discriminate	Open most mail, feel in control. Quick to filter out useful and not useful.
Adolescents	Negative	Dislike Pressure Attack & Rejection of Authority	Defensive and rebellious Feel threatened
Cynics	Negative	Scepticism Want to Prove It's a Con	Fear of being duped Want to show they can see through things.
Conscientious Objectors	Very Negative	Anger Dislike Intrusion	Fear of manipulation Justified by rational arguments Concern for other defenceless people

Table 8.1 Personality Typologies in Respect to Direct Mail

(Source: TQC/Ogilvy and Mather Direct, cited in Henley Centre 1991:83)

Advantages of Direct Mail

Direct mail offers the marketer a great deal of selectivity. As we have seen, targeting is crucial to direct marketing. Because direct marketers can select mailing lists with specific relevance for them and because they can further select the prospects that offer the greatest potential from within those lists, direct mail offers the direct marketer more in the way of tightly defined targeting than any other medium. Poor prospects can be removed from lists so that pinpoint targeting can be further improved. Direct mail is not a cheap medium to use. On a cost per thousand basis direct mail cannot compete with the likes of press or television. That said, the ability to target precisely those customers who offer the greatest prospects means that direct mail is more cost effective than other media.

Direct mail is also a particularly flexible medium. It can be utilized for a wide range of applications and with an equally wide range of different formats. It enables the direct marketer to choose whichever format best suits his or her purposes. Depending on the demands of the campaign, the direct mail piece can be used to convey as much or as little information as is required. If the campaign requires that the consumer receives a large quantity of information (as can be the case in highly technological markets), then there really is no substitute for direct mail. The medium can also be used with equal efficiency in prospecting for new business, in customer retention drives and in communicating with other organizational stakeholders. Direct mail's creative potential means that organizations can send almost anything in the direct mail package – videos, scratch and sniff, samples, vouchers, competitions and teasers. From a consumer perspective direct mail's flexibility means that they don't have to read it straight away; they can take their time over the mailing: they can read it at their leisure; they can revise any sections that they are unsure of; they can save the piece for future reference; and they can pass it on to friends or family who they believe may be interested in the offer (Roman 1988).

Direct mail also offers the opportunity for personalization of the message. However, personalization involves more than just putting the name and address of the recipient on the envelope. Personalization also means that the consumer receives an offer that is relevant to them. Many direct marketers have become engrossed in the minutiae of personalization (Hill 1993). True personalization involves adapting the product or service offer, including the means by which it is communicated, to the needs of the target audience. In achieving this, direct marketers need to make more effective use of the consumer information they have at their disposal. This information can allow them to tailor the whole package (offer and communication) and not just the name and address on the envelope.

When recipients open and read a direct mail piece, there is no direct competition for their attention. This happens because with other media the message has to compete with other programme or editorial content while direct mail does not have this problem.

Direct mail facilitates testing operations and lends itself to measurability. Organizations can quickly and easily identify who is responding to their mailings, and can use this information to further refine their targeting efforts. One of the main advantages of direct mail as a marketing medium is its accountability. Response rates are easily judged and the exact success of a campaign can be rapidly evaluated. Methods of measuring success inevitably depend on the initial objectives of the campaign. They also depend on different levels of direct mail expenditure.

Direct mail has a wide variety of devices at its disposal which can be used to engage the involvement of the recipient while he or she is making a decision about whether or not to respond. This is important in light of the fact that it is becoming ever more difficult to gain the attention of consumers who are exposed to thousands of marketing messages every week. Gaining attention of the recipient is made easier by the fact that it is difficult to ignore direct mail. While it is always possible to put direct mail straight into the bin, most people go as far as opening and reading the message before disposing of it.

Disadvantages of Direct Mail

Direct mail is not without its problems. For many organizations the costs of direct mail still prove to be the biggest barrier to its implementation. Despite its attendant advantages direct mail is not particularly cost efficient for organizations who produce low-cost products and whose consumers are spread over a wide geographic area. These organizations are better served by traditional mass communications techniques, such as advertising, or by door-to-door marketing. Furthermore, direct mail has to some extent failed to live up to its promise of increased response rates following the introduction of complex modelling procedures, geodemographic and lifestyle profiling, and the detailed consumer information to which direct marketers now have access. One reason for the stagnation of response rates is the failure by many direct marketers to include response devices in their mailings. According to the DMA census in 1996, 30 per cent of mailings do not incorporate a means for the consumer to respond. Furthermore, of those mailings that do include a response device, 40 per cent require the consumer to pay for postage (Darby 1997a). Increasing volumes of direct mail have also meant that the medium is developing a clutter similar to that experienced by traditional communications media. Such clutter only serves to alienate many consumers and the pressure is now on direct marketers to improve their targeting so that consumers only receive mailings which are of interest to them.

Catalogues

Mail order continues to play a major role within the UK direct mail sector. It accounts for nearly £5bn (Field 1997) annually and represents in the region of 15 per cent (*Marketing Direct* 1997) of all UK direct mail. However, it has experienced a slight downturn in its fortunes in recent years, falling from a total of 369 million mailings in 1995 to 321 million in 1996. In an effort to fight the decline many catalogue companies have extended their product lines to include financial services and in 1996 6 per cent (*Marketing Direct* 1997) of the sector's mailings were accounted for by such products as home insurance. This move has been made possible by the exploitation of customer databases and the extensive information which these organizations have held about their customers.

Mail order has had to change with the times. Not only does this involve the introduction of new product lines, but it also includes some fundamental changes in the way these organizations do business. The changing needs of society have perhaps had their greatest impact on the 'big book' catalogues such as Freemans, Littlewoods and Great Universal Stores. These big catalogues have traditionally depended on a network of agents for most of their business. These agents, cash-strapped housewives more often than not, earned commission by introducing others to the catalogue and ordering products on their behalf. However, today, these networks of agents are not as proficient as they have been in the past. The main reasons for this include the fact that there is an increasing lack of trust in society today, the population is generally more mobile than in the past and agents have begun to play the system. In order to encourage agents to work for their catalogue, the likes of Great Universal Stores offer them incentives such as discounts on purchases and free gifts. Attracted by these incentives many agents worked their way through the main catalogues collecting goodies as they went (Field 1997). Despite these problems 'big book' catalogues are likely to represent a large proportion of the mail order market for some time to come. The competitive advantage which these catalogues possess revolves around the easy credit terms which they have to offer and which customers cannot obtain elsewhere. Because the number of people in the UK existing on a below average income is increasing these credit terms are always likely to attract new custom.

One recent development of huge importance within the mail order industry has been the growth of more specialized catalogues or 'specialogues' (Slater 1996). Specialogues compete on the basis of being more tightly targeted than their big book counterparts, focusing on particular segments of the consumer market. The specialogue market includes players such as Next Directory, Racing Green and Land's End but also incorporates even more tightly targeted offerings such as Divertimenti who offer up-market kitchenware. Specialogues appeal to those consumers who are too busy to wade through huge catalogues and tend to focus on the more upmarket end of the consumer spectrum. They usually cater for the ABC1 market, while the traditional mail-order catalogues appeal to the C2DEs (Field 1997). Specialogues don't necessarily work on the basis of easy credit terms but concentrate more on convenience. ABC1 customers value convenience and quality, they are prepared to pay extra for these features, and this is what specialogues offer them. The high margins which specialogues earn mean that they don't have to worry too much about generating high volumes. Because specialogues are more highly targeted they tend to rely more on customer profiling (especially lifestyle profiling) than do the big book catalogues. When focusing on the specialized end of the market companies need to be aware of their customers' interests in order to ensure that what they are offering is relevant. Another of the advantages of specialogues is the speed with which they can deliver. While big book catalogues have traditionally taken 28 days to deliver, specialogues such as Next Directory can have the products at your door next day. If the big books are going to remain competitive, they too will have to improve the flexibility of their delivery systems.

Customer Magazines

Many organizations have added a new dimension to their customer loyalty programmes in the form of customer magazines. Originally used by the airline industry and financial services, customer magazines are now being utilized by retailers and fast moving consumer goods companies such as Heinz. By building up detailed profiles of their customers these organizations are able to tailor the magazines to tightly defined customer segments. Indeed, some organizations are moving toward the development of individualized magazines – the only thing holding them back at the moment is printing technology. Maintaining loyalty is the major focus of these magazines and this advantage has led to brand manufacturers using them in the fight against own-label competitors. A secondary feature of these magazines is that they can be utilized for data collection purposes. Customer information can be gleaned from vouchers, coupons and competitions and used to identify prospects for other direct marketing campaigns.

Customer magazines can be quite costly. It is rarely the case that production and distribution costs can be covered by advertising revenue. That said, in terms of the job they do such magazines can be cost effective and this effectiveness is easily quantifiable. Fostering customer loyalty comes at a price but does pay dividends in the long-term.

Card Decks

Card decks originally evolved from the market for business-to-business periodicals (Cobb 1993). Publishers extended the use of their circulation lists by mailing packs of advertising reply cards to industry readers. It wasn't until the late 1980s that card decks were used within consumer marketing. In the last couple of years they have come into their own as many organizations begin to recognize the useful role they can play within the field of direct marketing. The medium appeals particularly to advertisers in financial services, travel, and home improvement sectors (Cobb 1993). Experience has shown that card decks work best as a cost effective means of generating leads and enquiries or raising awareness of a brand prior to a mailing approach (*Direct Response* 1993). Response levels for card decks are not the greatest and there is a high degree of wastage. However, like everything else, response depends to a large extent on the nature of the offer. Despite low levels of response the card deck can still be relatively cost-effective.

Royal Mail's Mailsort Programme

Royal Mail's Mailsort programme offers direct marketers a number of options in terms of direct mail delivery. The programme includes a number of different discounted tariffs related in the main to the speed of delivery required (see Table 8.2). Mailsort 1 guarantees next day delivery on a minimum mailing of 4000 (Darby 1997b). Mailsort 2 delivers within three days and Mailsort 3 can take up to seven days. Mailsort light is designed for follow-up mailings. Provided each mail pack does not exceed 15 grammes up to 40,000 pieces can be posted at a cost of 4.5p per piece. Royal Mail also offer Customer Bar-coding (CBC) which utilizes electronic bar-code readers to sort large volumes of mail. CBC is designed to reduce delivery times and improve the cost effectiveness of the Mailsort programme. The bar-code incorporates household specific Delivery Point Suffix data (DPS) which helps to make delivery that much quicker and more accurate (Couldwell 1997). However, in using CBC direct marketers have to ensure that the lists they work from are extremely accurate (72 per cent of addresses must include DPS data and 90 per cent of the postcode information must be accurate). Set-up costs for the system can be quite high and organizations using it should view it as a long-term investment.

Table 8.2 Royal Mail's Mailsort Programme

Tariff	Delivery Time	Minimum Delivery	Discount
Mailsort 1	Next Day	4,000	13%–32%
Mailsort 2	3 Working Days	4,000	15%–32%
Mailsort 3	7 Working Days	4,000	25%–32%
Mailsort Light	As Mailsort 1,2,3	Up to 40,000 items	Cost 4.5p per item
Customer Bar-coding	As Mailsort 1,2,3	30, 000 per mailing	2% on top of Mailsort

Direct Spirit

Seagram UK has utilized direct mail in the past to recruit and retain drinkers of its products. In 1994 the company launched an award-winning customer acquisition campaign for Martell cognac. Run in conjunction with an above-the-line campaign, direct mail was used to target drinkers of rival brands.

The mailing tied in with the entertainment focus of the advertising and recipients were invited to enter a competition where they could win a plush dinner with their friends at the House of Martell. 24,000 new Martell drinkers were recruited.

Hot on the heels of the success of the Martell campaign, Seagram launched another mailing to support their whisky brand Glenlivet. The objective here was to target heavy users – the 15 per cent believed to consume two-thirds of all whisky in the UK. The use of direct mail was predicated on the belief that while advertising had its place, niche brands could achieve greater success through the use of a more personalized approach.

(Source: Burnside 1995)

Telemarketing

Telemarketing is becoming increasingly prevalent in the UK. Many organizations have recognized the power of the telephone and it is now being used across a broad range of activities. These activities include (Roman 1988; *Marketing* 1992):

▶ new customer acquisition;

▶ reactivation of past customers;

▶ consolidation of and cross-selling to existing customers;

▶ upgrading current customers;

▶ screening and qualifying leads;

▶ servicing marginal accounts that don't justify a personal sales call;

▶ covering a wide geographical spread;

▶ retailer and dealer support and traffic building;

▶ market research and database building;

▶ customer care, loyalty building and helpline provision;

▶ direct response enquiry and order handling.

The Growth of Telemarketing

The majority of outbound telemarketing calls made in the UK continue to be to existing customers to stimulate interest in and cross-sell other products and services and to enhance loyalty. A large proportion of outbound calling remains in the business-to-business sector where recipients tend to be more comfortable with the medium. That said, there is increasing incidence of the use of outbound telemarketing within consumer markets, though many remain sceptical of its utility. The major growth within the sector has been in terms of inbound services and the rapid growth of the medium owes much to the increased use of direct response television (DRTV) advertising in the UK (Slater 1997). In addition to the effect of DRTV, the expansion of service industries and contemporary service culture, the opening up of the telecommunications market and the introduction of freephone numbers and local-charge calls, have contributed to the rise of the telemarketing industry. Inbound telemarketing allows organizations to build and refine their databases. Such a process is invaluable to the success of an outbound telemarketing or other direct marketing programme which the organization might initiate.

Advantages of Telemarketing

Once it is carefully planned and controlled, telemarketing, like direct mail, is highly selective in nature. Targeting is carried out in much the same way as with direct mail and telemarketing provides a quick and accurate means of collecting up-to-date and pertinent information about contacts. It is usually possible to generate feedback from 80 per cent–90 per cent of telemarketing contacts, compared with about two to five per cent from direct mail. Future communications can thus be tailored to the needs of each contact: the information obtained can be used to build highly targeted consumer lists and follow-up strategies can be devised based on the media preferences of contacts. Telemarketing does suffer from high costs though these can be managed by maximizing the effectiveness of the targeting process. The flexibility of telemarketing ensures that the medium can be used to contact consumers across a wide geographic area and calls can be timed to suit the contact and to provide maximum response levels.

The personal nature of telemarketing means that any queries can be resolved quickly and efficiently. The call handler may be able to develop a rapport with the contact and it may even be possible for a close relationship to be developed over time. Customer loyalty can be maintained between sales by providing 24-hour access to the company and by using the telephone to check on customer needs and to make customers aware of new developments. Providing the customer with up-to-date information may also facilitate the achievement of programme objectives. Additionally, the two-way dialogue associated with telemarketing allows the call handler to quickly gauge the success of the marketing programme. It becomes possible to identify which techniques are working and which are enjoying less success.

Testing is also facilitated by telemarketing. The immediacy of telemarketing means that resources can be quickly deployed and elements of the marketing programme that are not working can be changed as the programme progresses. List accuracy can be also tested instantly and this helps to further improve targeting efforts and reduce wastage. Monitoring can take account of such factors as call rates, contacts reached, numbers unobtainable, positive and negative responses, etc. Even the effectiveness of call handlers can be tested through the constant monitoring of their activities.

One of telemarketing's greatest advantages is the proficiency it offers in support of other media. It has been shown that the use of telemarketing as a support medium boosts success rates and provides incremental effectiveness (Roberts and Berger 1989).

Disadvantages of Telemarketing

The personal nature of telemarketing provides one of its major disadvantages as well as advantages. Outbound telemarketing in particular has to carried out with care and aforethought. It is most useful when a relationship exists between caller and contact. A telemarketing call from an organization with which the contact already does business is likely to be viewed as a service and is welcomed. The very same call from an organization that has had no previous contact is much more likely to be viewed as an intrusion (Nash 1986). Proper training and monitoring of personnel is vital because when used incorrectly it is all too easy for telemarketing to annoy. Nothing will irritate a consumer quite as much as a poorly timed, poorly conceived or poorly executed telephone call (Nash 1986). Outbound calls, however well targeted, can be inconvenient for the contact (Murphy 1997). With direct mail an unwanted solicitation can be easily discarded but with telemarketing we find it much more difficult to let the phone ring without answering it. Because outbound telemarketing can be so intrusive, the initial part of a script must be geared to checking that the person is happy to talk at that moment (Murphy 1997). It is vital that telemarketing calls are carefully planned and controlled and used more often than not as part of a relationship building programme. A blatant sales pitch should never be the first call that a consumer gets from a company.

Telemarketing can be quite costly and it provides little in the way of economies of scale. Other media such as direct mail and media advertising are less expensive which places ever more emphasis on getting the targeting correct. Overheads, in particular the cost of maintaining a well-trained workforce, can be very high. Automated Call Handling (ACH) can reduce costs but cannot always be used. The medium is also limited in terms of the amount of contacts that can be made. While traditional advertising and direct mail, etc. reach large numbers of people in a short period of time, the number of telephone calls that can be made at any one time is restricted.

Telemarketing Technology

In an effort to handle the increasing number of telephone calls generated by the likes of direct response advertising, direct marketers have had to develop automated systems which dispense with the need for large numbers of live call handlers. To a large extent automated systems, such as Interactive Voice Response (IVR), are limited to inbound telemarketing campaigns. IVR provides telemarketers with the support necessary to capture excess calls and to provide 24-hour customer access. At its simplest, IVR can at least explain that the lines are busy and thus removes a great deal of the frustration of callers waiting to contact the organization (Sappal 1996a). IVR systems are interactive by using either touch tone, keying in numbers on the telephone using a key pad, or automatic voice response where it responds to 'yes' and 'no' or other simple words. IVR gives a caller control by giving them choices and navigating them through the system, so they don't have to wait around. If it's a complicated enquiry, or problem or sensitive issue, the caller should be automatically diverted to the relevant person (Sappala 1996a). The advantages of IVR include (Sappala 1996a):

▶ *Minimizes Call Abandonment.* Because automated systems can be set up to deal with a vast number of calls, the number of callers who cannot get through at peak times is reduced dramatically. This factor makes automated systems ideal for large campaigns.

▶ *Access.* Automated services provide access to the organization 24 hours a day. Customers value such a services and it goes a long way toward building and maintaining relationships with them.

▶ *Consistency.* The message which the customer receives is consistent. There is no problem with live operators who deviate from the script. Thus the organization can feel secure in the knowledge that their brands are being properly and consistently represented.

▶ *Flexibility.* It does not take very long to set up an automated system and it can be quickly and easily adapted. This allows the organization to respond to any changes in circumstances.

▶ *Cost.* Automated systems can be more cost effective than using live operators because they don't have to be trained and equipped.

The disadvantages of IVR include:

▶ *Artificial.* IVR can be cold and impersonal whereas it is generally conceded that live operators provide greater warmth and give a better impression of the product or service. Given the choice, most consumers would probably prefer to deal with a live operator and some simply flat out refuse to talk to machines. Furthermore, there are some situations in which there is no substitute for a well-trained operator and automated systems would be of little use. In sectors such as financial services and charities live operators are more beneficial. This is because people feel uneasy about discussing financial details on a machine and because donations are better acknowledged by another person. While automated systems certainly have their advantages, tasks such as giving quotations and customer care should still be handled by live operators.

▶ *Limited Data Collection.* Automated systems provide limited utility in terms of collecting customer data. Live operators are able to improvise to some extent and to get more information out of people. They can deal with *ad hoc* queries and can ask the caller to clarify information over which there is any doubt.

The Importance of Personnel

Although the role of technology with the telemarketing industry is increasing, the part played by people is arguably more important than ever (Darby 1996a). While technology has opened up the market for telemarketing expertise this has effectively led to a burgeoning in the number and variety of tasks which personnel have to perform. No longer is the medium restricted to hard-sell outbound promotions. Contemporary telemarketing encompasses areas such as customer service, consumer complaint handling and technical support. This places pressure on the skills required within the industry. Traditionally populated by bored housewives and students, telemarketing departments are now inhabited by well-trained personnel with much wider skill bases. Having the right personnel is essential for the successful implementation of a modern telemarketing programme. In planning any campaign, skill requirements should first be identified and then suitable personnel should be found. This is likely to produce a greater incidence of dedicated teams working on accounts than has been the case in the past and this is no bad thing.

Unaddressable Media

Direct Response Television Advertising

Perhaps the area of most dramatic growth with the direct marketing industry as a whole has been evident in the field of direct response television advertising (DRTV). In excess of one in five television commercials now carry a response device (Reid 1995). The 1996 Direct Marketing Association Census suggests 25.4 per cent of TV advertising carries a response element. Statistics such as this seem to imply that the insidious growth of direct response television advertising has the potential to swamp traditional TV advertising whilst the majority remain blissfully unaware of its move into the mainstream. For many, DRTV has given direct marketing an air of respectability that had thus far eluded the industry. One could be forgiven for thinking that television advertising is something that would not sit well with direct marketers. After all, it appears to be extremely wasteful, it is ill-targeted and costs are prohibitive (Fletcher 1996b). However, in this the last decade of the twentieth century, consumers have witnessed a veritable explosion in the communications network. There are now more television channels available through terrestrial, cable and satellite broadcasting than ever before. This revolution in television means that the various channels can now offer more tightly defined audiences. Direct response television advertising has also altered the direct marketer's perception of television campaigns. Traditional television advertising is subject to notoriously difficult measurement. DRTV, in contrast, provides instantly measurable results.

Types of Direct Response Television Advertising

Contemporary direct response television ads take on a number of different formats. Perhaps the most famous and best loved is the infomercial, a long, tacky, low-budget affair designed to exhibit products in the manner of an in-store demonstration. These advertisements, largely broadcast in the dead of night, hope to inspire insomniacs to dust off their credit cards and take advantage of the offer of the century. Whilst normal people enjoy the relative comfort of their beds, the insomniac is comforted by the knowledge that he or she is purchasing the *ultimate* gadget, *exclusively* available on a one-time offer only, complete with *inclusive* accessories at an *unbelievable* price of £9.99. Then there is the more sophisticated and respectable true direct response commercial which exists only to generate phone calls (Blackford 1997). Because of clever targeting the true direct response advert can side-step the expensive primetime slots so coveted by the traditional advertiser, and in so doing can avoid head-to-head competition for the viewers limited attention. Placements around low-interest programmes are used as this makes it that bit easier to motivate the viewer to call. Within minutes of screening, the telephone lines begin to ring. Next there is the traditional awareness ad with a last minute inclusion of a response device. In this case the inclusion of the phone number is simply a risk-free strategy designed to dispel the fears of clients, tacked on at the end. Finally, there is the most recent addition to the direct response advertising family, branding response television advertising (BRTV). Branding response television advertising, used increasingly by fast moving consumer goods manufacturers, combines the creative brand-building properties of traditional television advertising with the measurability of response. BRTV is more about eliciting a two-way communication with consumers and does not necessarily intend to sell the consumer a product or service immediately (Darby 1996b). Today, there are numerous approaches which cultivate the brand and integrate response in the same advertisement. In so doing, the clever brand response advert can actually use the response as a branding device. Unlike DRTV, brand response aims to reach the largest audience possible. Because BRTV utilizes peak viewing times it can cause problems in terms of call handling. However, it doesn't tend to generate the same level of immediate response as DRTV, the calls are shorter and they can usually be handled by automated systems (Darby 1996b).

Some direct marketers have criticised BRTV for failing to take advantage of customer response. They claim that many brand response advertisements don't take the opportunity to gather customer data when calls are made in response to the advertisement. Apple Tango, for example, no longer gathers details from callers. It has restricted itself to brand building activities of which the response is merely a part (Darby 1996b). On the other hand, some companies are making the best use afforded by brand response advertising. Oxfam have integrated their branded advertising with a response element in order to achieve the twin objectives of soliciting donations and building the brand (Darby 1996b).

Direct Response Press Advertising

Direct response advertising in newspapers and magazines present the direct marketer with a cost effective means of generating response from relatively large audiences. Both magazines and newspapers allow the direct marketer to provide substantial amounts of information though in the case of magazines this can be further supported by high quality photography and artwork. In addition the fragmentation of these media in recent years means that direct marketers can use them to reach more tightly defined audiences than was previously possible.

In looking in particular at magazines, Roberts and Berger (1989:342) suggest that the single most important criterion for selecting magazines to use in direct response advertising is the receptivity of the magazine's readership to such advertising. 'The direct marketer, then, must look not only for magazines that contain substantial amounts of direct response advertising, but also for those that continually feature direct response advertising for similar products.' Furthermore, according to Nash (1982:114–16) other considerations in using this medium will include:

▶ *Economics*. Because of the low cost per contact associated with magazines they may be suitable as a vehicle for direct response advertising if the margin is low or if the objective is to get information to a large number of prospects.

▶ *Credibility*. If the organization and/or the product or service on offer are not very well known they might benefit from the *halo effect* of the magazines own credibility. In other words the authority and credibility of the magazine may rub off on any advertisement placed in it.

▶ *Lack of satisfactory lists*. If no suitable lists exist for a particular type of offer (as may be the case with innovative products), then direct response advertising in magazines may be a suitable approach as it reaches a large number of prospects. The organization can then generate its own list as a result of the response generated by this element of the campaign.

Newspapers too offer a valuable means of direct response advertising to direct marketers and they also provide a number of distinct benefits (Roberts and Berger 1989:349–50):

▶ *Frequency*. Many newspapers are published on a daily basis and while they may only have a short shelf life, repetition serves to enforce the message of the advertiser.

▶ *Immediacy*. The deadline for submission of advertisements is usually pretty close to the day of publication. This allows the direct marketer to avail of up-to-the-minute information.

▶ *Reach*. Newspapers reach a high proportion of households in their primary geographical area. As explained earlier, access to such large markets comes with attendant advantages.

▶ *Local Shopping Reference.* Local newspapers are used by readers as the primary reference to local shopping opportunities and so represent an ideal media vehicle for local organizations.

▶ *Fast Response.* Because of the frequency with which they are published, newspapers offer the direct marketer an excellent opportunity for close monitoring and testing of their activities.

Direct Response Radio Advertising

Direct response advertising on radio offers the direct marketer many of the opportunities afforded by its counterpart on television. According to Book and Cary (1978:11) radio has a lot to commend it from a direct marketing point of view:

▶ *It is ubiquitous.* The high incidence of radio ownership in the UK means that the medium is available around the clock to almost every consumer.

▶ *It is selective.* Fragmentation of the industry and the stylising of programme format has meant that independent radio stations in the UK reach relatively homogenous groups of highly defined target audiences.

▶ *It is economical.* Radio provides direct marketers with cost effective reach, while production costs for radio advertising remain some of the lowest of any medium.

▶ *It offers rapid access.* Production times for radio advertising are relatively short compared to those for other media such as television. This means that the direct marketer can develop and air a direct response radio advertisement in a short period of time.

▶ *It is involving.* While many remain sceptical of the power of radio advertising, studies have shown that the personal nature of radio as a medium engages the audience. Listening to the radio, even when conducted as a secondary activity, has the ability to get the message across.

▶ *It is flexible.* The short lead times for production and airing of radio advertisements make it an ideal medium for testing purposes. Furthermore, should close monitoring of the campaign indicate that changes are required, these can be carried out quickly and with little cost.

Door-To-Door

Proponents of door-to-door direct marketing claim that its cost effectiveness and new found targetability bring it out of the basement of direct marketing media to take its rightful place alongside the likes of direct mail. Inexpensive and more accessible, geodemographic targeting systems have vastly improved the accuracy with which door-to-door can be accomplished while still leaving it cheaper than its direct media counterparts. The response levels it generates may not be as high as those for direct mail but its cost effectiveness ensures its survival as a major direct marketing force. Although retailers continue to be the greatest users of door-to-door, many fast moving consumer goods companies and financial services organizations are now using the medium to good effect.

Door-to-door marketing encompasses a number of options including leaflets, samples and coupons, though it seems that sampling offers the greatest advantages for direct marketers. Sampling allows the consumer to try the product for free, something that consumers are always going to like, and it takes the risk out of trying new products. 'Uniquely among marketing methods, sampling breaks down the adversarial psychological barrier between buyer and seller (Denny 1995:8).' Studies show that in the region of 95 per cent of samples are tried by consumers and thus go some way toward influencing subsequent purchase (Sappal 1996b). When launching new products, sampling probably works best if it's run in conjunction with a television advertising campaign and when the sample is coupled with a coupon or voucher. The television advertising helps to create awareness of the new product, the sample induces trial and the coupon encourages the consumer to buy the product for themselves if they like it. However, given the nature of sampling, it is better suited as a medium to products and services with wide appeal.

In recent years the remit of sampling has been widened by some organizations to include some element of market research (Derrick 1997). Data collection can be accomplished through the inclusion of data capture vehicles in prize draws, etc. It is the requirement by client organizations for more up-to-date information that has encouraged samplers to get involved in market research. New technology, such as hand-held computers, allows door-to-door marketers to collect detailed information as they work. The client organization can then access that information and use it to make decisions as the campaign is still running.

New Media

The Internet

❝ The Internet's secret: Internet is more about people than technology. Any direct marketer needs to be clear about this. The Internet is a relationship medium uniquely suited to providing low-cost, near instant dialogue . . .Simply transposing tradi-tional advertising and selling messages onto this new medium

*will not work. It is not the place for broadcasting image-building
messages or sending out prospecting mail in the hunt for new
business leads. But the medium is uniquely suited to developing
higher levels of relationships, to establishing dynamic customer
communities and allowing satisfied customers to become your
champions.* 🔟 (Cross 1994)

Originally used for scientific and military research in the US, the
Internet has evolved since the early 1970s into an elaborate
communications system comprising electronic mail, thousands of
specialized forums called 'newsgroups' and on-line 'bulletin boards',
offering everything from Joan Rivers Jewellery to access to the *Sunday
Times* Interactive Team Football. The Internet is an organic and
democratic entity, owned and operated by no single authority and not
covered on the whole by conventional legislation. Its rules of function
or 'Netiquette' are unwritten or preserved only in a type of verbal
precedence. Availing of this 'Marxist medium gone mad' is relatively
simple. An organization using the Internet must understand and truly
believe in relationship marketing, must appreciate niche marketing
and not just treat the medium as the marketing equivalent of soup du
jour.

Direct marketers who use the Internet must remember that as a
commercial environment it is highly democratic. Internet consumers
can and do exercise more power than in any other marketing situation.
They have ways of showing their disapproval of organizations who
cross the boundaries of netiquette. These range from aggressive posting
to blacklisting organizations who have defrauded customers, published
misleading product information, been guilty of too much hype or
simply advertised or sent direct communications where it was not
wanted. This power has major repercussions for direct marketers who
can no longer use shotgun mailings.

Internet consultants emphasize the importance of delineating the
objective for any proposed Web site (Darby 1996c). Marketers must
employ cross-marketing techniques and use other communications
media to drive traffic to their sites. In utilizing the Internet to the
fullest organizations should take steps to capture details from those
who visit the site. But just gathering information in a passive fashion
isn't enough. A site must be supported with interactivity through
the inclusion of offers, competitions and other means of data
collection.

Before the Internet lives up to its early promise a number of
potentially serious problems need to be overcome (Denny 1996).
Perhaps the most pressing problem is that of the speed at which data
can be downloaded. Current speeds can make it irritating and
expensive for users, although it is getting faster. A second problem
relates to the low penetration rates amongst consumers. For this
reason the Internet seems to be more suited to business-to-business
just now than to consumer marketing.

The Internet does have advantages over other direct marketing
media. It allows all but the smallest organizations to compete on what

is more or less a level playing field, as start-up costs are relatively low. However, direct marketers need to approach the Internet with care. As a marketing medium the Internet is still quite young and a little anarchic. Also hidden issues, such as the need for site development and support, can add to the cost.

Kiosks

Interactive information kiosks are one of the most recent introductions to the marketer's armoury. Using touch screen technology, kiosks allow consumers to search for and retrieve the information that they want, rather than having it forced upon them by overeager sales assistants. Kiosks have the ability to accomplish the following activities (Lord 1997:40):

▶ Extending brand presence beyond existing retail sites and reaching many more potential customers.

▶ Creating an unintimidating environment in which customers can make purchasing decisions.

▶ Freeing up staff from answering basic enquiries.

▶ Taking pressure off staff to make complex and under-informed recommendations.

▶ Providing a greater range of information than a human being can offer.

▶ Providing customers with a hard copy of the information they are after.

▶ Allowing customers to work within a budget and compare prices easily.

▶ Increasing awareness of complementary products and increasing average customer spend.

Kiosks also satisfy the need for specialist advice, a service which all too many sales assistants fail to provide. Furthermore, the interactive kiosk can reduce queues at checkouts as customers can find out in advance whether the product they wish to buy is in stock. Marketers need to be careful with the use of kiosks however. This involves understanding that kiosks need to provide added value to existing retail operations. It remains unclear whether the kiosk is simply a primer, readying consumers for the onslaught of interactive technology, or whether the medium is here to stay. Whatever its future, the interactive kiosk is already providing direct marketers with yet another means of communicating personalized marketing messages.

Television personality

Mitsubishi decided to go the direct route to persuade its customers to stay loyal to its brand. By Ian Darby

Ask people what product Mitsubishi makes and they will probably say cars. That's the problem faced by the marketing team at Mitsubishi Electric, which has become a top five player in the TV and video market without anyone really noticing. This could all change as Mitsubishi seeks to develop brand awareness, and gain new prospects while developing ties with existing customers.

Not easy on a total marketing budget of £3.5 million, says Paul Tittle, general marketing manager of the consumer products division at Mitsubishi Electric: 'Many of our competitors have a much wider product range, which they can use to finance greater marketing activity. We're significantly outspent by many of our competitors.'

Tittle says main rivals Sony, Panasonic, JVC and Toshiba spend up to ten times more on marketing. Traditionally, Mitsubishi Electric has relied upon consumer sales promotion and trade advertising to market its products. It attempted one TV campaign in the early 90s but, following a review; it decided to try more cost-effective methods.

Direct marketing was explored as a possible avenue. Mitsubishi holds a database of 250,000 existing owners, derived from data accrued via NDL Consumer Link cards filled in by buyers following a purchase. In spring 1996 it rolled out a trial loyalty mailing, through D4B, to 6,000 of its existing customers. This is the first of three mailings in the programme to date.

The major problem in the brown goods market is that purchases are relatively infrequent, so it is difficult to keep track of people over time. This was the first task faced by Mitsubishi. Then, after establishing some basic level of contact over time, the company sought to increase frequency of purchase and cross-sell TVs to video owners and vice-versa.

The mail packs contained vouchers incentivising future purchases and vouchers to be passed on to friends of the recipient in an attempt to develop new prospects. It asked people to respond if they wanted to hear from Mitsubishi again.

The D4B mailing produced a 47 per cent response. Of those who responded, 94 per cent said they'd recommend the products to a friend and pass on the vouchers.

Mitsubishi and D4B then had to build upon indications that its customers were willing to develop a relationship with Mitsubishi. 'We had to find something to harness that loyalty which we found existed with the tests,' says Tittle.

It decided to embark on a longer term loyalty programme called 3 Diamonds. This was a daunting task when you consider that Mitsubishi had never done any direct marketing before and D4B was better known as a design agency. Even more daunting with a budget of just £500,000 a year.

Mitsubishi sought to convey its brand values of reliability and quality with the loyalty mailings. Anything less would risk upsetting customers. This was reflected in the creative: '3 Diamonds came into the mix and gave it a more hi-tech look — the quality feel was very important,' says Sue Allsopp, a director at D4B. 'We wanted the customer to feel special and not just think of it as another piece of mail on their doorstep. This helped towards the response rate we achieved.'

By October 1996 a two-stage 3 Diamonds mailing was reaching selected customers. Prior to a roll-out to the full database, Mitsubishi targeted several cells of customers to test the two-stage mailing. 'We didn't want to roll this out to 150,000 people and get it horribly wrong. We weren't direct marketing experts and didn't want to make silly mistakes,' says Tittle.

Testing the water

The first stage was a basic letter with a survey attached. It asked customers if they were interested in joining the scheme and also asked for personal details and purchasing intentions to supplement the database.

Respondents were then sent the full loyalty pack complete with £20 and £30 vouchers for themselves and up to five friends, and a loyalty card displaying a helpline number ('the most important part of the mailing,' says Tittle).

Nottingham-based telemarketing agency APS was brought in to handle careline response. APS also monitors the influx of data and conducted market research on 600 customers sent loyalty packs prior to the full roll-out in January 1997.

'We found response to the pack to be good,' says Tittle. 'People found most of the content creatively striking and they said things like 'it smacks of quality' and 'makes me feel good about making a future purchase with you'.'

The two-stage mailing found ten per cent willing to buy a product immediately, and 48 per cent saying they would pass on vouchers to friends. Results indicated that 3 Diamonds was increasing frequency of purchase and keeping customers loyal, even in the face of a five or six year purchase cycle.

In January Mitsubishi mailed 182,000 customers from the 250,000 database. So far it has attracted 50,000 members to 3 Diamonds. 'We are in the process of re-mailing those who didn't respond,' says Tittle. He expects a further 15 per cent response. And the scheme is yielding practical results. Tittle is looking for an overall sales uplift of between 5 and 7.5 per cent as a result of the scheme.

● ● ▶

Mitsubishi is preparing to grow more sophisticated as 3 Diamonds progresses. The first stage of the two-stage mailing is adding additional data to that collected from the NDL survey. This will enable event timed mailings to fit in with consumer intention to buy.

It plans regular membership mailings, roughly every quarter. The first will be a Christmas push in September, and another option is a mailing to coincide with the World Cup next summer. The scheme is supported by an Internet site, also designed by D4B.

Mitsubishi intends to carry out some profiling of its data with a view to prospecting for new customers and it is working on a key initiative with two retailers. Though NDL has supplied data on 250,000 buyers who completed survey cards, Tittle estimates around 750,000 others didn't fill them in. In order to reach these owners he is talking to retailers who keep track of what customers buy and are willing to sell information on.

Tittle is clearly thrilled with the progress of 3 Diamonds: 'You can tell the success of the scheme by the way people react to it internally. It's been elevated in importance,' he declares.

(Source: *Marketing Direct*, September 1997)

Review Questions

1 What are the various uses to which direct marketers put direct mail?

2 What are the main determinants of consumer response to direct mail?

3 List the advantages and disadvantages of the following:

(a) direct mail;
(b) telemarketing;
(c) direct response radio advertising.

4 What are the pros and cons of using interactive voice response systems in telemarketing?

Discussion Questions

1 What, in your opinion, are the major reasons for the dramatic rise in UK specialogues?

2 Some commentators suggest that BRTV isn't strictly direct marketing. To what extent do you agree? Give reasons for your answer.

3 To what extent do you believe that the Internet will be a major force in direct marketing in the new millennium?

References

Blackford, A. (1997) 'Never Mind The Quality', *Marketing Direct*, April, pp. 46–51.

Book, A.C. and Cary, N.D. (1978) *The Radio and Television Commercial*, Chicago: Crain Books.

Burnside, A. (1995) 'Shots of Whisky', *Marketing*, August 3, pp. 30–32.

Cobb, R. (1993) 'A Full Deck of Cards', *Marketing*, August 19, pp. 26–7.

Couldwell, C. (1997) 'Dawn of the Machine Age at the Royal Mail', *Marketing Direct*, March, pp. 60–70.

Cross, R. (1994) 'Internet: The Missing Marketing Medium Found', *Direct Marketing*, 20(9), pp. 37–46.

Darby, I. (1996a) 'The Right Staff', *Marketing Direct*, November, pp. 55–60.

Darby, I. (1996b) 'Calling For Attention', *Marketing Direct*, September, pp. 58–64.

Darby, I. (1996c) 'Spinning A Web Site', *Marketing Direct*, September, p. 31.

Darby, I. (1997a) 'Marketers Suffer Lack of Response', *Marketing Direct*, July/August, p. 10.

Darby, I. (1997b) 'Mailsort! Is It a Help or a Hindrance?', *Marketing Direct*, February, p. 32.

Denny, N. (1995) 'Sampling Takes The Top Slot For Launches', *Marketing*, May 4, p. 8.

Denny, N. (1996) 'The Internet: Is It A Help Or A Hindrance?', *Marketing Direct*, December, pp. 18–24.

Derrick, S. (1997) 'Reaching A Captive Audience', *Marketing Direct*, June, pp. 37–40.

Direct Response (1993) 'Wanted! More Card Decks' July, pp. 43–4.

Field, L. (1997) 'Hail The New Order', *Marketing Direct*, July/August, pp. 60–6.

Fletcher, K. (1996a) 'Dawning of a New Daewoo', *Marketing Direct*, May, pp. 36–9.

Fletcher, K. (1996b) 'Vera Goes A-Wooing', *Marketing Direct*, December, p. 32.

Henley Centre (1991) *Positive Response*.

Hill, M. (1993) 'Delivering the Personal Touch', *Direct Response*, November, pp. 43–5.

Lord, R. (1997) 'Death of the Car Salesman', *Revolution*, July, pp. 38–40.

Marketing (1992) 'Telemarketing and What It Can Do For You', February 13, p. 20.

Marketing Direct (1997) 'A Catalogue of Failure?', June, pp. 20–1.

Nash, E.L. (1982) *Direct Marketing: Strategy, Planning, Execution*, New York: McGraw Hill.

Nash, E.L. (1986) *Direct Marketing: Strategy, Planning, Execution* 2nd edn, New York: McGraw Hill.

Reid, A. (1995) 'Can DRTV Really be the Advertising of the Future?', *Campaign*, July 14, p. 11.

Roberts, M.L. and Berger, P.D. (1989) *Direct Marketing Management*, Englewood Cliffs, NJ: Prentice Hall.

Roman, E. (1988) *Integrated Direct Marketing*, New York: McGraw Hill.

Sappal, P. (1996a) 'Smooth Operators', *Direct Response*, November, pp. 67–8.

Sappal, P. (1996b) 'Sampling The Market', *Direct Response*, November, pp. 63–4.

Slater, J. (1996) 'A Tightly Targeted Business', *Marketing Direct*, May, pp. 42–54.

Slater, J. (1997) 'You've Got My Number, Why Don't You Use It?', *Marketing Direct*, April, pp. 52–6.

Taylor, T. (1995) 'Direct Mail', *Campaign*, August 19, p. 27.

Further Reading

Stone, M. (1988) *Successful Direct Marketing Methods*, Lincolnwood, IL: NTC Business Books.

The Internet

Direct Marketing in the 21st Century: How Organizations and Consumers may Respond to the New Interactive Marketing Media

by Linda Peters

This Chapter:

▶ Introduces Students To The Benefits Of The Internet For Direct Marketers.

▶ Describes How The Internet Works.

▶ Discusses The Possibilities For Interactivity With Customers.

CHAPTER

9

The Internet

Uploaded cuts back on words, but not content

Loaded may have been overtaken by *FHM* in the off-line circulation race, but its webzine and alter ego, *Uploaded*, has taken and held onto the online lead.

For Chris Rayner, new media director at BMP Interactive, what impressed him most about the site is how it manages to produce online content without mirroring the printed magazine.

'They manage to do that, but not lose the incredibly strong brand of the magazine. I would say that 98 per cent of the content online is not only unique, but highly interactive and quite often is a foil for features that appear in *Loaded* itself. On this point I believe it is unrivalled in the consumer magazine market online', says Rayner.

High praise indeed, but not uncommon. BMP has run two banner campaigns on the Uploaded site since it was launched nine months ago, for clients UK Plus and BMG.

Uploaded editor Adam Porter says that, unlike many sites on the web, Uploaded has tried to literally stay away from words.

'We are not interested in putting lots of text on the site. What we have produced is a reflection of the magazine without the features. We have sought to create something different; something that works on the web', he says.

Uploaded also benefits from avoiding over-use of browser-slowing Java and Shock-wave technology, which is common on many similar sites.

'There are two reasons behind this', says Porter. 'A lot of people who access the site are either students or are at work, and it's time consuming down-loading bits of Shockwave and RealAudio. Secondly, it makes the site technology-led rather than content-led. If you are an entertainment site, or a leisure site, you should be content-led'.

Uploaded is currently in the process of getting an ABC audit which is likely to give it added creditability with advertisers.

Tel: 0171 261 7949
Web: www.uploaded.co.uk
Contact: Adam Porter
Rate: £20 to £35 per thousand impressions
Audited: talking to the ABC

(Source: *Revolution Magazine*, September 1997, p. 59)

An Overview of the Internet, its Origins and Features

The Internet may be defined as the interconnection of a number of computer networks on an almost global scale. The primary method of connection is through telephone and cable networks and it is this feature that contributes to the uniqueness of the Internet as a communication medium. Through both historical development and intentional efforts, the Internet is not 'owned' or 'operated' by any one particular body, be it governmental or commercial. The growth rate, accelerated greatly by the development of hypermedia capability and browser software in the early 1990s, seems to be accelerating more rapidly as commercial providers and users discover its potential for communication and information dissemination, and as the popular media focus more attention upon its possibilities.

Much of this commercial development is occurring on that portion of the Internet known as the World Wide Web (WWW, or simply 'the Web'). The Web is a distributed network environment within the Internet, and is characterized by the use of hypertext markup language (HTML), which allows text, icons, sound, or images in a document to be shared by users, regardless of the particular computer operating systems at the sending or receiving end of the communication. This development has had extraordinary, and unforeseen, consequences in the growth and popularity of the Web. The ability to locate content on a Web server, which is interconnected with other Web servers around the world, allows those who access it to share multimedia information globally. The connections are made through what is known as a hyperlink (which may itself be text or image based). Any hyperlink can point to any other document (often referred to as a Web page) anywhere on the Internet.

Because this hyperlink is based upon graphical user interface technology, there is no need for users to know specific commands in order to use the Web. Users simply 'point and click' on highlighted hyperlinks, thus making navigation of the system accessible to computer users of low or moderate experience. Already, many potential Internet users are gaining experience of travelling (or 'surfing') the Web through highstreet cybercafés, which offer access to the Internet. Users find that with a minimum of tuition, they are able to utilize the Web to seek information or engage in communication and commerce. The growth of the Internet (and in particular the Web) can be attributed mainly to the user-friendly consumer-oriented homepages (or Web pages) which utilize hypertext capability.

> ❧ The popularity of the WWW as a commercial medium (in contrast to other networks on the Internet) is due to its ability to facilitate global sharing of information and resources, and its potential to provide an efficient channel for advertising, marketing, and even direct distribution of certain goods and information services. ❧ (Hoffman *et al.* 1995:1)

The Web presents a fundamentally different environment – both as a medium and as a market – than traditional communication channels. Marketing activities, including advertising, pricing, word-of-mouth influence, distribution, and product development will need to reflect the unique characteristics of Internet-based marketing strategy. This is perhaps best summarized by the introduction of the term 'marketspace' (Rayport and Sviokla 1994) to describe a new arena of value adding activity, one which is parallel to but different from the traditional marketplace. While some companies may operate solely in the marketplace, others may operate solely in the marketspace, or they may straddle the two realms. Many believe that eventually the marketspace environment will dominate. 'Information-defined transactions are both inevitable and increasing in number and complexity, given the growing omnipresence of the microprocessor. As a result, companies must learn how to manage in – and take advantage of – this new arena.' (Rayport and Sviokla 1994:142). One example of a successful marketspace business is the Internet bookstore Amazon <http://www.amazon.com/>. Billed as the 'Earth's Biggest Bookstore', customers may order books, participate in discussions with selected authors through e-mail, take part in promotional contests, and generally gain information and insight into the products and services offered. Although these developments – and the new links which they forge between buyers and sellers – may seem impressive, the long-term impact of the Web on commercial activity will require firms to acquire an understanding of this unique environment.

A Glossary of Internet Terms

Bandwidth: Used to express the maximum possible throughput of a data link in bits per second. The higher the bandwidth of a communication line, the faster it may transmit data and the more data it may carry.

Cyberspace: a term coined by William Gibson in the novel *Neuromancer* to describe the sum total of computer-accessible information in the world. Often used interchangeably with the term 'virtual reality' to describe an alternative realm of experience to the physical world.

Flame: a deliberately abusive message in e-mail or posted to a discussion group.

Homepage: a personal web page which you control and can refer other people to.

HTML (Hypertext Mark-up Language) : a convention for inserting instructions into a text file which allows web browsers (software, such as Netscape) to display the file, and which may include links to non-text based communication (such as audio, video, or picture files).

Hypermedia: media such as video and audio, which go beyond the conventional text or picture based communications which were traditionally shared by computer networks.

Hypertext: a system of interactive text linking allowing the reader to choose any path through the text displayed.

Internet: a network of computer networks stretching across the world, linking computers of many different types.

Surfer: a user, or traveller, who navigates through the Internet.

Web page: a coherent document that is readable by a web browser. A web page may contain simple text, or may give the reader access to complex hypermedia presentations.

World Wide Web (or WWW or Web): the arrangement of Internet-accessible resources, including hypertext and hypermedia, which conforms to HTML format.

The Concept of Interactivity

Standard dictionary definitions of the term 'interactivity' refer to elements of a system mutually influencing and being affected by each other. The application of interactive capability to computer-communication services is seen as impacting upon three main classes: information services (e.g. databases), communications services (e.g. messaging, e-mail, etc.) and transactional services (e.g. teleshopping, Electronic Data Interchange, etc.). 'I recall one manager remarking that his service (Prestel) saw itself as selling interactivity rather than information' (Miles 1991:150).

Why should this new capability be considered so valuable in the design and delivery of modern-day products and services – indeed to the point of defining the firm's offerings in terms of their capacity for interaction? Two key principles which underlie the departure of interactive marketing from traditional marketing practices are put forward (Spalter 1995). First, the ability for computer networks to enable communication from anywhere in the globe at anytime removes the constraints of space and time associated with physical marketplaces. Second, traditional mass marketing media have consisted primarily of monologues, from the firm to the consumer. Commercial online services and the introduction of the Web have created the potential for a mass interactive dialogue between exchange parties. The shift is then from a 'one (firm)-to-many (consumers)' model of communication to the 'many-to-many' model where contribution to the medium and the message may come from both directions. The newer media are marked by increased user control, more specialized content, speed of transmission, and non-linear access.

> ❝ Typically these [e-mail, videotex] are not 'passive' media, like traditional publications or like familiar broadcast and recorded media, but are interactive. Interactivity makes the classic model of an originator and receiver of information rather suspect, since both parties are now playing a role in generating the final information output, even if this flows from the former to the latter. ❞ (Miles 1991:149)

Many of the current offerings to consumers via the Web are not designed to be interactive. While the possibility of consumer controlled, or even initiated, product design customization and information search is proposed, little evidence thus far has emerged that suggests how interactive capability will impact upon marketing practice. Relatively few firms have successfully oriented their product or service offerings to final consumers in the new interactive environments. 'Creating attractive interactive products is a challenge, as it currently usually requires combining skills from computing (to process information), and media (to package it is attractive forms), and also often telecommunications (to deliver it)' (Miles 1991:149). This is of significance because in the new interactive environment, consumers will increasingly target advertisers as opposed to advertisers targeting consumers

(Anderson 1996). The decision as to what content will be seen and when, and the opportunities for the manipulation of content, are in the hands of the consumer themselves.

> ❝ New media have made interaction possible, however, and have even turned the dialogue round. The initiative is now with the consumers. With interactive TV and CD ROM, consumers can choose the areas that interest them, and can then look more deeply into the varieties within those areas; they can ask questions and get answers in several rounds. Even if the answers are programmed, the range of alternatives can be very large, which makes for interaction verging on the dynamic. ❞
> (Wikstrom 1996:367)

One example is the use made by both Eagle Star Direct (<http://www.eaglestardirect.co.uk>) and Direct Line Insurance Ltd (<http://www.directline.co.uk/>), who solicit information from customers about their home or car online, and then offer an insurance quote based on the information given.

Characteristics of the New Interactive Media

The new interactive media may be seen to have significant differences to the more traditional marketing communications media (both personal and non-personal). We explore four key areas of differentiation; communication style, social presence, control of communication content and control of communication contact. With respect to each of these key areas, we compare the new electronic communication media with more traditional media.

Communication style

Communication style refers to the temporal (or time) dimension of communications, and can be seen to be either more synchronous or more asynchronous in nature. Synchronous communication styles, as the name implies, tend to have little or no time lag between the giving, receiving and responding aspects of communication between the parties. Examples would include face-to-face conversation and telephone conversations. Asynchronous communication styles would include such a time lag, examples being written communications (mail, e-mail) or even direct response advertising.

Social presence

Social presence, or perceived personalness, is the feeling that communication exchanges are sociable, warm, personal, sensitive, and active. Social presence is influenced by channel attributes; that is, channels that convey non-verbal information, such as facial expression, gaze and posture are usually rated higher in social presence. Channels that are considered useful for filling more personal communication needs should also be rated as higher in social presence (Perce and Courtright 1993). Closely related to the concept of social presence is the concept of medium richness, which is the perception that a medium is higher in immediate feedback, multiple cues, natural language, and personal focus.

Personal (face-to-face selling) and non-personal (telemarketing, direct mail, and electronic commerce) communications methods are seen as differing in the possession of these two attributes (see Figure 9.1).

Personal selling, because of the rich variety of cues available in face-to-face communication and the absence of a time lag in the interaction, is placed in the top left corner of the grid. Direct mail, with relatively minimal social cues and a distinctive time lag in the interaction, is placed in the bottom right corner. Because of the ability to transmit verbal cues and the immediacy of the response, telemarketing has been placed slightly above electronic commerce in the grid. However, with the increasing sophistication of audio and visual capabilities on the Internet and the development of speedier responses, its position may well move closer to that of personal selling. Shopping modes (TV, computers, radio, telephone, mail, interpersonal selling) differ along a range of dimensions and it must be recognized that these differences may affect consumer responses in areas such as involvement, intrusiveness and entertainment value. Increasingly, we find that the new electronic commerce media are in fact taking the 'person' out of personal selling!

> ❧ *New IT marks a break with the information and communication technologies of earlier eras. Microprocessors have brought cheap and convenient information-processing power to economic life. Activities that formerly required human mediation or massive mainframe systems, if they were economically and practically feasible at all, can now be performed by mass commodity 'chips'.* ❧ (Miles 1991:146)

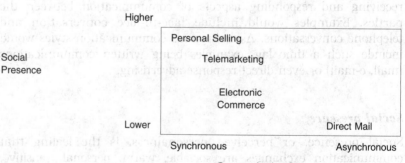

Figure 9.1 Social Presence and Communications Methods

(Source: TQC/Ogilvy and Mather Direct, cited in Henley Centre 1991:80)

Consumer Control of Contact

Early research into the willingness of consumers to utilize technology in shopping behaviour concludes that the ability to control the pace and presentation of product information has the strongest influence on willingness to engage in computer-mediated marketing activity (Carson *et al.* 1996). This ability to control communication contact is put forward as a key factor in the success of voice messaging services, an example of an industry that has successfully handled the transition to the marketspace. This replacement of the physical product (the answering machine) with an information-based service allows consumers to access voice storage and retrieval from any location, store messages for future delivery, and broadcast information to other users. These developments emphasize the need for firms to develop a new core competence – that of market-oriented computer interface development (Spalter 1995). By understanding what features of the interactive media induce trial, search and purchase behaviours, firms can begin to define the successful components of the online marketing mix.

Consumer Control of Content

The ability to customize message content is one dimension of interactivity (Anderson 1996). The content can be customized by either users or by senders. Where users are able to control the content, or presentation, of the message it is said to be interactive. If senders alone are able to customize the content, then the message is non-interactive. The new interactive communication media allow consumers to customize content by supplying content to medium (through their own homepages, posting messages on electronic bulletin boards, or supplying content which is included in corporate web pages).

These aspects of control, that over content and over contact, place differing marketing media in different customer interactivity relationships (see Figure 9.2).

One of the key features of the new electronic communication media is the ability for consumers to control both contact and content. It is interesting to note that direct mail, one of the cornerstones of 'one-to-

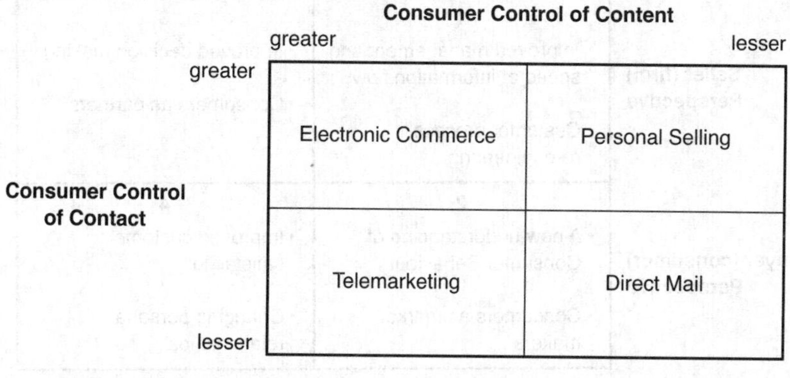

Figure 9.2 Consumer Control of Contact and Content

one' marketing media, is at the opposite end of the spectrum to the newer electronic commerce media, such as the Web, in this framework.

The New Marketing Landscape

Individuals, whether at a personal or organizational level, need to respond intelligently, flexibly and speedily to rapid changes taking place in marketplace environments. In the virtual marketplace the changing nature of marketing relationships is creating new challenges for both buyers and sellers. However it is increasingly being questioned whether IT is fostering new forms of trading and relationships or simply new tools to extend existing personal and organizational skills and practices. In Figure 9.3 these questions are viewed using a framework which investigates impacts at the personal/individual level and the organizational level of the use of IT to enable virtual relationships or to build virtual markets. Investigating these issues requires an appreciation of the intended purposes and benefits, and the realities and unintended impacts, at these levels from the perspective of both the buyer (or consumer) and the seller (or firm).

Organizational Level Impacts

Firm Perspective

From the point of view of the firm utilizing the new interactive communication media, a number of dynamic changes may be experienced (see Figure 9.3, cell 1). We concentrate here on two key areas of change, the utilization of information within the firm and the role of the consumer in designing and delivering product or service value.

IMPROVED MANAGEMENT AND SPEED OF INFORMATION FLOW

Electronic based commercial activities are available 24-hours a day. This makes computer mediated communications useful not only in the

	Organizational Level Impacts	Personal Level Impacts
Seller (firm) Perspective	**1** • Improved management and speed of information flow • Customer process re-engineering	**3** • Improved decision making • Consumers as partners
Buyer (consumer) Perspective	**2** • A new understanding of Consumer Behaviour • Consumers as market makers	**4** • Improved customer satisfaction • Changing personal relationships

Figure 9.3 Organizational and Individual Level Impacts of IT

realm of availability, but also allows users to stagger their communications to coincide with different time-zones across the globe. In addition, the asynchronous nature of many traditional marketing communication methods may be reduced, so that buyers and sellers carry out their communication in a way which more nearly reflects 'real-time' conversation.

Electronic markets are ubiquitous. The ability to reach a global audience has led to a shift in the economies of operating in the marketspace. As Internet accessibility increases, the opportunity for firms with global ambitions increases. This raises issues that impact upon the globalization of markets and the fragmentation of markets and imply an increased role for marketing communication content, which may be customized by the receiver through the use of interactive communications media, to conform to local cultural norms and expectations.

The creation and extraction of value from the new electronic marketing media will have profound consequences for firms as the influence of the information revolution is felt.

> ▨ *Specifically, when buyer-seller transactions occur in an information defined arena, information is accessed and absorbed more easily, and arranged and priced in different ways. Most important, the information about a product or service can be separated from the product or service itself.* ▨ (Rayport and Sviokla 1994:141)

The rapid growth in catalogue and cable shopping networks suggests that there are many products and services which meet the criteria for successful trading through electronic markets (low asset specificity and ease of description) (Wigand and Benjamin 1995). In the Marketspace, the content of the transaction is different – information about a product may replace the product itself. The context of the transaction in no longer 'face-to-face' but takes place within the arena of 'cyberspace', or a virtual reality. In addition, the infrastructure that enables transactions relies upon computers and communication lines rather than physical proximity. By giving prospective customers a 'taste' of the product offered, a guesthouse in central London now receives over 50 per cent of its bookings from customers who have viewed their web pages: The London Vicarage Hotel <http://www.deadlock.com/hotels/london/vicarage/>. This web site allows potential guests to view the facilities, find out what is on offer in local shops and theatres, and even sample some of the humour exhibited by the staff in their helpful hints for foreigners on ordering drinks in a British Pub:

> ▨ *When you've picked your spot approach the person in front as closely as you can without making it seem that you're pushing. Guard your position and don't let anyone get a shoulder in front of you. When you reach the 'second row', try to place yourself behind somebody who is currently being served (your 'live*

punter'). When a gap presents itself between the live punter and the person adjacent (a one inch gap is ample), set your prop [a £5 or £10 note] on the bar. Yes, go ahead and push your arm through the gap and stake your claim. As the gap widens, get your shoulder in sideways so that when the live punter has finished being served and is collecting his/her change, you're in the perfect position for the final phase. It's perfectly permissible to actually hang your prop over the far side of the bar obstructing the free movement of the bar staff, and to stand on the foot bar to gain extra height.

As the barmaid approaches the live punter to administer the change (if the live punter has tendered exact money this is a big setback, in which case all you can do is to scowl at him/her), it's absolutely vital to stare in the barperson's face to gain eye contact. You'll only get one chance and if you blow it, it could set you back ten minutes. The instant eye contact is attained, start talking. Order one drink, even if you have a list of ten. Once you've started the order you're home and dry and you can relax. In reply to your one-drink request, the barperson will always ask if there's 'anything else'. At this point, if it takes your fancy, you can turn around and smile smugly at the person who joined the battle at the same time as you but is still standing halfway back. **🔢**

CUSTOMER PROCESS RE-ENGINEERING

Another key to success is understanding the concept of 'consumer processes' (that is the tasks or steps that people go through to achieve a goal, as opposed to producer processes) and the fundamental ways on-line technology transforms them (Champy *et al.* 1996). The power of a global, interactive computer network lies in transforming the means by which consumers satisfy their critical desires. The focus on consumer processes represents a natural evolution of another type, or wave, or re-engineering. Previously, managers organized work around functions like sales, marketing and finance but the technology of the 1990s allows managers to rigorously examine end-to-end business processes such as order fulfilment, concept to market and customer acquisition, or indeed to focus upon the end-to-end tasks of end customers. There are a number of ways in which consumer processes vary, and where activities may be re-designed: first, by the type and number of steps involved for the customer in the process; second by the cost and time involved in doing each task; and third, by the complexity of the task (Champy *et al.* 1996.). As with re-engineering the business processes of a company, redesigning the consumer processes for an electronic community involves reducing time, costs and errors wherever possible.

Consumer Perspective

From the point of view of the consumer utilizing the new interactive communication media, a number of changes may be required of organizations in their dealings with consumers (see Figure 9.3, cell 2). We concentrate here on two key areas of change; the understanding the firm has of consumer behaviour and the role which consumers may play in the creation of marketing opportunities.

A NEW UNDERSTANDING OF CONSUMER BEHAVIOUR

The ability for consumers to customize the content of marketing communications is important to marketers since it allows consumers to self-select message content depending on their level of involvement (Carson *et al.* 1996). The desire for objective information content is an important attribute of what is termed 'technology assisted shopping' use by consumers, who may favour a controlled search for product information. However, the cause-and-effect relationships between products and their perceived benefits will be affected by the consumers' ability to view different renderings of content in a non-linear way, by choosing the order in which they view the information (through the use of hypertext links) (Anderson 1996:158). Marketers will therefore need to understand the dynamics of consumer involvement as it relates to the new media landscape.

The notion of involvement relates to the level of motivation (e.g. high or low) which consumers have and can affect the extent to which a consumer will process the information they are given. When we are involved we pay attention, perceive importance and behave in a different manner than when we are not involved. With respect to communications, recipients respond differently to the same message due to their personal characteristics. When recipients are more involved with a message they give more counter-arguments and form evaluations differently, depending upon how involved they are with the topic. There is a challenge for businesses wanting to utilize new information technology based communication media to understand how to transform the content communicated to encourage involvement in users.

The transformation of marketing activities in hypermedia environments relies, in part, on the fact that interactivity may incorporate contact between the user and computers as well as with other people. 'Thus, the Web is not a simulation of a real-world environment, but an alternative to real-world environments where consumers may experience *telepresence*, the perception of being present in the mediated, rather than the real-world, environment' (Hoffman and Novak 1996a:2). Within these virtual environments both experiential (e.g. netsurfing) and goal directed (e.g. online shopping, information search and processing) behaviours may compete for the consumers' attention and involvement.

In addition, these behaviours are mediated by competency issues, which relate to the capability of the user to meet the challenges posed by the environment and their ability to sufficiently master the technology needed to act in this new virtual environment. 'Interactive marketers capable of producing experiences that appeal to wide audiences will understand that the key to interactivity rests in involving and capturing users' attention by enabling them to control their own experience and communications' (Spalter 1995:175). This may be achieved by giving consumers the ability to express emotions and react to content by communicating through bulletin boards, chat features and e-mail. Thus a cycle of success may develop, where content attracts users, users create more content, new content enhances the value of the site and so more users are drawn to the marketspace. Such interactive capability also closes the time gap between exposure and response, allowing users to select ads and respond by placing orders or requesting more information instantly. Memory will be relevant to the extent that consumers can recall whether the transaction or service encounter was a positive or negative experience. Creating memorable advertisements will become a secondary issue and developing interactive dialogues that retain the attention of consumers and facilitate purchase behaviour will become the primary aim.

An important aspect of consumer experience in utilizing computer mediated environments is the concept of *flow*. Csikszentmihalyi (1978) defines flow experiences as those optimal and enjoyable experiences in which we feel a sense of exhilaration, and a deep sense of enjoyment. The concept of flow can be seen to be applicable to consumer or user behaviour in computer-mediated environments precisely because of the presence of machine interactivity (that is, the experience that the user has with the computer environment itself) in such environments. It has also been defined as a state occurring during network navigation [or 'surfing'] which is: characterized by a seamless sequence of responses facilitated by machine interactivity; intrinsically enjoyable; accompanied by a loss of self-consciousness, and self-reinforcing (Hoffman and Novak 1996b:57). In computer-mediated interactions flow involves a certain kind of intrinsic interest, the intrinsic interest that accompanies cognitive arousal and use of the imagination. When in the flow state:

> ❛ *Players shift into a common mode of experience when they become absorbed in their activity. This mode is characterized by a narrowing of the focus of awareness, so that irrelevant perceptions and thoughts are filtered out; by loss of self-consciousness, by a responsiveness to clear goal and unambiguous feedback; and by a sense of control over the environment . . . it is this common flow experience that people adduce as the main reason for performing the activity.* ❜ (Webster *et al.* 1993:413)

A new basis for market segmentation will be needed for Web-based marketing efforts. As consumers vary in their ability to achieve flow, they state that there exists a need to determine the variables that relate to a consumer's propensity to enter the flow state. 'Since 'repeat purchase', that is, repeat visits to a particular Web site, will be increased if the environment facilitates the flow state, the marketing objective on the first visit (i.e. 'trial'), will be to provide for these flow opportunities' (Hoffman and Novak 1996a:7).

It has been argued that flow will lead to increased quality time in a hypermedia computer-mediated environment such as the Web (Hoffman and Novak 1996a). The facilitation of flow will be an important factor in Web site design, where consumers need a balance of experience – neither boring (where insufficient challenge is presented) nor anxiety producing (when network navigation is too difficult, which would increase the likelihood of site jumping, or exiting from network navigation). This balance between situational challenges (the ease or difficulty with which users may interact with a web site) and personal skills (whether the user is experienced or not in the use of a particular computer software) is seen by Csikszentmihalyi (1978:339) as directly influencing the users' willingness to volunteer attention. He states that attention is a finite resource, and that its intensity and inclusiveness has narrow limits set by the relatively few bits of information that can be processed in consciousness at any one time.

The ability for the computer screen to stimulate and encourage users to become absorbed in the activity they are engaged in may be seen as an important tool for marketing. Not only does computer-mediation increase the capacity for interaction by allowing greater control over the communication context and content, but the medium itself may facilitate the experience of flow and thus help focus consumer attention in ways which more passive mass media cannot. When in the flow state, individuals find the activity intrinsically interesting and therefore engage in the activity for its own pleasure and enjoyment rather than for some utilitarian purpose. Exploring the opportunities offered through interactive computer-mediated environments can become an involving activity in itself. The ability to modify a computer-mediated environment to suit the users' particular needs or wishes may contribute to the flow experience, and facilitate use of the medium. In computer-mediated communications, the primary relationships may not necessarily be between sender and receiver, but may instead focus on the actual computer mediated environment with which they interact. In this new model, information or content is not merely transmitted from a sender to a receiver but, instead, mediated environments are created by participants and then experienced (Hoffman and Novak 1996a).

CONSUMERS AS MARKET MAKERS

The use of information technology can have unintended consequences for unwary marketers. An example is the introduction of ATM technology in the banking industry. Introduced initially to reduce transaction costs by automating teller transactions, consumers soon realized that ATMs were more convenient because they were available 24-hours a day. This market space began to take on a life of its own, and banks began to realize that their customers were responding to the ATM technology itself, not the individual bank which provided it.

> ■ *Their hard-won brand equity was swept away by the power of*
> *the marketspace transactions. The loyalty a customer felt for a*
> *particular bank threatened to evaporate entirely. Indeed, as banks*

*linked and branded their networks for added customer conve-
nience (for example CIRRUS or NYCE), the net effect was
further homogenisation of ATMs and declining consumer brand
loyalty to individual retail banks.* **"** (Rayport and Sviokla
1994:143)

In the past, interorganizational information systems, electronic data
interchange networks, shared databases, and other forms of electronic
links mainly connected firms. Today, on the other hand, information
infrastructures are extending to reach individual consumers (Saker *et
al.* 1995). The potential for transformations in the value systems of
many firms is thus far greater now than it has been in the past, as
technology begins to enable producers to directly interact with
consumers. One fundamental question, therefore, is to what extent
producing organizations would take advantage of direct electronic
links with consumers, and whether, in the process, intermediaries will
be eliminated from the value system. The opportunity for individual
consumers to become market makers themselves has never been
greater.

Important implications for consumer participation in the marketing
process result from such shifts in channel power. Consumers may
collaborate on idea generation, product design, or marketing
communication efforts directly. The ability for consumers to add
content to the medium, for instance by mounting their own Web page
or contributing to newsgroup discussions, brings new power to 'word-
of-mouth' advertising. Interactivity on the Web gives consumers the
opportunity for greater control of communication messages. 'Such
control may manifest itself in startling new ways: for example, it is
feasible for consumers interested in purchasing big-ticket durables
such as cars or appliances to broadcast their interest and solicit open
bids from different firms' (Hoffman and Novak 1996a:6).

Alternatively, because the Web increases the power of the consumer
and decreases the power of the firm (thus approaching 'symmetrical
power' between the two parties), the best communication efforts are
likely to be 'collaborative' rather than 'autonomous' (Hoffman and
Novak 1996b). This implies that firms utilizing such a collaborative
approach may find that they not only have the capacity to keep pace
with market change, but they may, indeed, accelerate it.

In addition to a new understanding of this unique environment,
there are other barriers to its development as a global arena of value-
adding activity. Foremost among these are the barriers which exist in
the infrastructure and technology needed to access mass markets.
Consumers must have access to technology in the home which allows
for interactivity with a user-friendly, feasible way to access the
marketspace.

" *Until then, the retailer will continue to be the traditional
consumer market, buying and displaying merchandise from
multiple suppliers. But the required technologies are evolving
rapidly, and the NII [National Information Infrastructure, a*

> *government initiative in the USA to improve communication network availability] represents the organizer of these technologies. There seems little likelihood of significant change until the NII connects consumers to the industry value chain.* 🔳
> (Benjamin and Wigand 1995:67)

It is therefore important to remember that a number of assumptions often underlie many of the predictions made about the new field of electronic commerce. These include: the interconnection of all consumers and organizations with each other; that these connections will be at very high bandwidth, able to support interactive multimedia transactions; that access and use will be affordable (in order to facilitate the implementation of low-cost co-ordination transactions); that the available technology will provide the interactive capabilities for making free market choices easily and intuitively; and that there will be no favouritism designed into market access (i.e. by government restrictions or legislation) (Benjamin and Wigand 1995:64).

Personal Level Impacts

Firm Perspective

Taking again the point of view of the firm utilizing the new interactive communication media, a number of dynamic changes in the ways in which employees undertake their duties may be expected (see Figure 9.3, cell 3). We concentrate here on two key areas of change; the decision making process, and the role of consumers as partners in value creation.

IMPROVED DECISION MAKING

The development of computer supported co-operative work within organizations is the focus of a great deal of attention in the current business environment. These systems allow multiple users to work together on the same document or database simultaneously –'where they can meet formally and informally in the ways in which they do in traditional continuous working environments, so that opportunities for social networking and meta-communication are not lost in the new media' (Miles 1991:163). The opportunity for a wider range of organizational members to be involved in the collection, interpretation and dissemination of information through the new media also implies an increase in process-based knowledge (that is, knowledge gained through the process of conducting the research itself (Menon and Varadarajan 1992)). This type of knowledge enhancement is characterized by a high level of involvement on the part of the participant and should therefore affect information utilization and decision outcomes within the firm. The importance of such opportunities is recognized by many organizations, with skill and effectiveness in the use of information seen as critical to becoming market-oriented, which is accepted as a major method of gaining success in an intensely competitive business environment. Speed and flexibility of decision-

making is of increasing importance in these new marketing environments, requiring both rational and intuitive abilities in formulating
insight on the part of decision makers (Eisenhardt 1992).

In the acquisition and use of information by individuals, the current
information search techniques allow users to select independent facts
and then create new patterns of organization of these facts (Chesbro
and Bonsall 1989:235). This promotes the use of isolated facts
without a consideration of the political-cultural context in which these
facts occur. They further state that knowledge is becoming a corporate
product rather than an aspect of personal comprehension, utility and
growth. Benefits may occur in computer mediated markets when the
production of knowledge is treated as a corporate asset. The
interaction between buyer and seller often starts with the solving of
problems, which provides an opportunity for much deeper interaction
and more advanced learning for those concerned. In these activities, it
is not only sales and service staff but also design and production
people who interact with customers, which means that all these people
learn directly from their often close and dynamic co-operation with
many of their clients. Where this information is recorded electro-
nically, it may provide an historical picture of the development of the
relationship which may be accessed by a variety of different actors
within the firm.

CONSUMERS AS PARTNERS

While the company is the dominating actor in design and production
and is still the main provider of information as part of the marketing
activities, the consumer seems poised to take part in product/service
design and in deciding what information to search for. The dynamics
unfolding as the Internet develops highlight questions which focus on
the heart of the source-message-receiver model of communication.
These dynamics also have implications for the nature of the marketing
exchange relationship itself. With higher information intensity,
channel power can shift in favour of consumers and a lessening of
the distinctions between producer and consumer may result (Glazer
1991). Firms utilizing the Web no longer broadcast a single
communication to address consumer needs as network navigation
allows consumers to choose what information (if any) to receive from
the firm. 'Thus, marketers must begin to examine the manner in which
these more collaborative communication efforts should proceed'
(Hoffman and Novak 1996a:6). They point out that in its simplest
form, the marketing concept states that to be successful a firm must
satisfy consumer needs and wants. In the rush to set up shop on the
Internet, they observe that few firms are expending the effort required
to identify these needs and wants. In other words, the capability for
interactivity has preceded the understanding of how to harness and
utilize such capability, and how to extract value from it.

Consumer Perspective

From the point of view again of the consumer utilizing the new
interactive communication media, a number of opportunities may

arise to improve the value which customers receive. We concentrate here on two key areas of change (see Figure 9.3, cell 4); improvements in the satisfaction customers experience, and the nature of the relationships which are potentially formed.

IMPROVED CUSTOMER SATISFACTION

In the marketspace, the traditional interaction between physical buyers and sellers is eliminated. The context of the interaction is now a 'virtual' world which may complement, contradict, clarify or confuse the parallel physical world experienced by both buyers and sellers. The concept of audience activity is a critical feature of commerce on the Web, and the link between the uses which are served and the gratifications which are sought is an important one. The rapid growth in catalogue and cable shopping networks suggests that consumers are willing to buy products through outlets other than retail stores, with the potential erosion of retail markets resulting. The cable home shopping channel QVC is said to move goods at the rate of $30 per second, and that there were 10,000 mail order companies in the United States in 1992 – turning over $51 billion worth of goods (Wigand and Benjamin 1995).

> ▨ *The interactive nature of the medium offers another category of firm benefits since it is especially conductive to developing customer relationships. This potential for customer interaction, which is largely asynchronous under current implementation, facilitates relationship marketing and customer support to a greater degree than ever before possible with traditional media.* ▨
> (Hoffman and Novak 1994)

In the long term, effective Internet marketers will be those which are actively involved in activities which: firstly, further the development of the medium itself and; secondly, work with consumers to develop a shared understanding of the consumer benefits offered by Internet-based commerce (Wigand and Benjamin 1995).

CHANGING PERSONAL RELATIONSHIPS

The user community on the Internet regards it as an omnipresent resource of knowledge and intercourse, and that an Internet culture has established itself for the purpose of maintaining this resource's integrity and efficiency. For example, Internet culture requires that information presented by commercial users must be of demonstrable value and interest. Direct solicitation of sales or the self-promotion of products and services may be met by a hostile and vocal response – known as 'flaming'. The ability to contribute content to the Web gives consumers an unprecedented voice, and they have been known to use it. The indiscriminate sending of e-mail solicitations may provoke an avalanche of hostile replies to the senders' system, thus forcing it to 'crash' and preventing genuine consumer contacts. Increasingly, firms must take a different role than that of the traditional paternal provider. Listening to customer input regarding topics of interest (e.g. product functionality, service availability, customer needs) and responding with helpful advice and/or information is one acceptable means of conducting marketing activity on the Internet. Suggestions may be made to customers regarding sources, both on the Web and elsewhere, where additional help or information is available.

Here is a classic example of what happens when a one-to-many mentality clashes with a many-to-many mentality. The legal firm, Canter and Siegel shot a crudely and offensively implemented mass marketing missile out to a highly fragmented and dramatically varied group of individuals by e-mail. Their actions were met with hostility and rage on a mass (and global) scale. Thousands and thousands of 'flaming' messages [i.e. angry responses] were sent by enraged consumers, resulting in the loss of their Internet access and a global reputation which was not to be envied (Wigand and Benjamin 1995). 'Consumers empowered to control, choose, and help create their own commercial experiences will wreak havoc on rigid, inflexible organizations unwilling or unable to adapt to the marketspace' (Spalter 1995:163).

A Framework for Developing Web Sites

Developing a web site draws upon many of the traditional elements of marketing management which characterize good marketing practice. The framework outlined below illustrates some of the more traditional planning activities, together with elements that arise in the development of web sites, which should be considered. There are six elements of importance, and five processes:

The six elements are:

1　Audience information – gaining knowledge about the target audience, as well as the current users of your marketing information. In what ways will your internet users be similar or different to your current target audience?

2　Purpose statement – the reasons for and the scope of the web site.

3　Objective statement – the specific goals which the web site is to accomplish.

4　Domain information – gaining knowledge about the subject domain which the web site will cover. What information will users value and which the firm may provide? What information *from* users will the firm want to collect?

5　Web specification – the elements that will go into a Web site, described in detail. What hyperlinks should be included, will there be audio and/or video content?

6　Web presentation – how will the information be delivered to the user? The use of logos and other design features needs to be considered.

The five processes are:

1 Planning – the process of defining the overall goals for the Web site, and how these relate to corporate marketing goals.

2 Analysis – the process of gathering and comparing information about the Web and its operation in order to improve the overall quality of the web site.

3 Design – the process whereby the web site designers build the site, the specifications which must be adhered to and the way in which the actual components of the web site should be constructed.

4 Implementation – the process of actually building the web site itself, using hypertext mark-up language (HTML).

5 Development – the process of ensuring that the other processes continue and that the web site itself is being presented well to Internet users. It involves directing the analysis of audience information, usability, and use patterns.

(Source: December, J and Randall, N. (1994) *The World Wide Web Unleashed* Sams Publishing.)

Types of Commercial Web Sites

The commercial activity presently taking place on the web may be organized into two main categories; traffic control sites (e.g. search engines, which direct users to the correct web site) and destination sites (the ultimate destination for the user which presents the firms' virtual counterpart) (Hoffman *et al.* 1995). Of particular interest to market-space retailers are the forms and functions which these destination sites may adopt. Three categories of destination site are identified as Internet Presence Sites, Online Storefronts, and Content Sites. The impact which these new communication media may have on business transactions may be usefully viewed in relation to the way in which they influence three key areas of uncertainty which consumers experience in relation to purchasing goods or services. These uncertainties focus on the buyer's perceived need for the product (need uncertainty); the buyer's perception of the reliability and consistency with which the firm will be able to carry through its commitments (transaction uncertainty); and the buyer's perception that differences or changes in the marketplace itself will impact the outcome (market uncertainty) (Hakansson *et al.* 1990). Table 9.1 summarizes how each of the three types of web site may impact these uncertainties.

Internet Presence sites provide a virtual signpost which informs net users of the firms' offerings. This may take the form of a home page equivalent to a conventional advert. It may concentrate on emotional appeals by presenting product information in an educational/ entertainment format (edutainment) – for example the Ragu home page <http://www.eat.com/> which includes its own on-going soap-opera ('As the Lasagne Bakes'!). Alternatively, it may rely on rational

Table 9.1 Impact of Web
Sites

	Reduction in Need Uncertainty	Reduction in Market Uncertainty	Reduction in Transaction Uncertainty
Internet Presence Sites	▶ Easy availability of production/firm information ▶ Use of Edutainment formats	▶ Contribution to the building and maintaining of brand equity ▶ Geographical constraints lessened ▶ Consumer may assume role of market maker	
Online Storefronts	▶ Online product trial possible ▶ Ease of purchase may encourage impulse purchase	▶ Medium facilitates relationship building and customer support availability ▶ Geographical constraints lessened	▶ Consumer has greater control over information search, ordering and product specification
Content Sites	▶ Consumer able to customise product or service itself and/or its form of delivery	▶ Disintermediation (the reduction of the number of intermediaries in the transaction) ▶ Geographical constraints lessened	▶ Direct distribution ▶ Time compression of order and delivery to consumer ▶ Consumer as partner is able to co-ordinate and carry out some of the ordering and fulfilment functions thus reducing errors, overheads and costs

appeals through the provision of detailed product or company related information (such as may be found on the homepages of many Universities). The provision of timely and relevant information can help to reduce the uncertainty consumers may have regarding their need for the product. In addition, because geographical constraints are lessened the firm may be able to reach a wider market. The building and enhancing of brand equity will also be an important feature, as it will highlight differences between product offerings. When product becomes place becomes promotion however, brand equity can rapidly evaporate. ATM users respond to the technology itself, not the bank 'brand' that provides it (Rayport and Sviokla 1994:143). This provides opportunities to develop brand loyalty in customers to the *context* of communication and therefore with the communication medium itself. Electronic communication media can be used by firms to create brand value because in the marketspace the firm can manage directly its interface with customers. However, these opportunities may be offset by the threats which rising consumer power may bring in this new medium. The ability for consumers to create their own marketplaces, and the ability to easily and cheaply compare product information, may lead to a situation where retailers who offer well-known branded products (about which consumers do not need a lot of information) may find themselves forced to compete on the basis of price alone. It is this threat that is often the driving force behind firms which utilize one of the other forms of internet site. These sites offer opportunities to add value through the medium itself.

Online Storefronts offer the opportunity for consumers to purchase directly from the firm, using the electronic equivalent of a catalogue. This marriage of direct marketing capabilities with the functional characteristics of the web as a communications medium (control of content, time and location availability, etc.) can provide an extremely attractive option for marketspace marketers. There are opportunities for customization and relationship building as well as reduced transaction costs. Not only are consumers able to conduct product trial online (for example, listen to music clips or use software), but they are able to order the product with greater ease.

> ❡ *Savings may also be realised from efficiencies in the marketing and selling functions. The Web shifts more of these functions to the customer; savings result through reduced brochure printing and distribution costs and reductions in order taking as customers use fill-out forms to prepare their own orders. As control is also effectively transferred to the customer, we speculate that customer satisfaction might actually be increased.* ❡ (Hoffman *et al.* 1995:8)

Content sites supply users with the actual information-based product. Such products may include online publishing (i.e. newspapers, books, magazines), graphic or audio based products (i.e. new music releases), or time sensitive information (i.e. stockmarket data). The scope for customization to the individual needs of consumers is great, and the ability to distribute directly reduces the number of intermediaries, thus making the relationship between producer and consumer more direct.

The Intranet

The real growth on the Internet may not be where you think it is. Internal computer networks within the world's large organizations are currently enjoying the dawn of a new age ... the age of the Intranet. One web consultant commented that while the Internet launch of the Web site for a major plastics company was seen as huge (1500 pages on-line), their Intranet site was gargantuan (over 10,000 pages available to employees of the firm, internally!). Why are Intranets stealing all the thunder? Companies are using these internal networks for strategic advantage in the following ways:

▶ As a replacement to paper for routine communications. Quality control procedures, staff memos, progress reports, all can be mounted on a web page which is available to users throughout the firm, no matter what kind of computer system they have on their desk.

> ► To foster group communications, especially in cross-business unit teams or where users are located in different geographical sites.
>
> ► As a uniform front-end for different types of computer applications. Don't want to train your staff in how to use a complex database package? Just design a user-friendly web page and let staff access it from the Intranet.
>
> ► To distribute software within the company. With an Intranet, you can download the latest application straight onto your desktop computer.
>
> So remember, next time you visit a company's Homepage, it is only the tip of the iceberg. Behind that glossy exterior may lie the real heart of the organization . . . its own 'internal Internet'.

Value Creation in a Virtual World

The direct relationship which may be facilitated by the new electronic communication media raises many issues in the realm of value creation as it has traditionally been conceptualized. The Web page has become an information mirror in the marketspace of an activity that traditionally has occurred in the physical world. The new 'many-to-many' model allows for consumer contribution to the development of the communication medium itself. Customers can support their own web sites, with content created by consumers for consumers. This places increased emphasis upon the ability of firms to 'listen' and respond appropriately to customers, and for this IT may also play a part. While many firms have established sites on the web in order to advertise goods and elicit consumer opinions, some have actually automated the interface with the customer. This allows firms to both lower the cost of customer response, and perhaps more importantly, to monitor the interactions it has with customers. In the future, 'Computers will function as the command-and-control centres of marketing campaigns, deciding when to hand-off individual consumers from one marketing tool to the next.' (Deighton 1994)

Traditionally, the value chain put forward by Porter consists of 'upstream' and 'downstream' value adding activities for any given point of activity within the firm (see Figure 9.4). In addition, in relation to the customer, value creation is seen as unidirectional (from the firm to the customer). The new electronic communications media radically alters this model. The firm is now in the centre of a 'whirlpool', where value may be added by both suppliers *and* customers. This means that the firm may take advantage of opportunities in both directions. This chapter has focused largely upon the impact which electronic communication media may have upon the firm-customer relationship. However, many of the dynamics discussed may be equally applied to business-to-business relationships. In fact, one of the fastest growing opportunities for business in cyberspace is not the World Wide Web, but the Intranet. That is, networks which parallel the Internet, but which are functioning at firm (or between firms) level. These Intranets provide many of the benefits of interactivity and interconnectedness,

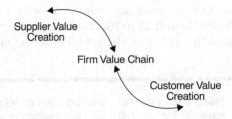

Figure 9.4 Firm Value Chain

but are far more secure and suffer less from the limitations of bandwidth that plagues the Internet.

In order to manage in the new marketing landscape, firms will need to apply the information they collect at each stage of the value creation process in the virtual marketspace to their corresponding activities in the physical world. This new value creation logic requires not only an understanding of how to integrate supplier and consumer input, but of how each realm of activity may operate and complement one another.

> ❝ *The economic logic of the two chains is different: a conventional understanding of the economics of scale and scope does not apply to the virtual value chain in the same way as it does to the physical value chain. Moreover, the two chains must be managed distinctly but also in concert.* ❞ (Rayport and Sviokla 1994:143)

Conclusion

In this chapter we have first defined and then explored the nature of the new electronic communication media. The similarities and differences with previous marketing communications media and methods have been highlighted, and the potential impact upon the nature of the relationship between buyers and sellers has been discussed. Many are heralding the dawn of the age of 'Interactive Marketing', yet few understand its essential nature, nor have they considered the potential problems or threats which such an age may bring. The ways in which this capacity for interaction may impact upon both the individual (be they employee or consumer) and the organization have been outlined, and the dynamics of buyer-seller relationships in an interactive environment have been reviewed.

In conclusion, the ways in which firms may make use of these new media have been introduced. The decision as to which one of the three types of internet site, or indeed what combination of their use, may be appropriate continues to be a key question for firms wishing to gain strategic advantage in the marketspace. In order to create value, the firm looking to practice Direct Marketing in the twenty-first century must develop and exploit a paradigm which rests not on the unidirectional nature of value creation which has been traditionally proposed – from firm to consumer – but one which recognizes the dynamic role which consumers in the interactive age may adopt, and which incorporates this role into the activities of the firm.

STUDY 2

The big boys: US full-service sites

Travel has come to be regarded as one of the most lucrative online industries, largely due to the success of large, full-service travel sites.

Most of these sites, which offer everything from information about destinations through to online search and reservation facilities, are based in the US.

The companies behind them come from a variety of backgrounds. Unsurprisingly, one organization which has zeroed in on selling travel over the web is Microsoft.

The software giant's Expedia service (*www.expedia.msn.com*) acts as an online

booking agent. Crucially, it undercuts other agents by charging only five per cent commission for flights, compared to the usual 10 per cent. It also aims to be quick and simple for users, with a direct link to an existing computer reservation system (CRS). The idea of taking a computer reservation system and building an internet front-end onto it is taken to its logical conclusion by one of Expedia's main rivals Travelocity (*www.travelocity.com*). The service is run by Sabre, owner of the largest CRS, which accounted for $40bn of travel agent sales in 1996.

Travelocity claims to have recruited more than 750,000 users in a year, and also runs sites in partnership with companies like Hilton Hotels and Budget Rent A Car.

Partnerships are the favoured means of growth for another of the big internet travel players, Preview Travel.

The company has recently amalgamated its existing reservations.com and vacations.

com sites into a combined Preview Travel site (*www.previewtravel.com*).

Preview, which provides a travel reservations area through AOL in addition to its web service, is working on joint sites with at least 10 prospective partners. It is reporting transactions of between $1.3m and $1.5m per week, and claims to have more than 1.5 million subscribers.

The nearest UK equivalent to the American internet travel big guns is EMAP Online, with its A-B Travel and Bargainholidays sites. However, EMAP Online joint managing director Roger Green is keen to point out that his company is focused on the general holiday market.

In contrast, the big full-service sites in the US tend to concentrate on business travel, with flight-only sales accounting for 88 per cent of total online travel transactions.

(Source: *Revolution Magazine*, September 1997, p. 37)

Review Questions

1   What are the key characteristics which differentiate marketing communication on the World Wide Web from other forms of marketing communications? How might these characteristics be utilized in developing other aspects of the marketing mix by firms operating in the marketspace environment?

2   How are the relationships between customers and firms being altered by the use of the Internet? What implications might this have for firms offering:

(a) financial services;
(b) cosmetics;
(c) daily news services?

3   If the customer is to become part of the value creation process for firms, what issues might this raise in relation to the way products or services are created and sold?

Discussion Questions

1 What in your opinion makes a good Web site?

2 Discuss the extent to which the Web presents a fundamentally different environment both as a media and as a market – to traditional communication channels.

3 How is value created through company-consumer interaction?

4 It has been argued that the Internet is uniquely suited to 'developing higher levels of relationships, to establishing dynamic customer communities and allowing satisfied customers to become your champions' (Cross 1994). To what extent do you agree with this statement?

References

Anderson, C. (1996) 'Computer as Audience: Mediated Interactive Messages in Interactive Marketing' in Forrest, E. and Hizerski, R. (eds) *The Future Present*, AMA Chicago, ch 11.

Benjamin, R. and Wigand, R. (1995) 'Electronic Markets & Virtual Value Chains on the Information Superhighway', Sloan Management Review, Winter, pp. 62–72.

Carson, S. Peck, J. and Childers, T. (1996) 'Preliminary Results on the Determinants of Technology Assisted Shopping: A Model, Measure Development, and Validation', AMA Winter Educators' Conference, pp. 229–39.

Champy, J. Buday, R. and Nohria, N. (1996) 'The Rise of the Electronic Community', http://techweb.cmp.com/iw/583/csc.html, accessed 25th June.

Chesbro, J. and Bonsall, D. (1989) 'Computing as Rhetoric', in *CMC: Human Relationships in a Computerized World*, U of Alabama Press, ch 9 pp. 213–37.

Cross, R. (1994) 'Internet: The Missing Marketing Medium Found', *Direct Marketing*, 20(a) pp. 37–46.

Csikszentmihalyi, M. (1978) 'Attention & Holistic Approach to Behavior', in Pope and Singer (eds), *The Stream of Consciousness*, London: Plenum Press, pp. 335–58.

December, J. and Randall, N. (1994) '*The World Wide Web Unleashed*', Sams Publishing.

Deighton, J. (1994) 'Brave new world – Future Issues in Marketing Communication', Marketing Science Institute Conference, Marketing Communications Strategies Today and Tomorrow: Integration, Allocation, and Interactive Technologies, report number 94–109, July, pp. 40–43.

Eisenhardt, K. (1992) 'Speed and Strategic Choice: Accelerating Decision Making' *Planning Review Special Issue*, Sep/Oct, pp. 30–32.

Glazer, R. (1991) 'Marketing in an Information-Intensive Environment: Strategic Implication of Knowledge as an Asset,' *Journal of Marketing*, 55(Oct) pp. 1–19.

Hakansson, H. Johanson, J. and Wootz, B. (1990) 'Influence Tactics in Buyer-Seller Processes', in Ford, D. (ed.) *Understanding Business Markets*, The IMP Group, London: Academic Press.

Hoffman, D. and Novak, T. (1994) 'The Challenges of Electronic Commerce', Intelligent Agent, Hotwired, December 29th

Hoffman, D. and Novak, T. (1996a) 'A New Marketing Paradigm for Electronic Commerce', *The Information Society* 13 (1).

Hoffman, D. and Novak, T. (1996b) 'Marketing in Hypermedia Computer-Mediated Environments: Conceptual Foundations', *Journal of Marketing*, vol 60 (July 1996) pp. 50–68.

Hoffman, D., Novak, T. and Chatterjee, D. (1995) 'Commercial Scenarios for the Web: Opportunities & Challenges', *Journal of Computer-Mediated Communication*, 1, (3) p. 1.

Menon, A. and Varadarajan, R. (1992) 'A Model of Marketing Knowledge Use Within', *Journal of Marketing*, 56 (Oct), pp. 53–71.

Miles, I. (1991) 'When mediation is the message; How suppliers envisage new markets', in Lea, M. (ed.) *Contexts of Computer-Mediated Communication*, Harvester Wheatsheaf, London, pp. 145–66.

Perce, E. and Courtright, J. (1993) 'Normative Images of Communication Media, Mass and Interpersonal Channels in the New Media Environment', *Human Communication Research*, l9 (4), pp. 485–503.

Rayner, C. (1997) 'Uploaded cuts back on words, but not content', *Revolution*, September, p. 59.

Rayport, J. and Sviokla, J. 1994 'Managing in the Marketspace', *Harvard Business Review*, 72 (6) pp. 141–150.

Sarker, M., Butler, B. and Steinfield, C. (1995) 'Intermediaries and Cybermediaries: a Continuing Role for Mediating Players in the Electronic market-place', *Journal of Computer Mediated Communication*, vol 1 no 3; http://www.usc.edu/dept/annenberg/vol1/issue3/sarkar.html.

Spalter, M. 1995 'Maintaining a Customer Focus in an Interactive Age', in Forrest, E. and Mizerski, R. (eds) *Interactive Marketing*, AMA Publication, pp. 163–87.

Webster, J; Klebe, L; Trevino, and Ryan, L. (1993) 'The Dimensionality and Correlates of Flow in Human-Computer Interactions', in Tennyson, R. (ed.) *Computers in Human Behavior*, Pergamon Press, New York, Vol. 9, no. 4, pp. 411–26.

Wigand, R. and Benjamin, R. (1995) 'Electronic Commerce: Effects on Electronic Markets', Journal of Computer Mediated Communication, vol 1 no 3 <http://www.usc.edu/dept/annenberg/vol1/issue3/wigand.html>

Wikstrom, S. (1996) 'Value Creation by Company-Consumer Interaction', *Journal of Marketing Management*, Vol 12, pp. 359–74.

Further Reading

Hoffman, D. and Novak, T. (1996) 'Marketing in Hypermedia Computer-Mediated Environments: Conceptual Foundations', *Journal of Marketing*, 60 (July) pp. 50–68

Hoffman, D. and Novak, T. (1996) 'A New Marketing Paradigm for Electronic Commerce', *The Information Society*, vol 13 (1)

Miles, I. (1991) 'When mediation is the message; How suppliers envisage new markets', in Lea, M. (ed.), *Contexts of Computer-Mediated Communication*, Harvester Wheatsheaf, London, pp. 145–66.

Rayport, J. and Sviokla, J. (1994) 'Managing in the Marketspace', *Harvard Business Review*, 72 (6), pp. 141–50.

Wigand, R. and Benjamin, R. (1995) 'Electronic Markets & Virtual Value Chains on the Information Superhighway', *Sloan Management Review*, Winter, pp. 62–72.

Wikstrom, S. (1996) 'Value Creation by Company-Consumer Interaction', *Journal of Marketing Management*, vol 12, pp. 359–74.

Creativity, Production and Fulfilment

CHAPTER

10

Creativity, Production and Fulfilment

Direct Mail Creative: CIGNA Parent Plan

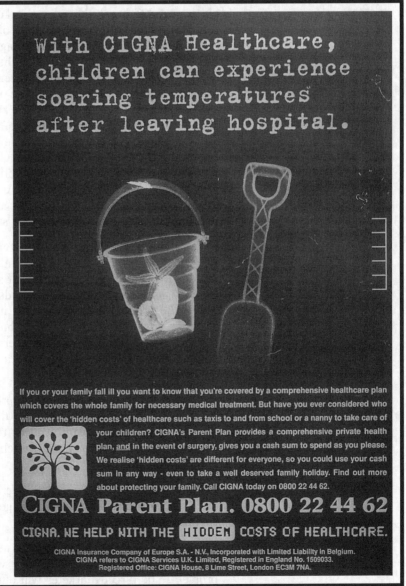

With CIGNA Healthcare, children can experience soaring temperatures after leaving hospital.

If you or your family fall ill you want to know that you're covered by a comprehensive healthcare plan which covers the whole family for necessary medical treatment. But have you ever considered who will cover the 'hidden costs' of healthcare such as taxis to and from school or a nanny to take care of your children? CIGNA's Parent Plan provides a comprehensive private health plan, <u>and</u> in the event of surgery, gives you a cash sum to spend as you please. We realise 'hidden costs' are different for everyone, so you could use your cash sum in any way - even to take a well deserved family holiday. Find out more about protecting your family. Call CIGNA today on 0800 22 44 62.

CIGNA Parent Plan. 0800 22 44 62

CIGNA. WE HELP WITH THE `HIDDEN` COSTS OF HEALTHCARE.

CIGNA Insurance Company of Europe S.A. - N.V., Incorporated with Limited Liability in Belgium. CIGNA refers to CIGNA Services U.K. Limited, Registered in England No. 1509033. Registered Office: CIGNA House, 8 Lime Street, London EC3M 7NA.

Introduction

Creativity is a difficult concept to define precisely. It is much easier to give examples of creativity than to explain exactly what it is. The marketing concept, in the form of a customer orientation provides the foundation upon which to build creativity. This is because creativity comes, first and foremost, from an understanding of the target audience. We must be familiar with what they view as important and what their feelings and emotions are. However, this understanding is not enough on its own. We must also be able to communicate this understanding in such a way as to be relevant to the audience and distinctive from our competitors. In creating distinctive messages there is often a need to break the rules or take risks. Constantly adhering to accepted rules leads to the production of me-too communications that are dull and lack impact. The message has to get through to the audience; it has to stand out from the crowd and be remembered. However, in taking risks the creative team must always be mindful of the objectives that have been set. 'One of the prime skills of the expert direct marketer is to communicate the right message in such a way as to attract the desired type of response.' (Holder 1993). Furthermore, creativity is about simplifying a complex world so that the message is accessible.

Creativity cannot occur in isolation. Rather it occurs against a backdrop of hard work and planning. As such Graham Wallas outlined a process whereby marketers can lay the groundwork for creativity which incorporates the following four steps:

1 *Preparation.* Conducting various types of research in order to provide background information about the marketing problem and to give meaning to subsequent stages. This not only involves more traditional research methods but also includes reading about the product and the market in which it operates, listening to what customers have to say about the product or service in the field, using the product or service and learning about the client's business first hand by visiting the organization (Moriarty 1986).

2 *Incubation.* Getting away from the problem at hand and using the information that has been gathered to help generate ideas. In order to develop potentially fruitful ideas the creative team will need to consciously avoid focusing too much on the problem and remain open to inspiration.

3 *Illumination.* This relates to the generation of ideas which might be later put to use creatively. This stage will make use of procedures such as brainstorming.

4 *Verification.* Refining the ideas generated and identifying whether or not they are workable and if they will provide a solution to the problem. The direct marketer will often rely on testing during this phase, using samples of the target audience to evaluate different

concepts and themes which have emerged from the illumination stage.

Creativity must also bear some relation to any marketing objectives which have been outlined. Of increasing importance in this area is the need to ensure that any communication takes account of the brand image the organization is trying to foster. Brand image refers to consumers' subjective perceptions of how a brand performs across a range of criteria, both functional and non-functional, which they consider to be important for evaluation purposes. These subjective perceptions are organized by the consumer into a succinct picture of the brand which will play a part in that consumer's consumption behaviour (Engel *et al.* 1986). The brand image is compiled by the consumer through direct experience of the brand, through exposure to marketing communications, through packaging, and even through observation of what kind of people use the brand and the occasions and situations in which the brand is used (Gordon 1991). From the organization's perspective brand image aids in the establishment of the brand's position (Park *et al.* 1986), can protect against competitive attack (Oxenfeldt and Swann 1964) and thus leads to enhanced market performance (Shocker and Srinivasan 1979). A brand image has in itself a number of inherent characteristics which include, among others, brand personality and user image. In many ways the organization lives or dies by the brand image it manages to foster and thus there is a distinct need in the creative process to be aware of these issues and to ensure that communications are consistent with them.

One of the points of discussion within marketing generally, is whether direct marketing is the poor relation in terms of 'creativity'. It has often been claimed by traditional above the line agencies that having to include direct response mechanisms in advertising stifles the creative effort and as soon as an 0800 telephone number is plastered across a TV commercial, any creative value is immediately destroyed. However, times are changing and contemporary direct marketing is fighting to be seen as creative in its own right. The marketing communications industry in general is also beginning to realize this fact and direct marketers are being recognized for their creativity with British Design and Art Direction Awards (Denny 1996).

Furthermore, the old above/ below the line distinction is being displaced by the concept of 'left' and 'right' of the line. This distinction between above and below the line was based on whether the agency received commission from media owners for their buying of time or space. If they did it was declared to be above the line, if not (e.g. traditional direct marketing and sales promotion), it was below the line. Now, this distinction has become blurred not only because many campaigns are paid for by fee rather than by commission but also because direct marketing employs media through the use of direct response advertising. It is now more accepted to speak of left ad right of the line which represents acquisition and retention strategies.

The Importance of Understanding the Audience

We have already touched upon the fact that good creative springs from a thorough understanding and appreciation of the target audience. Of particular importance here is an awareness of the things that motivate consumers and the benefits they seek from different products and services.

Motivation is a basic concept in human behaviour and thus also in consumer behaviour. Motivation can be described as the driving force within individuals that moves them to take a particular action. This driving force is produced by a state of tension, which exists as a result of an unfulfilled need. Individuals will strive both consciously and subconsciously to reduce this tension by fulfilling their needs. Every individual has the same need structure but different specific needs will be to the fore in different individuals at various points in time. Thus, our proposition is that marketing does not create needs, rather it encourages us to *want* brand X by associating its acquisition with the satisfaction of a latent need. On this basis, direct marketing creative can benefit from an understanding of the key aspects of motivation theory because specific message appeals can be based on such analysis. Perhaps the most widely acknowledged theory of motivation is that of Dr Abraham Maslow (1970) which is represented as a hierarchy of needs (Figure 10.1). Maslow's proposition is that needs at one level must be at least partially satisfied before those at the next level become important in determining our actions.

We assume that most readers will be familiar with Maslow's hierarchy and thus we will not dwell on its details. However, the significance of the hierarchy to marketing is great. It clearly demonstrates that a need refers to more than mere physiological essentials. Other forces driving our behaviour can come from a concern for our safety, social integration, personal recognition, learning, appreciation of our surroundings or from the perceived

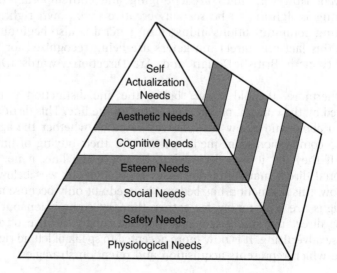

Figure 10.1 Maslow's Hierarchy of Needs

importance of spiritual satisfaction. We are less concerned about what products and services *are* than what they can *do* for us. In short, consumers do not buy on the basis of product and service features *per se*. Rather, they buy because of the benefits these features offer us. Recognition of this can be translated into message appeals and other aspects of direct marketing creative.

This point can be illustrated in many ways. A quotation often attributed to Charles Revson of Revlon Cosmetics is: 'In the factory we make soap, in the market we sell hope'. In other words it isn't the physical composition or features that are being purchased, but rather what they can do for consumers; the benefits consumers might derive from their purchase. The classic way of focusing in on benefits is to identify the needs of the target and to match one or more product or service features that are in some way relevant with each need. Then each feature can be converted, using a 'which means' approach, into a benefit that can satisfy that need (see Table 10.1).

Direct marketing creative often reflects the application of this approach. Playing to some extent on Maslow's safety level, direct mailings for pensions aimed at the 18–35s have shown that in order to secure an assured future, a second pension is increasingly desirable. Indeed, the campaign by Ogilvy and Mather Direct has won a variety of creative awards for its inserts in magazines, mailings and door drops. BUPA's DRTV creative was another award winner, based on safety needs: 'You're amazing, we want to keep you that way'. This and direct campaigns for life assurance, especially covering family members also relates to concerns for loved ones (i.e. social needs) and additionally to more personal esteem needs (our self esteem can be enhanced by feeling we are looking after those for whom we have some responsibility). Social needs are also portrayed by BT's 'Friends and Family' and 'It's Good to Talk' DRTV campaigns.

The direct marketer also has a number of specific appeals which he or she can utilize to strengthen the message. Basic appeals by and large

Needs Identify Needs	Features Select Relevant Features	Benefits Convert Features into Benefits that Satisfy Needs
Newly married couple who have just moved into a newly built house.	This drill-bit set includes a quarter-inch masonry and a quarter-inch wood/metal bit.	This drill-bit set can help you turn your house into a home by allowing you to personalize it by hanging shelves, pictures etc.
Shy and retiring 18 year-old who has just started university and wants to make some new friends.	Brightly coloured designer-label jacket.	This jacket will help you fit in and become part of the in-crowd.
A young woman who wants to experience life to the fullest and wishes to make a statement about her individuality.	A navel piercing service.	Piercing your navel makes a statement. It says something about who you are and you've never before experienced anything like the feeling it gives you.

Table 10.1 Needs-Features-Benefits

focus on the central idea to be contained in the message, what advertisers sometimes refer to as the advertising platform. Such appeals are generally aimed at a particular need of the target audience that can be met by the advertised product. No rules can specify which appeals to use in order to arouse a certain need. To a great extent, the effectiveness of an appeal depends upon the product and the situation. The most common appeals used in marketing communications include (Burnett 1993):

▶ projected savings;

▶ self-enhancement;

▶ projected harm;

▶ unique product feature;

▶ relative competitive advantage;

▶ perceived price advantage;

▶ major change or breakthrough;

▶ popularity;

▶ free samples.

Using the Hierarchy of Effects

There is a long-held belief in marketing that audiences respond to messages in a very ordered way: cognitively first (thinking), affectively second (feeling), and conatively third (doing). Based on this response sequence numerous authors have developed what have become known as hierarchy of effects models (see Table 10.2). These hierarchies of effects have received much criticism mainly because this is not necessarily a sequence that consumers follow in all situations. However, such models do provide a framework with which to guide

Table 10.2 Hierarchy of Effects Models

St. Elmo Lewis (1900)	Colley (1961)	Lavidge & Steiner (1961)	McGuire (1969)	Engel et al. (1986)
			Presentation	Exposure
Attention	Awareness	Awareness	Attention	Attention
	Comprehension	Knowledge	Comprehension	Comprehension
Interest		Liking		
Desire		Preference	Yielding	Yielding
	Conviction	Conviction	Retention	Retention
Action	Action	Purchase	Behaviour	Action

discussion of consumer responses to marketing actions and thus creativity. In looking at how hierarchies of effects might provide insights for creative effort we will utilize the model proposed by Engel *et al.* (1986)

Exposure

Exposure involves ensuring that the communication is placed in such a way as to make it accessible to the target audience. Thus there are implications here for list selection, media selection and indeed for distribution channel selection. The major focus at this stage is on reaching the target audience.

A number of years ago Lea & Perrins sauce ran a campaign which incorporated door drops of free samples, a small bottle of sauce banded onto magazine covers and sales of the bottle through Tesco for a loss leading price of 19p. In all cases targets were invited to send for a recipe book in exchange for providing data about themselves (nine questions-worth). The exercise was designed to gather data for targeting purposes. By matching the data collected with NDL lifestyle profiles it was found that Lea & Perrins customers were absolutely 'average', nothing peculiar to them seemed to emerge. However, one of the specific questions enquired about television viewing habits. Of the Lea & Perrins users 43 per cent said they watched morning programmes on ITV. Had the company relied solely on their demographic and lifestyle profiling they would not have selected this particular medium (i.e. off-peak television advertising) and thus they saved valuable resources and satisfied presentation criteria very effectively (Lovell 1997).

An example of how careful attention to detail during exposure sometimes doesn't occur concerns the launch of the Sunday colour supplement of the *News of the World*. A typical pattern at the time was for Sunday colour supplements to be packed with direct response, off-the-page advertisements. These provide a picture of the product or other descriptions together with a coupon to post in order to place an order. This was fine for those with cheque accounts or credit cards. However, the profile at that time of 'News of the World' readers suggested something of a mismatch. As Table 10.3 shows, the publication's readership is biased toward the C_2Ds, whereas those with the highest level of bank account ownership are the ABs.

Attention

Even if the marketing offering is in the right place, there is no guarantee that the market will see it. Consumers sometime discard mailings as 'junk mail' (even if it might be relevant to them if they opened it) and 'channel hop' when watching television if advertisements don't capture their attention. This is especially true of acquisition drives, as relevance is not necessarily immediately apparent to the audience.

Table 10.3 Bank Accounts and Readership Related to Social Grade

Social Grade	Bank Account Penetration	*News of the World* Readership
A	88%	7%
B	81%	10%
C₁	69%	22%
C₂	45%	38%
D	29%	43%
E	15%	28%
		JICNARS/TGI 1992

It has been estimated that every American consumer is exposed to at least 1,500 promotional messages a day but that they notice less than five per cent. Americans are also exposed to 18 million unsolicited telephone calls daily and receive 3000 coupons per year (Hallberg 1995). In the UK, Davidson (1997:464) suggests that the average consumer is exposed to 15,000 commercials per year and the figure in Spain and Italy is over 20,000. He also submits that £1m worth of advertising probably only buys 0.1 per cent share of consumer exposure. So there is a clear implication that once the communication is presented effectively, the next task is to ensure that it gets noticed. Four aspects of attention may be distinguished:

1 *Gaining attention.* This is especially important but difficult in the clutter of commercial messages.

2 *Holding attention.* Once gained the attention needs to be held in order for the actual message to be conveyed.

3 *Leading attention.* Attention must be guided toward the message and not to peripheral elements in the communication.

4 *Distracting attention.* This is usually ineffective, unless the arguments of the message are weak. Distraction might prevent consumers from discovering the weakness of the arguments. However, as a means of convincing the audience the use of distraction raises certain ethical questions.

Thus, during this phase direct marketers are concerned with attracting and maintaining attention and there are particular techniques that can be employed to accomplish this. Among these is the use of colour. On a general level, colour tends to arrest the attention more than monochrome and indeed different colours have different attention values. The warm colours (orange and red) advance toward us in our perception, having the effect of making whatever it is appear larger, whereas the cooler colours (blue) recede in our perception making the message appear smaller. On this basis red is often cited as having the highest attention value. Having said this there can be problems associated with the use of red. The Royal Mail's automated sorting machines cannot read addresses printed in black on a red background and this presents enormous difficulties every Valentine's Day when the use of red envelopes is commonplace.

Movement is another technique utilized to gain attention. Thus direct response advertising on television or in the cinema are often considered more efficient at generating attention than static press or direct mail messages. However, it is possible to simulate movement in a still picture and this is often done effectively with blurred backgrounds suggesting a moving foreground (e.g. a speeding sports car). Video cassettes which also allow the use of movement are becoming more popular for communicating direct messages, as are direct communications via the Internet. A variation on movement is the use of sound and modern technology enables the direct marketer to send 'speaking brochures' containing a 'chip' allowing personalization of each message.

The position of the message is also important in gaining attention. The back outside cover of a magazine, for example, means that the direct response advertising message can be noticed even without opening the magazine at all. Some direct marketers might include the main component of the message on the envelope of a mailing to increase the chances of it being noticed. Others, however, believe that by doing this, recipients might be more likely to discard the piece before opening because it would be clear it was a piece of direct mail. Variations on this theme include letting an enticing part of the creative (e.g. the incentive) show through the window of the envelope. Some believe that the right-hand page attracts more attention than the left because as we leaf through the pages from the beginning, it is the right page that is uncovered first. Those, however, who start with the sports page on the rear of a newspaper may well disagree and argue that the left hand page is the one that is usually noticed first. If a double-page spread is employed then there are no competing messages and so attention could be more likely because of this. A compromise is to cover a double page spread with just half of each page. The 'golden section' technique, or 'law of thirds', known by architects and artists can also be employed. This suggests that if a rectangle is divided into thirds, both vertically and horizontally, then the eye goes to the points of intersection (see Figure 10.2). Placing important parts of the copy or graphics at these points might therefore make them more prominent. Additionally, in the context of direct mail, if some of the message is moved to the postscript or 'PS', it is often the case that this will be the part of the letter that is especially noticed and remembered.

The size of the message has also been the focus of marketing discussion. This is not, however, a straightforward matter. Doubling the size of a message is unlikely to double attention. A suggestion is that attention increases as the square root of the message size (this is the 'square-root law' developed by Rudolph (1947)).

Yet another approach to gaining attention uses what might be described as known conditioned responses. We attend, almost automatically, to the sound of a telephone ringing and this approach is used to good effect in direct response radio advertising. Other

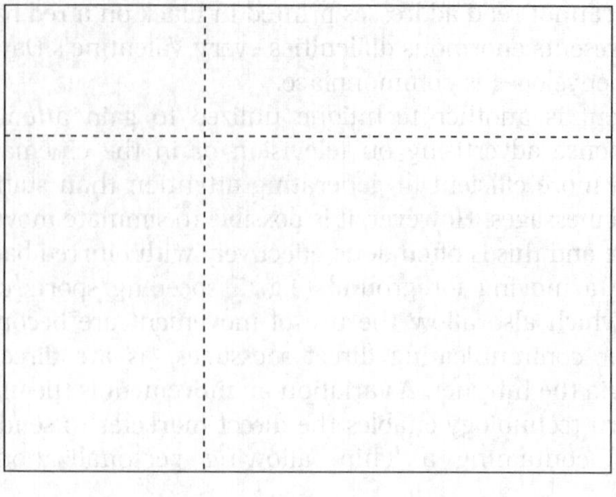

Figure 10.2 The Golden
Section

examples include the introduction to a radio advertisement with a statement such as 'Here is a news flash'. A major direct marketer, Avon Cosmetics, uses a ringing door bell and 'Avon calling' slogan, in its promotional approach.

If a message is in some way different then because of its distinctiveness it may stand out and thus attract more attention. In practice many marketers place the distinctiveness of their communications at the top of their priorities. Communications do need to stand out from the crowd but because many consumers may be risk averse, communications must also create a sense of familiarity. Thus, the direct marketer needs to be careful when using novel messages. Another problem of course is that novelty only lasts a short time, so the employment of this approach must be especially dynamic in order to maintain its distinctiveness. The direct marketer will need to constantly test different approaches because each will not be effective for very long. It is clear, though, that direct marketers are very proactive in this area and they do try different approaches (e.g. the use of envelopes of different shapes, sizes, colours and textures). An Oxfam mailing included a tape measure which could be used to measure whether one's child's arm was small enough that they could be classified as suffering from malnutrition. Posters for Disneyland Paris by Ogilvy Mather Direct are based on capturing images from 8mm cinefilm before production and end up as 3-D holograms which are expensive but attention grabbing (Stokes 1997).

Not only is it important to attract the attention of consumers, but the direct marketer must also hold the attention and convey the message. Attention-getting devices are numerous, but if attention is attracted by methods inconsistent with the message or the situation, this attention is readily lost. Attention may be held by encouraging the audience to participate. Messages which work in this way might be ambiguous or incomplete and for this reason the audience is encouraged to attend to the message more than would otherwise be the case, in order to complete the message and to make sense of it (this is called the Zeigarnik effect, after Zeigarnik 1927).

Comprehension, Yielding and Retention

Once noticed the message/offering should be perceived and understood in the intended way. Comprehension is an extremely subjective process and how a message is comprehended depends on a variety of factors such as needs, attitudes, expectations, personality (Engel *et al* 1986) etc. Crucial to comprehension is the notion of perceptions, in that messages can be comprehended in different ways depending on how they are perceived. In getting the audience to perceive a message in a particular way, direct marketers can utilize a number of techniques. One application concerns visual illusions and although space does not permit more coverage here, the reader will be familiar with line drawings which deceive the eye. An example for the direct marketer could include the design of welcome packs which appear taller or broader than they really are, by employing thin vertical stripes or broad horizontal bands respectively. 'Figure-ground' relationships can also be employed to change the perception of graphic images, depending on which is identified as the background to the image.

Because direct marketing targets individuals, messages can be tailored to be congruent with the 'frame of reference' of each target. Even when targeting segments, the message can be tailored (e.g. mailings can be written specifically and differently for men and women or for different ethnic groups etc.). In the case of gender specific mailings, Pidgeon (1997) has found, through exploring the issue in focus groups, that there are gender specific styles which lead to different perceptions. Essentially what we are saying is that perception is selective. That is, different individuals might perceive the same message differently, or selectively. The task for the direct marketer (who will be targeting customers as individuals) is to discover, through market research and database analysis, what the relevant 'fields of experience' of the intended audience are. Figure 10.3 shows that effective communication occurs where common frames of reference are used. If the sender of the message understands the experience and general frame of reference of the receiver and puts the message in terms that mean the same to both sender and receiver, there is a greater chance of effective communication. The receiver should then perceive and understand the message in the intended way.

Earlier we discussed the use of colour in attracting attention. Colour is also an important consideration during the comprehension stage because different colours can transmit different meanings. Most colours have both positive and negative meanings and of course different colours are more or less fashionable at different points in time. Furthermore, different colours can mean different things in different countries, thus making any generalizations almost impossible to make. However, in western cultures, red is often seen as being a fiery, passionate colour; white as being pure and virginal; black as being mysterious, perhaps wicked but sometimes smart. Yellow might be seen as being cheerful but also sometimes as associated with deceit and cowardice. In other cultures these colours may have entirely different associations. The funeral colour of black has no major taboo attached

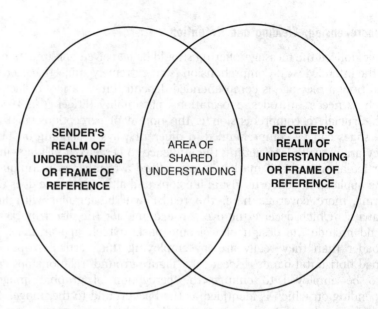

Figure 10.3 Schramm
Model of Communication

to it in the UK, but the funeral colour of other countries is not always black and sometimes should not be used outside the funeral context. It is therefore necessary to be cautious about international mailings and Internet communications which may be inappropriately homogeneous across national and ethnic boundaries.

Message comprehension is not the same as message acceptance. Thus, yielding is concerned with the degree to which the message persuades the target audience. In achieving such persuasion the direct marketer has a number of possible appeals he or she can draw upon. These will be discussed in detail in the next section of this chapter.

Assuming the direct marketing offering is interpreted appropriately, retention is concerned with ensuring it is remembered in the intended way. Marketing communication may be considered to be concerned with teaching consumers about various marketing offerings. If this is the case, marketing itself can benefit from a knowledge of how consumers learn about things. Two approaches to teaching customers to learn and remember are outlined here. First, Associationist learning theory, which is summarized in Figure 10.4 and second, Gestalt theory.

Associationist learning

This is based on the early work of the Russian physiologist Ivan Pavlov (1928) and on the work of Skinner (1938). Pavlov considered learning to be essentially concerned with stimulus-response relationships. His experiments included observation of dogs' responses to various stimuli. For example, when presented with food, dogs often salivate. There was nothing exceptional about this, it is a natural and even automatic response to that stimulus. Pavlov went on to present various other stimuli at the same time as presenting the food. Again the dogs

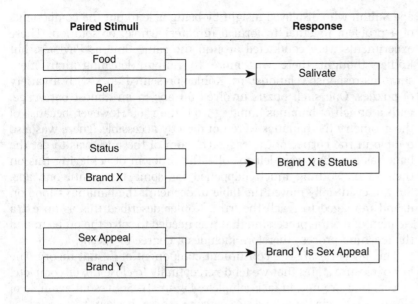

Figure 10.4 Associationist learning

salivated. When, however, this process of paired stimuli presentation was repeated very often, he then presented the other stimulus (the sound of a tuning fork, light bulb being flashed, etc.) by itself and the dogs salivated to that other stimulus even though no food was present. What he argued was that an unnatural response to the light or sound had been conditioned into the animals. This type of learning became known as *classical conditioning*.

Skinner's work resulted in the acknowledgement of *operant conditioning*. This recognizes that learning can be encouraged through the use of positive and negative reinforcers. By pairing rewards or punishments with certain behaviours Skinner showed that these behaviours could be reinforced.

Direct marketing might not operate precisely at the level of Pavlov's or Skinner's experiments but the principles are used every day. If the creative team understands what the intended market segment is interested in (e.g. status appeals or sex appeals), it can present the relevant appeal and thus the market is likely to respond favourably. Presenting a brand together with a benefit as paired stimuli in a repetitive fashion may mean that the market will learn to associate the brand with that particular benefit. The associations attached to a large number of well-advertised brands can be explained by this process. Marketing does not create needs, but rather encourages a want for a specific product because it associates its acquisition with the satisfaction of a need. This is the basis of the Associationist learning approach.

Gestalt theory

Another school of thought which considers how we learn is the *Gestalt* school. Gestalt theory is based on the work of Köhler (1927) and his ape Sultan who displayed insight by being able to put the components of a problem together to form a (greater) whole, or solution. These experiments were conducted around the same time as Pavlov's, but Köhler thought there was more to human learning than mere stimulus-response relationships. Köhler presented apes with a variety of puzzles. One such puzzle involved an ape in an almost bare cage, with a bunch of bananas hanging from the roof. However, because of the geometry the bananas were not directly accessible. There was also a table in the corner of the cage. The aim of the apes was to get the bananas but they were left to solve the problem of achieving this on their own. Nothing much happened for some time until one ape, Sultan, eventually moved the table underneath the bananas, stood on it and managed to reach the fruit. Köhler described this as an extra element of mental processing that was needed to solve the problem and the learning process therefore includes a degree of *insight*.

The *law of closure* is a constituent component of Gestalt theory. The law of closure states that we tend perceptually to close up, or complete, objects that are not, in fact complete. Figure 10.5 gives an example of closure, whereby we tend to perceive three broken rectangles as opposed to six individual shapes. The marketing implication of this is that by encouraging participation, because the problem is not solved at the immediate superficial level, marketers are tapping into this process of insight. Indeed, because of this the approach is often considered to be more effective in helping with the learning of a marketing message.

A useful summary of the Gestalt process is that 'the whole is greater than the sum of the parts' and there are plenty of examples of this in practice, especially in recent times. The direct mail example mentioned earlier, concerning the Oxfam tape-measure, is an example of real participation in the direct marketing message. Another example includes a blurred plastic pack mailed by Help the Aged to demonstrate the effects on older people of suffering from cataract problems. Other examples of Gestalt participation include the Tango advertisements encouraging people to call a telephone number for more information and the Mazda car advertisement which asked viewers to video record

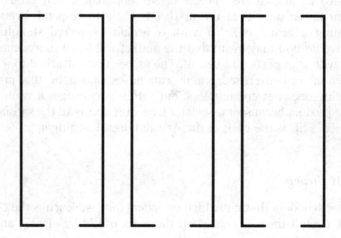

Figure 10.5 An Example of Closure

the ad and to pause it at places in order to make sense of the 0800 number.

Additional support for the use of participative gestalt approaches comes from research amongst Generation X (Ritson 1995; Ritchie 1995). 'Xers' have been variously described as lazy, indifferent and cynical. None of this would be a problem if only marketers knew how to sell them products. The inability of the tried and tested to work on this cohort has left many marketers exasperated. The problem, however, remains. This cohort represents a potentially lucrative source of income in the future and marketers simply cannot afford to dismiss it out of hand. What successful trend-spotters have found is that contemporary teenagers and twenty-somethings react best to playfulness, honesty and irony. Thus they may respond better to playful approaches such as the one used by Tango. Furthermore, DRTV advertising in particular may appeal to them because it gives them control over the solicitation of any further information and kitsch, low-budget 'infomercials', designed to exhibit products in the manner of an in-store demonstration are just the type of thing that appeals to this playful, ironic and anarchic postmodern television audience.

In the same way that we discussed selective perception earlier, there can be an equivalent at this stage as well; selective retention. The techniques and theory on which to base direct marketing creative approaches, however, provide potential means for ensuring a reasonable degree of uniformity of response even though there is equally the potential for individualistic responses – and in any case the direct marketer should be increasingly individualising not only the fact of targeting but the nature of targeting.

We are also concerned at this stage with developing favourable beliefs, attitudes and intentions toward the marketing offering. Coverage of attitude measurement in our chapter on marketing research explored this in greater detail, but it is worth a brief recap. These are components of the structure of attitude and the attitude–behaviour relationship which we discussed in that chapter. Attitude (A) consists of a set of beliefs multiplied by their evaluations. In a similar manner, the social norm (SN) consists of a set of normative beliefs multiplied by the motivation to comply with these norms. Normative beliefs are convictions about what is socially acceptable (i.e. how relevant others, such as the notorious mother-in-law, might evaluate the behaviour). The motivation to comply is the degree to which one accepts the evaluations of these relevant others. Behavioural intention (BI) is a weighted sum of attitude and social norm and is a useful predictor of behaviour.

Focusing on such a structure helps in the definition of communications objectives, message creation and campaign evaluation. Objectives can be defined by discovering the nature of perception with regard to the direct marketing offering, whether attitudes are favourable or unfavourable, what the antecedents of these attitudes are, and whether the target audience exhibit any intention to buy. Thus, messages can be tailored depending on what is discovered during this analysis. Campaigns may also be evaluated by measuring these same dimensions over the course of the campaign in order to identify if progress is being made.

Action

The previous stages of response move potential customers through pre-purchase events so that there is a better chance of conversion. However, in order for action to take place, direct marketing messages must include a 'proposition', a 'solution' and a 'mechanism' for facilitating response. Unfortunately, many such mechanisms are designed poorly and make it difficult for the target audience to respond (e.g. coupons which are too small to fill out completely or DRTV advertisements which do not provide ample time for the telephone number to be recorded).

Direct marketers will be especially interested in the nature of this stage; measuring response rates and the time of response according to individual profiles and so on. It has been found that if direct mailings are written using 'you' (the consumer) rather than 'us' (the company) response rates are significantly higher. Similarly, adding words like 'now' or 'instantly' at the end of sentences such as 'If you buy this/donate to that' will also usually increase response rates.

Response or purchase do not represent the end of the process. Direct marketing is concerned with satisfied customers, good relationships with customers, loyal and repeat purchasing and/or the spreading of goodwill. After purchase has taken place the provision of direct marketing information through packaging and labelling is important for consumers to structure their product experience. Consumers who buy a bottle of Moldavian wine like to learn about the country of origin of this wine, the type of grapes and other information. Indeed, the wine may taste better knowing all of this. The same is true for Scottish single-malt whiskies. Background information helps to structure the experiences with the product and to appreciate it more. Direct mailings via loyalty and retention schemes can help create the relevant relationships through which the consumer can achieve this structure.

Post-purchase activities can be better understood with reference to cognitive dissonance theory. Cognitive dissonance is a kind of psychological tension resulting from perceived inconsistencies in cognitions (Festinger 1957). For example, let us assume that you have just purchased a new car after a fairly extensive pre-purchase search and evaluation of alternatives. Your final choice is probably a bit of a compromise because no car is completely tailored to the requirements of each individual customer. Having said this, you are likely to view your choice as highly satisfactory. However, there may have been other cars available that you believed had some superior design features. These slightly contradictory cognitions can produce dissonance and you may ask yourself if you have made the correct choice. The level of dissonance is a function of the importance of the cognitions to the individual. So, if the point about other design features is very minor, the level of dissonance might be negligible. If, however, you drive your new car home and the next door neighbour, who you see as being especially knowledgeable about cars, says 'Why on earth did you buy that, that model has a terrible repair record?', your level of dissonance could be very substantial indeed.

Cognitive dissonance is a motivator in that the individual tries to reduce it. In the above example, a high level of dissonance over the car might lead you, the buyer, to seek supporting evidence for your decision, to reassure yourself that you have done the right thing. Indeed, much direct advertising is aimed at people who have already made a purchase, in order to help them overcome dissonance, reassure them of their purchase decision and to therefore ease the way for a repeat purchase or at least to spread positive messages to others. It is also worth emphasizing that dissonance is not the same as dissatisfaction. Dissatisfaction produces dissonance, yes, but a generally satisfying purchase may also produce cognitive dissonance if some of the cognitions over it are slightly inconsistent with each other. Take an example reported by Jones (1996) who claims to have been satisfied with his BMW for ten years until the ash tray went missing after a service. He contacted the garage the next morning to be informed that they had found the ash tray and he could collect it later that day. He was not too impressed with this because he felt the garage should do the work to rectify their mistake; it wasn't him who had mislaid the ash tray! Coincidentally, he had cause to talk to a Lexus dealer and they said they were delivering a car in his neighbourhood and would stop off at the BMW garage and collect his ash tray for him. He was not targeted after this event by the Lexus sales force but it is clear that incidents like this can help to increase dissonance over the current product and reduce it for competing products and potential purchases. As it turned out, Jones eventually purchased a Lexus.

Although we are discussing dissonance in the post-purchase phase, because it applies particularly well here, it can occur in the pre-purchase phase as well. We can usually perceive positive and negative cognitions whenever we are faced with alternatives, so the mental processing of these pros and cons can obviously lead to levels of confusion and doubt over the best choice. Therefore the onus is on the direct marketer to provide the target with information which will help the individual overcome such dissonance. It might appear obvious to suggest that we emphasize consonant cognitions (positive aspects of the product). However, there are occasions when a slightly negative set of points can be made as well. The use of two-sided arguments has been suggested as being effective for more educated audiences. Direct charity marketers often draw attention to the 'downside' of, for example, parting with one's hard earned money but for a very good 'cause'. The direct marketer might also emphasize how many satisfied customers there are. For example, in the mid 1990s a satellite broadcaster, in direct response advertising, used the copy headline 'half a million people can't be wrong'. Direct marketers can also extend this by targeting specific individuals as endorsers or opinion leaders. The targeting of opinion formers (e.g. journalists) is also a highly sophisticated business with the aim of securing positive and relevant 'editorial' coverage by those who are likely to be perceived as being independent, credible experts.

Related to this is offering reassurance through after-sales service and warranties. This is again very prominent in the car market and reflects the pragmatic view that cars are complicated pieces of machinery and that no car is (yet) tailor-made for each individual customer, so there are bound to be both consonant and dissonant cognitions. However, by emphasizing that if anything does go wrong, then it will be taken care of, dissonance can be reduced (Jones 1996). In the late 1990s Mitsubishi used the copy headline 'They would cost us a fortune if they were not so reliable'.

Moral Principles, Emotions and Logic

In trying to persuade the target audience we must first decide whether we are to appeal to their moral principles, their emotions or to logic (Aristotle's *Ethos*, *Pathos* and *Logos*).

Ethos

In focusing on ethos the message will essentially refer to the source; the organization sending the message. To this end source credibility becomes a major consideration. 'Credibility is the extent to which the recipient sees the source as having relevant knowledge, skill, or experience and trusts the source to give unbiased, objective information' (Belch and Belch 1990:189). Obviously, organizations seen to have expertise and knowledge are likely to be looked upon more favourably than those who aren't. One means of achieving source credibility on this basis is to use accepted experts in the field to endorse the product or service. Trustworthiness may, however, be rather more difficult to achieve. 'The variable most universally accepted as a basis for any human interaction or exchange is trust.' (Gundlach and Murphy 1993:41). Trust has been the subject of debate and discussion within a whole range of disciplines. Indeed, because of its centrality to social and economic life, an academic school has developed, whose primary objective is to understand and elucidate this single concept. Based on the work of Anderson and Narus (1990), we define trust as the consumers' belief that a firm will perform actions that will result in positive outcomes for him, and will not take unexpected actions that will result in negative outcomes. The more trustworthy an organization is seen to be, the more likely that consumers will have positive attitudes toward the ideas they put forward (Giffin 1967; Hovland *et al.* 1953). This may be especially true when consumers are negatively disposed toward these ideas in the first place (Sternthal *et al.* 1978). However, trust is not something that an organization can truly convey through their communication alone. Trustworthiness depends first and foremost on the actions of an organization as it conducts business.

Pathos

Messages which appeal to pathos 'involve creating an appropriate feeling in the receiver by appealing to feelings, values or emotions, by associating strong affective cues with the product or brand.' (Percy and Rossiter 1980:102) Humans are emotional creatures and the emotions we express can also form the basis of direct marketing creative appeals. Plutchik (1980) identifies eight basic emotions (see Figure 10.6) which occur in four pairs opposite each other in the circle. Emotions that are adjacent to one another combine to create a composite emotion (e.g. joy and anticipation combine to form optimism). The following are examples of how some of these approaches might be used in direct marketing communications.

▶ *Fear.* The intention here is to imply that something nasty or unfortunate might happen if the target does not take some action. Appeals such as 'Don't miss out on the opportunity of a lifetime' are often used.

▶ *Love.* Reflected in mailings for products and services associated with marriage or anniversary gifts, where the purchase of these items is an expression of the target's love.

▶ *Disgust.* Here the appeal is designed to shock the target so that they are mobilised into action. RSPCA pieces often use images of tortured or neglected animals in order to achieve this.

▶ *Anticipation.* The idea here is to engage the target and get them to seek more information. 'You could be the lucky recipient of £25,000. Just open this envelope for more details.'

A very different perspective is provided by the application of Sigmund Freud's psychoanalytic theory which distinguishes three basic

Figure 10.6 Plutchik's Emotion Wheel

structures of the mind: Id, Ego and Superego (Freud 1964:21). The *id* is the unconscious, instinctive source of our impulses, a source of psychic energy. It is a beast looking for immediate hedonic gratification (pleasure), self-interest and a short-term perspective. Freud argued that the libido, sexuality, is the driving force of the Id. The *ego*, on the other hand, responds to the real world and acts in a mediating role between the id and reality. Thus it controls our instinctive drives and tries to find a realistic means by which we can satisfy our impulses. The *superego* represents the internalised representation of the morals and values of those important to us in society. Thus it controls our behaviour by seeking to make it fit with these internalised norms.

It might be suggested that appeals to the id can be made in subconscious ways. Designs for mail pack inserts that spark off a subconscious set of associations might be based on phallic and other symbolism in the designs, shapes, textures and materials. Other messages might attempt to tap the subconscious id drives with what, superficially, would appear to be rather obscure references. It might go completely over or under the heads of the target market, at least at the conscious level, but if it reaches the id then it might well be achieving the intended objective. The problem with the subconscious of course is that it is very difficult to identify and research, even if it exists. Different psychoanalysts might well interpret research findings in different ways and so the whole approach attracts critical attention.

Consider the id a little further. When on holiday in a foreign country we are often unaware of the local norms and some people will deliberately ignore them to such an extent that there is little perception of social constraints at all. In such situations the id can be free and this might explain the misbehaviour of the lager louts in Spanish resorts. The proposition, then, is that there can be *good* and *real* reasons for behaviour. Direct marketers can use messages which reflect this to varying degrees. At one extreme would be the Club 18–30 approach where the real reason (i.e. sex on holiday) is barely disguised ('Beaver Espania', 'One Swallow Doesn't Make a Summer', etc.) and at another extreme might be a more subtle set of imagery for a direct mailing concerning a sports car in which the good reasons appear to revolve around speed being a safety feature. This might be converted into the benefit of being able to accelerate safely during an overtaking manoeuvre. However, the underlying real reason might be that the sports car helps attract the opposite sex or is even a substitute mistress (e.g. in a recent research programme between Bristol Business School and Target Direct it was found that men tend to be much more concerned about the appearance of cars than are women). Another example would be direct mailings for 'men's health' books; the name reflects the good reason (perhaps more acceptable to the superego) but the message inside the mailing is about 'unleashing animal magnetism' and the books are mostly concerned with improving one's sex life (an appeal to the id).

The use of entertainment may also be useful in pathos appeals. Entertainment can break through the clutter of contemporary marketing communications and captivate the target audience. It tends to be used to best effect with products and services that are not highly differentiated, are frequently purchased, elicit low involvement and are relatively inexpensive (Burnett 1993). Entertainment often involves the use of humour, hyperbole or borrowed interest. Devising a message which is considered humorous by everyone in the target audience is extremely difficult, and humour tends to wear out quickly. There is also a chance that humour may overwhelm the other aspects of the message and in particular draw attention away from the product. Hyperbole or exaggeration may also be entertaining in its own right, though its primary purpose is to present some fact about the product in a form that is larger than life and therefore attractive. Inevitably some products and services don't lend themselves too well to the use of entertainment. It is often the case, therefore, that the message will borrow interest by incorporating a focal point which has high inherent interest but which is not directly related to the product or service being sold.

Logos

> ▨ *Logos appeals require the receiver to deduce the desired conclusion from a message based upon certain general principles presented or implied within the message that the receiver accepts as true; or they may require the receiver to induce the required conclusion as a result of believable evidence in the arguments presented.'* ▨ (Percy and Rossiter 1980:103)

In other words, this is essentially a rational appeal that uses logic to develop a reason why, benefit, or position. Because the audience must follow through the logic, this strategy requires a moderate level of both interest and information-processing skills on the part of the audience. Such messages frequently make use of factual statements about the product or service which are used to introduce new products and to describe technical products. Alternatively, the direct marketer may focus upon product or service comparison, outlining the benefits of their offering in relation to those of competitors. Demonstration of the product in use may also prove beneficial, although this naturally requires the utilization of television, cinema or videos.

Symbolism

In addition to consideration of ethos, pathos and logos appeals the direct marketer will need to be mindful of the images and symbols incorporated in their communications. The study of signs such as these is referred to as *semiotics*. Semiotics comes originally from the work of Ferdinand de Saussure whose work was concentrated on linguistics but which is appropriate for the study of all signs. In looking at signs Saussure highlighted that every sign consisted of a *signifier* and *signified* – a typical Saussurian model is depicted in Figure 10.7.

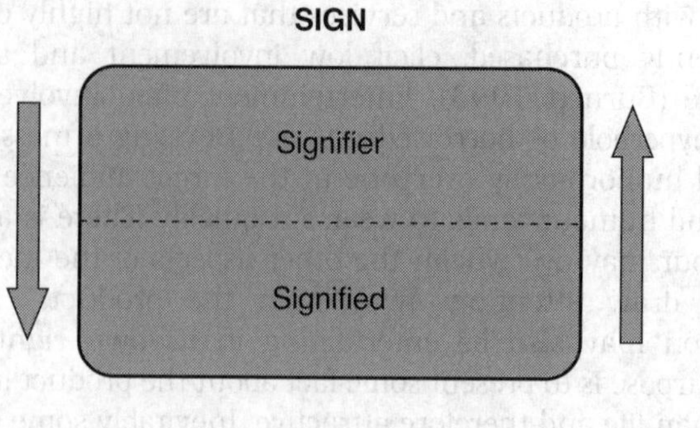

SIGN

Signifier

Signified

Figure 10.7 Saussure's
Signifier and Signified

The signifier is the form which the sign takes, while the signified is the concept it represents. So, for example:

▶ *Sign*: the written word 'house'.

▶ *Signifier*: the letters 'h-o-u-s-e'.

▶ *Signified*: the category 'house'.

It must be remembered that there is no necessary connection between the signifier and the signified. While in English the letters 'h-o-u-s-e' represent the category we know as 'house' in French there is a totally different signifier (i.e. 'c-h-a-t-e-a-u').

Other major developments in the study of signs have been offered by Charles Sanders Peirce who, in contrast to Saussure's dyad, proposed a triad depicted in Figure 10.8. Peirce's model is different in that he highlights that the meaning of a sign comes from the sense that is made of it by an interpreter. Therefore:

▶ *Sign Vehicle*: the form of the sign.

▶ *Sense*: the sense made of the sign by an interpreter.

▶ *Referent*: what the sign stands for.

Of particular interest to marketers in the use of signs are the notions of *metaphor* and *metonymy*. The purpose of using metaphors is to imply a resemblance between something which is essentially unfamiliar to the target audience (usually the product or service) and something which

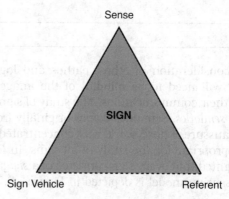

Sense

SIGN

Sign Vehicle   Referent

Figure 10.8 Peirce's Sign
Triad

is more familiar to them in order to convey a particular message. For example, in its advertising Solpadeine is portrayed using the metaphor of arrows shattering a pane of glass. This is done to signify both the ability of this drug to target pain and to overcome it. Interestingly, pain killers usually use one of two metaphors; strength in overcoming pain or soothing and relaxing properties. Thus, the use of metaphors, whether they be images or phrases, lends credence and strength to the message concerned. However, metaphors do rely upon the audience to make the connection and thus they must be used with care. Metonyms may also be visual or verbal and their purpose is to use an individual example to signify a related general category (e.g. the use of pictures of a starving child to represent the poverty and deprivation of the third world). Thus the associations brought about by the use of metonyms can also lend power to our message.

'The necessity of differentiating products motivates sign competition. The competition to build images that stand out in media markets is based on a process of routinely unhinging signifiers from signifieds so that new signifier-signified relationships can be fashioned (Goldman and Papson 1996:5).' To all intents and purposes signifiers, through constant use and appropriation, have become free-floating to the extent that marketers can now attach almost any signifier to their brands when communicating. For example, an image of a crawling baby might be used to signify a new generation of product, exploration, starting out on a new project and a whole host of other ideas and notions.

Deciding Upon Visual and Verbal Elements

The final consideration in designing the creative strategy is the creative mix; the manner in which visual and verbal elements are combined in a particular message. The following are a few general guidelines that help with developing the creative mix (Burnett 1993):

▶ *Product Facts*. When facts about the product are important in accomplishing the objectives outlined, verbal aspects of the ad become more important.

▶ *Product Appearance*. Where the appearance of the product is important in the ultimate purchase, then the visual aspect should be emphasized.

▶ *Product Newness*. The newer the product the more likely that verbal elements will be more effective. People naturally have questions about new products and ads should aim to answer these questions verbally.

▶ *Emotional Associations*. The more important it is to make emotional associations with the product, the more likely that the visual elements will be emphasized. Emotional appeals are often difficult to put into words and the visual approach offers a richer range of association.

▶ *Narration*. The more important narration is in making the point of the ad, the more important words will be to develop interest in the characters, the situation and the outcome.

▶ *Action*. If you wish the consumer to take a specific action then you are better off using words to do so rather than pictures.

Production

Although the creative concept gives direction to those who produce the desired direct marketing product, both the creative and production teams need to work hand in hand; 'the biggest bugbear is over-promising creativity without giving any thought to how it is done' (Baynes 1997:50). Creative designers need to be aware of the implications of including many different items in a mailing: Can these be controlled in the production process? What are the effects on costs? etc. Figure 10.9 summarizes the flow of the production process for a direct mailing.

While the creative concept might have been well formulated, it now needs to be converted from a mere concept into reality. Graphics (artwork and photography) and copy (the words and phrases to be used) will be identified as part of the creative process. These must now be subject to layout where the position and size of each element is determined exactly. This will then be ready for what used to be referred to as typesetting and although the term is still used, the old method of moving metal characters to the correct position in a template has been replaced by desk top publishing and other specialized software. Several detailed issues will be resolved here as well, such as the preparation for colour printing; four-colour printing produces every colour, shade and tone because that is what the combination of red, blue, yellow and black can produce. Because each colour needs to be applied as a separate overlay, it might be acceptable to compromise over the

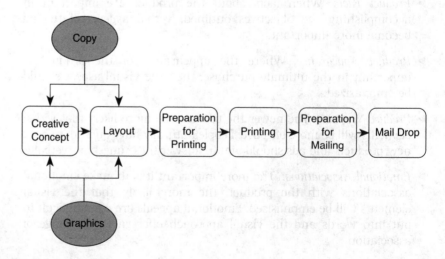

Figure 10.9 The Production Flow

number of colours used, as long as precise colour, tone and shade are not critical.

The gap between the creative and production teams is certainly narrowing as the importance of working together on these issues becomes critical (Darby 1997). Clients are asking for ever more unusual mailings as discussed in the context of developing 'novelty' creative treatment. This can be manifested in odd shapes, sizes and materials and although the creative team might come up with such ideas, it is the production staff who identify whether it can be achieved. Indeed, they will increasingly suggest methods based on their knowledge of ever-changing printing and production technology. In this synergistic sense, it is useful for them to work hand in hand. The example given earlier of the Disneyland Paris 'hologram' posters being a case in point.

Improvements in printing technology mean that it is now possible for campaigns such as 'Heinz at Home' to be personalized. Although improvements in database technology have promised the possibility of one-to-one marketing, print and production techniques have traditionally lagged behind. However, with the advent of digital printing one-to-one marketing is now firmly on the agenda.

> ❧ *In traditional litho-printing, you have to typeset your page, scan it, impose it, expose the plates, make your plates, make the process ready, run 'up to colour' (probably wasting a couple of hundred sheets) and then print. How much easier to have a digital file which is sent to print in much the same way as we send our day-to-day work to desktop printers.* ❧ (Bloom 1997).

Digital printing makes it possible to individualize every single print, thereby making its application in direct marketing extremely powerful. It is even possible to produce an individualized catalogue mailing for a responder to a DRTV advertisement within 24 hours. Digital printing, therefore, brings with it personalized and just-in-time mailings. Having said this, early experience of digital printing suggests that it can be expensive and of lower quality than litho-printing. However, as with most new technologies, it is likely that both these factors will improve as their use increases.

The next stage is for sample printings to be checked and then sent to print. We do not delve into the intricacies of the printing processes in this book because there are many good sources that concentrate on these mechanics, as listed at the end of this chapter. After printing, some items will need binding and finishing (e.g. folding, embossing, trimming and laminating, depending on the requirements of the mailing). Before mailing, also, items will be folded and inserted, envelopes will be labelled, personalized and sorted by postcode or other targeting variable and bagged for the mail deliverer. Once mailed, we await the response; but must be geared up to receive it and to respond appropriately and these are matters of *fulfilment*.

Before turning to the issue of fulfilment in detail, a specific issue is worth additional comment. This concerns the type of paper used for mailings. It is environmentally, as well as politically, correct to do what we can to safeguard the planet's physical environment, so does it make sense to use recycled paper? The answer is not straightforward because recycled paper is more expensive than virgin paper and recycled paper can be significantly poorer in quality unless it goes through a relatively expensive bleaching process. Sometimes this can be an advantage: some charity mailings might even be more appropriate if printed on paper which is not so overtly opulent. Another factor here is that virgin paper does not come from hardwood forests but from faster growing softwoods which are often managed especially for the paper industry. Thus, one argument put forward is that such forests actually add to the world's tree stock and provide useful habitats that otherwise would not exist.

In the late 1990s the direct marketing industry appeared to turn away from recycled paper perhaps because the 'green' lobby is less vociferous over direct mail's threat to the environment as it was in the late 1980s and early 1990s (Teather 1996). Another view is that recycling means fewer managed forests dedicated to paper production and because these contribute significantly to *increasing* the number of trees, many are happy to use virgin paper from what can be argued is a *more* environmentally friendly source. 'The pulp and paper industry is one of the major planters of new forest. If we keep recycling more and more material there will be less intensive forest management.'(Collins 1996:48) Another criticism of recycling comes from head of print production at Rapier Stead and Bowden, Bonnie White who says 'a lot of recycled paper is of no use to the environment. The chemicals they use to de-ink are like caustic soda. That's more damaging than chopping down trees from managed forests.' (White 1996:51) At any rate, recycled paper is not 100 per cent recycled, but contains at least 75 per cent recycled pulp, so even recycling requires a substantial input from virgin paper. The future is likely to see advances in how recycled paper is produced, resulting in quality improvements and cost reductions (Teather 1996).

A fairly typical number of different items to be included in a single mailing is half a dozen, but some mail packs can include more than 30. Any hiccup in the process which means that the odd item isn't ready at the time of mailing would disrupt the entire project. Each item also might need to be tracked, so codes need to be clear for the response handler. Additionally, the number of items obviously affects weight and therefore mailing costs. If costs turn out to be higher than estimated, the entire project can be dramatically affected: a ½p per mail pack can lead to an additional cost of £2500 for a mailing of 500,000 which would be a relatively small campaign.

Fulfilment

We have discussed some of the issues involved with developing direct marketing creative and with the production process. However well these are followed through, they must be backed by appropriate systems for fulfilling any request from the customer, whether it be for more information or the product/service itself.

Fulfilment is not the end of the process; rather it is a potential beginning of a relationship. As more attention is paid to the quality of service as well as to products, it is important for the direct marketer to ensure that responses to DRTV, mailings and telephone contacts are appropriate for the customer. In the past there were two industries; one catering for the handling of responses from sales promotions such as coupons and competitions and the other for direct marketing. These are now becoming increasingly integrated.

Booking Frenzy

A railway company offers direct booking of tickets and seat reservations via the telephone in addition to telephone based timetable enquiries.

Dr O'Pattervans is invited to a meeting in London in two day's time and contacts the telephone enquiry line. He is informed of train times and ticket prices and is told that if he books before 2pm on the day before departure the ticket would be less than half the full fare. However, this would be conditional on seat availability because these particular tickets are allocated according to quotas. He is also given the number for the ticket booking service, which he then calls. Unfortunately he is not successful in getting through; the line is either engaged or a recorded message tells him that 'all operators are busy, please try again later' and at that point the line is cut. Even when the line is engaged the 'ring back' facility is not available on that number. He tries again and again, over a four-hour period, but to no avail. The alternative method of buying the ticket was not open to him because he couldn't leave his desk that day to drive 10 miles to the nearest booking office.

Dr O'Pattervans needs to know if there are seats available at the cheaper fare but can't phone his nearest station because the entire rail enquiry service has been routed through one telephone number. He tries this again but is told that they are not able to divert calls to individual booking offices and neither can they check availability of seats. A 'Catch 22'!

The following day, with only an hour to the 2pm deadline, he has still had no success getting through to the direct booking number so he decides to leave his work (despite the fact that things were extremely busy) and drive to the nearest booking office. On arrival he is informed that the cheaper fare was not applicable on the train he would have to have taken to be on time for the London meeting. This contradicted the information the timetable enquiry service had provided. Dr O'Pattervans ended up paying the full fare which he could have done on the day of travel. Indeed if he had, it would have saved several wasted hours trying to get through to the booking number and a round trip of another hour to buy the ticket in person. To complain would involve collecting and completing a complaints form, which would take more time and, on the basis of one previous experience of complaining (over a delayed train which meant he missed a job interview), he decided it wasn't worth it because all he had received that time was a brief letter of apology and a voucher for £2.

This story of woe demonstrates that any direct service must be capable of delivering accurately, effectively and efficiently. In this instance, the customer would probably have been better off and certainly less stressed and annoyed if the direct service didn't even exist.

Fulfilment is mainly concerned with receiving orders or enquiries via the mail, telephone, Internet, or interactive TV. But handling complaints is also part of this aspect of customer service and carelines are becoming more prevalent and relevant (Hemsley 1997). Furthermore, as we discussed in our chapter on databases, fulfilment offers an opportunity to capture data on potential customers. Fulfilment is a process in its own right. Systems must be set up to deal with receipt of customer mail/calls, then to capture their details, produce personalized response output, enclose and mail information or products (which in turn involves order picking, packing and dispatch), analyse the statistics on enquiry nature, level, timing profiles, bank monies for orders and update stock control systems. Figure 10.10 summarizes some of the stages and components of this system (Roberts and Berger 1989:185).

Other fulfilment issues are concerned with planning for levels and timing of response. For example:

▶ Once a DRTV advertisement is broadcast, how many calls might we expect within half an hour of the broadcast? In reality the burst of inbound calls is almost instant and, if any one cannot get through, we might have lost them and their business forever.

▶ How long should we plan the time lag to be for responses to a poster campaign?

▶ What level of mailing response might we expect and have we liaised with the Royal Mail about this?

▶ How many catalogues should we print?

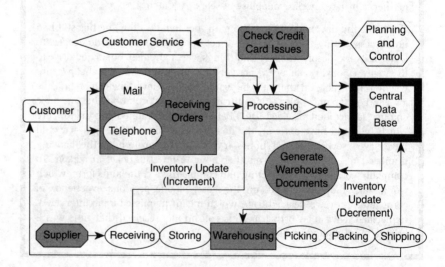

Figure 10.10 The Fulfilment Process

▶ What stock holdings should be considered for product orders? Remember the fiasco when Hoover could not meet demand for their sales promotion offer of free flights to America with the purchase of a vacuum cleaner!

There are other points which need to be addressed, such as the coupon itself; has it been designed to allow enough space for a consumer to complete their full address and other details? Many are not! Also, the media code needs to be included in order to track the response effectiveness of different media used. Order forms need to be designed to help both the customer and the fulfilment house. Product codes need to be easy to include and record. Payment terms (e.g. credit facilities), need to be in line with the Consumer Credit Act, 1974 and there should be appropriate provision for credit and debit card 'numbers' (16 'boxes' are needed). If insurance for order delivery is relevant, provision must be suitable and pre-planned. Forms should also be designed to facilitate data capture and data to be captured must be pre-determined and planned for. The type of analysis to be conducted on outcomes should also be planned for in advance, such as the production of response levels by media, cost per enquiry/order, geographic and geodemographic profiles of order/enquirers, stock control, financial reporting such as banking and credit card reports.

Data capture for use in the next stage, outbound contact, is a crucial component of the fulfilment process. Dedicated software (for example the Post Office Address tables) can check addresses for accuracy and this is important if we are to accurately target individuals. Otherwise we might be accused, justifiably, of sending 'junk mail'.

Response services also need to be determined. There are a variety of alternative approaches, including the *Business Reply* envelope or card and the *Freepost* system, both of which provide the responder with the means to reply free of postage charges. The *PO Box* system provides the marketer with a confidential delivery address but the responder has to pay for the postage.

As with our discussion of databases, there is a similar issue here, with respect to outsourcing a fulfilment specialist or keeping the operation in house. Conducting the fulfilment operation in-house can be disruptive because usually there are peaks and troughs of fulfilment activity and if managed internally there might be few economies of scale. If, on the other hand, response handling is required on a more even and regular basis, an in-house operation might be less disruptive. Also, if the business operates almost exclusively on a 'direct' basis, such as Reader's Digest, then gearing entire internal business systems around direct contact – inward and outward – makes more sense.

It is more likely, then, that the outsourcing of fulfilment is more appropriate for the majority of organizations. Fulfilment and response handling houses work for others so there are some economies of scale and concentration of expertise and equipment. This expertise and equipment can be significant and as technology changes the specialists are more likely to be at the cutting edge than would be the case with smaller internal operations. Also, there are often links between response handling and mailing operations. Response frequently involves some form of mailing, so again, those specialists who have the capacity for rapidly responding to clients' requirements for irregularly timed response activity, are often worth using. They will also be more likely to have access to state of the art printing and production equipment than the smaller internal operation is likely to be able to afford. The previous section on production gives some indication of what we mean by specialized equipment; folding machines, enclosing machines, printers, labellers, wrapping and strapping machines, weighing and counting machines, for mailing operations and for telephone based contact there can be fully automated digitized systems running to 2000 lines or more! In addition, the points mentioned on order picking and packing, stock control, banking of monies and data capture are all worth considering for outsourcing.

We mentioned complaint handling earlier and it has been found that customers who experience some level of dissatisfaction or concern and complain about this, are more likely to be retained as customers than those who do not complain (Jones 1996). Dr O'Pattervans might have been more likely to use the rail service again if he had complained and had a satisfactory response. It might even be suggested (only slightly facetiously) that it might pay marketers to create situations over which customers would complain! Related to this, it has been found that those customers who are 'very satisfied' are up to six times more likely to be retained than those who are just 'satisfied' (Jones 1996) so the importance of 'delivering' the direct marketing service is very important.

Conclusions

The main emphasis of the marketing concept is on customer orientation, satisfying and anticipating the customer's needs and wants. Thus, understanding customers needs, feelings, drives and emotions can provide the direct marketer with valuable clues to how the creative strategy should be structured.

People are not always aware of the real needs determining their behaviour and more subtle and indirect creative may appeal to unconscious needs. This chapter has also used a sequential model of customer responses to marketing actions to suggest the application of behavioural concepts to direct marketing creative. Furthermore, we have outlined different strategies depending on whether we are appealing to the target audience's moral principles, passion or sense of logic.

In addition, we have briefly reviewed aspects of the production process and issues involved with fulfilment. As with all systems, the creative, production and fulfilment processes are only as good as their weakest links and so the importance of all of the three topics covered in this chapter should not be underestimated.

CASE
STUDY 1

Planning screws you up

Once the Planner had reared its head from the amoebic soup the die was cast. Direct marketing was subverted as clients and creatives were bamboozled. Thank God consumers were too stupid to notice.

A copywriter, it is said, is someone who has failed at something else. I would extend the principle to planners: a planner is someone who has failed at everything. Including planning.

When I was a boy, planners were called Researchers. Their job was to go out and unearth evidence in support of whatever untenable hypothesis the account director had dreamed up after a four-hour lunch with his secretary.

The Researcher was like the driver in an armed robbery. He only had to provide a suitable vehicle for the job. His opinion was neither requested nor, if offered, respected. He hung around in Oxford Street with a clipboard, asking pre-ordained questions of people who vaguely resembled the Target and ticking the appropriate boxes on a form.

An horrific revelation

Then, in the early 80s, Researchers began to get ideas above their station. Just as, at the very dawn of time, a bolt of lightning must have struck a random mixture of chemicals and created the first spark of life, so a researcher somewhere must accidentally have entertained a Thought.

That Thought, however humble, must have divided, creating two new Thoughts and so on until the West End of London was a teeming, fecund soup of thoughts. At what point these began to conjoin and combine to form simple Ideas, it is impossible to say. But by 1985, the humble Researcher had evolved into a complex sentient organism, equipped with rudimentary intelligence.

What it lacked in cognitive skills, it made up for with cold, aggressive ambition and a monstrous self-esteem that had no basis in objective reality. These ruthless, parasitic creatures re-Christened themselves Planners implying a far more proactive role than that previously enjoyed by the passive Researcher.

The rest is history. Like razor-toothed raptors launching themselves on a herd of bovine herbivores, the Planners have completely usurped the role of the account handler, reducing him to a mere bag carrier, a mental eunuch whose timorous contributions to the intellectual debate will rarely prompt more than a derisory snigger from his new masters.

The planners have emasculated the creatives too. Those once proud hot-heads have been finally subdued, forced to march beneath the yokes of Logic and Statistic. The pub stands empty at 4pm. The lonely, rusted typewriter remains unhurled through fifth-floor window.

Creative work, if the sterile and mechanical product of modern direct marketing deserves the name, is a Stepford Wife: a perfect, plastic data-driven replica of passion, devoid of any real warmth or humour or humanity. The planners would rejoice over their three Perrier lunches, if only 'Rejoice' were part of their vocabulary.

Planning to fail?

So what does your Planner actually do? He will write your Brief, elevating his own prejudices to the status of objective truth by means of a few, quite arbitrary assumptions, disguised as empirical facts.

Then he will evaluate your creative response by exposing your ideas to an unsophisticated marketing illiterate audience under conditions so artificial that the so-called 'target' feels obliged to offer destructive criticism as proof of her intelligence and so alien that she flees for comfort to the most depressingly familiar, undemanding and anodyne execution on offer.

Then he will invoke random sets of statistics from whichever contradictory and equally questionable academic source happens best to perpetrate his favourite myth, then toss them casually to your client as a feudal baron might toss red-hot pennies to his serfs. The result is a mindless, self-imitating dirge, in which no hint of originality is allowed to disturb the monotony of the entirely expected.

The Planners are responsible for a conspiracy of mediocrity that perpetuates itself by protecting our clients from having to say boo to geese.

In the end, of course, it doesn't matter. With or without castrated Creatives, vicious Planners, cowardly Clients or stupid Account Men, one truth remains. People buy stuff.

(Source: *Marketing Direct*, September, 1997, p. 82.)

Review Questions

1   Using the 'needs-features-benefits' framework, devise direct marketing creative for a new direct banking service, a charity for battered husbands and an up-market mail order clothing catalogue.

2 How might theories of motivation be applied to the development of direct marketing messages?

3 Freud identified the Id, Superego and Ego. What are these and can they contribute anything to marketing? What is meant by 'good' and 'real' reasons for behaviour and what are the implications of such a distinction?

4 Of what value to direct marketing messages are 'sequential models' of customer response to marketing activity?

5 Discuss 'Gestalt' psychology and its role in 'participative' direct marketing messages.

6 How might direct marketers use human emotion to develop their creative appeals?

7 What is involved in the direct marketing production process and how is new technology affecting the process?

Discussion Questions

1 'Fulfilment is not the end of the process – it is a potential beginning of a relationship'. Discuss.

2 Produce a typology of message 'appeals' based on underpinning theory from the behavioural sciences.

References

Anderson, J.C. and Narus, J.A. (1990) 'A Model of Distributor Firm and Manufacturer Firm Working Partnerships', *Journal of Marketing*, 54(January), pp. 42–58.

Baynes, S. as reported in Dye, P. (1997) 'Don't be Frightened of the Press Gang', *Marketing Direct*, March, pp. 49–59.

Belch, G.E. and Belch, M.A. (1990) *Introduction to Advertising and Promotion: An Integrated Marketing Communications Perspective*, Chicago: Irwin.

Bloom, J. (1997) 'Digital Revolution?', *Marketing Direct*, June, pp. 46–8.

Burnett, J. (1993) *Promotion Management*, Boston: Houghton Mifflin.

Colley, R.H. (1961) *Defining Advertising Goals for Measured Advertising Results*, New York: Association of National Advertisers.

Collins, L. as reported in Teather, D. (1996) 'Recycled Paper: A Cause that's Gone to Waste?', *Marketing Direct*, October, pp. 47–53.

Darby, I. (1997) 'Printing Gets All Creative', *Marketing Direct*, January, pp. 52–6.

Davidson, H. (1997) *Even More Offensive Marketing*, London: Penguin.

Denny, N. (1996) 'Can We Win Creative Respect?', *Marketing Direct*, November, p. 12.

Engel, J.F., Blackwell, R.D. and Miniard, P.W. (1986) *Consumer Behaviour*, 5th edn, Chicago: The Dryden Press.

Festinger, L. (1957) *A Theory of Cognitive Dissonance*, Evanston, Ill: Row Peterson.

Freud, S (1964) 'New Introductory Lectures', in *Standard Edition of the Complete Psychological Works of Sigmund Freud*, London: Hogarth (Original work published in 1933).

Giffin, K. (1967) 'The Contribution of Studies of Source Credibility to a Theory of Interpersonal Trust in The Communication Process', *Psychological Bulletin*, 68(August), pp. 104–20.

Goldman, R. and Papson, S. (1996) *Sign Wars: The Cluttered Landscape of Advertising*, New York: The Guildford Press.

Gordon, W. (1991) 'Accessing the Brand Through Research', in Cowley, D. (ed.), *Understanding Brands*, London: Kogan Page, pp. 33–56.

Gundlach, G.T. and Murphy, P.E. (1993) 'Ethical and Legal Foundations of Relational Marketing Exchanges' *Journal of Marketing*, 57(October), pp. 35–46.

Hallberg, G. (1995) *All Consumers are Not Created Equal*, New York: John Wiley.

Hemsley, S. (1997) In the Line of Fire, Marketing Week, August, pp. 39–42.

Holder, D. (1993) 'Customer Acquisition and Retention', *Direct Response*, June, p. 40.

Hovland, C.I., Janis, I.L. and Kelley, H.H. (1953) *Communication and Persuasion*, New Haven, CT: Yale University Press.

Jones, T.O. (1996) 'Why Loyal Customers Defect', *KeyNote Presentation*, IDM Symposium, June 6th, London.

Köhler, W. (1927) *The Mentality of Apes*, New York: Harcourt Brace.

Lavidge, R.J. and Steiner, G.A. (1961) 'A Model for Predictive Measurements of Advertising Effectiveness', *Journal of Marketing*, 25, pp. 59–62.

Lovell, C. (1997) IDM Guest Lecture, University of the West of England, January 30th, Bristol.

Maslow, A.H. (1970) *Motivation and Personality*, 2nd edn, New York: Harper & Row.

McGuire, W.J. (1969) cited in Barry, T.E. and Howard, D.J. (1990) 'A Review and Critique of the Hierarchy of Effects in Advertising', *International Journal of Advertising*, 9, pp. 121–35.

Moriarty, S.E. (1986) *Creative Advertising: Theory and Practice*, Englewood Cliffs, NJ: Prentice Hall.

Oxenfeldt, A.R. and Swann, C. (1964) *Management of the Advertising Function*, Belmont, CA: Wadsworth Publishing Co.

Park, C.W., Jaworski, B.J. and MacInnis, D.J. (1986) 'Strategic Brand Concept-Image Management', *Journal of Marketing*, 50(October), pp. 135–45.

Pavlov, I.P. (1928) *Lectures on Conditioned Reflexes: The Higher Nervous Activity of Animals*, 1, London: Lawrence and Wishart, translated by H. Gantt.

Percy, L. and Rossiter, J.R. (1980) *Advertising Strategy: A Communication Theory Approach*, New York: Praeger.

Pidgeon, S. (1997) 'The Success and Future of Gender-Specific Fund-raising Propositions', *Journal of Not for Profit Marketing*, Spring, pp. 22–34.

Plutchik, R. (1980) *Emotion: A Psychoevolutionary Analysis*, New York: Harper and Row.

Ritchie, K. (1995) *Marketing to Generation X*, New York: Lexington.

Ritson, M. (1995) 'Marketing to Generation X: Strategies for the Measurement and Targeting of Advertising's Lost Generation', *Proceedings of the Henry Stewart Annual Conference on Advances in Targeting, Measurement and Analysis for Marketing*, June, London, pp. 63–79.

Roberts, M.L. and Berger, P.D. (1989) *Direct Marketing Management*, Englewood Cliffs, NJ: Prentice Hall.

Rudolph, H.J. (1947) *Attention and Interest Factors in Advertising*, New York: Funke Wagnalls.

Schramm, W. and Roberts, D. (eds) (1971) *The Process and Effects of Mass Communication*, Urbana, IL: University of Illinois Press.

Shocker, A.D. and Srinivasan, V. (1979) 'Multiattribute Approaches for Product Concept Evaluation and Generation: A Critical Review', *Journal of Marketing Research*, 16 (May), pp. 159–80.

Skinner, B.F. (1938) *The Behaviour of Organisms*, New York: Appleton-Century-Crofts.

St. Elmo Lewis, E. (circa 1900) cited in Barry, T.E. and D.J. Howard (1990) 'A Review and Critique of the Hierarchy of Effects in Advertising', *International Journal of Advertising*, 9, pp. 121–35.

Sternthal, B., Dholakia, R.R. and Leavitt, C. (1978) 'The Persuasive Effect of Source Credibility: Tests of Cognitive Response', *Journal of Consumer Research*, 4(March), pp. 252–60.

Stokes, D. (1997) cited in Darby, I. (1997) 'Printing Gets all Creative', *Marketing Direct*, January, pp. 52–6.

Teather, D. (1996) 'Recycled Paper: A Cause that's Gone to Waste?', *Marketing Direct*, October, pp. 47–53.

Wallas, G. cited by Belch, G.E. and Belch, M.A. (1995) *Introduction to Advertising and Promotion: An Integrated Marketing Communications Perspective*, 3rd edn, Chicago: Irwin, p. 272.

White, B. as reported in Teather, D. (1996) 'Recycled Paper: A Cause that's Gone to Waste?', *Marketing Direct*, October, pp. 47–53.

Zeigarnik, B. (1927) 'Uber das Behalten von erledigten und unerledigten Handlungen', *Psychologische Forschunnge*, 9, pp. 1–85.

Further Reading

Engel, J.F., Blackwell, R.D. and Miniard, P.W. (1986) *Consumer Behaviour*, 5th edn, Hinsdale, IL: The Dryden Press.

Evans, M. J., Moutinho, L. and Van Raaij, W.F. (1996) *Applied Consumer Behaviour*, Harlow: Addison Wesley.

Percy, L. and Rossiter, J.R. (1980) *Advertising Strategy: A Communication Theory Approach*, New York: Praeger.

Thomas, B. (1996) *Royal Mail Guide to Direct Mail for Small Businesses*, Oxford: Butterworth Heinemann.

The Law of Direct Marketing

by Paul Sampson

Eversheds Solicitors

This Chapter:

► Introduces Students To The Relevant Legislation In The Area Of Direct Marketing.

► Describes Some Of The Relevant Legislation.

C
H
A
P
T
E
R

11

The Law of Direct Marketing

Introduction

Direct marketing professionals have a problem. There is no Direct Marketing Act, where all of the relevant law can be found in one convenient place. Instead, there is a proliferation of statutes, regulations, directives and precedents which have to be analysed. To make matters worse, the position is always changing as new legislation comes from Parliament and Brussels, and the courts continue to interpret and re-interpret the legislation.

This chapter is an outline of some of the laws affecting direct marketing. It is not an exhaustive treatment of direct marketing law. It cannot be: every situation is different and different laws apply in different ways to each situation. Anyway, practising marketers are not interested in abstract legal principles but in the application of those principles to their particular circumstances. The direct marketer wants to know: Can I do it? What is the risk? What are the consequences?

Many of the statements in this chapter are simplistic. Unfortunately this is essential. The laws, procedures and terminology all have numerous exceptions, but this is not a book for lawyers and to deal fully with these would be to condemn the direct marketer to death by boredom. I have decided that it is more useful to make the essential point than to pursue legal correctness.

In short, this chapter is an outline of some of the risks direct marketers face but it is not a substitute for professional advice from a specialist solicitor.

What are the Relevant Laws?

I shall consider the law of two elements of direct marketing: (a) communication with individuals, to persuade them to buy goods or services and (b) the use of database lists.

Where Does The Law Come From?

The law is the rules which are applied and enforced by the courts. There are various sources of these rules and there are a number of people who can enforce these rules through the courts.

Each country has its own legislative body which passes legislation. In the United Kingdom, our Parliament passes statutes ('Acts of Parliament'). A statute may delegate to a Government Minister the authority to make detailed regulations covering a particular subject.

The courts, and the judges who sit in them, have to interpret and apply Parliament's legislation, and sometimes their interpretation is quite different from the ordinary meaning of the words of the statute. In reaching their decisions, the courts must state the reasons for those decisions. Those reasons then become binding on other courts according to certain rules. Consequently, it is always necessary to look not only at the wording of the statutes, but also at the way in which that wording has been interpreted by the courts.

Since the United Kingdom joined the European Community in 1972 Parliament has agreed to be bound by Community law. This takes effect mainly in two ways.

First, the European institutions (the European Commission, the European Parliament and the Council of Ministers) introduce 'Directives' and 'Regulations'. Regulations are effective immediately in the same way as our Acts of Parliament and our courts must enforce them. Directives, on the other hand, are instructions to the member states to pass their own legislation to implement the principles described in the Directive. Member states are usually given a few years in which to do this, and they are often given some flexibility as to how they must implement the Directive.

Second, our Parliament has agreed that the parties to a dispute can appeal to the courts of the European Union (the highest of which is the European Court of Justice) and that our courts are bound by the decisions of those courts.

The result is that it is becoming increasingly difficult to determine what the law is, as the number of sources of law increases and the interactions and conflicts between them have to be worked out.

But whatever the law is – and of course it is constantly changing – it has two quite distinct functions: (a) to deter and punish the wrongdoer and (b) to compensate the injured.

Punishment or Compensation?

The law can be divided crudely into two distinct parts: the criminal law and the civil law. This is reflected in the way that the court system itself is divided into two parts: the criminal courts and the civil courts.

Criminal

The criminal law is the primary way in which the State regulates the behaviour of its citizens. Particular behaviour is identified as undesirable and is made an offence. A number of enforcement agencies, including the police and local authorities, have a duty to prosecute those suspected of offences. But it is an important principle of the legal system in England and Wales that, in general, private citizens may also prosecute and this appears to be happening more and more.

The penalties for committing an offence include imprisonment and fines. Fines go to the State, not to anyone harmed by the offence.

In many instances, where an offence is committed by a company with the consent or connivance of anyone who acts as a director, manager or secretary of the company, or where the offence is committed due to the neglect of such a person, that individual is guilty of the offence as well. The individual can be prosecuted and punished as well as, or instead of, the company itself.

Depending on the nature of the offence and (sometimes) the choice of the defendant, the case may be brought either in the Magistrates' Court or the Crown Court. It is the more serious offences which are tried before a jury in the Crown Court, where the judge is able to impose much greater sentences on a guilty defendant. Generally there is no limit on the size of the fine a Crown Court judge may impose.

Civil

The civil law is a body of rules which gives us all certain rights and remedies if anyone interferes with our rights. However, it is up to us (as companies or individuals) to sue the wrongdoer in the civil courts.

With the exception of libel and slander, these cases are heard by judges without a jury. The person wronged who brings the case to court (the *plaintiff*) has to prove that it is more likely than not that the other person (the *defendant*) breached the plaintiff's rights and then the court will provide various remedies. The primary remedy is financial compensation, but there are other important rights. One of these is an 'injunction', which is an order of the court that the defendant should do something or restrain from doing something. Anyone who disobeys an injunction is likely to be fined or even imprisoned.

The cost of court proceedings is another factor to consider. Each party can easily incur legal costs of tens of thousands of pounds and the general rule is that the loser has to pay the majority of the winner's costs. This can make losing very expensive.

Having reviewed where laws come from and the way they work in general, I shall now explain how some specific activities of the direct marketer are affected.

Description of Goods and Services

Voluntary Descriptions

It is an offence to use a false or misleading description in relation to goods (S1 of the Trades Descriptions Act 1968). Similar provisions apply in respect of services and accommodation (S14, Trades Descriptions Act 1968). The maximum penalty under the Trade Descriptions Act is two years' imprisonment plus a fine.

Almost anything counts as a description, including the quantity, size and origin of the goods, any approvals they may have received, and their fitness for any particular purpose. Furthermore, the Secretary of State for Trade and Industry has the right to pass regulations with the effect that any words and expressions used in relation to goods should be understood as having a specific meaning.

> A watch was described as being a 'diver's watch' and as being 'waterproof'. This was a criminal offence as when the watch was placed in a bowl of water the water leaked in and the watch stopped. (Sherratt v Gerald's The American Jewellers Ltd (1970) 68 LGR 256)

There is an important defence for direct marketers under the Act. The defendant will not be guilty if he can prove that he committed the offence due to a mistake, or because he relied on information supplied to him, provided he can show that he exercised due diligence and took all reasonable precautions to avoid committing the offence. Although this defence is not limited to such situations, it will be particularly valuable to 'middlemen' who pass on goods or services provided by others. However, it is not enough simply to rely on those others and, depending on the particular circumstances, it may be necessary for the defendant to show that he undertook his own tests and made his own enquiries.

There is rather better protection for those who only arranged for the advertisement to be published, such as direct marketing agencies and advertising agencies. They can be prosecuted for their involvement but they have a special defence if they can prove that they did not know or suspect, or have any reason to suspect, that an offence would be committed by publishing the advertisement.

Compulsory Descriptions

So far I have considered statements which direct marketers choose to make. But the Secretary of State has the power to pass regulations requiring that any advertisement of goods should contain, or at least refer to, particular information (S9 Trade Descriptions Act 1968). These regulations may specify the form this information must take and the manner in which it must be included in any advertisement. Anyone who publishes an advertisement which does not comply with these regulations commits an offence.

The Trade Descriptions Act is enforced by local trading standards officers who have very wide powers to investigate apparent offences. There are very many prosecutions each year: in 1995 there were 1761.

Price Indications

It is an offence to give to consumers any misleading indication of the price at which goods, services, accommodation or facilities are available (S20 Consumer Protection Act 1987). It does not matter whether the indication is misleading to all of the consumers to whom it is given, or only to some of them. The penalty is a fine.

Indications can be misleading in many ways.

> They might indicate that the price for the goods or services is less than it really is.

> A picture or description which includes, or refers to other goods or services might lead a consumer to believe that those other goods and services are included in the quoted price when in fact there is an additional charge for them.

> It might not be clear to a consumer that the price quoted only applies if the consumer buys something else as well, or only if he buys the advertised goods or services through a particular outlet.

> The publishers of a newspaper published an advertisement for a wristwatch. The watch was described as 'a £50 watch' and was being sold at under £5. The publisher was prosecuted because at the time the watches were advertised they had not been available for sale in the United Kingdom at £50. Although the watches did subsequently go on sale shortly afterwards, the publisher was prosecuted and convicted of using a misleading price indication because the advertisement suggested that the watches were already available for sale on the open market (MGN Ltd v Northamptonshire County Council).

In some circumstances it is a criminal offence to include a statement that the price indication should not be relied on.

It is possible for an indication to be correct when it is given but subsequently to become misleading. If this should happen, it is necessary to take all reasonable steps to prevent consumers to whom it was given relying on it. This might mean a follow-up mailshot must be sent or that an advertisement must be published in an appropriate place.

The astute direct marketing agency will quickly realize that this last provision is not only a potential risk, but also a potential benefit. It could be used to convince a client that he should pay for a repeat mailing to correct the now-misleading price indication, so generating extra revenue while avoiding liability for the agency!

Direct marketers will in most cases have a defence if they can show that when the advertisement was published (e.g. when a mailshot is sent out) they did not know that it contained a misleading indication *and* that they had no grounds for suspecting that this was the case.

Similarly, direct marketers will have a defence if they can show that they exercised all due diligence and took all reasonable steps to avoid committing the offence. However, it may not always be enough simply to rely on information supplied by someone else.

The Act allows the Secretary of State to pass regulations covering the way in which price indications must be given, and to make it an offence not to comply with these regulations. This allows the Government to deal quickly with any new undesirable practices which might develop.

For example, any mailshot which invites consumers to place orders for goods, services, accommodation or facilities, whether by post, telephone or the Internet, must make it clear if the indicated price does not apply to any particular method of payment (e.g. by credit card) and must state the difference between the indicated price and the price which is payable if that method is used (The Price Indications (Method of Payment) Regulations 1991).

The Act also allows the Secretary of State to approve codes of practice which contain practical guidance on giving price indications. An example is the Code of Practice for Traders on Price Indications. Where codes of practice have been approved, direct marketers do not have an automatic defence to a prosecution under the Act simply by showing that they have complied with the code, but it is a factor which the court can take into account.

Making Comparisons

One of the most effective ways of promoting a company's goods or services is by making a favourable comparison with the products or services of a competitor. However, there are dangers in using comparisons in promotional materials.

Trade Marks

The name of a company, its products and its services are usually trade marks and in many instances they are registered trade marks. When a trade mark is registered for particular goods or services, it is unlawful for anyone other than the trade mark owner to use that trade mark in connection with those goods or services. The obvious example of this is where one company fraudulently applies another company's trade mark to its own goods in order to sell more of them or in order to sell them at a higher price.

It is also used to cover comparative advertising, where the registered trade mark is used to refer to the genuine goods or services of the trade mark owner. This made it almost impossible to use comparative advertising, although in some industries (such as the car industry) there was an 'understanding' between manufacturers and it became the norm for them to compare specific features or performance levels with each others' models. However, the Government was persuaded of the benefits to consumers of comparative advertising and it was legalized in the Trade Marks Act 1994. Even so, in order to be lawful the comparison must be in line with honest commercial practices. In addition, the comparison must not unfairly exploit the other person's trade mark or damage its reputation or distinctive character.

All of the particular facts and circumstances must be taken into account when assessing whether a comparison is lawful. It should not be assumed that competitors will concede this quietly. The Royal Bank of Scotland sent out a mailshot which included a leaflet. In the leaflet was a table which compared the various charges applicable to different credit cards, including Barclaycard. BARCLAYCARD is a registered trade mark of Barclays. Barclays sued because it believed that the mailshot did not compare like with like and implied that the Royal Bank of Scotland's Advanta card was better than Barclaycard in every respect. The judge said that a reasonable member of the public expects marketing people to be reasonably selective in the points they choose to compare against competitors' products, expects them to use a certain amount of hyperbole, and expects them to poke fun at competitors or their products. Provided the direct marketer does not go too far, all of this is allowed (Barclays Bank plc v RBS Advanta).

But the direct marketer must get his facts right. If he says something which is incorrect, not only might he lose the special defence under the Trade Marks Act for comparative advertising, but he might also incur liability for other reasons irrespective of whether he has used someone else's trade mark.

False Statements

If a direct marketer improperly makes a false statement about someone's goods, that person could sue the direct marketer for compensation if they suffer any losses – such as a loss of sales.

Once again, the courts expect people to hype their own products and to exaggerate to a reasonable extent, so it is not libellous of someone's products simply to say that your own products are the best. Nevertheless, if specific figures are given, or the statement is dressed up as a scientific report, it might cease to be hype and could lead to a claim being made.

Of course, by libelling someone's goods the direct marketer might also libel that person. This can be much worse for several reasons. First, the plaintiff does not have to prove that the statement was false: the defendant must prove that it is true and this can be difficult to do. Second, the plaintiff does not have to prove that the statement was made improperly: he only has to prove that the statement was made. Third, the plaintiff does not have to prove any specific losses – such as contracts which have been lost because of the untrue statement (although these can be claimed if they can be proved) – and the court can award a general sum as compensation for the damage to the plaintiff's reputation. It is worth noting that it is not only individuals who have reputations and companies can sue for damage to their reputation. Fourth, the plaintiff may be entitled to have a jury award the compensation and juries are notorious for awarding very large sums.

The plaintiff does not have to show that the statement explicitly identified the plaintiff: it is enough that the plaintiff can show that some people believed the statement referred to the plaintiff, so simply omitting the name of a competitor company in a comparison does not mean that it cannot sue.

Economic Marketing Ltd sends out a mailshot promoting the beef products of its client. The copy describes how 'these products are 100 per cent high quality, organic beef guaranteed to be from herds which are certified free of BSE, unlike the products of its competitors'. What the copywriter meant to say was that his client's products are made from beef from herds certified to be free of BSE, and unlike its competitors his client uses only high quality, organic beef.

If the competitor can show that the statement was made improperly – for example deliberately to deceive consumers – there will be a claim for libelling the competitor's beef products. The agency, the copywriter and his client could be sued by a competing manufacturer for the value of any drop in sales which result from this. The competitor could also sue if its reputation for quality and safety had been damaged by the suggestion that it was using beef from herds which might be contaminated with BSE. The competitor would not have to show that it had lost any sales at all, and the damages awarded by the jury could easily be six figures.

It is worth noting that the directors of the competitor company could also sue, as their reputation as caring businessmen and men of integrity might have been damaged!

When all of the legal costs are included, this could prove to have been a very expensive slip of the pen. In one case the net award of damages was £110,000 but the legal costs were estimated to be £5 million.

Financial Services

All advertisements relating to investments must be clear and must not be misleading (Financial Services Act 1986). For these purposes many mailshots are advertisements. They must also be approved by an 'authorized person' (i.e. someone who is authorized according to the provisions of the Act to conduct investment business) and anyone – including a direct marketer – who issues an unapproved advertisement commits an offence. It is not just a criminal offence: anyone who relies on the advertisement and suffers any loss as a result can sue the direct marketer for compensation. Obviously the direct marketer's potential liability is enormous.

Promotions

Direct marketers use all manner of devices to promote goods and services. Special offers are common, with a discount or 'two for the price of one' for a limited period of time. These offers are subject to the laws on misleading prices (see page 395).

Another type of promotion is the offer of something for nothing. The 'something' ranges from very small gifts (in practice nearly always alarm clocks which do not work) to more substantial prizes such as holidays, cars, houses, and even millions of pounds in cash. These promotions are subject to the Lotteries and Amusements Acts 1976.

Direct marketers use these promotions because they appeal to the natural greed in us all, which means we cannot resist the idea of something for nothing. This legislation is the latest in a long line of statutes which were introduced to protect us from our own greed. It is important to keep this in mind. The legislation itself is not especially precise and the courts have had to apply it to many different promotional schemes. The decisions are often difficult to reconcile with each other but the touchstone is nearly always the protection of the public.

The Act does not prohibit all 'something for nothing' promotions. Whether such a promotion is lawful or unlawful depends on whether the participants make any contribution to participate and the extent to which the skill of the participants contributes to the outcome.

No Skill Involved

Where prizes are to be distributed by pure chance and not according to the skill of the participants, the legality of the promotion depends on whether or not the participants make a contribution for participating.

If anyone can participate *completely* free of charge, it is a lawful prize draw.

Reader's Digest Association Ltd sent out a personalized mailshot addressed to each recipient. In addition to containing promotional material for Reader's Digest magazine (and some other goods) it contained a list of six-digit numbers and two envelopes – one marked 'yes please' and the other marked 'no thank you'. The recipients had to return their application form to participate in the prize draw. Depending on whether or not they also wished to take the magazine or other goods they had to use either the 'yes please' or the 'no thank you' envelope. This made them eligible to receive

> one of 2103 prizes being offered, depending on whether or not the
> participant's numbers matched any of those drawn at random by Reader's
> Digest. Reader's Digest was prosecuted but the court decided that it was a
> lawful prize draw because the participants did not have to contribute
> anything in order to participate. Their chances of winning one of the prizes
> was unaffected by which envelope they returned their application in and
> was not dependent on them purchasing anything from Reader's Digest.
> (Reader's Digest Association Ltd v Williams [1976] 3 All ER 737).

However, if there is any charge (either direct or indirect) it is a lottery
and unlawful unless it is one of the specifically permitted types of
lottery. As these permitted lotteries will not generally be of interest to
the direct marketer I shall not discuss them further.

Is there a Charge for Entry?

A critical test is whether or not a substantial number of participants
have to make some contribution in order to participate in the prize
draw. If they do, it becomes an unlawful lottery.

But it is not only the payment of money which amounts to a
contribution. Nor does everyone have to contribute something for it to
be an unlawful lottery. It is enough that a substantial number of
participants have to do something in order to participate.

In practice, one of the most common conditions for people to
participate is that they have to buy something. If this is the case, it is
irrelevant that they do not have pay anything above the usual price for
that thing and that it is worth the price which is charged.

> A promotional mailshot invites people to send in the application form
> together with a token from the top of a special promotional packet of corn
> flakes. These packets are the same price as the usual packets. The forms are
> to be entered in a prize draw. This is an unlawful lottery as a purchase is
> necessary.

It does not make any difference that some people can participate free
of charge. In a case decided by the House of Lords, the cards which
were necessary to participate in the prize draw were inserted in
packets of cigarettes. Although 2¼ million entry cards were
distributed free of charge to anyone who asked for one, the House
ignored those and focused on the 'sale' of the remaining 260 million
cards. Although the special packets were sold at the normal price, the
House decided that a substantial number of people did make a
contribution in order to participate in the prize draw and that made it
an unlawful lottery (Imperial Tobacco v Attorney General (1981)
ALL ER 866).

A newspaper distributed numbers free of charge by putting them through letter boxes. The recipients had to check each day to find out if their number appeared in the newspaper, and if it did they won a prize. The court recognized that the participants did not have to buy a newspaper to find out if they had won. Instead, they could have read someone else's or they could enquire of the newspaper proprietor. However, the court decided that most people would have bought a newspaper and although the newspaper continued to be sold at the normal price this meant that a substantial number of the participants did contribute to the prize draw. This made it an unlawful lottery. (Willis v Young & Stembridge [1907] 1 KB 448)

Although some judges in later cases have doubted whether this last decision was right, it has not been overruled and it would be safest to treat it as correct.

In conclusion, direct marketers considering a prize draw where the skill of the participants does not contribute to the outcome should obtain legal advice before proceeding or they could find themselves in court.

Skill is Required

If the distribution of prizes is determined by the skill of the participants, the promotion is not a lottery but a competition. The important point to note is that if it is a *lawful* competition it is perfectly permissible to charge participants for entry, whether in the form of cash or tokens from promotional packets of corn flakes!

However, in practice the level of skill required is seldom very high. No doubt the average consumer would be deterred from participating if it were. This means that chance still plays a significant part in determining which participants win and it will depend on the precise circumstances whether it is a lawful competition or an unlawful lottery. This is recognized in Section 14 of the Act which prohibits any competition in which success does not depend *to a substantial degree* on the exercise of skill.

There have been very many instances of promoters attempting to dress up an unlawful lottery as a lawful competition. There will of course be many shades of grey and the courts have reached different decisions on similar (but not identical) facts. However, some fictitious examples will usefully illustrate the principle.

A holiday company offers to all those who book a holiday with the company during the month of October the chance to win their holiday free of charge. After the holiday is booked the company sends its customers a difficult crossword puzzle with only one known solution. In January, any customer who has returned a properly completed crossword wins their holiday free of charge. This is a lawful competition.

In the above example, most of the crossword puzzle clues are easy but there are a few difficult ones. It is likely that this is a lawful competition.

In the above example, most of the clues in the crossword puzzle are easy, and where the clues are difficult more than one answer will still complete the puzzle. The chairman of the company completes the puzzle himself and the entries are compared with his solution. Those customers who completed the crossword using the same answers as the chairman receive their holiday free of charge. This is probably an unlawful lottery (Coles v Odhams Press [1936] 1 KB 416).

Forecasts

Although proper competitions, where the skill of the participants does substantially affect the outcome, are lawful and a charge may be made for entry, this does not apply to all competitions.

In particular, any competition in which prizes are offered for forecasting the result of a future event are prohibited no matter how much skill is required.

Database Lists

It was Francis Bacon who said: *'Knowledge is power.'* Had he been born a little later, and pursued a career in direct marketing, he might have said: *'Heuristic data mining within an information warehouse can enhance competitive advantage.'*

The use of computers to gather, analyse and use information about customers and prospects has almost certainly contributed more to the growth of direct marketing than any other single factor, and possibly more than all other factors put together. It is this which allows the direct marketer to communicate one-to-one with a customer or prospect in a meaningful way.

This means that the database list is one of the direct marketer's single most important assets. It was widely reported that one of the former public utilities spent in the region of £100 million on its customer database system following privatization.

Although the accountants have been slow to recognize this, and database lists do not appear on balance sheets as an asset, the law does protect them. And it is only because database lists are protected by law that list brokers are able to recover the enormous sums of money required to gather the data (plus a profit of course!) by licensing them out to direct marketers.

However, it is not only those who create databases who are protected: so are the individuals about whom data is collected. Consequently there is a complex interaction of different principles and laws.

The Protection of Databases

Databases are protected by copyright and there will soon be changes to this protection under forthcoming legislation and new database rights will be introduced.

Copyright

Most databases are protected by copyright, which makes it unlawful for anyone to copy a substantial part of the database without permisssion from the copyright owner (SS3 and 16 Copyright, Designs and Patents Act 1988).

It is important to realize that copyright does *not* protect the raw information – for example, the names, addresses, ages, etc. of the individuals in the database. What copyright does protect is the database itself: the selection and structure of the data in it. And copyright only prevents someone copying the database. It does not prevent someone creating their own similar, or even identical, database.

> A fictitious agency, Economic Marketing Ltd, has written to every business in London which manufactures widgets and asked them to complete a questionnaire. From the questionnaires which have been returned it has compiled a list of the names of the companies, their addresses, the names of the heads of their purchasing departments and their telephone numbers.
>
> This list is automatically protected by copyright. Anyone who uses a copy of that list to telephone or write to all those heads of purchasing without permission from Economic Marketing would infringe its copyright. However, anyone is free to repeat the same exercise by finding out for themselves which companies manufacture widgets, sending out their own question-naires and compiling their own list.

Computerized database lists receive even greater protection. With these it is not only telephoning or writing to the people on the list which infringes copyright. Merely loading the database list onto a computer infringes copyright unless the copyright owner has given permission.

The Database Directive

The law in this field is set to change. There is now an EC Directive on the legal protection of databases which is intended to harmonize the protection of databases throughout the European Community (Directive 96/9/EC). The member states must implement this by passing legislation before 1 January 1998.

Under the Directive, all member states must protect databases and they must do so by a combination of copyright and two new rights: the extraction and re-utilization rights. The interaction between these three rights is complex and beyond the scope of this book (for further reading see Sampson, P. (1994) 'Electronic Databases – A legal Perspective', *Engineering Management Journal*, October). However, in practice the result will be that all computer database lists will be protected throughout the European Community for at least 15 years.

There are two ways in which these rights can be used. First, the rights owner can keep the database list to himself in order to obtain an advantage over his competitors. Alternatively, the rights owner can allow others to use the database on payment of a fee. This permission is called a *'licence'*.

The Licensing of Databases

The law and practice of licensing database lists is extremely complex and a full treatment is beyond the scope of this book. The important point is that in the licence the rights owner may specify the purpose for which the database list may be used and how many times it may be used. The consequence is that if the user (known as the *'licensee'*) should use it for any other purpose, or on more occasions than is permitted, then that unauthorized use is unlawful.

Rights owners often insert traps into their database lists. For example, they will often insert names and addresses which ensure that they receive a copy of every mailshot made using the list. This allows the rights owner to monitor usage of the list and to take legal action if the user exceeds the terms of the licence or if someone is using an unlicensed copy of the list.

In practice, list brokers often bring together data which has been collected by other organizations so as to offer a more comprehensive service. The owners of the rights in the underlying lists often retain those rights and this leads to complex licensing, cross-licensing and sub-licensing arrangements. A consequence of this is that a database list will often contain trap addresses planted by more than one person as each of the rights owners attempts to monitor the usage of their own list.

The consequences of ignoring database rights can be very serious. A direct marketer who takes a copy of a database list, either in the form of a photocopy or on disk, knowing that he does not have permission to do so commits a criminal offence. The company could be fined an unlimited amount. The person responsible, as well as the directors and managers involved, could also be prosecuted and if convicted they could be imprisoned for up to two years and be fined an unlimited amount. The courts are beginning to treat copyright infringement as seriously as theft, which in reality is what it is: the theft of someone else's work.

The rights owners (as there could be more than one) can also sue for compensation.

The Protection of Individuals

The individuals about whom direct marketers collect information have various legal rights, and they will soon have even more when new legislation is introduced.

The Data Protection Act

The main legislation in this field is the Data Protection Act 1984. The purpose of this Act is to protect the rights of individuals when other people, such as direct marketers, collect information about them and store or process it on computers.

Under the Act, any direct marketing organization which stores information about individuals on a computer must register with the Data Protection Registrar. It is a criminal offence to store or use personal information without being registered. The organization must register various information, including:

▶ the sort of personal information which is held;

▶ the sources from which it is obtained;

▶ the purposes for which it is used;

▶ to whom it might be disclosed.

It is important to supply full details when registering, and to keep the registered details up-to-date, as it is a criminal offence to operate outside the terms of the registration.

The Data Protection Principles

Having registered with the Data Protection Registrar the organization must comply with the data protection principles. These provide, amongst other things, that the personal information must:

▶ be obtained and processed fairly;

▶ be adequate, relevant and not excessive in relation to the purpose for which it is held;

▶ be accurate and up-to-date;

▶ be held for no longer than is necessary for the purpose;

▶ be adequately protected.

It is not automatically a criminal offence to break these principles, but it can give rise to liability to pay compensation to the individual concerned. Furthermore, if anyone reports the breach to the Data Protection Registrar an enforcement notice can be issued and it is a criminal offence not to comply with one of these notices. If an organization ignores an enforcement notice, the Data Protection Registrar will remove the organization from the register and the organization will then be unable to continue storing or using personal information at all.

Although there are some exceptions, in general individuals are entitled to be supplied with a copy of all information relating to them. If that information is inaccurate, they can obtain a court order that it be corrected or deleted.

Unless the user of the information can prove that all reasonable care was taken to ensure that the information was accurate, individuals may be entitled to compensation for any injury, loss or distress suffered by them as a consequence of being inaccurate. For example, if information is collected about someone's health or lifestyle, but it is entered on to the computer incorrectly with the result that they are denied insurance cover, that individual may have a claim.

Similarly, unless the user of the information can prove that all reasonable care was taken to prevent the loss of information relating to an individual, that individual may be able to claim compensation for any loss or damage suffered as a result of that information being lost. For example, an individual may reply to a mailshot to register with a company which provides financial services in order to be informed of suitable investment opportunities which arise. If the details are accidentally deleted, and as a consequence the individual is not notified of a particular investment opportunity, he or she may be able to claim the profit that would have been made out of that investment.

Similarly, unless the user of the information can prove that all reasonable care was taken to prevent any unauthorized disclosure as information relating to an individual, that individual may be able to claim compensation for any unauthorized disclosure of that information.

Perhaps the most troublesome of these for the direct marketer is the principle that personal information must be obtained and processed fairly and held for no longer than is necessary for the purpose.

STUDY 1

Data law requires industry scrutiny

The new Data Protection Bill is designed to give more protection to consumers in an increasingly data-oriented age.

This is an admirable motive. The more protection consumers have against the misuse of personal data, the happier they will be to hand over information to direct marketers.

And in spite of the costs involved in its implementation, the Bill will make the transfer of data across Europe much easier by standardising data laws across the EU.

But the Bill also gives greater powers to the Data Protection Registrar, Elizabeth France. Under her new title of Commissioner, she will be able to stop-and-search companies on suspicion of data misuse.

France has already proved herself deeply suspicious of the direct marketing industry. She has made life difficult for utilities which use customer lists for direct marketing. And she attempted to stop Tesco mailing its own customers with information on its own financial products.

The industry must prepare to defend its use of consumer information in the face of the Commissioner's anti-direct marketing stance.

One way to do this is to continue the Direct Marketing Association's work of building a comprehensive system of self-regulation. If direct marketers solve their own problems they are less likely to suffer outside interference.

And the Mailing Preference Service, which has been one of direct marketing's best kept secrets, must be more widely promoted. Far better to let consumers opt out of direct mail before they complain, than to encourage the attentions of an increasingly powerful Elizabeth France.

(Source: *Marketing Direct*, February 1998, p. 4)

Industry faces £1bn bill for changes to data law

The UK direct marketing industry faces estimated costs of £1 billion to meet the requirements of the Data Protection Bill. Introduced in January, the Bill will be phased in over three years.

Costs will be incurred by some companies holding manual records, which previously did not fall under the rules of data protection.

Making data more easily accessible to consumers, as required by the new Bill, will also require substantial investment by some organizations.

Other changes include new powers for the Data Protection Registrar Elizabeth France, to be known as the Commissioner.

France no longer needs to have a consumer complaint before she investigates a company. She can now take action against a company she suspects of misusing data.

Also, under the 1984 Data Protection Act only registered data users could be subject to enforcement for breach of the principles. In future the Bill will apply equally to all data controllers — whether they register or not.

New Bill: Key Points

► The Data Protection Bill will be phased in over three years from 24th October, 1998.
► The Data Protection Registrar will become the Data Protection Commissioner and have wider powers.

► Even companies not registered with the Commissioner will fall under the power of the new Bill.
► The Commissioner will be able to request information about a company's data processing operations where there are 'reasonable grounds' for believing that the principles of the Bill are being breached. Previous legislation required a complaint to be made first.
► Consumers will have greater access to personal information and be able to prevent companies processing it for direct marketing.
► Consumers will also have greater scope to seek 'financial compensation and other redress' for breaches of the Bill.

(Source: *Marketing Direct*, February 1998, p. 3)

Information Must Be Obtained and Used Fairly

The direct marketer should be open and honest about the fact that the information is being collected, who he or she is, why the information is being collected, the purpose for which it will be used and the identity of anyone to whom it may be disclosed. This information should be given to the persons concerned before any information to be used is collected from them (Data Protection Tribunal Decision: Innovations (Mail Order) Ltd v The Data Protection Registrar).

It is essential to understand that this requirement does not apply only to information which is going to be disclosed outside the organization which collects it. It applies to all information about living individuals which is stored on computer.

A fictitious company, Decrepit Homes Ltd, is a large estate agency. The company sends out a mailshot to everyone living on an estate offering a special law commission on the sale of their house. Mr and Mrs Smith reply and complete the form with details of their name, address, number of children, the area they want a house in, the price they are willing to spend and the number of rooms they require. This information is then entered into Decrepit Homes' computer system. Unless anything is said to Mr and Mrs Smith before they complete the form, this information is only obtained fairly if it is to be used only for selling their house, for searching for suitable properties for them and sending Mr and Mrs Smith details of those properties and ancillary matters such as invoices.

If Decrepit Homes wishes to write to Mr and Mrs Smith with details of mortgages it can arrange through a building society, it must make this clear to Mr and Mrs Smith at the time the form is completed and Mr and Mrs Smith should be given an opportunity to require the information not to be used for that purpose. (Commonly referred to as an 'opt-out').

If Decrepit Homes wishes to pass Mr and Mrs Smith's details to a building society or insurance company so that they can write direct to Mr and Mrs Smith, the information will only be obtained and used fairly if this is made clear to Mr and Mrs Smith when they complete the form. If the identity of the building society is known at that time, Mr and Mrs Smith should be given this information. Once again, Mr and Mrs Smith should be given the opportunity to opt out of this. Furthermore, the notice should make it clear which information taken from the form will be passed on: whether it is simply Mr and Mrs Smith's name and address or whether it will also include their telephone number, the area in which they are looking and the price they wish to spend.

Of course it is not only Decrepit Homes which must worry about this. The direct marketer working for the building societies and insurance companies which receive this information should also be concerned as to whether the information was obtained fairly and whether they will be processing it fairly.

Two developments which help to deal with the use of database lists are the Mailing Preference Service and the Telephone Preference Service. These services allow individuals to notify the service that they do not wish to receive unsolicited direct mail or unsolicited marketing telephone calls. There is no explicit legal requirement that direct marketers must make any use of these services. However, both the British Codes of Advertising Practice and Sales Promotion and the Direct Marketing Association Code of Practice require that database lists are 'cleaned' by comparing them against the most recent version of the records held by these services and removing names and address as appropriate. This will obviously be a factor which is taken into account by the Data Protection Registrar when deciding whether or not information has been processed fairly.

It might not always be enough to use an opt-out mechanism whereby people have to object to information about them being used for other purposes. In some circumstances it might be necessary to use an opt-*in* mechanism, so that the information is not used for other purposes unless the individual has specifically consented to this.

Direct marketers prefer to use an opt-out rather than an opt-in for the simple reason that – human nature being what it is – people often cannot be bothered to object. However, it is for this very reason that at the time this chapter is being written the Data Protection Registrar is considering legal action against some of the privatized utility companies for the way they are using their databases.

The Registrar's particular concern is that these companies have acquired vast amounts of information about customers who previously had no choice about where they obtained their gas, electricity and water, and no choice about the information they had to supply to what was at the time a state-owned organization. The Registrar believes that these companies can now only use this information in order to market other goods and services if their customers have opted-in. The Registrar believes that in these special circumstances it is not processing information fairly if these companies rely on opt-out and the inertia of their customers.

Only you will know whether your organization is for some reason a special case as well, and that therefore you should use opt-in too.

The Data Protection Directive

The law in this area is due to change following the introduction of an EC Directive on data protection (Directive 95/46/EC). As with all Directives, it is not in itself generally binding on direct marketers but the Government must pass legislation to implement it in UK law by 31 October 1998.

The Directive will lead to several changes in our data protection law. The following are probably the most important for the direct marketer who uses information about people.

Direct marketers can only collect and process information about people if those individuals have given their clear consent. This will give people the right to object to the collection and processing of information about them unless the direct marketer can show that it is *'necessary'* for the legitimate interests of the direct marketer or of any third party to whom the information is disclosed (such as the client). It will seriously hamper the activities of direct marketers if they have to obtain everybody's consent, so it has to be hoped that the alternative justification is available.

Unfortunately, the Directive does not explain what is meant by *'necessary'*. The usual meaning of *'necessary'* is something which is essential. Although it may be highly desirable to process marketing information on computers, and indeed it may be impracticable to do it any other way, can it be said to be *essential*? We will have to wait to see how the Directive is implemented here in the UK and how the courts interpret it in the light of the Directive.

The Directive introduces a specific provision relating to direct marketing. However, it gives the Government an option as to how the provision might be implemented in UK law. The first option is that people must be given the legal right to stop information about them being used for direct marketing purposes. The effect of this would be to introduce a legal right equivalent to the Mailing Preference Service and the Telephone Preference Service. This is the least objectionable option as far as the direct marketing industry is concerned.

The alternative option for the Government is to oblige direct marketers to notify each individual before using information about them for direct marketing purposes on behalf of a client and before disclosing any of that information to anyone else. They would also have to tell those individuals that they have the right to object to that use or disclosure. This option would cause less problems for direct marketers working in-house because they would not have to notify people unless they intended to disclose the information outside of the organization. But it could be very expensive, and an administrative nightmare, for direct marketing agencies who will always have to notify people of their rights.

If the direct marketer is going to collect information about someone from that person, he must tell them whether or not they are obliged to provide that information and any possible consequences of not providing it. He must also tell them of their right to see the information about them which is held, and their right to have it corrected if it is wrong.

There is no doubt that data protection is an increasingly important area, of which direct marketers must take heed.

Other Reasons For Not Writing to People

The Data Protection Act is not the only reason for not writing to people. In 1993 a solicitor received faxes from three companies advertising their services. He wrote to them asking them to remove him from their distribution list but he continued to receive further faxes from them. He sued and the court agreed that the unsolicited faxes were a misuse of his fax machine and his paper. He was awarded £5 compensation and £50 towards his costs. It is clear that a mailshot using unsolicited faxes could cost much more than planned!

The Internet

The Internet – and the World-wide Web in particular – has been heralded by many as the perfect tool and delivery mechanism for direct marketers. Already users of Internet e-mail are regularly deluged by unsolicited e-mails advertising a full spectrum of products and services from suppliers all around the world. Of course there are direct marketers using the Internet in a much more sophisticated manner. There are a number of legal issues which must be taken into account.

Law On The Internet

Direct marketers who use the Internet for promotional purposes must ignore the siren voices which still persist in proclaiming that the Internet is unregulated. The truth is quite the reverse, and there has probably never been a more regulated medium.

The main problem is the very thing which makes it so attractive to direct marketers: its global reach. Everything which the direct marketer puts on an Internet site is accessible from anywhere in the world unless access controls are put in place, and of course this would defeat the objective of mass distribution. Email can be sent more selectively, but has other problems.

Every Country's Laws Apply

Because Internet sites can be accessed from anywhere, the courts in many countries (including the UK and the USA) are treating things done on the Internet as within their jurisdiction no matter where the computer hardware is sited. Worse still, they are applying their own laws, not the laws of the country where the computer hardware is. One example is the issue of misleading price indications. Virgin Atlantic Airways maintained a Web site which included details of its transatlantic airfares. The Web site described a return airfare of under $500, but when a prospective passenger asked for one of these tickets he was told that this special price was no longer available and the alternative was a ticket costing a little over $500. Under US law the airline was obliged to keep the information up-to-date and as it had inadvertently failed to do so it ended up paying the US Department of Transport $14,000.

The result of this is that direct marketers must consider the legality of what they wish to do under the laws of every country, not just their own. And just in case some direct marketers believe this doesn't matter because foreign courts cannot get at them, it is worth noting that in many cases the judgments of foreign courts can be enforced very easily through our own courts.

One topic which has received a lot of publicity is that of trade marks.

Trade Marks

Unconnected businesses in different countries may have developed using the same trade marks for the same products, and may have registered those trade marks in different parts of the world. However, as soon as anyone uses a trade mark on the Internet they will be using it in every country of the world. This means that direct marketers using the Internet may well infringe someone else's trade mark rights overseas and could be sued, even if they have never heard of that other person before. It is also important to realize that not every country has a special defence for comparative advertising as we do in the United Kingdom (p. 396). One useful procedure to avoid this problem is to undertake a trade mark search before making marketing material available on the Internet. A specialist solicitor can help with this.

It is worth noting that the trade mark used does not have to be identical to infringe someone else's trade mark.

> Playboy Inc – the publisher of the well-known glamour magazine 'Playboy' – sued Tattilo Editrice SpA, the Italian publisher of a glamour magazine called 'Playmen'. The court decided that the use by Tattilo of the name PLAYMEN infringed Playboy Inc's US registration of the PLAYBOY trade mark because Tattilo's Internet site was used to market erotic pictures to US citizens in the US. This was so even though Tattilo's Web site was based in Italy. The court ordered Tattilo to hand over to Playboy all of the profit it had made from customers based in the US, and either to ensure that its Web site could not be accessed from the US in future or to close down its Web site altogether. The court threatened to fine Tattilo $1,000 per day if it did not comply with this order. (Playboy Enterprises Inc v Chuckleberry Publishing Inc and Others, DC SNY, 79 Civ 3525.)

In this case the court treated Tattilo's Internet address itself as part of the trade mark infringement.

Domain Names

Every Internet user must have an Internet address. This is a number attached to each message sent to that user which enables the computers and telecommunications equipment which constitute the Internet to route those messages through to that user. These numbers are very long, and it is quite impracticable for people to remember them or use them in that form. To overcome this, the user can choose a name and that name is associated with the user's address number. For example, my e-mail address is paul.sampson@eversheds-west.co.uk.

The part which is *'eversheds-west'* indicates the name of our firm and because it is our name it is (for us) the most important part of my address. Of course every company wants to register an Internet address which has as its domain name either the name of the company or the name of one of its important trade marks. The problem is that there can only be one domain name 'eversheds-west.co.uk'.

Some people, not being slow to recognize a business opportunity, have registered the names of well-known companies as their own Internet address. These people are known as *'cyber-squatters'* because they have occupied someone else's address in Cyberspace. These cyber-squatters usually offer to sell the address to the well-known companies at an exorbitant price. However, in an American case the court decided that an Internet domain name is itself a trade mark, and that the company should be allowed to evict the defendant from the Internet address *intermatic.com* and to have the address for itself (Intermatic Inc v Toeppen). The English High Court adopted the same approach in a case involving the Harrods name (Harrods v Lawrie and others (9 December 1996)).

Conclusion

The task of the direct marketer is to gather information about customers and prospects, analyse that information and to communicate to an appropriate group a message which will sell goods or services. As I have tried to indicate in this chapter, each of these activities involves legal traps for the unwary direct marketer to fall into.

No one would seriously suggest that the direct marketer should take legal advice on every mailshot. But the need for specialist advice should be kept in mind. An in-house training programme, or even a set of guidelines which should be followed, can go a long way towards reducing the risk of expensive mistakes and criminal prosecution. These will also enable the direct marketer to identify those occasions when he should seek specific legal advice. Perhaps he should take a leaf out of the book of his 'peers' in the advertising profession, where copy is often cleared by lawyers before it is released. After all, the direct marketer working in an agency should remember that it is not only the cost and embarrassment of being sued or prosecuted which is important. The relationship between the agency and its client is unlikely to be strengthened if the agency has to admit it has gaffed!

STUDY 3

A racket about data protection

A new data protection bill aims to bring UK legislation in line with that of Europe. What effect will it have on the direct marketing industry? By Karen Fletcher

The Data Protection Registrar, Elizabeth France, has had a very active few months. She is on the warpath against most of the UK's utilities companies.

In July, at the DPR's annual conference, France voiced concerns about the use of the electoral roll for marketing purposes — particularly companies which provide the data on disk with additional lifestyle data.

Now she is moving in on Tesco for mailing to its own Club Card customers.

If that weren't enough, the government is introducing a Data Protection Bill this Autumn which will, among other things, extend the powers of the DPR.

The Bill is part of the process of bringing the European Community data protection directive into UK law by October 1998. The EC data directive has sat in the background since 1995, having little effect on the way data is gathered, stored or analysed by UK companies. That could soon change.

Changing the rules

Although the EC directive is similar to current UK data protection law, it goes beyond the present legislation in a number of respects. It sets detailed conditions for processing personal data which could have an impact on the way companies use their databases for analysis and marketing. It also sets new rules for the transfer of individual data outside the European Union.

Although France could be accused of being a little hard on the direct marketing industry, the government seems to be more sympathetic. Jack Straw, Home Secretary, says: 'The proposals build on our existing data protection law. They attempt to achieve the right balance between individuals' entitlement to privacy in the handling of information about them, and the information users' needs in processing information to provide the services which individuals require.'

Direct marketers will be relieved to know that the government's proposed bill enforces the practice of allowing consumers to opt out of mailings. A statement from the Home Office on the new bill says: 'The government intends to provide for data subjects to be able to object free of charge to their personal data being used for direct marketing purposes (ie to opt out).'

This is an improvement on the 1984 Data Protection Act which was more vague — saying the data must be collected 'fairly'.

● ● ▶

Colin Fricker, director of legal affairs at the Direct Marketing Association, gives a cautious welcome. But he points out that the proposals do make a significant change to the opt out principle.

'Under the 1984 act, companies who collected data only had to give consumers the opportunity to opt out if the information was going to be used for a different purpose – for example if they were going to sell the data on to another company. Now companies must give consumers the chance to opt out from all other mailings.'

This closes a loophole in the 1984 legislation which allowed companies to diversify from their core areas, and then mail consumers about these new business areas without obtaining prior consent.

Fricker's main concern is how consumers will learn about their new rights. The government says: '[We are] still considering how best to give effect to the requirement for data subjects to be made aware of their right to object.'

Know your rights

Fricker says: 'Perhaps the DMA might like to take quarter page ads in three or four newspapers explaining these new rights.'

But interpretation of data protection legislation will still be in the hands of the DPR – or Data Protection Commissioner as the role will be known.

And, while she may not be against direct marketing in principle, France's interpretation of the law will always be heavily in favour of the consumer – that is, after all, her job. Her interpretation could lead to more confrontations with some of the UK's biggest users of direct marketing.

As Fricker warns: 'There are still battles to be fought. They have simply been deferred.'

(Source: *Marketing Direct*, September 1997, p. 12)

PART II

Right to prevent processing for purposes of direct marketing.

(4) The failure by a data subject to exercise the right conferred by subsection (1) or section 10(1) does not affect any other right conferred on him by this Part.

10.—(1) An individual is entitled at any time by notice in writing to a data controller to require the data controller to cease within a reasonable time, or not to begin, processing for the purposes of direct marketing personal data in respect of which he is the data subject.

(2) If the court is satisfied, on the application of any person who has given a notice under subsection (1), that the data controller has failed to comply with the requirement, the court may order him to take such steps for complying with the requirements as the court thinks fit.

(3) In this section 'direct marketing' means the communication (by whatever means) of any advertising or marketing material which is directed to particular individuals.

Compensation for failure to comply with certain requirements

11.—(1) An individual who suffers damage by reason of any contravention by a data controller of any of the requirements of this Act is entitled to compensation from the data controller for that damage.

(2) An individual who suffers distress by reason of any contravention by a data controller of any of the requirements of this Act is entitled to compensation from the data controller for that distress if —

(a) the individual also suffers damage by reason of the contravention, or

(b) the contravention relates to the processing of personal data for the special purposes.

(3) In proceedings brought against a person by virtue of this section it is a defence to prove that he had taken such care as in all the circumstances was reasonably required to comply with the requirement concerned.

Rectification, blocking, erasure and destruction.

12.—(1) If a court is satisfied on the application of a data subject that personal data of which the applicant is the subject are inaccurate, the court may order the data controller to rectify, block, erase or destroy those data and any other personal data in respect of which he is the data controller and which contain an expression of opinion which appears to the court to be based on the inaccurate data.

(2) Subsection (1) applies whether or not the data accurately record information received or obtained by the data controller from the data subject or a third party but where the data accurately record such information, then—

(a) if the requirements mentioned in paragraph 8 of Part II of Schedule 1 have been compiled with, the court may, instead of making an order under subsection (1), make an order requiring the data to be supplemented by such statement of the true facts relating to the matters dealt with by the data as the court may approve, and

(b) if all or any of those requirements have not been complied with, the court may, instead of making an order under that subsection, make such order as it thinks fit for securing compliance with those requirements with or without a further order requiring the data to be supplemented by such a statement as is mentioned in paragraph (a).

Extract from draft Data Protection Bill.

Review Questions

1 Which laws control those communications with individuals which aim to persuade them to buy goods or services?

2 What are the Data Protection Principles as given in the Data Protection Act (1984) and how do they affect direct marketing?

3 Which laws control the use of database lists?

4 How does the law of copyright affect marketing databases?

5 Some of the regulations contained in laws such as the Trade Descriptions Act also relate to direct marketing. Which ones and how do they apply?

6   How can a) EU Directives and b) EU Regulations affect direct marketing in the UK?

7   How is direct marketing via the Internet regulated?

Discussion Questions

1   Do you think there is a need for legal controls of direct marketing? Why?

2   What are the relative contributions of legal and voluntary controls with respect to data protection in a Direct Marketing context? Should the industry be controlled by predominately voluntary controls?

3   Should there be a Direct Marketing Act? Why?

4   To what extent do you think a) consumers and b) direct marketing organisations appreciate the role of the EU in shaping direct marketing legislation?

Further Reading

Consumer Protection Act 1987, The Stationery Office, London.

Copyright, Designs and Patents Act 1988, The Stationery Office, London.

Data Protection Act 1984, The Stationery Office, London.

Data Protection Bill 1988, The Stationery Office, London.

Financial Services Act, 1986, The Stationery Office, London.

Laddie, Prescott and Vitoria (1995) *The Modern Law of Copyright and Designs*, Second Edition, London: Butterworth.

Perri 6 (1998) *The Future of Privacy*, Volumes 1 and 2, London: Demos.

Sampson, P. (1994) 'Electronic Databases – A Legal Perspective', Engineering Management Journal, October.

Trade Descriptions Act 1968, The Stationery Office, London.

Direct Marketing and Social Responsibility

This Chapter:

▶ Introduces Students To The Issue Of
Social Responsibility Within The
Context Of Direct Marketing.

▶ Discusses The Issues Which Are
Relevant To Direct Marketers Including
Privacy, Accuracy, Control And
Environmental Issues.

▶ Describes The Ways In Which Direct
Marketers Can Respond To These
Issues.

**C
H
A
P
T
E
R

12**

Direct Marketing and Social Responsibility

A Step Too Far

In 1991 in the US, Lotus Development announced the launch of what they considered to be an innovative new product. Lotus market-place: Households was a CD-ROM containing both demographic and lifestyle information on individual American households. For the first time, data which had traditionally been used by large organizations in their efforts to target customers was to become widely available. The announcement drew protestations from privacy advocates in the US who saw it as a breach of their rights. A stream of negative publicity was directed at the product to such an extent that it became a matter of discussion in governmental committee meetings. In the meantime 30,000 people telephoned Lotus complaining about breaches of privacy and demanding that their names be removed from the database. Following a nine month period of debate, Lotus were forced to admit that the adaptations necessary to make market-place: Households acceptable to the public and to privacy advocates would be far too costly and they were forced to withdraw the product. The strange thing is that the information contained on the database is in fact routinely used by large organizations to communicate directly with consumers.

(Sources: Bessen 1993; Cespedes and Smith 1993)

Marketing as a Societal Enterprise

The field of marketing ethics, although of immense importance, has traditionally proven to be a difficult one. Any discussion of ethics also requires an understanding of social responsibility and quite often the distinction between the two terms is unclear. Ethics essentially relates to individual decision-making based on individual or organizational values. Social responsibility, on the other hand, refers to the impact of those decisions on society.

While marketing ethics must not be overlooked, the judgement of whether a decision proves to be unethical or ethical, lies more or less with the individual concerned. In making ethical decisions, individuals must first be aware of the moral dimension of a particular situation. As such, there may be much to be gained by discussing social responsibility as this should go some way towards identifying the moral dimensions of particular situations. This chapter will deal with the issue of social responsibility in terms of how it pertains to direct and database marketing. Some of these issues also have legal implications, and these have been outlined in Chapter 11. Some organizations interpret and implement this legislation to the letter of the law (i.e. do the minimum required to be within the law). However, adhering to the spirit of the law will go much further in terms of taking these social issues on board.

In order to identify and maintain socially responsible behaviour, an organization must continually monitor trends in the values held by society. This results from the fact that as consumers are exposed to, and gain a greater understanding of, organizational practices, their values and expectations may change. Indeed, this is particularly relevant to the direct marketing industry in the UK. As the industry has grown, consumer values and expectations have evolved, so that practices which would have once been viewed as legitimate and responsible by organizations, may no longer be so.

Many so called ethical decisions made by organizations are based purely and simply on related legislation without any real recognition that ethics and social responsibility often go beyond the realm of legislation. In their headlong pursuit of profit many companies, while keeping within the law, are forced to keep the notions of ethics and social responsibility firmly in the background. Camenisch (1991:246) points out that marketing 'occurs in society, with society's permission and support, and purportedly, in part for society's benefit.' On this basis, it may be true to say that marketing managers should have to take into account the moral expectations of society. In truth this also makes good business sense because, if organizations continue to disregard the moral expectations of society they are putting themselves on a collision course with consumer dissatisfaction and alienation.

Despite this it appears that most managers have given little thought to the social impact of direct and database marketing (Cespedes and Smith 1993). Those who have given it any degree of thought have dismissed it. They seem to think that if they continue to believe that concerns do not exist, then they will not exist. Furthermore, they argue that discussions of social responsibility are all fine and well in academia but they have no place in the competitive world of business. Even much academic literature seems to have satisfied itself largely with the practical problems faced by industry participants, at the expense of the consumer and social implications in general (Whalen *et al.* 1991). While this type of approach may have been possible in the past when related social values were as yet unformulated, it is unlikely to be so in the future. Consumer concerns are very real, and any direct marketer that wants to experience long-term success will have to take these concerns into account. For example, a 1995 survey revealed that many respondents considered unsolicited direct mail and telemarketing to be unethical and were also concerned with the practice of selling and sharing mailing lists between organizations (Evans *et al.* 1995).

STUDY 1

Before all the pats on the back make the direct marketing industry over-confident, there are some serious issues that need to be addressed

Direct marketing enters 1998 in rude good health. Investment by clients continues apace. Given that well over £6,000 million has been spent in 1997 (the most recent DMA estimate), a growth rate of at least ten per cent seems a safe bet. Across all sectors and in all media, direct communications are spreading.

Digital and Web TV in the home will boost distance selling. The Government's commitment to putting educational establishments on-line will also produce more home shoppers. Not that traditional media are losing out. Direct mail volumes increased by 13 per cent in the first half of 1997 alone.

What underpins this ongoing investment in DM is no longer just the desire to make advertising more accountable. That may have been what drove the industry forward in the early 1990s, as clients sought to measure exactly what they were getting for their ad spend. But now the direct philosophy has become more deeply embedded in the new business credo of being 'customer-focused'.

To orient a business around its customers requires a database. To demonstrate that the business now puts its customers first requires a combination of telephony and the computer — as each individual's

records, purchasing and communications history must be on hand for the operator at the start of the call. And to get the message across that this really is how the company wants to do business requires good DM.

But before all the pats on the back make the industry over-confident, there are some serious issues that need to be addressed. If DM wants to end 1998 in as good shape as it begins the year, then some broad objectives need to be considered. Boiled down to their essence, they can be summed up in these three New Year Promises.

▶ Take the consumer with you. Marketing is nothing without the consumer, and DM cannot function at all unless the general public allows it to. This means that people must give permission for personal data to be used, as well as being willing to be mailed, phoned or e-mailed. Undercurrents suggests this patience may not last for ever.

While registrations with the Mailing and Telephone Preference Services remain low, 37 per cent of the population has now gone ex-directory. Even if a marketer gets the phone number through legitimate channels, such as a lifestyle database, consumers may not recognize or remember the source. This means they could get very upset about being contacted, which might rapidly lead to a backlash.

The irony of this, of course, is that consumers quite happily engage in DM all the time — it's just that they don't call it that. When they pick up the phone to order from a catalogue, respond to a mailshot requesting a test drive, or log on to a Website, they do not describe any of those actions as marketing. That is a word for the practitioners, not their targets.

For this reason, the Direct Marketing Association's long-delayed generic campaign is badly needed. It has certainly got its work cut out — in any market research survey, there is strong antipathy towards 'junk mail' and 'cold calling'. Highlighting the fact that companies want

to carry out more of these activities is a bit like trying to get salmon to think of bears as their friends (an image used by one data owner in trade ads, incidentally).

Sources within the DMA recognize there is probably a six-month window of opportunity to get the campaign up and running — and to bring the national media on-side. The previous launch date was delayed by the postal strike of 1996, but this may have been a blessing in disguise, given how much has changed even since then.

But to really reinforce the message that the DMA is seeking to put across, the industry also needs to get behind the campaign, both on a company and an individual level. It is still a striking feature of DM that it lacks any representatives of national stature. When advertising came under pressure in the late 1980s, it wasn't difficult to find admen such as John Hegarty or Winston Fletcher to defend it. You can count on the fingers of one hand those in DM with the same qualities. Which brings me to the next pledge.

▶ It is time for the industry to grow up. The most obvious sign of maturity has been the growing stature of the DMA. But given how much it has achieved, why does it still engage in a turf war with the Institute of Direct Marketing? Both sides may rebut that suggestion, but they still put each other down, both publicly and privately.

The good of DM would be best served by a more mutual outlook. After all, the Advertising Association and the Institute of Practitioners in Advertising do not compete with each other. Senior direct marketers, especially on the client side, also need to stand up and be counted.

Higher visibility, not just in the trade press but in the national media, will be to the good of all. A history of secrecy, stemming from DM's tactical role as a secret weapon, still informs many marketers' outlook. It is time to acknowledge the responsibility that

● ● ▶

practitioners bear in creating a positive, sustainable public climate of opinion.

▶ Defend the right to use public domain information. This is probably going to be *the* battle of 1998. Having introduced a revised Data Protection Act, which enshrines the principle of opting out, the Data Protection Registrar has not made peace with the DM industry. She has already announced her intention to look into use of the Electoral Roll for marketing purposes.

Despite the growth of high-volume, individual-level databases, direct marketers cannot afford to lose access to the voting register. But they will only sustain this access if they make a strong, mature and well-argued case for their right to do so. In other words, to enjoy the benefits of winning resolution number three, they need to commit heavily to numbers one and two. But then, Father Christmas only gives presents to those who have been good.

David Reed is a freelance journalist.

(This article first appeared in *Marketing Business*, the magazine for The Institute of Marketing, January 1997/1998, p. 22)

Diseconomies of Growth

In Chapter 1 we discussed the growth of UK direct marketing. While such growth opens up a host of opportunities for marketers in this country, it also poses many difficulties. The rise in direct and database marketing has been mirrored by a rise in consumer concern in relation to companies involved in these fields (Patterson *et al.* 1996). The sheer pace of growth of the direct marketing and database industries in Britain, and the volume of direct communications they have produced, have alerted public attention to the actions of industry participants. Some proponents of direct marketing suggest that consumer fears have arisen largely as a result of increased media coverage during recent years. Media owners may have good reason to be critical, because to some degree their income, through advertising revenue, may be threatened by direct marketing. However, it is likely, as has been shown in the US, that public concerns had evolved and were evident in the UK even before media coverage became widespread (Phelps *et al.* 1994). Indeed, public salience is more likely to be a factor of consumers' experiences of direct marketing than of anything else.

A number of consumer concerns with regard to direct and database marketing have been identified in the literature. The majority of these fears centre around the issue of privacy although environmental and exclusion issues may also be of concern. Since much of this literature is based within a US context, the extent to which these issues concerned UK consumers was until recent years uncertain. Initial studies conducted in the UK seem to indicate that the issues highlighted in this chapter are of direct concern to UK consumers at this present time.

Privacy Issues

The issue of consumer privacy has been particularly slow to come to prominence in the UK. While legislators began to give it serious thought from around the mid–1960s, consumer concern over threats to privacy remained at a low level for a number of years. This is quite possibly due to the fact that abuses in individual privacy continued to be rare until the recent explosion in direct marketing practices. Indeed, it is interesting to note that privacy legislation in this country was enacted more as a consequence of pressure from the business community than from consumers (Petrison and Wang 1995). It was the business community that forced statutory recognition of privacy rights because British companies were becoming increasingly worried about the possibility of losing trade with organizations from countries where privacy legislation had been enacted and was thus restrictive.

The term 'privacy' is deceptively simple. However, we cannot really talk about 'privacy' as a generic concern. In reality, it encompasses a number of specific issues. With regard to direct and database marketing, the privacy issues include:

▶ Information privacy (control over one's personal information).

▶ Physical/interaction privacy (control over the physical intrusion of direct marketing).

▶ Accuracy (control over accuracy of data).

In the US privacy concerns are very specific and focus primarily on physical/interaction privacy issues. This is probably as a result of the sophistication of the American direct and database industries. In the UK the focus tends to be on information privacy, primarily because UK consumers have traditionally guarded their privacy and find it undesirable that anyone else should possess personal information about them.

Meet Some of our Participants and See What They Said

Ken: Age 36, married with two young kids. Has had a maildrop for Next catalogue which he responded to. Was a member of a book club which he came across in a magazine insert. Says he receives quite a bit of direct mail but responds to very little – only if he is looking for something in particular. Recently, he does seem to be getting more telesales calls. He gets his kids to answer the phone and that tends to put them off. He also gets a lot of glossy promotional literature from his bank with his statements. He believes telesales is a real intrusion, he doesn't mind leaflets, etc. coming through the door but telesales annoys him especially as it usually comes just when you're beginning to relax.

Lloyd: Age 37, married with three children. He recently received a mailing which incorporated promotions for a number of different companies, which he found quite useful. Usually gets lots of mail and free samples which all tend to come together in one drop. Has bought dolls' houses, electrical equipment, etc. but it depends on what he is looking for and what is on offer. He buys from catalogues as well – usually small electrical goods catalogues. Doesn't get many phone calls. Has got one for insurance but it was linked to the company he presently deals with. Phone calls do his head in. They won't accept no for an answer. If you say no they should accept it. If he ever found out the name of the company he would refuse to do business with them. His definition of 'junk' is when the company doesn't use their intelligence – they can see you've got double glazing and yet they still try to sell you some. Mailings are just indiscriminate.

Nigel: Age 30, lives with his girlfriend. Get lots of 'junk' mail but doesn't normally reply to it and often he doesn't even read it. He recently got some for Bettaware household goods from which he bought a pet hair remover for his dog – it was one of the best products he has ever bought. He will buy products from catalogues if it suits him, but he won't consciously look for them. His definition of 'junk' is if the company doesn't know him but send material such as – 'If you are under 75 years of age come to us and get cheap car insurance!' That's just a waste of paper. He lives in a fairly young community but they all get the same type of direct mail. He believes that if direct marketers used the electoral register they could improve their targeting. Recently, he has noticed more direct mail and TV shopping channels. Thinks QVC is good because you can trust the company and it's your choice to buy. If you don't want to watch it then you don't have to.

Dave: Married. Receives lots of mail and catalogues, and with two young children tends to get a lot of free samples. Obviously the companies that send you free samples pass your details on because you get inundated with certain offers that are child related. Gets quite a few book offers and Reader's Digest stuff. Buys some products from catalogues because some of it is interesting, but most of it gets binned. His definition of 'junk' mail is the repetitive mail from the same companies which you haven't replied to. Has noted that many companies are using freephones which is good, because you've got control.

Source: Previously unpublished description of participants in one group discussion carried out by the authors on privacy issues in direct marketing. The names have been changed to protect the identity of respondents, but otherwie these are the descriptions of participants and their general attitudes.

Information Privacy

Information privacy refers to the extent to which individuals can control who holds their data, and what is done with it (Westin 1967). Basically, it incorporates three issues:

▶ who controls consumer information;

▶ how information is collected and used;

▶ Data security.

Information privacy has been the subject of debate for some time. On the one hand, there is the argument that consumers should have a right to determine what happens to their personal information. This is closely related to the notion of control. For example, in the US many consumers already believe that they have lost all control over how information about them is used, with some even suggesting that if they could, they would add privacy to their constitutional rights to life, liberty and the pursuit of happiness (Schroeder 1992).

On the other hand, many organizations argue that they should have the right to access consumer information for business purposes. Indeed, many marketers believe that because they have committed valuable resources to the development of databases, the information held on them is their property to do with as they see fit (Cespedes and Smith 1993). They also argue that they have no interest in highly personalized information, but it is clear that they have a growing appetite for individual level behavioural and lifestyle data. Despite this, as we saw in earlier chapters, few marketers are using the full capacity of the data they already have. Indeed, they may not yet have any great or immediate use for some of the information which they hold, but they are reluctant to have it removed from their databases in case it may prove to be of benefit in the future. While this is understandable from an organizational point of view, it suggests a worrying trend for consumers.

There is also the issue of how organizations acquire data. In the past much data acquisition has been covert, with consumers unaware that data is being collected for marketing purposes. The growth of direct marketing has created the need for data on a massive scale, and there seems to be some controversy over the extent to which consumers are happy to provide their personal data (see Figure 12.1). For example, studies in the US have claimed that consumers are generally quite happy to supply information in order to facilitate a specific exchange. However, many consumers believe that the data is necessary to facilitate the transaction, and give limited consideration to uses outside the specific transaction concerned (Cespedes and Smith 1993; Gandy 1993). In other words, they may not expect their information to be shared with other organizations.

> **▟** *For the large majority of consumers (80 per cent) in the UK, concerns and fears about information provision are currently balanced by a pragmatic understanding of the need to play ball with companies. However, we believe that this balance is relatively fragile and should not be taken for granted.* **▟** (Henley Centre 1995:3)

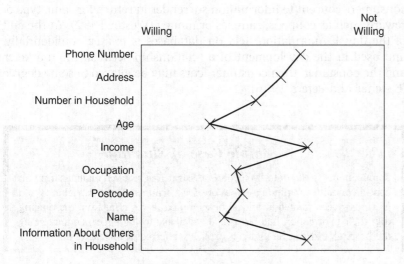

Figure 12.1 Consumer Willingness to Divulge Personal Details to Direct Marketers

The UK may pose different problems to the US in that traditionally consumers here have been very protective of their personal details and thus are more likely to be concerned with information privacy issues. For example, suggestions in recent years that the National Blood Service would share its database of blood donors with other organizations was met with public outcry.

In reality consumers will have different thresholds of information privacy which will be determined largely by the kind of the information being collected, the organization responsible, how data is collected and the subsequent uses to which that information will be put.

The Office of National Statistics is only just beginning to consider the inclusion of questions relating to income and religious affiliation and as a governmental authority it is likely to be open to less suspicion than commercial organizations. Because perceptions of information privacy abuses are so dependent on these situational variables, it would be true to say that it is very much interaction-specific and therefore any regulation in the area is likely to be problematic. This is where the role of advisory bodies is invaluable.

Further complicating the issue of information privacy are increasing concerns regarding data security. As technology improves, and as greater numbers of individuals gain access to desk-top computing facilities, the ability to control data security becomes more difficult. Consumers gauge for themselves whether or not they view a particular company as trustworthy, but it is impossible to determine the trustworthiness of individuals within that company. Many firms have been proactive in setting up data security measures, but it is literally impossible to ensure 100 per cent protection. The consequences of a breach in security in many organizations would be serious. Indeed, the consequences could be disastrous for consumers if there was unauthorized access to an insurance company's database, particularly when we consider the degree of detailed stored about individuals' home security measures.

Thus, it seems that as marketers' appetite for information grows, consumers may become more protective of their data. As a result, Westin envisages a rise in what he calls 'consensual databases', where consumers consent to information surrender in return for some type of reward such as coupons, samples or money (Westin 1992). At the end of the day, if information held on databases is treated confidentially, and used in the development of a relationship between the marketer and the consumer, then consumer fears may be allayed to some degree (Fletcher and Peters 1996).

A Simple Case of Sharing?

Complainants to the Data Protection Registrar had received mailings from an appeal committee requesting donations for a scanner. The complainants had previously been treated at a local hospital and it was clear from the mailing that their information had been made available to the appeal committee by the hospital. Indeed, the mailings explicitly referred to this fact.

The complainants had a case. Under the Data Protection Act, personal data must be processed 'lawfully'. The term 'lawfully' applies not only to criminal law but also to civil law including, for example, common law duties such as confidentiality. When a patient provides information for the purpose of his or her treatment a duty of confidence arises.

The health authority decided that patient data would not be used for appeal purposes in the future.

(Source: Case 3, *The 10th Annual Report of the Data Protection Registrar*)

Physical/interaction privacy

Physical/interaction privacy relates to the physical intrusion of marketing communications (e.g. direct mail, telesales, e-mails) into the daily lives of consumers. It is generally deemed to be of less direct concern to consumers in the UK than the issues related to information privacy. However, this situation may be changing as consumers are exposed to greater volumes of direct communications. Indeed, outbound telemarketing may face severe difficulties in the UK due to the fact that we do not possess the same kind of telephone culture here in Britain as exists in the US. UK database marketing in general differs greatly from its American counterpart in that it remains very much an industry in its infancy, and as such many mistakes continue to be made. Many marketers have yet to perfect their targeting techniques and this has contributed much to consumer dissatisfaction with database marketers in this country (di Talamo 1991). List brokers have also been criticised in this regard, as payment is generally based upon the number of names supplied, not response rates. While it is difficult to conceive paying list brokers by any other way, there is currently little financial incentive for them to develop smaller, more tightly targeted lists. That said, clients are now requesting more tightly targeted lists and, as a result, the situation may change in the future.

Much of the direct communication received by consumers in the UK is used by companies in prospecting for new business. New business is the lifeblood of any company and consequently marketers are constantly trying to recruit new customers. However, consumers have little or no control over the prospecting efforts of companies (Waldrop 1994). In terms of traditional marketing communications, consumers have the ability to screen out unwanted communications by means of zapping, zipping and nipping, and they possess control over the solicitation of further information (Kitchen 1986). Direct communications are likely to cause far greater difficulties in this regard, although the degree to which this is manifested in consumer concern is uncertain. Opt-outs are available, but when consumers opt-out 'what they really mean . . . is that there are certain things they want and certain things they don't want (Waldrop 1994:48).' The situation as it stands does not allow for consumer selectivity, because organizations *not* consumers determine who shares the data.

Accuracy

If consumers are concerned when organizations utilize their data for commercial purposes, or pass on that data to third parties, then these concerns may be compounded further when their data is inaccurate. This may be especially true if the consumer suffers in some way as a consequence. 'With the amount of data in use by direct marketers it is not surprising that mistakes happen.' (Fletcher 1995:58). The problem is, however, that as direct marketing practices increase and as direct marketers handle even greater amounts of data using more sophisticated technology, the likelihood of errors being made may rise. Consumers for their part are distrustful, especially when basic details such as name and address are incorrect.

Concern with respect to the accuracy of data held may be heightened in certain circumstances. If, for example, the data relates to the credit history of the consumer then the possibility for negative consequences are high. Inaccuracies in financial data may result in the consumer being turned down for a loan or mortgage. Indeed the practice of linking County Court Judgements (CCJs) with addresses (via postcodes) has resulted in new residents experiencing difficulties with getting credit, not because of their own actions, but because of those of the previous household resident. Failure to update data held on a regular basis may lead a marketer to be unaware of changes in circumstances. Fortunately this rarely has any significant effects. However, should a consumer have died and yet continue to receive direct communications, then other family members may be very upset.

And All This Because of One Ice-Cream

'In the summer of 1984, the Selective Service dispatched a curt letter to an eighteen-year-old boy in California who was several months' delinquent in registering for the draft. As it turned out, there was no boy by that name at the address used. The name was fictitious. It had been invented by two teenagers who had, some seven years before, filled out a card at a local ice cream store which was offering free birthday treats to its young customers. The name went into the store's computerized mailing list. The company which owned the store then sold its list . . . to one of the country's main direct mailing businesses, which, in turn, made it available to Selective Service.'

(Source: Roszak 1986:185)

Some consumers believe that the large amounts of unsolicited and irrelevant direct communications they receive come as a result of inaccurate data. However, consumers themselves may be unwittingly contributing to the problem. In an attempt to minimize abuses in both information and physical/interaction privacy, consumers may knowingly provide false information (Gandy 1993). Indeed, many UK consumers readily admit to such behaviour. For example, consumers may say that they earn more than they really do – simply to get more upmarket direct mail, others may lie about the number of people in their household for security reasons (especially when they live alone), finally there are those who simply attempt to make it difficult for any organization to process their data by writing illegibly, or giving false names or postcodes. While this may indeed solve the immediate problem of abuses in other areas, in the longer term it is likely to cause problems with direct transactions, or even contribute to abuses in physical privacy issues as the subsequent relevance of offers diminishes.

Maintaining data accuracy should be of paramount importance to industry participants. Accurate data facilitates the building of consumer relationships (Smith 1994). The point is that if organizations are going to utilize personal details on consumers for marketing or other purposes, then the onus is upon them to ensure that the information they hold is correct, and consumers themselves this feel that this should be the case.

I've Left, But We Seem To Be Keeping in Touch!

Another complainant to the Data Protection Registrar had held a subscription to receive a work-related publication until January 1995. After the subscription finished, the complainant started to receive mail at his home address, addressed not to him, but to various employees at his former job. It appeared that the publishers had traded their mailing list to a number of companies resulting in the complainant receiving about 60 mailings addressed to his ex-colleagues.

The publishers were contacted and it was established that the error had been caused by a software problem. The company has since rectified the problem and is no longer running the programme to amend addresses and is making changes manually. The publishers have confirmed suppression of the complainant's details, and have contacted all companies the lists were rented to in order to achieve the same.

(Source: Case Study – Example 10, 12th Annual Report of the Data Protection Registrar)

Privacy's Antecedents

In the previous section we discussed different privacy concerns, including those relating to information, physical intrusion and accuracy. One of the biggest problems in dealing with privacy issues is that not everybody is concerned with the same issues, at the same time, to the same extent, or in the same way. Simply put, privacy means different things to different people. This is one of the reasons why legislating for privacy protection is particularly problematic. Indeed, legislation is even more difficult when dealing with international direct marketing, and when attempting to regulate across different countries, as is currently the case within the EC.

Privacy issues do not simply exist. Privacy concerns develop as a result of other factors and influences. In an attempt to increase understanding of privacy, the authors have developed a model of privacy's antecedents (i.e. the factors which influence privacy concerns).

We conceptualize three levels of antecedents, which interact, influence and are influenced by other antecedents and privacy concerns themselves (see Figure 12.2). These include:

▶ the cultural environment;

▶ the ideological environment;

▶ the interaction-specific environment.

The Cultural Environment

The cultural environment is the macro-environment in which direct and database marketing operate. Using Milne *et al.'s* (1996) conceptualization, this includes country level direct marketing technology and infrastructure, adherence to individual rights (norms), consumers' experience of direct marketing and individual demographic background.

Infrastructure is important because the state of the direct marketing infrastructure within a country will, by consequence, dictate the level of direct marketing activity in that country. Structural statistics such as those in Table 12.1 would seem to suggest that the UK is highly

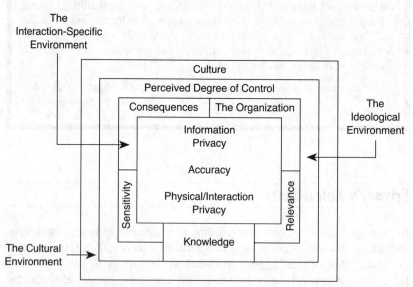

Figure 12.2 Privacy and Its Antecedent Variables

(Source: Patterson *et al.* 1997)

Pieces of domestic mail received each year per capita	519
Percentage penetration of radios	99%
Percentage penetration of television sets	98%
Percentage penetration of telephones	90%
Gross National Product	£706 billion
Literacy Rate	100%
Percentage of employed women	66%
Direct mail's share of the letterbox	29%
Consumer volume of direct mail	2015 million pieces
Percentage of press ads carrying response device	92%
Percentage of companies using telemarketing	39%

Table 12.1 UK Structural Statistics

(Source: compiled from Office of National Statistics, IDM and Royal Mail sources 1996)

developed. Despite these figures it may indeed be true to say that the UK industry is not as highly developed as its US counterpart. Consequently consumer experiences of direct marketing in the UK are more limited. This may in turn explain the fact that although UK consumers have traditionally been protective of their individual privacy, concerns in relation to direct and database marketing have been slow to evolve here (Patterson *et al.* 1996; Petrison and Wang 1995).

Demographic factors also have an important influence in that age, education and to some degree income have been found to be particularly good predictors of consumer attitudes (Milne *et al.* 1996). This probably comes as a result of the fact that because such demographic factors will determine the degree to which consumers are exposed to direct marketing, they will consequently influence their attitudes toward direct communications.

The existence of different cultural environments explains to some degree the different attitudes to both privacy issues and direct marketing in different countries. The cultural environment will also have an impact upon the existence of privacy protection legislation, and the effectiveness of self-regulation in each country. For example, in contrast to some other European countries, the UK has traditionally favoured self-regulation over legislation in marketing communications.

The Ideological Environment

The ideological environment comprises consumer perceptions with regard to the level of control they have and should have in the exchange process. Also of importance here is the level of knowledge which consumers possess in relation to database and direct marketing practices in general, existing legislation and the process of seeking redress when privacy intrusions occur (Patterson *et al.* 1997).

Marketing, by definition, is supposed to involve a mutually profitable exchange. While organizations may have traditionally enjoyed greater power in the exchange process than consumers, there is a growing danger that the consumer's position will be further eroded. Thus, in addressing the issue of social responsibility in direct marketing, the notion of control becomes central. This is a consequence of the fact that consumers tend to see the loss of their influence on the exchange process as a major factor in patterning other concerns. Many direct communications in the UK continue to be unsolicited in nature, that is they do not come as a direct consequence of requests from the consumer (di Talamo 1991). Consumers themselves really do not have any great input into how their personal details are being utilized and managed; information, once in the hands of organizations is firmly and totally under their control. In many cases, although the consumer is offered incentives designed to engender co-operation, information surrender is conducted with some reluctance. These factors play a large part in unsettling consumers, as they see their independence falling away. Unfortunately, studies have all too often failed to focus on the aspect of control, preferring instead to deal with the more emotive issue of privacy. However, it may simply be that 'invasions of privacy' are manifestations of the loss of control. Lenk supports this view, believing that the concentration on privacy masks the real problem; that possession of personal details on consumers affords the organization greater power at the expense of the individual (Lenk 1982). Where individual consumers are unconcerned about the balance of control shifting in favour of organizations, they are unlikely to be sensitive to privacy issues. However, when consumers who have attempted to correct misinformation, amend their details, remove their names from a mailing list, or attempt to influence the use of their information in some other way, they become aware of the difficulties. Usually, such attempts are influenced by a critical event, probably in the course of dealing with a particular organization (interaction-specific environment). When individuals become concerned with perceived invasions of their privacy in one context or interaction, this tends to influence their awareness of privacy issues generally. This in turn is likely to make them more sensitive to perceived invasions of their privacy.

In considering how direct marketing may be used to foster relationship marketing, the notion of control is of even greater importance. Using a database to get close to customers has been described as 'customer intimacy' (Treacy and Wiersema 1993). However, such 'intimacy' has also been heavily criticised for amounting to little more than a means of gathering enough information on customers so that the organization can market at them (Barnes 1994). This does not really foster relationship building as it centres on the interests of the organization to the exclusion of those of consumers. Furthermore, the consumer may not be committed to the relationship and may even be unaware that one is being developed. Increasing organizational power may diminish the role which the consumer has to play, allows the organization to engage in manipulative behaviour, and as such does not represent a move towards relationship marketing (O'Malley *et al.* 1997).

Consumer knowledge of direct and database marketing practices in general is also an important mediating variable. This knowledge may come as a result of exposure to or experience of these practices. Concern is likely to be exaggerated when the consumer is largely ignorant of the demands placed on direct marketers for detailed consumer information, is unaware of legislation designed to protect the consumer body, or is not conversant with the means by which consumers can protect themselves. On the other hand, concerns are likely to be allayed when the consumer is cognisant of why direct and database marketers use the methods they do, why they collect personal information, and the purposes to which that information is put.

The Interaction-Specific Environment

As we identified earlier privacy concerns tend to be interaction-specific. That is, perceived invasions of privacy are a function of the company involved, the knowledge which consumers possess about this particular instance of data collection and the specific uses to which the information will be put. It will also include the extent to which the consumer believes the offer/request to be relevant, the degree of sensitivity they associate with the particular information being collected and any negative consequences likely to result from information collection (Patterson *et al.* 1997).

Your Name is in the Book!

A number of complaints were received by the Data Protection Registrar from members of the public who where concerned about the receipt of unsolicited mailings promoting a family surname book. The mailings stated that their details had been featured in the book. The marketing literature failed to identify the name of the company responsible for the mailings and also failed to give prior notice to the individuals that they may ask for deletion from the book. Also a number of individuals who had previously asked for suppression of their details continued to receive further marketing literature.

It was established that the company behind the mailings was based in the USA but the mailing lists originated from the UK. It was considered that the data were being unfairly processed in the USA. The Registrar served a preliminary Transfer Prohibition Notice on the UK company to stop transferring data to the USA unless changes were made to the literature by the US company. The list brokers in the UK gave an undertaking to the Registrar that no further data would be transferred, unless the company responsible for the mailings amended the literature to comply with the requirements of the First principle. The US company also gave an undertaking to the Registrar to make the necessary changes.

(Source: Case Study – Example 9 12th Annual Report of the Data Protection Registrar 1996)

If the consumer has a history of dealing with a particular organization, and believes that organization to be trustworthy, the likelihood of that offer/request being considered intrusive diminishes. Therefore, marketers must be seen as trustworthy in order to successfully communicate with and obtain information from consumers. However, because many marketers acquire consumer data through covert means, the result is a reduction of trust towards firms in general.

When consumer knowledge of a specific instance of data collection or data use is reduced, control will also be reduced as the consumer will not be in a position to prevent his or her data from being collected, to decide what information is shared with or sold to others, or to agree with the utilization of that information. Thus, lack of interaction-specific knowledge is likely to aggravate privacy concerns.

Consumers may also question efforts by companies to collect information if that information does not appear to be relevant to the transaction at hand.

So Tell Me What You Need, What You Really, Really Need!

The Data Protection Registrar received a complaint about the loyalty card application form issued by a large supermarket chain. The form gave no indication that some of the information being requested was optional and was to be used only for future marketing purposes. The supermarket chain agreed to revise the form when reprinted to fully meet the *fair obtaining element* of the First Principle.

(Source: Case Study – Example 4 13th Report of the Data Protection Registrar 1997)

Furthermore, the relevance of the direct communications which a consumer receives is likely to affect the degree to which that consumer is concerned. One possible way to circumvent many of the concerns which consumers have is to ensure that they only receive communications which are of interest to them. 'If a person is interested in a subject and receives an unsolicited telephone call or piece of mail about it, he is not likely to view its receipt as an invasion of privacy ... It is relevant (Sherman 1991:40).' However, this relevance can only be achieved through improvements in targeting, improvements that require the use of personal data on individuals by companies. Placing restrictions on the uses to which companies put information may only serve to increase the amount of 'junk' consumers receive, and consumers themselves recognize this.

The degree of sensitivity which the consumer attaches to a piece of information will also determine the level of concern involved. Most consumers will be quite happy to surrender personal details such as name and address although they could be troubled by the fact that profiling may 'produce sensitive information from that which was not sensitive in its original form (Gandy 1993).' Ideally, marketers should only be using such information as is directly relevant for their marketing purposes, and 'information that by any reasonable standard would be considered personal, confidential or private should not be used in an inappropriate way' (Sherman 1991:41).

In supplying personal information, consumers are likely to pay regard to the possible consequences for them of such information surrender. This is especially true if those consequences are negative (Gandy 1993: 139). In an effort to minimize the effects of this, consumers may actively avoid situations in which they would be required to give information, they may refuse to give information, or they may provide false information.

Because of the influence of the interaction-specific environment on perceptions of privacy, regulation in the area is potentially problematic. Ideally, the solution lies in companies conducting their business with the concern due to customers, and to ensure that those customers have some say in what happens to their data. Self-regulation guidelines are discussed later in this chapter.

Implications of Privacy Concerns

Many commentators believe that direct marketing is in a fortunate position. As the marketing world evolves with the information age, direct marketing is in the ideal position to profit from social change. Clearly there are obvious benefits to both consumers and companies of the growth in direct and database marketing. However, we cannot expect that the successful history of direct marketing will be mirrored in the future. Indeed, given the increase in the use of direct marketing it is something of an indictment of the industry, that attitudes are not more favourable. In the light of consumer concerns action must be taken to protect the future.

Improving technological capabilities may pave the way to solving many of the problems outlined. Indeed, technology may allow direct marketers to get a firmer grip on data accuracy and security, may help them maintain the relevance of their offers, and facilitate relationship building. Although technological advances may have the potential to make a more positive contribution by increasingly allowing more complex profiling of customer information, it should not be viewed as a panacea for all direct marketing problems. It must be used wisely, as it can allow direct marketing to have both the power and the capability to become more intrusive. Thus, it may be that consumer concerns over privacy will become more and not less important in the wake of advancing technology.

Given the relative cost effectiveness of direct marketing, response rates in the region of six per cent to nine per cent are considered acceptable by industry participants. While this may constitute a large enough return on investment for direct marketers it gives little consideration to the consumer, especially those consumers who have not responded to direct approaches. The common response from the industry is to suggest that response is closely related to the timing of the offer, and those who do not respond today may do so tomorrow. This argument of course also validates the repeated targeting of certain consumers. A young industry can be forgiven for such complacency, but tolerance will eventually wane.

Another explicit benefit of direct marketing, as perceived by the industry, is that it can overcome the clutter which has become increasingly more obvious within traditional media. In particular, the proliferation of new media alternatives has led to consumers being continuously bombarded with advertising. Their defence has been to become more adept at screening out unwanted communications. Direct marketing was thought to overcome this problem given that it is more personal, more directly targeted, and is not competing directly with numerous other offers. However, the fact that direct marketing continues to be seen in 'junk' terms highlights that this is not necessarily the case. Furthermore, a significant number of consumers believe that they are victims of excessive targeting. They realize that this is probably because they have favourable demographic characteristics, but it still bothers them. What this implies is that direct marketing is developing a clutter all of its own among heavily targeted segments.

It has also been claimed that consumer attitudes toward direct marketing is a factor of age, in that younger consumers are more tolerant and accepting of direct approaches. This may be a source of encouragement for the industry. Alternatively, it may just be that younger consumers are more unlikely to receive as many direct marketing offers as their older counterparts, and their attitudes may become more critical as the frequency with which they are targeted increases. In this sense, the focus on age may be misleading.

Other Issues

There are a number of other issues of social responsibility also associated with direct marketing. In this section we will deal with only two. These are:

▶ environmentalism;

▶ exclusion.

Environmentalism

The last three decades have seen a progressive increase in world-wide environmental consciousness. Recession tends to divert interest in environmental issues, but underlying concerns appear to be strengthening with the recognition that business has been responsible for many of the problems associated with the environment. Consumers appear to be very cognisant of the environmental impact of direct mail and

leafleting in particular. While industry participants satisfy themselves
with low incidences of response, consumers recognize this as a waste.
Denny (1995) draws an analogy between direct mail and the battle of
the Somme in that vast quantities of direct communications are used
to win a small number of sales sufficient to make the exercise
profitable. Adding to the problem is the fact that many direct mail
pieces incorporate glossy paper which cannot be recycled. Yet as Bloom
et al (1994) point out, environmental groups are slow to react as they
are heavy users of direct mail themselves. Many UK consumers do have
very real concerns about the environmental impact of direct mail.

As we outlined in Chapter 10, the use of recycled paper, for example
may not be substantially more friendly to the environment because of
the chemical processing involved. However, consumers are unaware of
this. Their opinion is based upon not only the type of paper used in
direct marketing, but also the vast quantities that move swiftly from
the letter-box to the bin. Clearly, this does little to improve consumer
perceptions. The solution to this problem may lie in the ability of direct
marketers to utilize information in such a way as to produce smaller,
more tightly defined and relevant communications which reduce the
wastefulness of their operations.

Exclusion

By its very nature targeting means that some members of society will be
excluded from direct marketing offers. Cespedes and Smith (1993:13)
argue that as 'people from different races, religions, and ethnic groups
tend to live in distinct areas' and as geography is one of the major
variables used in targeting then some sections of society will effectively
be discriminated against. Although, in Britain there does not appear to
be the same degree of ghettoization as in the US, it may yet occur that
as companies increasingly target neighbourhoods with high spending
power, lower income groups will find their choices increasingly limited.

Also as direct marketing changes with the information age, and as
more highly developed technologies and media are utilized for direct
marketing purposes, those within society without the resources to keep
pace will suffer as they will be virtually unable to purchase goods
through this medium.

Yet another aspect of exclusion according to Cespedes and Smith
involves the ability of smaller companies and non-profit organizations to
compete with larger organizations. Initially, it was these smaller
organizations which first took advantage of the fact that direct marketing
enabled them to use niche marketing as a means of combating companies
with large mass media budgets. As we have mentioned previously stricter
controls, legislation, and consumer backlashes may only have the effect
of making the situation untenable for these smaller companies. The cost
of acquiring and using personal information would inevitably rise
effectively driving smaller operators out of business. All this would serve
to do is place consumers once more in the hands of the larger
corporations and consequently reduce consumers' freedom of choice.

CASE
STUDY 2

There should be a new data principle in business – in order to build, maintain and enhance a customer relationship, every possible data collection opportunity must be used

How are you going to populate your database this year? This may sound like an odd question if you already have a customer and prospect file. But, unlike other forms of capital equipment, databases are not a once-and-for-all solution to a problem. They need constant replenishment and feeding, otherwise what looks a sound investment now will be a rusting hulk in 12 months' time.

As part of an ongoing data strategy, direct marketers needs to identify ways to acquire new information on their marketplace in a dynamic way. For most companies, that will mean sizeable volumes of names and addresses being added on a monthly or quarterly basis.

Fortunately, there have probably never been more ways available to meet this demand. A prime candidate for data acquisition has to be the sponsored question on a lifestyle survey. ICD is now mailing the entire country on a regular basis and receiving double-figure response rates.

That offers direct marketers the opportunity to ask for exactly what information they require from the broadest possible sample. Ownership of that data rests with the client for anything up to a year, offering the chance for competitive advantage. And using these records for direct marketing presents no problem, since respondents have clearly opted in to having their data used.

In some industry sectors this has been almost the only way to build a database. Tobacco companies have spent the past four or five years buying space on lifestyle questionnaires and now have a good fix on the universe of smokers. If the DM industry has to confront the loss of public domain universal data sets such as the electoral roll, then these data collection mechanisms will be critical.

Of course, those smokers' files are not static either. Tobacco companies have gone further by turning their packets into data gathering mechanisms. If you smoke and have sent off for a lighter or wine cooler, you are on the database. Continually refreshing such offers helps to keep track of customers as they move around.

This is one channel open to most manufacturers that has long been overlooked. Despite the continuing high level of sales promotion activity, data capture still doesn't play a part in the thinking. Is your warehouse full of response coupons, waiting to be thrown away?

You might think nothing of it now, but what would your finance director say if you left the company fleet of cars in a field to rust? As data slowly creeps onto company accounts as an asset, more questions will be asked about how well it is being maintained. And if some channels of communication get shut down, either through privacy legislation or industry-specific bans, it will not be possible to continue to be so careless.

DRTV is likely to become an ever more important engine for data collection. It is still the quickest and fastest way to pull high volumes of responses. Here again, it will be crucial to have planned how to capture and use that data before embarking on a campaign.

Last year saw one of the worst examples of profligate direct marketing. A major cable and telephone operation ran a nationwide, high-profile campaign asking people to take part in a survey about its services. It was only after the campaign had been running for some months that business units within the company began to ask if they could access some of the respondents' data.

Yet this should have been part of the objective from the beginning. Why ask the public to tell you what they want from your company if you are not really listening? Of course, it requires a considerable cultural shift to decide to let the market really define your offer. But that is what direct marketing is ultimately about.

This year is also likely to see a big breakthrough in the penetration of the Internet. According to lifestyle survey company NDL, during 1997 Internet usage underwent a significant shift from being predominantly affluent, male and professional towards being far more mass market.

As cable penetration grows, and digital, interactive services are launched, use of the Net will accelerate. Every click on a Website leaves a trace. You may not be able to use that information for marketing but it forms a basis for management, decisions. Creating attractive interactive services that encourage people to give you their personal information will help to build the database fast. And those Web users will be good prospects because they will have come looking for you.

Telephone costs will continue to fall as competition rises and the regulator begins to bite harder on profits. That is good news for telebusinesses, since it reduces the potential barrier to consumers of the cost of making a call. At the same time, consumers are becoming ever more willing to transact their business by phone.

That level of direct contact is a perfect opportunity to solicit more information or

● ● ▶

to capture personal data for marketing purposes. While the legislators may worry about individuals giving their consent, those same people are getting on with talking to companies and happily providing their personal data.

Nowhere is this more evident than in the robust response rates to direct mail. Yet again, the volume of items being sent by advertisers rose by well over ten per cent during 1997. Despite this increase, average response rates appear to have risen, to stand at just under seven per cent.

Some years ago, it suddenly dawned on marketers that consumers were now advertising literate. They understood the role of ads and the language they used. It is fair to say that the general public has probably become 'response ready' as well. If it suits them, they will pick up the phone, fill in a coupon or visit a Web site.

Reaping that positive disposition by gathering data as often and as carefully as possible should be top of every direct marketer's strategy. It is not just a case of following the principles of the Data Protection Act. There should be a new data principle in business in order to build, maintain and enhance a customer relationship, every possible data collection opportunity should have been harvested.

David Reed is a freelance journalist.

(This article first appeared in *Marketing Business*, the magazine for The Chartered Institute of Marketing, February 1998, p. 25.)

Facing the Challenge

Looking to the future, direct marketers are going to have to do a better job of facing their responsibilities if the industry is to achieve its potential. With this in mind there are a number of ways that they can tackle these difficult issues.

Self-Regulation

Privacy and social responsibility issues, for companies, customers and legislators may be alleviated by increased attempts by the industry to police itself. Self-regulation 'goes beyond the minimum requirements of legislation and has to be adhered to in spirit as well as to the letter' (Titford 1994:341). A number of new authorities and codes of practice have been introduced by the industry over the last few years (for a more detailed description of the roles of all self-regulatory bodies see Titford 1994). Indeed, in terms of the policy of self-regulation the UK industry is considered one of the most successful. The introduction of the Mailing Preference Service and more recently the Telephone Preference Service are a clear recognition of consumers' rights and concerns. Unfortunately, unless more proactive measures are instigated more and more people may register their wish not to be contacted. This will only serve to reduce the size and potential of the market available.

The Direct Mail Services Standards Board (DMSSB) was set up in 1983, with the objective of maintaining and enhancing high standards of practice in the direct-mail services industry and direct mail generally (Titford 1994). The main function of the DMSSB is to administer an accreditation scheme for all types of supplier within the direct mail arena. Criteria for recognition are stringent: an established trading record has to be demonstrated along with evidence of financial probity. Applicants must abide by British Code of Advertising Practice (BCAP) and other relevant codes, and only work for clients who do likewise. Furthermore, they are required to pay a levy on advertising mail. This supports the Advertising Standards Authority's (ASA) work overseeing direct marketing complaints and funds the Mailing Preference Service (MPS). In addition, the UK List and Database Suppliers (LADS) group will refuse to provide mailing lists for any advertising or promotions which breach the codes. Similarly, the Data Gatherers and Response Handlers (DAGAR) group formed in 1994, will only supply fulfilment and response services for advertising which meets the code.

Telemarketers are governed by the Direct Marketing Association's Code of Practice which provides voluntary guidelines on when it is reasonable to call consumers at home. The recently adapted Code recommends only ringing between 8am and 9pm Monday to Saturday.

The industry response in terms of establishing new authorities and detailing codes of practice is clearly important. However, self-regulation will only succeed if direct marketers, at individual company level, are committed to making it work. In order to promote the spirit of self-regulation, alleviate consumer concerns over privacy, reduce the threat of further restrictive legislation, and generally further the interests of the industry, organizations involved in direct marketing should become more open, honest, and accessible. In order to adhere to the spirit of self-regulation, companies should find the following guidelines of some use (adapted from Evans *et al.* 1995):

▶ If running a campaign using an external agency, use only companies recognized by the DMSSB. The handbook of registered agencies is freely available and should be consulted by advertisers seeking to use third-party services to produce their direct marketing campaigns.

▶ If internal direct mail or telemarketing campaigns are being undertaken, ensure that the mailing preference and telephone preference lists are consulted regularly. Do not, under any circumstances, cold call or mail consumers who have registered their wish not to receive unsolicited marketing communications.

▶ Never use the telephone book for indiscriminate cold calling. If you receive such calls yourself, report the offending company to the DMSSB.

▶ Regularly clean and update your own internal databases. Be particularly careful with mailing lists which you have purchased, and cross-reference them with the Postcodes Address File (PAF) and the Deceased Register to ensure that they are correctly targeted and addressed.

▶ Do not sell or swap lists without first ensuring that the proposed campaigns meet the BCAP requirements of being legal, decent, honest and truthful. If in doubt, consult the DMSSB.

▶ Do not attempt to sell to consumers either via mail or telephone under the guise of market research. Such practices serve to undermine both the market research and database industries in the long-run and in any case contravene the Market Research Society's code of Conduct (Fletcher and Peters 1996).

▶ Monitor and evaluate campaigns, not just in terms of response per 1000, but also in terms of consumer attitudes.

The success of self-regulation will also be dependent upon consumers using the facilities provided to them (e.g. MPS and TPS) and registering complaints on offending companies. To this end, consumers and direct marketers will need to be better educated as to what is acceptable and what is not acceptable in the future.

Consumer Education

On an industry level, it is important that consumers are made aware of their rights. Given that consumer knowledge of direct marketing practices is a factor in how they perceive the industry, direct marketers need to allow the consumer greater access to information. Consumers should be made aware of what constitutes acceptable and unacceptable behaviour in terms of data collection and utilization by organizations. Additionally, they need to know how to protect their information, how to query information held on a company's database, and how to remove their information if they so desire. As the saying goes, a little knowledge is a dangerous thing. Without comprehensive knowledge on how direct marketers operate, why they need information and how they use it, consumers are likely to jump to their own conclusions and to be susceptible to scare-mongering by the media.

Protecting Information

Direct marketers need to be more protective of their consumer lists. List sharing is encouraged within the industry, indeed, direct marketers argue that there is no point in protecting lists in a country where the electoral register is on the market. However, it may be that this practice is contributing to many of the consumer concerns already outlined. The last thing companies want is for the relationships which they have built with customers to be damaged by unscrupulous marketers to whom they have sold their lists. Even if third parties are respectful of codes of practice, it still leads to increased volume of direct mail which may in itself serve to alienate consumers. Thus, companies should be wary of sharing lists because of problems associated with over-use, misuse, and abuse of lists (Patterson *et al.* 1996)

Over-use

Over-use of customer lists, although not the most serious problem, is likely to be the most prevalent. As such it also contributes greatly to problems associated with physical/interaction privacy. The first and obvious result of data sharing is clutter as certain segments of the consumer population will be continuously targeted by a number of competing companies, selling a myriad of products and services. Second, in order to avoid unwanted and unsolicited communications consumers may become more protective of their data. They may opt out, refuse to provide information, or provide inaccurate information. The widespread withdrawal of information by consumers would clearly be something which the industry would wish to avoid.

Misuse

Misuse of customer information is also problematic and usually occurs as a result of incorrect or inaccurate data. Consumers may be targeted inappropriately, thus creating waste and contributing both to physical/interaction privacy and environmental concerns. They may be appropriately targeted but with inaccurate details, thereby aggravating information privacy concerns.

Abuse

Abuse of customer data is potentially the most serious problem. We include any activity which results in consumer distress in this category. This may be unintentional – for example because of failure to ensure information accuracy, the parents of a baby who has recently died are targeted for baby products. The more serious cases are likely to be those which are deliberately unprofessional or indeed illegal. For example, a former student of one of the authors was targeted by a funeral undertaker to purchase a coffin for her father. It seems that the hospital had given the names of patients in intensive care to this undertaker. The problem in this case, was that the student was approached while the father was alive, making a difficult situation far more stressful. In any case, abuse results in negative perceptions, which may prove very difficult to alter in the future.

Direct Response

In the future, marketing communicators will need to devote greater attention to direct response mechanisms, particularly for customer acquisition purposes. These allow consumers who are interested to initiate meaningful dialogue with organizations and to retain some modicum of control over the interaction. As such, direct response is unlikely to be the focus of consumer concern. Equally, it is less intrusive for consumers who are not interested and is therefore unlikely to engender negative perceptions. Additionally, direct response advertising facilitates the development of consensual databases, which should be of greater use in building relationships.

Taking on the Big Boys: Opt-in or Opt-out?

In 1997 the Data Protection Registrar served preliminary notices on two utilities under the UK's Data Protection Act. The British Gas case attracted a great deal of attention in the trade press. According to the Registrar, the issue at stake is a 'fundamental human right – the right to have personal information protected and to be left alone. It may sound petty but people worry about it a lot.'

The utilities are clearly upset with the Data Protection Registrar, so much so that they are planning to take the case to a tribunal. For example, British Gas is reputed to have spent £100m on developing its customer databases, and are clearly concerned that they may not get the full benefit from this (Martinson 1997b). In particular, they argue that they already have their own, up-to-date detailed (and generally accurate) databases, and to have to purchase external databases would be costly, and they would be far less accurate and useful in any case. Furthermore, their ability to compete effectively after the industry is liberalised in April 1998 will be seriously undermined if they are not in a position to capitalise upon the customer database.

The Data Protection Registrar believes that mailings by the utilities are unlawful under the principles of lawfulness and fairness as detailed in the Data Protection Act. In terms of the legality of the situation, the Registrar believes that the use of customer databases is unlawful under the acts which privatized the utilities. The Gas Act says that if the utility wants to use its database to market other services, it must gain customers' consent to make the offer. Although this position could be legalized by the addition of an amendment, she argues that this still leaves the issue of fairness. 'The point is that information obtained from you must be taken with the clear understanding of what it's going to be used for.' The utilities initially collected the data for billing rather than marketing purposes, and consumers had no choice given their monopoly status, the question now is whether new uses of this data are fair.

British Gas did ask customers for their permission. In March 1995, British Gas began sending out a booklet to all of its 19 million customers entitled 'Your Data Protection Rights – the right to choose the information you read.' This informed customers that British Gas wanted to send them information about products offered by other organizations and to pass on information about consumers to other companies within the group. Those who did not wish to receive such information or who did not consent to the disclosure of their details were asked to contact British Gas via FREEPOST or FREEPHONE. Almost 100 customers complained to the Registrar about this booklet, in particular at the fact that unless customers responded to the mailing it would be presumed that they were happy for their personal details to be disclosed.

The Registrar considered the complaints to be valid, on the basis that customers had been asked to opt-out rather than opt-in. That is customers had to write back if they did not wish to receive further information from them. 'The opt-out enables British Gas to benefit from inertia selling. A lot of people don't read things that come with their bill and that's all to British Gas's advantage.'

Rather than engaging in a long drawn out battle, the Registrar believes that the utilities should write to customers asking their permission to receive extra information. This is effectively the 'opt-in' option. However, the Direct Marketing Association's legal advisor believes that the 'opt-in' if applied to the whole industry, could have potentially disastrous consequences. As a result, the utilities are planning to go to a tribunal, and if that fails, to lobby government. However, there are also those in the industry who agree with the Data Protection Registrar's stance in this case. One managing director said 'Other companies have to spend millions to collect information before they can do things with it. From the Data Protection Registrar's point of view, it's important that the customers have the opportunity to opt in.' (Fletcher 1997).

Questions

1 Do you believe that British Gas made a 'fair' attempt to get consumers' consent?

2 What do you think would be the consequences for the direct marketing industry if 'opt-in' became the norm?

3 In this case, would you support British Gas or the Data Protection Registrar?

4 What would you do now, if you were managing director of one of the other utility companies?

(Source: All quotations from the Data Protection Registrar are from Martinson 1997a)

Review Questions

1 What concerns do UK consumers exhibit in relation to direct marketing? Outline the main foundations for each concern.

2 What do you understand by the following terms:

   (a) cultural environment;
   (b) ideological environment;
   (c) interaction – specific environment.

3 What other issues should a socially responsible organization consider?

4 What is the difference between legislation and self-regulation guidelines?

Discussion Questions

1 Marketing '*occurs in society, with society's permission and support, and purportedly, in part for society's benefit*', (Camenisch 1991:246). To what extent do you think direct marketers should have to take account of the moral expectations of society?

2 What are the implications of social responsibility issues for the direct marketing industry in the UK?

3 As technology improves, what direction do you think consumer concerns with regard to direct marketing will take?

4 How should UK direct marketers tackle the issues raised in the chapter?

5 To what extent does the information in Case Study 2 marry well with the general sentiment of this chapter?

References

Barnes, J.G. (1994) 'Close to the Customer: But is it Really a Relationship?' *Journal of Marketing Management*, 10, pp. 561–70.

Bessen, J. (1993) 'Invasion of Privacy: When is Access to Customer Information Foul – or Fair?', *Harvard Business Review*, September–October, pp. 154–55.

Bloom, P.N., Adler, R. and G.R. Milne (1994) 'Identifying the Legal and Ethical Risks and Costs of Using New Information Technologies to Support Marketing Programmes', in Blattberg, R.C. Glazer, R. and Little, J.D.C. (eds.) *The Marketing Information Revolution*, Boston MA: Harvard Business School Press, pp. 289–305.

Camenisch, P.F. (1991) 'Marketing Ethics: Some Dimensions of the Challenge', *Journal of Business Ethics*, 10, p. 239–48.

Cespedes, F.V. and Smith, H.J. (1993) 'Database Marketing: New Rules for Policy and Practice', *Sloan Management Review*, Summer, pp. 7–22.

Denny, N. (1995) 'The Quest for the Best Messenger', *Marketing Direct*, November, pp. 21–28.

Evans, M., O'Malley, L. and Patterson, M. (1995) 'Direct Marketing: Rise and Rise or Rise and Fall?', *Marketing Intelligence and Planning*, 13(6), pp. 16–23.

Fletcher, K. (1995) 'Dear Mr Bastard . . .', *Marketing Direct*, July/August, p. 58.

Fletcher, K. and Peters, L. (1996) 'Issues in Customer Information Management', *Journal of the Market Research Society*, 38(2), pp. 145–60.

Fletcher, K. (1997) 'Putting the squeeze on data use' *Marketing Direct*, June, p. 10.

Gandy, O.H. (1993) *The Panoptic Sort: A Political Economy of Personal Information*, Boulder CO: Westview Press.

Henley Centre (1995) *Dataculture*, Henley Centre, p. 3.

Kitchen, P. (1986) 'Zipping, Zapping and Nipping', *International Journal of Advertising*, 5, pp. 343–52.

Lenk, K. (1982) 'Information Technology and Society', in Friedrichs, G. and Schaff, A. (eds.) *Microelectronics and Society: For Better or Worse*, Oxford: Pergamon Press, pp. 273–310.

Martinson, J. (1997a) 'The Data Protection Registrar Explains Why She is Curbing Utilities' Mailshots to Their Customers', *Financial Times*, May 9.

Martinson, J. (1997a) 'Watchdog Snaps at Utility Database Plans: Data Protection Registrar Prepares for Fight Over Use of Customer Information', *Financial Times*, April 3.

Milne, G.R., Beckman, J. and Taubman, M.L. (1996) 'Consumer Attitudes toward Privacy and Direct Marketing in Argentina', *Journal of Direct Marketing*, 10(1), pp. 22–33.

O'Malley, L., Patterson, M. and Evans, M.J. (1997) 'Intimacy or Intrusion: The Privacy Dilemma for Relationship Marketing in Consumer Markets', *Journal of Marketing Management*, 13, pp. 541–59.

Patterson, M., O'Malley, L. and Evans, M.J. (1996) 'The Growth of Direct Marketing and Consumer Attitudinal Response to the Privacy Issue', *Journal of Targeting, Measurement and Analysis for Marketing*, 4(3), pp. 201–13.

Patterson, M., O'Malley, L. and Evans, M.J. (1997) 'Database Marketing: Investigating Privacy Concerns', *Journal of Marketing Communications*, 3(3), pp. 151–74.

Petrison, L.A. and Wang, P. (1995) 'Exploring the Dimensions of Consumer Privacy: An Analysis of Coverage in British and American Media', *Journal of Direct Marketing*, 9(4), pp. 19–37.

Phelps, J.E., Gozenbach, W.J. and Johnson, E.A. (1994) 'Press Coverage and Public Perception of Direct Marketing and Consumer Privacy', *Journal of Direct Marketing*, 8(2), pp. 9–22.

Schroeder, D. (1992) 'Life, Liberty and the Pursuit of Privacy', *American Demographics*, June, p. 20.

Sherman, R.L. (1991) 'Rethinking Privacy Issues', *Direct Marketing*, April, p. 40.

Smith, R. (1994) 'Setting and Maintaining Data Quality: An Overview', *Journal of Database Marketing*, 1(3), pp. 247–53.

di Talamo, N. (1991) 'Private Secrets', *Direct Marketing*, April, pp. 42–44.

Titford, P. (1994) 'Self-regulation in Direct Marketing', *Journal of Database Marketing*, 2(2), p. 335–50.

Treacy, M. and Wiersema, F. (1993) 'Customer Intimacy and other Value Disciplines', *Harvard Business Review*, 71(1), pp. 84–93.

Waldrop, J. (1994) 'The Business of Privacy', *American Demographics*, October, pp. 46–54.

Westin, A. (1992) 'Consumer Privacy Protection: Ten Predictions', *Mobius*, February, pp. 5–11.

Westin, A. (1967) *Privacy and Freedom*, New York: Atheneum.

Whalen, J., Pitts, R.E. and Wong, J.K. (1991) 'Exploring the Structure of Ethical Attributions as a Component of the Consumer Decision Model: The Vicarious versus Personal Perspective', *Journal of Business Ethics*, 10, pp. 285–93.

Further Reading

Rothfeder, J. (1992) *Privacy For Sale*, New York: Simon & Schuster.

6, P. (1998) *The Future of Privacy: Private Life and Public Policy*, London: Demos.

6, P., Lasky, K. and Fletcher, A. (1998) *The Future of Privacy: Public Trust in the use of Private Information*, London: Demos.

Cases and Clippings

This Chapter:

C
H
A
P
T
E
R

13

Cases and Clippings

The launch of the new Range Rover – as told by Craik Jones

The launch of the new Range Rover was one of the most significant steps in Land Rover's history. The objectives of the launch were to establish the new Range Rover as the true successor to the classic Range Rover.

Land Rover's vision was to launch the car in a way that no other car had been launched before. The plan was to simultaneously involve, excite and inform customers, dealers, Land Rover staff and key influencers around the world about the new Range Rover. The desire was to create an intimate global experience and interactive satellite TV was to provide the world-wide link.

The only advertising activity prior to the launch event was to be direct mail. Our job at Craik Jones was to reach 12,000 wealthy individuals in the UK, including Range Rover owners, past and present, and owners of other luxury cars and invite them all to their local Land Rover dealership for the launch of the new car.

There was just one teeny-weenie creative constraint. We couldn't mention the car. We

were working under a strict press embargo which forbade us from saying anything that might be taken as confirmation of the car's existence. Of course, it goes without saying that we couldn't show a picture of it. Not even the merest hint of wing mirror.

Oh yes, and one other thing. We were asked for 'Something that's never been done before, please.'

The Solution

At first, it seemed like the press embargo was going to make our life impossible. But then we discovered that there was one thing – and only one thing – that we could hang our hats on. As part of the celebrations, Land Rover would be sending the new car and teams of drivers (some of whom would be celebrities, but we couldn't mention that either) on epic expeditions in various parts of the world, which were expected to include Vermont, Patagonia and Japan. So we found out what we could about those places and what usually happens there in September, and here's what we came up with.

First, a series of three-dimensional teaser postcards to fix the dates of the launch in

recipients' minds. The first teaser contained an autumn leaf and said 'As green turns to gold in the villages of New England, what was merely glorious becomes spectacular. Witness the transformation on September 28th/29th'. Next, we sent a seashell from Patagonia. Thirdly, we sent a chrysanthemum from Japan. Our theme was a season of change around the world.

In the fourth week, the invitation, which echoed the postcard design, arrived. Showing through the window envelope was the specific date of the invitation (which could be either the 28th or the 29th) and inside was a letter and highly personalized RSVP card. A day before the launch a booklet was sent out as a reminder and as a means of drawing all the previous elements together. Now, at last, we could hint at the car.

Budget & Results

Finding 12,000 autumn leaves in the middle of summer was just one of the production challenges of this ambitious campaign. But was it expensive to produce? Not when you compare the £340,000 spend for this campaign with the typical above-the-line spend for a new car launch

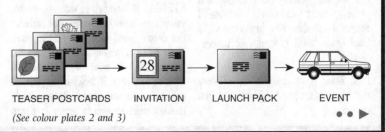

TEASER POSTCARDS   INVITATION   LAUNCH PACK   EVENT

(See colour plates 2 and 3)

of well over £6 million. Remember too, that a large part of the budget went, not on creative fripperies, but on co-ordinating the vast amount of dealer information and the 4,000-odd lasering variables.

Given that our work had to be something very different and intriguing, it actually delivered excellent value for money. Even more so, when you set the final cost of £30 per attendee — every one a top quality, ready primed, hotter-than-hot lead — against the average purchase price of £40,000 or more for a new Range Rover. Every penny was directly accountable.

It was a mould-breaking campaign and a rare example of a client who, faced with the most important launch in the history of the company, eschews advertising and dares to commit body and soul to the unique strengths of direct marketing: The risk paid off.

Some dealerships reported 100 per cent response to the invitations (the average was over 94.3 per cent). Certainly, over two days of the preview, the dealerships were packed — and with the right people.

Most dealers reported strong sales on the day and Land Rover believe that it was their most successful new product launch ever (e.g. Land Rover's Coventry dealership sold three months supply of Range Rovers at the launch).

Before we get into the campaign, I'd like to give you a sense of where this launch fits into Land Rovers vehicle and brand strategy. Firstly, to help you understand how customers and prospects in the UK perceive this well known and well loved brand. Secondly, because the strategy behind the new Range Rover is an extension of Land Rover's on-going product and marque strategy. And thirdly, and perhaps, most importantly, because I believe it will show how fundamental the Land Rover brand is to all our communication.

Land Rover is an amazing success story that began in the late 1940s with a chance remark.

Maurice Wilks was the head of engineering and design of the Rover car company. He owned an American Army Jeep left over from the second world war which he used to get around his country estate. In 1947, it finally shuddered to a complete and unrepairable halt. As he stared at the immobile hulk of the vehicle, one of the workers on the estate noticed the demise of the jeep and remarked 'If you can't build a better vehicle than that — you should get out of the car business.'

The comment struck home. One year later, the Rover car company launched the Land Rover — a lightweight but powerful four by four vehicle with supreme off-road capability. It was designed to be a proper farm machine, one which could be used as a general purpose vehicle, as a power source and even occasionally as a tractor. It was able to go anywhere and everywhere. It was also rather Spartan. Optional extras at the time included luxuries like: seat cushions, doors, a heater, side windows, spare tyre and starting handle.

To Rover's great surprise it became a huge success and their best selling vehicle. The product was exported to every continent and literally became the workhorse of the world.

Today, that workhorse is now called the Defender and Land Rover is the name of the company. Though the vehicle has gone through a continuous and unrelenting process of improvement and development, it still looks pretty much the same as it always did.

As Land Rover are keen to remind their customers — their vehicles will safely take you anywhere you're prepared to go.

Land Rover's best selling vehicle is currently the Discovery. Priced around $35,000, it competes with executive saloons on one hand and 4x4 vehicles like Jeep's Grand Cherokee on the other. While it's been around in Europe since the late eighties, it was only launched in America last year. It took seven years to get here, because Land Rover simply couldn't make enough to satisfy European

demand, let alone a market the size of the US.

Discovery is a spacious, comfortable family car with superb performance on and off the road. It is positioned as 'The family car that's also a Land Rover'. It's Land Rover's heritage and marque values that make the car the premium product in its class.

Discovery appeals to a very particular type of customer. Picture this — a young couple, no kids — with an active, sporty lifestyle. They attach great importance to their choice of car and what it says about them. As such, they tend to own a convertible, a GTi or a sportscar. However, once they begin to have children, they are suddenly faced with an awful dilemma. They need a practical car for all the paraphernalia of family life, but are horrified by the prospect of buying a mini-van or a station wagon. Discovery allows them to fulfil both their rational needs for space and their emotional needs for a car that reflects their self-image.

The Range Rover is Land Rover's flagship. At around $50,000 it's a luxury car and competes with the likes of Mercedes, BMW and Jaguar. When it was first launched in 1970, it created the luxury 4x4 market single-handed.

With leather seats, walnut burr trim and all the amenities you'd expect from a grand tourer it's impressive both on and off the road. One of Europe's most authoritative car magazines calls it 'The worlds best 4x4 car and by a huge margin'.

Before Land Rover launched the Discovery, they conducted extensive clinics with potential prospects to get their reactions to the car. When prospects first saw the vehicle it had no badges or logos on it. It was unbranded. While most people were quite impressed with the styling, every single one thought it too 'elegant' to be a serious four by four that would probably flounder off-road. However, the minute the Land Rover badge was placed on the

● ● ▶

vehicle, any doubts about its capability instantly evaporated.

We never forget that direct marketing must embody the brand and deepen the relationship with every communication. So, in the five years that we've worked for Land Rover, we've learned a lot about our customers and all of this learning helped us to prepare the ground for the launch of the new Range Rover.

So who are these people, these Range Rover owners who have such a strong emotional attachment to the vehicle? Many of them buy Range Rovers again and again. In fact 80 per cent of Range Rover owners go on to purchase another.

The old Range Rover was a much loved and timeless classic. So why was Land Rover going to go against their customers wishes and launch an entirely new Range Rover? Simple, they had no choice.

Change was driven by a number of factors. First of all, crash, emissions and fuel consumption legislation in Europe and America meant the car had to be re-engineered to meet new tougher laws. The original Range Rover was, of course, designed before these concerns even existed.

Moreover, the car was designed before the advent of modern manufacturing techniques. In its current form it was becoming too expensive to manufacture. Car technology too had also taken great strides since the original was launched. There were limits on what could be done to improve the existing car — particularly in the area of aero-dynamics. Finally, although a classic design, it was perhaps beginning to show its age.

It was simply uneconomic to act on all these things with the existing car. Land Rover needed a new vehicle to take it further and win a wider customer base.

It was no small challenge. Land Rover spent close to a half a billion dollars on developing the new car.

The new Range Rover, it was an all new car and a major step forward in all areas. Land Rover created a vehicle which drives like a luxury car on the road and competes on equal terms with the likes of Lexus, Jaguar and Mercedes. But it also provides the world's best performance off the road. The design is modern and up-to-date, but even unbadged it is instantly recognisable as a Range Rover.

With that level of investment — for a company the size of Land Rover — they were essentially betting the store on the new vehicle. The fundamental objective of the launch was to establish the new Range Rover as the true successor to classic Range Rover. Above all, the launch had to convince the most important people in the world — our existing Range Rover customers.

The internal name for the launch was 10 days that shook the world. It was to be like no other car launch before. Land Rover's vision was to simultaneously involve, excite and inform: customers, dealers, Land Rover staff and key influencers around the world about the new Range Rover.

The entire world-wide launch from the initial delivery of the car to dealerships — through to showing it to customers — would be condensed into a ten day period. On day one, the cars would be secretly delivered to the dealerships. For most people in the dealership this would be the first time they had ever seen the vehicle. Over the next week the dealers salesforce and service staff would be comprehensively briefed and trained on all aspects of the vehicle. It would be a massive logistical operation.

On the ninth and tenth days, small groups of selected customers and prospects would experience the car in the dealerships — through a series of events.

For the ten days of the launch all of Land Rover's dealerships around the world would be linked to each other and to Land Rover's headquarters with interactive satellite television.

At the same time, groups of celebrities, scientists and other people of note would be driving the new Range Rover on expeditions called 'Epic Adventures' to the four corners of the world. These groups would also be on the satellite link and would send back live reports to the dealerships while the customers were experiencing the car.

There was to be no advertising prior to the launch. And in contrast to all the media hype and PR that would usually surround such an important event, Land Rover did their best to stifle all rumours and thwart all media attention, In fact, there was a strict press embargo which meant that nothing could be printed until the day of the launch.

Of course, even the direct marketing had to observe this embargo.

OK, so we know we want to make twelve thousand customers and hot prospects feel party to privileged information — we just can't tell them anything. And we know we have to get the date into their diaries as soon as possible, we just don't know exactly what we are inviting them to or when.

What we do know however, is that it's all happening on one of two days in late September. And, as part of the launch celebrations, Land Rover would be sending the new car and teams of drivers (some of whom would be celebrities but we couldn't mention that *either*) on epic expeditions in various parts of the world. The list of possible locations changed almost daily but three of the most likely destinations were thought to be Vermont, Patagonia and Japan.

OK. So now we're getting somewhere. We have three probable places and we have a definite time of year — Autumn.

Autumn. What does Autumn mean to you? *We* thought, with all the mists and mellow fruitfulness, that Autumn could be called the season of change — which would certainly fit in well with the launch of a new model.

● ● ▶

So, what sort of changes happen in autumn in our three locations?

Well, Vermont was easy — autumn leaves.

Now, Patagonia . . . Where *is* Patagonia? . . . oh . . . it's in Argentina . . . oh no, it's spring there when it's autumn here . . . never mind . . . a mountain of guidebooks . . . something must happen . . . yes! that'll do! . . . the southern right whales come back to the waters they were born in to breed . . .

. . . and finally, Japan. More desperate searching through guidebooks and what do we find . . . *'In the land of the chrysanthemum throne, to mark the passing of summer and the coming of winter, they hold chrysanthemum shows in the imperial gardens.'* Sold.

We had us the makings of a creative idea. To start with, we would send out some sort of teaser postcard from each place, bearing the two launch dates.

Actually, to represent Vermont, our first thought was to laminate an autumn leaf in a clear plastic postcard and take as our theme 'Soon all will become clear'. Then we would encapsulate some sand in clear plastic sheets to represent the beaches of Patagonia and, for Japan, three perfect pink chrysanthemum petals, arranged and laminated in a suitably artistic Japanese pattern.

It was not to be. And we lost a lot of time in the production schedule, experimenting with these ideas.

Of course, for the leaf, we knew it wouldn't be easy finding 12,000 autumn leaves in the middle of summer. But it turned out that the real problem was the lamination. For some reason, nobody could make the postcard airtight enough to stop the leaves withering and mouldering.

The sand was a *total* nightmare. Quite understandably in retrospect, nobody would let us anywhere near their precious rollers with buckets of the gritty yellow stuff. When we gave up on that, we went in search of a large quantity of glossy green seaweed but all we could find was shredded and dried and pretty brownish . . . and then we went to shell shops and we investigated all sorts of starfish and seahorses and tropical shells which were simply too expensive and too fragile and too precious to even consider sending through the post.

And as for the flower petals — what an insight into human nature they gave us. Like most enclosing houses, the one we were using employed teams of little old ladies to turn creative's dreams into realities. In all seriousness, it turns out that — even with step-by-step diagrams to follow — little old ladies cannot be expected to make an artistic Japanese pattern out of three flower petals. Apparently, it's some sort of genetic thing and quite beyond their control.

But give them three of anything and they automatically make a triangle.

What? But even if this baffling geometric compulsion could somehow be side-stepped, there was still the issue — as with the leaves — of trying to encapsulate organic material without it decomposing en route.

(I should explain that we couldn't cheat and use silk or plastic for any of these items because authenticity is an important marque value for Land Rover. They all had to be the real thing.)

So it was back to the drawing board.

By now the creative department was starting to look like a nature study class and the production people were up to their eyes in bits of plastic moulded every which way. But our persistence paid off and, although we had to drop the 'all becoming clear' idea, what we ended up with was not a million miles away.

Colour Plates 2 and 3 shows what our three-dimensional teaser postcards eventually looked like . . . the first postcard contained a petrified red beech leaf (a cunning choice as it very conveniently holds its autumnal colour all year round.) The copy says:

As green turns to gold in the villages of New England what was merely glorious becomes spectacular.
Witness the transformation on September 28th/29th.

In the end incidentally, the postcards were constructed for us by a firm who make packaging for children's toys. They consisted of a piece of card printed on both sides with a window containing a made-to-measure box for the specimen, all enclosed in two pieces of plastic welded together.

So, next, we sent a seashell to represent Patagonia, with the words

Close to these beaches come the whales
returning to the same waters every year to breed and raise their young.
Be there at the birth of a new generation on September 28th/29th.

Thirdly, for the Japanese postcard, we sent a freshly dried chrysanthemum:

They call it the flower of autumn, the crest of the Mikado, the chrysanthemum.
Bathed in the glow of the autumn sun, where heaven and mountain meet.
Achieve true enlightenment on September 28th/29th.

Although we would have preferred to have lasered the address directly onto the card before encapsulation, we were now in danger of falling behind schedule and we had to settle for transparent labels. It didn't seem like a big deal because we often use transparent labels on closed face envelopes and they're virtually undetectable. But we'd never used them on plastic before. We should have tested the labels first and, with all the other shenanigans

● ● ▶

that were going on, we didn't. The first I saw of the finished effect was when my seed list sample landed on my doormat. I mean, I know it wouldn't really matter to customers and I don't want to sound precious here, but it does bother me that, in some lights, the glue of the label shows up as opaque against the clear plastic. It's definitely something I would change if I could do this job again and I just hope that this warning about so-called invisible glues might stop the same thing happening to you.

Originally, of course, we talked about actually posting the cards from the real destinations, but once again logistics and timings and post office regulations about mailing organic matter defeated us. We did, however, design special stamps for each location to give the cards a sense of place and more exotic feel to the compulsory Royal Mail postage paid impression. We had also wanted to design a special frank for them but the Post Office – who gave us quite a hard time over the legalities of the stamps – put their foot down on that one.

Actually, I do have another cautionary tale here for any art directors in the audience. I blush to remember but, you know, that stamp artwork was lying around for *weeks* while we sorted out other details of the campaign. After all, it only needed perfing. And surely, we thought, a perf is a perf is a perf . . .

We thought wrong. It turned out that only a few specialist printers in the UK hold the right die for the perfs and, since they were all busy printing stamps of the realm, they needed massive lead times . . .

All we could do was find a friendly printer who could *approximate* the perfs for us. But, as you can imagine, it's not as convincing as we would have liked . . . if *only* we'd thought ahead a little more. At the very beginning of the job we would have had the time – we just never imagined the perfs would be a problem. My message here would have to be: beware prioritising a job into big

problems and little ones. You really don't know which is which until the job is in the post . . .

Anyway, the postcards arrived one a week for three weeks. In the fourth week, we sent an invitation mailing which echoed the postcard design. By this time, each of the 125 dealers had been through the lists and told us who they wanted to invite to what and when. So showing through the window envelope was the specific date of the invitation, which could be the 28th or the 29th and inside was a letter and highly personalized RSVP card, which was lasered with details of the event – which could be breakfast, lunch, dinner, cocktails . . . you name it.

With all that out of the way, we still had another two weeks to go. So immediately before the preview, as a reminder to those invited, we sent this booklet.

The front cover said 'September 1994.' The copy tells you that, all over the world, a change is in the air. It goes on . . . *In Vermont, the leaves are turning fifty shades of gold.*

In Patagonia, the whales are swimming in on the spring tide.

Look, I have a confession to make here. A lot of people have complimented us on the clean, very graphic design of this booklet. I have to tell you that, when we were working on it, *my* baby was twelve months old, my art director's baby was nine months old and we were both spending inordinate amounts of time turning the pages of baby picture books. Hmmm. Big bold shapes and not a lot of words. I recommend the study of under-fives literature as a source of inspiration for creatives everywhere.

In Japan, the chrysanthemums are coming into bloom.

Now, at last, we could mention the car.

At your Land Rover dealer, the new Range Rover has arrived.

See it. (The leaves, the whales and the chrysanthemums can wait until next year.)

For those customers not among the top 12,000 to be invited to the launch celebrations, the dealers were planning various open weekends and follow-up days. Those customers also received this booklet on the day of the launch with a letter tactfully inviting them to one of these later events. Finally, this booklet was also used as the basis of a 'for your information' mailing to those people who were not good enough prospects to be invited to an event but whom we wished to keep informed out of politeness on the off-chance that they would one day return to the fold.

So, that was how we got the right people to the right dealerships on the right days. Of course, it was only when they got there and saw the Land Rover Live satellite transmissions from the various epic expeditions that the mailing campaign really made sense to them.

Well, at least we'd got the customers to the dealership. But, of course, another very important part of the brief was to generate test drives.

Now some people would simply sign up on the night, in which case – since this was a brand new vehicle which did not yet exist in large numbers – they would face anything up to a three month waiting list. But there would be other, equally important people, who were not able to make it on the night, who we also wanted to sign up for a test drive. For the first group we needed something to keep them going while they waited. For the second group, we needed something exciting enough to communicate the atmosphere of the launch and fill them with desire and longing.

As you might have guessed, money was by this time running out. So we came up with one pack to do both jobs. A week after the launch, Land Rover had compiled a video of the live footage from the epic

● ● ▶

expeditions, so we ran off several thousand copies of that as the base for the mailing.

It arrived in a box which said *'Now it's your turn'*.

Inside, there was the video and a series of perforated colour postcards from each of the epic locations.

The postcard strip was printed with two different perforated reply cards, one at the top which said *'Your test drive is confirmed'* and one at the bottom which said *'You are invited to take a test drive'*. Depending on which one of the two groups we were sending it to, we ripped off one or the other card before mailing it – thus saving a sizeable amount in printing costs.

There was one more pack in the communications cycle. This was for the dealer's use to send to new customers in the months ahead or to people who, heaven forbid, had somehow been omitted from the rest of the mailing. Since it was put together several weeks *after* the launch, this pack was able to move the communication forwards by including several press reviews of new Range Rover.

The envelope features a quote from Autocar magazine:

'A wondrous car and an utterly worthy successor to the legendary Vogue SE'

and underneath the headline says:

The new Range Rover: it really has arrived.

And inside the brochure unfolds from A5 to A4, revealing a different quote at every turn.

Well, that was it. The new Range Rover was well and truly launched. But what I haven't told you yet was about all the lasering variables – around 4,500 at last count – or about the results of the programme.

The total direct marketing budget was $750,000. Which works out to about $60 per customer. That's not a lot of money for a car that sells for $50,000 and which customers tend to buy every two years.

It's certainly not a lot of money if you bear in mind that there was no launch advertising and that a typical new car launch in the UK would usually be

supported with an advertising budget of about 10 million dollars.

So what happened? Were Land Rover right to trust direct marketing to launch the most significant new vehicle in their history?

Some dealerships reported 100 per cent response to the invitations – the average was over 94 per cent. Certainly, over the two days of the launch, the dealerships were packed – and with the right people.

Like the Land Rover dealer you just saw, most dealerships reported strong sales on the day and a three month waiting list was instantly created. And to this day, demand still exceeds supply.

Land Rover believe that this launch was their most successful new product launch ever.

Yes, there are a few remaining die hard Range Rover owners who still haven't made up their minds on the new vehicle, but for the vast majority the mantle has been successfully passed on.

© Craik Jones Watson Mitchell Voelkel Ltd.

■

Attention seeking

Off-the-wall thinking can result in some weird and wonderful campaigns, discovers Emily Booth. But they still have to pay their way

How do you get the attention of the 55 most powerful hotel groups in the world? You send them a ransom note threatening to put a mouse on their premises. Then you send a beautifully crafted mouse cage,

complete with one of the pesky little creatures (of the computer variety) sitting inside.

This was the approach taken last year by Leisureplan Live, an Internet service to help travellers select and book hotel accommodation. Its direct mail campaign, run by MSB+K was targeted at a database segmented according to business potential. While the top groups received the mouse cage, the next 2,800 received a computer mouse in a box, and another 36,500 hotels and chains had a teaser mailer.

The campaign won both the Direct Mail UK (High Volume) and International categories in the DMA/Royal Mail Direct Marketing Awards 1996. More importantly, the recruitment target of 5,000 hotels was smashed by the 14,218 hotels that signed

up within the first month. The conversion rate for the UK mailing ran at 59 per cent.

Creative mailings can give a campaign its edge. They can be wacky (carrots, fishing rods, juggling balls), weird (perfumed bus tickets, Star Trek figures) and wonderful (filled vodka bottles). But what about the practicalities? Do agencies or clients realize the mailing costs involved? Can the joke fall flat?

Keep it relevant

Ian Smyth, director of MSB+K, says: 'The objective is to get noticed. But you have to make sure it's relevant. Individually tailored, high-impact mailings are only appropriate in certain circumstances. It's

● ● ▶

the law of diminishing returns.' This is the notion that to be exclusive you have to keep adventurous mailings exclusive. Swamp customers and they become bored. 'You can do unusual mailings that aren't effective,' he adds. 'For instance, the mouse joke didn't translate well in some languages (those spoken in Latin America) and were re-worded.'

For Bob Nash, creative director at WAVV Rapp Collins, 'appropriateness' is the byword: 'Wacky mailings can have a place if you need to stand out in a market. The danger is not to let the wackiness of an idea cloud the proposition.' With the 3D Renault Espace mailing campaign behind him and fond memories of sending manuscripts in clear plastic tubes through the post, Nash is not afraid of the unusual. 'The important thing is the strength of the proposition and the ability to dramatise it properly,' he emphasizes. He accepts that sometimes standard letter mail-outs are appropriate, especially when speed is vital, such as charity campaigns.

So do clients initiate unusual campaigns, or do they need coaxing? Marc Rigby, associate director of Interfocus, has just finished working on the latest Thomson campaign, where families with young children are sent a video. 'Clients are keen to see conceptual thinking,' he explains. 'Thomson was prepared to back a hunch, but many companies tend to have a formulaic marketing approach. People know that about 75 per cent of what they receive on their doormat every morning is unsolicited. Something off-the-wall is likely to attract their attention. We have a responsibility to make things happen.'

At the extremes of fresh thinking is Explosive, a small agency which deals with business-to-business mailings. Last year, its 40° campaign for Emap Fashion's trade show had a three-stage approach. First, customers were mailed a plastic washball. Then they received a vodka bottle (lots of scope for puns: '40° proof, if you still want proof call this number'). The final approach involved posting stress balls emblazoned with: '40° will help take the stress out of selling.' The campaign achieved 12,400 pre-registrations against a target of 4000. For this year's show, Sindy and Action Man invited you to 'come shopping in London town', while some (surely collectable) cigarette cards informed you of the show's change of address.

Making an impact

Cute, but necessary? 'The aim is to make an impact,' says Paddy Barnes, managing director of Explosive. 'Even if a mailing is relevant it can be binned, so we try to do it in a more interesting way. We put ourselves in the shoes of the recipient. Our mailings cost between £1 and £2: a unit price that is not prohibitively high. For small runs it is cheaper than leaflets.'

Creative campaigns often require complicated packaging however, and no one knows more about the practicalities of posting than mailing houses. 'The number one thing for a successful campaign is a well-targeted list,' explains Ian Hughes, sales and marketing director at Mail Marketing. 'Standing out in the post is important, but cost/benefit is the issue. Creativity doesn't mean you have to put a bottle of whisky in every box. There are other ways of being creative.' He has found the elusive middle ground between creativity and cost-effectiveness lies with getting printing technologists, the agency and sometimes the client to discuss proposals together. 'There is this idea of a wall between the technologist side and creative side. But when they sit in a room together they understand what they can achieve, with interesting results. For example, when Maxwell House wanted a 3D pop-up house, we found out how to do it on a folding machine. Once there was a power chain from client to agency to technologist, now there is a virtuous circle.' The result is a creative solution that takes advantage of superior technological knowledge.

When problems arise, it is often because agencies have not thought about practicalities: 'Some mailings have up to six personal items,' says Hughes. 'And personalization always causes classic issues. The personalized items often arrive sealed down, so we don't know who to send them to and have to open them all up. The creative is often not bothered about the production process. However, it's a two-way street. We need to find an interesting way of getting across the information and tell them what we need.' To solve the problem, Mail Marketing has training sessions for customers every month. It seems to have a positive effect: nowadays more than 60 per cent of business is conducted direct with the client.

Fifteen minutes to save £15,000

Neil Shotton, group marketing manager of Mailcom, has seen the range of mailing pitfalls and has written copious guides on how to avoid them. 'Design has as much to do with practicalities as aesthetics when the resultant product has to survive a journey through the mail,' he explains. 'With printed material, there are two potential costs if something goes wrong: money and brand image. Remember that 70 per cent of the impact will occur at the moment the recipient opens the pack. Put as much effort into the design of the wrapping and presentation as you do into producing the print or choosing the gift/incentive.'

Common mistakes include up-grading the brochure paper to make it look more impressive and accidentally lifting the postage weight into the next price brand; not talking to the fulfilment house before placing the order for incentives (a cautionary tale concerns audio tapes which arrived in packs of three, to be dispatched in pairs); and putting coupons on glazed paper which refuses to hold the ink of a ball-point pen. As Shotton advises: 'Fifteen minutes on the phone to your fulfilment house can save £15,000 in service costs.'

It seems as though the agencies are responding to the mailing houses pleas. 'Creativity has to meet practicality,' enthuses Rigby. Nash agrees: 'We'll have

● ● ▶

priced the project beforehand so we're not surprised by the cost. What is important is a return on investment.'

In terms of industry awards, which are an incentive for unusual campaigns, Nash is adamant: 'Anyone who tells you that winning awards isn't important is lying. What should win is effective communications.' Since the DMA/Royal Mail awards judge on response and result, it seems that effectiveness is all.

Sue Whitmore, direct mail and international divisional director at SR Communications, is one mailing house representative convinced of the power of unusual campaigns. 'I'm in favour of anything that pushes our industry away from junk mail. We like working with agencies that are prepared to do something different,' she says.

Making a statement

Whitmore's memorable jobs include Barraclough Hall Woolston Gray's mailing for Ski Direct, comprising a bright orange mock-up of Radion washing powder, renamed Radical, with straplines proclaiming 'Bringing powder to the people!' and opens to reveal a polystyrene snow block; then there's the miniature high-jump pole stuck inside The Royal Bank of Scotland Business Direct mailing ('See for yourself how much higher we can go'); and Tambrands' Pillow Pack containing a personalized letter and Tampax sample. 'The cost is higher, but the impact is greater. An agency is creating a statement. It can't be too rushed,' says Whitmore.

She adds: 'The direct marketing industry is changing. The more sophisticated the industry gets, the more creative the agencies must become. We work with agencies or clients directly and put forward quotations well before the job is scheduled. Such work is more difficult to do, but the overall impact outweighs difficulties in production.'

(Source: *Marketing Direct*, November 1997, pp. 49–55)

STUDY 3

Dawning of a new Daewoo

With customer care as its USP, the Korean car company's UK debut proved to be a phenomenal success. By Karen Fletcher

Daewoo has taken one per cent of the UK car market in 12 months. It could haven't done this without direct marketing.

Since its launch into the UK in April 1995, the Korean car manufacturer has sold 18,000 cars — smashing previous records for new car launches.

And next year Daewoo will extend its range, adding three new models to the existing Nexia and Espero. All this from a company which doesn't even claim to make the greatest cars in the world — but just treats its customers the best.

There was a time when the company's marketing director, Patrick Farrell, thought this level of success could never be achieved in so little time. 'When the management team first came together, Daewoo's chairman challenged us to win one per cent of the UK car market — as soon as possible,' he says. 'We thought this was impossible. But the chairman said, 'Don't tell me why it can't be done. Tell me what you need to do it.'

The new Daewoo management team cut out the middlemen, bought its own network of sales outlets and branded itself as the UK's most customer-focused car manufacturer — and the only one to use direct marketing to such a large extent.

The launch campaign was originally budgeted at £16 million but the final cost of above-the-line direct response television advertisements was £11 million.

Farrell says: 'When you say to the average Brit 'We have cut out the middleman, and we give good value for money', it rings a bell with them. We offer a better deal.'

The Daewoo deal includes a three-year warranty on every car, three-year or 60,000 mile servicing and three years' membership of the AA. The cost of a Daewoo car (between £8,000 and £13,000) includes road tax and delivery.

Although many consumers reacted favourably to Daewoo's direct selling methods, the cars received a cool reception from the motor trade press, which felt the cars lacked glamour. Farrell himself was quoted in *Marketing* (January 11) saying: 'They are not earth-shattering cars, but they are very reliable and tremendous value for money.'

Farrell stands by the design of the Nexia and Espero, yet he believes the image of the company as a whole is more important. 'We do realize the importance of image,' he says. 'We are trying very hard to build up our position and branding. But the image we want is of a customer-focused company When you think of Volkswagen you think reliability; Volvo means safety. We want to be the ultimate in customer care.'

The Daewoo customer is a particularly niche market. Farrell says: 'The Daewoo buyer tends to be very rational, not driven by emotional reasons for purchasing one of our cars. They are not BMW badge hunters.'

● ● ▶

The customer focus of Daewoo was established from the beginning. The company ran a direct response television advertisement early last year (devised by Duckworth Finn Grubb Waters) offering 200 year-long test drives.

'We originally designed two DRTV ads — one with the test drive incentive offer and one without. We had intended to run the non-incentive ad on Channel 4 first, but they mixed up the tapes and ran the ad with the incentive.' explains Farrell.

The response was phenomenal. 'The switchboard at our telemarketing agency was swamped, as was Daewoo's UK head office,' says Farrell. 'BT told us that after the ad ran there were 40,000 attempts to get through in one hour.'

Daewoo built a list of 200,000 individuals who responded to the ad. They were mailed a follow-up questionnaire which received a 60 per cent response rate.

Discovering what consumers want

The questionnaire was designed to discover what consumers wanted from a car company. Four main points were identified and used by Daewoo to build its strategy: direct selling to the consumer, hassle-free buying, peace of mind and courtesy.

The 200 consumers who received a free, year-long test drive were asked to keep diaries recording the car's performance, interactions with any Daewoo service staff and even how often they refuelled their vehicles.

'Since we didn't have a dealer network we could market the cars directly to the consumer. We sent out invitations to people on our database to come along to our showrooms for the launch and got a 20 per cent response rate,' says Farrell.

Farrell claims although Daewoo tried using outside list sources to identify potential customers. this wasn't as successful as its own database. 'We don't use lists because then we just go back to the old two per cent response rates,' he says.

Daewoo continued to build its database through information gathered at its showrooms (known as Motorshows). Consumers are encouraged to come in and look at the cars, unmolested by salesmen. They can fill in questionnaires or use interactive media to answer questions on what they think of the vehicles and the service they receive.

In January Daewoo began a campaign to identify the 100 individuals who had received the worst treatment from competitor car dealers. The DRTV ad, which featured a crash test dummy taking the place of the typical unhelpful car salesman, elicited 125,000 telephone calls.

These people were sent questionnaires, narrowing down the database to 51,000. A panel of specialists then built a shortlist which was credit checked. The 100 consumers picked up their Daewoo cars on April 1 this year and, like the first set of guinea pigs, will keep a diary of their experience with a Daewoo car.

Farrell adds that Daewoo is working with four or five affinity groups to build up a list of potential buyers. The company has established service centres within Halfords out-of town stores. Daewoo is also experimenting with selling its cars through Sainsbury's supermarkets (*Marketing* April 4).

Next year Daewoo will roll out three new models, extending its range up and down market. But Farrell stresses Daewoo will not relinquish its positioning as the UK's most consumer-oriented car company.

Farrell believes Daewoo's share can only grow. 'A lot of ads show cars speeding along wide, empty roads — but how often do drivers experience that? We offer reliability and excellent service. That's what people want.'

(Source: *Marketing Direct*, May 1996, pp. 36–9)

CASE
STUDY 4

Proposal for the Provision of a Consumer Marketing Database to Scandinavian Seaways

Introduction

Firstly we would like to take this opportunity to thank Scandinavian Seaways for inviting The Database Group to present its proposals for the provision of a Consumer Marketing Database with added value for its UK based passengers.

After having digested the brief and established the business case we have compiled the following document to present you with a detailed plan of the methodology we will employ to assist in reaching the defined objectives.

We believe we can exceed both the technical requirements and service levels required by Scandinavian Seaways, as well as being able to provide other additional services and consultancy to ensure you reap maximum benefits from your database investment.

Executive Summary

Having established your requirement we feel that the optimum solution would be to provide our mainframe bureau manage-

● ● ▶

ment service with on line access using our fast counting, profiling and analysis system Swift, which would be held by Scandinavian Seaways at their offices.

This solution would be fully supported by a dedicated account management team and would be further enhanced by our analysis team and support staff, enabling us to identify marketing opportunities and achieve your direct marketing objectives.

Our aim is to provide Scandinavian Seaways with a fully integrated service combining knowledge acquired collectively within marketing and IT over the past 20 years, and to apply previous experience gained within the travel sector. We look forward to the opportunity of working with Scandinavian Seaways on this project.

The following diagram 'the database wheel' graphically provides an outline of the process involved in construction and management of a strategic marketing database.

The Database Group Credentials

The Database Group is one of the UK's foremost providers of database management and marketing information systems, built upon over 20 years' experience of working with clients from a spectrum of industries – Financial Services, Automotive, Travel and Retail, Publishing, FMCG, Leisure.

Our reputation has been established by our service, integrity and technical skills in the areas of both mainframe support and PC marketing systems.

Recent developments include the expansion of our consumer data sources of lifestyle, geodemographic and financial information, presenting a unique blend of consumer information available for customer and prospect analysis and modelling.

With our strategic partner Syntax Spa/ Olivetti S.A., we have significant computing resources to deliver solutions for Data Driven Marketing.

Overview of Products and Services

Over the years we have developed a comprehensive synergistic product and service portfolio to provide a complete range of database marketing services to include:

- ▶ Database Management
- ▶ Analytical Services
- ▶ Marketing Software and Systems
- ▶ Provision of Consumer Data

Database Creation and Maintenance

There are a number of techniques available to us in the development and maintenance of a marketing database and the enhancement of consumer data. These processes will assist in maintaining household information which is accurate and up-to-date.

Receive and Convert Data

Receive an estimated 584,000 records and convert into The Database Group specified format. Initially fields to include those supplied in appendix 1 of the brief.

Personalization

Check salutation on all records by examining names and titles (Mr, Mrs, Miss, Ms, Dr, Sir etc) and place where titles have been omitted incorrectly added or partially added.

Postcode and PAF Enhance

Check all records for validity and accuracy of existing postcodes, match up address to existing PAF files and apply updated postcode data and complete abbreviated address components (ie. Ave to Avenue) and complete or replace any other irregularities within the address.

Deduplication

Apply The Database Group's highly developed deduplication and intra-file merge purge modules which enables a multiple pass, multiple variable key deduplication to be carried out.

For each pass, a deduplication key is built from one or more fields extracted from the source data. The number of characters extracted from each field may be varied, and several options are available in extracting the data.

- ▶ Byte for byte extraction, where the exact number of bytes specified are carried over to the dedupe key with no space or punctuation removal.
- ▶ Squeezing, whole punctuation and spaces removed from the data.
- ▶ Squashing, similar to squeezing but in addition vowels are reduced to '∗' and multiple alphabetic characters compressed to single.
- ▶ 'Soundex' where the source field is converted to a phonetic string.

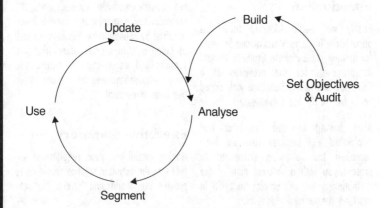

●● ▶

Where a record has been a member of a duplicate group in more than one pass, every record occurring as a member of each of these groups, becomes a member of the same overall group.

Suppression

The suppression file will effectively recognize goneaways, deceased's and do not mails as well as people registered with the mailing preference service and will extract matching records from a client file thus avoiding wasted mailings. A significant development at The Database Group has been the combining of the suppression file with client data to provide a cost effective stop list against sourced prospect data.

Data Updates/Counts/ Selections

Updates

Weekly or monthly updates to existing records or addition of new records could be added to the database via modem link or by magnetic media and can be matched back to the file using the unique customer number.

It is estimated that around 70,000 records are added to the database each year.

Selections and Counts

Counts can be performed on the database using either our Swift software or can be operated on the mainframe dependant upon the complexity of selections required. Once the count is completed and we have matched the required quantity of records needed for your campaign we can initiate the campaign processing procedure.

Campaign Processing

The typical producers for producing a campaign would be:

- ► Confirm counts, select data.
- ► Run against suppression files.
- ► Select into any test packs and code data.
- ► Flag mailing history for selected records with promotion code.

- ► Mailsort.
- ► Create laser image tape.

Reporting

Ad-hoc Reporting

Ad-hoc reports can be produced as and when required and would normally take between 24 and 48 hours to process from receipt of a faxed/written request.

Reports can also be produced using our Swift system which enables detailed profiles and reports to be carried out quickly, as a desktop campaign management tool.

Your account team will provide reports for any designated member of Scandinavian Seaways at their request.

A detailed description of Swift is provided. (See appendix 2).

See also selections, counts and updates.

Monthly Reports

Monthly reports to Scandinavian Seaways can be produced and will take the format of either personal presentation and/or written report.

The details of these reports are to include:

(i) Summary of main segments
(ii) Summary of additions and deletions
(iii) Geo-graphic demographic and travel history
(iv) Summary of the ICD survey
(v) Conversion analysis enquiry v booking.

Analysis – A Phased Approach

Our standard method of Analysis has been developed in a phased approach, to allow clients to identify and establish the 'Business Care' to continue, or 'opt-out' at given stages.

As this proposal incorporates a number of elements and objectives, it will become apparent that they are related in part in their consistency and evaluation of the data.

Therefore a phased approach provides milestones towards the ultimate objective of achieving a Long Term Value Model.

However, it should be noted, that at the outset clear objectives must be defined, in terms of what learning and benefits are required by Scandinavian Seaways across their range of products.

e.g. Are we looking to determine?

>   Campaign response
>   Frequent traveller
>   Source/media
>   Customer types
>   Prospect selection
>   Acquisition cost/rates

Phase I

Exploratory Data Analysis

As the existing customer records have selective histories and consumer data sources, this exercise now needs to be addressed in full, to evaluate the predictive power across all relevant data fields, by appending a significant number of data items from The Database Group's extensive UK consumer sources, to those provided by Scandinavian.

Effectively this stage of the process is designed to give us an initial look and establish:

I The relative importance of each customer characteristic in predicting responsiveness, financial stress, investment, lifestyle, demographics, profitability etc.
II Identifying the interactions between the characteristics.

Data Sources

The critical elements of the project will be drawn from two primary sources.

Namely Scandinavian Seaways and The Database Group.

● ● ▶

- Existing customer characteristics.
- Responder data – not converted.
- Responders/Recent conversions to customers.
- Lapsed customers data.
- Data from prospect universe.

Specifically we require details of:

- Response data.
- Method of payment.
- Value of booking.
- Media code.
- Promotional code/product/histories.
- Product derivatives, cabin etc.
- Destination.
- Tariff.

The Database Group

As stated previously the extensive UK consumer data sources of The Database Group Limited will be applied in all cases. (Please see Appendix for full details)

Establishing the 'Business Case'

Upon completion of the Exploratory Data Analysis phase of the project a clear picture will be present to identify which elements hold discriminatory power.

At this stage Scandinavian Seaways will be in a position to progress with subsequent phases, based upon the level of potential benefits now available.

Phase II

Once it has been agreed that the statistical 'raw materials' and business case are strong enough, we can enter into a Scorecard Development stage. The objective of this phase of the programme is to create a predictive mechanism which typically can be used to score names from the client's customer and prospect databases.

Optimization techniques will be used to create a scorecard which is the best possible predictor given the input data. Again, a milestone checkpoint would allow us to review the results of the process before deciding to move into the next phase of the work.

Phase III

Once the Scorecard has been constructed, a software module will be developed which allows for its application to score records from a prospect database or applied to 'cold lists' rented for specific campaigns. The module could be applied to the entire prospect and customer databases, or it could be used to score subset and cold lists etc.

Phase IV

Prospect Data Overlays

The creation of the Scorecard will have taken Scandinavian Seaways customer data through all of the necessary stages to identify relevant consumers variables, that appear predictive.

Effectively one would now be in a position to acquire, under licence, these external characteristics for application to the existing prospect and customer databases, thus providing the ability to rank and segment data accordingly.

Phase V

Prospect Data Provision

Additionally, this same methodology can be applied to external data sources, ie. in the UK Electoral Roll, Lifestyle, and Demographic List etc., to create a 'scored' prospect database.

In effect creating a cost efficient tailored 'prospect pool' of consumer data – on a multiple use – annual licence basis to be held at The Database Group for ongoing selections and usage.

Phase VI

'Long Term Value' Modelling

As stated previously one of the ultimate objectives must be to create an effective 'Long Term Value' model.

To achieve this we must assimilate all of the learning from the previous phases and across an agreed timeframe, incorporate actual customer histories and events, to create an effective model, which can then be applied to marketing initiatives.

This process will be undertaken on an ongoing basis to refine the model, based upon past and present performances of campaigns. (The typical lifespan of such a model is 18 months – 2 years).

Consultancy and Account Management

Your Account Director will act as the central point of contact and will be available for discussion as and when required, and by adopting a pro-active approach and combining both technical and marketing knowledge will advise on the best approach to reap maximum benefits from your Marketing Database.

Account Management

It is our policy to ensure that all clients have a high level of account support and that all members of an account team are fully versed in the client business. This will be confirmed once we have established the needs and objectives of Scandinavian Seaways.

A typical account team structure is as follows (see opposite).

Project Costings

These costings are supplied given our current understanding of your requirements.

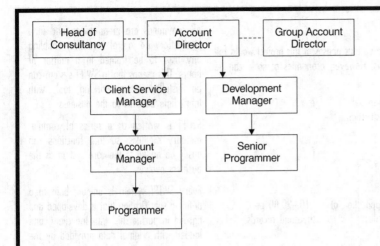

Database Load and Design

1 Database design and construction.   (one off fee)

2 Load 584,000 records including conversion
   from existing formats deduplication and
   forename and title processing.   £8 per 1000

3 Postcode and postcode validate.   £5 per 1000

4 Provision of tailored Swift campaign
   analysis tool.   (one site) a

Database Maintenance

1 Postcoding and postcode validation
   (if required)   £5 per 1000

2 Addition of new records including conversion
   deduplication and forename and title
   checking via magnetic media   £8 per 1000

3 Suppression   25p per match

4 Additions of responses and update
   by URN   £3 per 1000

5 Additions of responses and updates by
   address   £8 per 1000

6 Swift updates   £750 per update

Selections & Outputs

1 Records selected and flagged with
   campaign history   £8.00/1000

2 Outputs   Magnetic tape   £20.00 per tape
              Diskette   £5.00 per diskette
              Self-Adhesive Labels   £8.00/1000 labels

3 Mailsort allocation Sortation and Royal Mail
   documentation   £4.00/1000 records
     Creation of laser tape   £4.00/1000 records

Reporting

   Ad-hoc and fixed reports.
   (dependent upon complexity)   b per report

Account Management

   Provision of dedicated account
   management for three days per month.   c per day
   (This cost to be reviewed after an initial (Estimated 3 days
   six month period).   per month)

   Training.   d per day

Timings

We estimate that from receipt of Scandinavian Seaways data to the production of a working mailing database which has been fully tested and signed off will be a maximum elapsed time of 12 weeks.

Phase 1	Data audit and design	3 weeks
Phase 2	Create and load mailing database	9 weeks
Phase 3	Develop SWIFT using a selection of existing modules plus tailoring to suit the clients data	3 weeks
Phase 4	Testing and evaluation	2 weeks
Phase 5	Install the clients SWIFT system on our bureau network	1 week
Phase 6	Train staff on their database	2 days

We can concurrently develop the SWIFT system should this be required from the start of the project. This should be completed shortly after the database goes live.

● ● ▶

Analysis Project Costings

Based upon current information, the costs for the various phases of this project would fall into the following ranges on an individual basis. However, economies of scale can be derived for multiple scorecard development.

PHASE I   *Exploratory Data Audit and Analysis*   e
Sample extractions, database construction, data processing analysis.

PHASE II   *Scorecard Development*   f
Creation of scorecard development

PHASE III   *Scorecard Application*   g
Software module development. Application of score: dependent upon key variables   £10–20.00 per thousand records.

OR

PHASE IV   *Prospect Data Overlays*   h
Provision of key variables, under licence. (Dependent upon variables and volume of records).

PHASE V   *Prospect Data Provision (UK)*   i
Provision of scored records, on annual multiple use licence basis.   (typically 500,000 records)

Account Management   j per day

N.B.   Phase III –   Application charges for partial file or cold list scoring.

Phase IV –   Alternative option for complete file overlay. Negating Phase III costs.

Appendix 1 – Client List

Clients using similar services from The Database Group include:-

American Express
Arjo Wiggins Fine Papers
Bristol and West Building Society
Brittany Ferries
British Airways Holidays
Cigna Insurance
Citroen
Colleges Direct Marketing
Family Assurance Society
Fiat
Golden Wonder
ICD
J Rothschild Assurance Plc
Microsoft
Nat West Insurance
NORWEB
Shearings Holidays
Sun Life Direct Marketing
Tropical Places
United Airlines
Volvo

Appendix 2 – Swift

All of the requirements of the system as outlined in the brief can be provided by our SWIFT software. This is a modular system. The appropriate modules will be selected and fully customized to suit the clients requirements.

SWIFT is an extremely powerful database management system, which will effortlessly control huge amounts of data traditionally stored on a mainframe, using a sophisticated PC platform. It has been developed specifically for the marketing industry, and is designed to be used by marketers rather than IT professionals.

All commands are menu-driven and in a straightforward logical sequence, enabling any user to be trained in a matter of hours. This means that a SWIFT system can be installed as a working tool, with immediate benefits to the business.

SWIFT is written as a series of complementary modules, so that functions can easily be added to the core system as the business evolves.

Every SWIFT system is unique; built to a detailed specification that is developed and agreed in partnership with the client, and loaded with original data provided by the client.

The database will have the ability to:

– Receive data from external sources via magnetic media, tape or diskette, modem link or inputted manually
– Extract data for mailing runs onto tape or diskette.
– Maintain a mailing file selection history.
– Receive and maintain all responses/orders history.
– Provide seed names/suppress records for any campaign or run.

Functionality

The database will:

▶ Maintain a consolidated set of all customers providing:
– Name and Address
– URN
– Home Delivery Records
– Competitions/Reader Offers
– Mailing History
– Response History
▶ Have pre-determined analysis routines on specified fields to view on screen or to print.
▶ Have a menu led operation.
▶ Enable ad-hoc analysis to view on screen or print – including graphics.
▶ Allow selections of records meeting specifiable criteria.
▶ Enable output of user specified records (and allocation of activity codes for selections).

● ● ▶

Scandinavian Seaways – Estimated % Breakdown of Year One Operating Costs – (Not including analysis or data acquisition or reporting)

	AUGUST	SEPT	OCT	NOV	DEC	JAN	FEB	MARCH	APRIL	MAY	JUNE	JULY
Set up and design	33											
Load records and processing	17											
Postcoding of existing data	16											
Development of SWIFT	16	60										
Account Management	8	30	52	00	00	00	00	00	00	00	00	00
Selections Est. 33,300 records per month @ 8.00 per 1000* see notes		4.5	9.5	00	00	00	00	00	040	00	00	00
Creation of laser tape		2	5	00	00	00	00	00	00	00	00	00
Mailsortation		2	5	00	00	00	00	00	00	00	00	00
Addition of new records Est 55,000 records monthly @ 8.00 per 1000		1	2	00	00	00	00	00	00	00	00	00
Postcoding of additions		0.5	1	00	00	00	00	00	00	00	00	00
Addition of responses by URN. Assume 20% 6,600 monthly			0.5	00	00	00	00	00	00	00	00	00
SWIFT update			3.5	00	00	00	00	00	00	00	00	00
Monthly Totals	100	100	100	100	100	100	100	100	100	100	100	100

% Costs for Data Analysis and Scorecard Application

	AUGUST	SEPT	OCT	NOV	DEC	JAN	FEB	MARCH	APRIL	MAY	JUNE	JULY
Exploratory data analysis		100										
Scorecard development				50	98							
Data overlays				50	2							
Scorecard Application @ 10 per 1000						100	100	100	100	100	100	100
Totals		100		100	100	100	100	100	100	100	100	100

- Allow inputs by diskette or tape of new/amended customer records.
- Provide the facility to export data directly onto standard outputs.

SWIFT System For Marketing Management

A user friendly marketing analysis tool designed to give marketers information on campaign response, sales trends and customer profiles.

There are six functional facilities within SWIFT:

- Campaign Analysis
- Count
- Profile
- Cross Tabulations
- Graphics
- Output

Campaign Analysis – Designed to record the response over time for different campaigns, driven by campaign codes, with additional codes selectable to group multiple campaign responses together.

Count – This function allows the integration of a marketing, response or prospect database to identify mailing audiences and produce a selection from the overall file. The selection criteria can be altered and calculated until the desired mailed audience has been selected.

Profile – This facility allows for any subject to be compared against the total or subset of the database – with frequency counts on each variable, with indices to highlight under or over representation.

Cross Tabulation – Will examine the relationships between two different variables – on either subsets or across the complete database.

Graphics – Providing a pictorial representation of campaign results, profiling and cross tabulations.

Output – Once the target audience has been selected, URN's can be output to the bureau processing routines for matching and the file provided.

Overall SWIFT provides a hands-on desktop analysis and campaign management tool to the marketer.

The SWIFT data is normally refreshed after each main update of the Bureau SWIFT system.

The Database Group Consumer Data Sources

The Database Group currently holds in-house at both the Bristol and Liverpool offices extensive data sources for use in:

I. Data analysis – customer and prospects
II. Development of prospect scorecards/models
III. Customized geodemographic/lifestyle segmentation systems
IV. Clustering analysis
V. Creation of prospect databases

There is an on going programme of acquisition and licensing of additional data to further enhance the existing information sources of:

UK Electoral Roll – Household, Composition, Occupancy, Attainers, Gender

Lifestyle Information – Facts of Living, NCD

Investment/Shareholder Data – Top 650 UK Companies

Geodemographics – (Mosaic, PiN, FiNPiN, ACORN, Financial ACORN, Define, Super Profiles)

Financial Data – County Court Judgements

Census Data – Individual key variables

P.A.F. – Postal Address File

FIND – Income/Financial Indicator

Lifestyle Information
Lifestyle Database

In 1988 ICD Marketing Services started a consumer questionnaire distribution programme gathering detailed lifestyle information from individuals. To date over

150 million *Facts of Living* and *Consumer Research Bureau* surveys have been distributed throughout the UK.

As at July 1994 this database had grown to over 4 million records and is used as one of the main sources of targeted list rental, as well as generating data which can be used both for highly qualified leads and as a source of strategic information.

National Consumer Database

The Database Group has available one of the largest consumer databases currently available, the National Consumer Database (NCD). The NCD has been developed from a range of sources including the Electoral Roll, over 650 Share Registers and the information gathered from the Lifestyle Questionnaires (see above).

All of this data is available for analysis and is divided into 5 main sections:

- Geographics
- Household Composition
- Wealth
- Home
- Lifestyle

and within each section there are individual areas that are analyzed and reported on.

Geodemographic Systems

Given the number of geodemographic codes available identifying which one best meets a company's requirements is often left to initiative or familiarity.

The Database Group has access to all the major geodemographic coding systems and can perform analyses which takes the 'guess work' out of choosing a coding system.

Geodemographic profiles are produced through matching the postcode of each record with the postcode directory which contains the relevant geodemographic

● ● ▶

code. There are several classifications available all with their unique selling points, however all are based upon the Census of Population which was conducted by the Office of Population Census and Surveys (OPCS) in April 1991.

At The Database Group we hold, in-house, several of these systems:

System	Supplier
ACORN	CACI
PiN	CACI
MOSAIC	Experian
DEFINED	Equifax Europe
SUPER PROFILES	CDMS

The basic methodology involved in a comparative test of the systems is to take

a sample of customer records and profile/code each record with each system. The system which allocates most customers to the fewest number of clusters/types can be thought of as being the 'best' or most suited for the individual client.

STUDY 5

Scandinavian Seaways

The Database Group Consumer Data Sources

The Database Group currently holds in-house – at both the Bristol and Liverpool offices – extensive data sources for use in:

I.   Data analysis – customer and prospects

II. Development of prospect scorecards/models

III. Customized geodemographic/lifestyle segmentation systems

IV. Clustering analysis

V.   Creation of prospect databases

There is an ongoing programme of acquisition and licensing of additional data to further enhance the existing information sources of:

UK Electoral Roll – Household, Composition, Occupancy, Attainers, Gender

Lifestyle Information – Facts of Living. NCD

Investment/Shareholder Data – Top 650 UK Companies

Geodemographics – (Mosaic, PiN, FiNPiN, ACORN, Financial ACORN, Define, Super Profiles)

Financial Data – County Court judgements

Census Data – Individual key variables

P.A.F. – Postal Address File

FIND – Income/Financial Indicator

Lifestyle Information

Lifestyle Database

In 1988 ICD Marketing Services started a consumer questionnaire distribution programme gathering detailed lifestyle information from individuals. To date over 150 million *Facts of Living* and *Consumer Research Bureau* surveys have been distributed throughout the UK.

As at July 1994 this database had grown to over 4 million records and is used as one of the main sources of targeted list rental, as well as generating data which can be used both for highly qualified leads and as a source of strategic information.

National Consumer Database

The Database Group has available one of the largest consumer databases currently available, the National Consumer Database (NCD). The NCD has been developed from a range of sources including the Electoral Roll, over 650 Share Registers and the information gathered from the Lifestyle Questionnaires (see above).

All of this data is available for analysis and is divided into 5 main sections:

- ▶ Geographical
- ▶ Household Composition
- ▶ Wealth
- ▶ Home
- ▶ Lifestyle

and within each section there are individual areas that are analyzed and reported on.

Geodemographic Systems

Given the number of Geodemographic codes available identifying which one best meets a company's requirements is often left to initiative familiarity.

The Database Group has access to all the major geodemographic coding systems and can perform analyses which take the 'guess work' out of choosing a coding system.

Geodemographic profiles are produced through matching the postcode of each record with the postcode directory which contains the relevant Geodemographic code. There are several classifications available all with their unique selling points, however all are based upon the Census of Population which was conducted by the Office of Population Censuses and Surveys (OPCS) in April 1991.

At the Database Group we hold, in-house, several of these systems:

● ● ▶

System	Supplier
ACORN	CACI
PiN	CACI
MOSAIC	CCN
DEFINE	Equifax Europe
SUPER PROFILES	CDMS

The basis methodology involved in a comparative test of the systems is to take a sample of customer records and profile/code each record with each system. The system which allocates most customers to the fewest number of clusters/types can be thought of as being the 'best' or most suited for the individual client.

Thanks to Scandinavian Seaways for granting permission to reproduce these cases.

Introduction

The BMW reputation has grown over the last 25 years to represent prestigious performance cars and fine engineering. This successful recent history has helped BMW (GB) to consistently generate a profit in the UK.

The success of BMW is a fascinating case study combining diligent brand management and the conception and production of class-leading cars to create one of the most desirable ranges today. However this is only part of the story as BMW also faces new challenges. Indeed this is perhaps best summarized in Charles Handy's quote from 'The Empty Raincoat': 'What got you where you are isn't what's going to keep you there.'

The management of the BMW brand has contributed to BMW (GB)'s growth from a specialist car importer of the 1970s to a dealer network of 157 today with a healthy market share of three per cent. Significantly BMW's market share and profits have been maintained throughout the recession in comparison to its competitors, a factor largely due to sustained customer demand which eliminated the need to pursue a strategy of heavy discounting.

The role of direct marketing too has played an ever increasing important role in the success of BMW. Within the motor industry BMW's direct marketing activities are among the most respected. The success is in part due to the strong creative developed for each campaign and tightly targeted communications which have helped BMW achieve campaign response rates up to five times those experienced by competitors.

The continued success of direct marketing campaigns has led to the discipline achieving a high profile within BMW and its recognition as an important strategic marketing tool over the next few years. The BMW (GB) Board has accepted the development of a comprehensive Customer Relationship Marketing Programme which will assist the development of the car company in the future by building the loyalty of its customers.

Part of this programme is the development of the 'BMW Card', a customer benefits card exclusively for BMW owner/drivers.

A number of agencies are now being briefed to develop a direct marketing launch campaign for this new initiative.

The development of BMW

BMW is an international brand with offices and sales networks across the world. Initially all BMWs produced were manufactured in Munich, Germany where the original company Bayerischen Motoren Werke was established in the 1920s. Today BMW has manufacturing plants in South Africa and its most recent plant in Spartanburg, South Carolina where amongst others the exciting new BMW Z3 is produced.

In addition to a desirable range of cars, BMW is also well-known for its motor-cycles, producing some of the best touring motorbikes available.

In 1995 BMW hit the headlines in the motor industry following its audacious take-over of the bastion of British motoring; the Rover Group. Despite close links on the technical development aspects of the business, BMW and Rover remain clearly distinct in terms of their identities and marketing activities.

Since its inception BMW has come a long way from many of its early model such as the well known and idiosyncratic 'Bubble Car' of the 1960s. Today BMW cars are most succinctly described through their famous advertising strap-line: 'The Ultimate Driving Machine'

The statement 'The Ultimate Driving Machine' is far more than a mere strap-line, it summarizes the ambition of their corporate philosophy. BMWs are built for the driver by the driven. In reality this means that every BMW model is optimized to offer the best driving experience available regardless of whether the actual model is an estate (Touring), Saloon, sporting coupe or the new class of the BMW Compact.

Perhaps the turning point for BMW in its quest to create the Ultimate Driving

● ● ▶

Machine was the introduction of the 1502 model in the 1960s. Today this car is still recognized as having introduced new standards in the driving experience and helped to define BMW as the 'sporting saloon'. These same values have continued to be applied since then and are obvious in the painstaking attention BMW has paid to the development of each model. Many of these product features and innovations which contribute to the driving experience have been the focus of some of the most famous car advertising ever.

At the heart of BMW's driving philosophy is also the fact that all BMWs are rear wheel drive. Described by engineers as 'Standard Drive' (engine located at front, driven wheels at the rear) this formation does not only have certain benefits, it is also viewed by BMW as the best solution in the interests of customers and the all round driving experience. The easiest comparison of the increasingly popular front wheel drive against the standard drive set-up is that of fast food against a carefully chef-prepared meal. The pressures of marketing and business have led to an increase in front wheel drive cars (cheaper, less space) whereas BMW has consistently produced standard drive (rear wheel drive) as it is believed to deliver the best driving experience available.

There is yet further demonstration of BMWs sporting heritage in that there is a separate division of BMW simply known as 'M'. 'M' means Motorsport and the distinct badging appears on some of the BMW range most notably today on the M3 – a motorsport developed derivative of the 3 Series.

BMW have also demonstrated their sporting saloon capabilities with a list of championship victories throughout the world in the Touring Car Championship (essentially race-bred saloon cars). BMW achieved much of this success through the 1980s and early 1990s. However despite not having an official team during recent years in the UK championship, BMW is set to return to motorsport having announced a partnership with the Williams Formula 1 team as their main engine supplier from the year 2000.

Another increasingly important part of the BMW organization is that of BMW Financial Services. Although BMW Financial Services has been in existence for many years (supplying finance agreements for leasing, hire purchase and insurance) it has recently gained bank status (in Germany) thus allowing it to offer its own range of financial products including savings products and credit cards. BMW Financial Services also exists in the UK, however, they do not currently have bank status but they are likely to follow the trend set in Germany. In the case of BMW Financial Services UK, any finance products developed currently have to be underwritten by another organization with bank status.

BMW (GB) Ltd

BMW (GB) Ltd is a wholly owned subsidiary of BMW. Based in Bracknell, Berks and with approximately 300 staff, BMW (GB)'s role is that of an importer and sales office for the UK. As part of this role, BMW (GB) will assess market conditions and estimate its car sales accordingly. Through the support of the dealer network, BMW (GB) will then market these products to its UK customers. This is a carefully balanced process, any excess stock or lack of demand and BMW could be forced to discount prices in order to sell the cars. Any excess demand and lack of supply then BMW are at risk of losing customers to competitors and possibly also losing their goodwill and loyalty.

BMW (GB) is also supported by a number of other organizations in addition to its dealer network. Organizations of significance to its marketing operation and its customer service include the following:

Mondial Assistance

Operate the BMW Emergency Service. A service free to all new and used BMW owners for 3 years and 1 year respectively. BMW Emergency Service covers drivers and their BMW for almost any eventuality, including; breakdown and accident recovery throughout Europe, car rental, health cover and repatriation.

Mondial Assistance also operate the BMW Warranty. Again a complimentary addition to all new and used BMWs.

Mondial Assistance essentially operate as an administration centre for these services which are then handled by the customer's BMW Dealer.

BMW Call Centre

The Call Centre is also administered by Mondial and offers 24 hour information on the BMW range specifically covering pricing details and brochure requests generated by ads, direct marketing and Internet enquiries.

BMW Marketing Services Agencies

BMW retain a number of marketing services agencies which work closely together on specific projects to provide an integrated approach to all of BMW's communications. These agencies include:

► WCRS – main advertising agency responsible for the development of the brand and production of TV and press advertising. WCRS have retained the account for 17 years and recently won the IPA (Institute of Practitioners in Advertising Grand Prix award)
► Evans Hunt Scott – BMW's direct marketing agency responsible for all direct mail (customer communications and product launch communications) as well as the development of relationship marketing activities.
► Dunn Humby – responsible for the maintenance and development of BMW's customer database of drivers, owners and prospects from which much of the direct marketing activity originates.

● ● ▶

▶ EMO – responsible for all BMW Dealer communications from internal marketing within the dealer network to production of specific BMW Dealer ads which appear throughout the country in the regional press.

▶ BGA – BMW's design agency responsible for Point of Sale material within dealerships and product brochure design.

▶ The Russell Organization – responsible for organizing BMW customer events such as driving events at motor racing circuits.

▶ The Travel Organization – responsible for internal BMW events such as national dealer conferences.

BMW (GB) Ltd has recently undergone significant staff changes which has had important implications for the development of future marketing activities.

In the autumn of 1996, Kevin Gaskell was appointed as Managing Director of BMW (GB) Ltd following an impressive tenure at Porsche as Managing Director. Kevin Gaskell's appointment was closely followed with that of Phil Horton who joined in April 1997 from Renault UK to head up the marketing department.

In addition to these appointments there were also significant changes in responsibilities for many in the marketing department. Significantly Richard Downes, previously Direct Marketing Manager, was given new responsibilities as Customer Marketing Manager. Rather than just a title change these new responsibilities also signalled a renewed commitment to 'Relationship Marketing' and customer management – at the heart of which may be the BMW Card.

These changes represent an exciting period for BMW as it looks to move forward to a position where it can be recognized as one of the UK's leading customer service companies.

The BMW database and customer information

As with all good direct marketing and particularly the more sophisticated use of relationship marketing a good database is central to the planning and success of campaigns.

With BMW (GB) this is no exception. BMW recognized many years ago the importance of a good database both in terms of improving its targeting as well as supplying important management reports to BMW marketing and sales staff.

Today the BMW Customer Database (CDB) is supported by a thorough infrastructure which feeds in new information on customers and prospects as well as updating existing information. The data sources which are fed into this database can be summarized as follows:

New Car Sale Data (P55)

This supplies information on which car is sold to whom and includes model details, owner (eg: finance company for leased cars), driver (the actual user) and keeper (eg: a company who is running the car as part of a fleet). In the case of a privately owned car bought outright these details will be the same in most cases.

BMW Call Centre

Any person whether they are a current customer or prospect who makes an enquiry via the BMW Call Centre is logged onto the CDB. The nature of their enquiry is logged which may then be used for future marketing activity.

Data Cleansing

All databases need to be kept up to date to ensure that communications are tightly targeted and relevant. Data cleansing can take many forms and the following is a summary of the types employed on the CDB:

▶ Suppressions – anyone who does not wish to be mailed by BMW is included here.

▶ Address verification – addresses are automatically validated to ensure that the mailing information is correct. People who have moved house can be identified and their new address added to the database

▶ Campaign responses – any response to a campaign from a customer or enquirer provides the opportunity for people to update their information/areas of interest. This may range from changes to their name/address to when they are considering changing their car and what sort of car they intend to buy next.

NB: A summary of the information held against each individual on the CDB is included in the appendices.

The diagram overleaf provides an overview of this information flow:

The UK car market – a summary

BMW's position in the UK car market is very healthy. Not only is the health of the BMW brand very good, but car sales are at a record level. The recession of the early 1990s had a lesser influence on BMW than it did on its competitors. This environment has helped BMW to consistently build its market share throughout the 80s and 90s to a level today where it holds approximately three per cent of the total industry volume of car sales.

The BMW range is sold to a mix of private, business and finance/leasing companies. Leasing companies are then likely to sell on the BMW via their own finance packages.

Although BMW is still considered a niche brand, there are in fact over 470,000 BMWs in the UK Car Parc (i.e.; the total number of BMWs on the road). The size of the BMW car parc and product ubiquity is essentially undermining the exclusive brand status which BMW has traditionally enjoyed.

Despite the fact that BMW enjoys 'only' three per cent market share, this is a significant volume for what is a niche manufacturer. The following table draws a comparison against other niche car importers in the UK:

● ● ▶

BMW DATABASE

1. **SALES**
   V55 SALES REGISTRATION FORMS – NEW AND APPROVED USED SALES

2. **ENQUIRERS**
   ADVERTISING ENQUIRIES
   DIRECT MARKETING CAMPAIGN RESPONSES
   EXTERNAL RENTED DATA SOURCES – RESPONDERS
   INTERNET ENQUIRERS
   VALIDATED ADDRESSES
   EVENTS/PROMOTIONS LEADS
   DEALER CAMPAIGN NOMINATIONS
   BMW CALL CENTRE LEADS/ENQUIRERS
   LEADS FROM PRODUCT PLACEMENT ACTIVITY

3. **POLICY RENEWALS**
   EMERGENCY SERVICE/WARRANTY RENEWALS
   THIRD PARTY PROMOTION LEADS

4. **PRODUCT RECALLS**
   VEHICLE RECALL DATA FROM DVLA

1. **CAMPAIGNS**
   DIRECT MARKETING CAMPAIGNS: PRODUCT (TACTICAL) APPROX 10/YEAR
   ENQUIRY FOLLOW UP (PROSPECTS AND CURRENT CUSTOMERS) 4X/YEAR
   INVITATIONS TO EVENTS/PROMOTIONS
   AFTERSALES CAMPAIGNS: EG FOUR PLUS STYLING ACCESSORIES PROMOTION
   TARGETS FOR OUTBOUND TELEMARKETING

2. **BMW MAGAZINE**
   BMW MAGAZINE MAILING 4X/YEAR

3. **RENEWAL CAMPAIGNS**
   EMERGENCY SERVICE/WARRANTY POLICY RENEWAL PROMPTS
   AFTERSALES CAMPAIGNS: EG. FOUR PLUS STYLING ACCESSORIES PROMOTION
   TARGETS FOR OUTBOUND TELEMARKETING

4. **RECALL ACTIVITY**

5. **RESEARCH QUESTIONNAIRES/CALLS**

Current BMW Market Share in comparison to key competitors

Make	Share YTD
BMW	3.11%
Lexus	0.10%
Mercedes	1.92%
Honda	2.57%
Audi	1.63%
VW	5.61%
Saab	0.80%
Rover	8.86%
Land Rover	1.00%
Jaguar	0.41%
Mazda	1.49%
Volvo	1.82%
Toyota	3.31%
Porsche	0.11%

The chart below demonstrates BMW sales performance and corresponding market share.

The BMW Dealer network

BMW (GB) sells its cars both to the public and to businesses and fleet companies through a network of dealers. Dealers are third party business partners acting as franchises for BMW (GB), selling BMW branded products and services, such as cars, motorcycles, accessories, financial services and insurance. BMW Dealers are independent trading entities (i.e. they are not owned by BMW GB). Often the owner of a BMW Dealership will operate franchises on behalf of other manufacturers and importers from the same site. There are 157 authorized BMW dealers in the UK.

Whilst BMW dealers retain considerable financial autonomy, they are regulated to a large extent by the terms and conditions of their franchising agreement. These cover such areas as the cost of servicing work, the retail price of products, and the layout of the site. Dealerships are also subject to a quota system which regulates the number of vehicles they are allowed to sell. Applications are submitted to BMW (GB) by dealers based on the number of vehicles they believe they can sell within their territory. BMW (GB) then returns an allocation quantity which itself will be a function of the total number of vehicles allocated to the UK market by the parent company, BMW (AG).

Dealerships are supplied with sales leads through a computerized viewdata system which is operated by BMW (GB). The leads are generated by central marketing activity, paid for by BMW (GB) which may consist of a direct response freephone telephone number or a direct marketing reply device. This process is regulated by a territory system which divides the country up by postcode. Dealerships will also carry out local marketing campaigns for which they may use a local supplier, or BMW's own dealer marketing Agency.

Other functions of dealers are to carry out pre-delivery inspection work in advance of the delivery of a new car to a customer, issuing warranty documents with new cars, and maintaining quality control for BMW approved used cars. This is a scheme underwritten by BMW whereby a used vehicle which has been either traded in or purchased by a dealer must fulfil certain quality control standards in order to be branded as 'approved' by BMW. Dealers effect any work on a vehicle which may be necessary within the terms of the manufacturer's 3 year guarantee. Dealers are also able to arrange finance packages for customers as well as insurance cover through BMW Insurance.

The BMW product range in detail

The BMW car range spans from a compact hatchback to an executive luxury saloon, with prices ranging from £13,930 to £72,840. BMW also manufacture a range of motorcycles from the K1200RS Sports Tourer to the retro-styled Cruiser, along with clothing and accessories.

A profile of BMW customers

The average age of a BMW driver, including Compacts, has remained at 46 years. However, excluding the Compact, it has reduced slightly to 45 years. The average age of a Compact driver is the highest for any of the model variants at 53 years.

Source: BMW

● ● ▶

Model	Derivatives available	Comment
3 Series	Compact hatchback Saloon Coupe Convertible Touring	The 3 Series is the highest volume seller in the BMW range, accounting for 74% of sales. As the 3 Series has evolved over the last 20 years it has encompassed a touring, a small hatchback and a convertible, as well as the classic saloon and coupe. With its front engine, rear drive layout it has long been considered the sporting driver's choice in its class. The range is headed by the 321bhp M3 with a performance envelope which will blow your mind. Engines range from 1.6 to 3.2 litres.
Z3	1.9 Roadster 2.8 Roadster Z3M Roadster	The Z3 roadster is a 2 seater convertible sports car with the emphasis placed firmly on fun. Roadsters have experienced a renaissance over the last 5 years and the Z3 has enjoyed huge media interest and favourable press coverage. The imminent launch of the Z3M will leave BMW as the high performance leader over its German rivals, Porsche and Mercedes Benz. Engines range from 1.9 to 3.2 litres.
5 Series	Saloon Touring	The 5 Series is the benchmark saloon in its class. Since its launch in 1995 it has consistently been praised by the motoring press for setting new standards in the executive saloon sector. On more than one occasion it has been described as the best car in the world.
7 Series	Saloon	The 7 Series is BMW's flagship saloon and offers a combination of luxury and driving dynamism unrivalled by its competitors. With such options as satellite navigation, and the most sophisticated active safety system available on a road car (Dynamic Stability Control — DSC3), the 7 Series is one of the most desirable cars in the world.
8 Series	Coupe	The BMW 8 Series is a grand tourer in the GT mould with effortless performance and classic coupe design. Developed over the last 7 years, it now features BMW's sophisticated V8 engine and wind-cheating exterior styling. The 840 is powered by a 4.4 litre V8.

The number of women driving 3 Series has declined since the last survey with more women now choosing to drive a Compact. However, the number of women choosing to drive a convertible has remained high.

5 Series drivers are the most likely to have children in their household, especially younger ones.

There has been an increase in the number of retired people driving BMW cars since the last survey, due mainly to the number of retired people choosing the Compact. There has also been an increase in the number of owners of small businesses whilst there has been a decrease in the number of company directors driving BMW cars.

Golf remains the most popular hobby for BMW drivers, increasing in popularity even since the last survey.

Over 70 per cent of BMW drivers have one or more other cars in their household with this number rising to over 90 per cent amongst 7 Series drivers. The second car is most likely to be a Ford, with Rover and BMW also high on the list.

There has been a slight increase in the number of BMW cars owned privately since the last survey and also in the number of cars owned by a company rather than acquired as a business expense.

The average annual mileage of a BMW car reduced to 15,700 miles, down from 16,900 in the last survey. The average for all new cars is now 15,300 down from 16,000.

Loyalty

Information from customer surveys has demonstrated a gradual increase in their loyalty (repurchase) over the last few years.

BMW gained the most sales from GM and also Ford.

Those BMW customers who choose to leave the brand and go on to buy a competitor's car tend to go to Mercedes-Benz.

Jaguar drivers claim the highest satisfaction levels with their new cars, with BMW drivers rating their car next highest. In terms of quality, Mercedes drivers are the happiest with their cars.

Purchasing

The majority of purchasers take a test drive prior to purchase. Six per cent of BMW drivers did not take a test drive, but would have liked one. This was a much lower level than the mass manufacturers, but not as good as the Jaguar dealers achieved (1.3 per cent).

Reliability and style are main reasons for BMW drivers choosing their BMW, whilst

● ● ▶

top speed performance is also a consideration. This is the main difference between BMW and Mercedes drivers who do not choose their car for its top speed performance, although they do rate reliability and style very highly.

Occupation of principal driver

There has been an increase in the number of retired people driving BMW cars, influenced mainly by the Compact purchasers and a decrease in the number of company directors driving BMW cars.

Hobbies of principal driver

Golf remains the most popular hobby for BMW drivers, having increased slightly in popularity over the last year. More people now enjoy walking as a hobby than in the last survey.

The role of BMW communications

Direct communications

BMW's direct communications have evolved over the years to a position where they are considered a key element in any product launch or on-going marketing activity. These communications can be simplified into two categories:

Customer communications:

Those direct marketing campaigns which are not necessarily product based but may involve promoting a service, an event or an offer. Examples of these include:

▸ BMW Emergency Service: Renewal communications sent out to customers whose BMW Emergency Service is about to expire.
▸ 'Packington Hall': an invitation only event to a selected range of customers inviting them to the Motorshow as guests of BMW, including hospitality at a nearby stately home.

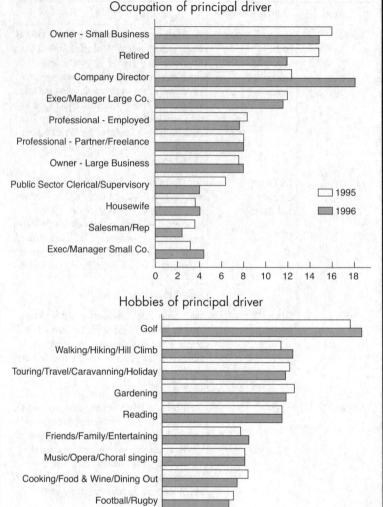

▸ Brands Hatch: a campaign sent out to attendees of the BMW Nigel Mansell Driver Training school.
▸ BMW Magazine: a complimentary subscription to BMW Magazine sent to all new car customers for a period of three years (their likely ownership period).

Product campaigns

Product campaigns typically coincide with product launches to provide additional support to the launch campaign. These

● ● ▶

campaigns target both customers as well as prospects/enquirers. The aim of these campaigns is to generate interest in the new car being promoted and elicit a response which will then be followed up via the dealer network, hopefully concluding with a sale.

In developing these campaigns, there is usually an incentive to reply. These incentives are usually not the common prize draws experienced with typical mail order companies. Instead BMW prize draws always attempt to underpin the understated values of the BMW brand as well as enhancing the proposition of the communication. An example of this would be the launch of the 840 Ci Sport, an indulgent and very exclusive Grand Tourer. This prize draw offered a weekend at a top hotel in Cannes together with an 840 Ci Sport to enjoy the roads and countryside around Cannes.

Historically BMW has rarely employed the use of press inserts in any direct communications. This is mainly because it was felt inappropriate for a brand like BMW to employ these techniques, nor did it have much requirement to prospect for customers which is a common use of inserts.

In much the same way BMW does not endorse the use of complicated paper formats which are used simply for their own sake. The format and presentation of each communication must support the proposition and communicate it clearly and uncompromisingly.

Advertising

BMW's advertising has made a great contribution to the success of the brand over the last 17 years. The advertising has until recently consistently lauded the central brand values of exclusivity, advanced technology and performance.

In recent years BMW's advantage over competitors in terms of brand perceptions has been eroded. Many of BMW's rivals have begun to stake a claim on the traditional BMW attribute of performance, most notably Volvo's recent campaigns which have overtly focused on the performance element of their cars to overcome their tired safety-first image.

The advertising of late has begun to widen the gap between BMW and its rivals. This is not simply a perceived gap, it is an actual difference in the very nature of the cars. This advantage which BMW is now attempting to highlight is that of 'Driving'. Driving is at the heart of all of BMW's communications. 'Driving' is not simply another word for 'motoring', it is about dynamism and the entire experience of driving a BMW which cannot be easily imitated through any of its rivals.

These dynamic driving qualities are prevalent throughout all BMW communications, both advertising and direct marketing. These different executions of 'dynamic driving' range from the TV ad 'Soundtrack' to the press ad '50/50' which highlights BMW's near perfect balance which it tries to achieve with each car's weight distribution.

Creative Guidelines

In developing any creative work for this case study, adherence to the BMW brand guidelines is essential. For all direct BMW communications, illustrations of the new brand guidelines are shown in the copies of previous direct marketing campaigns, notably the BMW Emergency Service campaign and the 5 Series Touring campaign.

The basic principles are as follows

- ▶ Headlines set in BMW Neue Helvetica bold in sentence case.
- ▶ Headlines can be set inside or outside the picture (usually inside if headline supports the picture).
- ▶ Colours in the typography are always set in the colour of the predominant tint of the main picture (i.e.: red car against sun set: red type).
- ▶ The BMW symbol (the 'roundel') is always set in three-dimensional form with the claim 'The Ultimate Driving Machine' printed in black (10 pt size) and centred below the roundel.
- ▶ The line 'The Ultimate Driving Machine' is NEVER used in headlines or bastardized in any way i.e.: 'The Ultimate Credit Card' — the line is sacrosanct.
- ▶ All communications both in their tone and use of photography should enhance the appeal of dynamism of the BMW brand. However care must be taken with the copy not to exaggerate this through use of superlatives in place of well crafted copy.

The future for BMW

The future looks very exciting for BMW both in terms of product development and through its marketing.

The new marketing structure and philosophy has been detailed in this case study already and demonstrates a commitment to a customer-focused strategy. The product innovations themselves are just as exciting.

Not one month passes when 'spy shots' are seen in the motoring press of the latest BMW or a BMW concept car which is being considered for production. Obviously not all of these models will reach the showroom, but two new product launches of particular interest include the Z3 Coupe and the C1.

The Z3 Coupe builds on the popularity of the Z3 Roadster and is due to be launched in 1998. The C1 is an exciting innovation in the interests of 'urban mobility'. The C1 offers the mobility of a motorbike with some of the comfort of the motorcar by incorporating a protective hood over the riding compartment.

BMW is also at the forefront of developing alternative forms of technology to power cars; hydrogen and battery power being amongst the most well-known attempts.

Perhaps of more significance to the way in which BMW has to protect its customer franchise will be the future changes to Block Exemption.

● ● ▶

Block Exemption is a piece of legislation which allowed motor manufacturers to sell their products through a restricted distribution network (Dealers). This practice of employing a regulated dealer network allowed motor manufacturers to control much of the marketing process from price to the way in which their products were promoted. It also allowed manufacturers to insist on 'best practice' guidelines which in turn ensured consistent customer service and protected their brand and reputation.

However the relaxation of Block Exemption rules and effective deregulation of the sales channel will mean that in the future any established company can sell and service cars from a chosen manufacturer. In this scenario it might not be uncommon to see a 'dealer' selling just 'German cars' or focusing its efforts on 'Estate cars' from any manufacturer.

The implications of this might mean that the distance between a customer and the manufacturing brand will widen. In the case of relationship and direct marketing efforts this may mean a loss of customer information which forms the key to any on going relationship.

For any manufacturer wishing to bridge this gap, they must start now while this privileged relationship is still intact. An appropriately conceived 'customer card' could perform a central role in any future relationships.

The Team Brief

As an agency invited to pitch by BMW (GB) Ltd you have been asked to take an overview of BMW's marketing operation, with particular attention to the renewed focus on relationship marketing and customer service elements and prepare a strategy document which will demonstrate specifically how direct marketing can be used to launch and sustain the introduction of a BMW Card to build increased loyalty among BMW customers.

Main task:

To launch the BMW Card

The detailed plan must take into account the launch activity and then the development of customer communications throughout the typical ownership period of three years.

Your proposals should consider:

1 The positioning and definition of the BMW Card, eg: an exclusive card for customers?

2 The type of benefits or rewards which may be associated with the card. This is an important aspect to the brief. Attention should be paid to existing research extracts provided and what is appropriate to the BMW brand.

3 What would be the technology for the card, eg: swipe card or smartcard?

4 A customer communications programme which will support the relationship marketing programme.

5 What implications would this have for any existing infrastructure with particular attention to the BMW Customer Database?

6 How would loyalty be built by using the card?

7 Indications as to how loyalty might be measured and the setting of appropriate targets.

8 A clear budgetary breakdown will be required to support your proposals.

NB: Attention must be paid to all forms of direct customer communications, do not restrict your thinking to direct mail only.

Budget availability

The budget must be able to include activity for all BMW customers who have purchased a new or used BMW within the last three years.

As a guide BMW sells approximately 60,000 new cars and 30,000 used cars each year.

The budget for Year 1 has been set as £1 million. For Years 2 and 3 a budget of £500,000 has been allocated.

The proposals should consider the following:

► Creative/Agency fees
► Production, print, lasering and mailing costs (including postage)
► Media costs
► Datacapturing information and additions to the database
► Campaign reporting eg: increases in customer satisfaction, increased spend on BMW products, increased repurchase or loyalty rates
► Customer and Dealer communications
► Incentives and offers (NB: it should be assumed that many incentives can be sourced free such as 2 nights for the price of 1 at an 'exclusive' hotel on the basis that they may want to be associated with BMW. 'BMW-only' incentives must be estimated)

List of appendices

I.   Database overview – details of records held on the BMW Database
II. Useful reading
III. BMW Card – research extracts
IV. Target group Index of BMW customers
V.   Sample EHS Creative brief

Permission to use this case study was granted by EHS and BMW (GB) Ltd.

● ● ▶

I. Database overview – details of records held on the BMW Database

Data held on customers

Vehicle Details

Product type	Car/Motorcycle
Chassis	
Registration number	
Model	
Selling Dealer	
Colour	
Upholstery	
Interest Type	Keeper/Owner/Driver
Interest Start Date	Start of ownership
Interest End Date	
Sale Type	New/used
Registered Keeper	Y/N (Y if sold by a dealer)
Main Use	
Finance Type	
Buying Purpose	Additional vehicle/replacement
Previous Vehicle	

Customer Details

Sex	Male/Female/Joint
Title	
Initials	
Surname	
Address 1	
Address 2	
Address 3	
Town	
County	
Postcode	
Tel – home	
Tel – work	
Tel – Car/mobile	
Works for Company	Employer
Occupation	
Job Title	
Age Group	

Data held on Prospects

Campaign Code
Date dd/mm/yy
Assigned Dealer
Title
Initials
Surname
Company name
Address Line 1
Address Line 2
Address Line 3
Town
County
Postcode
Telephone
Reply device   (Eg TEL, DMC)
Current Car Make
Current Car Model
Current Car Reg Year
Purchase intent Month, Year

NB Prospects and customers are held on the same central database allowing us to track leads through to sales.

II. Useful reading

▶ The BMW Breakthrough – 15 years of BMW advertising

▶ The Loyalty report, Professor Steve Worthington, 1996 (Commissioned by The GM Card)

▶ The Customer Loyalty Report 1997, SJB Services

▶ Hallberg, G. (1995) All consumers are not created equal, New York: Wiley.

▶ The Loyalty Effect, Reichfield (chapters 1,2,8)

III. BMW Card Research – extracts

IV. BMW Target Group Index profiles

BMW Target Group Index profiles – 'BMW was the most recent car I bought'

Sex	(000)	Vert %	Index
Sex			
Men	324	55.44	114
Women	260	44.56	87
Age			
15–19	57	9.79	114
20–24	14	2.32	334
25–34	161	27.6	140
35–44	115	19.7	116
45–54	108	18.55	116
55–64	61	10.51	86
65+	67	11.53	59
Social Grade			
AB	279	47.78	221

● ● ▶

Sex	(000)	Vert %	Index
C1	149	25.48	94
C2	92	15.76	70
D	43	7.39	44
E	21	3.58	31
Employment			
Full Time	264	45.20	114
Part Time	86	14.80	130
Retired	72	12.31	63
Not Working	162	27.68	95
Marital Status			
Single	118	20.27	91
Married	436	74.62	120
Separated/Divorced/Widowed	29	4.88	31
Household Income			
£35,000+	210	35.97	343
£25,000–£34,999	82	13.97	115
£20,000–£24,999	40	6.84	72
£15,000–£19,999	48	8.28	77
£11,000–£14,999	56	9.64	88
£5,000–£10,999	21	3.67	25
£4,999 OR LESS	4	0.68	8
Family Unit			
Single person	50	8.60	47
Adults Only (16yrs+)	291	49.88	104
Adults and Children	243	41.52	122
Home Ownership			
Own Home Outright	138	23.55	94
Buying Home	389	66.50	137
Rent from Council	24	4.18	25
Rent from someone else	27	4.63	56
Standard Region			
Scotland	40	6.88	76
North West	60	10.18	91
North	46	7.90	139
Yorkshire & Humberside	24	4.14	48
East Midlands	21	3.65	55
East Anglia	8	1.42	37
South East	144	24.68	129
Greater London	137	23.42	191
South West	39	6.68	80
Wales	17	2.88	55
West Midlands	48	8.17	81
Presence of Children			
Yes	243	41.52	121
No	339	58.02	88
Child(ren) under 1	28	4.72	198
Children – 1–4 years	101	17.28	138
Children – 5–9 years	74	12.71	87
Children – 10–15 years	126	21.60	121

Source: BMRB Target Group Index (rolling 96–97); Base: All Adults

V. Sample EHS Creative Brief

1. What is this brief is about? (include creative requirements)

In March 1997, BMW will launch the 840 Sport (it is badged 840Ci and this is how it should be shown in any visuals). The task is to communicate the overall 8 Series offering (ie the lifestyle aspects of the Grand Tourer) and how the product specifics of the 840 have combined to make it the superbly capable car that it is today. Cars in this price bracket, eg Jaguar's XK8 and the Porsche 911, are not rational purchases, due to their impracticalities, depreciation rates etc. They are bought by wealthy individuals, who may well be disloyal to specific marques/models, but who have the means to lay out a large sum of money on a car if they are convinced it should be on their shopping list.

The 8 Series has been described variously by the press ranging from a 'problem child" to 'an iron fist in a velvet glove". This ambivalence was largely down to the V12 850 CSi, which was priced at over £70,000 and did not have the rawness and sporting performance of the Ferraris etc which were its price competitors. The 840Ci launched in 1994 led to perhaps the most rounded appraisal of the 8 Series: 'BMW's 8 Series, a car of outrageous good looks and extravagant mechanicals devoted to the same utterly self-centred task" (Top Gear, March 1994).

The task is to communicate the 840 Sport as the quintessential Grand Tourer, using the product enhancements and beauty of the car's design as the substantiation of the claim.

2a. What is the single most important thing we are trying to achieve with this communication?

Ensure the recipients consider the 840 Sport when they change their current car.

● ● ▶

the
creat*i*ve
brief

CLIENT:	BMW (GB)
BRIEF NAME:	840 Sport
JOB NO:	32 119
VISUAL REQUIREMENTS *Please choose from scamps / AD visuals / highly finished visuals:*	Finished Visuals
COPY REQUIREMENTS *eg headline, subs, full copy:*	Headlines, subs
BUDGET *Including all originated & print, excluding postage:*	
MAILING/PRINT QUANTITY *Or attach media schedule*	

PROJECT TEAM		TIMINGS	
Deputy MD/Grp AD	**Kate Wheaton**	*Brief to Creative Controller:*	
Account Director		*Brief to Team:*	
Account Manager	*Andy Patton*	*Creative Review:*	
Media		*Internal Review:*	
Account Planning	*Bob Udale*	*Work Required on:*	*27/11/96*
Targeting	*Oli Janus*	*Time (am or pm)*	*am*
Production	*Eve Toomey*		
Creative Director	*Terry / Ray*		
Creative Grp Heads	*Mark / Graham*		
Art Director			
Copywriter			

APPROVAL		
ACCOUNT DIRECTOR	Signature	Date
ACCOUNT DIRECTOR	Signature	Date
ACCOUNT DIRECTOR	Signature	Date

Evans Hunt Scott

2b. Is there anything else we need to achieve?

They drive the new 840 at their local/ preferred dealer.

Give them the evidence and information to enable them to (re)appraise the car.

Suggest how our piece might integrate with other activity (eg placement at BMW events etc).

3. Describe who we're talking to. What do they currently think and feel about the product/brand? What data supports this?

Current owners of an 8 Series model, plus prospects owning direct competitor vehicles.

Current owners may feel it is time for a change, based on the performance of the current product. We should encourage a REAPPRAISAL of the car: 'This car is hugely better than it used to be, taut, precise, interactive and easy to fling from bend to bend" (Car, November 1996).

There is currently a battle for their custom, especially from the high profile launch of Jaguar's XK8. The 8 Series is a very capable car from an engineering point of view. We should inject more emotional (and fun) appeal for the car.

Owners of this type of vehicle tend to be enthusiastic and knowledgeable about driving – hence emotional imagery and details of the 8 Series' dynamic performance, will be a key area in which to entice the recipient of the pack to (re)appraise the car.

4. How are we going to reach them? (Consult media and targeting planners)

By direct mail. We have owners', prospects' and 8 Series enquirers' details on the database. It is proposed that we supplement these with externally rented names – from lifestyle and wealth lists.

5. What do we want them to do, and what is the *one* most persuasive reason why they should do it?

They should . . .

(Re)appraise the BMW 8 Series via a test drive

Because . . .

the sum of the changes to the 8 Series make it the quintessential Grand Tourer.

6. Why should they be convinced of this?

The 840 Sport is a classic Coupe and benefits from the following aesthetics changes:
- front apron
- M3 style wing mirrors
- rear diffuser
- Motorsport derived wheels
- sports seats
- sports suspension

These combine to give the 840 Sport £3,000 worth of equipment at no extra cost to the customer and give the car a fresh sporty look.

Other technological developments in-creasing the driveability and fun of the car introduced over the last couple of years are:

- 4.4 litre V8 engine, launched March 1996 with torque levels of 310 lb/ft 25 per cent higher than the previous 4 litre engine and improved the fuel economy.

- The Steptronic sequential gearbox, which allows much greater driver involvement than a conventional automatic.

- ARAK, rear axle kinematics (passive rear wheel drive), and ASC+T help underline the claim of technological excellence in the area of driving dynamism.

7. How do we want them to then think and feel? (Rational and emotional key words and phrases)

THINK: The 8 Series is more muscular than it was, looks like a piece of modern art and the recently introduced technology make it an even better drive.

FEEL: This is a self indulgent purchase, but the car is very sexy and it performs, so who cares?

8. What else can we do to encourage action? (Include offers/incentives etc here)

An incentive could encourage action. This action might be two stage.

Stage 1: the return of a reply device registering the recipients' interest in the 840 Sport.

Stage 2: those who meet our selection criteria, receive a loan car delivered to their home/office, so they can take an extended test drive.

Another opportunity to consider is that there will be two Motorsport Days (Oulton Park 14 May; Brands Hatch 26 June) where BMW owners and prospects will be able to drive their own cars and the range of sporting BMW models (M3, 328i and 8 Series) on the track. Attendance at the events will cost c£150. We could consider offering a quantity of free places to winners drawn from the reply device returns.

9. What is the mood and tone of voice of this piece?

Self indulgent. Sexy. Evocative. Alluring. Convincing.

10. Are there any restrictions and why? (eg size, photography, spend etc)

Total budget will not stretch to new photography.

The existing photography will be of the 850CSi as this appears visually the same as the 840 Sport externally.

11. Checklist of things creative must achieve (at internal review)

Suggest a strong, incentivised call to action – bearing in mind the profile of the potential customers and the extent to which they will need motivating to reply.

Display a clear understanding of the technological content of the 8 Series – a video, brochures etc covering this will be available at the briefing session.

Convince recipients that the 8 Series has changed.

The 8 Series is one of the most sexy (and expensive: £56,000) non vintage cars in the world. The creative should reinforce the image and reputation of this awesome model. A visit to a local dealer/BMW (GB) can be organized to show the 8 Series in the flesh.

◼

Permission for use of this case has been granted by EHS and BMW (GB) Ltd.

CASE STUDY 7

Getting the goods to a global market

What started as a small lump of Plasticine in a studio somewhere in Bristol has grown into a world-famous partnership with a following that crosses continents and time zones – and at the same time winning three highly coveted Oscars® and earning creator, Nick Park, international acclaim.

The sheer skill and creativity of the work of Aardman Animations has delighted television and film audiences all the way from the cheeky character, Morph, star of the children's programme Vision On, to the imaginative 'Creature Comforts' and the flagship characters Wallace and Gromit – not to mention a selection of evil penguins, remarkable trousers and hair raising adventures.

Small wonder, then, that Aardman's creations have become so popular throughout the world. And small wonder that people all over the planet are keen to own Wallace and Gromit merchandise – from fridge magnets and watches to Christmas

cards and baseball caps! But success on this scale called for a completely new way of servicing the marketplace – both in terms of receiving orders and of fulfilling them.

Wallace and Gromit go online

The task was to find a cost effective way to present a wide range of merchandise to an international audience – including all the mechanics necessary to receive orders and payments and manage despatch to fans as far apart as Brazil, China and the Czech Republic. It had to be a solution that would work across time zones and national

● ● ▶

boundaries and could show off the merchandise without the need to produce brochures in hundreds of different languages, quite apart from the logistical nightmare of distribution on such a huge scale.

The answer came from an expert team from Mail Marketing working with key personnel from Hewlett Packard. The one medium that could 'talk' to the world at all times – indeed, at any time – was the Internet. It would allow Aardman to display any number of products, keep the site updated as necessary and act as a springboard for all the transaction management needed to service a marketplace anywhere in the world.

Aardman Animations already had a site on the World Wide Web – http://www.aardman.com/ – which recorded a very high hit rate and which also provided a Visitor's Book for comments and requests. This proved what a massive demand there was for access to Wallace and Gromit merchandise from fans around the world and that prompted the next step – The Aardmarket.

The Aardmarket – global commerce made simple

The new website – http://www.aardman.com/aardmarket – has been designed and configured for global trade with all the elements required for speed, accuracy and security. Visitors can call on the site direct or link to it from Aardman's existing site. Once they've arrived, they can browse through the offerings from the Aardshop – featuring studio merchandise as worn by the Aardstaff – or the sumptuous Wallace and Gromit selection of T-shirts, resin figures, cards, bags, and much more. They can order on the spot, using Visa, Delta, Mastercard or American Express, even a cheque drawn on a UK bank via what has come to be known as 'snail mail'.

Once people have begun the order process they are connected automatically to a separate and secure server so that all sensitive information, such as name, address and credit card details, can be subjected to military grade encryption to guarantee security. This information cannot be read from the Internet and isn't even accessible from any Internet socket. It's held on a secured file system before being transferred to Mail Marketing where the orders are batched, fulfilled and despatched.

Order tracking is performed by the generation of a unique Reference Number for each order, automatically created by the secure commerce server.

Perfect partnership

There will be more for fans to enjoy as Aardman is planning to open more shops within the Aardmarket for merchandise from Creature Comforts, Pig and Pog and oodles of other characters from the Aardman Studio.

Like Wallace and Gromit, the partnership between the electronic expertise needed to set up the website facility and the skill and experience in transaction management is a perfect combination. Mail Marketing has built up an excellent relationship with the Royal Mail over the years and this has enabled them to set up to mail Wallace and Gromit products to 53 European countries and 183 non-European countries.

That means that Wallace and Gromit fans from Isleworth or Israel, Camberley or Canada, can go electronic shopping for their favourite merchandise any time of the day or night at the touch of a button. All they need is access to the Internet.

Author Index

Subject Index